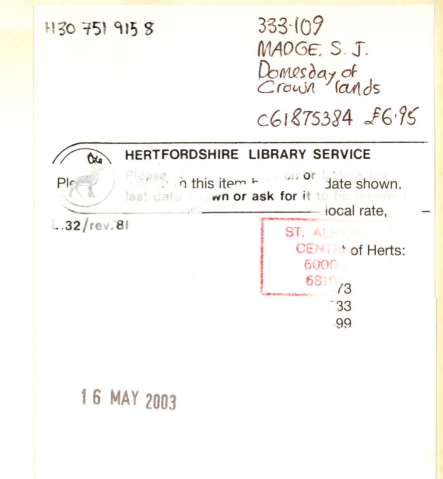

THE DOMESDAY OF CROWN LANDS

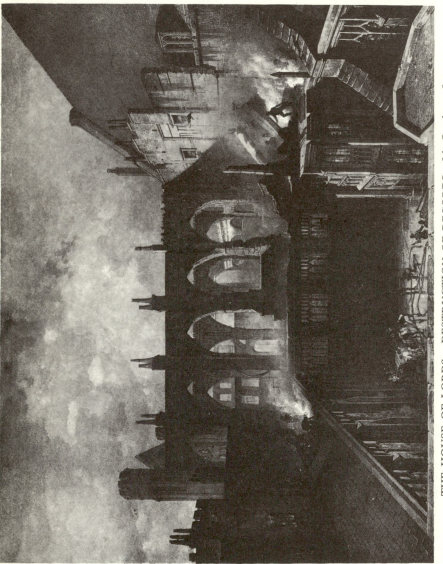

THE HOUSE OF LORDS : DESTRUCTION OF RECORDS, 16th October, 1834

THE DOMESDAY OF CROWN LANDS

A Study of the Legislation, Surveys,
and Sales of Royal Estates under the Commonwealth

SIDNEY J. MADGE

REPRINTS OF ECONOMIC CLASSICS

Augustus M. Kelley, Bookseller
New York 1968

Published by

FRANK CASS AND COMPANY LIMITED

67 Great Russell Street, London WC1

by arrangement with George Routledge & Sons Ltd.

Published in the U.S.A. by A. M. Kelley,

24 East 22nd Street, New York, U.S.A.

First edition   1938

New impression   1968

Library of Congress Catalog Card No. 67—31560

Printed in Holland by
N. V. Grafische Industrie Haarlem

TO
ARTHUR I. ELLIS, M.A., F.S.A.
IN TOKEN OF OLD
AND LOYAL FRIENDSHIP

PREFACE

The Domesday of Crown Lands, now happily completed, owes its existence to a combination of most fortunate circumstances : its title, for instance, to Mr. Leadam's *Domesday of Inclosures* ; its preparation to suggestions made between 1918 and 1920 by the late W. J. Corbett, of King's College, Cambridge, and Dr. Lilian Knowles, of the London School of Economics ; its progress to advice, introductions, and many official courtesies received at Oxford, Cambridge, and in London ; and its completion to the care bestowed upon the work by the printers and publishers. I greatly fear, however, that when the suggestion was first made, we none of us realized the magnitude of the task that lay ahead ; but the hours spent in research remain among the treasured recollections of the past, owing to the interest taken in the work by Dr. Hubert Hall, Dr. R. H. Tawney, Dr. Claude Jenkins, the late Sir Charles Firth, Professor H. S. Foxwell, and H. E. Malden. To the officials (so many of whose names might be mentioned) of the Public Record Office, British Museum, Duchy of Cornwall Office, and the Society of Antiquaries of London, I am particularly indebted, for without their aid this single-handed piece of work could not have been accomplished within a lifetime. It is a privilege and a pleasure to pay a tribute to the faithfulness with which the old tradition of friendly service to scholars is maintained by the present generation of the staff, especially in the departments of the British Museum and the Public Record Office. In an especial degree my thanks are due to Mr. A. I. Ellis, who has added to his many kindnesses by reading the proofs ; Mr. A. E. Stamp, for permission to photograph the original record of Domesday ; Mr. Marchant, and the staff of the British Museum, for numerous photostats and photographs of records ; Mr. Jenkinson for the use of his block to illustrate exchequer tallies, and the Commissioners of Crown Lands for advance information relating to the revenues of the present year.

That so many discoveries have been made in the present work is largely due, I feel, to the ease with which one may follow the clues provided by the official calendars. King James I declared that he would make his State Paper Office " the rarest office of that quality in Christendom " ; and it was acknowledged by the Master of the Rolls in 1855 that the records in his charge undoubtedly constituted " the most complete and perfect series of their kind in the civilised world." But, as the Deputy Keeper, Sir Francis Palgrave, admitted in his letter to the Master of the Rolls, 27th October, 1848 : " I acknowledge, and with regret, that the Calendars are not so complete, in many respects, as they might be, if a perfect classification were effected. The imperfection, however, cannot be helped : it is not a figure of speech, but a matter of fact, to state that the duration of human life scarcely affords any probability of bringing the vast mass into that state of arrangement required by the theory, that a perfect classification of the whole store of records should precede the operation of calendaring." Even as late as 1889, when records of Northamptonshire first awakened my interest in the subject, there was no official " Guide ", and no " Lists and Indexes " Series ; but modern " Calendars " now supplemented the older Series of Records (1783), the " Chronicles and Memorials " (1858), and the " Reports " of the Deputy Keeper (1839) and Historical Manuscripts Commissioners and Inspectors (1870). The Commonwealth State Papers, moreover, had been completed, so that it was possible to note, in 1886, that from these records " a second Domesday Book of the seventeenth century " might be compiled—the germ of an idea, which has unconsciously developed into the present work, *The Domesday of Crown Lands*, fifty years later. It is only necessary to compare the latest list of publications, March, 1937, with the earlier issue of 1st May, 1896— the year in which I first met at the Record Office the present Deputy Keeper, Hubert Hall, Scargill Bird and Trice Martin—to realize the progress made in the last forty years in organizing and preserving the national records. Of no other country in the world is it possible to say that its records " excel all others in age, beauty, correctness, and authority " : in no other land can one pay so great a tribute to the efficiency of its public service.

Three other circumstances, fortunate beyond measure, may be recorded here as a footnote to history : the attempt in 1662 to complete this investigation, now for the first time accomplished ; the escape, with little loss or damage, of the Parliamentary Surveys in the fire at the House of Lords on 16th October, 1834 ; and the further escape (by mere chance) from utter destruction of the present study and the " Crown Lands Collection ", in the appalling disaster to the Dutch airliner on 9th December, 1936, when fifteen lives were lost and Numbers 23 and 25 in this road were destroyed by fire. The Collection is now preserved in the London School of Economics, where it has been very skilfully arranged by Dr. W. C. Dickinson for the use of research students and historians, who in the future will be able, with the aid of the special indexes I have given in this book, to start new lines of inquiry concerning the history of Crown Lands in this country.

S. J. MADGE.

" HARBLEDOWN,"
22 HILLCREST ROAD,
PURLEY, SURREY.
7th October, 1937.

CONTENTS

PART IV

THE PARLIAMENTARY SALES OF CROWN LANDS

PART V

THE RESTORATION OF THE CROWN LANDS

APPENDIX

I

THE AVENUES AND INSTRUMENTS OF RESEARCH

II

ADMINISTRATION, SURVEYS, AND SALES OF CROWN LANDS

III

THE PARLIAMENTARY SURVEYS OF CROWN LANDS

APPENDIX

IV

Documents Relating to the Survey and Sale of Halliford Manor, 1633–1652

V

Valuation of Crown Lands, 1649–1659

VI

The Audit of the Restoration Officials in 1662 :

LIST OF TABLES

xiii

LIST OF ILLUSTRATIONS

xvi

THE DOMESDAY OF CROWN LANDS

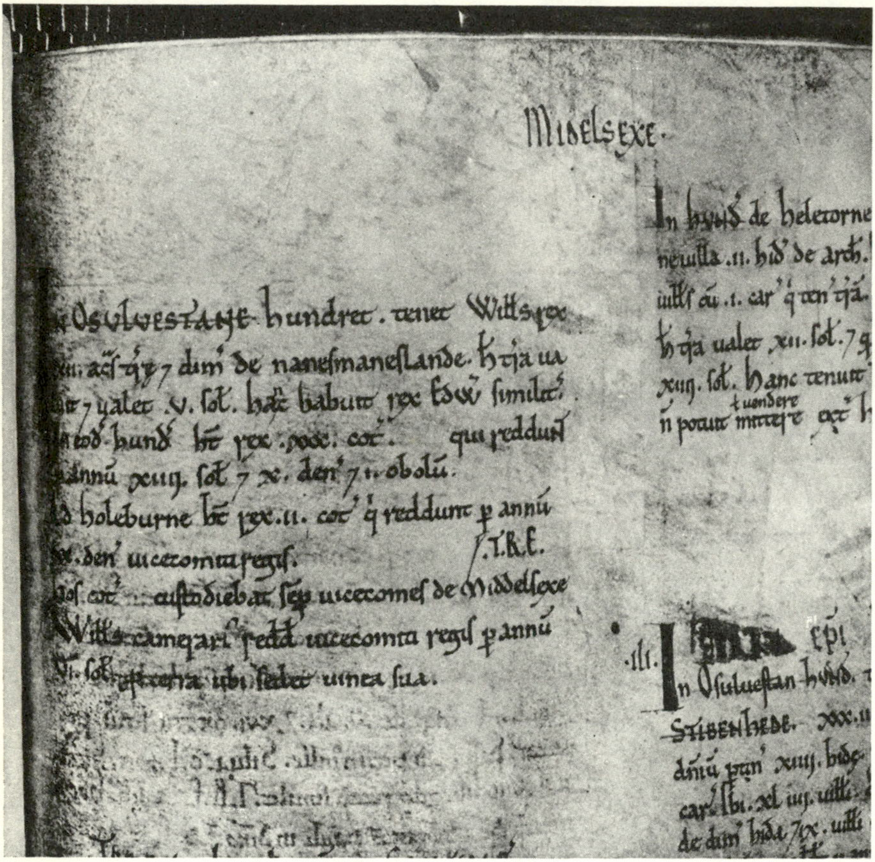

DOMESDAY BOOK: THE CONQUEROR'S MEAGRE SHARE OF MIDDLESEX

[*face p.* 1

PART I

STATE LANDS AND NATIONAL OBLIGATIONS

CHAPTER I

STUDIES OF CROWN LANDS

It is a singular circumstance that no one has ever made a comprehensive study of the Crown lands of England and Wales in the critical
period of their history under the Commonwealth.[1] At times, it is
true, curiosity has been aroused and some little interest shown in
particular aspects of the subject; but the Parliamentary surveys as
a whole, extending to all the counties of England and Wales, and the
special legislation passed in readiness for the sales, together with a
great mass of material relating to the contracts and conveyances,
have remained almost entirely unexplored by the student of seventeenth
century affairs. This is the more to be deplored because calendars and
indexes have been in existence for some years, and although their
inadequacy was recognized by the Commissioners of Public Records
between 1800 and 1812, the publication of an official calendar of
surveys in 1846 and 1847 made the study of the subject at length
possible. In the past, general historians have been content to quote
short statements of fact from the works of Scobell or Thurloe, or the
opinions of Dr. Walker in regard to Commonwealth finance. Hume's
sole contribution is a single sentence, which although casually written
is frequently quoted, namely that "Crown Lands yielded also considerable sums, but very difficult to be estimated". Historians of the
Stuart period and writers of special monographs on the reigns of
Charles I and Charles II, have likewise added little to the researches
of Sir Charles Firth, Dr. Gardiner, and Dr. Shaw upon this subject;
and it is not until we come to the work of Mr. Lennard, who, under
the guidance of the late Professor Vinogradoff and Sir Charles Firth,
revealed the economic importance of the parliamentary surveys of
Northamptonshire, that any further advance was made in this
direction.[2]

[1] Throughout this work the calculation of the year as beginning on 25th March is
adopted, and double reckoning of years after 31st December is thus avoided. The accession
of James VI of Scotland to the throne of England on 24th March, 1602–1603 is regarded
as having taken place therefore on the last day of the year 1602. The first two Stuart
kings will also be referred to as James and Charles instead of James I and Charles I, until
the events of the Restoration period are mentioned.
[2] See the *Reports of the Commissioners of Public Records*, 1812, App. E. 2, p. 54, and
D.K.P.R., reports 7 and 8, App. ii. Hume, *Hist. of England*, vol. iii, ch. 62, pp. 500–501
is often quoted, but is almost as useless as the general statement in Fletcher's recent history
of England, vol. ii, pp. 447–8, to the effect merely that "money was raised by the sale
of church, crown, and cavalier lands". Gardiner was the first to reveal the total proceeds
of the sales of fee farm rents in his *Hist. of the Commonwealth*, vol. i, pp. 280–281. Sir C. H.
Firth's great work on the Acts and Ordinances of the Commonwealth has been of the

But although the Commonwealth surveys are said to have been frequently consulted, there is little evidence in the published account of searches at the Public Record Office that those relating to Crown lands were being used : in the lists for the years 1835 to 1840, for example, it is the surveys of Church property that searchers want. And even after the publication of the important calendar of Parliamentary Surveys in 1846 and 1847, it was possible for Edw. Peacock as well as " G. B. A." to make fruitless inquiries in *Notes and Queries* as to where the records of the surveyors of Crown lands were preserved and whether the Parliamentary Surveys of Kent had been printed— queries, indeed, that have never been answered in those columns from that day to this. The request of E. H. W. Dunkin as to whether the surveys of Crown lands ordered by the Act of 16th July, 1649, had been printed was more fortunate in that two replies were received in the following months, "K. P. D. E." intimating in one of them that he was " in a position to state pretty positively that the Parliamentary Surveys of Crown lands have never been published ", and W. D. Cowper adding that twenty-six of the fifty-one surveys for Sussex had just appeared in print. But apart from such queries and their replies, the subject has never been discussed in *Notes and Queries* throughout the years of its literary life. Nor can it be said that the *Gentleman's Magazine*, in an even longer career, has shown the slightest interest in the subject, for only two notes, many years apart, occur among its volumes, one suggesting in the year 1762 the necessity for the immediate sale of the Crown lands to help pay for the Continental wars, and the other referring to the second report of the Commissioners of Land Revenues issued in 1803.

In other ways the amount of interest shown by readers and the extent of research accomplished by writers in connection with the surveys and sales of Crown lands during the Commonwealth may be tested. In the years 1901 to 1905, for example, an average of five historical works bearing in some degree upon this period appeared annually, yet the information they reveal in connection with this subject would barely fill a page of print. Again, in the *Victoria History of the Counties of England*, an important work which has been in progress since 1901, the parliamentary surveys of not more than a dozen counties are quoted, never at any length, while the certificates of sale and conveyances are scarcely noticed at all.[1]

greatest possible value in the preparation and completion of the present work. Lennard's essay on the Northamptonshire surveys deserves praise for the pioneer work accomplished in this direction. Scobell's volume of *Acts* is now superseded by the new publication of Firth and Rait. Thurloe's *State Papers* and Walker's *Independency*, furnish contemporary evidence of legislative changes and both works are frequently quoted.

[1] In *D.K.P.R. Report* 1 (1840), see App. 3, p. 22. The works referred to will be found in the Subject Catalogue of the British Museum for the period 1901-1905 ; but there is a larger range of publications which the student can examine and test at his leisure in the recently issued *Bibliography of Stuart History*. The only references in *Notes and Queries* are to be found in series iv, vol. i, p. 414, and vol. viii, pp. 167, 255, 269, 486, the

If, moreover, we examine the monumental works of the great county historians that line the shelves of the topographical section in the reading room of the British Museum, we shall discover that very little attention has been paid to the Commonwealth surveys and sales of royal property during the past three centuries. Classifying the references as " brief " or " extensive ", and selecting one work for each county of England, omitting Monmouth, we find that local historians of the period 1656 to 1856 gave short references to the subject in ten of their works, and somewhat longer accounts in six other publications, leaving the rest of the county histories, twenty-three in number, without any discernible reference to these important records.[1]

With the execution of Charles we stand on the threshold of revolutionary changes, just as men a century before had done when they witnessed the fall of the monasteries. On the very eve of both of these changes we find appointments being made for the purpose of valuing the property of the victims : Royal Commissioners in the earlier case, whose returns described minutely the revenues of the Tudor Church ; and republican surveyors in the later period, whose surveys revealed the values of the Stuart Crown lands. " No one," says Dr. Savine, " has ever made a careful study of this Survey, neither general historians of the Tudor age, nor historians of the English Church, nor authors of the very few monographs on the Dissolution.

dates being 2nd May, 1868 to 9th December, 1871. For the *Gentleman's Magazine*, see vol. 32 (1762), p. 135, and vol. 73, part i (1803), p. 279. The *Victoria County Histories* are disappointing, for the only counties that contain material worth noting are Bedford, Berkshire, Buckingham, Derby, Hampshire, Hertford, Lancashire, Middlesex, Northamptonshire, Surrey, Worcester, and Yorkshire. In other counties the references are either casual or non-existent. See App. I, sect. viii (KI.), p. 300.

[1] Taking one publication for each of the counties of England, excluding Monmouth, we may divide the thirty-nine works into three classes, as follows : (*a*) six containing Parliamentary Surveys of an extensive character, three of them recording full transcripts in particular cases : these six relate to the counties of Gloucester, Rudder, 1779 ; Hereford, Duncumb, 1804 ; Hertford, Clutterbuck, 1815 ; Kent, Hasted, 1778 ; Surrey, Manning, 1804 ; and Wiltshire, Hoare, 1822. (*b*) In the second class we have ten more containing brief references to Parliamentary Surveys : these concern the counties of Bedford, Lysons, 1813 ; Berkshire, Lysons, 1813 ; Buckingham, Lipscomb, 1847 ; Cambridge, Lysons, 1808 ; Cornwall, Lysons, 1814 ; Derby, Lysons, 1817 ; Huntingdon, Brayley, 1808 ; Middlesex, Lysons, 1802 ; Stafford, Harwood, 1844 ; and Suffolk, 1846. (*c*) Lastly we have the remaining works which contain no reference whatsoever to the Parliamentary Surveys : these are the histories of no less than twenty-three counties, namely, Cheshire, Omerod, 1819 ; Cumberland, Nicolson, 1777 ; Devon, Polwhele, 1797 ; Dorset, Hutchins, 1773 ; Durham, Surtees, 1816 ; Essex, Wright, 1836 ; Hampshire, Warner, 1795 ; Lancashire, Britton, 1807 ; Leicester, Britton, 1807 ; Lincoln, Allen, 1834 ; Norfolk, Blomefield, 1805 ; Northants, Bridges, 1791; Northumberland, Hutchinson, 1778 ; Nottingham, Thoroton, 1677 ; Oxford, Dunkin, 1823 ; Rutland, Blore, 1811 ; Shropshire, Eyton, 1854 ; Somerset, Collinson, 1791 ; Sussex, Horsfield, 1835 ; Warwick, Dugdale, 1656 ; Westmorland, Nicolson, 1777 ; Worcester, Nash, 1781 ; and Yorkshire, Allen, 1828. In this last section Williams' *History of Monmouth*, 1796, might find a place. Of these works, two were published in the seventeenth century, 11 in the eighteenth, and 26 in the nineteenth century, but only two of the works published prior to the year 1802 are found to contain references to these Surveys, and not more than fourteen other works published subsequently. The Suffolk volume is by Suckling, 1846.

But as a proper understanding of the Dissolution is impossible without a study of the Valor, I shall attempt to struggle through this labyrinth, however great may be the danger of losing the right way in the wearisome and unattractive maze of names and figures." [1]

What Dr. Savine has so well stated may be applied with equal force to the Commonwealth land surveys of the Crown, for it has already been shown that no one has ever made a complete and careful study of these records, and that such research work as scholars, general writers, or historians have hitherto attempted has been singularly inadequate to the importance of the subject. Although, as Dr. Savine admits, " critical examination of evidence is the dullest kind of historical research, and the analysis of surveys is the dullest kind of critical work," yet in spite of the fear that " only a very incredulous or a very patient reader will have the courage to wade through " such tedious but necessary evidence, an attempt will be made in the present work to explore this unique region of unexamined material relating to land finance.

The order in which the subject will be developed in the present study may be very shortly stated. Consideration in the section which follows will first of all be given to the constitutional position and changes of the Crown lands in days preceding the Commonwealth period. Next, the treatment of the royal estates during the great crisis will be examined in some detail, in order to discover the characteristic features of the legislation, surveys, and public sales sanctioned and directed by the republican government and its officials. Lastly, the reaction of the Government policy of sales will be considered in connection with the restoration of monarchy.

In Part I, for the more adequate treatment of the subject, discussion will turn on the origin, nature, and development of the Crown lands, the derived revenues and the various methods of accounting for them at the Exchequer. Part II will examine closely the nature of the republican legislation, the army schemes, committee work, and departmental activity connected with the surveys and sales of Crown lands and fee farm rents, the additional and amending acts providing for the exemption and subsequent sale of premises, and the disafforestation and sale of royal forests and chases. Part III will describe the calendars, reveal the planning of the surveys, and analyse in considerable detail the whole of the seven sections which compose

---

[1] Dr. Savine, *English Monasteries on the Eve of the Dissolution*, indicates the scope of his inquiry on p. 1, the results of his critical examination of the Valor Ecclesiasticus on pp. 73–5, and the limits of his inquiry into the monastic economy on pp. 96–100. In his appendix, pp. 269–288, he gives a valuable table of monastic income based on the Valor Ecclesiasticus. The minimum amounts were below £10 in eight counties, but there were twice as many counties in which the net income exceeded £1,000. The extreme limits of variation in the " net monastic incomes " recorded by Dr. Savine appear to be 18*s*. 2*d*. in the case of Huntingdon, and £3,311 15*s*. 2*d*. in Somersetshire, while the total amount of such income in England is given as £136,361 12*s*. 9*d*. Cf. Fisher, *Political Hist. of Eng.*, vol. v, p. 369–370 for earlier confiscations.

the Parliamentary Surveys; it will for the first time record complete statistics, and relate not only the existence of an entirely new calendar but the discovery of notable documents, some of which were prepared expressly for the methodical and accurate working of the parliamentary surveyors. Part IV will deal in a complete manner with the sale of Crown lands, a whole mass of newly discovered material being analysed for this purpose. Part V will show the outcome of the republican experiment and the difficulty of restoring the property of the Crown after 1660—in which connection an estimate will be attempted as to the extent of restoration on that occasion; and finally an endeavour will be made to summarize the main changes that have occurred in connection with the control of the Crown lands by Parliament since the seventeenth century.

So great was the abundance of material at the command of Dr. Savine that he was compelled to limit his study of the Valor Ecclesiasticus in a number of ways. Thus his inquiries were con-fined to England, and while they included all the nunneries, he was obliged to exclude some of the monasteries, most of the hospitals, all the colleges, and every one of the friaries; to this extent, therefore, his work remains incomplete.[1] So, too, in the present instance, the amount of material in existence is so enormous, and often so conflicting and perplexing, that completeness in a limited time is quite out of question; for these records, be it remembered, kept an army of officials busy for years in the many departments of Worcester House, the Treasury, and elsewhere, so that the student to-day, compelled to work single-handed, would need a number of years to digest even a portion of the evidence abstracted, and a literary lifetime to reach the ideal set up by a methodical and thorough mind. The limit of time sets a limit to useful inquiry, so in the analysis of the Parliamentary surveys, in order to preserve clearness of general outline in the present study, the main illustrations are drawn from the counties of Middlesex, Sussex, Surrey, and Northamptonshire, but in special matters, such as leases, rentals, and reprises, examples are taken from every part of the land. The statistics relating to the calendars and surveys are complete in that they embrace the whole of the counties of England and Wales, and the section dealing with the sales is likewise complete, since it embraces every type of property as well as every county throughout the land.

For the purpose of comparative study in connection with the present work, the materials relating to the surveys and sales of Crown lands have been arranged on a methodical plan which will permit of consistent interpretation from an economic point of view. The possibility of establishing territorial divisions must ever depend upon the purpose in hand, for this may be accomplished in a variety of ways. Thus, the divisions of the country might be arranged on

[1] Savine, op. cit., limits of the inquiry, p. 96.

the basis of the suggested circuits of the Domesday Commissioners, in which case we might follow Eyton's arrangement of nine groups of counties, or Ballard's rearrangement of six; or indeed we might try division of the country into ten areas of relative density of population in accordance with the Domesday evidence. Again, Ramsay's divisions of from three to seven groups of counties in connection with the judicial " iters " of Henry II's reign might prove acceptable as a working basis, or the areas of the seven auditors of the office of Land Revenues might prove more useful still. But the one scheme of territorial division in connection with the Crown lands which has most in its favour for present needs, is that which divides the country from north to south in such a way that three main political areas result. If two lines be drawn, one on the east from Hull, through Newark, Leicester, and Reading, to Southampton, the other on the west from York, through Manchester, Stafford, Gloucester and Bristol, to Exeter, then (1) south and east of the first line we have the main Parliamentary area, protected in the Civil War; (2) north and west of the second line we shall find the main Royalist area, likewise protected; but (3) between the two lines will be found the main battle area, in which most damage to property must have occurred. By arranging that the lines follow the boundaries of counties instead of cutting through them, we have sixteen central counties in the battle area, namely :—

1. Bedford.	9. Northants.
2. Berkshire.	10. Nottingham.
3. Buckingham.	11. Oxford.
4. Derbyshire.	12. Rutland
5. Dorset.	13. Somerset.
6. Hampshire.	14. Stafford.
7. Leicester.	15. Warwick.
8. Lincoln.	16. Wiltshire.

To the east of this group will be found ten counties, largely protected and controlled by the Parliamentary forces during the Civil War, while to the north and west of the group lie the remaining English counties with those of Wales and Monmouth, loyal in the main to the king.[1]

Across these two groups of central and eastern counties other lines may now be drawn from east to west along the county boundaries, so as to form two subdivisions that lie partly within and partly without the contested region. These may be called the metropolitan and extra-metropolitan areas, the former consisting of ten

[1] Eyton's *Notes on Domesday*, p. 10 ; Ballard, *Domesday Inquest*, p. 12 ; Stanford's *Compendium of Geography*, Europe (1902), vol. ii, pp. 273-6 ; Ramsay, *Revenues of Kings of England*, vol. i, under the years 22-35 Henry II, 1175-1189 ; Keating and Fraser, *History of England*, p. 393 ; Rogers, *Hist. of Prices*, vol. v, pp. 73-4 ; Traill, *Social England*, vol. iv, p. 223 ; with maps of the Civil War in Gardiner's Atlas and in Historical Assoc. Atlas.

counties whose land values should be greater because they lie mainly in the protected region of the Parliamentary troops, whereas the majority of the counties in the latter area lie in the harassed battle zone. The remaining English counties lying to the north and west may be called the Borderlands; hence we may expect values to be lower in these areas, as well as in Wales, not so much on account of military raids as on account of the undeveloped condition of this part of the country, although Cheshire certainly suffered from both causes. The full arrangement of the area is displayed below in tabular form for the sake of clearness.[1]

The relative importance of these areas throughout the centuries may very briefly be considered. In reference first of all to distribution of population in 1086, we find Essex in Area I, Norfolk and Suffolk in Area II, and Gloucester in Area III with the chief positions in the Domesday list; thereafter come Somerset, Cornwall, and Devon, and most of the counties in Area III, with Yorkshire last of all. Area I is prominent in all the assessments recorded by Thorold Rogers. Middlesex is always first, on account of London, between 1341 and 1693. Oxford claims second position in wealth per acre according to the assessments of 1453 and 1503—a position taken by Hertford in 1636 and Surrey in 1693, while Sussex was second only in the Danegeld assessment of 8 Henry II (1161). Oxford also had the third position in 1341, Bedford in 1636 and 1660, Surrey in 1649 and 1672, and Hertford in 1693, so that this area during many centuries has been well populated and prosperous. In Area II Norfolk ranks either second or third in the assessments from 1161 to 1503, but between 1649 and 1672 the second place is taken by Suffolk, and then Norfolk drops to the middle of the list. Northamptonshire was fifth in the " Shipmoney " assessment of 1636, Leicester seventh, Huntingdon eighth, and Somerset ninth, while Rutland took the eighth position in the assessment of December, 1649, and the seventh in 1341. The position of Somerset between 1636 and 1693 varies from eighth to fourteenth. But the lowest positions are always to be found among the counties which compose Area III. Gloucestershire stands out best in this group, being twelfth in Domesday, but twenty-third in 1660, rising two places in 1693. Lancashire is last in 1341, last but one in 1636, and only a trifle higher between 1660 and 1693. After 1341 Cumberland remains at the bottom of every list. The Border Lands area, therefore, is one of low assessments,

---

[1] Table I. This is the arrangement adopted in recording the Valuations of Church and Crown lands, and the detailed analysis of research work accomplished in connection with the Parliamentary Surveys. The arrangement here shown agrees well with Eyton's groups for Domesday circuits, Nos. 1, 3, and 5 mainly corresponding to area i, Nos. 2, 6, 8, 9, with area ii, and Nos. 4 and 7 with area iii. Ramsay's lists of judicial circuits of 22–35 Hy. II, 1175–1189, similarly agree, area i including circuits 1, 2, 5, area ii, Nos. 4 and 7, and area iii, Nos. 3 and 6.

and slender prosperity. Among the Welsh counties Monmouth stands first and Merioneth last after 1641.[1]

---

[1] Ramsay, op. cit., vol. i, p. 194 ; Rogers, op. cit., vol. i, pp. 104–107, vol. iv, pp. 74–89, vol. v, pp. 66–76, 104–123. The relationship of the above areas to the Field Systems and Corn prices may be ascertained from the maps and tables in Gray's *Eng. Field Systems,* and Gras, *Evolution of the Eng. Corn Market,* pp. 46–55. The average medium-price area of the Lower Thames (6*s.* 3½*d.* in the period 1301–1500) became the highest of all areas three centuries later (47*s.* 6½*d.* in 1672–1702).

I. AREAS OF LAND VALUATIONS

A. Parliamentary Region	Battle Area	Protected Area
I. *Metropolitan Area* .	1. Bedford. 2. Berkshire. 3. Buckingham. 4. Oxford.	5. Essex. 6. Hertford. 7. Kent. 8. Middlesex. 9. Surrey. 10. Sussex.
II. *Extra Metropolitan Area*	11. Derby. 12. Dorset. 13. Hampshire. 14. Leicester. 15. Lincoln. 16. Northants. 17. Nottingham. 18. Rutland. 19. Somerset. 20. Stafford. 21. Warwick. 22. Wiltshire.	23. Cambridge. 24. Huntingdon. 25. Norfolk. 26. Suffolk.

B. Royalist Region	North Area	South Area
III. *Borderland Area* . .	27. Cheshire. 28. Cumberland 29. Durham. 30. Lancashire. 31. Northumberland. 32. Westmorland. 33. Yorkshire	34. Cornwall. 35. Devon. 36. Gloucester. 37. Hereford. 38. Shropshire. 39. Worcester.
IV. *Welsh Area* . . .	40. Anglesey. 41. Carnarvon. 42. Denbigh. 43. Flint. 44. Merioneth. 45. Montgomery.	46. Brecon. 47. Cardigan. 48. Carmarthen. 49. Glamorgan. 50. Monmouth. 51. Pembroke. 52. Radnor.

CHAPTER II

THE ORIGIN OF THE CROWN LANDS

The Crown lands of Charles the First, administered by the State upon the abolition of monarchy in January, 1648, were of ancient origin. Like the manor, these specialized lands appear to have developed through contributions from British and Continental sources, the ancient customs of which were confused in the course of time by conquests of Romans, Jutes and Saxons, Angles, Danes, and Norsemen within the realm of Britain. During many centuries the Crown succeeded in uniting the rival principles of private and collective ownership in land, but of the ultimate claims to ownership, that of the sword received recognition earlier than the other and more competitive claim of the spade.[1]

When we gaze into the mirror of the historic past we see, but very faintly, successive societies of primitive folk who, in the infancy of those early times, struggle to sustain their culture upon the soil of southern Britain; and though the outline is assuredly dim, we can recognize the institutions of land ownership and kingship, which emerge and develop with the needs of later days. That these Celtic communities perceived the economic force of kingship is apparent, since they not only supported the ruler by the payment of regalian dues, but attached to his royal office (though not to his private estate) certain portions of tribal lands, called " mensal lands ", which may be regarded as forming the earliest " royal estates " known to history.[2]

Four centuries of intrusion followed in which the subtle but powerful civilization of Rome modified in some degree the Celtic process of social evolution; yet the occupation of Britain, in spite of its essentially military character, failed to achieve the thorough Romanization accomplished by its arms in lands nearer home. So incompletely, indeed, did her culture absorb Celtic nationality that the subservient elements proved capable of emerging once again in the Celtic revival of the fifth and sixth centuries that followed the collapse of the imperial rule of Rome. Nevertheless, abiding results of that conquest are still to be found in the customs relating to land

---

[1] Slater, " Hist. Outline of Land Ownership in England " (*The Land*, vol. i, pp. lxi, lxiii). For the records of Crown lands and Rents, see Scargill Bird's *Guide*, pp. 66–74, and Giuseppi's *Guide*, vol. i, index, p. 369. The former divides his references into six parts, viz. (1) Accounts, etc., relating to Crown lands; (2) Bargains and Sales of Crown lands and of Fee Farm Rents; (3) Concealed lands; (4) Fee Farm Rents; (5) Purchases and Exchanges; (6) Resumed Lands. Giuseppi's references are scattered throughout the volume.

[2] Ramsay, *Foundations of England*, vol. i, p. 5; Vinogradoff, *Growth of the Manor*, p. 3.

tenure and cultivation, a domain in which, as Sir James Ramsay points out, use and wont exhibit a surprising vitality. As the conquered province of Britain was a personal domain of the Emperor, absolute ownership of its soil was barred to private persons, so that under Roman law, occupiers could only cultivate the land and enjoy the possession or usufruct of it subject to imperial rights. Officials with military titles administered the State lands, and during their journeys the landowner was bound to entertain them, being liable also to find corn for such troops as might be on the march.

Three class of agriculturists were settled by the imperial officials upon the lands, namely, the *tributarii*, or early settlers, whose heritable holdings or allotment strips in the common fields with appendant pasturage were assigned by ballot; the *contributi*, or original native owners, whose irregular patches of land were exchanged for newly measured strips in the common fields; and the *coloni*, or original free cultivators who were now the tillers of the soil, men with rights and capable of acquiring property, paying a rent for such unassigned lands as were brought into cultivation and leased to them, but inseparably attached to the soil by the fourth century and represented by the agricultural worker of a later date, neither serf nor yet freemen. For their lands, State rents were paid to the imperial officials by all except the *contributi*. In early times the *tributarii* made a payment of a tenth of the annual produce, an amount which would appear grievous as a State rent; but in later times they might pay in money or kind an amount varying from a fifth to a seventh of the estimated value of the land, and this proportion would also prove in practice to be heavy as a land tax. The payments of the *coloni* appear to have been customary rents of money, service, or kind. One very important principle has come down to us from those distant days—a legacy more lasting than even the bridges, fortifications, and admirable roads bequeathed by the Romans to their successors—namely, the necessity of making the maintenance of all these works a primary burden on land.[1]

But the period of Roman imperial power passed, and with it the theory of absolute state-ownership based on forfeiture of conquered land in Britain. In the centuries which follow, when the strongly revived Celtic spirit was finally crushed, the theory of a three-fold scale of land-ownership—of royal, public, and private lands—arose, based, in the absence of definite records, upon the consideration of the character of the English conquest and the consequent introduction of Teutonic institutions. This view of primary ownership rests, however, upon the hypothesis that during the period of Teutonic migrations the victorious leader of an invading tribe, disposing of

---

[1] For the Roman period, see Ramsay, op. cit., vol. i, pp. 5, 16; Vinogradoff, op. cit., pp. 15–47; Sharpe, *Middlesex in Roman Times*, pp. 63–4, 92–4. See also the two essays on administration and agriculture by Jones and Heitland in *The Legacy of Rome*, 1924.

the spoils of war, divided the conquered territory into three portions, one of which, the royal lands, he retained for his own needs ; the second he shared among the armed followers who composed the "host" and the "hundred", a share ever after to be known as the private lands ; and the third portion he reserved, under the name of the public lands, for the constitutional needs of the newly established community. In the development of such a primitive State variations in the respective shares would result from differences in the efficiency of the forces concerned : the activity of a tribal king, constantly extending the margin of conquest, would carve out new estates for the Crown and at the same time enlarge the private lands of his adherents, while the passivity of the new state would increase the extent of the public lands at its disposal.[1]

It is clear, however, that in the course of time the proportionate shares themselves would vary, owing to extension or diminution in one direction or another, until at last the three-fold scale of ownership would become but a two-fold scheme, in which case the lands of the people would probably be the first to vanish, leaving only the royal and private shares of land. This, in fact, is what actually occurred, though the period when it happened cannot be stated with certainty. Yet to conclude that the rights of the nation in the public lands were wholly lost would be incorrect, for the rights of the local public still exist in commons and wastes, just as surely as those of the general public exist in highways and common streams ; and it is of particular significance that to-day the Crown lands are administered by a State department under Commissioners, and are thus in a very special sense in public ownership.

The point raised by Dr. Round, as to when the folk land became Crown land, has been considered by Bishop Stubbs, Professor Freeman, and Dr. Hubert Hall, and although a definite date is, of course, impossible, an approximate one has not been difficult to determine. It was Freeman's opinion that the two kinds of lands were confounded after the Norman conquest, and that under William I folk land became King's land and was registered as such in the record of Domesday under the title of *terra regis*. This suggestion Dr. Round refused to accept because he thought it was "coloured by political prepossession". Stubbs, on the other hand, put forward the view that the change occurred in days earlier than the Norman conquest, asserting in one passage that from the moment kings of Wessex began their rule over the entire English nation "the folk land was virtually becoming

---

[1] For the Saxon period, see Ramsay, op. cit., vol. i, pp. 102–5 ; Vinogradoff, op. cit., pp. 52–87 ; Cotes, *Social Britain*, vol. i, pp. 271–2 ; Freeman, *Norman Conquest*, 1st edition, vol. i, p. 94 ; Jeudwine, *First Twelve Centuries*, pp. 213–214, 225–7 ; Stubbs, *Constit. Hist. of England*, vol. i, pp. 71, 428, and cf. ch. vi, p. 59, ch. vii, p. 75, ch. ix, p. 95 ; Davis, *Med. England*, pp. 319–322. For the Crown lands of this period, see Round, *Antiquary*, vol. vi, p. 256 and vol. xiii, pp. 85–6, and especially Hubert Hall, *Antiquary*, vol. xiii, pp. 1–2 ; also the reports of the Commissioners of 1792, vol. xii, part i, p. 5.

King's land", thus placing the date of the change about the year 830. In a second and conflicting passage Stubbs stated, however, that the rights of the Crown over the public lands of the kingdom appear to have merged in the Crown demesne after the reign of Ethelred, so that by this statement he moved the period of the change from the ninth century to the eleventh, a date later than the year 1016, but probably during the rule of Danish kings in England.

The view of Dr. Hall, which Round commends on account of the scholar's caution with which it is expressed, and for the lack of sanction which it gives to Freeman's ill-considered statement, rests upon the thesis that the acquisition of an extensive royal demesne by the Crown was in the nature of an indirect bargain with the nation, whereby the former undertook duties of a more definite and extended character than the mere regulation of the royal household. No longer a mere tribal leader, the king had now to meet the immediate needs or prospective wants of a more complex community, and the Crown, therefore, enlarged its responsibilities by having the care of the national defence, the establishment of justice, and the maintenance of law, religion, and order. Dr. Hall argues that the Crown had shown a tendency from very early times to treat the folk lands as its own for purposes of State; that the existence of a theoretical check on the part of the Witan upon this pretension nevertheless failed to prevent alienation of national property; and further that owing to appropriation and feudal grants the residue of the folk lands had become not only unattractive, but of small extent and little value. Indeed it is arguable that owing to the nature of the physical structure of these lands, they had never been really valuable; for if we consider the state of the residual public lands, after their more attractive portions had been seized by earlier rulers, it is certain that wild districts of pathless woods, wastes, and forests would prove a refuge for lawless marauders as well as for beasts of the chase, so that like the highways and great rivers, these waste lands would become a source of actual danger to the community, and even a positive inducement to crime. The existence of these evil conditions and the persistence of anxiety and even fear led, in all probability, to the late discovery that the claims of the Crown in regard to the public lands were neither wholly interested nor entirely disadvantageous from a national point of view. The conclusion therefore reached by Dr. Hall is, that the change which Stubbs and others supposed to have been in progress since the Battle of Ellandune in 827, occurred " somewhere about the end of the ninth century ", when the Crown undertook the management and order of the folk land because it alone was qualified by the possession of equivalent territorial jurisdiction to do so—a change, he adds, which is " known to have been accomplished before the Conquest by the evidence of Domesday Book. Here we find the Crown actually in possession of the ancient folk land, which passes under the generic title of *terra regis*. There is not much evidence to show to what extent the latter benefited by this appropriation ", he admits, " and there is none at all to show when or how it took place." [1]

The acquisition of the folk lands by the Crown may perhaps be regarded as a " not very solid concession" because, as Dr. Hall reminds us, " the Sovereign was required to enter into that Constitutional contract with his subjects which runs through our history as an expansion of the Anglo-Saxon coronation oath, which guaranteed the liberties of all in matters of religion, laws, and justice." But for all that there was a profitable side to the undertaking. Bishop Stubbs groups the revenues of the Wessex Kings under two main heads, those essentially due to land, and those arising from sources other than land. In the first class he places the king's private estate, then the demesne of the Crown, and lastly the rights of the Crown over the folk lands. Now we may assume, with Dr. Hall, that the various component parts comprising the physical structure of the folk lands were transferred from public ownership to that of the Crown, as royal demesne, " in trust " for the natural rights of the subject, and that the exchange included an absolute jurisdiction over forests, wastes, highways, and river-courses (formulated in a later period as forest-law, conservancy, and " defence "), as well as a definite proprietorship in the case of existing farms and vills. In addition, therefore, to the farms cultivated by the Crown, there were others leased out to tenants, whose rent emerged in the shape of produce in kind, often in stock, rendered by the farmers or bailiffs. King Alfred, for example, had manors and lands under cultivation in several counties, and, as we know from his will, about £2,000 in money, besides the cattle which formed so large a share of property in those early times. Then there were the profits to be obtained from those sources other than land which Bishop Stubbs had in mind, namely the tolls and fines as well as the market and other dues paid by the travelling merchant ; the proceeds from courts of justice, national and perhaps forestal ; occasional escheats and forfeitures from time to time ; the net receipts in connection with mines and salt works, and shares of wrecks or treasure trove. In addition to all this there was a steady income to be derived from heriots and other payments of a semi-feudal kind ; but above all there was " the infinite vista of sport opened up to the Saxon monarch ", who so greatly loved the chase within the forest glades of so many of the southern shires of England. Such were the inducements that probably led to the acquisition of an extended royal demesne, and the assumption of greater responsibility for the preservation of peace. We may agree, therefore, with the Commissioners of Woods and Forests, who in 1792 expressed the opinion that, while in very early times the rents

[1] Hubert Hall, Introductory Note on the History of the Crown Lands, *Antiquary*, vol. xiii, pp. 1-2.

or produce of lands formed the principal source of revenue of all European sovereigns, in no country could it be so well ascertained as in England, what share of the land property was allotted for that purpose.[1]

Alienation of the royal lands, commencing at an early date, continued through the centuries, each sovereign making grants of lands to those who served or pleased him best, and although from time to time forfeitures doubtless redressed the balance, there was a tendency for the proportionate share of the nobles to increase. As will be seen from the list of early grants made by kings of the separate kingdoms of Essex, Kent, Mercia, and Wessex, between 660 and 870, and by those who were sole rulers of the realm in later days, the Church shares to a considerable extent in the alienations of royal property that occurred before the Norman Conquest. The recipients named in the early grants which follow include the Archbishop of Canterbury, the Bishops of Rochester and Winchester, the Abbots of Peterborough and Westminster, and the Priors of Lyminge and Reculver :—[2]

II. Early Grants of Royal Lands in England, 660–1060

Dates.	Kings.	Counties.	Places.
664	Wulfhere	Northants	Peterborough
679	Hlotharius	Kent	Isle of Thanet
c. 685	Caedualla	Sussex	Pagham
697	Wihtred	Kent	Wilmington
704	Suebred	Middlesex	Twickenham
732	Aethilberht	Kent	—
734	Aethilbald	,,	—
c. 757	,,	Middlesex	Yedding Green
c. 765	Eardulf	Kent	Perhamstede
774	Offa	,,	Lydd
778	Egcbert	,,	Bromley
778	Cynulf	Wiltshire	Bedwyn
c. 781	Ethelberht	Kent	Rochester
798	Coenuulf	,,	Hremping wiic
805	Cuthred	,,	Bocholt
822	Ceolwulf	,,	Mylentun
831	Wiglaf	Middlesex	Botwell
833	Ecgberht	Kent	Sandtun
839	Aetheluulf	,,	Canterbury
c. 860	Aethelberht	,,	Rochester
869	Burgred	Worcester (?)	Upthorp
895	Aelfred	Suffolk	Freckenham
931	Aethelstan	Wiltshire	Ham
940	Eadmund	Kent	Oswaldingtune
947	Eadred	Surrey	Merstham
956	Eadwig	Oxford	Cuddesdon
960	Eadgar	Berkshire	Ashbury
978	Aethelred	Middlesex	Lohtheres leage
986	,,	,,	Hampstead
987	,,	Kent	Bromley
1018	Cnut	,,	Haesel ersc wood
1042	Harthacnut	Hampshire (?)	Seolescumb
c. 1043	Edward Conf.	Kent	Cliffe
c. 1044	,,	Middlesex	Chalkhill

[1] *Reports of Commissioners of Woods and Forests*, vol. xii (1792), part i, p. 5.
[2] The List of Early land grants of the Saxon and Danish periods is based on Ellis's *Index to Charters and Rolls*, vol. ii, pp. 226–233. The earliest grant known in connection

It is quite probable that much of the folk land found its way by means of these grants into the possession of the Church, but the extent to which the nobles and clergy shared in the " stripping " of the public lands will never be known. Yet the fact remains that by the tenth century nothing remained of the folk lands but tracts of woodland, moor, and marsh, the highways and river beds, and those narrower tracts of soil that served as boundaries between parishes, hundreds, shires, and ancient tribal lands. Often the king conferred great rights and privileges upon the Church by his charters, and some of these gifts of " bocland " were passed on to individuals in the shape of leases, perhaps for two or three lives, the tenants discharging military service in return for their " laenland ", and paying *Church-scot* and other dues of the Church. Bede shows that some grants made by kings were due to weakness or to a desire to oblige favourites, and that when exemptions from military service accompanied these grants of land, they were a source of national danger, because persons having no claims to monastic character lived in some monasteries in a state of evil owing to idleness and sinful conduct, thus leaving the land to some extent undefended. Moreover, he reminds Archbishop Egbert of the numerous tracts of country which were of use neither to God nor man. In consequence of such practice on the part of the Crown the supply of secular militia tended to decrease, for so many persons appear to have had estates of this character under their control that there was little opportunity of bestowing grants of land upon veteran soldiers or the sons of nobles. In this way, as Cotes points out, the converse was reached from the early position of land grants as rewards for war service, a disintegrating tendency of feudalism which the Norman Conquest speedily checked.

Before the Norman Conquest, therefore, it is possible to find a feudal edifice of at least four stages—first, the King as supreme lord ; then the holders of " bocland " with their " courts ", and the power of making separate grants ; next the owners of " laenland ", rendering military service and special dues ; and lastly, the cultivators of the land, of two types, free and unfree. But in the making of that structure many races played a part, and beyond question the arrival of the Northmen had a most disturbing effect upon the existing division of the land, since, as conquerors of territory east and north of the Thames, and in the west of Mercia, they must have distributed the Crown lands very much to their own advantage, and at the same time confused the relationship between the classes by their settlement

with each of the separate kingdoms and for the realm as a whole under the later Saxon and Danish kings is recorded in the table, mere " confirmations " being excluded, except in two cases connected with Middlesex grants of the years 978 and 986, the first of which refers to a purchase of land made by Archbishop Dunstan.

of landless men, in an age when no social condition apart from land existed, except in ports such as London.

The proportionate shares of land held by the Crown, Church, and Baronage immediately before the Norman Conquest, are revealed by an analysis of the evidence recorded in Domesday Book. The late C. H. Pearson, in his *History of England*, 1867, placed the total valuation of recorded lands at £46,000 in the time of Edward the Confessor, but of this sum less than half related to lands in the possession of the Crown and the Church. This was still true after the Conquest when the total valuation had risen to £50,000, an increase of over 8 per cent, as the following table shows :—

III. TRIPARTITE DIVISION OF ENGLISH LANDS, 1065–1086

	Years	The Crown £	The Church £	The Barons £	Totals £
(a). Values	1065	9,363·3	13,176·1	23,204·7	45,744·1
	1086	9,900·6	14,703·2	25,054·1	49,657·9
(b). Per cent	1065	20·5	28·8	50·7	100·0
	1086	19·9	29·6	50·5	100·0

This division of the land before and after the Conquest, worked out so carefully in 1867, but expressed in percentage form for the first time above, reveals the curious fact that the Church alone gained by the Conquest, relatively speaking, the Crown and the Baronage showing proportionate losses in the new triangular balance of power. The proportionate share of the Crown is still least, but owing to its recent losses it is now less than a fifth of the total.

We may pursue this matter more closely if we examine the detailed valuations which Pearson gives for twenty-one counties, and rearrange them in such a way as to show the values for each of the areas (though nothing can be recorded for Wales) adopted in the present work. We then see that both before and after the Conquest the lands of the Barons exceeded in value those of the Crown and Church combined in seventeen of the twenty-one counties, the share of the Crown being least of all. But in the Borderland area this was not the case under Edward the Confessor, and it was even less true under William the Conqueror. Here the Crown made a slight gain and the Church a greater one. The lands of the Baronage, however, declined in value as a result of the Conquest. In the following table the first section (A) indicates the values for 1065, and the next section (B) those for 1086, as recorded in Domesday Book [1] :—

---

[1] The calculations shown in this table are based on the work of C. H. Pearson, *Hist. of England*, 1867, vol. i, app. D, pp. 665–9.

IV. TERRA REGIS AND OTHER LANDS IN DOMESDAY

(A) *Areas.*	*Cos.*	*The Crown.*	*The Church.*	*The Barons.*	*Totals.*
i. Metropolitan . .	10	3,007·1	6,433·5	14,728·9	24,169·5
ii. Extra-Metropolitan . .	7	2,141·3	2,187·9	4,837·6	9,166·8
iii. Border-Lands . .	4	2,437·1	1,717·6	3,402·3	7,557·0
Totals . . .	21	7,585·5	10,339·0	22,968·8	40,893·3
(B) *Areas*	*Cos.*	£	£	£	£
i. Metropolitan . .	10	3,461·6	7,181·1	14,903·9	25,546·6
ii. Extra-Metropolitan . .	7	2,964·0	2,694·9	6,417·0	12,075·9
iii. Border-Lands . .	4	2,444·4	1,882·2	3,374·5	7,701·1
Totals	21	8,870·0	11,758·2	24,695·4	45,323·6

CHAPTER III

THE NATURE OF THE CROWN LANDS

Three kinds of property in land were owned by the kings of the Heptarchy. There were the lands, first of all, that composed the private estate of the monarch ; these, with other lands that were acquired by him through the exercise of certain royal prerogatives, he might dispose of freely by will or otherwise. Next there were the demesne lands of the Crown, to alienate which required the consent of the Witan ; and thirdly, there were recognized rights which the sovereign enjoyed over his folk land. At the time of the Norman Conquest the royal demesne was extensive and of great value, consisting as it did not only of lands previously held by Edward the Confessor and his relatives, but of others that had been acquired by Edward and Harold in turn from the Saxon nobility by reason of escheat or forfeiture. After the Conquest, such lands as were in the immediate tenure of successive kings still consisted of three definite classes, but these were differently distinguished :—

(1) Lands regarded as " ancient demesne " of the Crown,
(2) Lands administered as " acquired demesne ",
(3) Residual lands, largely unenclosed.[1]

The extensive estates of Edward the Confessor which, in all probability, represented the remains of the ancient property enjoyed by the kings of the Heptarchy, appear to have been originally set apart as a special category of allodial lands for the purpose of maintaining the king and his household. Being recorded in Domesday under the title of *terra regis*, they became known for all future time as demesne land of the Crown, final appeal to that record deciding the question whenever it arose as to whether particular lands were ancient demesne or not. Yet the title " terra regis ", as Ballard observes, included other elements, since the Domesday officials had

[1] For the Norman period see Munro's article on Crown Lands in Palgrave's *Dict. of Polit. Econ.*, vol. i, p. 468 ; Slater, op. cit., pp. lxii–lxiii ; S. Bird's "Notes on Crown Lands", in *Antiquary*, xiii, pp. 89 *et seq.*, with Hall's introductory note, pp. 2–4 ; also Cotes, op. cit., vol. i, pp. 178, 271–4; Madox, *Hist. of Exchequer*, vol. i, and Ellis, *Introduction to Domesday*, vol. ii ; Davenant, *Discourse on Grants*, p. 105 ; Ballard, op. cit., pp. 85–8, and table C, p. 264. Ramsay's *Revenues of the Early Kings* deals with the reigns from Wm. I to Ric. II. Pearson's *Historical Maps of England* illustrate notes on Crown Lands and Church lands, pp. 56–61, 70 ; also his *History of England*, i, appendix D, pp. 661–670, contains valuable data concerning the rentals in numerous counties in Domesday. For references to this period in the Commissioners' Reports of 1792 and 1793, see vol. xii, part i, p. 5 ; vol. xv, app. No. 1, p. 21, No. 5, p. 31.

to register lands which came into the possession of William I under two main claims, namely, as heir to the estates which had belonged wholly or in part to the Saxon royal house, and as ultimate owner of those escheated lands formerly belonging to rebellious owners, some of whom were actually Normans. Ballard considered that the Commissioners made no distinction between the king's private possessions and the Crown lands because they found the differentiation too subtle for them to understand and use, but in certain passages which he quoted in regard to lands in Norfolk and Suffolk described as " terra regis de regione ", a contrast is made between the ancient demesne and other lands, perhaps those forfeited in recent years to the king. Scargill Bird, moreover, quotes other passages from the Exeter Domesday, as well as from the general survey of the Exchequer, which referring to lands described as " Dominicatus Regis " or " Dominicatus Regis ad Regnum pertinens " appear to sanction the suggestion that the demesne lands were regarded as the property of the nation, and not the private property of the king, who had the usufruct only of those lands. It was, therefore, considered a matter of grave national injustice for the monarch to dispose of any portion of the ancient demesne ; but although Cotton definitely states that the king might alienate escheats and not ancient demesne, there appears to be no authority whatever for such distinction in the actual practice of the Exchequer officials.[1]

Many cities and boroughs were vested in the Crown as part of the royal demesne, and most of these were committed to the care of custodes or farmers, but occasionally they were placed under the control of the citizens and burgesses themselves. Domesday records, for example, several in Devonshire, such as Barnstaple, Lidford, and Totnes, as well as the City of Exeter, in which the Conqueror held nearly three hundred houses. Ballard and Ellis both give a total of 7,968 burgesses recorded in the Survey, though why they should agree is not at all clear since Ballard's figures, tested in a group of seven counties,[2] show a total of 5,209, as compared with 4,261 in the case of Ellis, which indicates an excess for that group of over 20 per cent.[3] Under Henry I the Crown was seized of many of these Domesday boroughs, and in subsequent reigns their number was largely increased. Cambridge, Colchester, Exeter, Huntingdon, Ipswich, Malmesbury, and Northampton, all Domesday boroughs with their own mints, were in the hands of Henry I, as well as Carlisle (later, a chartered borough), Tamworth, and Winchcombe. With the exception of the

---

[1] S. Bird, op. cit., p. 89 ; Hall, op. cit., pp. 2–4 ; Reports of Commissioners, 1792, vol. xii, part i, p. 5.

[2] Devon, Hampshire, Lincoln, Norfolk, Nottingham, Suffolk, and Yorkshire.

[3] These figures are the results of computations by Ballard and Ellis ; the former records 1 thousand more burgesses than the latter in the seven counties indicated, but the two writers agree in regard to the figures for the rest of the country.

last two, all these towns were recognized as Chartered and Parliamentary Boroughs before 1307.[1]

In addition to the ancient demesne there was a class of royal property which, being acquired from time to time and held by virtue of certain prerogatives of the king, may be called the acquired demesne. These royal estates were in the main of two kinds, the tenures of the Crown being in the one case of a permanent, and in the other of a temporary character. The first kind, escheats proper, comprised lands which through want of heirs devolved upon the Crown as ultimate owner, or had been seized because of forfeitures for traitorous conduct or delinquencies of a feudal character. The temporary tenures, on the other hand, consisted of lands which were vested in the Crown for a short space by reason of the king's feudal superiority or because of the exercise of his prerogatives : these estates included the possessions of wards and minors, and occasionally those of abbeys and bishoprics during vacancies, sometimes enforced, in their sees. In course of time these miscellaneous possessions of the Crown became very numerous and profitable, for as long as they remained in the hands of the king they were treated as part of the royal demesne, but a wide distinction appears to have been made from an early date, namely, that while the lands of the ancient demesne were inalienable, those acquired in the above manner, being regarded as the king's private property, might be freely disposed of. While this theoretical distinction may be upheld, some justification for alienation at will is afforded by the recognition that, had the king not exercised his authority fully and frequently in this direction he would, beyond question and at no very distant date, have become absolute owner of the soil of England, thus regaining the position once held by the imperial rulers of Rome in regard to their conquered provinces. But that was not to be.

During the reigns of Henry I and Henry II between 1120 and 1184, the Crown was in possession of several important honours, baronies, and lands, with a number of hereditary offices and serjeanties of a miscellaneous kind, all of which were inscribed upon the Great Rolls of the Exchequer under their owners' names. Sometimes the words were added, " quae est in manu Regis," but seldom was there any indication of the cause whereby such escheats or forfeitures became vested in the Crown. The Estates of Dapifer, Peverell, and others were recorded in the rolls of 31 Henry I, while the lengthy list of forfeitures entered in 31 Henry II included the possessions of the Earls of Arundel, Gloucester, and Leicester.[2]

---

[1] These towns are recorded in Scargill Bird's list, op. cit., p. 90 ; Ellis, *Introd. to Domesday* ; Parliamentary Writs of Edw. I ; Ballard's *Dom. Inquest, Dom. Boroughs, and Brit. Bor. Charters.*

[2] The lists of 31 Hy. I and 31 Hy. II may be compared, for they show the honours, baronies, or lands of various families seized by those kings by reason of escheats or forfeitures. The property of the Earls of Boloigne, Leicester, Conan, and Giffard, and the

The greater escheats were usually committed to the care of particular bailiffs, though at times they were let to farm in the same way as the royal demesnes. Indeed, as Madox in his work on the Exchequer indicates, after long holding by the Crown these acquired estates could hardly be distinguished from the ancient demesne itself.[1]

Besides the ancient and acquired demesnes, national and private, of the Crown, there were other lands, of great antiquity in many cases, but largely unenclosed. These were the royal forest lands, the chases, and the parks, the distinctions between which will presently appear. From very early times the forests of England appear to have been regarded as the special property of the monarch, whose prerogative of unfettered jurisdiction was guarded with the utmost care. Although little is known of their origin, it may reasonably be surmised that they were portions of the public lands which before the Norman Conquest had remained uncultivated and unenclosed. Such portions of the Crown lands, therefore, not being objects of assessment, seldom appear in Domesday, where the only forests mentioned are those of Berkshire, Dorset, Hampshire, Oxford, and Wiltshire.[2]

Distinctions between forests, chases, and parks inevitably turn upon the essential facts of enclosure, administration, and, in a lesser degree, custody or ownership. Forests at no time were enclosed, being portions of territory of a woody and pastoral character, clearly circumscribed by well-known meets and bounds, within which the right of hunting was reserved for the exclusive use of the king. Being exempt from the ordinary law of the land, forests were subject to a special code of royal regulations, some of which were of great severity, administered in special courts by specially appointed officials. The Courts of the Forest were three in number, one superior, the Court of Justice Seat, and two inferior, namely, the Courts of Swainmote and Woodmote; these were held, the first every three years, the second every four months, and the Woodmote Court or Court of Attachments every forty days. Two Justices in Eyre of the Forests, one for the district north of the River Trent and the other for the larger territory south of that stream, were created early in the reign

lands belonging to de Curci, and Fitz-Alan were seized as early as 19 Hy. II. Those of Peverell were in the king's hands in 31 Hy. I, as well as 19 and 31 Hy. II. See Scargill Bird, op. cit., p. 90.

[1] For the Crown lands during the Plantagenet period see Davenant, op. cit., pp. 114–127, 148–150, 208, 249, 257–263, 281, 309, 316–353, 395 ; St. John, *Land Revenue*, pp. 48–60 ; Sinclair, *Hist. of Pub. Revenue*, pp. 51, 62–99, 229. See also Rolls of Parliament for many references for the period 18 Edw. I to 1485 in vol. i, pp. 42–311 ; vol. ii, pp. 10–440 ; vol. iii, pp. 8–625 ; vol. iv, pp. 46–373 ; vol. v, pp. 26–572 ; vol. vi, p. 71.

[2] Scargill Bird, op. cit., pp. 89–90 ; Hall, op. cit., pp. 2–4. It is remarked by the Commissioners of Woods and Forests that " the origin of none of the forests belonging to the Crown is to be found mentioned in any history or record ". See Commissioners' Reports, vol. iii, pp. 7–8. For Waste lands between 1306 and 1338 see Rolls of Parliament, vol. i, p. 194, vol. ii, p. 101 ; and P.R.O. List 37, Special Commissions and Returns in the Exchequer.

of Henry II, and these officials were specially appointed by each successive sovereign for the express purpose of presiding over the forest courts within their respective circuits. Here they tried offences presented by the two inferior courts, and decided pleas and all other matters that were concerned in the application and enforcement of the forest laws. The principal officers of the forests were six in number, of whom the verderers were of particular importance since they supervised all the others by reason of their position as judges of the Swainmote Court. Next in importance came the regarders and foresters, the first of whom were required to make a regard or survey of the forest every three years and to pursue inquiries into alleged offences concerning assarts or purprestures, and the second were charged with the preservation of the vert and venison, and also with the duty of attaching offenders and presenting them in the Woodmote Court. Then there were the agistors, men who regulated the agistment or pasturage of cattle within the forests, the woodwards and the stewards, and others of lesser degree.

As to the question of ownership, strictly speaking a forest could only belong to the king, for he alone had the power to create a Justice in Eyre of the Forests. And yet occasionally we do find a forest held by a subject, but in such cases the authority of the Crown was delegated by Special Commission. Edward II, for example, granted the Forests of Lancaster and Pickering to the Earl of Lancaster, and Richard II did the same with the Forest of Dean, which he granted to the Duke of Gloucester, but such kings were notoriously improvident, wasteful, and unpatriotic.

The royal forests are said by Scargill Bird to have been sixty-nine in number, only four of which, if we except the New Forest, are mentioned in Domesday. The formation of the New Forest, as he observes, added much obloquy to the Conqueror's memory, since it was by his order that Hampshire was largely laid waste for that purpose. Henry I, Richard I, and notably John made changes in the bounds of the forests, but, as Dr. Hall remarks, our knowledge of the domestic policy of the Norman kings fully prepares us for the encroachments in the direction of afforestation which they made, since these kings " undertook the administration of the national resources for ensuring law and order in return for a territorial enjoyment and profit becoming more and more invidious and absolute, and a territorial jurisdiction verging on tyranny, even as it is seen under the milder rule of the first Plantagenet ". In the Chartae de Foresta of the second and ninth years of Henry III, however, an attempt was made to remedy some of the evil consequences of the Assize of the Forest (1184), for it was now enacted that not only should the forests be restored to their ancient limits but that all portions definitely ascertained not to be ancient demesne of the King should be disafforested ; and to carry out the provisions of these Acts several perambulations of the forests were made during the reigns of Henry III and Edward I, the results of which were confirmed by the Statute of 1 Edward III, cap. 1.[1]

Like the forests, but unlike the parks, the chases were ancient unenclosed lands of a woody and pastoral character intended for the " infinite vista of sport " enjoyed so thoroughly by the monarchs of old. Unlike the forests, however, the chases had no special courts, and few special officers—keepers and woodwards only—consequently the special regulations of the forests did not apply. When, therefore, persons were punished for offences committed in the chase they paid the penalty under the milder code of laws which governed the rest of the kingdom. As there was no Justice in Eyre to be appointed to enforce decision in such cases, the ownership of a chase was not necessarily vested in the king. Altogether there appear to have been not more than thirteen chases in the kingdom.[2]

Parks and chases were of the same nature, being woody and pastoral lands, but they differed in the matter of enclosure, the park alone being enclosed within a wall or a pale. Like the chase, but unlike the forest, parks might be owned by any subject of the king. So large was the number of parks in the kingdom that, according to the computation of Scargill Bird, they exceeded seven hundred before the Commonwealth period.[3]

From all these various sources, then—ancient demesne, acquired demesne, and residual lands—with subsidiary sources of revenues acquired through the ingenuity of departmental officers in different reigns, the revenues of the crown were derived. In the following table we see how the valuations of crown lands and revenues varied in the reigns of Edward the Confessor, William I, Henry I, and Henry II. The number of counties involved in these calculations, is, however,

---

[1] Scargill Bird, op. cit., part ii, pp. 91–2 ; Hall, op. cit., p. 2 ; Ellis, op. cit., vol. i, pp. 103–116 ; Pearson, *Hist. Maps,* pp. 44–8. For the history of the Forests, see Cox, *The Royal Forests of England.* The Commissioners of Wood and Forests detail the legislation of three periods, namely, prior to 1535, then to 1700, and 1700 to 1792. See the Commissioners' Reports for grant of custody temp. Henry II of the forest of Essex, vol. xv, app. No. 5, p. 31 ; exemplication of a Charter of disafforestation of part of the same forest, 25th March, 5 John, confirmed 8 Edw. IV, vol. xv, app. No. 1, p. 21 ; the forest laws of various periods, from 9 Henry III to 9 Geo. III, *c.* 41, vol. iii, pp. 7–10, and vol. xi, pp. 12–16 ; land measures and the Statute of Forests, 2 Hy. III, vol. xiv, app. No. 12, pp. 35–6 ; inquisition concerning the forest of Sherwood, 35 Hy. III, vol. xiv, app. No. 13, pp. 37–8 ; various perambulations of the forest of Salcey, Northants, 27 Edw. I, vol. vii, app. No. 1, p. 21 ; Whittlewood, 27 Edw. I, vol. viii, app. No. 1, pp. 27–9 ; Aliceholt and Woolmer, 28 Edw. I, vol. vi, app. No. 1, pp. 33–4 ; Bere, Hants, 28 Edw. I, vol. xiii, app. No. 1, p. 19 ; and of the forest of Sherwood, Notts, 28 Edw. I, vol. xiv, app. No. 1, p. 21 and app. No. 12, pp. 35–6 ; also a grant of common of pasture and pannage in Sherwood forest, 8th September, 37 Edward III, vol. xiv, app. No. 14, p. 38. For references to forest lands in the Rolls of Parliament between 1306 and 1314, see vol. i, pp. 200, 317, and the Index Volume under Woods and Forests.

[2] Cox, op. cit., p. 2, and the various Chases recorded under the different counties of England. For free chase and free warren see Rolls of Parliament, vol. i, p. 178, under date 33 Edw. i, 1305.

[3] Cox, op. cit., p. 2, and the various references to parks among the counties of England.

not uniform. For the period 1065–1086 it is twenty-one, and for the year 1130 there is an increase to twenty-four, but for *c.* 1180 no less than thirty-six of the thirty-nine English counties are represented.[1]

V. VALUATIONS OF CROWN LANDS AND REVENUES, 1065–1180

Areas.	1065.	1086.	1130.	c. 1180.
(i) Metropolitan . .	3,007·1	3,461·6	2,234·5	3,612·5
(ii) Extra-Metropolitan	2,141·3	2,964·0	3,254·9	5,218·5
(iii) Border-Lands .	2,437·1	2,444·4	1,195·8	2,574·1
Totals . .	7,585·5	8,870·0	6,685·2	11,405·1

[1] The table is compiled from Pearson's figures for 1065 and 1086, and Ramsay's *Revenues of the King of England*, vol. i, pp. 61, 192.

CHAPTER IV

THE REVENUES DERIVED FROM CROWN LANDS

The revenue of the Crown in early feudal times was to a large extent derived, as we may readily see, from lands in the immediate tenure of the king, and as such lands varied in extent and composition throughout the centuries the natural income of the Crown expanded or contracted with the thrift or improvidence of the various sovereigns. Sir James Ramsay has very carefully distinguished between the land revenues of the period 1065–1485 and the total revenues enjoyed by the individual sovereigns during that period.[1] From the calculations which follow in the next table it appears that the natural income from land varied from £600 under Stephen to £25,000 in the reign of Richard II, and that considerable reductions occurred through the improvidence of Richard I, John, and Edward III. The proportion of land revenue to total revenue, which reached 60 per cent between 1066 and 1272, subsequently declined owing to its relative unimportance and barely exceeded 30 per cent in 1485. Even in the reign of Elizabeth, whose income from land amounted to more than £182,000 in 1601–2, the land revenue formed only 36 per cent of the total revenue of the Crown.[2]

Apart from the evidence of Domesday, we find the land revenue of the Crown derived from three elements which, as set forth in the Pipe Rolls of Henry I, and Henry II, were called (*a*) the farms (*fundi regii*), (*b*) the feudal acquisitions, and (*c*) the forestal lands.[3] Now

---

[1] For the revenues of the various kings from Wm. I to Ric. II see Ramsay, op. cit., vol. i, pp. 1, 5, 53, 62, 64, 197, 228, 262; vol. ii, pp. 1, 91, 150, 296; also Commissioners' Reports, vol. xii, part i, pp. 5–6; and Rolls of Parliament, Index Volume, vii, under " Crown lands ". The revenues of the Prince of Wales, Earl of Chester, and Duke of Cornwall are recorded for Edw. III and 44 Eliz. by St. John, op. cit., pp. 75–6, who quotes a curious treatise by Sir Jn. Doderidge; cf. Sinclair, op. cit., vol. i, p. 229 for Edw. I and the Black Prince. Ramsay's accounts of Edw. V and Ric. III will be found in the *Antiquary*, vol. xviii, pp. 241–6, tables ii and iii referring to the income of the latter king between 1483 and 1485. P.R.O. List 37, revised from D.K.P.R., report 38, contains a large number of documents relating to special Commissions and returns in the Exchequer, issued for the purpose of instituting inquiries into matters affecting Crown revenues; some of them are surveys of royal castles, manors, and parks, and certificates relating to the spoil of Crown woods.

[2] This table is based on Sir J. H. Ramsay's *Revenues of the Early Kings*, vol. i, pp. 1–4, 7, 53–5, 60, 63, 105–6, 232–4, 274; vol. ii, 81, 86, 144, 146, 293, 427; also the *Antiquary*, vol. 18, pp. 241–6. The account for the year 44 Eliz. 1601–2 is referred to in the *Account of Manors, etc.*, 1787, app. ii, pp. 79–80. The figures for Edward I and Edward II are described as " Hereditary Revenues ", and those of Edward III to Richard III as " Old Crown Revenues ".

[3] Scargill Bird, op. cit., part ii, pp. 89–92; Hall, op. cit., p. 3; and see the notes in Commissioners' Reports, vol. xii, p. 5.

VI. THE LAND REVENUE OF THE EARLY KINGS, 1086–1485

Reigns.	Land Revenue. £	Percentage of Total Revenue.
William I	12,000	60
William II	15,000	60
Henry I	11,180	42
Stephen	600	30
Henry II	11,040	58
Richard I	3,500	35
John	8,930	36
Henry III	14,635	59
Edward I	20,000	29
Edward II	20,000	22
Edward III	7,360	5
Richard II	25,100	21
Richard III	17,900	31

the farms were those ancient allodial estates already referred to as having been originally assigned to the monarchs of early Saxon England, or else acquired by them by the exercise of their prerogatives in later Saxon times—all of which were known in days subsequent to Domesday as ancient demesne of the Crown. As these lands, and such boroughs as were established upon them, had been set apart at first for the purpose of maintaining the king and his household, the rents paid for them by the tenants consisted in the earliest period of the produce of farms, and sometimes cloth, silks, and other necessary goods. After 1100 it was more usual for these fixed rents of the demesne lands and manors to be paid in money.[1]

As most of these cities and boroughs, the lordship of which was vested in the Crown, were under the control of custodes or farmers or in exceptional cases of the citizens or burgesses themselves, certain fixed rents known as " fee-farm rents ", generically defined as the *firma burgi*, had to be rendered for them annually at the Exchequer.[2]

From the second of the elements, the feudal acquisitions, collectively composing the Crown Lands, as indicated in the entries of those early Pipe Rolls, arose a variety of rents and profits, for all such feudal estates, knights' fees, honours, or baronies as were occupied by the Crown, either as lord of the fee, or in the last resource as lord paramount, by reason of escheat, forfeiture, or resumption. During the period these lands were retained, the king enjoyed the reliefs, wardships, marriages, and other profits connected with them, putting the greater fees to farm, and placing the lesser fees and the smaller forfeitures in the care of responsible officers. From all of these sources of profit the Crown derived a considerable income, for the sums received included not only the annual values of the lands, hereditary offices, and serjeanties for the period, sometimes prolonged, they devolved upon the Crown, but the varying fines

[1] Jacob, *Law Dictionary*, art. " Ancient Demesne ". The income from ancient demesne after the Conquest is estimated by Ramsay, *Revenue of Early Kings*, vol. i.
[2] Hall, op. cit., p. 3 ; Jacob, op. cit., art. " Fee-farm Rents of the Crown ".

which their former owners more or less willingly paid to have them restored.[1]

No considerable revenue might be expected to emerge from the third source, the Residual Lands, because the forest lands were reserved to the king for the express purpose of pleasure and sport. But important sums, nevertheless, came into the Exchequer from rents, licences, and assessed fines, and these find expression in the entries in the Pipe Rolls of accounts periodically rendered for purprestures and assarts, in connection with encroachments of various kinds, or such clearings of forest growths as were permissive by royal licence with the intention of reducing the land to cultivation. There were also fines and amercements imposed by the forest courts, and the various sums received for the agistment of cattle.[2]

In this way the Crown derived its " land revenues " ; but these were only a part of the royal revenues enjoyed by the early kings of this country. Amongst the numerous payments rendered, chiefly by the Sheriff, into the Exchequer were the sums arising from the assessments known as tallages, which, whenever the royal necessities demanded, were made by the king's Justices Itinerant or other specially deputed officials upon all demesne lands, with their cities and boroughs, and all honours and lands acquired by the king through resumption, forfeiture, or escheat. This right of tallage was of such importance, that whenever manors were demised or towns granted in fee farm, it was almost invariably reserved to the king and his successors ; and even, on those rare occasions when tallage was included in the grant, it could only be utilized by the grantee at the time when the king himself tallaged his own demesnes. When these assessments are compared, moreover, it is found that the tallages paid by the tenants of the ancient demesnes of the Crown were heavier than those paid by others in the country at large, so that petitions were not infrequent from those who held their estates by different tenures to be tallaged with the rest of the shire instead of with the tenants above mentioned. Sometimes the tallages assessed upon the men of the demesne lands or the citizens and burgesses of the associated towns were indicated by a gross sum (*in communi*) which the custos or farmer, or the mayor and bailiffs rendered to the Exchequer, the sum being subsequently apportioned amongst the tenants and burgesses in proportion to the extent of their tenures ; but at other times the tallage was distributed as an amount *per capita*, or in the form of a poll tax.[3]

Tenants of lands held in ancient demesne, of course, escaped the payment of scutage, since this liability rested not upon those who

---

[1] Jacob, op. cit., art. " Forfeiture and Resumption ".
[2] Jacob, op. cit., art. " Agistment, Assart, and Purpresture ". Hone, *The Manor*, 176, 206, 219.
[3] Jacob, op. cit., art. " Tallage ".

had been responsible for the maintenance of the royal household but upon those whose tenure by knights service provided for the king's defence. As if in compensation for this practice, tenants of ancient demesne, upon the commencement of military operations, were called upon to pay an auxilium or voluntary aid to meet the expenses connected with the feeding of the king's host—a demand which, upon refusal, led to the assessment of a tallage, amounting at the most to a tenth of their goods, sometimes before (though usually after) the expedition had returned. As the assessments levied on the knights' fees were variable and the contributions of the other tenants were distinguished by their fixed amount, these two payments are sometimes called *escuage variable* and *escuage certain* respectively.[1]

During the Tudor period the land revenues of the Crown continued to expand in spite of grants and numerous sales, for the confiscations, especially of monastic property, were on an extensive scale during that period. The revenue derived from land in the reign of William I has already been given as £12,000, an amount which was more than doubled under Richard II. In two generations, after 1540, the Crown revenues from this source rose rapidly from £38,260 in Henry VIII's reign and £86,690 in that of Mary, to £182,146 at the close of Elizabeth's reign. A more detailed statement of these revenues appears in the following table :—

VII. Valuations of Crown Lands and Revenues, 1086–1555 [2]

Areas.	Counties.	William I, 1086. £	Henry VIII, 1541. £	Mary, 1555. £
(i) Metropolitan	10	3,461·6	5,989·6	20,751·3
(ii) Extra-Metropolitan	16	2,964·0	9,725·9	34,405·1
(iii) Border-Lands	13	2,444·4	16,234·2	26,210·5
(iv) Wales . . .	13	—	6,310·7	5,323·9
Totals . .	52	8,870·0	38,260·4	86,690·8

[1] Jacob, op. cit., art. " Scutage, Escuage, and Tallage ".
[2] This table is compiled from several sources. The figures for the reign of William I are based on Pearson's calculations, 1867. Those recorded for Henry VIII are obtained from the writer's analysis of the very choice and hitherto unquoted volume, Add. MS. 32469, in the British Museum. The remainder are based on material recorded in the *Account of Manors*, 1787. Of the counties twenty-one are represented in the column for 1086, but the others include forty-nine and fifty-one respectively.

INCHES.

EXCHEQUER TALLIES : SURREY

[*face*

CHAPTER V

VARIATION IN EXCHEQUER METHODS OF ACCOUNTANCY

Having considered the origin, nature, and profits of the Crown lands, reference may now be made to the various accountants at the Exchequer, and the different methods by which the revenues arising from Crown lands were controlled. The chief agents for the collection of the land revenue were, as we have seen, the sheriffs of the different Counties of England and Wales, accounting as custodes or as farmers, though there were various bailiffs, reeves, feodaries, and other ministers and receivers of importance who were accountants also at the yearly audit of the Exchequer. Subsequently, district officers known as escheators, later still as General Surveyors and Auditors of the Land Revenue, were appointed to manage the large revenues that accrued during the centuries within their respective territorial jurisdictions.[1]

To the sheriffs were committed the manors and lands within their bailiwicks, either as custodes or bailiffs (in which case the issues of each estate were accounted for separately) or as "fermers", which was the usual plan. The entire rents of the king within the county limits being thus "let to farm", the sheriff rendered a fixed sum for these annually, the Exchequer officials deducting amounts for lands no longer in the king's possession, the issues of which were now beyond the responsibility of the sheriff. This fixed annual payment was called the "firma comitatus" or "corpus comitatus", the farm or body of the Shire.[2]

It was usual every year to record upon the sheriff's account the various items of the "terrae datae". As this involved almost endless repetition in regard to the alienations of Crown Lands, it was enacted by the Statute of Rutland, 2 Edward I, that in future a separate roll should be provided in which the "corpus comitatus" and the "terrae datae" up to that period should be entered, the labours of the clerks of the Pipe being greatly lessened by this "Rotulus de corporibus comitatuum". After this date, therefore, the sheriff's

---

[1] Scargill Bird, op. cit., part ii, pp. 92–5, quoting Madox, *Hist. of Exchequer*, vol. i ; Hall, op. cit., p. 3, quoting *Dialogus de Scaccario*, vol. ii, 10. A very full account of the system of the Exchequer, based on the same record, is given by Ramsay, in his *Revenues of the Early Kings*, vol. i, pp. 8–52 ; this account is divided into four parts, which relate to (1) the Abacus, tallies and Lower Chamber, (2) the Upper Chamber, (3) the Audit, and (4) the Branches of the Revenue.
[2] Jacob, op. cit., art. "Sheriff".

account began with the words, " Corpus hujus Comitatus annotatur in Rotulo . . .", and then proceeded to the " Remanens firmae post terras datas ".[1]

Seldom were the fee farm rents of cities and boroughs placed upon the sheriff's account, for these were rendered separately by the custodians or farmers within whose jurisdiction they lay. When the work of the Exchequer was of comparatively small extent, as in the early days of public finance, these items appeared on the Pipe Rolls or the Chancellors' Rolls ; but as the rolls became more and more unmanageable in size they were supplemented by the " Rolls of Foreign Accounts ", upon which were recorded the fee farm rents, as well as those accounts of the collectors of Customs and of various keepers (as of the Wardrobe and the royal mints) which were regarded as foreign to the ordinary jurisdiction of the sheriff.[2]

The method of accounting for the escheats varied with their importance, the profits arising from the lands of inferior persons being returned at first by the sheriffs of the counties in which these lands were situated, under the title " De escaetis et purpresturis ". But as the greater escheats, like the fee farm rents, were seldom left in the jurisdiction of the sheriffs, the usual practice was for the accounts to be rendered at the Exchequer by the particular persons to whom they had been let to farm or by the actual custodians themselves. These entries of escheats appear at an early date upon the Pipe Rolls, but later the accounts were enrolled upon the Rolls of Foreign Accounts.[3]

At an early period, too, district officers called at first " custodes escaetarum ", and later escheators, were specially appointed to manage the Crown revenues arising from escheats and forfeitures, the entire kingdom being subdivided about the middle of the reign of Henry III into two escheatries for this purpose, styled " Citra Trentam " and " Ultra Trentam ", in much the same way as were divided the two provinces of the Archbishops of Canterbury and York. This arrangement, with a short interval, continued for almost seventy years until 17 Edward II, from which year until the close of the reign the system of escheatries underwent frequent changes. Eventually it was superseded by a more elaborate scheme, the district north of the Trent, with the exception of Lancashire, remaining as before, while the rest of the kingdom was divided into seven separate districts, each consisting of a group of counties,[4] namely :—

---

[1] Jacob, op. cit., art. " Alienation ". See also the various items relating to " Terrae Datae " for early kings in Ramsay, op. cit., vol. i.

[2] Hall, op. cit., p. 3 ; Jacob, op. cit., art. " Borough ".

[3] Jacob, op. cit., art. " Escheat and Purpresture ".

[4] These Escaetorial divisions of the period 1250-1334 were finally abolished between 1645 and 1660. See Scargill Bird, *Guide to the Principal Classes of Documents preserved in the Public Record Office*, 1891, p. 108 ; and Giuseppi, *Guide to the Manuscripts preserved in the Public Record Office*, vol. i, p. 92.

1. Kent, Middlesex, Surrey, and Sussex.
2. Bedford, Berkshire, Buckingham, Hampshire, Oxford, and Wiltshire.
3. Cambridge, Essex, Hertford, Huntingdon, Norfolk, and Suffolk.
4. Derby, Lancaster (for a time), Leicester, Nottingham, and Warwick.
5. Lincoln, Northampton, and Rutland.
6. Gloucester, Hereford, Shropshire, Stafford, Worcester, and Marches of Wales.
7. Cornwall, Devon, Dorset, and Somerset.
8. Cumberland, Northumberland, Westmorland, York (and for a time Lancaster).

In 8 Edward III, 1334–1335, therefore, the revenues from Crown lands were controlled by these eight escheatries and their officials. The rolls of accounts known as " Escheators' Accounts ", together with the inquisitions which accompany them, contain very full particulars of the extent and value of the lands which from time to time were seized by the king, and the reasons for which they were taken into his possession.[1]

Subsequently the Sheriff of each county (or group of two counties) was appointed Escheator, and the arrangement of the Escheatries thereby became identical with that of the Counties at the Exchequer. At the beginning of the reign of Richard II, in 1377, the country was divided into nineteen Escheatries, each of two counties—with the exception of Lincoln, Worcester, and York, which stood alone, the joint county districts of Gloucester and Hereford, Shropshire and Stafford, which shared the Marches of Wales, and the three-county group of Cumberland, Northumberland, and Westmorland. The officials of the palatine counties of Chester, Durham, and Lancaster did not account at the Exchequer with the other counties.[2]

The early practice of accounting for forest rents through the sheriff on the Pipe Rolls was followed subsequently by the plan of making the several foresters responsible, the accounts of these " custodes forestarum " appearing in consequence upon the Rolls of Foreign Accounts. These Rolls, supplemented by a large series of original forest accounts in the *Miscellaneous Accounts of the Exchequer*, cover the reigns from Henry III to James I. After the establishment in the reign of Henry VIII of the two special Courts of the Augmentations and the General Surveyors,[3] the forest management was entrusted to special officers who accounted for the revenues to those courts.[4]

[1] Jacob, op. cit., art. " Escheator ". For the records dealing with Escheats, attainders, and forfeitures, see Scargill Bird's *Guide*, pp. 107–113, and Giuseppi, *Guide to Public Records*, vol. i, index, p. 374. The division of the country into Escaetorial districts between the reigns of Henry III and Henry V is shown in Bird's *Guide*, p. 108 ; the subsequent division into Auditor's Districts is indicated by Giuseppi, p. 170.

[2] For the methods of controlling the Land Revenues of the Crown after the reign of Henry III see Scargill Bird's note in the *Antiquary*, xiii, pp. 92–5.

[3] For this Court and its records see Giuseppi, *Guide to the Public Records*, vol. i, index, p. 378.

[4] Jacob, op. cit., art. " Forests ". For the Forest records see Bird's *Guide*, pp. 125–8, and Giuseppi's *Guide*, vol. i, index, p. 377.

With the accession of Henry VII the practice began of taking lands out of the direct survey or control of the Exchequer, the reason being that the new king desired to ensure a more speedy payment of the revenues due to him. For this purpose he appointed Sir Robert Southwell and others as Special Commissioners [1] to take the accounts of such lands orally and pay in the revenues to the king direct in his chamber or to some person expressly appointed to receive them for his use. The Treasurer of the King's Chamber kept the necessary bills or books, signed with the royal sign manual, but the books themselves were not regarded as a sufficient discharge to the accountants, who were still required to follow the ordinary course of the Exchequer.

This new scheme of Henry VII was utilized by his successor, who in 1510 appointed Sir Robert Southwell, and Westby, one of the Barons of the Exchequer, surveyors of the lands of the Crown,[2] naming them in 1511 " General Surveyors and Approvers of the King's Lands ", and giving them at the same time authority to call accountants before them to render their accounts in the " Prince's Chamber " at Whitehall. By this means Henry VIII improved upon the hitherto cumbrous method which, to be lawful, required process issuing from the Exchequer. In the year following he took the further step of including in a special Act a schedule of the lands and revenues which were henceforth to be under the control of the General Surveyors, whose powers were confirmed and amplified in five subsequent Acts between 1514 and 1535. The greatest change of all, however, occurred six years later, in the statute of 33 Henry VIII, cap. 39, when the king placed the General Surveyors in a position which made them independent of any other external authority or jurisdiction in regard to the estates under their control, namely those specified in the schedule of the Act of 1522-1523, which included all the lands accruing to the sovereign by attainder, escheat, or forfeiture. Provision was made by this statute for the erection of a court of record, henceforth to be known as the " Court of the General Surveyors of the King's Lands ",[3] composed of the King's Surveyor and Attorney, the Treasurer of the King's Chamber and a Master of the Woods. This court possessed a privy seal, and included such auditors and receivers as were appointed from time to time by the king, but its life was of short duration for in 1546 the court was abolished.

Some years earlier, by the statute of 27 Henry VIII cap. 27, another court had been established for the purpose of controlling the revenues

---

[1] The duties of the " Special Commissioners ", created c. 1485, were modified in 1510.
[2] The style of the " Surveyors of King's Lands ", 1510, was improved the following year.
[3] The Court, with its schedules of 1522-1523, only lasted from 1541 to 1546. The office of Surveyor-General of Crown Lands, and of Woods and Forests, originally dating from c. 1552, was abolished in 1809 in favour of Commissioners of H.M. Woods, Forests, and Land Revenues.

arising from dissolved monastic estates, as well as the lands acquired by purchase or exchange. This "Court of the Augmentations of the Revenues of the Crown"[1] was composed of a Chancellor (who was empowered to make grants under the Privy seal of the Court), Treasurer, Attorney, and Solicitor (with specially appointed auditors and receivers). In 1546 it was superseded by a new Court of the Augmentations with many officials: a Chancellor, empowered as before to make grants, two surveyors, and two Masters of the Woods for the districts north and south of the Trent, ten auditors of the revenues and two others of the prests and foreign accounts, eleven receivers of revenues, an attorney, as well as a solicitor and clerk. The new authority,[2] which in turn was abolished at the commencement of Queen Mary's reign, had complete jurisdiction over the whole of the revenues hitherto under the survey of the two earlier courts (the Augmentations and the General Surveyors), and the prospective revenues that might ensue from future acquisitions by the Crown of honours, castles, seigniories, manors, and lands within England, Wales, Calais, and the recognized Marches, obtained by Acts of Parliament, gifts, grants, surrenders, bargains and sales and attainders, escheats, and forfeitures. One exception to these extensive powers occurred in the case of the Duchy of Lancaster property, the honours and manors remaining as before within the survey of the Court of Exchequer.[3]

Another of the Courts of Henry VIII arose in 1540, perhaps from a desire to conciliate tenants whose complaints in the Exchequer were frequent concerning the injustice and partiality of the escheators, but more probably because the king desired to be "better served" with the incident profits of the various tenures *in capite*, a considerable portion of the land revenue of the Crown being derived from this source. To this "Court of Wards"[4] the liveries of lands were added in the following year, and the "Court of Wards and Liveries" thus established continued until its virtual suppression in 1645 and its complete abolition in the reign of Charles II.[5]

In the first year of Queen Mary's reign, by the statute 1 Mary, cap. 10, the business formerly transacted by the powerful Court of the Augmentations was transferred once again to the control of the Exchequer; but as the Act directed that the future collection of the revenues should be either by the ancient mode through individual sheriffs, or the more modern method through persons specially appointed by the Lord Treasurer, it would appear that the latter mode

---

[1] This Court lasted from 1535 until its abolition in 1546.
[2] The second Court of the Augmentations, 1546, was abolished in 1552.
[3] For the records of this Court, see Giuseppi, *Guide*, vol. i, index, p. 359.
[4] The Court of Wards, 1540, was enlarged in 1541; its successor was abolished 1645–1660.
[5] For the records of this court see Bird's *Guide* ("Wards and Minors"), pp. 336–8, and Giuseppi's *Guide*, vol. i, index, p. 407.

was considered to be the better plan and accordingly prevailed. The rents and profits were therefore collected and the accounts rendered in the same form as before the abolition of the Court, though not quite in the same manner since the payments were now made into the Receipt of the Exchequer. The sheriff, however, continued still to be responsible for such rents as were charged upon him in connection with the " firma comitatus ". Under the new arrangement the accounts were rendered before the " Auditors of the Land Revenue ", seven officials of the Exchequer, reduced from their former number of ten.[1] By this arrangement there were six auditors for England and one for Wales, the officials of course being distinct from the Auditors of Imprest (who were subsequently merged in the Office of the Commissioners for auditing public accounts), while the Counties within their respective divisions were grouped as follows :—

1. Cambridge, Essex, Hertfordshire, Huntingdon, Middlesex, Norfolk, and Suffolk.
2. Bedford, Berkshire, Buckingham, Kent, Oxford, Surrey, and Sussex.
3. Cornwall, Devon, Dorset, Gloucester, Hampshire, Somerset, and Wiltshire.
4. Cumberland, Hereford, Lancaster, Leicester, Northampton, Rutland, Shropshire, Stafford, Warwick, Westmorland, and Worcester.
5. Durham, Northumberland, and York.
6. Chester, Derby, Lincoln, and Nottingham.
7. Monmouth, North and South Wales.

[1] For the records of the Auditor's office see Giuseppi, *Guide,* vol. i, index, p. 385, also the special section in vol. ii, pp. 114–118. The seven auditors of 1552–1553 were reduced to three in 1706 and finally the title of " Auditors of the Land Revenue " was abolished. In 1832 the office of " Land Revenue Records and Enrolments " was established. Commissioners of H.M. Woods, Forests, and Land Revenues had been appointed since 1809, but in 1924 the title was changed to Commissioners of Crown Lands.

Chapter VI

SALES OF CROWN LANDS BEFORE THE STUART PERIOD

The expedient of selling royal estates and fee farm rents after the execution of Charles I was not entirely a departure from the ordinary practice of alienations adopted by the State in previous reigns. In the solitary Pipe Roll of 31 Henry I it is possible to see the process of alienation of the royal lands in operation by means of grants to officials or sales to the king's subjects, and the same kind of evidence is available as to sales of Crown lands under Henry II. In the reign of Henry III, when the first of the Resumptions of royal property took place—a precedent which the Parliament of Charles II attempted to follow in 1660—the adherents of Simon De Montfort were allowed to procure their lands at the rate of five years' purchase under the terms of the Dictum of Kenilworth. The fatal expedients of Resumptions—a plan whereby " bankrupt monarchs discharge through the graces of Ministers of Parliament "—proved to be the consequence of the feudal concessions made by such weak kings as Stephen, Henry III, Edward II, Richard II, and Henry VI, and the parliamentary remedy thus provided began to play an important part in the administration of the Crown lands during Plantagenet times, being frequently set in motion. Nothing indeed was easier to accomplish, because the principle involved was simply this : What the Nation through the King had bestowed, the Nation through Parliament might take away.[1]

The process involving the transference of the ownership of landed estates in England, begun by the collapse of the Baronage after Bosworth Field and continued by the fall of the Monastries and the attack on the Church,[2] was accomplished in part by the land sales of

---

[1] See Appendix, Bibliography, ZA to ZC, for the period 1100–1485.

[2] Dr. Savine gives a list of monastic revenues appropriated by the Crown between 1536 and 1540 in the appendix to his work on the Fall of the Monasteries. The " net monastic income ", based on the figures of the Valor Ecclesiasticus of 1534, is shown to have varied in the Metropolitan area from £9 in Hertford to £2,433 in Kent ; in the Extra-Metropolitan area from £1 in Huntingdon, to £3,312 in Somerset ; and from £7 in Worcester, to £1,650 in Yorkshire, in the Borderlands. Wales is not mentioned in the summary of incomes. The differences between maxima and minima in each county may be arranged according to areas as follows : *Area I* : Kent, £2,393 ; Middlesex, £2,345 ; Herts, £2,093 ; Berks, £1,919 ; Sussex, £892 ; Surrey, £888 ; Essex, £871 ; Oxford, £642 ; Bucks, £423 ; Bedford, £352. *Area II* : Somerset, £3306 ; Northampton, £1,716 ; Suffolk, £1,649 ; Hunts, £1,642 ; Hants, £1,465 ; Dorset, £1,136 ; Cambridge, £1,069 ; Lincoln, £941 ; Leicester, £927 ; Norfolk, £869 ; Wilts, £778 ; Warwick, £522 ; Staffs, £414 ; Notts, £320 ; Derby, £248 ; Rutland, £40 ; (only one). *Area III* : Yorks, £1,643 ; Gloucs, £1,329 ; Durham, £1,304 ; Worcester, £1,290 ; Cheshire, £963 ; Devon, £872 ; Lancs, £785 ; Shropshire, £465 ; Cumberland, £465 ; Northumberland, £386 ; Cornwall, £343 ; Hereford, £253 ; Westmorland, £155 ; (only one).

the Tudor monarchs. In the Letters and Papers of Henry VIII between 1539 and 1547 there is abundant evidence of the extent to which this was carried on. In the years 1539 to 1543, for example, sales were authorized of lands which had a yearly value of at least £17,000; while in the next year, 1544, four amounts are recorded showing that the land sales produced no less than £237,226. The Policy of sale was continued after Henry VIII's death, as we see from the State Papers of Edward VI's reign, 1547 to 1553.[1]

Liljegren in his work on the Fall of the Monastries, thought that it was only natural that Mary should " put a stop to a process which was so injurious to the Catholic Church, though she had to suffer the poor land question to remain in *statu quo*. Her treasury accordingly was empty ". He gives a dozen references from the Calendar of State Papers, but does not appear to have examined any of them, or he would have discovered that at least four of the entries refer to Commissioners of Sales,[2] and that in one case the Queen writes to the Lord Mayor and Aldermen of London expressing a desire to borrow. 100,000 marks in the City, on the security of the Crown lands, promising to dispense with the Act of Usury in favour of those who will lend money to her.[3]

Liljegren also came to the conclusion that " it was equally obvious that the reign of Elizabeth should continue the policy initiated by her father, just where her brother had left off ". In explanation of this he adds a footnote with an imposing array of references to the Calendars of State Papers—over 270 pages are cited— but unfortunately he omits to test the entries, with the result that he commits himself to a rather bad blunder when he declares that " Elizabeth, however, had often ample revenues without having to ask parliament for money, or being obliged to sell Crown lands ".[4]

The magnitude of the alienations of Crown lands under Elizabeth has been perceived by few writers, consequently the subject is worthy of separate investigation. There appear to have been three periods of sales during her reign, one before and two after the destruction of the Spanish Armada. These periods were as follows :—

(*a*) *First Period*: 1558–1568.—The sale of Crown lands pro- ceeded very slowly at first, Sir Nic. Bacon and other Commissioners writing to Cecil on 28th July, 1559, complaining, that as so few suitors attend the sitting of the Commission there is little expectation of raising much money in this way. A certificate showing the clear yearly value of lands sold since 14th July, 1558, accompanies this statement. Yet the total recorded, however imperfectly, by the

---

[1] S.P. Dom., 1547–1580, pp. 5, 51, 53, and Addenda, pp. 367, 370, 400. For sales of Crown lands from 1509 to 1558 see Bibliography (Appendix, ZD–ZF).
[2] S.P. Dom., 1547–1580, pp. 55, 100, 102, 108.
[3] S.P. Dom., 17th March, 1558, p. 100. See Bibliography (Appendix, ZD–ZF), for land sales under the Tudor monarchs. Also Liljegren, op. cit., pp. 126–7.
[4] Liljegren, op. cit., pp. 127–8. See also Bibliography, ZG, for sales under Elizabeth.

Auditors, proves that from the sales authorized between 1561 and 1563 no less than £176,648 was received.[1]

(b) *Second Period* : 1588–1592.—Extensive sales of Crown lands, due probably to the cost of defence in connection with the Spanish Armada, occurred a generation later. According to an entry of 4th February, 1591, in the Calendar of State Papers, where an account is given of the clear yearly value of all lands sold and of the money received or expected from this source, the sum obtained from the sales in a single year, between 14th November, 1589 and 26th November, 1590, reached £126,305. This amount is increased in the Auditors' Accounts [2] for the period 1589–1592 to £131,842 7s. 7¾d. Sixteen entries in the Calendar of State Papers for 1590 and 1591 record the clear yearly values of the premises sold as £653 and the amount received from their sales as £20,952.

(c) *Third Period* : 1596–1603.—The third series of sales followed closely upon the second, and this may have been caused partly by the expedition to Cadiz under Lord Howard in 1596, and partly by the troubles in Ireland at the close of the reign. On 8th December, 1598, we find Elizabeth approaching the City of London for a loan, with Crown lands to the yearly value of £5,000 as security, just as Mary did thirty years before, and as Charles I will do thirty years hence.[3] In August, 1601, we find Lord Buckhurst recommending Cecil to sell Otford and Deptford mansions as the cost of victualling the forces in Ireland is very great ; and the artful suggestion is made that such sale would bring in £3,000 of ready money and at the same time " save £3,000 to her Majesty ". The eagerness with which men suggest the sale of Crown lands to pay for national needs will be remembered at a later time, when another Irish expedition eats through the Treasury store of the Commonwealth, and the exhaustion due to the Seven Years' War threatens a further raid on the fragments left in 1762.[4] In the present instance two accounts among the State Papers show that Crown lands of the clear yearly value of £2,628 9s. 3d. were exposed to sale before 27th October, 1599, from which date the sales continued, the yearly value amounting to £5421 4s. 5d. by 25th April, 1600. As to the amount realized by these sales; it is recorded that £105,916 was received by the date first mentioned, and that the entire sum paid for Crown lands by 17th May, 1600 was not less than £212,614 15s. 8d. Moreover, it was computed about March, 1603, that the amount obtained from land sales towards the cost of wars in Queen Elizabeth's reign

[1] Audit Off., Declar. Accounts, Bun. 593, roll 1.
[2] S.P. Dom., 1591–1594, p. 8, vol. 238, No. 30, and Audit Office, Declared Accounts, bundle 593, roll 2.
[3] Cal. S.P. Dom., 1547–1580, p. 100, vol. 12, No. 52 ; 1598–1601, p. 130, vol. 269, No. 6 ; and *Antiquary*, vol. xiii, p. 195.
[4] Hist. MSS. Com., Salisbury MSS., vol. xi, p. 373 ; Act of 16th July, 1649, Firth and Rait, *Acts and Ordinances*, vol. ii, p. 168–9 ; *Gentleman's Magazine*, vol. xxxii, p. 135.

exceeded £817,350.[1] Liljegren's contention, therefore, as to need-less sales of Crown lands in this reign is undoubtedly wrong.

There are a score of entries in the Calendar of State Papers which, like those already mentioned for the years 1590 and 1591, are of special interest by reason of the comparison made between the yearly values of the premises and the amounts realized by their sales. They are included in the table below for comparison with the values recorded for the years 1596 to 1600 :—

VIII. SALES OF CROWN LANDS, 1590–1600

Dates.		Items.	Yearly Values. £	Sale Values. £
1590	July 12	3	67·0	1,378·3
,,	July 14	1	15·4	539·6
1591	Jan. 18	3	54·3	1,964·9
,,	Jan. 22	5	371·0	12,095·8
,,	Feb. 8	1	48·1	1,477·6
,,	Feb. —	2	97·6	2,546·6
,,	Nov. 18	1	—	948·9
1596	Aug. 3	1	30·3	1,213·3
1599	June 16	2	57·6	2,845·0
,,	June 24	3	84·7	4,148·3
,,	July 5	1	3·7	183·3
,,	July 14	2	95·2	3,691·8
,,	July 24	1	41·0	2,008·6
,,	Nov. 10	3	99·7	4,373·2
,,	Nov. 29	1	68·0	2,720·0
1600	Jan. 15	2	65·3	2,581·0
,,	Jan. 20	4	240·1	9,091·6
	Totals	36	1,439·0	53,807·8

Concealments of land appear to have been widespread during the reign of Queen Elizabeth,[2] although to some extent they were checked by the activity of the Commission for inquiry into concealed lands in 1567.[3] John Caley, Secretary of the Record Commissioners, prepared an index [4] which contains some 2,500 entries relating to these concealments, the rolls to which he refers recording particulars from which grants or leases were made by virtue of warrants issued by the Commissioners for Compounding of Defective Titles. In Middlesex there were discoveries of this nature in Hackney, Haliwell, Hillingdon, Isleworth, Islington, Kentish Town, Laleham, Littleton, Marylebone, South Mimms, Shoreditch, Staines, Stanwell, Tottenham, and Uxbridge. The index records forty-two entries for London alone.[5]

---

[1] Cal. S.P. Dom., 1598–1601, pp. 334, 425, 438, vols. 273, No. 17, and 274, Nos. 117, 146 ; also 1601–1603, p. 304, vol. 287, Nos. 59–60.
[2] S.P. Dom., 1560–1589. See indexes, and particularly pp. 290 and 702 in vol. i.
[3] S.P. Dom., 12th April, 1567, Certificate of the Clergy of Berkshire.
[4] Caley MS. (25), Cat. 2250, No. xii ; subsequently Sir Thos. Phillipps' MS., No. 6815, and Madge MS. 1935, which was presented to the British Museum, 5th February, 1937. The Index is an original and unpublished MS. of 256 pages, dated 1802.
[5] The references to London and Middlesex entries (Index, pp. 104–256) occur in the following Rolls : A 6, 8, 14, 30 ; B 5 ; C 10, 20 ; D 6 ; F 13 ; G 8, 18 ; K 7, 15–16 ; L 3 ; O 7, 14 ; P 16 ; Q 23, 25 ; S 4 ; T 3.

By means of these discoveries titles were amended as new grants were made, and the revenue of the Crown was thus improved.[1] From the evidence just considered the conclusion is inevitable that sales of Crown lands, although intermittent during the Plantagenet period, were systematic and frequent under the Tudor sovereigns ; and we shall presently see that such sales continued in the Stuart period owing to financial difficulties experienced by the first two kings of the new dynasty. There were, therefore, well-established precedents for the action taken by the Parliamentary Commissioners for the Sale of Crown lands during the Commonwealth.

If we examine the accounts of revenues derived from Crown lands and other sources during the last five years of her reign, 40–44 Elizabeth, 17th November, 1597 to 16th November, 1602,[2] we can estimate the average income of the queen at the close of the sixteenth century, and thus realize what expectations James I must have formed when he ascended the throne four months later. The average income reached a total of £502,000, of which less than £183,000 was derived from land revenues. Deductions, however, amounted to nearly £47,000, the largest proportion of which, quite 67 per cent, was associated with land management. In this way the " Ancient Revenue " was reduced from £54,660 to £50,317, the " Annexed Revenue " from £102,450 to £80,315, and the " Associated Revenue " (from Chester, Wales and the two duchies of Cornwall and Lancaster) from £25,035 to £20,195. At the close of Elizabeth's reign, therefore, the Crown Revenues amounted, on the average of the last five years, to the clear sum of £455,367, of which £150,827 was derived from departments dealing with Crown lands, as we see in the table which follows :—

IX. The Land Revenues of Elizabeth, 1598–1603

Revenues.	Gross. £	Deductions. £	Clear Amount. £
(i) *Ancient Revenue.*			
Certainties of Fee Farms, etc.	14,068·4⎫	4,343·6	50,316·7
Casualties of Goods, etc.	40,591·9⎭		
(ii) *Annexed Revenue.*			
England	94,488·0	18,880·6	75,607·4
Wales	7,962·6	3,255·0	4,707·6
(iii) *Principality and Duchies.*			
Principality of Wales	2,146·7	909·4	1,237·3
Duchy of Cornwall	4,606·7	548·6	4,058·1
Duchy of Lancaster	17,309·4	2,848·0	14,461·4
County Palatine of Chester	827·3	534·1	293·2
Houses of the King	145·5	—	145·5
(iv) Total i	54,660·3	4,343·6	50,316·7
ii	102,450·6	22,135·6	80,315·0
iii	25,035·6	4,840·1	20,195·5
Total of Land Revenues	182,146·5	31,319·3	150,827·2
Total of Crown Revenues	502,231·7	46,864·8	455,366·9

[1] Cf. the Cathedral Churches erected by Henry VIII, since they had been " called into question for want of the records of that time, and the lands of most of them being purchased covertly at a small rate, as concealed " (S.P. Dom. Eliz., vol. cxlvi, No. 128 (1580 ?), Cal., p. 702).

[2] See *Account of Manors*, printed in 1787, app. ii, pp. 79–80.

PART II

CROWN LANDS AND THE LEGISLATURE

Chapter I

A CHANGE OF DYNASTY

The eve of the vernal equinox of 1601 came upon a troubled land in which two monarchs, offspring of a notable marriage which united the once rival " Roses ", awaited the fateful events of the morrow : one, a king whose realm lay in the north, the other a queen who long had ruled the south—third and fifth of the generations that sprang from Owen Tudor. Within the palace at Greenwich, as the century neared its close, the dynasty of a second son and childless or unmarried queens was on the point of failing ; but in the north at Dunfermline the second son of the Scottish king had just been born—he who was destined to renew the strife of nations. Who had vision to see that two years hence, this very eve, the northern king would be seated on the southern throne, founding a second dynasty of second sons and failing daughters, and complicating still further the problems of a troubled land ? [1]

With the dawn, that Wednesday morn, a century full of hope and yet of fear opened upon a wondering world, as the first rays of sunlight sought out the rooms wherein two babes lay sleeping—one, a child scarce four months old in the royal apartments of his Scottish home, the other not yet of years aged two in an English farmer's dwelling—both unconscious of the coming strife, when each would be called in turn to rule and one at length be slain. And in other homes throughout the land the fitful rays lit up the features of those who were fated to play strong parts in the days of tragedy that lay ahead : two boys of six, two lads of seven or eight, a youth of twice that age, and one, the oldest of them all, approaching twenty-eight —all destined suddenly to die, upon the battlefield or in the Tower, by sword, assassination, or the headman's axe.

Thus came the seventeenth century upon the awakening land of Britain, with a Tudor still enthroned in the south but a Stuart

[1] Queen Elizabeth of England, aged 68 at this time, and James VI of Scotland, whose age was then 34, were the grand-daughter and great-great-grandson of Henry VII of Lancaster and Elizabeth of York. Prince Arthur and Prince Henry, the eldest sons of Henry VII and James I, both died before their respective fathers ; had they succeeded to the throne there is a possibility that neither the dissolution of the monasteries nor the Civil War might have taken place. Henry VIII, Charles I, and Charles II were second sons, Edward VI, third child and unmarried, and James II third brother and twice married. Elizabeth was unmarried, and the marriages of Mary I, Mary II, and Anne were unfortunate in regard to succession. Moreover, the children of Charles II and the son of James II by a subsequent marriage were not recognized by the nation. Thus the tragedies of the two dynasties were due in a measure to the succession of second sons and unfortunate daughters. In our own time, George V and George VI were likewise second sons.

47

expectant in the north, while the royal babe Charles slept unaware of his destiny. A few months later the Queen was dead, a new king proclaimed, and the Scottish infant then entered upon his career as a prince of England.[1]

King James I ascended the English throne on 24th March, the last day of the old year, 1602. Whatever expectations he may have formed in regard to the Crown lands and their revenues, the proceeds proved quite inadequate in the very first year of his reign; for after the alienations of the Tudors had ceased, a greatly impoverished inheritance was all that remained to sustain the dignity of the first Stuart sovereign of England. We may therefore " indulge ", with Dr. Hall, " in a faint pity for the luckless descendant of Henry VII who inherited a beggarly account of grants and leases in place of the joint possessions of the two greatest landowners by repute of the Middle Ages (the Crown and the Church), and who, being thus left dependent on a diminished and low-rented patrimony was easily starved into submission by his loving subjects." [2] That is the reason, which Liljegren does not fully understand, why James I returned so gladly to the " old stratagem " of selling Crown lands—perhaps more readily because of his " greed and greater need for money ". It is indeed wholly on the ground of need and avarice that Liljegren accounts for the king's " inconsiderate policy " of securing for himself the temporary advantage of ready money by methods which left his son even more entirely at the mercy of Parliament. " Instead of leasing Crown lands as had been the practice of previous kings, in this way keeping a great many families and boroughs dependent on the king and getting fines and rents, James managed to sell the estates for ever, thus depriving himself of much fixed revenue and authority in order to procure money at once." [3]

If the average income of Elizabeth, so far as her Landed Revenues for the period 1597–1601 are concerned, had been fully sustained, James might reasonably have expected a clear annual sum of not less than £150,000 from this source ; but the latest years included in that period revealed the fact that diminishing returns were in operation and that the tendency was still unchecked at the close of the reign. Sir Robert

---

[1] The victims of the Stuart period referred to were first of all King Charles, born 19th November, 1600, and executed 30th January, 1648, and his great opponent Oliver Cromwell, born 25th April, 1599, vindictively " executed " after exhumation on the anniversary of the death of the " martyr king ", 30th January, 1660 ; next the Duke of Buckingham, born 1592, who met his death by assassination 23rd August, 1628 ; then the five great statesmen, arrayed in the order of birth : Archbishop Laud, 1573, executed on Tower Hill, 10th January, 1644 ; " King Pym," 1584, who died peacefully in December, 1643 ; Strafford, 1593, executed 12th May, 1641 ; Eliot, 1594, dying as a prisoner in the Tower of London in 1632 ; and Hampden, 1594, slain at Chalgrove Field, 18th June, 1643.

[2] Antiquary, vol. xiii, p. 5. See Appendix I, Bibliography, ZH, for sales under James I. Cal. S. P. Dom., 1603–1610, pp. 45, 320, 360, 380–1, 386, 393, 439–441, 493, 509–510, 523, 578 ; and addenda vol. 1580–1625, p. 457, 497–8.

[3] Liljegren, op. cit., pp. 128–9.

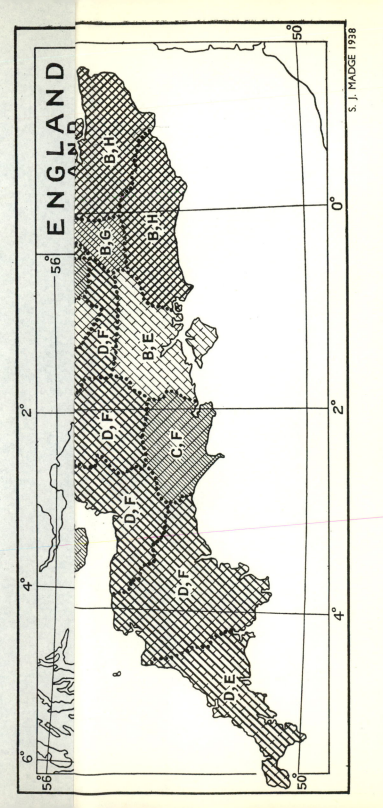

ENGLAND
AND

B, H

B, G

B, H

D, F

B, E

D, F

C, F

D, F

D, F

D, F

D, E

56°

56°

6°

4°

2°

0°

50°

50°

S. J. MADGE 1938

[face p. 48

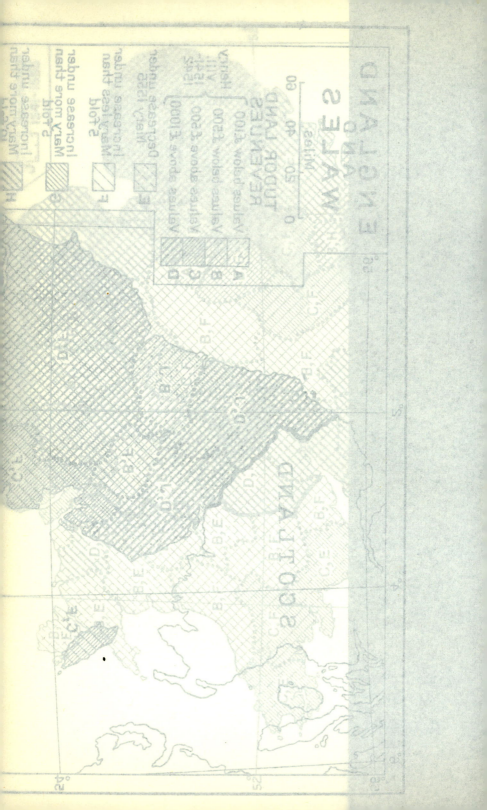

ENGLAND
and
WALES

SCOTLAND

TUDOR LAND
REVENUES

Values below £100

Values £100 & £500

Values above £500

{ Henry VIII 1541–1547 }

Decrease 1535 under Mary 1558

Increase 1535 less than Mary 5-fold

Increase under Mary more than 5-fold

Increase under Mary more than

A
B
C
D

Miles
0   20   40   60

Cotton has stated that the entire revenue from all the Crown lands, royal residences, forests and parks, did not exceed £32,000 at the beginning of the reign of King James. But this does not appear to be correct, if we accept the evidence given in two schedules prepared for the king in 1604 and 1609. In the first of these, " a summary collection of the annexation of 100,000 marks yearly to the Crown " [1]—a statement which shows " the yearly value, rent, and revenue of the Crown, with the exception of tithes, and all lands of 5 marks yearly and under, also all Custody lands "—the lands alone produce £64,371, and the Exchequer rents another £16,947. In the second schedule,[2] which records the names and values of " all manors, lands, fee farm rents, etc., annexed to the Crown of England," 8th May, 1609, the rents are slightly lower than five years before, but the lands only amount to £56,836. By setting aside £4,000 for Prince Charles and rendering £64,086 annually to the king, there would be a residual sum (according to the 1604 statement) of £13,231, in addition to the " Mortgage Lands ", making a total amount of more than £16,400 available for the use of the Crown.[3] The detailed figures are shown in the following table :—

X. The Land Revenues of James I, 1604–1609

Revenues.	1604.	1609.
	£	£
Exchequer Lands . .	49,344·9	40,054·5
Exchequer Rents . .	16,946·6	16,781·6
Duchy of Lancaster Lands .	11,816·1	10,034·0
Mortgage Lands . .	3,210·0	—
Totals . . .	81,317·6	66,870·1

In the " Instrument and Schedules of Annexation " of 1609 the first schedule records the names but not the values of the royal mansions, castles, forests, chases, and parks. It is a larger list than that incorporated in Add. MS. 38444, where agreement is only found in the number of chases recorded, while the Exchequer and Duchy of Lancaster Estates are separated throughout. The main differences are shown below, the " Instrument " list being indicated by (a) and the British Museum Manuscript by (b) :—

XI. Schedule of Annexation, 1609

		Duchy of	Totals.	
Premises.	Exchequer.	Lancaster.	(a)	(b)
Mansion houses	26	—	26 ⎫	93
Castles and forts	67	16	83 ⎰	
Forests . .	55	13	68	73
Chases . .	7	2	9	9
Parks . .	77	40	117	104
Totals .	232	71	303	279

In Add. MS. 38444, f. 97. The date is 29th November, 1604.
[2] St. John, Observations on Landed Revenues, pp. 78–9. Two Schedules, dated 8th May, 1609.
[3] The scheme for " Annexation " failed because the proposals proved unacceptable to Parliament. Republican control was the sequel under the Commonwealth.

The sales of Crown lands were resumed immediately upon the accession of James I as the State Papers sufficiently show. In 1610, between Michaelmas and Easter, the amounts received as "Extraordinaries" were very large, for they included the following sales [1] :—

XII. SALES OF CROWN LANDS, 1610

Premises.	Sales. £	Defective Titles. £	Totals. £
Manors and Lands . .	50,000	247	50,247
Mills	3,000	—	3,000
Parsonages and Chantries .	12,500	—	12,500
Woods	781	—	781
Assarts and Purprestures .	1,220	—	1,220
Totals . . .	67,501	247	67,748

In 1612 James received £6,500 from alienations and another £8,000 in 1614. Indeed, Scargill Bird, in his notes on the Crown lands, shows that the king used his power to alienate royal property on such a liberal scale that lands to the value of £775,000 were disposed of during his reign.[2] Liljegren gives the usual footnote of pages cited from the Calendars of State Papers, without indicating which of the entries relate to sales, though thirty-five at least of the references to sales of Crown lands are contained in the first of the volumes dealing with the period 1603–1610 alone. The extensive character of the transactions concerning Crown lands under the early Stuart kings is apparent from the fact that more than 1,630 "Surveys and Rentals" dating from 1603 to 1640 are still preserved in the Public Record Office.[3] That there were abuses in connection with the landed estates of the Crown is equally clear, and it is certain (as we can see from a table in Add. MS. 38444, f. 98), that such abuses were widespread, for the record of 18th May, 1607, gives particulars of "true values" and "false deductions" drawn from no less than nineteen counties. Even Sir Robert Cotton did not escape suspicion of having purchased the manor of Glatton and Holme "at a great undervalue, upon false suggestions by him made to the deep defrauding of His Majesty and the Commissioners of Treasurers." [4]

Some admirable comments were made by Sir Robert Johnson to Cecil, 18th April, 1602, a few months before the death of the Queen, which have a bearing on other suggestions which he made

[1] Add. MS. 38444, f. 63.
[2] Add. MS. 38444, ff. 62, 63, 65 ; *Antiquary*, vol. xiii, p. 195. For Sales of Crown lands under James I, see Bibliography, ZH. The total receipts from fee farm rents, the receiver-general, alienations, hanaper, and Duchy of Lancaster, 1610–1614, range from £295,726, to £461,606, with "Inequalities", when compared with the issues, of from £60,050 to £101,934. Clearly James failed to balance his land revenues during the first ten years of his reign.
[3] An Analysis of PRO. List xxv, reveals a total of more than 7,200 documents, of which only about 400 are later than the Commonwealth period, whereas 1,500 are earlier than Richard III, and about 3,700 are Tudor records.
[4] Petition of tenants, 14th July, 1613, Privy Council Acts, pp. 137–140.

to King James a few years later. As his earlier memorandum to Cecil throws a curious light on the position of the Crown lands only about forty years before the drastic action taken by the Parliamentary Commissioners, it deserves to be quoted in full.[1]

"Whenever I have heard of the sale of Her Majesty's lands," Sir Robert writes, "I have observed that the value was seldom known, and the pig was sold in the panier, as the proverb is, and have wished that either the Commissioners had been better informed, or there had been a suspension of that service. It might be objected that the necessities of the realm would not permit of such, and that of two evils the least was to be chosen. I know not how to answer the word necessity, but with a wish that it had not been a denizen in England; I should have thought that Her Majesty's own estate, if properly managed, would have proved a sufficient bulwark against the arrival of that stranger.

"The question whether, to maintain a defensive war, one Sovereign should be forced to part with the kingly ornaments of a crown to defend, whilst her subjects are able to supply, is rather political than arithmetical, far above my reach, etc. I will point out where reformation seems needed.

"The chief foundation of mischiefs has been the want of authentic surveys and the preservation of Court rolls, by which there has been the loss of many rents, the confounding of tenancies, the change of tenures, perverting of customs, concealing of fines, fines arbitrary made, certain heriots lost by uniting tenants, demesnes and wastes passed into copyhold or customary estates, and sometimes those estates made hereditary, and thus the value of the inheritance obscured; albeit the nature of the soils may be quickly seen to the skilful surveyor, yet the other points are no less necessary in sale or demise.[2]

"I believe that of every ten manors there is not one perfect survey, and not one court roll of 100, and few or none (unless it be for Duchy lands) are to be found. Much of Her Majesty's land stands leased as manors, and the lessees, as lords for the time, keep courts and have stewards, careless save for the present profit, not troubling their heads with preservation of ancient customs, nor their pens with engrossing records, but keep rough pay books, which are commonly lost or embezzled on the death or change of the steward, and suppressed at the change of the Queen's tenant. What simple scrolls are kept even of those manors and courts in Her Majesty's actual possession is no secret, but a common evil, and there is much deceit in orders for fines to be paid according to court rolls, or for rents to be paid as they have been before."

[1] S.P. Dom. Eliz., Cal., 1601–1603, pp. 176–8 (vol. 283, No. 80).
[2] The extraordinary success of the Commonwealth Surveys of Crown lands is due to the skill of the surveyors and the directing ability of Colonel Wm. Webb, the Surveyor-General, who must have paid close attention to all the considerations named in this paragraph.

Six suggestions made by Sir Robert Johnson follow by way of remedy for these evils :—

" (1) A building might be allotted, wherein all the surveys and court rolls of Her Majesty's lands might be methodically placed, and for their keeping an officer appointed, whose fee might be a rate for search or copies, and £10 a year.

" (2) All the ancient and other court rolls touching Her Majesty's lands might be called into the said office by a time limited, six or nine months, and every steward enjoined to send them in, engrossed on parchment, or at least so many as have been made by the now stewards, and the rest as they find them, and this on oath that none are withholden.

" (3) Either Her Majesty's surveyors or other sufficient men should be authorized by commission, within one year, to certify all the present customs of the several manors.

" (4) Some learned persons should be appointed to peruse and report upon such customs as to which are reasonable and which prejudicial, etc., comparing the modern with the ancient, that such as appear controllable by records may be put in their ancient course, and such as appear uncertain may be settled before the Barons of the Exchequer."

Before proceeding with the fifth and sixth suggestions, Sir Robert acutely observes : " The reason why Her Majesty should more strictly examine these things than her predecessors is, that the cunning devices of these later times, as compared with the ancient simplicity of the overworn world, and the great losses which have happened thereby, make it needful. Within these sixty or eighty years, and chiefly forty or fifty, the wit-craft of man is more and more extended, to obscure ancient customs, and pervert them to private profit. Tenants in these days, when inquisitions of survey or inquest of office are taken, do not study so much to answer what is true, as to set forth such customs as are profitable for themselves. If any say the succeeding age may shift for itself as this does, it is folly, for the controversies that have grown though want of preservation of records need no agreement." He then continues his suggestions for preventing such abuses in the future :—

" (5) The Queen's tenants (being lords of manors), and all the stewards of her lands, should, every Hilary term, deliver in court rolls of the year ending at Michaelmas, subscribed and sealed.

" (6) Every steward should take an oath before a Baron of Exchequer, to maintain the ancient rights and customs of the manor, and to observe his instructions."

Suggestions in regard to such instructions were on the point of being formulated when Sir Robert suddenly recalled to mind the existing position of the Crown lands. " I once thought of walking into the forests, parks, chases, etc., to consider of some good improvement," he adds, " but I remembered that in some Her Majesty is only owner of the royalty, having no soil or wood; in others of like royalty, with some part of the soil; and in a third sort, of all, which diversities would move sundry considerations. For the several parks preserved for deer there is no difficulty of improvement, and the moors, heaths, and wastes, in many places, with the good contentment of the commoners, may also be improved, but these I will leave until I hear what is aimed at." [1]

Nine years later, 22nd January, 1611, Sir Robert Johnson again wrote, reminding Salisbury of his former projects for advancing the King's profits on forests, and reminding him further that a certain book which he had recently sent to the king was composed of the contents of letters which that minister had previously approved. The new project which he now advanced, and which he thought was good, consisted of four plans for improving the royal revenues, the last of which he preferred personally because it would tend to improve the fee farm rents whenever renewals of leases of Crown lands occurred. Incidentally, Sir Robert begs for occupation in connection with these schemes.[2] His notes relating to particulars and exact surveys " humbly submitted to the Hon'ble consideration of such as have management of the affairs of the Crown of England " are in the British Museum.[3] " Hitherto," he sadly says, " my best endeavours (based on imperfect groundwork) for His Majesty's service have effect more mischief and frowns to myself than all the other business of my life, of which if I should say all that I would I might perhaps hear that I would not." The king's service, however, greatly needs assistance and he desires to " proceed to lend a helping hand to that great work " even though it should prove that he was " but like a torch in the business which consumeth itself in giving light to others ".

Johnson's memorandum of " Considerations " contains seventeen articles, each with the Auditor's observation and the reply to objections raised by that official. His suggestions that Surveyors should sit in person with the Auditor at his annual audit was considered by the auditors to be " altogether derogatory to the Auditor's authority ", and this was met in reply by the rebuke : " What derogation it may be to the auditor to have the Surveyor sit with him at his audit is not suddainly understood when as it cannot be denied but that the Surveyor is the ground and foundation of the Auditor's office unless happily they may fear somewhat may be thereby discovered whereof

---

[1] This memorandum of eleven pages is endorsed, apparently by Cecil, " Concerning subsidy ". Although it was printed in the Calendar of S.P. Dom., Elizabeth, in 1870, I have not seen it quoted subsequently, in spite of its interest and importance.
[2] Cal. S.P. Dom., James I, 1611–1618, p. 3 (vol. 61, No. 25).
[3] Add. MS. 38444, ff. 91–2. Signed Robert Johnson. The date seems to be 28th February, 1609.

they desire none to take notice." [1] In reply to objections of the Auditors in regard to Articles 3 to 7, which suggested that Surveyors should confer with stewards of manors on " matters not already ordered by the printed book or decrees ", the somewhat caustic remark is made : " Though the printed book [2] hath in it worthy directions not to be excepted against and the use of a perfect Surveyor thereby intended yet it will appear that amongst the thirty-six Surveyors or more of particular Counties not one of them hath ever laboured to perfect his understanding concerning his office,[3] and how commodious it is to have a neighbour Justice to assess fines we leave to be imagined and further to be enquired." The final consideration,[4] which urged that the Surveyors should do everything in their power to preserve the king's possessions and revenues, met with the Auditors' objection that " the revenues are better ordered and answered than the Surveyor can tell how to direct ". This objection was quickly and decisively overruled.[5] " If the revenues have been and are so well ordered how cometh it to pass that there hath been of late so many abuses discovered followed and many punished when the Auditors knew not how to defend the same, and many more would be and of several kinds but modes by [6] restraineth them to do hurt which have no power in themselves to salve the same again. But if it be now so good and perfect as it seemeth they avowe, it must be concluded that necessity enforceth amendment of continued errors, and yet if the beginning of order and Instruction be respected it will be approved the Surveyor the first in that service."

The concern showed by James over the state of his revenues from Crown lands in 1609, only forty years before the execution of his son, reveals some of the difficulties which Charles had to face after 1625, when a much diminished income forced him to take desperate measures which eventually led to rebellion and defeat, and the regrettable republican decision to regulate and sell the whole of the Crown lands. The position in the years 1608 and 1609 is, therefore, worthy of the closest study. There is the memoranda, for instance, which John Hercye submitted to Salisbury, 21st November, 1609, in order to further the king's scheme for the composition of copyhold tenants.[7] In the list enclosed by him are the names of such manors and lands, with the total of their rents, " as are likely to make most money " if

---

[1] This is the first article, with its consideration, and the reply.
[2] The reference may be to Norden's The Surveyor's dialogue, 1607, as Rathborne's The Surveyor in four books did not appear until 1616.
[3] The Commonwealth Surveyors, on the other hand, were remarkably skilled men.
[4] Article 17 with its consideration and reply.
[5] For further details relating to sales of Crown lands and rents under James I see Cal. S.P. Dom., 1603–1610, p. 404, Nos. 28–9, and S.P. Dom., vol. 51, No. 20, which is a book of values (1609), relating to two contracts of £5,000 and £4,524 19s. Add. MS. 38444 is invaluable.
[6] BY: "private, privy, covert." (N.E.D., sense III 3 (d).)
[7] S.P. Dom., vol. 49, No. 50 ; Cal. 1609, p. 561.

brought to sale: from his surveys he records 91 estates, situated in 23 counties, the rents of which exceed £4,182. Then there is the important " Book of the King, Queen, Prince, and Duke of York's copyhold lands of inheritance or for lives ",[1] also dating from 1609, of which an analysis is given in the table which follows. Only 50 out of 217 copyhold manors are in the counties which were held by the Royalists in the Civil War; the rest will be found in the Parliamentary areas in and beyond the metropolis. The copyhold manors of inheritance are in the majority, 161 altogether, the rest being " copyhold manors for lives ". Of the former 131, and of the latter 42, are in hand, the remaining 44 manors being granted in lease, some for long periods, as for example, the coppices of Barton, Lincolnshire, which still had 80 years to run. As to the distribution of these manors 116 belonged to the King, 12 to the Queen, and 63 to Henry, Prince of Wales, while the remaining 26 were set apart for Prince Charles, the Duke of York, few of whose manors were either " for lives " or granted in lease. The incidence of fines, shown only in connection with the " Copyhold Manors of inheritance " in hand, is remarkable. Of 131 instances recorded, 86 concern the king's manors, six those of the queen, and the remainder refer to the possessions of the two princes in practically equal shares. Most of these fines had hitherto been " arbitrary ", and of these 13 had of late become " fixed " by decree, while 79 were awaiting a similar decision; but in the case of the " certain " fines, of which 33 were alleged to be " pretended ", only six were confirmed by decree.

XIII. Crown Copyhold Manors, 1609 [2]

Areas.	Inheritance. Held.	Lease.	Lives. Held.	Lease.	Totals. King.	Queen.	Prince.	Duke.
(i) Metropolitan	54	5	11	—	48	3	19	—
(ii) Extra-Metropolitan	50	14	20	13	40	7	31	19
(iii) Borderlands .	27	11	11	1	28	2	13	7
Totals .	131	30	42	14	116	12	63	26

There is, as a further test, the evidence contained in the remarkable series of Crown estates taken during the reign of James,[3] some of which are summarized in Johnson's memoranda already quoted.[4] Here we find some astonishing examples of inadequate revenue derived from Crown lands through inefficient management on the part of officials.[5] In Yorkshire, for instance, a survey of twenty manors made in 1605 discloses the fact that while seven fee-farmers

[1] S.P. Dom., vol. 51, No. 19; Cal. 1609, p. 578.
[2] The counties in each area number 9, 14, and 10 respectively, or 33 out of 39 English counties, excluding Monmouth.
[3] PRO. List 25 contains references to over 1,340 rentals and surveys of this reign. Every county in England and Wales is represented.
[4] Add. MS. 38444, p. 87.
[5] The Improved values (additional to the " ancient rents ") in the Commonwealth Surveys, upon which the sales were based between 1649 and 1660, show a three-fold increase on the average. James and Charles both failed to secure the improvements in value which the Commonwealth government obtained, and Charles II largely retained.

paid less than £40 for the collective property granted to them, 221 freeholders paid a total rent of only £51 in acknowledgment of their services, and 505 leaseholders merely contributed a sum of £609 annually for premises that should have produced £2,012 or more. As for the copyholders, 328 in number, these paid on the average only 11s. a year, their combined rents being less than £190 for property now valued at £1,050 annually. Three years later, in the same county, we find 523 owners of some small portions called " Quillets " paying an annual rent of £860 for land worth at least £2,500 per annum, the freeholders and copyholders both paying an average rent of 3s., the fee-farmers 15s., and the leaseholders less than £3 each per annum. And if we analyse the evidence concerning the rents of tenants in 111 manors scattered over nine counties, including Yorkshire, in surveys of the year 1608, the inadequate returns from Crown lands will be acknowledged to have been an indisputable factor in the discontent shown by James and his successor. Not only were freeholders in this widespread area paying an average annual rent which did not exceed 3s., but copyholders, customary tenants, and tenants " at will ", nearly 4,000 altogether, contributed no more on the average, than 9d. a month to the king's revenues by way of rent for the estates which they held. The total amount paid by freeholders of these manors came to less than £135; the fee-farmers contributed only £567, but £86 more came from an unrecorded number of " tenants of inheritance " in Pembroke—making a total of not more than £788. What the real value of all these lands, especially those of the fee-farmers, amounted to is not stated. We do know, however, that there were over 1,300 leaseholders on these manors, that their combined rents were only £3,144, and that the real value of the lands thus held in lease was approximately £10,340. The king got even less consideration from the copyholders, for whereas they paid a total sum of £1,660 in rents, their lands were valued by surveyors at £13,375. It follows, therefore, that if the full " Improved Value " of all these estates was to be obtained from the tenants, the rents of the leaseholders would have to rise from 10d. a week, on the average, to 13s. a month, while the average rent of the copyholders would need to be increased from 9s. to £3 10s. per annum. If we assume, what indeed is unlikely, that the values of lands in the hands of freeholders, fee-farmers, and tenants-at-will show no improvement over the rents they pay, the critical position of the revenues from Crown lands in Cumberland, Devonshire, Dorset, Somerset, Westmorland, Wiltshire, Yorkshire, Carmarthen, and Pembroke, in the year 1608, is revealed without exaggeration in the Analytical statement which follows.[1]

[1] If the " Improved Values " of all these types of tenants were known, the total would be larger ; and if the unrecorded leaseholders and copyholders of Wales were known, as their rents and values are, these numbers would be increased, causing a (slight) fall in the averages mentioned above. See Table XIV.

XIV. ANNUAL RENTS AND VALUES OF CROWN LANDS, 1608

Areas.	Manors.	Free.	Copy.	Lease.	Farms.	Rents. £	Values. £
(i) Metropolitan . .	—	—	—	—	—	—	—
(ii) Extra-Metropolitan .	22	14	639	55	11	746·0	6,826·4
(iii) Borderlands . .	75	672	3,047	1,262	23	4,514·4	16,596·5
(iv) Wales . . .	14	212	—	—	—	332·1	1,079·3
Totals . .	111	898	3,686	1,317	34	5,592·5	24,502·2

In spite of the king's inadequate revenues from the Crown lands, James made very liberal allowances to his two sons, the Prince of Wales and the Duke of York. Sinclair [1] shows that Prince Henry, until his death in November, 1612, was in receipt of a clear revenue of nearly £52,000,[2] a sum which was greater than any heir-apparent had previously received. John Chamberlain, writing to Sir Dudley Carleton concerning the death of the young prince, mentions that " his revenue of £60,000 returns to the king, till Prince Charles is older. The Duchy of Cornwall is said to revert to the Crown, as being entailed only on the king's firstborn ".[3] Ten years later the full allowance granted to Prince Henry was in the hands of his brother Charles, whose " annuall revenew certen in lands and other things " exceeded £59,000 when his father's reign drew to a close.[4]

It was during Easter 1603 that the young prince Charles, Duke of Albany, first met the English subjects of King James. Created Duke of Cornwall at the age of twelve, he became Prince of Wales four years later upon the unexpected death of his brother, and at the early age of twenty-four he ascended the throne of England, meeting his first parliament on 18th June, 1625, within a week after his marriage to Henrietta Maria, sister of Louis XIII, King of France. A contrast to his ungainly father, Charles was handsome and dignified, and he began his reign with an earnest desire to rule well. Possessed of tenacity, shrewdness, and a singular subtlety in intrigue, his subsequent failure as a monarch was very largely due to obstinacy, faithlessness, and ingratitude.[5] For in truth, as Macaulay says, he was impelled by " an incurable propensity to dark and crooked ways. It may seem strange that his conscience, which on occasions of little moment, was singularly sensitive, should never have reproached him with this great vice. But there is reason to believe that he was perfidious, not only from constitution and from habit, but also on principle ". The

[1] Sinclair, *History of the Public Revenues*, 1803, vol. i, p. 229.
[2] In 1937 an income of £25,000 for the late Prince of Wales, ex-King Edward VIII, is being discussed with some anxiety; and on the very eve of the coronation of George VI there is correspondence in *The Times* on the subject of the hereditary revenues of the Crown, by Lord Hugh Cecil, Lord Strickland and Mr. A. Beesly.
[3] Cal. S.P. Dom., 12th November, 1612, p. 155.
[4] Add. MS. 33469, f. 30, under date 18th January, 1621–1622.
[5] Madge, *England Under Stuart Rule*, pp. 44–5, 92–3, Charles became Duke of Cornwall, 6th November, 1612, Prince of Wales, 4th November, 1616, and king, 27th March, 1625. He was married to the sister of the French king, 13th June, 1625.

son, even more than the father, failed to understand the nature of Englishmen. Yet it must be confessed that many of the difficulties which Charles had to face in 1625 were not of his own seeking, for his financial troubles had their origin in the state of the Crown lands, the improvement of which necessitated an increase in the rents of tenants and consequently provoked a considerable section of his subjects to acts of disloyalty and revenge. A more careful consideration of the new king's efforts to improve the landed revenues, and a fuller appreciation of the attitude of his tenants towards this desirable economic change, would have caused the older historians to modify in some degree the harsh judgment they have pronounced on the second Stuart king.

The consequences of the inconsiderate policy of compositions and alienations adopted by James I and his predecessors fell sternly upon his successor who, perceiving that there was little to collect from " the scattered wreck of the ancestral revenue of the Crown ", owing to the aggrieved attitude of his relatively more prosperous subjects, was compelled to seek new and exacting methods of raising revenue rather than continue at the mercy of Parliament in the matter of ungracious grants. In this way he laid himself open to the charge which Hallam [1] has made of imposing illegal taxation or obsolete and vexatious exactions.

The sales of Crown lands were quickly resumed, as we learn from the Salvetti [2] correspondence and the State Papers. Liljegren [3] has little to say in connection with these pre-Commonwealth Sales beyond recording two sums, amounting to £150,767, derived in this way in the first three years of the reign. Writing to the Grand Duke of Tuscany at Florence, 24th July, 1626, Salvetti shrewdly observes : " We shall soon hear more on this subject " because, since it was considered that " the Royal Revenue might be better and more profitably managed than is at present the case ", eight commissioners had recently been appointed, charged with the duty of " reducing the number of parks and forests which are the property of the Crown in different parts of England to a state of profitable cultivation, or even of selling them to whoever offers most money for them ". Writing later, 14th September, a day earlier than the king's letter to the Commissioners, Salvetti mentioned that Charles, in order to relieve his " most pressing wants ", had given orders to sell a number of estates " reserving only small returns from them as acknowledgement of homage ". It was calculated that large sums would be obtained, but Salvetti doubted if ready money would be available for some time. On 2nd October his letter to the Duke of Tuscany contains some

[1] Hallam, *Hist. of England*, ch. viii.
[2] Amerigo Salvetti, more correctly Alessandro Antelminelli, Tuscan Resident at Whitehall ; Skrine MSS., Hist. MSS. Com., 11 Rep. vol. i, pp. 79–85, 135–143.
[3] Liljegren, op. cit., pp. 129–130.

significant admissions. " The Royal Commissioners met on Wednesday last for the first time to make a beginning of the sale of the landed estates of the Crown, this plan of raising money having been adopted in consequence of the determination of the inhabitants of the provinces not to contribute except through the action of Parliament." Few have consented to pay, yet the necessity for obtaining revenues is pressing. Nevertheless, the king's subjects " will not submit to taxation on any other terms, whilst he is wholly averse to it, and will not yield, unless he is reduced to extremity and pulled by the hairs of his head, so much does he dread returning to school with such inflexible masters ".[1]

The Minute Book of the Commissioners of Sales has been preserved.[2] It opens with a reference to the meeting at Westminster, Saturday, 2nd December, 1626, and closes with sales effected to 26th June, 1627. The items relating to sales of lands in fee farm or otherwise number 276, of which 14 concern groups of counties; the remainder are single entries which embrace most of the counties of England and Wales.

XV. SALES OF CROWN LANDS, 1626–1627

Areas.		Counties.	Items.	Largest Number of Items.
(i) Metropolitan	.	8	106	Berks, Bucks, Herts.
(ii) Extra-Metropolitan		11	46	Northants, Suffolk, Warwick.
(iii) Borderlands .	.	8	63	Durham, Gloucs, Yorks.
(iv) Wales .	.	6	47	Carnarvon, Montgom., Pembroke.
Totals .	.	33	262 [3]	

The record, however, is imperfect, for nothing is known as to sales of Crown lands after June, 1627. Only two items relate to Norfolk.[4] Yet it is to this period that a curious manuscript relating to land speculators belongs.[5] " There is a societie or Combination lately sprang upp called the Land buyers. Theis lay their purses together and as they cane light on a manor a Gentlemans seat or a good quantity of lande they buy it in grosse and make pr'fit of it by retailing it in p'cells even to single acres as a purchaser will buye and by making other waste thereof," with detrimental effects on hospitality, depopulation, commodity prices, and above all social distinctions—" the making of a parity between Gentlemen and Yeomen and them w'ch before were laboringe men."

---

[1] On 28th December, 1627, Salvetti refers to the City of London Loan " secured upon landed estates of the Crown which the citizen may hold or sell as they think fit ". On 3rd April, 1628 he comments on the speech of the Keeper of the Great Seal in reference to the sales of royal estates, jewels, and plate " sacrificed solely to maintain the honour and reputation of this kingdom ".

[2] S.P. Dom., Chas. I, vol. 69. For Sales in this reign see Bibliography, YJ–YL and ZI.

[3] With fourteen items from " Various Counties ", combined.

[4] S.P. Dom., Chas. I, vol. 69, pp. 43, 64.

[5] Gurney MSS. (vol. xxii, ff. 82–93), Hist. MSS. Com., 12 Rep. App. ix, p. 135 ; Rye, Norfolk Archæology, vol. xv, pp. 1–3.

Liljegren asserts, in reference to the sales of Crown lands during this reign, that "about 1630 this source of revenue seems practically to have run dry. And so Charles had recourse to other means of a somewhat desperate character". But Prynne in his " Account of the King's late Revenue and Debts ", 1647, shows that the sales continued for some time longer, since the extraordinary receipts of the Exchequer from 1625 to April, 1635, were as follows : —

XVI. SALES OF CROWN LANDS, 1625-1635

Premises.	Individual Sales. £	Corporate Sales. £	Defective Titles. £	Totals. £
Lands and assessments	241,058·5	339,599·2	8,415·6	589,073·3
Woods . . .	62,085·2	—	—	62,085·2
Totals . .	303,143·7	339,599·2	8,415·6	651,158·5

The amount recorded for wood is also given in Add. MS. 20078, f. 45, under the date 18th April, 1635, but the total is increased on f. 53 to £70,816 8s. 3d. From the City of London the King borrowed over £300,000 on the security of the Crown lands to carry on the war with Scotland ; the extensive grants made to Edw. Ditchfield and others, as trustees for the City, under his arrangement, occupy three entire patent rolls, each consisting of three parts. To this evidence may be added Newburgh's confession to the Earl of Middlesex that the treasury was empty, " all the great farms being so clogged with the anticipations " connected with the City grants, 13th January, 1636 ; also the decision of the Lords to borrow £200,000 more from the city on the same security, 25th September, 1640 ; and finally the note of despair which creeps into the record six days later, when the Lords " offered for supplement that they would be all bound for the repayment (of £200,000), the king giving the best security he could ", for he " offered he would sell himself to his shirt for their indemnity ".[1]

Even as late as April, 1640, the plan of extending the sales of Crown lands was under consideration, as we see from a paper preserved among the records of this year.[2] This document unfolds a project for raising money by selling, in the first place, all copyholds, with their woods and timber, all parsonages, tithes and sheafs, all houses of the king in cities, boroughs, and towns, all cottages elsewhere, and all mills in his possession ; next, all farms, granges and small manors, as well as all the king's forests and parks, with their woods, timber, land, and soil. The first group consisted of estates that were a yearly charge to the king, and the suggestion was made that after they had been surveyed, they were to be sold either in fee farm or in fee simple. The second group had to be " carefully surveyed and valued ", and then sold likewise, but there were certain

[1] Cal. S.P. Dom., 1640-1641, pp. 97, 128 ; Hist. MSS. Com., Earl de la Warr MSS. rep. 4, p. 292.
[2] S.P. Dom., Chas. I, 1640, vol. 451, No. 123 ; Cal. S.P. Dom., p. 101.

reservations to be made for the king's use, viz. " only choice and necessary lands, manors, castles, and royalties," such forests and parks as were " near any of his houses of access ", and such timber as would be useful to the king personally or to the navy. This project, made on the eve of the revolution, provided the Commonwealth Commissioners with whatever excuse they may have needed for carrying out their own schemes for the survey, valuation, and sale of the Crown lands of the late monarch,[1] whom fate had delivered into their hands.

There is little need in connection with the present study to follow the fortunes of the ill-fated Stuart king, either in the periods of ministerial and personal rule between 1625 and 1637, or during the phases of resistance, reform, and revolution which preceded and followed the inevitable Civil War. It is clear that in the hour of victory the army officers turned upon the Parliamentary leaders and by means of " Pride's Purge " prepared the way for the final act of tragedy. On 13th December, 1648, the " Rump " resolved that the king should be brought to trial, and a High Court of Justice was constituted for this purpose early in the following month, sixty-seven of the 135 members being present when Charles was brought from Whitehall to the Court on 20th January, and arraigned as " tyrant, traitor, murderer, public and implacable enemy of the commonwealth of England ". Sweeping aside the king's objections to the lawfulness of the tribunal, Bradshaw urged Charles to plead, otherwise, said he, " the Court will regard you as confessing the charge." But the king replied : " I see no Lords here. Where are the Peers who alone have power to try the king ? I tell you this Court is no Court before which a king can be tried. It has been appointed by a Parliament which is not a Parliament. A true Parliament consists of King, Lords, and Commons ; was this Court appointed by such a Parliament ? " So the trial became a mere formality, and within seven days he was condemned to death, the sentence being carried into execution outside the royal banqueting hall at Whitehall on 30th January, 1648–49.

The execution of Charles has long been regarded not only as an error, but also as a crime, for even if the theory of political necessity be admitted, it is clear that the revolutionary tribunal under which he suffered, had no authority under the law or the constitution, and there can be no question that the occasion gave the king an opportunity for displaying certain latent qualities which, by their very nature, commended themselves to the admiration and affection of large numbers of his subjects. In misfortune the king was seen to possess moral greatness, as Ranke shows, though Hallam declares his inability to perceive any circumstance tending to alleviate the guilt of the

---

[1] His last letter, which concerns the disposal of forests, chases, and parks, is dated 1st June, 1642, and the reply of the Commissioners, 3rd August. A list is sent, but valuation is impossible. Cal. S.P. Dom., 1641–1643, pp. 334, 365.

transaction. The responsibility for this deed of violence rests, therefore, entirely upon a small, but extremely active group of partisans whose reign of power did not end until monarchy was restored in 1660. Well may one marvel at the political strategy which placed so small a body at the head of affairs, and still more at the remarkable stability of its power during all the years that followed; but in truth the reason is not difficult to discover, for every condition necessary to sustain the rule of a small minority was fulfilled in England at that time. Such conditions, as we see in all instances furnished by history, are never more than three : first, that the State shall have become weary with unceasing contention and civil strife, and eager therefore to find repose under any government powerful enough for administration; second, that the party proposing to rule shall have the power to do so, thus providing a prospect of prolonged peace; third, that the majority shall remain in opposition hopelessly split into factions unable to reconcile their divergent views. This was precisely the case in England after seven years of civil war, when Cromwell's assumption of power undeniably carried with it the consent and approval of the armed forces of the realm, while the opposition—in all probability five-sevenths of the whole nation at that time—remained so confused with irreconcilable points of difference that episcopalians and presbyterians, covenanters, and other partisans, found themselves incapable of combining to destroy the new government.[1]

The possibility of an experiment of this kind being tried in this country was apparently foreseen, if we may judge from the existence of a remarkable document preserved among the records of Elizabethan England. Writing ten years before the Armada left the shores of Spain and less than fifty years before the coronation of Charles, Henry Killigrew drew the attention of William Davison, the Ambassador to the Low Countries, to recent activities on the part of the Sorbonnists, one of whom had publicly maintained for five days on a recent occasion certain political propositions of a highly contentious character. Three of these propositions were specially noted by Killigrew, the first asserting that kings chosen by the people govern with more benefit to the Commonwealth than those who rule by succession; the second contending that it is lawful to depose and kill a king who oppresses his subjects and overrides the laws of the realm; and the third, while rejecting the legality of private action against the person of a wicked prince or tyrant, nevertheless affirmed that such action was rightly reserved for states and magistrates. Within the lives of two generations of Englishmen these propositions, feared by Elizabethan statesmen, found acceptance in this country, and England saw her " wicked prince and tyrant " deposed and slain,

[1] State Papers, Domestic Series, Commonwealth, 1649–1650, p. xxvi.

and a Commonwealth established for the governance of the land instead.[1]

Without delay the new government proceeded to establish its authority by means of parliamentary decisions. In January, 1648, provision was made for the omission of the king's name in public documents, and the prohibition of proclamations concerning his son. In the following month came the constitution of a Council of State of the Commonwealth of England, the appointment of Commissioners for the custody of the Great Seal, the regulation of proceedings in Courts of Justice, and the repeal of relevant clauses in the Acts of 1 Elizabeth and 3 James, in connection with the difficult question of the oaths of allegiance, obedience, and supremacy. In March, the House of Peers and the office and title of king were abolished, and on 19th May, 1649, Parliament passed an act declaring and constituting the people of England to be a Commonwealth.[2]

It was not long before serious financial difficulties—arising in part from a disorganized Exchequer and a declining revenue, but chiefly from the rising cost of public administration, especially in the matter of defence—compelled the Council of State to seek new methods of taxation whereby the national income might become enlarged. In the parliamentary efforts made at this time to broaden the basis of taxation, we may detect, as Dowell shows, the very germs of that successful fiscal system so thoroughly established in this country in later days. Taxation alone, however, could not meet the whole of the requirements of the State during those unsettled years, nor was it expedient that it should; but in spite of the numerous methods adopted, the average annual deficit on the total expenditure of the realm, according to the calculations of Dr. Shaw, proved to be in excess of £400,000.[3]

Notwithstanding the vast expenditure upon the military forces, the pay of the soldiers constantly fell into arrears. Even at the commencement of the Civil War the cost of the army and navy appears to have exceeded £100,000 a month, and upon the death of Charles the

---

[1] S.P. Dom., 1566–1579, p. 533, being No. 74 of vol. 25 at the Public Record Office. The date of the letter quoted is 22nd February, 1578.

[2] The Acts of 1648 referred to were those of January 29th, 30th, February 8th, 9th, 13th, 17th, March 17th and 19th followed by an Act of 19th May, 1649. See *Commons Journal*, vol. vi, pp. 123, 125, 135, 138, 144, 166, 168, 212; also Firth and Rait, *Acts and Ordinances of the Interregnum*, vol. i, pp. 1262, 1263; vol. ii, 1, 2, 6, 18, 24, 122; vol. iii, 64. In a speech made in Parliament about May, 1649, much of it unfit for publication, Alderman Atkins referred to the many great works "carried on by us worms" in connection with religion : " the late tyrant " had been slain and the Commonwealth established, the House of Lords being very properly abolished " when it would serve our turn no longer ". This is quoted in part in S.P. Dom., Commonwealth, vol. i, No. 100, Cal. for 1649–1650, p. 167.

[3] For a discussion on these various financial topics see Dowell, *Hist. of Taxes*, vol. ii, p. 4; Shaw, *Camb. Mod. Hist.*, vol. i, ch. xv, 454, 457; Gardiner, *Great Civil War*, vol. iii, 192, 216, and *Hist. of Commonwealth*, vol. ii, 311–313. An historical sketch of the Land Tax will be found in Cox-Sinclair's *Land Values*, pp. 1–12.

army alone cost not less than that amount, while the expenses of the navy rose suddenly to £1,300,000 in 1652. It was therefore a matter of vital concern to the new state that these arrears of pay should be met, for the stability of its power depended so largely upon the continued good will of the troops that the gravest possible consequences might be feared if the causes of discontent were not removed. In order to reduce the annual deficit and at the same time meet the urgent claims of the armed forces, Parliament now decided upon a change of policy in regard to the land revenues—a decision which had tremendous consequences in the days that lay ahead.[1]

[1] Lennard, *Rural Northamptonshire*, pp. 9–10.

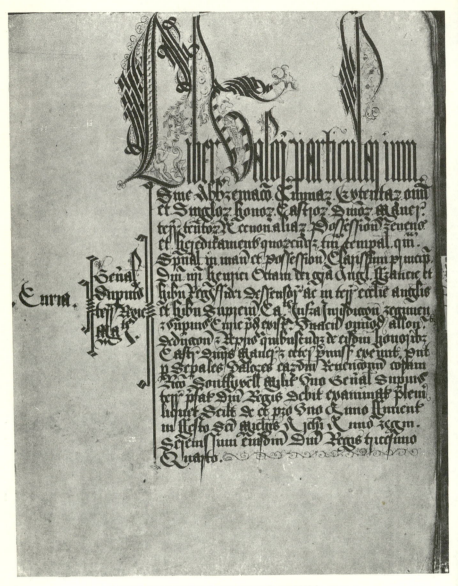

LIBER VALORUM PARTICULARIUM, 1541-2

[face p.

Chapter II

REPUBLICAN LAND TRANSACTIONS

The decision of the Commonwealth Government not to retain but to sell the various estates that came into its possession as a result of victory was a reversal of its earlier policy of deriving an annual income from land. Hitherto the government had contrived to subsist upon the ordinary revenues at its command, supplemented by special impositions such as the Excise, which provided an additional £200,000 a year, and augmented by the rents, fines, and profits derived from extensive territorial possessions. In its attempt to meet the financial claims of the army, the legislature was compelled to abandon the plan of administering the various Estates, first of the Bishops, by the Act of 17th November, 1646, then of the Deans and Chapters, 30th April, 1649, and finally of the Crown, 16th July, 1649, until at last there was little left from which an annual income could be derived at all. Little justification can be found for the extension of the new policy, for it involved the necessity of living on capital—a practice ever favoured by those in financial distress—and this plan was so essentially unsound that the plea of political expediency alone can be urged in its defence, the government having the utmost need for ready money to fulfil its extraordinary obligations. For the moment, however, the policy proved a success.[1]

The policy of selling land now adopted by the legislature assumed a variety of forms few of which had novel features. Mr. Lennard finds a ready parallel for the sale of royal pictures and plate in the use made of melted plate by royalists during the Civil War; but a better instance might have been quoted in the authority given to the Commission of December, 1625, to dispose of Crown jewels and plate. He quotes as a precedent for the confiscation of private lands the Irish Act of 1640, but instances might also have been given in connection with forfeited lands under the Tudors. The seizures of lands belonging to bishops and deans and chapters he regards as " almost parallel " to the use made by Henry VIII of the lands of suppressed monasteries, although he omits to mention that the scheme for the sale of bishops' lands was first put forward in the reign of James I, when it received the immediate support of the Duke of Buckingham.[2]

[1] Lennard, *Rural Northamptonshire*, pp. 21–3.
[2] Shaw deals with the government policy in regard to episcopal and capitular lands in his *History of the English Church*, vol. ii, 206, 211–214. Lennard's views will be found in his essay, pp. 10–16. He overlooks the commission and inventory of 1625 and 1635 in connection with the Crown jewels and plate : the former will be found in D.K.P.R., 43 (1882), app. i, No. 1, pp. 16, 48 : the latter is preserved in Land Revenue Office, Misc. Bks., vol. 123.

Mr. Lennard finds a precedent for the sale of Crown lands in the similar sales of Charles, yet other instances can be found in the alienations of Elizabeth and James. When, however, he seeks more venerable antecedents and declares that " parliament was following the example of William the Conqueror " in its " confiscation of the Crown lands ", he raises a debatable point, for the two instances are by no means comparable. In the Norman period the transference of power was clearly due to foreign conquest, and in consequence the wholesale confiscation of land adversely affected the entire nation. But this was not the case in the Stuart period, for the victory of Parliament was the outcome of civil strife, so that a section only of the community was affected by the confiscations that followed, namely, those made notorious by their active support as partisans of a now defeated royal cause. As for the Crown lands of the Stuarts, they were no less " State lands " under the Commonwealth than they had been before the change of government ; the main difference lay in this, that the control of Parliament over these estates, hitherto limited in extent, was now made absolute. Confiscation, apart from those lands which had been in the private ownership of the monarch, was hardly in question so far as the Crown lands were concerned, hence the tenants, in spite of changes, continued to pay their rents and fines into the Exchequer as before, thus contributing their customary share towards the sum total of the public revenues. Had the Civil War ended in favour of Charles, the Crown lands in the day of triumph would have become enlarged by numerous confiscations of property belonging to the disloyal section of his subjects, just as the royal estates of the Tudors grew at the expense of the Yorkists when the Wars of the Roses came to an end. But fate decided otherwise, and it was now at the command of Parliament and not of the Crown that the State lands of Charles became enlarged, though the sufferers were necessarily delinquents together with dignitaries of the Church.[1]

These various transactions of the Commonwealth government at the bidding of the army, indicate the change of policy in regard to land transfer caused by the increasing financial difficulties of the State. The two-fold character of this policy receives little emphasis

[1] On this subject see also Hist. MSS. Com. rep. 5, p. 148, rep. 8, vol. i, 553, and rep. 11, vol. i, 76, 77 ; S.P. Dom., Charles I, 1628–9, pp. 571–2, 582–3 ; 1640–1, pp. 33, 146, 151, 1641–3, p. 292, and addenda, pp. 66, 82, 88, 125, 161, 241, 257 ; Proc. for Adv. of Money, pp. 78, 553, 1142, 1547 ; Com. for Compounding, p. 3364. There is a good deal to be obtained from the Journal of the House of Commons, index, p. 331 ; also Bibl. Lindesiana, vol. i, Nos. 2158, 2174 ; and Rawlinson MSS. at the Bodleian Library, A.1 (65–71) and A. 414 (68, 101, 102). Firth and Rait, op. cit., is invaluable for the treatment of the various estates. Thus for the surveys of episcopal lands see vol. i, pp. 881, 894–7, 902–3, 910–911, 1029, 1232, and vol. ii, p. 435, while the ordinances are summarized in vol. iii, pp. 18–19. Surveys of capitular estates will be found in vol. ii, pp. 85–6, 89, 93–4, 96, 98, 204, 435, 894, and the summarized ordinances in vol. iii, pp. 45–6. Surveys of forfeited estates in England, Scotland, and Ireland are recorded in vol. i, pp. 1152–4 ; vol. ii, 331, 524–7, 533–4, 723, 729–730, 743–8, 885, 888, 928, 1103, 1105, 1261 ; and vol. iii, p. 61. For the legislation concerning delinquents and sequestrations see vol. iii, pp. 48 and 123.

at the hands of Mr. Lennard, although he recognizes differences in the treatment of the various kinds of estates, and records his conviction that the policy of sale was both a political and financial success. Parliament had been engaged since the opening of the Civil War in a policy of land acquisition which had now assumed proportions so vast that not even the augmented Crown lands of Henry VIII were equal to the State lands of the Commonwealth, whether in extent, variety, or value.[1] On the other hand, the later policy of Parliament involved alienation of estates on an equally unprecedented scale, the dispersion of an enormous amount of property being accomplished in a manner so systematic and complete that nothing since the days of Henry II, when the Crown lands assumed their greatest proportions, can compare with it. The records indeed of these remarkable land transactions are so numerous, and the particulars and valuations so important and precise, that it is hardly yet realized how possible it would be for scholars to compile an entirely new Domesday Book of State lands. The original orders and papers relating to compositions of delinquents, which concern a large proportion of the landed gentry of the country, alone fill a quarter of a million pages of the material at our disposal to-day, and in addition, there are twenty-four volumes relating to the estates of archbishops, bishops, deans, and parochial clergy, and more than a thousand surveys relating to the royal lands.[2]

In considering the financial success of the new land policy of the Government it is necessary to distinguish between the revenues derived from the sale of the various kinds of lands placed upon the market. Broadly speaking, the State lands fall into two main classes, of which one consists of lands already in possession of the State, but transferred from the control of the Crown to that of Parliament, and the other of lands newly acquired from royalists as a result of confiscation. The first of these divisions was composed entirely of Crown lands, held until recently by Charles, and now in the power of Parliament. Of a more varied character, however, were the acquired lands of the State, for they included not only the royal lands privately owned by the late monarch, but the forfeited estates of royalist peers, delinquent gentry, officials of the Church, and rebels of Ireland and Scotland. The financial gain arising from the alienation of lands, in the first category is clearly more apparent than real, since many of these lands had been in possession of the State for centuries, and had provided a regular though fluctuating income in the shape of rents, fees, and fines ; therefore an important source of national revenue was abolished by reason of such sales. But in the case of

---

[1] As to the financial results of the government policy reference may be made to Sinclair, *Hist. of Public Revenue*, vol. i, p. 245, wherein Hume and Macaulay are quoted.
[2] S.P. Dom., Commonwealth, 1649–1650, pp. x–xi ; and 1659–60, p. xxii. See also Lennard, op. cit., pp. 11–23, 25–6. The ecclesiastical documents are mostly at Lambeth Palace Library, while most of the Surveys of Crown lands are preserved in the Public Record Office.

lands recently acquired through forfeiture, the revenues accruing from their sales undoubtedly represent a gain to the Commonwealth, for these were unexpected " windfalls ", and the expenses connected with administration and custody of these miscellaneous acquisitions were in some cases curtailed and in others altogether avoided by the policy of selling such lands to private individuals. Hence, the entire gain to the State from the whole series of transactions involves subtraction as well as addition of amounts, some of which are difficult to determine owing to the perplexity of Commonwealth finance.[1]

Early in September, 1642, the principle was recognized by Parliament that delinquents ought to contribute towards the cost of the Civil War, and to this end special provision was made under the Ordinance of 27th March, 1643, for the disposal of revenues derived from the periodic rents and profits of sequestered estates. A change came when Parliament, after 16th August, 1643, authorized the realization of capital sums by means of the compositions of delinquents, who, being thus saved from absolute ruin, were induced not infrequently to desert the royal cause. Occasional sales of lands also occurred under the order of 10th July, 1644, and especially in connection with the forfeitures enforced by the Ordinance of 9th June, 1646. But it was not until the abolition of monarchy that special Acts provided for the sale of these estates in large numbers.[2] Seventy-three delinquents, for example, were named in the Act of 16th July, 1651, a further twenty-nine persons in that of 4th August, 1652 (the proceeds in this case being assigned to the Navy), and no less than 678 in the Act of 18th November, 1652.[3] The policy therefore of the Government in regard to the lands of private individuals appears to have been, first of all, to draw annual sums of rents and profits from the sequestration of the estates, next to derive capital sums from compositions on an increasingly large scale, and finally to authorize the actual sale of lands expressly declared to have been forfeited for treason.[4] The table which follows [5] records some significant figures in connection with these transactions, although

---

[1] The financial history of the Interregnum period remains unwritten, so for the present, generalizations on this perplexing subject can only be of a tentative character. A university thesis in preparation at the London School of Economics (1929) may eventually throw considerable light on the financial transactions that occurred between 1640 and 1660. The present work reveals the nature and extent of the sales of Crown lands and rents in this difficult period of history. For 1558–1641, see Dietz, Eng. Pub. Finance, 1932.

[2] See Firth and Rait, op. cit., vol. iii, pp. 48–9, for the classes of persons regarded as delinquents, the authorities empowered to act, the penalties imposed, and above all the particular ordinances and acts ; also vol. iii, pp. 123–5, for the subject of sequestration of delinquents' estates in general, and for particular instances of such confiscations.

[3] The general Acts relating to the three special sales of forfeited estates in 1651–2, as well as references to payments of a miscellaneous character will be found in vol. iii, p. 61. The compositions quoted in S.P. Dom., 1649–1650, pp. x–xi, were computed in 1875 to be equivalent to the sum of about £5,000,000.

[4] See also Lennard, op. cit., pp. 11–14 on the policy of Parliament in regard to the estates of delinquents. Reference may also be made to Hume, Hist. of England, vol. iii, ch. 62 ; Sinclair, op. cit., pp. 283–5 ; and Stevens, Royal Treasury of England, pp. 289–296.

[5] See Table XVII, p. 69.

the results must be read with caution.[1] Hume, quoting Thurloe, states that the lands of delinquents were worth over £200,000 a year, and the figures given by Stevens in regard to sequestrations seem to bear this out. Stevens also records the total receipts from compositions, but the amount of £1,277,226, which he gives, appears to have been exceeded, for it is now known that at least £1,305,000 was received in the eight years ending August, 1652. Sinclair agrees with the total given by Stevens of £2,245,000 received from the sales of delinquents lands in England, but the latter gives an additional sum of £7,760 received from the sale of naval timber out of the woods of delinquents, and estimates that the government obtained £1,000,000 from compositions and £1,322,500 from three successive sales of lands belonging to Irish delinquents. How much was derived from similar transactions in Scotland is unknown.

XVII. Sequestrations and Sales, 1643–59[2]

(A) Sequestrations; (B) Sales; (C) Compositions.

Note.—The amounts given for the Sequestrations and Sales represent thousands (£'000), during the period 3rd November, 1650, to 5th November, 1659.

	Years.		Amounts.	
Sources.	A.	B.	A. £'000.	B. £'000.
(i) The Crown Revenues.				
Crown Lands	4	13	280·0	9,152·0
Prince of Wales' Lands	4	13	80·0	260·0
Houses and Castles	—	—	—	600·0
Forest Lands	4	13	16·0	56·0
Fee Farm Rents	4	8	1,054·4	1,908·8
New River Water	—	8	—	8·0
Court of Wards (C)	14	—	1,400·0	—
Public Services (Officers' Income)	15	—	850·0	—
(ii) The Church Revenues.				
Bishops' Lands	4	10	884·1	2,420·2
Dean and Chapter Lands	4	10	564·7	1,411·9
Inferior Clergy Lands	4	12	2,077·8	6,203·6
Tenths of Clergy	4	8	400·1	1,200·2
(iii) The Royalists' Revenues.				
Temporal Estates	4	—	280·0	—
Vintners' Delinquency	—	—	4·0	—
English Delinquents (C)	—	—	1,277·2	—
Irish Delinquents (C)	2	—	1,000·0	1,322·5
Craven Estates, etc.	—	13	—	700·0
Gifford Estates, etc.	—	13	—	900·0
Stawell Estates, etc.	—	5	—	560·0
Pr. Palatine Settlement (171 persons)	—	—	—	85·0
Naval Timber (Delinquents)	—	—	—	7·8
(iv) Total (i)	—	—	3,680·4	11,984·8
(ii)	—	—	3,926·7	11,235·9
(iii)	—	—	2,561·2	3,575·3
Grand total	1 *to* 15		10,168·3	26,796·0

[1] For an estimate of the Land Revenues for the period 3rd November, 1650, to 5th November, 1659, under the three heads of Crown, Church, and Royalists' Revenues, with separate amounts for sequestrations and sales, see Table No. XVII, in which the figures given by Stevens and others are recorded.

[2] Estimates of John Stevens and other early writers on Commonwealth sales, combined in one table as shown, but the legislation covers the years 1643–59.

A comparison between the pre-war values of sequestered estates and the later valuation in connection with compositions reveals a great decline in the value of land and tenements in some of the counties of England. In Wiltshire, where parks were much decayed, and the county seriously disturbed in recent years by royalist forces, the letting value of six premises was only two-thirds of earlier values. In Cheshire, where values are sometimes omitted owing to war damage, the valuation is often less than half of the pre-war amount, and at times it is only one-third, as is the case not infrequently in Gloucestershire. The following instances of depreciated values in 1647 are taken from counties in the war area [1] :—

XVIII. PRE-WAR AND POST-WAR VALUATIONS, 1640–1647

Counties.	Total No.	Under £100.	Above £100.	Pre-War Value. £	Later Value. £	Range.
Cheshire .	31	22	9	4,143	2,247	£3 to £262
Gloucester	27	18	9	6,542	3,142	£7 ,, £600
Wiltshire .	23	9	14	3,799	2,218	£14 ,, £680
Totals .	81	49	32	14,484	7,607	£3 to £680

In eighty-three cases taken from Buckinghamshire, ranging from £1 to £2,750, the pre-war value of which is not stated, forty-three were below £100 and four above £1,000.

The month of September, 1642, witnessed also the decision of Parliament to abolish episcopacy and arrangements were made for the sequestration not only of the lands of bishops, but also of deans and chapters of cathedrals and collegiate churches, the object being to provide security for the payment of the Scottish forces. By an Ordinance of 9th October, 1646, the episcopal estates were vested in trustees and ordered to be surveyed, and on 17th November following, the speedy sale of these lands was authorized, the minimum rate allowed being ten years' purchase of their full values in the year 1641. Such sales served their immediate purpose, and Parliament postponed further action in regard to Church lands, advowsons, impropriations, and the expected *jura regalia* of the bishoprics of Durham and Ely, although the capitular estates were referred to in the king's propositions of October, 1647, and in the military projects advanced by Ludlow. Not until the execution of the king did Parliament resolve to abolish the deans and chapters, and by the Act of 30th April, 1649, their lands were seized, surveyed, and sold, the minimum rate of purchase in this case being twelve years. This decision was undoubtedly hastened by the most urgent needs of the

[1] Table XVIII with values of sequestered property in 1647, showing the effect of war conditions in the counties named, is based on particulars obtained from the Calendar of the Committee for Compounding, 1643–1660, vol. i, pp. 60–2, 66–8, 76–9, 85–6. With care and patience no doubt a greater amount of evidence might be forthcoming from this source in regard to pre-war and post-war valuations. The values given in this table are calculated to the nearest pound.

army, whose departure for Ireland was delayed by the failure of a deputation from Parliament at the Guildhall, on 12th April, when the citizens professed doubts as to the security then offered in the shape of fee farm rents and assessments. Eventually large sums were realized from the sales of Church lands. Hume, quoting Dr. Walker as his authority, states that these lands were sold for a million pounds. Mr. Lennard, following Dr. Shaw, says erroneously that nothing is known of the amount of money brought in by the sale of episcopal lands, but he considers that the estates of the deans and chapters produced £980,724 between 1649 and 31st August, 1650, and possibly £503,178 afterwards. Very different figures are available in the table already given,[1] which shows that Stevens records a total of £884,089 16s. 7d. received from sequestrations of bishops' lands and a further sum of £2,420,224 11s. 6½d. derived from their sales. Sinclair, although critical of the methods of computation adopted by Stevens, nevertheless endorses these figures. Mr. Tatham industriously traced 727 of these sales of bishops' lands among the enrolments upon the Close Rolls, and thus accounted for fully £662,600 received from this source between 1647 and 1659; but it is certain, just as in the case of the Crown lands, that not all the sales were enrolled. Most of the money appears to have been received before 1650 as will be seen from the analysis given below[2] :—

XIX. Amounts Received from the Sales of Bishops' Lands, 1647-1659

Period.	No. of Sales.	Amount received. £
1647–1649	459	463,302·6
1650–1654	234	186,812·5
1655–1659	34	12,485·5
Totals .	727	£662,600·6

From the whole of the sequestrations of Church lands the Government received, according to Stevens, £3,526,632 16s. 4d.—an amount which Sinclair, whose addition is erroneous on this occasion, records as £3,528,632. The receipts from the sales of all the Church lands are shown by both writers to have reached a total of £10,035,663 1s. 11½d. though in view of the researches of Dr. Shaw and Mr. Tatham, these figures must be received with caution. Sinclair agrees with Stevens that the tenths of all clergy and other exactions from the Church during this period amounted to £1,600,320.[3]

[1] See Table XVII, p. 69.
[2] Table XIX records the number of sales and the amounts received in connection with bishops' lands in each of three periods between 1647 and 1659, based on the figures recorded by Mr. Tatham. The values are given to the decimal of £1. See also Table XIX B and the fuller table (No. XIXA) relating to Church lands.
[3] See Lennard's account of the treatment of episcopal estates and the lands of the Deans and Chapters in his essay, pp. 15–17 and 22. For the list of ordinances relating to these lands reference must be made to Firth and Rait, op. cit., vol. iii, pp. 18–19 and 45–6. For other points connected with this subject see Firth ,Ludlow's Memoirs, vol. i, p. 231 ;

Considerable interest, as Mr. Tatham recognizes, attaches to the character of persons who purchased ecclesiastical property, and as all the twenty-four trustees appointed by the Ordinance of 9th October, 1646, were either aldermen or citizens of London, it is not surprising to find that nearly 60 per cent of the purchases were made by Londoners. The figures furnished by Professor Savine and Mr. Tatham form an instructive comparison in respect to the grants and purchases of Church and monastic lands during the sixteenth and seventeenth centuries. Excluding the grants to Welsh monasteries, Savine classified altogether 1,593 monastic grants of Henry VIII, involving approximately £90,000 in yearly values and £779,000 in money payments. Of these grants forty-one are classified as gifts, sixty-one as exchanges, and 1,186 as sales, while the remainder are merely variations of these three methods of alienation. As a result he finds that Crown officials, the Court of Augmentations, and king's servants, 230 persons in all, account for at least 267 of the sales and 484 of the whole number of grants, and that thirty-eight peers and several corporations, spiritual as well as lay, received 193 grants between them. Leaving out all doubtful cases, we find the remaining grantees consist of eighty-six industrials with 140 grants to their credit, twenty-one lawyers and eleven physicians who account for another sixty-two grants, and eleven yeomen and eight clerks who share twenty-one grants between them, the annual value not exceeding £500 in their case. That is to say, the percentage of grantees outside the Court and peerage, numbering 137 out of a total of 405 (if we put aside corporations and all uncertain cases), is slightly under 35 per cent for the reign of Henry VIII. Mr. Tatham's analysis of the Commonwealth purchasers shows that the country gentry represent 30 per cent, and important citizens of London 20 per cent of the whole ; moreover, provincial clergy and tradesmen, with three corporations, form 4 per cent, and London tradesmen and merchants 29 per cent ; while yeomen and lawyers make up the remaining 17 per cent in almost equal proportions. In view of these figures the yeoman appears to be a person of over-rated importance.[1]

The separate values of capitular and episcopal lands, recorded in some detail in the next table, are of particular interest and importance because they have been calculated from a return made to Parliament

Baillie's Letters, vol. ii, 411 (quoted by Shaw) ; Shaw, op. cit., vol. ii, pp. 206, 211-14, and app. viii, pp. 558-569, also *Camb. Mod. Hist.*, vol. iv, p. 457 ; Hume (quoting Walker and Thurloe), op. cit., vol. iii, ch. 62, pp. 500-1 ; Gardiner, *Hist. Commonwealth*, vol. i, pp. 44-5, also *Civil War*, vol. i, p. 19 ; vol. iii, p. 145, and *Constitutional Documents*, p. 343 ; Sinclair, op. cit., pp. 283-5 ; Stevens, op. cit., pp. 289-296. Mr. Tatham's valuable calculations are contained in his contribution to the *Eng. Hist. Review*, vol. xxiii, pp. 91-108 ; cf. Whetham's note in the same journal, vol. xxii, pp. 553-4.

[1] For Tatham's figures see *Eng. Hist. Rev.*, vol. xxiii, pp. 101-2, 108. These have been compared with Savine's calculations, recorded in a table quoted by Fisher, *Political Hist. of England,* vol. v, app. ii, pp. 497-9.

in November, 1642, and compared with the receipts for each diocese which Mr. Tatham records in connection with the sales of bishop's lands between 1647 and 1659. It will be seen that Canterbury stands highest in the valuation of episcopal lands in 1642, but that York had

XIX*A*. VALUATION OF CHURCH LANDS, 1642–1659

The Annual Values of Capitular and Episcopal lands in November, 1642, and the amount realized by the Sale of Episcopal Estates between 1647 and 1659.

| | Annual Values. | | Episcopal Sales. | |
	Bishops' Lands. £	Deans' Lands. £	No.	Amount. £
Areas and Dioceses.				
(i) Metropolitan.				
Canterbury . .	3,093·9	300·0	82	73,031·7
Chichester . .	677·1	58·5	23	16,524·2
London . .	1,119·4	210·6	72	57,594·9
Oxford . . .	354·8	100·0	14	4,152·1
Rochester . .	358·2	100·0	8	9,958·1
(ii) Extra-Metropolitan.				
Bath and Wells .	533·1	116·4	27	22,176·5
Ely . . .	2,134·9	120·0	37	29,875·6
Lichfield . .	703·3	40·0	20	25,123·0
Lincoln . .	893·9	196·5	21	14,761·4
Norwich . .	899·4	102·0	28	20,259·1
Peterborough . .	415·0	100·0	12	7,633·5
Salisbury . .	1,367·6	204·5	25	33,985·9
Winchester . .	2,491·5	199·7	65	89,343·3
(iii) Borderlands.				
Bristol . . .	383·4	100·0	11	4,214·0
Carlisle . . .	531·2	120·4	10	7,386·3
Chester . . .	420·1	100·0	11	5,297·3
Durham . .	1,821·1	266·6	38	76,213·1
Exeter . . .	500·0	158·0	15	13,020·2
Gloucester . .	315·4	100·0	10	3,741·6
Hereford . .	768·5	38·3	18	8,285·9
Worcester . .	1,049·6	133·3	31	25,043·9
York . . .	1,610·0	308·5	103	67,274·6
(iv) Wales.				
Bangor . . .	131·8	22·4	2	795·2
Llandaff. . .	154·7	—	7	3,775·2
St. Asaph . .	187·6	45·6	3	1,500·1
St. David's . .	457·1	—	12	6,024·2
(v) Combined Dioceses .	—	—	22	35,609·7
Total [1] . .	23,372·6	3,607·1	727	662,600·6

the greatest number of sales and Winchester the largest receipts; on the other hand, apart from the Welsh dioceses, which are invariably low in position in the table, Gloucester had the lowest valuation in England and provided the smallest returns from sales, while Rochester had less than a dozen sales enrolled. York and Hereford have the highest and lowest valuations respectively of English capitular lands. Analysing

[1] The Deaneries of Westminster, £232·5, and Windsor, £133·3, are included in Area I. See Table XIX*B* for regional totals.

the figures given for each of the divisions indicated in the table we obtain the following comparative results [1]:—

XIXB. REGIONAL VALUATION OF CHURCH LANDS, 1642–1659

		Annual Values.		Episcopal Sales.	
Areas.	Dioceses.	Bishops.	Deans.	No.	Amount.
		£	£		£
(i) Metropolitan	5	5,603·4	1,134·9	199	161,261·0
(ii) Extra-Metropolitan	8	9,438·7	1,079·1	235	243,158·3
(iii) Border-lands	9	7,399·3	1,325·1	247	210,476·9
(iv) Wales	4	931·2	68·0	24	12,094·7
(v) Combined Dioceses	—	—	—	22	35,609·7
Totals	26	23,372·6	3,607·1	727	662,600·6

The average number of sales of bishops' lands in the four areas indicated above is seen to vary from six in Wales to forty in the Metropolitan area, the average amount received per diocese ranging similarly from £3,000 to £32,000. It appears also that on the average each sale produced £504 in Wales, £810 in Division I, £852 in Division III, and the largest amount of all, namely £1,035, in Division II.[2]

By these various stages we have seen the government policy in regard to land developed, first in the treatment of delinquents' lands and then in connection with the estates of bishops and the lands of deans and chapters. Only the Crown estates remain to be considered, and these in some detail as a special study; but for the moment it may be noted that the estimate of £1,993,951 which Mr. Lennard gives, is merely a repetition of Dr. Shaw's statement of the receipts from the sales of those lands. We shall see presently that this total is the result of an inaccurate addition, and that it does not in any case represent the true gain to the legislature from the sales, since the concurrent loss of revenue from rents, fees, fines, and other incidental profits, eventually amounting to £120,000 per annum, is not considered.

However much one may be disposed to criticize the Commonwealth government for its attitude in these matters, especially on the

[1] Table XIXB is based on two sets of calculations, namely, those of Rogers, *Hist. of Agriculture*, vol. vi, document xvii, p. 710, and Tatham, op. cit., as above. The annual values given of lands of bishoprics and deaneries are recorded in a special return made to the order of Parliament in November, 1642. Rogers' list includes twenty-six bishoprics with an equal number of deaneries, four of the former, and two of the latter being in Wales. Eleven of the bishoprics—Bath, Chichester, Exeter, Hereford, Lichfield, Lincoln, London, Salisbury, York, Bangor, and St. Asaph—are called " Pre-Reformation Foundations ", and the remaining fifteen " Novae creationes ". His totals of £23,372·553 and £3,632·056 for bishops' lands and those of deans', yield gross average incomes of £898·946 and £139·694 respectively. The net average income for bishoprics, deducting £2,289·569 for tenths, is shown to be £809·346.

[2] Tatham's figures show the number of sales and the produce for each diocese year by year between 1647 and 1659. In this table the results of both sets of calculations are summarized and displayed for comparative purposes, the values being expressed in decimals of £1, correct to the nearest florin. The figures for each diocese are given in greater detail in the table of Church lands set out in Table XIXA. The arrangement of the list and its division into areas is in accordance with a scheme for the Crown lands already explained. See Table I.

ground of political expediency as dictated by army needs, there can be no reasonable doubt that the policy was a financial success. While it is true that political opposition was intensified by the sequestrations and sales, it must not be forgotten that the ranks of irreconcilable opponents were not unduly filled, for the opportunity given for compounding and the merciful provision of one-fifth for the maintenance of delinquents' families, undoubtedly won the support of many former antagonists, the more so since in their case the policy of sale was not urged as the primary purpose of parliament. Nevertheless, as Gardiner shows, every acre sold became a firm bond between the purchaser and the Commonwealth, so that the various means adopted for attracting purchasers (who thereby became pledged to support the revolutionary government) created vested interests that were strong enough to defy Royalist intrigues throughout this period; and these were found to be effective enough after 1660 to prevent the restoration of many of the lands thus dispersed, just as the measures adopted by Henry VIII proved an obstacle to the return of monastic lands under Mary.

The amounts received from the various sequestrations and sales are shown by Dr. Shaw and others to have been very great indeed. Sinclair considers that the sequestrations of estates and compositions with private individuals in England amounted to £4,564,986. Stevens places the total of sequestrations of every kind at £6,044,924 17s. and says that from the sales of all English lands the large sum of £25,380,687 was received. In addition, there was a considerable revenue derived from assessments, the produce of the Land Tax between 1640 and 1659, according to Sinclair, being as much as £32,172,321. Hume came to the conclusion that in the most prosperous years of Charles, namely from 1637 to 1640, the revenue of the monarch had reached £900,000, though perhaps £200,000 of this might be declared illegal. But in 1651 the public expenses, as Montague points out, were thrice that amount, or £2,750,000 altogether, owing to the great increase in the cost of defence. The sales of land together with the royalist compositions provided extraordinary sources of income which did much to relieve the urgent needs of the Government in a time of financial crisis. Dr. Shaw's considered opinion is that these sources of income made up the yearly deficit and kept the Commonwealth somewhat solvent for about four years, but that after 1654 the excess of expenses over the regular income became a permanent debt of ever-increasing proportions.[1]

Summing up, we may conclude that the abolition of episcopacy on 9th October, 1646, followed shortly after by that of monarchy, 17th March, 1648, fulfilled in its entirety the prophecy " No Bishop,

[1] See Lennard, op. cit., pp. 21–2 ; Sinclair, op. cit., pp. 283–5 ; Stevens, op. cit., pp. 292–4 ; Hume, op. cit., vol. iii, ch. 62, p. 500, n. 2 ; Montague, *Political Hist. of England*, p. 382 ; Shaw, *Camb. Mod. Hist.*, vol. iv, pp. 457–8.

no King ", uttered years before by James. Financial necessity had compelled the Government to place the estates of the bishops immediately upon the market, in accordance with the ordinance of 16th November, 1646, and, as we have seen, the sales of the lands of the deans was not long delayed. It was natural, therefore, that Government supporters should expect the royal estates to be treated in a similar manner, and when, upon the execution of the king, Parliament acceded to the wishes of the army in this respect, it was certainly able to make a virtue of necessity, having been logically consistent in its attitude towards State lands of every kind. Nevertheless, the urgency of its financial problem was admittedly great.[1]

Within a few months, therefore, of the death of the king, we find the legislature engaged in the serious task of formulating measures for the dispersion of the royal possessions. Orders were early given for the seizure and speedy sale of the personal estate of the late king Charles, his queen Henrietta Maria, and the young prince, afterwards Charles II. From the existing inventories of the pictures, plate, and other treasures of the royal family, and the accounts furnished by Treasurer Jones in connection with the sales, it is possible to realize the importance of this new source of supply to a government so sorely pressed for money. Nor was it long before the landed estates of the royal family came under review, an Act of 16th July, 1649, being eventually passed which authorized their immediate survey, valuation, and sale. In succeeding sections we shall see how completely and successfully the contractors and other officials of Worcester House carried out their formidable task.[2]

[1] Firth and Rait, op. cit., vol. i, pp. 879–883.
[2] The act for the sale of the royal treasures is given in Firth and Rait, op. cit., vol. ii, pp. 160–8. Inventories of the pictures, plate, and other goods will be found in Harl. 4898 and 7352 at the British Museum. The account of H. Jones, treasurer under the Act, is preserved in the P.R.O. under the reference Decl. Accounts, Pipe Office, roll 569.

CHAPTER III

THE ACT FOR THE SALE OF CROWN LANDS, 1649

Early in the period of Civil War, Parliament had made provision for the receipt of rents and other revenues arising out of royal lands in the respective areas then controlled by its forces, several ordinances being decreed after 21st September, 1643, in reference to such matters as the payment of rents, preservation of game, felling of timber, and even the cutting of turf to supply the needs of the poor in the neighbourhood of the royal estates. But as the struggle proceeded the area under control of parliament grew larger and the revenues received from this source considerably increased in amount, so that by the ordinance of 29th July, 1648, it was found possible to arrange for the payment of the northern forces out of the revenues collected from royal possessions in Yorkshire, and at the same time to organize the collection of rents, issues, and profits in other parts of the country.[1] The amounts collected in this way improved between 1649 and 1651, after which, owing to the effect of land sales, the rents and miscellaneous payments decreased considerably. This is proved from inspection of the accounts kept by receivers of revenues, one of those books is preserved in the University library at Cambridge.[2] Of the total shown in the following table £1,055 was collected in 1649, £2,178 in the following year, and £2,831 in 1651, leaving £773 and £868 in the hands of receivers during the next two years. The amounts received from the Metropolitan area rose from £112 in 1649 to £815 in 1650, and then fell to £258 and £120 in the succeeding years, rising once again to £258 in 1653. In the Extra-Metropolitan area the revenue rose from £517 to £1,766 in 1651 and then fell back to £508. The Borderlands also varied in the same period, increasing from £427 to £868 in 1651 and falling back to £102 two years later.

XX. Rents and Revenues from Crown Tenants, 1649–1653

Areas.	Counties.	Items.	Amounts. £
(i) Metropolitan .	10	38	1,502·6
(ii) Extra-Metropolitan	13	51	4,368·5
(iii) Borderlands . .	10	23	1,834·6
Totals .	33	112	7,705·7

[1] See Firth and Rait's *Acts and Ordinances of the Interregnum*, vol. iii, pp. 42–3.
[2] Camb. Univ. Lib., Dd. 13.20 (2). The total recorded for the period 1649–1653 is £7,758 5s. 2½d., but I have not been able to account for £52 10s. of this amount.

Now was the time ripe, since the king was dead, for putting into operation the scheme of the army leaders for surveying and selling the lands of the Crown. The first hint of progress in this direction is found in the appointment on 23rd February, 1648–9, of a Committee of twenty-four Members of Parliament, Cromwell, Ireton, and other regicides being among the number, for the purpose of bringing in an Act which should empower Commissioners to survey parks, forests, chases, and manors of the Crown and the Duchy of Lancaster, and subsequently to dispose of them in such manner as would prove advantageous to the Commonwealth.

In February, then, this Committee set to work with results that were quickly seen, for in the following month Parliament discussed a suggestion from the Council of State that £40,000 required for army purposes might be easily raised by putting up the revenues of the Crown for sale, or as an alternative, disposing of the lands then in the custody of the Commissioners of the Star Chamber. Out of this suggestion came the decision of Parliament on 18th April, 1649, that the sum of £600,000, hitherto charged upon the Excise, should now be transferred as a charge upon the Crown lands, the speedy sale of which was eminently desirable in order to provide funds for the payment of the soldiers' arrears.[1]

Arrangements were immediately made for the preparation of an Act authorizing the sale of the parks, houses, manors, lands, and farms of the Crown, and on 9th May, this Act was read for the first and second time, after which it was entrusted to the care of a committee of twenty-five members, fifteen of whom were new, Cromwell and several others no longer serving now that the initial work was done. Additions were made from time to time to this " Committee for the Act ", and sub-committees of from five to eight persons appear to have been formed to deal with provisos or other amendments arising out of the reports made to Parliament. The Journals of the Commons show that by the time the Act received its third reading on 12th July, 1649, at least seventy persons, of whom twenty were regicides, had taken an active interest in the measure, notably such men as Boone, Corbett, Danvers, Garland, Harrington, Harrison, Holland, Martin, Say, and Weaver, most of whom made reports, while Alderman Pennington and Sir Peter Wentworth acted as tellers for the " yeas ", and Colonel Martin and Sir John Danvers for the " noes " on the occasion of the one division taken on 12th July. Meetings of the committee were held in the Court of Wards at first, but afterwards in the Speaker's Chamber, usually in the afternoon, though on one occasion (7th July) as early as six in the morning, the Serjeant being specially instructed to see that Mr. Attorney-General was present at that early hour. Petitions from the Earl of Pembroke, Sir John Danvers, and the freeholders of Gillingham, Dorset, were

<hr>

[1] House of Commons Journals, vol. vi, p. 150; Cal. S.P. Dom., 1649–50, p. 28.

referred to the three Committees of Sale, Revenue, and Complaints, respectively.

In May a division of opinion occurred among members, the Council of State eventually deciding to report its opinion that certain houses and parks ought to be kept for the public use of the Commonwealth and not sold. Next month an effort was made to complete the work, the Council considering that the Act should be passed before the intended recess. Debates began in earnest on 28th June when amendments to the Act were read for the first and second time, On the 29th and 30th, various officials were appointed, and the Committee was ordered not only to prepare instructions for the guidance of trustees and contractors, but to confer with the Committee for the Navy as to the best manner of preserving all the timber that might prove fit for shipping, if growing in accessible places upon the royal lands.[1]

July opened with the Act prepared for engrossing, a clause being accepted for inclusion on the 3rd in reference to the preservation of castles, and also public buildings that might be of use for the Navy or for the administration of justice. On 9th July came the warning from the Council of State : " To report to the House that the Act for the sale of the King's parks, for securing the soldiers' arrears, ought to be speedily passed, it being of very great importance." Three days later the Act was read for the third time, and after certain provisos had been accepted, two others amended and two more rejected during the debates which followed, it was finally decided on 16th July, 1649, " that the Act, with the several provisoes and amendments made at the table do pass." [2]

Within the short space of five months the first Act for the disposal of the royal estates had been considered, amended by successive committees, and finally passed by Parliament, a score of army leaders having eagerly watched the measure through the whole of its critical stages. The Act thus passed is one of the most important in the history of land legislation, its perfection of detail being due to the experience previously gained by Parliament in framing the ordinances relating to the sale of episcopal and capitular lands.[3]

Reference is first made in the Act to the financial needs of the State and the desirability of reducing the debts contracted for the Army. " Whereas," runs the preamble, " the late King, the Queen, and their eldest son, have been the chief authors of the late Wars and troubles," it is therefore meet and right, " in all Justice and Equity,"

---

[1] *Commons Journals*, vol. vi, 189, 205, 207, 225, 240–1, 244–6, 249, 258 ; and S.P. Dom., 1649–50, p. 155.
[2] Ibid., vol. vi, 249, 254, 258–61 ; S.P. Dom., 1649–50, p. 227.
[3] Firth and Rait, *Acts and Ordinances*, vol. ii, pp. 168–191. For the most active members who were responsible for the passing of the first Act for Sale of the Crown lands see the list of regicides and other republicans in Appendix III. sect. iv.

that they should bear the burden of the debts thus incurred.[1] For this reason, Parliament in its wisdom decided that the estates of the royal family should be " applied to take off and discharge the same, it being the duty, and especial care and endeavour of the Parliament, that the people should not in any sort be taxed and charged, but in cases of inevitable necessity, and when other ways and means are wanting ". Finding the office of King in this nation " unnecessary, burdensome, and dangerous ", it had already been abolished, and it was now expressly enacted that the sum of £600,000 for the payment of soldiers' arrears should henceforth be charged upon the security of all honours, castles, houses, messuages, parks, and lands, other than those excepted later, that were in possession of the royal family, on 1st April, 1635, and all lands found by survey of the chases to be rightly held by the Crown since 26th March, 1641.

The administrative work connected with the Act devolved, as in the case of the ordinance of 16th November, 1646, upon the Surveyor-General, Colonel William Webb, and his assistants. On 18th April Parliament had ordered the Lord General and Council of War to name six persons to act as trustees, and upon the resumed debate of 30th June seven other names were added by Parliament. Not all these names appear in the Act, for Thos. Blunt, Jn. Cleypool, and Jn. Ireton begged to be excused, and in their places Wm. Bosseville, Jn. Hunt, and Wm. Scott agreed to serve. With these thirteen trustees were twelve contractors, a comptroller, two registrars dealing with entries and debentures respectively, and four treasurers acting in conjunction with the Treasurers for War. None of the officials were regicides, and it is indeed significant that the four treasurers were Aldermen of the City of London, one of them, Thomas Andrews, being also Mayor at the time, so that the question of reprisals upon the restoration of monarchy in 1660, quite apart from the doubtful prospect of restitution of the lands themselves, presented very great difficulties.

All the officials were to receive payment for their services. Thus each of the trustees received threepence in the pound for all lands conveyed ; and although this appears to be but a small commission the actual amount received must have been considerable, for Holcroft, Steele, and Scott were the only trustees who sealed less than a hundred conveyances, whereas the names of Hunt and Harrison appear on nearly 460 of these documents.[2] The contractors, too, received another threepence in the pound for all the lands they sold. The treasurers, moreover, were authorized to deduct a penny in the pound from all the money received from purchasers for their own salary and the payments of their clerks and tellers. Fixed sums were allowed to

---

[1] A seventeenth-century example of a " War guilt clause ".
[2] Analysis of Cambridge University MS., Dd., 13.20. Jn. Hunt and Ralph Harrison were among the Trustees who sealed conveyances for Enfield Park and Lodges.

From a Drawing by Hollar

In the Pepysian Library at Cambridge

DURHAM HOUSE.

The three Houses above represented, stood on the banks of the Thames, nearly adjoining each other. DURHAM HOUSE, the first occupied the spot called DURHAM YARD, now the ADELPHI, and was built by Ant.d Bec, Bish.p of Durham, as a town residence for the Bishops of that See.

SALISBURY HOUSE.

SALISBURY HOUSE was erected by Robert Cecil, Earl of Salisbury, in the reign of James I. and covered the site of the present Salisbury and Cecil Streets. WORCESTER HOUSE, originally belonged to the See of Carlisle. It afterwards came into the possession of the Earls of Worcester, Edw.d the last Earl of Worcester died here in 1627.

WORCESTER HOUSE.

his son Hen.y being created, Duke of Beaufort, it was called Beaufort House, and the site is now called Beaufort Buildings. The above View was taken about the year 1650.

Published for Beckett, by W.m Herbert, Lambeth, and M.r Wilkinson N.o 58 Cornhill, London

WORCESTER HOUSE, STRAND, 1650

the Surveyor-General and the comptroller, the former receiving £150 per annum for himself and clerks, and the latter £300 for the same purpose, the amounts to be paid half-yearly for a maximum period of three years. To the registrar the trustees were to pay a yearly fee of £100, but he was permitted to receive in addition " reasonable fees " for writing, rating, and signing particulars, the amount not to exceed twopence per sheet of fifteen lines, whenever records were required to be copied.

Parliament ordered that all officials should take their respective oaths before commencing duties. The contractors were required to promise that they would, according to their best skill and knowledge, faithfully discharge the trust committed to them by the Act, and that on no account would they break their promise, " for favour or affection, reward or gift, or hope of reward or gift." Three or more of the trustees were empowered to administer a very carefully worded oath to each surveyor appointed by them, in order to secure that these officials should execute their office under the Act, using their best endeavour and skill to discover every part of the estate given in charge, thus finding out the true values and improvements, and making true surveys according to their " best skill and cunning " ; and afterwards the surveyors were to deliver their surveys closely sealed to the registrar, with a true copy or duplicate likewise to the trustees. By their oath these officials undertook that the work should be justly and faithfully executed, without gift or reward, directly or indirectly, from any person whatsoever, other than the amounts allowed for their duties by the trustees. In the same way the trustees were to call upon the registrar, his deputy, and clerk, to take the oath presented in the ordinance of 5th March, 1646, and thus execute their respective offices and places without fear, favour, malice, or reward.

The trustees were required by the same Act to perform a variety of duties by reason of the fact that Parliament had vested the honours, manors, and other royal possessions in their " real and actual possession and seisin ", in order that these estates might be an effectual security for the purpose which the Government had in view. They were to hold such premises as of the manor of East Greenwich in free and common socage, by fealty, and by no other tenure whatsoever, completely free from all payments of tithes. Officials such as the registrar of debentures and the various county surveyors were to be appointed by them, the requisite oath being duly administered to contractors and other responsible persons in connection with the sales. Whenever vacancies occurred, the trustees were to make appointments of stewards, bailiffs, and keepers of manorial property, and in order that the progress of the surveys might not be impeded or the sales delayed they were empowered to call upon sheriffs, mayors, and justices of the peace to render every assistance in their power.

Difficult legal questions might be met by the employment of counsel, the usual fees being allowed whenever this course was necessary. Property unsold might be leased for a year or less, and then continued from year to year so that the leases might terminate whenever sales were effected ; but the rents reserved were to be the best obtainable, while the custom of copyholds in any honour or manor was to be most carefully preserved. Accounts were inspected and revised by the trustees, arrears being certified to them from time to time by the registrar of debentures.

Any five of the trustees had authority to convey premises to the purchasers, and this might be accomplished either by bargain or sale enrolled upon the Close Rolls, or by any other good and sufficient legal method of conveyance, provided that the persons concerned had completed their contracts with the contractors. Such bargains of sale and conveyances of estates in fee simple were declared by the Act to be good and effectual in law, and purchasers, whether individuals or associates, were empowered to hold the premises fully discharged of all trusts and accounts, and entirely free from encumbrances, being entitled under the Act to all the advantages and benefits of possession hitherto enjoyed by the former royal owners. Should any purchaser desire to be even more fully assured in regard to his acquired rights of ownership, the Act provided that letters patent under the great seal of England, would be available, and that if necessary one or more Acts of Parliament would be passed, but that the requisite fees must be paid as directed by the ordinance of 23rd September, 1647. On the other hand, should a purchaser find himself evicted from his newly acquired premises by reason of some existing right, title or interest, the whole of the purchase-money would be refunded as directed in another ordinance of 21st November, 1648, for purchasers of Bishops' lands. Of the important services rendered by the trustees in connection with the issue of debentures at Worcester House it will be necessary to speak later. They were expressly required to observe such general or particular directions as were received from time to time from the Lord General and Council of War ; and as a final enactment they were required by Parliament to " forthwith cause this present Act to be printed and published ".

The work of the surveyors was of the utmost importance, and provision was made for this to be done correctly and speedily, for none of the contractors could commence operations until surveys had been returned to the trustees and the registrar. Any five or more trustees were empowered to appoint fit and able persons to survey the premises in all the counties of England and Wales, such surveyors being authorized to keep courts of survey for the better discovery of the premises and their values. The surveyors were required to observe the same rules, directions, and instructions as were given to the surveyors of the late Bishops' lands in the ordinance of 16th

November, 1646. They were now expressly authorized to demand, require, receive, and put into safe custody all charters, deeds, books, accounts, rolls, writings, and evidences relating to the premises, and in case of need to call to their aid sheriffs and justices of the peace. Should the trustees find surveyors "deficient, negligent, or unfaithful", they were to call them to account and if necessary remove them.

It was expressly ordered that each of the Parliamentary surveyors should before commencing duties take the following oath :—

" I A.B. do swear, That I will by the help of God, faithfully and truly, according to my best skill and knowledge, execute the place of Surveyor, according to the purport of the Act Entituled, *An Act of the Commons in Parliament assembled for sale of the Honors, Manors and Lands heretofore belonging to the late King, Queen and Prince* : And shall use my best endeavour and skill, to discover the Estate herein mentioned, and every part thereof, which shall be given me in charge ; and to finde out the true values and improvements thereof : And thereof shall make true Surveys according to my best skill and cunning, and the same from time to time to deliver, or cause to be delivered in writing close sealed up, unto the Register for the time being in that behalf appointed ; and also a true Copy or Duplicate thereof close sealed up, unto the said Trustees, or any two of them : And this I shall justly and faithfully execute, without any gift or reward directly or indirectly, from any person or persons whatsoever, except such allowances as the said Trustees, or any five or more of them shall think fit to make unto me for my pains and charges in the executing of the said place and office." [1]

The Surveyor-General, Colonel William Webb, who had served in the same capacity in connection with the Bishops' lands, now assumed control under the present Act, and in order to facilitate his work, " to the end the surveys may be speedily perfected," it was enacted that the surveys returned to the registrar by the different surveyors, together with the copies or duplicates forwarded by them to the trustees, should immediately upon their receipt be noted and then sent to the Surveyor-General. Within six days Colonel Webb was required to peruse the surveys, and if he thought them quite trustworthy he was to return them to the trustees and registrar with his observations and approbation signed thereon. But in cases where surveys were found insufficient to contract upon, he was to transcribe within the same period the imperfect portions and forward them with his comments to the surveyors responsible, requiring them to amend the faulty particulars, or if they were unable to do so to certify the cause of their inability : in this case the surveys were to be returned to

---

[1] The Act for Sale of the Crown lands, 16th July, 1649 (Firth and Rait, *Acts and Ordinances,* vol. ii, 172–3). The Registrar is styled " the Register " above.

the trustees and registrar so that the immediate tenants of any portion of the premises concerned might proceed to purchase.

The Surveyor-General was allowed by any three trustees to rectify or amend mistakes, errors, and other matters of slight importance, where credible information or proof was readily forthcoming, without notifying the surveyors. There were of course cases where persons were unable to enter their claims before the district surveyors returned the surveys to London; these persons were allowed to produce proof of their claims upon oath before the Surveyor-General and three trustees, and provided that this was done within forty days of the return of the survey, Colonel Webb was authorized to enter the claim, and certify his allowance to the registrar and trustees. It was left to the Surveyor-General to appoint the day and time when the surveyors should begin their work and also when it should be completed, though upon just cause he might be willing to extend the time; but they were to certify their proceedings and keep in touch with Colonel Webb by correspondence, so that he might know where they were employed and what work they were at the moment doing.[1]

After the Surveyor-General's allowance of claims and his delayed approval of surveys which had needed correction, the trustees and registrar were certified that the surveys in their hands formed a good and sufficient ground for the registrar to make out his " particular ", and for the contractors and trustees to open negotiations for sales and conveyances. As registrar and keeper, Hy. Colbron was required to have the custody of all records, charters, evidences, court rolls, ledger-books, writings, books of survey, rentals, certificates, and all other necessary documents relating to the premises about to be sold. He was to receive duplicates of all surveys made by any three surveyors in the different counties, and when these had been approved by the Surveyor-General he was to enter all the surveys, certificates, and other proceedings in his register. Like the surveyors he was to observe the instructions recorded in the ordinance of 16th November, 1646, particularly those drawn upon for the guidance of the official known as the registrar for the sale of Bishops' lands. He was to make forth, value, rate, and sign, according to the surveys returned to him, all particulars of premises, so as to provide good and sufficient ground for the contractors to proceed to sell. He was to see that entry was made of all contracts and other proceedings connected with the sales, and afterwards to deliver from time to time to purchasers such records, writings, and evidences as were concerned with the premises they had purchased. For the better conduct of the service Colbron was required to provide " one able and sufficient clerk, such as the contractors approve ", to attend their meetings, enter all orders and proceedings, and observe their directions concerning the premises

---

[1] The duties are recorded in full in Firth and Rait, op. cit., vol. i, pp. 894-6. The surveyors of Dean and Chapter lands were required to observe the same instructions.

exposed to sale; but while the books of entries were to remain in the custody of the contractors, the registrar and his deputy or clerk were allowed to peruse them in order to extract copies of entries relating to the contracts.[1]

District surveyors having been appointed by the trustees, and their surveys being returned with the endorsements of the Surveyor-General, the registrar thereupon issued to the public detailed particulars " grounded upon the surveys ". It was now the turn of the contractors or any five of them, to proceed to sell the premises. Three of their number had been appointed on 30th June, doubtless at the instigation of the Army Council, but unlike the trustees, none of these, nor even the other nine appointed in July, desired to be excused from what, after all, was bound to be a profitable though an adventurous under-taking, and the twelve contractors duly appear among the officials named in the Act, with duties very precisely laid down for their observance. In the first place, it was enacted that they should have " power and authority to treat, contract, and agree with persons or bodies, for sale of premises, upon any particular or certificate and values delivered to them " under the hand of the registrar or his deputy; and it was further ordered that they should observe the instructions and exercise the powers mentioned in the ordinances of 16th November, 1646, and 2nd December, 1647, in connection with the earlier appointment of contractors for the sale of Bishops' lands. The immediate tenants of lands and tenements, excepting parks and chases, were to be first consulted in the matter of sale, the contractors having no power to contract with any others during the space of thirty days following the return of the surveys; but if such tenants had no wish to purchase, or did not agree and failed to subscribe their contracts within the period allowed, then the contractors were to allow other persons who desired to purchase these premises to do so.

The rules governing the contracts were few and quite simple to understand, even when they referred to minimum rates of purchase for lands in possession, and to proportionate minimum rates when leases for lives or years were involved. Two rules were framed in connection with lands and premises in possession : first, that the minimum rate of purchase was to be fixed at thirteen years; and second, that in exceptional cases, such as the sale of castles, houses, and palaces, the provisions of the ordinance of 2nd December, 1647, applied. Two further rules concerned leases granted for lives or years, the minimum rates of purchase for lands and premises in reversion being fixed as under :—

(a) Leases for Lives.		(b) Leases for Years.	
1 life : 6½ years' purchase.		7 years : 6½ years' purchase.	
2 lives : 3½ „ „		14 years : 4½ „ „	
3 lives : 2½ „ „		21 years : 3 „ „	

[1] Firth and Rait, op. cit., vol. i, pp. 903-4.

Where tenants of premises claimed a customary estate in reversion, or where by custom leases for lives might be granted, the reversion was to be sold at rates proportionate to the above rules ; and all other reversions upon leases, either for more years or fewer than those expressed above, were likewise to be sold at proportionate rates.

It was definitely recorded that no contractor might, directly or indirectly, purchase any of the premises, under pain of forfeiture, both of the lands thus procured and of the purchase money ; but, should insufficient money be forthcoming from sales to pay the salaries allowed by the Act to the contractors, trustees, and treasurers, such officials might then receive part of the premises, as arranged by Parliament, in lieu of salary. It was expressly stated, that in spite of any law, statute, or charter to the contrary, all corporate and other bodies in England and Wales might purchase any of the royal estates without the necessity of licences of alienation or mortmain.[1]

Any two of the treasurers were empowered to receive and acknowledge sums payable into the treasury by virtue of the Act, but all entries, receipts, payments, and discounts made by them were to be supervised by the comptroller, Henry Robinson, a merchant of London. The instructions for the guidance of the comptroller and his deputies were, as usual, those contained in the ordinance of 16th November, 1646, relating to the sale of episcopal estates. No rents, issues, or profits of the premises were to be allowed by the treasurers without a warrant issued by the trustees, the receipt of the persons named upon the warrant being a good discharge to the treasurers ; and while the registrar of debentures, another official appointed by the trustees, kept a watchful eye upon the certificates he received and registered, as well as the accounts and evidences concerning arrears that were transmitted from time to time to the trustees, the comptroller was ordered to rigidly check all debts in order that they might be registered and charged.[2]

Under the Act of 26th November, 1646, and the later ordinance of 22nd June, 1649, all certificates relating to the arrears of officers and soldiers had been returned to the Committee for the Army or to the Commissioners of Accounts sitting at Worcester House ; they were now required under the present Act to be transmitted to the trustees for the sale of Crown lands, and as a first step the trustees appointed a registrar of debentures to receive, register, and secure the certificates transmitted in this way. The trustees were required by the Acts to examine the accounts, either personally or by means of auditors, and to revise periodically the arrears certified by the registrar. Preference was to be given to such officers and soldiers as were engaged for service in Ireland : in their case care was to be taken not only in the casting up of the account but in the deductions

[1] Firth and Rait, op. cit., vol. i, pp. 901-2, 1029-30.
[2] Firth and Rait, op. cit., vol. i, 901.

for free quarter authorized by the ordinance of 24th December, 1647, so that when the arrears were clearly established the trustees would be in a position to issue debentures to the persons concerned or their assigns.

The debentures were in the nature of bonds or bills, the form and time of payment being left to the convenience of the trustees. By this means the Commonwealth undertook to pay the creditor concerned such sums as were then due, either in one debenture or in several, provided that the trustees did not give " to any one creditor more than one debenture for any sum of £10 value or under, and so as for any sum to the value of £10 or upwards, they set down not less time for payment than at two twelve months from the date of the debentures ". But in every debenture thus given the trustees were to " charge the sum thereof to be allowed immediately in the purchase of any lands given for security of arrears ". All such debentures, suitably sealed, were to be signed by two or more trustees, and attested by the registrar of debentures, who was required to enter in his register the sum charged, the creditor's name and regiment, the times limited for payment, and the names of the trustees who signed the debenture. Thus perfected, the debentures were to be delivered to any of the field officers for their respective regiments, to the captains for the troops or companies, or to particular individuals notified to the colonels or captains.

Next to be considered were the arrears of officers and soldiers not engaged for service in Ireland. The examination and revision of claims in this case was of a much more searching character, the trustees being instructed to examine closely the validity of the grounds and evidences for these claims, comparing them with the accounts and other documents remaining with the Army Committee or the Commissioners and auditors at Worcester House—any or all of whom were required to be in attendance to assist the trustees and to correct accounts " so as the state may not be wrongfully charged ". Afterwards, debentures for the clear arrears of officers and soldiers who were in service in the month of January, 1647, were to be issued to the individuals named and registered. For such accounts as were taken and stated, under the Ordinance of 22nd June, 1649, by the Committee of the Army or the Commissioners of Accounts, it was only necessary for any three of the former or any two of the latter to certify the names and arrears of persons to the trustees, who might then proceed to issue the required debentures.

Arrangements were next made for the Trustees to call in and cancel, within six months from 1st July, 1649, all earlier issues of debentures ; new debentures or bills were then to be issued for existing arrears due to officers and men, or to their assigns, the registrar making the usual entries and the comptroller keeping a careful check on the debts thus charged. In this way it was possible to organize an efficient service, adequately protected by its two watch-dogs, the registrar and comptroller, and with a distinguishing date, namely 1st July, 1649, to examine and control all debentures issued by the trustees for the arrears of troops in the service of Parliament in January, 1647, whether engaged at the moment in Ireland, disbanded, discharged, or deceased, or even continued in any other public employment for which the State allowed pay. Debentures for any other individuals were to date from 1st December, 1649. Further, all debentures so perfected, registered, and issued were deemed to be sufficient and effectual to become a charge upon the Commonwealth for the payment of such arrears, since they were to be satisfied out of the Crown lands, rents, issues, and profits and the proceeds of authorized sales. To prevent misunderstanding it was to be always understood that any such principal debts not satisfied in this manner or not utilized in the purchase of lands and premises would be allowed to bear interest instead.[1]

From the proceeds of the sales paid to the treasurers in money, and the rents, issues and profits of the premises paid into the Treasury, after deducting all allowances to officials under the Act, the trustees were ordered to issue warrants for sums sufficient to satisfy, first, one-half of such debts and arrears, according to the sum of money in hand, and then the second half, when more money came in, always taking care to satisfy claims of original creditors, or assignees, in the following order :—

(1) Those who were deceased.

(2) Such as are disbanded, or lawfully discharged from military service, and are not receiving pay in any other public office or State employment.

(3) Others in military service in Ireland, or employed by Parliament abroad.

(4) Those in military service, or employed in other public office at home.

For the more public and certain proceeding in the satisfaction of these moieties to the several sorts of original creditors and assigns indicated above, it was left to the trustees to evolve a plan for establishing a public and open registry of the debts and arrears, so that any person concerned might at any time see " in what course and order the payment of the debts is to be expected, and what debts or moieties thereof are to precede the satisfaction of that or those he looketh for ". As a special favour the Act provided that such of the original creditors or their heirs who desired to become purchasers of Crown lands with the debentures immediately held by them, and

---

[1] Firth and Rait. op. cit., vol. i, pp. 1048–9. For the subsequent form of a debenture see the copy printed in Part IV, Section ii, p. 202.

not by way of assignment from others, were allowed liberty of pre-emption for ten days, upon the expiration of the period of thirty days set apart for the immediate tenants, and before any other class of prospective purchasers whatsoever.

A further enactment provided that it was lawful for any creditor to assign his right, title or interest to any other person. Every such assignee might continue the process, but the last assignee for the time being of any sums of money due, or of debentures issued in lieu thereof, alone possessed " the like liberty, right, title, benefit and advantage " enjoyed by the original creditors or assigns. It is worthy of note that the privilege of pre-emption for ten days allowed to the original creditors did not extend to the holders of these assigned bills.

Creditors or assigns who decided to purchase Crown lands with their debentures were entitled to deduct sums due to them from the purchase price, and pay the difference only, or if the amount exceeded the price then any difference in their favour was to be allowed. An important provision enabled purchasers to pay to the treasurers in ready money " so much per pound of his or their whole purchase, as the allowances for the trustees, contractors, treasurers, comptroller of entries and registrar of debentures amount to " (being 7d. in the pound for the first three, as recorded in the Act), the registrar of debentures being required to ascertain and certify to the treasurers the principal debt and interest allowed. Certificates issued in this way, combined with the delivery of debentures or bills, provided a sufficient warrant for the treasurers to permit deductions to be made upon purchase of the premises, after which the debentures were to be returned to the registrar of debentures to be cancelled, the entry in the register showing that the arrears of the individual concerned had at last been satisfied and discharged.

In regard to the payment made by purchasers the Act required all those who contracted for premises to pay in the first moiety of the purchase money within eight weeks of the date of the contract, and the second moiety six months after the first payment. They were then to proceed with their transactions and procure conveyances from the trustees within eight weeks, or incur penalties provided in an Ordinance of 23rd March, 1647, concerning the Bishops' lands, unless in the meantime they were able to persuade the contractors to grant a certificate for further time in which to perfect their conveyances.

Parliament had contemplated the appointment of a special committee to deal with obstructions to the sale of royal lands, but this for the present was deferred. Several honours, manors, mansions, public buildings, parks, and garrisoned castles were expressly exempted from sale by the Act, the intention being to reserve all the property so indicated for the use of the State. These specified premises were situated in Middlesex and nine other counties, but many of the buildings naturally were in London and Westminster. Some of these exempted properties were reconsidered and rejected the same year, as for example Theobalds House and Park; others, such as Hyde Park and Cornbury Park, were rejected three years later and then exposed to sale; but places like Somerset House and Greenwich Palace remained to the end unsold, and were restored to Queen Henrietta, as part of her jointure estate, in June, 1660. We can trace the decisions made by Parliament in respect to these various exemptions in the references made to the following premises in the Journals of the House of Commons between 3rd June, 1649 and 31st December, 1652 :—

XXI. Crown Property Reserved for the Commonwealth

Notes :[1] (A) Exemption named in Act of 16th July, 1649.
      (B) Exemption rejected 1649.
      (C) Exemption maintained, 1652.
      (D) Exposed to sale by Act of 31st December, 1652.

Counties.	Premises.
Berkshire	Windsor: Castle, Office of Works, and Timber Yard (A, C).
	,, Little Park (A, D).
	,, King's Meadows (D).
Cornwall	Scilly Islands (C).
Hertford	Theobalds: House and Park (B).
Kent	East Greenwich: Honor and Manor (A, C).
	Greenwich: Castle, House, Park, and Queen's Buildings (A, D).
	,, The Tiltyard (A, C).
Middlesex	Hampton Court: House, Bushey Park, House Park, and Middle Park (A, D).
	,, Hare Warren and Meadows (D).
	Hyde Park (A, D).
	London: Old Artillery Ground, Ordnance House (Heydon's), The Tower, Tower Hill, Tower Wharf, and the Wardrobe (A, C).
	Westminster: The Cockpit, the Mews (Scotland Yard), the Tennis Courts, St. James' House and Park, Scotland Yard, Spring Garden, Westminster Palace, and Whitehall (A, C).
	,, Somerset or Denmark House (A, D).
	,, New Artillery Ground (B).
	,, Savoy, Slaughter House (Millbank).
	,, Wallingford House (C).
Norfolk.	Stockton Socon: The Manor (A, C).
Oxford.	Cornbury Park (A, D).
	Woodstock: Honor, Manor, and Parks (B).
Surrey	Richmond: New Park (A, C).
	Vaux Hall (A, D).
Wiltshire	Clarendon Park (B).
Yorkshire	Pontefract Castle and Parks, and York Manor House (A, C).

Timber trees within fifteen miles of a navigable river were also reserved, as well as forests and chases throughout the land. Fee-farm rents and other rents due to the Commonwealth were likewise

---

[1] The references in the Commons Journals are as follows : (A) 3rd, 5th, 30th June, 3rd, 7th, 12th, 13th July, 1649; (B) 15th August, 5th and 28th September, 1649, and 29th March, 15th 30th April, 14th May, 1650; (C) 2nd September, 15th October, 18th, 27th November, 6th, 28th, 29th, 30th December, 1652; (D) 31st December, 1652.

left out of the Act; but, as will be shown hereafter, these various exemptions were not long permitted by Parliament.

There was one provision of great importance which Parliament inserted for the protection of the officials concerned in administering the Act. This was to the effect that should any future action be brought against the trustees, contractors, or treasurers "for any act done in execution of this Act or instructions unto which it relates, then they are hereby enabled to plead the general issue, and to give this Act in evidence". If judgment should pass in their favour they were authorized to recover double costs by way of retaliation.

CHAPTER IV

WORCESTER HOUSE AND ADDITIONAL ACTS

The Act of 16th July, 1649, in reality made provision for three distinct needs. There was the necessity, first of all, for obtaining and registering accurate surveys of the whole of the royal property in the different areas of England and Wales, in order to ascertain the values and thus secure the highest possible prices when the sales began; then there was the utmost need to attract purchasers so as to make speedy sales, a matter of some difficulty now that the maximum rate for lands in possession had been raised to thirteen years' purchase; and above all, urgent beyond question, there was the financial necessity not only of meeting all claims arising out of army arrears of pay, but of providing a balance for future needs of the State. It was therefore enacted " that Worcester House, or some other place, as the trustees shall think fitting, shall be the place where the said several persons shall transact the said service, and put in execution this Act ". Three departments were immediately set up to deal with administrative details, Colonel William Webb directing the department dealing with surveys and valuations, Colbron the registrar supervising that of contracts and sales, and the trustees, comptroller, and registrar of debentures jointly controlling the section devoted to claims and accounts. Later two other departments were created at Worcester House to deal with the fee-farm rents and forest lands.

The six months that followed the passing of the Act were utilized by army and parliamentary leaders in perfecting the measure. On 7th September, 1649, a Bill was introduced into Parliament to provide for " further instructions to the treasurers, trustees, contractors, registers, surveyors and other persons employed in the sale of the honours, manors, and lands belonging to the late King, Queen, and Prince ", and after it had been read a first and second time this was committed to the care of Alderman Allen and the Committee of Obstructions in the sale of capitular estates. In the meantime another committee had been formed to consider the whole question of the issue and use of debentures for paying off the arrears of soldiers, and various orders and amendments followed the reports of Colonel Jones and his committee during the months of September and October. On 12th October it was decided that the contractors and trustees should suspend the publication of surveys and delay the sales for two or three months, taking care that the interests of immediate tenants and original creditors were not in any way jeopardized; and in the meantime all stewards of hundred courts, sheriffs' turns, courts-leet, and baron, and all bailiffs and other court officials in the different counties, were required to "subscribe the engagement of the Commonwealth ".

New resolutions followed in November, especially after the report of Colonel Venn on 15th November, in reference to a petition of the Council of army leaders, wherein we find reflected the uneasiness of officers and soldiers lest any action should be taken giving preferential treatment to the immediate tenants; and at length it was resolved " that this House doth declare that if sale should be made of the late King's lands, according to the opinion delivered in to the committee by the trustees, that thereby a greater benefit will be afforded to the immediate tenant and a lesser benefit to the original creditor, than is intended then by the Act ". Accordingly, five days later it was ordered that a Bill should "with all speed" be brought in to provide not only for the " speedy sale " of the royal property but for " the removal of all obstructions in the sale thereof"; and the haste with which this was done may be judged from the fact that on 23rd November the bill was read the third time, and after some amendments had been made at the table, it was passed and ordered to be at once printed and published. At the same time it was declared that the rights of tenants were in no way prejudiced by the suspension of the sales, the benefit of pre-emption for thirty days being assured to them " after the time limited for stay of the said sale, as by the Act they are to have after the return or publication of the survey ".[1]

The new Act begins by referring to the terms of authorization provided by the Act of 16th July, 1649, and then proceeds to instruct the trustees as to the manner in which debentures were to be issued to the forces in future, the form of the new debentures being very precisely set out in this Act. Provided that the trustees observed the substance and effect of the declaration, they might vary the form of the debenture as circumstances required, but afterwards they were required to sign, stamp, and register the perfected debenture in order to make it effectual, and then cause delivery to be made to " such persons as shall bring to the trustees the respective original debentures, accompts or certificates, upon which such perfected debentures shall be made ".[2]

Trustees were ordered to rectify such mistakes and errors as were detected in accounts or debentures, taking every care that nothing should be done to the prejudice of the Commonwealth. For greater accuracy a Committee of Accounts was appointed to receive lists, accounts, certificates, muster rolls and all other evidences relating to the claims of military men, in accordance with an Act of 28th May, 1649, which provided for " the present examining and stating of accounts of the officers and soldiers now in the parliament's service

[1] House of Commons Journals, vol. vi, pp. 292, 298–301, 304, 306–8, 320, 322–5.
[2] Firth and Rait, op. cit., vol. ii, pp. 282–5.

within this Nation ". This committee was empowered to administer an oath to such persons as desired to have their accounts stated, upon receiving from them certificates, vouchers, or other testimony sufficient to enable the committee to issue debentures for the clear arrears due to them. All muster-masters, treasurers, auditors, registrars, and other officials concerned were required to produce muster rolls, books of payment, accounts, and all necessary vouchers in their custody; and instructions were also issued to the registrar of the late committee for Accounts to deliver all the records in his keeping to the new committee at Worcester House. Similar orders were sent to the Committee for the Army and the commissary for the musters of the army under the conduct of Thomas Lord Fairfax to immediately deliver to the trustees all the rolls, lists, certificates, and duplicates of debentures in their possession, so that it might be possible to ascertain with accuracy what persons were within the establishment of the army on 24th December, 1647. But as the accounts for the arrears due to many officers and men in the service of Parliament during December and January, 1647, were not yet fully audited, or confirmed, the contractors for the sale of the Crown lands were authorized to allow such individuals, when signing agreements, an extension of time (not exceeding six months in connection with their first payment, or three months for their second), beyond the limit originally provided in the act for other persons. For the services thus rendered the trustees were to allow the Committee of Accounts such salary as they considered reasonable, provided that the Committee for Obstructions approved; and provision was made at the same time for an assistant to the Surveyor-General, at a salary not exceeding £80 a year for a period of at least two years, the treasurers being instructed to pay such salaries and allowances accordingly.[1]

In the previous Act a clause had been inserted to show that it was originally the intention of Parliament to appoint " a Committee for removal of obstructions in the sale and conveying of the said premises ", so that they might effectively " execute all powers and authorities concerning the premises as the committee for removing of obstructions in the sale of Bishops' lands " had previously done. The first committee to undertake this work under the Ordinance of 21st November, 1648, consisted of thirty-three members, ten of whom appear in the enlarged committee of forty-seven persons appointed on 20th June, 1649, to remove obstructions in the case of the capitular lands. It was this later committee which proceeded to sweep away obstructions also in the sales of royal lands under the Act of 18th February, 1649–50. As early as 15th November in that year it had been ordered " that the Act for a committee for removing obstructions in the sale of the late King's lands " be reported as first business on the morrow, and a further order five days later mentioned

[1] Firth and Rait, op. cit., vol. ii, pp. 125–130.

the need for "speed" in bringing forward the measure. In later orders still, those of 17th January and 2nd February, the bill is referred to as "the supplemental" or "additional Act for sale of the lands of the late King, Queen and Prince", but the form in which the Act finally passed was clearly due to the efforts of Colonel Jones and his friends. By the subsequent Act of 1st April, 1652, the powers of the various committees concerned with the removal of obstructions were vested in seven commissioners—Rob. Aldworth, Josias Berners, Francis Mussenden, Jn. Parker, Hy. Pitt, Sir Wm. Roberts, and Matthias Valentine, all of whom appear in the surveys of Crown lands in connection with decisions recorded by the Surveyor-General.[1]

[1] *Commons Journals*, vol. vi, 323, 324, 348, 366 ; Firth and Rait, op. cit., vol. i, pp. 1227-8 ; vol. ii, pp. 152-3, 187-8, 338-42, 581-2. For the cost of the various services at Worcester House, see Appendix, pp. 398, 403-4.

Chapter V

THE FEE-FARM RENTS, 1649–59

When the Act of 16th July, 1649, came into operation it was found that Parliament had specially reserved certain classes of property, such as castles, mansions, and forests, from its operations. It was also expressly stated that there was no intention of granting to the Trustees any impropriation or parsonages appropriate, any advowsons, right of patronage, or presentation to any living whatsoever, or " any reversion or remainder in the Crown, expectant upon estate tail ". Nor indeed did the Act extend to any fee-farm rents, or other rents now due and payable to the Commonwealth, or to "any such Manors, Lands, or other Hereditaments, where there hath not been reserved in the Crown any Right or Propriety in or to such Manors, Lands, or other Hereditaments, other than the Rents reserved ".

But these exceptions in regard to rents were not long maintained, for even as early as 9th March, 1648, it had been decided that all the fee-farm rents belonging to the Crown and the Duchy of Lancaster should be sold, and that the money raised thereby should go " towards the payment of the £30,000 per mensem, to make up the £120,000 per mensem, for the forces in England and Ireland " ; to which end a committee was to meet in the Exchequer Chamber at 2 p.m. on the following day and consider the question fully and then prepare an Act, an order of Parliament five days later requiring this to be done " with all speed ". Very speedy indeed was the action taken, for in less than a month, on 3rd April, 1649, a measure was reported by Mr. Garland, read for the first and second time, and immediately committed to a special committee of thirty members. Eighteen of these members were already actively engaged in promoting a bill for the sale of Crown lands, but the remaining twelve were new, the latter including Sir Wm. Armyn, Sir Gregory Norton, Sir Gilbert Pickering, Serjeant Nicholas, and Colonel Ludlow. Any five of the committee formed a quorum. Their powers were comprehensive, for not only were they to appoint trustees and fix the number of years' purchase as a basis for sales, but they might send for judges to confer with them, or clerks of any of the courts and any other persons likely to be of service. In addition they had power to order records, papers, writings or anything else that would serve their purpose, to be placed before them. Other members were added to this committee in April, one of whom, Sir Henry Vane, senior, later reported that the committee were of opinion that the arrears of fee-farm rents due for the years 1646 to 1648 should be immediately levied, a course of action which Parliament promptly endorsed.

FEE FARM RENTS : BARFORD HUNDRED, BEDFORDSHIRE, 1650
(Damaged 1834)

This proposal appears to have been regarded as sufficient for the moment, for nothing further was done until the order of 2nd October, 1649, when Mr. Long was directed to " bring in the Act touching fee-farm rents, on Wednesday next, the first business ". Even then no progress was made ; and when on 17th January following another resolution appears it is merely to the effect " that the Committee for the Bill for selling the fee-farm rents be revived " and enlarged. After this, reports were presented and amendments made, a sharp hint being given on 28th January to " bring in the Bill with all speed ". Thus it came about that on 16th February an " Act for the selling the fee-farm rents belonging to the Commonwealth of England, formerly payable to the Crown of England, Duchy of Lancaster, and Duchy of Cornwall " was read the first time ; but even then, opposition was so strong that when the question was put for the Act to be read a second time " it passed with the negative ", as did the further proposal " that the order for the Committee to name trustees for sale of fee-farm rents do stand ". In consequence of the day's debate the committee was instructed to amend the bill, considering in the meantime the best method of selling the rents with least charge and most advantage to the Commonwealth. This done, Mr. Garland reported amendments, which were duly read on 21st February, when the Attorney-General was directed to take charge of the bill, the committee on this occasion being further instructed to " bring in the Bill for sale of all the fee-farm rents, tenths, dry rents, and pensions except what is already contained and settled in the Act for providing maintenance of preaching ministers and other pious uses ", which had been passed by the House on 8th June, 1649. The amendments of the Attorney-General, considered in committee, on 4th March, were read for the first and second time on the following day, and as a result it was decided that the trustees, contractors, and treasurers for the sale of Crown lands, as well as the registrar and comptroller, should be appointed to posts with similar titles in connection with the sale of fee-farm rents ; but on this occasion the provision was made of a uniform rate of 3d. in the pound for their salaries. The debate upon the amendments was resumed on 7th March, the most important decision that day being the acceptance of the committee's view that eight years should be substituted for the proposed ten years' purchase. Mr Lennard is puzzled by the fact that in subsequent enactments the period is fixed at ten years, and he suggests that the law was not being kept ; but he evidently did not know, what the Journals of the Commons make quite clear, that the original intention was ten years and not eight, and that Parliament subsequently threw over its committee's declared opinion.

Four days later, on 11th March, 1649–50, the third reading of this important measure took place, the only alteration that day being to delete the words " The Isles of Jersey and Guernsey ". It is also worth noting that three provisos, tendered at the last moment, were rejected : one of these proposed that the Act should not extend to fee-farm rents issuing from lands of archbishops, bishops, and deans ; another, that fee-farm rents amounting to £58 0s. o½d. should be excepted in the case of the manor of Bishop Wilton, in the East Riding of Yorkshire ; while the third proviso, namely, " that all fee-farm rents and other premises afore mentioned shall not be liable to any rates, payments, or taxes whatsoever, without the same be by particular name expressed by Act of Parliament," was immediately rejected. Next day it was ordered that the Act be proclaimed in every market town throughout England.[1]

Thus into the market came the fee-farm rents of the Commonwealth, with such other financial items as dry-rents, rents reserved, hundreds, bailiwicks, franchises, and non-appropriated tenths and pensions, arising out of royal manors and other premises, with the exception of those already granted away by the late monarch before 1st January, 1641. Vested in the same Trustees, and with the same contractors and officials conducting the sales, it was enacted that these rents should be offered to purchasers in order to provide funds " for the supply of the assessments lately abated by Parliament ", and for other urgent needs.

The trustees, having received from the respective auditors and the clerk of the Pipe, particulars or certificates of the rents and issues, were required " to put to sale, contract, sell and convey " the same by means of deeds or conveyances signed and sealed by them, in manner and form provided by the earlier Act ; and all persons purchasing these rents were to have the same liberties and advantages formerly possessed and enjoyed by the late owners. Tenants had the usual right of pre-emption for a period of thirty days, but this was to be exercised from 1st April, 1650. The custody of certificates and particulars, contracts and counterparts of conveyances, formed part of the duties of the registrar, who was authorized to deliver true copies to the purchasers ; and when they had been testified under the hands and seals of five or more trustees, these copies were deemed to be " a sufficient testimony in evidence, as any deed enrolled by the statute of 27 Henry VIII for enrolment of deeds is or ought to be ". No trustee was allowed to purchase any part of the premises unless he happened to be the immediate tenant at the date of the passing of the Act. The usual oath was to be administered to officials by the trustees. There were no new functions to be undertaken by the

---

[1] *House of Commons Journals*, vol. vi, pp. 160, 163, 178, 185, 195, 301, 348, 350-1, 353, 358, 365-7, 369, 376-80 ; Firth and Rait, op. cit., vol. ii, pp. 171, 190 ; Lennard, op. cit., pp. 19-20. The minimum rates of purchase were likewise fixed at ten years in the Acts for sale of bishops' lands, and capitular lands and forfeited lands between 1646 and 1652—although twelve years' purchase was at first demanded for capitular lands—then thirteen years in the case of royal lands sold in 1649, and even fourteen years in connection with disafforested lands in 1653. See Firth and Rait, op. cit., vol. i, p. 902 ; vol. ii, pp. 87, 103, 155-6, 176, 184-5, 360, 499, 528, 584, 594, 616, 644, 796.

treasurers or the comptroller; but while the Committee for removing Obstructions in the sale of capitular lands was authorized to exercise its powers in connection with the sale of fee-farm rents, it was left to the Committee for the Public Revenue, not for the trustees or treasurers, to gather and receive all fee-farm rents of premises unsold,[1] " as formerly they were used to do." And finally it was enacted that Worcester House should be the place where the appointed officials should transact all their business, so that a fourth department in connection with the sales of Crown lands was now created in that hive of Commonwealth activity.[2]

Other Acts followed in due course, that ot 13th August, 1650, being intended to remove some doubts that had arisen owing to lack of clearness in the language of the last Act. Reprises, where proved to exist, were of course to be allowed. Provision was also made for the recovery of rents, with the notification that fee-farm rents set apart for the maintenance of grammar schools, scholars, or preachers, or for the reparation of churches, chapels, schools, almshouses, highways, and bridges were to be continued as before. Fee-farm rents which, owing to defective titles or suggested concealments, had not been paid since 25th March, 1630, were not to be granted out by the trustees. In all transactions where sales were effected, fee-farm rents were not to be sold under eight years' purchase, proportionate rates being allowed for reversions upon lives or any number of years; also where hundreds, bailiwicks, liberties, and reservations were concerned the trustees were to impose a value and rate " according to their best judgments and such informations received as to the time and real value thereof ". They were, moreover, directed to make searches among records and take copies without payment of fees. Other provisions related to enrolments of conveyances, which were to be certified upon oath administered by the trustees, and to the method of paying for purchases, a special arrangement being made for the settlement upon purchasers of small rents below the yearly value of forty shillings.[3]

Yet another Act for the sale of fee-farm rents was passed in 1650, in the preamble of which the admission occurs that although the trustees have made several contracts and sales, a great part of the premises remains unsold; for which reason, " finding themselves pressed with an urgent necessity of raising with all speed a considerable sum of moneys for carrying on the Public Service," Parliament had determined that the sum of £250,000 should be borrowed upon the security of such part of the premises as remained on 6th February unsold. The method of accomplishing this was by way

---

[1] This may be the reason for the preservation at Cambridge of the book of rents and revenues for the period 1649–53, already referred to (*Camb. Univ. Lib., Dd.* xiii, 2, 20 (2)).

[2] Firth and Rait, op. cit., vol. ii, pp. 358–62.

[3] Firth and Rait, op. cit., vol. ii, pp. 412–19.

of " doubling "—a singular invention of Dr. Burgess, already put into practice by the ordinance of 13th October, 1646. By this plan original creditors of the Government who advanced an additional sum, equal in amount to that of the old loan and any interest then due upon it, might secure both the old and the new debts out of the proceeds arising from the sale of the fee-farm lands. This Act is noteworthy for the appointment of Colonel Rob. Manwaring as registrar-accomptant for the premises involved in these transactions. After 6th February, 1650, no sales were to be under ten years' purchase, and where interest was allowed to purchasers it was to be at the rate of 8 per cent. Twopence only in the pound was to be allowed to officials whenever doubling occurred in the contracts. Economy in management had begun to assert itself at Worcester House.[1]

Two years later, another attempt was made to persuade creditors to double their loans ; only a modest amount was required on this occasion, namely £25,000, the security being the residue of unsold fee-farm rents. Liberty to assign public faith bills freely was again acknowledged, and " doubled bills " of creditors were to be admitted and allowed by all officers in their respective transactions, but the interest was now reduced from eight per cent to six. All moneys intended for doubling were to be paid within ten days of the certificate being received by the treasurers, otherwise the lender would " forfeit his moneys allowed to be doubled ", unless good cause was shown to the treasurers for this neglect. The usual directions concerning manors and lands charged with fee-farm rents, the minimum rate of sale (still placed at ten years' purchase), the enjoyment of rights by the purchaser and the confirmation of all sales and conveyances—all these duly appear in the Act. But there are others, some of them being very detailed, in regard to rents reserved in special cases, small rents under 50s. (not 40s. as in the original Act), fee-farm rents issuing out of delinquents' estates, and other rents whereof grants could not be found, the survey and sale of hundreds and liberties, the allowance of special fees, and the requisition of rentals from all sheriffs, bailiffs, collectors, and receivers. By this Act the registrar-accomptant was entitled to receive £100 for his own services and those of his clerks, and as the officials were allowed twopence in the pound for their work, the clerk of the Pipe was now instructed to charge " 6s. 8d. by the press and 3s. 4d. the half-press, and no more " when making out certificates or particulars. Lastly it was ordered " that all moneys called Creation Moneys, charged upon any Honours, Manors, Lands, Tenements, or Hereditaments, or upon any Body Politique and Corporate, or payable out of the Public Revenue of the late Crown, unto any Duke, Marquis, Earl, Viscount, or Baron, shall from 30th January, 1648, cease, determine and be utterly void." [2]

---

[1] Lennard, op. cit., p. 15 ; Firth and Rait, op. cit., vol. ii, pp. 498–500.
[2] Firth and Rait, op. cit., vol. ii, pp. 583–8.

Two further "additional Acts" call for consideration, after which the complicated legislation relating to the sale of fee-farm rents comes to an end. One of these, dated 9th September, 1652, is very similar to the Act last named, for its purpose was to raise a second sum of £25,000 upon the security of the fee-farm rents, of which, it is again admitted, "there is yet a considerable remainder" unsold. The rate of interest remains at 6 per cent and the minimum rate for purchases continues to be ten years. A new feature is the sale of a moiety of the rents and profits of the New River, as provided in an indenture of 18th November, 1631; but as some doubt had arisen whether the sum of £500 per annum, the value of this moiety, was comprehended within any of the previous Acts for sale of fee-farm rents, it was now expressly enacted that the share should be vested in the trustees, and that the purchaser should have the full benefit of all conditions and covenants, with ample power to recover the rent and all arrears.

The final Act, passed 8th September, 1653, is called "an explanatory additional Act for the sale of the remaining fee-farm rents, and the finishing of that whole affair". It begins by passing the different Acts in review, and declares that although sales have been effected, "purchasers cannot receive and enjoy the same according to their contracts and purchases, but the same are detained and withheld from them by the owners, tenants, and occupiers of the manors, lands, tenements and hereditaments," (out of which the said fee-farm rents issue), upon various pretences. In consequence of these obstructions it was now ordered, by way of remedy, that lands charged with fee-farm rents exposed for sale should remain for ever thus charged, and that conveyances and assurances made by the trustees should be as good and effectual as if they had been duly enrolled. Purchasers desiring to enrol their conveyances might do so even though the time had lapsed,[1] provided that this was accomplished within the next six months, at the end of which time all salaries payable to officials must cease. Within that period, too, the granting of Reprises would discontinue. This Act was confirmed 26th June, 1657, but even as late as 19th May, 1659, a clause was inserted in the Act for constituting a Council of State which made provision for warrants to be issued in connection with the residue of the moneys arising out of the various sales of fee-farm rents. The whole business had proved exceedingly troublesome to the officials at Worcester House.[2]

---

[1] This is an indication that the enrolments upon the Close Rolls are incomplete.
[2] Firth and Rait, op. cit., vol. ii, pp. 614–18, 720–2, 1137, 1275.

CHAPTER VI
THE EXEMPTED PREMISES, 1652

During the preparation of the original Act for sale of the Crown lands, the question had arisen as to the desirability of retaining certain of the royal possessions by reason of their utility for national purposes ; as a result the Council of State decided on 24th May, 1649, to report its opinion to Parliament that the houses and parks of Greenwich, Hampton Court, St. James, Theobalds, and Windsor, together with Whitehall, Somerset House, and Hyde Park, " ought to be kept for the public use of the Commonwealth, and not sold." A month later, on 30th June, Holland reported this view, and Parliament at once decided to refer the list, with the inclusion of Westminster Palace, to the Council of State in order that they might " consider of such Castle, Houses, and other buildings that now are, or may be thought to be employed for the public use of the State ", and report on the following morning. In consequence of the debates which occurred in July it was ultimately resolved that thirty-five or more premises should be specially named in the list of exceptions attached to the forthcoming Act, to be reserved for the present or future uses of the State.[1]

The premises to which the Act of 16th July, 1649, did not extend were ordered to remain in the custody of the Commonwealth, so that they might be utilized or disposed of in any way that Parliament might think fit. Briefly stated, the various kinds of property reserved by the State under the successive Acts for sale of the Crown lands may be classified as follows [2]:—

(*a*) *Manors and Lands.*—Those of East Greenwich, Kent, and Stockton Socon, Norfolk, and the Manor house of York.

(*b*) *Forests and Chases.*—Several of these had been considered by Parliament, but none were expressly named, and eventually most of them were excepted, together with all timber trees fit for naval needs, provided these were standing and growing in accessible woods within 15 miles of a navigable stream.

(*c*) *Parks.*—Many of the parks were indicated by name, but most of these were attached to mansions or castles already referred to ; the remainder consisted of Cornbury Park, Hyde Park, and the New Park at Richmond, Surrey.

[1] S.P. Dom., 1649-50, p. 155 ; Firth and Rait, op. cit., vol. ii, pp. 188-91.
[2] See the decisions in respect to the exempted premises in nine counties already recorded under the Act of 16th July, 1649, and the references in the *Commons Journal* between June, 1649, and December 1652. Compare Table XXI.

(*d*) *Mansion Houses.*—Residential places of importance at Greenwich, Hampton Court, St. James' House, Somerset or Denmark House, Vauxhall, Westminster Palace, and Whitehall.

(*e*) *Castles and Fortified Places.*—The castles of Greenwich, Pontefract, and Windsor, the Tower of London, and all castles garrisoned by the troops of Parliament throughout England and Wales.

(*f*) *Places for the Navy.*—All houses, storehouses, buildings, yards, docks, barge-houses, and other grounds and places which within the past twenty years had been used by the navy. These included the Tower Wharf and Scotland Yard.

(*g*) *Places for Public Justice.*—All Courts of Justice and prisons.

(*h*) *Other Public Offices.*—All buildings used in connection with Customs and Public Revenue, the Office of Ordnance and all other public offices belonging to the service of the State. These included the Old Artillery Ground, Bishopsgate, the house of Sir John Heydon in the Minories belonging to the Ordnance, the Wardrobe, Blackfriars, the Office of Works and Timber Yard, Windsor, and other miscellaneous property at Greenwich and Westminster.

Although some of the proposed exemptions were rejected by Parliament during the progress of the first Act for sale of the Crown lands—as for example Clarendon Park, Theobalds House and Park, and the honour, manor, and parks of Woodstock—most of them were included in that measure, and the majority of these premises, especially in London, were not permitted to be sold when the second Act was passed in 1652. The New Park of Richmond was intended to be settled on the City of London " as an act of favour from this House, for the use of the City, and their successors ", in accordance with a resolution dated 30th June, 1649. The Castle, House, and Park of Greenwich, as well as the Forest of Leighfield and the Island of Sark were also included in an Act for settling lands amounting to £1,000 per annum upon Hy. Martin, until their removal was ordered on 15th August, 1649. Sir Jn. Hippesley's interest in the Mews at Charing Cross was easily satisfied by the grant of a lease for twenty-one years from 29th September, 1649, at a nominal rent of £1 per annum. For the late king's slaughterhouse and yards upon the Mill Bank at Westminster a new use was found, inasmuch as it became a storehouse for coal and other fuel required by Parliament. Somerset House, the Duchy House, and the Savoy were recommended to the trustees for the sale of the King's Goods for use in connection with their work.[1]

The interest taken by members in the passing of the various Acts for sale of the Crown lands may be easily tested. Between 1649 and 1652 there were nine divisions taken in Parliament, all being concerned with proposals for the exemption of royal property at Hampton Court, Somerset House, Stockton Socon, Theobalds Park,

[1] *House of Commons Journals*, vol. vi, pp. 246, 279, 290, 300, 388.

Wallingford House, Windsor Castle, and York Manor. On none of these occasions did the combined votes reach a total of sixty, though it was rare to find the number below forty-five. Once the " yeas " and " noes " were equal in numbers, but only fourteen members in this instance voted, and the decision of the chair alone gave an affirmative result. Majorities were seldom greater than ten, and as a rule it was the " yeas " who were defeated. In the case of Stockton Socon, Norfolk, twenty-five votes were in favour of exemption and fifteen indicated a preference for sale. The proposal to reserve Somerset House was definitely defeated by thirty-four to nineteen votes ; but the future of Wallingford House was not so easily determined, for whereas on the first count " ayes " had a majority of one, fifty-five members then voting, " noes " next day obtained a majority of three out of a total of forty-three, so that it was eventually decided to exclude the property from sale. On the balance these decisions resulted in four exemptions and four sales, so the parties engaged in the struggle appear to have been very evenly matched. The results of these divisions are recorded below [1]:—

XXII. PARLIAMENTARY DIVISIONS ON CROWN LANDS, 1649–52

Date.		Premises.	Ayes.	Noes.	Result.
1649, July	12	Stockton Socon	25	15	Exemption
1650, Apr.	15	Theobalds Park	7	7	Sale
1652, Nov.	27	Somerset House	19	34	Sale
1652, Dec.	28	Hare Warren	28	31	Sale
1652, Dec.	29	York Manor	19	35	Exemption
1652, Dec.	29	Hampton Court	18	30	Sale
1652, Dec.	29	Windsor Castle	19	29	Exemption
1652, Dec.	30	Wallingford House	28	27	Exemption
1652, Dec.	31	Wallingford House	20	23	Exemption

As long as any of the Crown lands or fee-farm rents remained unsold, petitions from army leaders for consideration of their claims constantly reached the House. One of these had been received on 24th September, 1650, from the attorneys attending the sales at Worcester House, " on behalf of themselves, the army, and Super-numeraries " ; this had been referred, as usual, to the Committee of Obstructions, with orders for such action to be taken as would be for " the benefit and best advantage of the Commonwealth ". Another " humble petition "—this time from the Northern Officers who, not having been in service during December or January, 1647, were outside the scope of the original bill—contained a claim for £23,566 for arrears of pay, and when Colonel Downes reported from his Committee that their debentures could not be accepted in the purchase of Crown lands, a bill was introduced, with the aid of the Army

[1] Table XXII. This record of Parliamentary Divisions between 12th July, 1649, and 31st December, 1652, is compiled from the statements contained in the *Journals of the House of Commons*, vol. vi, pp. 258–398 ; vol. vii, pp. 222, 236–9. The total votes recorded ranges at different times from fourteen to fifty-nine, and of the nine occasions referred to, the number of votes cast exceeded fifty only four times. Compare the five divisions of November, 1653, given in Section VII, when the votes numbered from 68 to 87, the majorities being very small. See Table XXIII, p. 111.

Council, to remedy this defect, 7th September, 1652. To the petition of the train of artillery in the following month, Parliament made reply that satisfaction for the non-fulfilment of their contract (which amounted to £3,005) for the Hare Warren at Hampton Court should be speedily made out of the other lands forfeited to the Commonwealth for treason.[1]

But the needs of the navy were even more urgent at this time, and Sir Henry Vane's report on the estimates for the ensuing year so seriously alarmed Parliament, 27th November, 1652, that it was immediately resolved, that not only Hyde Park and Enfield Chase should be sold for ready money, but that Hampton Court, Windsor Castle, and all the houses, parks, and lands at Greenwich should likewise be exposed to sale, and on 6th December the trustees were authorized to administer the oath to Sylvanus Taylor and Colonel Wm. Webb, so that the premises might be surveyed without delay. That the matter was urgent is clear from that fact that the Bill " for the exposing to sale divers castles, houses, parks, lands, and hereditaments belonging to the late King, Queen or Prince, excepted from sale by a former Act ", was introduced by the Solicitor-General on 6th December, read the first and second time on that day, and in less than a month was ordered to be engrossed and published.[2]

The new Act of 31st December, 1652, intended, as the preamble states, " for raising of money for the use of the Navy," exposed for sale all the castles, houses, parks and lands specifically named—though expressly reserving the " water-courses, conduits, pipes, pounds, sluices, bays, dams, or other instruments and things used for carrying or conveying water in or through the houses, lands, or premises"—which on or after 1st April, 1635 were in the possession of the royal family. As usual the premises were vested in trustees, the only difference being that, so far as officials were concerned, one of the original contractors, Jn. Humphreys, and two of the trustees, Sir Hy. Holcroft and Sylvanus Taylor, no longer served in the same capacity —the reason in Taylor's case being that he had been appointed assistant to Colonel Wm. Webb, the Surveyor-General. The Act was careful to specify that all rights of persons, other than the late king and his heirs, were to be saved as from 26th March, 1641, but claimants were to appear before the Committee of Obstructions and enter their titles not later than 1st February, 1652. Allowances were even authorized in connection with offices previously held by persons, but now no longer required. The trustees and contractors, as in the original Act of 16th July, 1649, held the premises as of the manor of East Greenwich in free and common socage, by fealty only, absolutely unfettered by tithes. They were to give public notice of sale within ten days of the delivery of surveys, taking care to " contract with

[1] *Commons Journals*, vol. vi, p. 471 ; vol. vii, pp. 191, 216–17.
[2] *Commons Journals*, vol. vii, pp. 222, 226, 236–40 ; cf. Index, p. 619.

persons or bodies, who will give most for the same, not selling any land under thirteen years' value, and selling the houses, wood, and timber at the best advantage for the Commonwealth " ; and upon making such contracts they were to pay to the treasurers one moiety or more of the purchase money within twenty days, securing the residue by means of a " Conveyance of bargain and sale ", which, being duly sealed, executed, and enrolled in Chancery, " shall be good and effectual in law to such purchasers " for all time. A special clause in this Act provided for persons who, having made a contract, failed to carry it through : such persons were to forfeit the fourth part of their contract-money, their estates being sequestered until the amount was forthcoming. The registrar and the four treasurers named in the first Act, continued to serve in their respective offices under the arrangements now made for selling the castles and parks of the Crown.[1]

Besides the castles, mansions, parks, chases, and forests, the Act of 16th July, 1649, had expressly reserved all Crown advowsons, presentations, and reversions. It was now enacted " that all reversions, remainders of honours, manors, castles, houses, messuages, chases, parks, lands, tenements or hereditaments, with appurtenances, and of all royalties, franchises, privileges and immunities belonging ", which on 26th March, 1641, were held by the late king, in right of the Crown of England or Duchy of Lancaster, or at any time since that date " expectant upon any estate tail ", were now to be vested and settled in the trustees and contractors by virtue of the present Act, and to the same uses. These officials were authorized to contract for, bargain and sell by means of deeds sealed and enrolled in Chancery, all such reversions and remainders to the respective tenants who before 28th February, 1652, expressed a desire to purchase ; after that date the trustees were to admit other persons " that shall buy or purchase and give most for the same, at such values and prices as the Trustees and Contractors shall think meet and convenient, for the best advantage of the Commonwealth ". All such contracts, bargains and sales, conveyances and assurances were declared to be good and effectual in law, any fine, recovery, conveyance or other Act to the contrary notwithstanding, the purchasers and officials being as fully protected as the late king under the statute of 34 Henry VIII, cap. 20. The premises as usual were to be held of the manor of East Greenwich, in free and common socage, by fealty only and not otherwise.[2]

[1] Firth and Rait, op. cit., vol. ii, pp. 691–6.
[2] Firth and Rait, op. cit., vol. ii, 694–6. The subject was debated in the House on 28th–30th December, 1652, and the clause referred to was drafted by Lord Chief Baron Wilde.

CHAPTER VII

DIS-AFFORESTATION AND SALE OF ROYAL FORESTS

AND CHASES, 1653-54

As the impropriations, advowsons, and rights of patronage belonging to the Crown were involved in the various sales of Church property, two only of the numerous exceptions in the Act of 16th July, 1649, remain to be considered. One of these referred to the royal timber growing within the woodlands of England and Wales. In this case Parliament took the view that the Act did not extend to any of the " timber trees fit for the use and service of the public Navy of this Commonwealth " that were growing at that time in parks, chases, or other premises, provided they were situated within fifteen miles of a navigable stream. Surveyors appointed by the navy were to survey and mark all trees they considered suitable for this purpose, and in their surveys, which were to be returned to the trustees not later than 10th December, 1649, they were required to state the number of timber trees marked, the places where they could be found, and other proceedings relative to their work. Timber trees which had thus been "surveyed, marked, and returned", were then to be cut down and carried away by order of the Commissioners of the Navy, the latest permissive date for doing so being 10th July, 1657.

The remaining exemption was contained in a proviso which stated that the Act " did not extend to grant to the Trustees any forests within this Commonwealth ", but a very significant clause was added in reference to the exemptions : " In case, upon surveys made and returned, it appears there is not sufficient to satisfy the arrears of the soldiery mentioned in this Act, then there shall be further provision made for the remaining arrears not satisfied, as abovesaid, out of the forests of the said late King, Queen or Prince, or otherwise as the Parliament shall direct." [1]

Several orders of Parliament, issued in the months preceding the passing of the first Act for sale of the Crown lands, reveal the anxiety of the Government in regard to the preservation of timber for shipping. Thus the Committee for Obstructions had already been directed, 3rd January, 1648, to find compensation for the owner of an ancient hedgerow in the parish of Stoke, part of the lands of the late Bishop of Winchester, because the elms, which he was not allowed to cut

[1] Firth and Rait, op. cit., vol. ii, pp. 189-190.

down, formed a landmark to guide ships on their return from the sea. In the following February the Council of State was authorized to take all possible care to prevent spoil, waste, or embezzlement in the woodlands of the Commonwealth, and in order that timber might be cut at the proper seasons and in proportion to the needs of shipping, surveyors, woodwards, and other officials and workmen were appointed. During March of the same year the Committee for the Revenue was instructed to find some way of letting the parks for one year, so that the State might benefit, and at the same time the Council was to give directions for the sale of decayed trees in forests and parks belonging to the Crown. As there had been great waste committed in the Forest of Dean, a stern order was next issued forbidding all persons—notwithstanding any sale, grant, or order then in force— to cut down trees, or remove those already felled, and this was followed later by the issue of a commission to find out not only what wastes and spoils had occurred, but who was responsible, and how great was the damage already done. When, therefore, Sir James Harington reported on 30th June, 1649, during the debate on the sale of the Crown lands, that the Council of State considered it necessary for some provision to be made in the bill, Parliament decided that the Committee of the Navy should express its opinion, and in consequence the two exceptions relating to forests and timber trees found a place, as already shown, in the original Act.[1]

In October, 1649, we find the Council of State endorsing the opinion which had been expressed by the Navy Commissioners, that as the trust to be reposed in the purveyors of timber was very great they ought to act under an oath ; but it was added, that " as it cannot be given but by Act of Parliament, and you know best what their employment is to be, we desire you to draw up an Act for that purpose, and send it to us ". By the following December, the Commissioners for the Forest of Dean had completed their investigations, and the surveyors appointed by the Navy Commissioners had marked all the trees they required throughout the land ; whereupon reports were read in the House on 1st January, 1649–50 by Colonel Martin and Wm. Bond in reference to the state of timber in the forests. So impressed were members by the disclosures then made that the House at once resolved that the contractors should suspend their sales of timber on royal lands ; that the power of the committee dealing with Irish affairs, in so far as it concerned the cutting down and selling of trees, should cease ; and that the Committee of the Revenue should recall and revoke all warrants issued by them " for cutting, selling or disposing of any wood, or timber, within any forest belonging to the Commonwealth ". As for the Forest of Dean, not a single tree was henceforth to be cut down, " upon any pretence whatsoever ", without direct order from the House, and those already cut were to

[1] *Commons Journals*, vol. vi, pp. 109, 148, 167, 172, 179, 247, 249.

be strictly preserved for the service of the State. Since the ironworks were considered to be responsible for the extraordinary waste of wood which had occurred in the forest, the order was also issued that these should be immediately " suppressed and demolished ", the Council of State being required to take care that this was effectively done. Doubtless it was due to these reports that the Council decided to report to Parliament (7th January) that some more ships ought to be built, " which will be best done now, because of the great stores of timber cut down." How seriously Parliament regarded the destruction of woods may be judged from the fact that a proviso was inserted in the Act of General Pardon and Oblivion, which was passed 24th February, 1651–2, stating, " that this Act do not extend to pardon any wastes or spoils committed or done since 31st December, 1631, in any of the forests, chases, or lands belonging to the late King, Queen or Prince, or in any other lands that have been disposed of by Parliament since 1641 or are now belonging to the Commonwealth of England." But the abuses continued, in spite of repeated orders, throughout the period, nor did they cease even at the Restoration.[1]

By the close of the year 1651, Parliament had decided to refer these matters to a Committee who were to consider and report how forests and chases might best be improved for the advantage of the public, " having special regard to the poor and to the just rights of all persons claiming anything therein." This instruction of 12th March, 1651, was followed by another on 2nd September, 1652, requiring the Commissioners of the Navy to specify the things which they desired to see reserved in connection with the forthcoming Act for the sale of exempted Crown premises ; but in the meantime the trustees and contractors were to take care not to sell or convey any of the lodges and enclosed grounds within the forests which the keepers or rangers had hitherto occupied. A further resolution of 15th October, directed that all State forests, parks, chases, and walks should be employed and improved to the uses intended, " and as may be best for the honour and benefit of the State." By 6th December a bill for the sale of forest lands was ready to be reported to the House (a duty undertaken by Strickland on 8th January following), after which it was read twice and committed to the care of the Attorney-General, Lord Chief Baron, the Lord General, Major General Skippon, and eight officers, Sir Henry Vane, Sir Hy. Mildmay, and four other knights, together with Strickland, Lechmere, Long, and a score of other members of the House. In this way the interests of the soldiery were strongly represented when the committee met a week later in

---

[1] Cal. S.P. Dom., 1649–50, pp. 347, 472 ; ibid., 1651, p. 45 ; ibid., 1651–2, p. 107 ; ibid., 1652–3, p. 320. See also *Commons Journals*, vol. vi, p. 342, vol. vii, p. 225 ; Firth and Rait, op. cit., vol. ii, p. 575. In the particulars of the warrants issued by the Committee of the Revenue for the sale of wood in the coppices of Whittlewood Forest, Northants, an appeal by Lord Grey secured the support of the House and the sale of these woods was then agreed to (*Commons Journals*, vol. vi, p. 368).

the Exchequer Chamber, armed with power to send for persons and all necessary records.[1]

It is probable, though not certain, that the committee appointed by the House in January, 1652-3 was too large for its purpose and that serious disagreements ensued; for when next we hear of action being taken in Parliament, 20th September, 1653, the projected bill is evidently dead, and it is found necessary to refer the consideration of the sale of the forests to a new and smaller committee, consisting of the Commissioners of Inspections, together with Major-Generals Desborow and Harrison, Alderman Titchborne and eight other members of the House. That unexpected difficulties had arisen is clear from an entry in the proceedings of the Council of State dated 7th May, wherein the " petition and remonstrance " of the contracting farmers was ordered to be " considered when the bill concerning forests and chases is renewed " ; and there is a further entry on 25th July, when Carew was instructed " to present to the Committee for Inspections the draft of an Act for the sale of forest lands.". There is also a very significant entry relating to petitions from the army in the proceedings of the Council for 21st September, on which action was taken in parliament two days later.[2]

On 23rd September we have the report of Alderman Titchborne from the newly-constituted " Committee for the Improvement of the Sale of Forests ", in which the opinion is given " that the only way in view for improvement of the sale of the forests to the best advantage of the Commonwealth is by the accepting of the propositions annexed, viz.:—

" The humble proposals of the late farmers of the customs (Sir John Jacob, Sir Job Harby, Sir Nic. Crisp) to the Parliament of the Commonwealth of England :—

" 1. That the Debt presented in May 1645 to the Committee of the Navy, being £276,146, as by their humble petition is expressed, may be made public faith upon the sale of the forest lands.

" 2. That, upon security of the said forest lands, they and their creditors propound to pay, for the sale of the Commonwealth, these sums following, that is :—

1st December next	£100,000
1st February next	100,000
1st May next	50,000
1st September next	26,146

£276,146

And that an Act pass for the doubling thereof with all convenient speed."

[1] *Commons Journals*, vol. vii, pp. 104, 174, 191, 217 ; cf. the Index, pp. 226, 240, 245, 1138.
[2] S.P. Dom., 1652-3, p. 311, and 1653-4, pp. 47, 161 ; *Commons Journals*, vol. vii, p. 322, and index, p. 1138.

This opinion of the Committee was shared by the House, Parliament expressing its willingness to accept the proposals, provided that three payments instead of four were made, and that the final payment of £76,146 was dated 1st May instead of 1st September. Instructions were then given to refer the matter to the same committee, with a view to bringing in an Act for the sale of forest lands.[1]

Accordingly, the committee set to work to prepare a bill for the sale of these lands, and with such speed was this done that on 22nd October, 1653, it was read for the first time, and when the second reading took place four days later, Sir Arthur Ashley Cooper, Col. West, and five other members agreed to assist the committee. Many amendments were proposed during November, four of which were withdrawn or " laid aside ", and more than twenty rejected. Among the latter were the petitions of the freeholders and others of the forests of Rockingham and Salcey in Northamptonshire. In connection with this measure five divisions were ordered, with the following results [2]:—

XXIII. PARLIAMENTARY DIVISIONS ON FORESTS, 1653

1653.	Proposals.	Ayes.	Noes.	Result.
Nov. 9	Stowood and Shotover forests, Oxf.	32	43	Rejected
„ 18	Salary of Trustees, £200 p.a. . .	27	41	Rejected
„ 18	Salary of Trustees, £300 p.a. . .	41	35	Accepted
„ 19	1st payment Dec. 1 next . . .	37	43	Rejected
„ 22	Petition of Anne Henshaw . .	40	47	Rejected

It will be seen that only one of the these divisions was favourable to the " yeas ", the majority secured even then being very small, and it is worthy of note that on this occasion Col. Cromwell and Alderman Ireton were " Tellers for the Noes ", Barebone and Sir Gilbert Pickering acting in a similar capacity for the " Yeas " when their previous motion for the adoption of a lower salary was defeated. The salaries of the treasurers and the register-accomptant, fixed at £200 and £150, respectively, were not challenged, but the clause relating to the " Brigade of Foot, raised within the County of Chester, for the late engagement at Worcester " was rejected after the second reading on 22nd November, when the bill as a whole was read for the last time, and the usual order went forth to print and publish the measure.

The Act " for the dis-afforestation, sale and improvement of the forests and of the Honours, Manors, Lands, Tenements and Hereditaments within the usual limits and perambulations of the same, heretofore belonging to the late King, Queen and Prince ", which had

[1] *Commons Journals*, vol. vii, pp. 322–3, 331, 338, 340.
[2] Table XXIII.   This is based on the record of votes entered in the *Journals of the House of Commons* during November, 1653 (vol. vii, pp. 347, 349, 352–5). The majorities are never less than six nor more than fourteen out of votes that range from sixty-eight to eighty-seven ; cf. the divisions of 1649 to 1652 given in a previous section, No. VI (Table XXII, p. 104).

thus been passed on 22nd November, 1653, is a very lengthy measure. In the preamble the declaration occurs that " the Parliament of the Commonwealth of England, considering it to be their duty to assert and maintain the honour, liberty, and safety of this Nation against all attempts ; and that such undertakings unavoidably draw great expense of Treasure ; and being equally sensible of the pressures and exhaustings they have lain under ; and desiring by all means to give what ease possible the necessity of affairs will permit ", of necessity " require the supply of very great sums of money to carry them on, the which can be raised by no way with more advantage to the public, than by the de-afforestation, sale, and improvement of the forest lands ". Accordingly, all the forests, with such manors and lands as then lay within the limits defined by an Act of 17 Charles, which had belonged to the Crown on 25th March, 1635, together with all their royalties, privileges, and rights, were declared henceforth to be vested in Rob. Aldworth, Josias Berners, Edw. Cressett, Francis Mussenden, Jn. Parker, Hy. Pitt, and Wm. Webb, as trustees, to be held as of the manor of East Greenwich, in free and common socage, freed from tithe. The trustees were authorized to enclose and improve the forest lands for the common good and public advantage, and definite directions were given for their enclosure, having due respect to such rights of commoners as were claimed within thirty days of the " public summons " which the trustees were to issue. As one of the objects of the Act was to provide for the necessitous people who dwelt in the neighbourhood of the forests it was enacted that there should be an allotment called " The Poor's Ground ". Then when all these claims were satisfied, the remaining parts of the forests were to be sold, with full freedom from forest laws but proper recognition of existing patents.[1]

Owing to the " absolute necessity of preserving a competent quantity, fitting for the Navy ", surveyors were ordered to take special note of all thriving timber of oak or elm, certifying six things in each survey of the premises :—

(1) Where any such timber grows.

(2) The number of such trees.

(3) How many loads of clean timber the trees contain.

(4) The value of the lop, top, and bark of such trees.

(5) How far are the trees from the nearest part of any navigable river.

(6) What price by the load such timber is then and there worth.

After the surveys had been completed the trustees were to order an abatement in favour of purchasers of the premises, and at the

[1] See S.P. Dom., 1653–4, pp. 265–6 ; also Firth and Rait, op. cit., vol. ii, pp. 783–812. The Act referred to occupies fifty-eight pages in vol. i, No. 78 of the collection of Acts in the Public Record Office Library, 489 F.

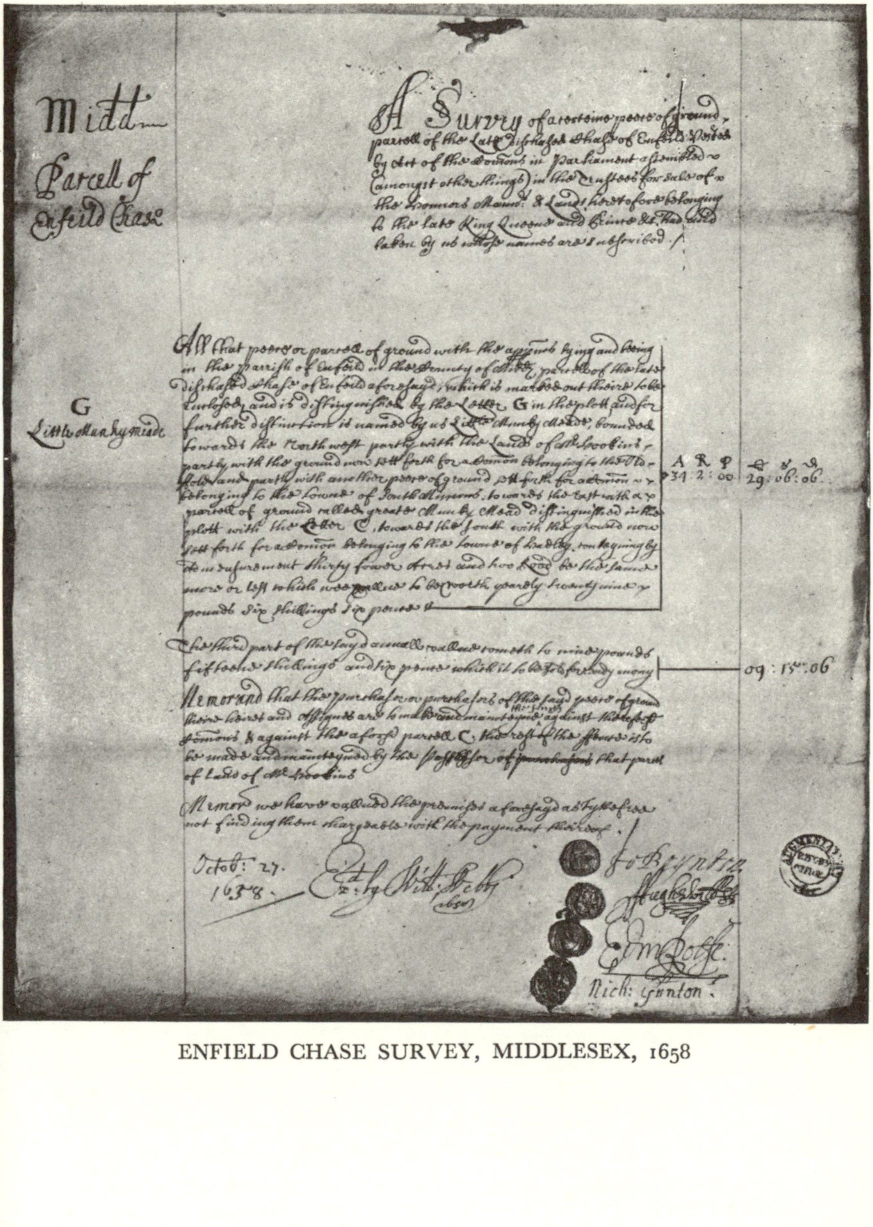

ENFIELD CHASE SURVEY, MIDDLESEX, 1658

same time they were to make provision for the delivery of the timber to the Council of State. Effective steps were to be taken to prevent spoils and encroachments.

In the new Act Col. Wm. Webb appears among the seven trustees, his place as Surveyor-General being taken by Ralph Hall, who is described as " Register, surveyor-general and keeper of all original surveys of premises ". Before estates were sold they were to be surveyed by fit and able persons appointed by the trustees, who were to administer to them an oath similar to the one provided in the original Act of 16th July, 1649. Their duties, too, were similar, though they were more elaborately specified in the latest Act. They were to keep courts of survey, and were empowered to take evidence on oath, every assistance being given by the civil power in case of obstruction. Their surveys, however, need only be signed by two surveyors, but the usual rule for forwarding duplicates had to be observed. Counsel in London and stewards of manors in the different counties were to be appointed from time to time whenever assistance was required by the trustees and surveyors.

Oaths were to be taken by the trustees, treasurers, and registrars before assuming the duties assigned to them and set down with so much detail in the Act. The trustees were to proclaim their summons in every market town within or near the forests, commencing with Windsor and Waltham. The Surveyor-General was to examine all surveys, make notes in the margin, and return them signed within four days (not six as in the original Act) to the trustees. He was also to certify weekly, as registrar, and to post up on the wall for public inspection a statement concerning all surveys and certificates returned to him ; and every week he was required to forward certificates to the treasurers and the register-accomptant showing :—

(1) All rates of particulars.
(2) All moneys payable upon any contract.
(3) The amount to be paid in hand.
(4) The amount to be forborne.
(5) The time involved in these payments.

The instructions to Wm. Benson, the register-accomptant, were no less precise. He was to keep a ledger book, and sign every leaf of the treasurers' book, keep every bill or receipt allowed by him, sign all vouchers connected with moieties of payments, and audit all the accounts transferred to him from the trustees. Two treasurers were appointed to act in conjunction with Charles Doyly and Matthew Sheppeard, the two registrars ; they were required to see that the " quick money or doubling money " was paid within twenty days, and should any case of fraudulent dealings with forged bills arise, the persons concerned were to forfeit treble the amount and be imprisoned, half the fine inflicted being bestowed upon the discoverers.[1]

It was the intention of the government to raise £400,000 " for the present use of the Navy " upon the security of the lands and premises now offered for sale. In order to encourage persons to advance money, notice was given that all persons who had advanced money, plate, arms, or horses upon the public faith bills, or who had lawful bills or receipts relating to such loans assigned to them, would be permitted to double their amounts in connection with this Act. Thus, for example, any person who possessed bills for £100, the interest on which for five years at 6 per cent would equal £30, by advancing £130 more, would be able to secure £260 in all ; and so proportionately for a greater or a lesser sum. Further, as the sum of £276,146 had been allowed by Parliament as a public faith debt to Sir Nic. Crisp, Sir Job. Harby, Sir Jn. Harrison, Sir Jn. Jacob, and other late farmers of Customs, on condition of their advancing the like sum in three instalments between 1st January and 1st May next, these sums were likewise to be secured upon the forest lands, as part of the £400,000 ; but as the executors of certain deceased persons formerly holding securities in connection with the Customs were unable to double their amounts, in this particular case it was provided that should they decide to double such debts, either out of deceased estates or their own, they " shall not be considered a waster of the estate of the deceased ".

Some special regulations provided for the payment of salaries to officials, each of the trustees receiving £300 a year, the treasurers £200, and the registrar-accountant, £150 ; and in addition to these amounts, sums of £100 and £50 were given to specified officials for managing the £400,000 loan. For the expenses in carrying on the work necessitated by the Act, a shilling in the pound was set aside. As an inducement to purchasers it was declared that no part of the premises would be liable to tax for three years, and that no greater sum than the £400,000 proposed would be secured on these lands until that sum and the doubled moneys were paid off. All purchasers not paying their money in due time were to forfeit one-third of their contract money, and in such cases the lands were to be sold again. It was also expressly stated that no officer or other person concerned in the actual working of the new statute might directly or indirectly purchase any part of the premises under pain of forfeiture of the money paid and the estates procured. As a final decision, it was arranged that all moneys advanced upon public faith debts for the purpose of doubling were to be paid into the Treasury before 2nd May, 1654. As to office accommodation, the trustees, being required to choose a convenient building, selected Worcester House as the place wherein

---

[1] Nevertheless, bills and debentures were forged, and fraudulent dealings occurred, as will later be shown, on a large scale. See Part IV, Sec. IV, " The Discovery of Frauds."

their work might most advantageously be done. One other matter contained in the Act concerned Joachim Mathews and Jn. Brewster, who were permitted by an order of Parliament dated 9th September, 1653, to retain an acre of ground in Waltham Forest, in the parish of Barking, for their " meeting-place for the public worship of God ", and lands to the value of £100 were also allowed at the same time to Mathias, son of Benjamin Valentine, deceased, in accordance with a grant of Parliament dated 27th August, 1652. The exemptions connected with this Act will be referred to later.[1]

[1] Firth and Rait, op. cit., vol. ii, pp. 811–12. See Chapter VIII which follows.

CHAPTER VIII

THE AMENDED ACTS OF THE PROTECTORATE,
1653-8

The Act for sale of the forest lands was passed at a critical time in the affairs of the nation, for Parliament, having fixed its dissolution to take place on 4th November, 1654, had secretly made plans for passing its own Perpetuation Bill, by means of which members would be able to retain their seats without re-election. Just as the bill was about to be read the third time Cromwell appeared on the scene with a troop of musketeers and dissolved the " Rump " by force. A provisional Council of State, with Cromwell as President, had already been appointed at the instigation of the army, and on 4th July, 1653, a convention was summoned to meet at Westminster. To this assembly came 122 English members, with six others from Wales, five from Scotland and six from Ireland. All were " godly men ", selected, on the advice of Harrison, from lists sent up by the separatists or congregational churches.

As the Council of State consisted at that time of eight officers and four civilians, the influence of the army was very strong. When therefore the assembly in September prepared its own bill for the sale of forest lands, members took care to insert a clause ensuring the non-payment of tithes, and another providing a free gift of 100 acres for a meeting house in Essex. But when it came to the question of deciding upon what service of the State the loan of £400,000 should be bestowed it was the navy that secured preferential treatment, and in addition several exemptions appeared in the Act. So the " daft little Parliament " composed of these " godly men " turned out to be " the most crotchety and unpractical set ever gathered together ", and the army again came to the rescue on 12th December, three weeks after the bill had been passed, expelling all those who would not support Sydenham's motion for resignation. Thus " the nominees sank again into private life, as little regretted by the nation as the Long Parliament had been regretted before them ". Then the personal rule of the Protector Cromwell began.[1]

No little anxiety was caused by these occurrences, even though it was found that in the " Instrument of Government ", dated 16th December, 1653, provision had been made for all lands, rents and royalties as yet unsold, to be vested in the Lord Protector, for

[1] Madge, *England Under Stuart Rule*, pp. 120-2.

116

this clause did not apply to forests and chases, nor to the honours and manors situated within their borders. Hence we find Sir Jn. Jacob's petition addressed to Cromwell in reference to the undertaking of the late farmers of Customs, to which the Council replied on 20th December with the assurance that the government intended to make no change in the Act recently passed, and in order that he might feel satisfied with this reply, a copy of that part in the Act which concerned him was ordered to be delivered, after it had been attested by Thurloe as a true copy. Alderman Jn. Fowkes in the following month forwarded another petition in connection with the sales of forest lands for the consideration of the Council of State. How many such petitions were received is unknown, but it is quite possible that the number was large; and in any case we know that finally it was a petition from the army officers which caused Cooper, Montague, and Sydenham to prepare a fresh ordinance to dispose of the forest lands.[1]

Now the recent Act had declared that nothing was contained therein which should be construed to apply to any of the manors exposed to sale under the original Act of 16th July, 1649; and it proceeded to state that seven forests were to be exempt from the new provisions, namely :—

(1) Ashdown, with Lancaster great park, Sussex.

(2) Dean Forest, Gloucester.

(3) Isle of Wight Forest.

(4) Kingswood, Gloucester.

(5) Needwood, in Stafford and Derby.

(6) New Forest, Hampshire.

(7) Sherwood, in Notts and Derby.

Of these, the first, fourth, fifth, and seventh, were to be exempt because they were reserved as collateral security to the officers and soldiers " whose arrears have not or cannot be paid and satisfied by the premises to that purpose intended " in the Act of 1649. In the other three cases not only were the honours, manors, and lands within the forests limits to be reserved, but the whole of the trees growing upon any part of the premises.[2]

That the government had definitely resolved to amend the Act for sale of the forest lands is clear from the orders of Council given in April to Cooper and Mackworth, and the " notes of alteration and amendments suggested in the ordinance for surveying forests " which have been preserved. In May, action was taken in Council, an Ordinance " for satisfying the arrears of officers and soldiers by the sale of several forests " being read on 3rd May, and again eight days later, when

[1] S.P. Dom., 1653-4, pp. 301, 360, 363 ; Firth and Rait, op. cit., vol. ii, p. 820. Act of 16th December, 1653, art. 31.
[2] Firth and Rait, op. cit., vol. ii, p. 811.

it was " recommitted to the Committee which brought it ". In the
following August, Council considered yet another ordinance " for
selling the four forests as a further security for the solders' arrears ".
This appears to be the first time these exempted forests are referred to.
By 21st August " An Ordinance for appointing Commissioners to
survey the forests, honours, manors, lands, tenements and hereditaments within the usual limits and perambulations of the same, heretofore belonging to the late King, Queen and Prince " had been amended
and passed.   The Commissioners, who were to be nominated by
Cromwell, were armed with extensive powers.   They were to enter
upon and survey all the forests in England and Wales, with their
attendant honours, manors, and lands, keeping courts of survey
whenever necessary in order to examine persons and find out a variety
of particulars relating to the nature and extent of the forests, the
existence of parks, the duties of officers, the amount of profits, the
extent of boundaries, as well as the woods and timber, the claims of
Commoners, and the questionable matters arising out of enclosures,
encroachments, wastes, and spoils of woods.   How extensive was the
range of inquiry under those heads may be judged from the particulars
set out in the following summary, which shows the kind of information
the Commissioners were required to obtain by means of their examination of claims and the verdicts of their Courts of Survey :—

(*a*) *The nature and extent of the Forests.*
    (1) The best means of improving the forest lands for the benefit of
the Commonwealth.
    (2) The quantity of acres and equality of soil belonging to the
Commonwealth.
    (3) Their situation.

(*b*) *The Parks, Officers, and Profits.*
    (4) The game or deer preserved.
    (5) The parks situated within the forests.
    (6) The officers belonging to the premises.
    (7) The proceeds taken by officers and upon what grounds.
    (8) The proceeds accruing to the Commonwealth.

(*c*) *The Divisions.*
    (9) The parcels claimed by persons, and by whom enjoyed.
    (10) The acreage of these parcels.
    (11) The estates in possession or reversion held by claimants.
    (12) The yearly profit made by claimants.

(*d*) *The Woods and Timber.*
    (13) The quantity, quality, and values of all timber and woods belong-
ing to the Commonwealth.
    (14) The condition of the fences.
    (15) The profit yearly made for the Commonwealth or legally enjoyed
by others.
    (16) The quantities of timber or wood claimed by others.
    (17) The extent to which they are subject to the liberty of the forests.

(e) Commoners and Encroachments.
(18) The number of commoners who challenge rights.
(19) The estimated number of cattle yearly fed therein.
(20) the number of questionable purprestures, enclosures, late erections, or encroachments.
(21) The name and number of acres of every fallet within the premises.
(22) The state of their fences, and the persons in default.

(f) Waste and Spoil of Woods.
(23) The loss accruing to the Commonwealth from lack of fences, cutting down timber or woods, undue browsing, or suffering cattle in the coppices.
(24) The persons causing such loss.
(25) The value of such detriment.
(26) The means to be adopted for making satisfaction in such case.

The Commissioners were further authorized to hear and determine claims, to set out proportions of land to meet rightful claims, to allow for all necessary highways, and permit persons to compound for the dis-afforestation of the premises. They were to observe all instructions issued by the Protector, and within ten days of the completion of their commissions they were to certify the surveys taken by them and other proceedings to the Court of Exchequer, a duplicate being delivered at the same time to the trustees.[1]

Meanwhile the Council of State was occupied with the consideration of " an Ordinance for sale of four forests or chases reserved for collateral security to the soldiers ", and within a few days this also was passed. The premises now to be exposed to sale were four out of the seven [2] previously excepted in the Act of 22nd November, 1653, that is to say the forests of Ashdown and Sherwood and the Chases of Kingswood and Needwood : these had been reserved for the benefit of officers and soldiers who were in service on 24th December, 1647, and whose arrears had not since been satisfied. The premises were now to be vested in ten of the trustees named in the original Act of 1649, and these, with Sir Wm. Roberts and the surviving contractors, were to contract for the sale of the forests after surveys had been completed. Enfield Chase, the sale of which had been suggested on 27th November, 1652, was now to have one-third of its area sold to provide ready money, but not under ten years' purchase. From these proceeds the arrears of Col. Edw. Montague and other officers were to be paid. All contracts made by the last Act for sale of the forest lands were now confirmed ; but the warning was issued that any purchases under the first Act which were not cleared within forty days of the return of the requisite surveys, or within four months of the passing of this ordinance (six months where the lands had not

---

[1] S.P. Dom., 1654, pp. 93, 98–9, 146, 166–7, 291, 300, 307, 309, 318 ; Firth and Rait, op. cit., vol. ii, pp. 946–9.
[2] Leaving the Forest of Dean, New Forest, and a forest in the Isle of Wight in reserve.

yet been surveyed), would be declared void, and the contractors debarred in consequence from renewing the claims of such purchasers. This ordinance was followed on 15th December, 1654, by an important resolution : " That the Acts and Ordinances of Parliament, made for the sale or other disposition of the lands, rents and hereditaments of the late King, Queen and Prince," including the forest lands, " shall no way be impeached or made invalid, but shall remain good and firm ; and that the security given by Act and Ordinance of Parliament, for any sums of money by any of the said lands " shall remain " firm and good and not be made void or invalid upon any pretence whatsoever ".[1]

Two subsequent Acts, both passed in June, 1657, remain to be mentioned. One of these was intended to mitigate the rigour of the forest law within the Forest of Dean, and to preserve the wood and timber in that forest from waste and destruction. The other, while recording the instructions agreed on in Parliament in connection with the survey of the four forests and Enfield Chase, confirmed the ordinance of 1654 for their sale. The Commissioners were to ascertain the bounds of the forests, inquire into claims, appoint juries for trial of claims, respect all rights enjoyed before 25th March, 1641, allow proportionate waste grounds for common, disallowing all claims expressed by " general words " in grants. They were to make inquiries concerning the yearly value of the lands and timber, and in due course to certify their findings to the Trustees. Various detailed provisions relating to diaries, messengers, and labourers are recorded. Sydenham and five others were to form a committee of appeal to examine matters on oath, their decision being regarded as final, except in case of equal votes, when Lord Commissioner Fiennes was to make the settlement. It only remains to add that these Acts of 9th and 19th June were confirmed, though partially, in the general Act of 26th June, 1657, after which the legislation dealing with the Crown lands came to an end.[2]

---

[1] S.P. Dom., 1654, pp. 323, 328, 341-2, 401-2 ; Firth and Rait, op. cit., vol. ii, pp. 993-9. The Act is preserved in vol. ii, No. 92, among the collection at the Public Record Office, 498 F.

[2] S.P. Dom., 1657-8, p. 16 ; Commons Journals, vol. vii, pp. 503, 527-8, 563, and index, p. 1138 ; Firth and Rait, op. cit., vol. ii, pp. 1114-15, 1116-22, 1138-9. There are references to a projected bill for the further sale of Forests and Chases, 8th June and 4th October, 1659 ; see Commons Journals, vol. vii, pp. 676, 791. The restoration of monarchy, however, was near at hand, and republican legislation now abruptly ceased.

PART III

THE PARLIAMENTARY SURVEYS OF CROWN LANDS

CHAPTER I

CALENDARS OF THE SURVEYS

In each of the Acts relating to the sale of the royal property—whether concerning the honours and manors, castles, mansions, and parks, or the fee-farm rents, forests, and chases—it was expressly declared by Parliament that surveys of all the premises must precede the announcement of the sales, so that we find in consequence an important department of Worcester House entirely devoted to this great undertaking, under the undoubtedly able administration of Col. Wm. Webb, the Surveyor-General. As the county surveyors were ordered to forward duplicates with their surveys, two series were formed, one consisting of originals intended for the registrar, the other of duplicates for the use of the trustees and the public. Under this arrangement many thousands of documents must have been prepared for the convenience of purchasers in London, and for the special service of the State. At the Restoration these records were collected and distributed, the originals (it was thought) being retained in the Augmentation Office, and the duplicates placed in the custody of the Surveyor-General. To-day, there exist four series of Parliamentary Surveys, namely, the Augmentation Office Series, which is the most important, that of the Land Revenue Office, which is more important than the official guide leads one to suppose, and those of the Duchies of Cornwall and Lancaster, which are almost entirely overlooked. In addition there is a scattered series of surveys, the majority of which repose in the Public Record Office or the British Museum, the remainder being either in the University libraries of Oxford and Cambridge or in private collections.[1]

The most extensive collection of surveys, and therefore the one most frequently consulted, is that belonging to the Augmentation Office, a calendar of which has long been in use. When Sir Jos. Ayloffe, Dr. Ducarel, and Thos. Astle made their " further report " to the Lords of the Treasury on 14th July, 1764, concerning the progress they had made in methodizing, regulating, and digesting the records in this office, they stated that " the original Surveys of the

---

[1] Three of the great collections of Parliamentary Surveys are referred to in Giuseppi's *Guide to the Public Records,* vol. i, viz. Records of (1) the Exchequer, Augmentation Office, pp. 159–160 ; (2) Office of the Auditors of the Land Revenue, pp. 168, 172 ; (3) the Duchy of Lancaster, p. 332. The fourth collection is preserved in the Duchy of Cornwall Office, but the index of surveys is unprinted. S. Bird's *Guide* refers to the Parliamentary Surveys of the Augmentation Office, and to the corresponding " Oliver Cromwell's Surveys " of the Duchy of Lancaster, pp. 311, 314. Cf. Hall, *Repertory,* vol. i, p. 52.

honours, hundreds, manors, etc. belonging to King Charles I, his Queen, and the Prince of Wales, have been put into 58 large and strong portfolios, each lettered on the back with the name of the county and placed in a press ; the calendar of which is now completed ". These portfolios are still in use, though the Calendar has been superseded. In the years 1846 and 1847 the Deputy Keeper of the Public Records reported the completion of a new calendar and inventory of Parliamentary Surveys preserved among the records of the late Augmentation Office, which had been prepared and examined by Charles Cole, under the directions of Henry Cole, Assistant Keeper. This calendar was issued in the seventh and eighth reports, the first part containing the section Bedfordshire to Lancashire, a series of 445 surveys with a total of 3,662 leaves; and Part II, the remainder of the series, Middlesex to York with the Welsh Counties, 779 further surveys, written on 6,095 sheets—making a total officially stated to be 1,224 surveys and 9,757 folios. The completion of the task of examining and calendaring these records deserves more than a passing word of recognition and praise, for the work was well done, the calendar containing " a full view of the contents of such of these valuable documents as are in the custody of the Master of the Rolls ", and in addition the Deputy Keeper inserted " a reference to those which are in other repositories, not yet brought under the regulations of the Public Record Act ". The revision of 1908 was not sufficiently thorough to detect the errors and omissions of Cole's calendar, in spite of the claim that the Parliamentary Surveys had been " entirely revised and incorporated ".[1]

A more searching examination of the various lists, as well as the whole of the documents in the Augmentation Office Series, recently completed in connection with the present work, revealed the following differences [2] :—

XXIV. Contents of the Augmentation Office Series, 1739-1927.

Dates.	Lists.	Documents.	Total Items.
c. 1739	Add. MS. 21328	—	1284
c. 1764	Add. MS. 21327	—	1285
1787	Printed List	—	1276
1847	D.K.P.R. Nos. 7 and 8	1224	1289
1908	P.R.O. List 25	—	1310
1927	Revision (Madge)	1320	1461

[1] See D.K.P.R., No. 7 (1846), p. 20, No. 8 (1847), pp. 9, 11, No. 20 (1859), pp. 91-2, No. 30 (1869), App. vol. vii, p. 260.
[2] Table XXIV is based on the various lists and calendars prepared since 1739 for the Augmentation Office series, all of which have been examined and their contents analysed. Two of the earliest inventories are preserved in the British Museum, viz. Add. MSS. 21327 and 21328—the second being the older of the two lists—and it was from one of these that the printed list of 1787 was prepared. See Madge, *Rural Middlesex*, pt. i, p. 279. The P.R.O. List of Surveys, No. 25, was incompletely revised. The Calendar of 1846-7 is contained in D.K.P.R. report 7, App. i, No. 28, p. 23, No. 51, p. 47, No. 52, p. 48 ; App. ii, No. 6, pp. 224-238 ; and report 8, App. i, No. 15, pp. 14, 17, No. 27, p. 35 ; App. ii, No. 2, pp. 52-80 and 80-1. See also D.K.P.R. report 20, App., pp. 91-2, where the portfolios are now stated to be fifty-six instead of fifty-eight, and reference is made to an index in one volume.

Only ninty-five of these items were found to refer to Wales and Monmouth, while the number of duplicates discovered did not exceed sixty-three. Fourteen were transfers from one county to another, and seven were discoveries among other classes of documents now brought into this series, while 224 related to the hundreds of each county and were thus connected with the fee-farm surveys and sales. No. 36 in Sussex referred to lands that proved not to be Crown lands, and No. 49 in the same county, a document which contained two items, belonged to the surveys of Dean and Chapter Lands of Chichester. Eight entries in early lists could not be traced at all : it may be that some of these documents perished in the fire at the Houses of Parliament in October, 1834; some of those preserved to-day indeed are soiled with mud or badly stained with water, showing how great was the risk these records ran on that occasion.[1]

A second series of Parliamentary Surveys, with inventories and calendars of even earlier date, is that preserved among the records of the Exchequer as belonging to the office of the Auditors of Land Revenue. It is an extensive series of which little has hitherto been known. When the Deputy Keeper issued the second portion of his calendar in 1847, he added references to Parliamentary Surveys in the custody of other officials, giving an ingenious reply which the Keeper of the records in the Duchy of Cornwall had made to his inquiries, and then stating that " no list had been furnished of Parliamentary surveys in the office of the Land Revenue ". Half a century earlier the Select Committee on Public Records had stated in its report (1800) in reference to the office of the Surveyor-General of Crown lands that " some further indexes to the surveys and other documents concerning the property of the Crown, would be useful, but no extra assistance beyond the present establishment of the office is deemed necessary for the purpose of preparing them ". On 31st January, 1804, an order was issued to prepare such indexes, but although the order was repeated on 22nd May, 1806, and again on 21st January, 1812—when inquiry was made " respecting a state of the Indexes, and whether the same are complete, or in what progress they are towards completion "—the Commissioners of Public Records had to confess as late as 1819 that " no answer has been as yet received ". It was not until 1841 that the Deputy Keeper of the Public Records was able to record a short note stating that the Parliamentary Surveys in the newly constituted office of Land Revenue Records and Enrolments were " well bound in 19 volumes ". Yet there was little need for secrecy, for West, one of the Auditors of the Land Tax, certainly had in his custody a " catalogue " of the Parliamentary

---

[1] For the new Calendar see later in this section. The narrow escape from destruction of these records, with the probability that some were lost and others of the Augmentation thrown into confusion when the Houses of Parliament were destroyed by fire on 16th October, 1834, is referred to by Thomas, *Materials*, p. 145.

Surveys in his department in the year 1793. And, as we know from the fifth report of the Historical MSS. Commission, the Marquis of Lansdowne not only possessed an original volume, signed by the surveyors Gibbon and Cartwright in 1726 (which contained a list of all the entry books and surveys in the office of the Surveyor-General in that year), but an older folio manuscript still, namely, "a schedule of the ancient surveys or rentals before the Rebellion, the surveys made in the time of the Rebellion, and the surveys since the Restoration, etc.," preserved in the same office, the list bearing the signatures of Elphinstone and Munday and the date 1713.[1]

This series of Parliamentary Surveys has been almost entirely ignored by students, probably because there is no reference to them in Scargill Bird's *Guide*, and of late years because in the new *Guide to the Public Records* they are dismissed in a single line as " copies ". A careful examination of these volumes and the various lists from 1713, enables one to say with confidence that they contain material of the utmost importance, the existence of which hitherto had been unsuspected. The following differences emerged during the course of the investigation [2] :—

XXV. Contents of the Land Revenue Office Series, 1713–1927

Dates.	Lists.	Dupli-cates.	New Material.	Total Items.
1713	Add. MS. 30206	—	—	415
1726	Add. MS. 30207	—	—	411
1793	Add. MS. 23749	—	—	243
1927	Revision (Madge)	645	118	763

It will thus be seen that although this collection of Parliamentary Surveys is only half the size of the Augmentation Office Series, and admittedly contains many duplicates, yet one in every seven of its items is new, and cannot be found elsewhere.[3]

[1] Reports from the Select Committee on Public Records, 1800, p. 12 ; Do. of Public Records Commissioners, No. i (1812), app. E. 2, p. 54; No. ii,(1819), p. 358; D.K.P.R., report 2, p. 23, and report 8, app. ii, No. 2, p. 81 ; Land. Rev. Office List, ff. 39–40. All these volumes are now accessible in the P.R.O., under the reference Exch., L.R. 2, Misc. Bks., vols. 276–302, for England, and 303–4 for Wales. See also Hist. MSS. Com., report 5, p. 259, in reference to the volumes in the Lansdowne collection : they have been acquired by the British Museum since the report of 1876.

[2] Table XXV is compiled from three eighteenth-century calendars as well as the actual documents, as in the case of the Augmentation Office series with which these surveys have been individually compared. The calendars were formerly in the Lansdowne collection and now bear the press-marks Add. MSS. 23749, 30206–7, in the British Museum: they are the work of the Surveyors Gibbon and Munday between 1713–1726, and West, in 1793. This is the first time the documents have been closely examined and their value ascertained. Thomas, *Handbook*, p. 239, referred to these surveys as " probably duplicate of those among the Augmentation Records ", and Giuseppi's *Guide*, vol. i, 172, dismisses them in a single line : " Miscellaneous Books, volumes 276 to 304. Parliamentary Surveys, copies of. Commonwealth." These two statements, equally misleading, are of interest as showing that the Land Revenue surveys had not been properly examined between 1853 and 1923.

[3] The new material now discovered among the documents of this series has been incorporated in the new Calendar of revised surveys presented by the author to the P.R.O. in July, 1927. See the reference at the end of this section, p. 131.

A third series of Parliamentary Surveys, deposited in the office of the Duchy of Cornwall, is mentioned in the Report of the Select Committee on Public Records (1800). When the Deputy Keeper's calendar was being prepared, Henry Cole made some inquiries concerning these surveys, with the result that he was furnished with a list by J. R. Gardiner, keeper of the Duchy records, which is printed in the Appendix to Part II. The list, however, was deceptive. It deceived the Deputy Keeper of the Public Records, who reported that there were "a few (duplicates) in the Duchy of Cornwall Office ". It has since deceived the general public, for Gardiner's list was ingeniously confined to the County of Cornwall instead of the Duchy. Even then his list was incorrect, as will presently be seen. There was no necessity, however, for an evasive reply, although it must be confessed that even that was better than to ignore the request, as the Keeper of the Land Revenue Office Records had done, and refuse to supply any list at all.[1]

The Parliamentary Surveys of the Duchy of Cornwall Office were formerly part of the records kept in the custody of the Surveyor-General. As they are mentioned in his list of 1713 but excluded from the list prepared thirteen years later, it is clear that they were transferred to the Duchy of Cornwall Office during the reign of George I.[2] In Add. MS. 30206, dated 1713, no less than 116 surveys connected with the Duchy are recorded, eleven being earlier and eleven later than "the Rebellion ". The ninety-four Parliamentary Surveys referred to Duchy property in the eight counties of Berkshire, Cornwall, Devon, Dorset, Hertford, Somerset, Surrey, and Wiltshire. A memorandum states that " all these Surveys are in paper Books and were made and examined by Wm. Webb, Surveyor, and others by Direction of the pretended powers, and are very particular in expressing the Nature of the Lands and Tenements and the Rents and Improved Values thereof, with Rentals to most of the Manors at the end of each Survey ". A comparison between the lists of 1713 and 1726 shows that these surveys were not retained long in the custody of the Surveyor-General [3] :—

XXVI. COMPARATIVE LISTS OF DUCHY OF CORNWALL SURVEYS, 1713-26

Surveys.	1713.	1716.
1. Before the Rebellion	11	3
2. During the Rebellion	94	4
3. After the Rebellion .	11	0
Total . .	116	7

[1] Report of Select Committee on Public Records (1800), p. 81 ; D.K.P.R., report 7, p. 224, and No. 8, p. 81.
[2] But see the warrant to the Clerk of the Pipe relating to Duchy records in Treasury Books, vol. i, 196. (*Early Entry Books*, vol. vii, p. 130.)
[3] Table XXVI gives an analysis of two lists for the reigns of Anne and George II, signed by Gibbon and Munday in 1713 and 1726 ; these inventories are now in the British Museum. Add. MSS. 30206-7, and the items referred to are entered in the section relating to the Duchy of Cornwall, p. 129.

Of the four Parliamentary Surveys mentioned in the second list, only one appears in 1713, and it may be remarked that this Survey of the Scilly Isles, preserved in the Duchy Office to-day, was much more complete than the one (No. 39) included in the Augmentation Series. The other three were Nos. 7 and 20, together with a Survey of Pengelley hitherto unknown. Several surveys of Dorset, Somerset, and Surrey are described in the first list as being " stitched together ", and in this condition they may still be seen, showing that the surveys of the Surveyor-General's department were undoubtedly transferred to the custody of the Duchy of Cornwall. No. 6 in the Augmentation List was also recorded in 1713 among the Surveyor-General's collection, but it was missing in the Duchy Office in 1915, and the writer's recent search also failed to find it. The survey of Pengelley likewise proved to be missing in 1927.

A very useful " Index to Extents and Surveys before 1700 ", prepared by the late Mr. R. L. Clowes, carefully records the Parliamentary Surveys now preserved in nine bundles at the Duchy Office. But upon examination of the surveys themselves during the progress of this work, it was discovered that the Series is much more extensive than this, since it contains not only bundles, but bound volumes of transcripts and miscellaneous volumes, beside a roll and a number of abstracts, as well as an important volume of *Baynes Papers* containing important surveys, some of which relate to lands outside the Duchy of Cornwall.[1] Instead, therefore, of the meagre list furnished by Gardiner in 1846, we have evidence of a much more extensive series, though its importance as a whole is not great, since it consists so largely of duplicates or copies of surveys already known to exist in the Augmentation Office collection; but its interest is increased by the chance discovery of new volumes of transcripts, and in particular of the unique volume of *Baynes Papers* to which special reference will be made later. Gardiner's list contains forty-seven entries, the names being arranged in alphabetical order, whereas the Augmentation Office arrangement is numerical and the omissions are not immediately perceived. It is now known that fifty surveys for Cornwall exist, two of which, Bucklawren and Treverbyn Courtney, are not included among the fifty-four in the Augmentation Series; while in addition to these there are twenty-four others for Somerset, fourteen for Dorset, eight for Devon, three each for Surrey and Wiltshire, two each for Berkshire and Northants, and single surveys for the counties of Hertford, Leicestershire, Middlesex, Sussex, and Warwick, as well as

---

[1] Table XXVII contains an analysis of the various lists preserved in the British Museum and the Duchy of Cornwall office, as well as the results of an examination of the individual surveys and transcripts. The list drawn up by the late Mr. Clowes is dated 1920, and within its limits it is thoroughly reliable. But much material has since come to light—even as recently as 26th September, 1927. Clowes discovered a Parliamentary Survey of certain tenements in the Strand belonging to Somerset House in 1650, which does not contain the usual signatures of the surveyors.

COLONEL WILLIAM WEBB, SURVEYOR-GENERAL, 1649-60

[face p. 128

a survey of the manor and soke of Kirton in Lindsey, Lincolnshire, which is not to be found at the Public Record Office. Leaving out of consideration for the present the *Baynes Papers*, we have the following result for the Duchy of Cornwall Series, with the addition of an item relating to Somerset House tenements, and a large collection of " Abstracts of Parliamentary Surveys ", found very recently [1] :—

XXVII. CONTENTS OF THE DUCHY OF CORNWALL SERIES, 1713–1927

Date.	Lists.	In Bundles.	In Rolls.	Bound Vols.[2]	Total Items.
1713	Add. MS. 30206	—	—	—	94
1726	Add. MS. 30207	—	—	—	4
1847	D.K.P.R. No. 8	—	—	—	47
1920	Office Index .	108	1	—	109
1927	Revision (Madge)	108	1	168	277

There is yet another collection [3] of Parliamentary Surveys, which was formerly in the custody of the Duchy of Lancaster Office at Lancaster Place, Waterloo Bridge, but transferred to the Public Record Office in December, 1868. Its existence was discovered by Henry Cole, who printed in the Appendix to Part II of his Calendar a list furnished by W. Hardy in reply to some inquiries. These " few similar surveys ", as the Deputy Keeper styled them, included copies procured as recently as 1838 ; but collectively they made an imposing array of ninety-two files and 989 folios, when identified, numbered, stamped, and packed in bundles by the officials in 1871. They were at first distinguished from the " Parliamentary Surveys " of the Augmentation Series by being called " Oliver Cromwell's Surveys ", but when the Public Record Office List No. 14 appeared this distinction was dropped, though the special calendar with its separate system of numeration was preserved, the records being referred to as " for the most part transcripts, in many cases of recent date ". Several of them, however, are not surveys at all, but particulars grounded upon

---

[1] An entirely new list has been suggested as a result of the discoveries made in connection with the present work. The chief sections of which it is composed are shown in the table as follows : (1) Parliamentary Surveys in Bundles, Nos. 1–9, with titles given in Clowes' index ; (2) Roll of Liskeard Manor, being a second copy of that survey ; (3) Bound volumes of Transcripts, vols. i to xx, eight of which were newly discovered ; and Miscellaneous Volumes, vols. i to iii, the first (labelled " Surveys not Duchy, temp. Jas. I, Divers Counties ") containing a survey of Northamptonshire, No. 35, the second (" Old Shoreham Accounts "), a survey of Sussex, No. 50, and the third (" Baynes Papers ") a number of important items and surveys that do not relate to Duchy lands. The bound volumes in Section 3 appear to be of various dates : vols. 19 and 20 may belong to the year 1698, a lease of that date being recorded in connection with the Scilly Isles, and the watermark on p. 163 certainly belongs to the reign of William III. The arms on the covers of these volumes are those of Frederick, Prince of Wales, or possibly George II. Some of the transactions which are included refer to the period 1753–63. (Notes from a suggested New List, presented by the author to the Duchy of Cornwall Office, dated 16th June, 1927.)
[2] This includes two " Miscellaneous Volumes ": items of the " Baynes Volume " are excluded.
[3] See the Warrants relating to records in Treasury Books, vol. i, p. 125.

the surveys preparatory to the sale of the premises. The counties concerned number twenty-two, compared with fourteen in the Duchy of Cornwall collection, namely, Berkshire, Cambridge, Cheshire, Derby, Essex, Hampshire, Huntingdon, Lancashire, Leicester, Lincoln, Middlesex, Norfolk, Northampton, Nottingham, Oxford, Stafford, Suffolk, Sussex, Warwick, York, with Glamorgan and Monmouth. An examination of other classes of records within the Duchy classification, such as maps and plans, special commissions and rentals and surveys, makes it clear that this collection of documents relating to the Parliamentary Surveys and Sales, is both large and important, as the following analysis shows, the particulars for sale being not included in the " revision " figures[1] :—

XXVIII. Contents of the Duchy of Lancaster Series, 1847–1927

Dates.	Lists.	Dupli-cates.	New Material.	Total Items.
1847	D.K.P.R. No. 8	—	—	91
1869	D.K.P.R. No. 30	58	33	91
1871	D.K.P.R. No. 32	—	—	92
1901	P.R.O. List 14 .	83	4	87
1927	Revision (Madge)	86	16	102

An inspection of the various lists made between 1713 and 1920, a careful comparison of the entries in each of the official calendars, and above all a close examination of the whole of the folios of the actual documents themselves, confirms the belief that much additional material existed that had been previously overlooked or perhaps deliberately withheld, as in the case of the Land Revenue Office Series. As a result of this investigation a new and more comprehensive calendar has been prepared, embracing the entire contents of the four great collections belonging to the Augmentation and Land Revenue Offices and the Duchies of Cornwall and Lancaster. Of the total number of items examined, now found to exceed 2,600, less than one-half appear in the important calendar of the Deputy Keeper in 1847, and of the remainder more than 300 items refer to new and original material not hitherto accessible for study. Even the Augmentation Office Series of surveys was found to contain sixty-three duplicates.[2]

[1] Table XXVIII. This is based on the various lists indicated in the table, and a complete examination of the documents themselves. See D.K.P.R., report 7, p. 224, No. 8, pp. 80–1, No. 30, pp. 2, 40–1, No. 32, p. xxv ; P.R.O. List, No. 14, pp. 90–3 ; S. Bird's Guide, p. 314 ; Giuseppi's Guide, vol. i, p. 332, where they are described as " transcripts, in many cases of recent date ", of the Augmentation series of surveys.
[2] Table XXIX. Madge Calendar, P.R.O. This is an analysis of the contents of the new calendar in 11 volumes, presented to the Public Record Office in July, 1927, upon the completion of the research work connected with the present investigation. Volumes 1 to 9 refer to English counties, arranged alphabetically, vol. 10 to Wales, and vol. 11 contains new material discovered during the progress of the work. See P.R.O. references, Press 14, No. 82, vols. 1–11. A second Calendar, in 12 vols., dealing with Sales, was presented to the P.R.O. in January 1937.

XXIX. CONTENTS OF THE NEW CALENDAR OF PARLIAMENTARY SURVEYS, 1927

Series.	Items. 1847.	Dupli- cates.	New Material.	Total Items.
Augmentation Office	1289	—	172	1461
Land Revenue Office	—	645	118	763
Duchy of Cornwall	—	274	3	277
Duchy of Lancaster	—	86	16	102
Totals . .	1289	1005	309	2603

Besides the documents comprised within the four official series already mentioned, there are a number of others, not always duplicates or copies of Augmentation Office Surveys, both in public and private collections. The British Museum has several relating to Berkshire, Derby, Devon, Gloucester, Hereford, Kent, Lincoln, Middlesex, Norfolk, Northampton, Nottingham, Somerset, Stafford, Surrey, and Sussex. At the Bodleian Library surveys exist of Edmonton and Enfield, dated 1650, but a much more important certificate of Enfield Chase, prepared for the Committee of Appeal in September, 1656, has been found in the Cambridge University Library, together with a mass of hitherto unexplored material of exceptional value concerning the sales of Crown lands in England and Wales. At the Duchy of Cornwall Office is a separate series of Abstracts of Parliamentary Surveys, prepared by Thomas Clark about 1750, to which later leases of the premises have been added. Even at the Public Record Office there are various documents connected with these surveys preserved among the Miscellanea of the Exchequer (Kings Remembrancer), the General Series of Rentals and Surveys, Special Commissions, and the State Papers of the Commonwealth period. At the Guildhall Library no surveys have been found, nor have any relating to Crown lands been discovered at Lambeth, although on the other hand one or two relating to Church lands in Bedford and Sussex are now discovered to have been included by mistake among the surveys of Crown lands at the Public Record Office.[1]

Various transcripts of Sussex surveys by Dr. Burrell, and similar ones for Surrey by Mr. Clowes, are now among the collections deposited in the British Museum and the Duchy of Cornwall respectively. One very important series of original papers remains to be mentioned, namely, that recorded in the seventh report of the Historical Manuscripts Commission as forming part of the collections of the Rev. Thomas Webb, and its importance consists in the fact that it includes surveys and documents that were once in the possession of Col. Wm. Webb, the Surveyor-General, and of Col. Jeremy Baynes, one of the Parliamentary surveyors. These documents have since been dispersed, the Baynes correspondence being acquired by the British Museum, but the important volume of surveys, sold in 1913,

---

[1] See Appendix II, Section i, " Parliamentary Surveys ", items XA—XZ.

has only lately been discovered to be in the possession of the Duchy of Cornwall, as already shown.[1]

Abstracts of Parliamentary Surveys, as a rule very incomplete, have occasionally been printed, but very seldom have transcripts been published in full. A few isolated surveys, such as Cambridge No. 4, Gloucester No. 2, Somerset No. 7, and Worcester No. 5 are available for the purpose of study; to these may be added Kingsford's surveys of Piccadilly and the writer's survey of Halliford manor. There are are also thirteen Surrey surveys contributed by Mr. Giuseppi and others between 1871 and 1914. But the most notable collection of transcripts is that of J. R. Daniel Tyssen, who published the entire surveys of the County of Sussex in 1871-1873. It is a most surprising fact that not a single writer in the past half century has hitherto examined this important mass of material for economic purposes, and that until quite recently the Surrey surveys as a whole had not received attention. Mr. Lennard's economic study of the Northamptonshire surveys includes a detailed account of Grafton Manor, but there is not a single transcript in the volume.[2]

[1] Hist. MSS. Com., report 7, app. i, MSS. of Rev. Thomas Webb, pp. xv and 688; British Museum, Add. MSS. 5705, and Baynes' Correspondence in Add. MSS. 21417-27.
[2] For printed transcripts of Parliamentary surveys see Daniel Tyssen's Sussex surveys in *Sussex Arch. Soc. Collections*, vols. 23-5; Surrey surveys, by Giuseppi, Hart, and others in *Surrey Arch. Soc. Collections*, vols. 5, 15, 18, 27, and the article by the writer in vol. xxxvii, part ii, pp. 200-210, for 1927. For individual surveys see *London and Middx. Arch. Soc. Trans.*, N.S., vi, parts iv and v, for Halliford Manor; Kingsford's *Piccadilly*, pp. 59-60; and various references in *Archæologia*, vol. 40, pp. 119-137, *Evesham Jour.*, 17th November, 1906, *Som. Arch. Soc.*, vol. 30, p. 78, and *Glouc. Arch. Soc. Trans.*, vol. iii, pp. 354-5.

CHAPTER II

THE PLANNING OF THE SURVEYS

The surveys prepared by the county surveyors under the direction and control of the Surveyor-General, Col. Wm. Webb, extend to all the possessions of the Crown throughout England and Wales. They are seen at their best in the record of the manor of Barton-upon-Humber, Lincolnshire, upon the survey of which Webb has recorded his special approval : " This (as to forme and order) is a most compleate survey." But they are seen, at their worst, in the survey of the Lordship of Bromfield and Yale, Denbigh, on one of the folios of which Webb has written : "Welcome Hodge Podge I understand you not." We shall see another example of his ready wit presently in connection with the Surrey surveys. It has been urged that the surveyors, particularly in Wales, were ignorant men, and further, that the Exchequer was too disorganized by the flight of its officials to Oxford to permit the " mysterious knowledge " of that ancient department of State to be readily acquired and utilized by the new men appointed at Westminster. Yet the surveys as a whole exhibit so great a skill and the penmanship is often so exquisitely performed that the charge of ignorance on the part of the officials cannot for one moment be sustained. Nor does it follow that the officials were entirely new men, for the number of those who fled to Oxford may have been exaggerated, and of those who remained at their posts few may have been superseded or dismissed. The surveys show quite clearly that the work was undertaken by experienced men, and that they were completed with the greatest possible care.[1]

One remarkable feature of these Commonwealth surveys is the extraordinary uniformity of construction they exhibit throughout the entire range of counties; this feature, accompanied by a most astonishing precision in the intricate details of valuation, strongly suggests that the county surveyors must have worked to a specially prepared pattern, in the form of a model survey, with definite instructions concerning procedure and particular directions whenever doubt or difficulty arose. Even the most casual examination of the printed Sussex surveys suggests the use of a specimen survey and the

---

[1] The best and the worst surveys are those of Lincoln, No. 6, and Denbigh, No. 1*A*. The latter was partially corrected in No. 1*B*. See Shaw, *Camb. Mod. Hist.*, vol. iv, ch. xv, p. 454 ; also the criticism as to " Ignorant Scribes " and Surveyors in Tyssen's notes, *Sussex Arch. Soc. Collections*, vol. xxiii, pp. 220, 302, and vol. xxv, p. 25.

deliberate guidance of surveyors in their work ; while a closer examination of some hundreds of surveys in other counties indisputably confirms this view. Yet no such model survey has been found in the four great collections already named, and no detailed instructions other than those of a general character recorded in the ordinances and acts are preserved at the Public Record Office. The possibility of preparing such a model for the use of the Surveyors, in spite of any disorganization of the Exchequer, can scarcely be doubted, for even if some officials fled, the documents themselves may never have been disturbed at all, and the recently completed surveys of royal possessions in the reigns of James and Charles in any case would serve as precedents and examples for the Commonwealth officials to follow.

XXX. SURVIVING RENTALS AND SURVEYS OF PRE-COMMONWEALTH DATE [1]

Periods.	England.	Wales.	Totals.
Pre-Tudor	1,430	59	1,489
Tudor .	3,549	177	3,726
James I .	1,276	67	1,343
Charles I .	269	23	292
Totals	6,524	326	6,850

Even now, some three centuries later, upwards of six thousand surveys and other analogous records of an earlier period remain in the Public Record Office, and there is hardly any doubt that a large proportion of these were available for immediate use when the Commonwealth surveyors began their work. Nor would it be a very difficult task for the officials, whether new or old, to examine and compare existing rents and former values of Crown lands in any county of England and Wales, back to the reign of Edward VI, and in the majority of counties even as far back as Edward I. Kent is especially well served to-day, its series of surveys, which commences with John, including seventy-nine medieval and 104 Tudor documents, with 176 others relating to the reigns of James and Charles. The probability therefore of abundant material being available in 1649, is reasonably strong and the expectation that advantage would be taken of this material during the progress of the new work is undoubtedly well-founded ; moreover, the remarkable uniformity in regard to language and form shown by the Parliamentary Surveys

[1] Table XXX.   This is based on an analysis of the entire contents of P.R.O., List 25, Rentals and Surveys, obvious duplicates being eliminated.   The total number of entries for Middlesex between Edw. I and Wm. IV is 244, and in addition there are two undated, and seventeen others among the " divers counties ".   Of the total, forty-four are of earlier date than the Tudor period.   Of the Tudor documents sixteen and 142 belong to the successive reigns of Henry VII and Henry VIII, while those of Edw. VI and Elizabeth are represented by six and twenty respectively, but of Mary's reign there are none.   The Stuart records preceding the Commonwealth period number thirty, most of them belonging to the reign of James I.   Only seventeen are of later date, between the Restoration and the death of Anne.

proves that originally there were in existence special instructions for the guidance of surveyors, and a " model " survey for each of them to observe when preparing their own returns.

During the progress of the present investigation the discovery was made that several documents originally in the possession of Col. Wm. Webb, the Surveyor-General, were included, as we have seen, among the manuscripts of the Rev. Thos. Webb. Amongst other items of interest in that collection were four of special significance. One of these referred to a breviate of instructions for ingrossing surveys ; a second mentioned some instructions for a method of drawing up and ingrossing surveys ; the third showed the existence of an index to a book of precedents ; while the fourth drew attention to a survey of the " imaginary manor " of sale in Surrey. When the Webb collection was subsequently dispersed all the four items just mentioned were missing. During the writer's search at the Duchy of Cornwall two of the four items were discovered in a volume marked " Baynes Papers ", all of which proved to be of exceptional interest. One document, which consisted only of five folios, was headed " Instruc'ons for a method in Drawing up & Ingrossing surveyes ", but the endorsement described it as " Further Instrucc'ons f'r ingrossinge and drawing up surveyes ". The second document, which is of greater length, is however, not complete, for folios 14, 15, and 19 are missing. The endorsement refers to this item as " A president for Returne of our Surveyes ", but as the title states that the document is " A Survey of ye Imaginary Man'or of Sale " in the county of Surrey, we have the satisfaction of knowing that the actual model survey created as a " precedent " for the surveyors' guidance has at length been found.[1]

It should be borne in mind that not all the Parliamentary Surveys at the Public Record Office are actually of the same kind, and further that some of the documents included in the different series are really not surveys at all. The distinction between the surveys themselves is set forth with clearness in their respective titles. In one case, which

[1] It was the search, long continued, for papers relating to the work of the Parliamentary surveyors that led eventually to the discovery of the documents in the Webb collection, referred to in the seventh report of the Historical Manuscripts Commission, but upon inquiry it was found that the manuscripts had been dispersed before the War. Not all the volumes, however, were acquired by the British Museum, and it was only by the chance discovery of a bookseller's invoice that the most important book of all was found, the Duchy of Cornwall having purchased the volume of surveys in 1913. The " Instructions for Method " and the " Precedent Survey " were both found in this volume. See Hist. MSS. Com., report 7, app. vol. i, p. 688, and the " Baynes Papers " in the office of the Duchy of Cornwall. The survey of the manor of Sale, Surrey, is now described in the official list, in consequence of this discovery as " a fictitious manor : Specimen survey for Commissioners to work to ". The Instructions for Method will be found in the appendix, where it is printed from a certified copy prepared under the direction of Sir W. Peacock, the Keeper of the Duchy Records. The " Precedent Survey ", certified in the same way, is summarized owing to its length, in the text of this work. Both certified copies have since been presented by the author to the British Museum, Department of MSS., Feb., 1937. Other copies are preserved in the Library, London University.

may be illustrated by Sussex No. 26, the authority cited is the Act of 16th July, 1649 : "A survey of the manor of Dudleswell and great park of Lancaster with the rights, members, and appurtenances thereof, lying and being in the County of Sussex, late parcel of the possessions of Charles Stewart, late King of England, as part and parcel of the Duchy of Lancaster, made and taken by us whose names are hereunto subscribed (viz. Jeremy Baines, John Lobb, Thos. Bridge, and Joh. Haddocke) by virtue of a Commission granted to us by the Honorable the Trustees appointed by *Act of the Commons assembled in Parliament for the sale of the Honours, manors and lands heretofore belonging to the late King, Queen and Prince*, under their hands and seals." This survey is dated 1st June, 1650. Surveys numbered 9 and 10 for Bedfordshire, formerly in the Augmentation Office, are of this kind, and examples are to be found in every county except Rutland. As an instance of the second type Bedford No. 2 may be quoted, where under authority of the later Act of 11th March, 1649, three surveyors, Wm. Dawgs, Alex. Rowley, and Thos. Tanner, prepared a survey of the hundred of Biggleswade in February, 1651, "by virtue of a Commission grounded upon *an Act of the Commons of England in Parliament assembled for sale of the fee-farm rents belonging to the Commonwealth of England, formerly payable to the Crown of England, Duchy of Lancaster and Duchy of Cornwall*, under the hands and seals of five or more of the Trustees in the said Act named and appointed." Similar surveys occur in the portfolios of Bedfordshire, numbers 5 to 8, and in other counties. As a rule not only may the two types be distinguished by the employment of different sets of surveyors, but the titles are characteristically different, those of the first kind being elaborately spaced in the form of an inverted triangle, sometimes with designs in colours, while the others are usually set out in rectangular formation. A third kind is occasionally found, but it is entirely out of place in a collection of surveys of Crown property and should be removed from the series. This may be illustrated by Sussex No. 49, which contains two documents signed by the surveyors, Wm. Eden, Benj. Okeshott, Thos. Newberry, and Jn. Smith, the first relating to "a survey and particular of the manor of Sharenden with the rights members and appurtenances thereof situate lying and being in the parishes of Mayfield, Rotherfield and Wadhurst within the Rape of Pevensey in the county of Sussex, parcel of and belonging to the late principal and commonalty of the vicars choral of the cathedral church of Chichester"; and the second, which bears the date 28th May, 1650, refers to the Manor of "Combe cum Gregories".[1]

Then again, certain of the "surveys", so called, are entirely misnamed inasmuch as they are really short statements signed by the surveyors in response to inquiries made by the Surveyor-General,

---

[1] See Bedford Surveys, Nos. 2, 5 to 10, and Sussex, Nos. 26 and 49. Madge, *Rural Middlesex*, pt. i, pp. 288–90. The surveys of forest lands form a fourth group.

or in obedience to definite orders from the trustees of Crown lands or the Committee for Obstructions. Bedfordshire provides examples of two kinds of certificates, Nos. 1, 3, and 4 illustrating what may be called " certificates of value " which the surveyors prepared from time to time, while Nos. 11 and 12 record short statements or " evidences " in regard to premises submitted by claimants and others to the surveyors during the progress of their inquiries. Middlesex No. 65 is of a similar character, the surveyors certifying the " perusing of evidence to us produced concerning the Stone Tower in the old palace yard, Westminster." Folio 1 of No. 17 in the same county is also a separate document relating to a petition of the " borderers " of Enfield Chase. In the Augmentation Office Series of Parliamentary Surveys for Middlesex, ten of the 159 documents are in reality certificates, and to these may be added eight others styled " additional surveys ", since they merely consist of single sheets with contracted titles wherein the surveyors certify information sought by the trustees or other officials. Nos. 33 and 57 of Middlesex, both dated 1650, refer, for instance, to meadows belonging to Hampton Court, and a roadway bordering Marylebone Park. No. 41 of Sussex is a good instance of a prepared abstract, showing the complicated character of Thomas Threele's title to certain lands belonging to the Duchy of Lancaster in Pevensey, the documents quoted extending back to 24th April, 1582. No. 43 in the same county is an example of a tabulated " certificate or breviat of the marsh lands claimed by Mr. Thomas Threele and returned in the survey of the Manor of Pemsey as claimed by one Maurice Aubert, the said Threele producing neither any grant from the Crown nor any title or assignment from his father, brother or mother, who were all legally interested successively in the said Lease granted to Mr. Edward Ferrers " ; this is dated 3rd February, 1606, and it may be added that No. 44 is a copy of Threele's grant 25th October, 1637 to Maurice Aubert. On the other hand No. 24 is styled " an additional by way of certificate " to the surveys of Chesworth, Colstaple, and Ashley Mills, and this is of interest because it clearly shows that " additional surveys " were recognized as belonging to the class now called certificates.[1]

With very few exceptions the entire collection of Parliamentary Surveys preserved in the Augmentation Office is in perfect condition, although here and there leaves are waterstained and covers are sometimes mud-splashed owing to damage done on the occasion of the fire at the Houses of Parliament in October, 1834, on which occasion part of survey No. 25 of Sussex appears to have been destroyed. But such damage is for the most part slight, and gaps are infrequent, while the existence of duplicates of many surveys in one or other of the series makes it possible to supply deficiencies in almost every case. For instance the whole of Part III of the huge survey of Spalding

[1] Madge, op. cit., pt. i, pp. 286–7.

(Lincoln No. 32) is missing in the Augmentation Series, but this deficiency may be made good from the Land Revenue Office copy.

The number of documents preserved in the county portfolios varies considerably, although as far as Wales is concerned only two counties have more than ten surveys or certificates, Carmarthen being the only one with as many as twenty-four. In England, however, twelve counties have more than thirty documents, Surrey and Middlesex heading the list with 72 and 159 respectively. Anglesey, Glamorgan, Montgomery, and Rutland on the other hand have but a single document each. The surveys, however, vary greatly in size and completeness. Mr. Hunter, the Deputy Keeper of 1846, said that " the series throughout is uniformly written on paper of foolscap folio size, each page being 15 inches long by 12 inches wide " ; but there are instances in the Middlesex collection of larger and smaller sizes of paper being used (as in Nos. 5 and 19), while in a few cases, Middlesex No. 85 being one, folded sheets of quarto size are employed. There are examples in nearly forty counties of single leaves forming complete documents. In Wales no survey is of greater extent than twenty folios, most of them being less than half that size. In England, however, the documents vary considerably, sixteen counties having surveys of from twenty to forty folios each, and sixteen others have an even greater number, the surveys of Grafton, Northants, and Duddleswell, Sussex, consisting of 101 and 132 folios respectively. The survey of Spalding, Lincolnshire, which was completed in February, 1650, is of such an enormous size that the surveyors had to divide it into six parts, its 816 folios exceeding in extent the entire collection of nearly 160 documents relating to Middlesex.

The surveys vary, moreover, in respect to the time taken to complete or " perfect " them. The earliest surveys were commenced immediately upon the passing of the Act of 16th July, 1649, when surveyors visited at least thirty-four of the counties, the work being completed in a very few months in Northumberland, Denbigh, Flint, and Radnor. In Middlesex only six of the documents were ready by January, 1649. Next year the surveyors had completed their work in Cumberland, Worcestershire, Anglesey, Glamorgan, and Montgomery. Gloucester, Rutland, and Shropshire do not appear to have been visited until 1651 or 1652, but the surveys as a whole were steadily continued so that by 1656 no less than thirty-nine counties were entirely completed, the remainder requiring another three years before the whole of the work was done. Most of the surveys are endorsed with the dates when they were received, and frequently they are numbered so as to form part of a consecutive series. Thus Middlesex No. 4, referring to two tenements near Charing Cross, received on the 16th September, 1650, and transmitted to the Surveyor-General the same day, was returned two days later and marked with

the name of the surveyor, Ralph Baldwin, and the number 524. The
remaining surveys of Middlesex bear the names of Jn. Brudenall,
Richard Heiwood, and Rowl. Brasbridge in 1649, Thos. Tanner,
Wm. Dawgs, and Alex. Rowley two years later, Ric. Sadler in 1653,
and Hugh Webb, Jn. Boynton, Nic. Gunton, and Edm. Rolfe after
1657. Several of these surveyors were also employed in other counties.
Heiwood and Dawgs for example sign Essex No. 11, Baldwin and
Brasbridge, Herts No. 15, Sadler and Webb, Sussex No. 45. As
Rob. Stafford and Benj. Jones alone signed surveys of Cumberland,
Colonel Webb wrote : " I forbear to sign this Survey (No. 8) because
I find but 2 hands to the same " ; but subsequently he added : " I find
this Survey to be returned by the two Surveyors aforesaid upon
particular instructions from the Trustees ". In some few cases, as for
example, Herts No. 28 and Sussex Nos. 41, 44, 45 the signature of
surveyors for reasons unknown are not recorded.   Most of the
documents bear the signature of the Surveyor-General, often with
comments and marginal notes, and it is seldom that his endorsement
is withheld.   Seals are attached to a number of the surveys dated
1657 and 1658, particularly in regard to Enfield Chase (Nos. 17D,
17K, and 17KK), special endorsement in such cases referring to the
reservation of premises as " collateral security to the soldiers ".
    Maps or plans are rare among the surveys, but one of them will
be found in Middlesex No. 25, a survey of premises in St. Giles in
the Fields, while the " plot " of Enfield Chase is often referred to and
appears to be now in the Bodleian Library, Oxford. In some of the
surveys of Essex and Surrey, moreover, the titles are ornamented
with coloured designs, but the arms of the Commonwealth when
shown in these designs have not always escaped mutilation. Very
seldom are the names of purchasers recorded or the amounts they
paid for their premises ; on the other hand the names of
" discoverers ", by whose aid the premises were recovered and
surveyed, are frequently given. In Middlesex, for example, the most
active of these persons were two officials, Colborne and Robinson,
and Captain Daniell, Matthew Scarborough, Nic. Elton, and John
Phelpes.[1]
    In the instructions relating to method, returns were ordered to
be made in English, and the surveys and duplicates were to be " fairly
ingrossed " without any sign of blotting or scraping. The valuations
were to be summed up with care and exactness, all copies being
compared so as to agree in both number and content of folios. The
penmanship of these surveys is often remarkably good, giving every
indication that the work was accomplished in a most leisurely manner,

---

[1] Madge, op. cit., pt. i, pp. 282–4. Exch., L.R. 2, vol. 285, ff. 163–248. *Sussex Arch.
Coll.,* vol. xxiii, p. 293. The Sussex surveys as printed are readily accessible and are seldom
found to be inaccurate. Essex, Nos. 10, 12–15, 17, 18B. Middlesex, 1, 2, 11, 12, 15,
19, 70. Several other surveys are indicated by numbers in the text.

and that the advice had been carefully followed, namely, to " keep close to the Precedents " where they would answer the purpose, " and to this method where they come short." [1]

[1] " Instructions for Method," henceforth to be quoted as " Method ", ff. 3 and 5. The reference to the " Precedents " is a reminder of the existence of the model or specimen survey prepared for the guidance of the surveyors.   The " Precedent Survey " will be quoted in these notes as " Precedent ", for brevity and clearness. Several examples of the finely ingrossed titles of Middlesex surveys will be seen in the photographs given in Madge, op. cit., pt. i, pp. 273, 278, 286, 299, and pt. ii, p. 403.   The cost of the survey can be ascertained from the Accounts in the Appendix (No. VI, sect, i–iii, pp. 397–405). The surveyors in England and Wales received sums of £30,487 17s. 10½d. and £3,458 10s. for Crown Lands and Fee Farm rents respectively (pp. 398, 403).   The payments to Col. Wm. Webb include two amounts of £1,457 2s. 7d. and £408 12s., but his clerks had to share these amounts.

CHAPTER III

ANALYSIS OF THE SURVEYS

If we examine a typical Parliamentary Survey, such for example as that of the manor of Barton-upon-Humber, Lincolnshire, highly praised by the Surveyor-General, or those of Middlesex and Sussex manors, since printed in full, we shall find that as a general rule each survey consists of seven distinct sections—though of course with variation in regard to order and even omissions at times. Each of them begins with an elaborate title and concludes with the signatures of the Surveyor-General and other officials. These seven divisions of the surveys are as follows :—

(i) First of all, precise statements in reference to the annual perquisites and profits of the manor surveyed.

(ii) Then particulars of all premises, either in possession or known to be demised.

(iii) Next, calculation of the values of timber upon the various estates.

(iv) Enumeration of patents, leases, and especially reprises.

(v) Memoranda relative to manorial customs, commons, boundaries, and waste lands.

(vi) Rental of manorial tenants with an indication of their premises.

(vii) Lastly, a comprehensive abstract of the values of the whole survey, summing up its characteristic features.

When the " instructions for method " are closely examined, it is found that these seven special sections, occur in precisely the order named, their importance being emphasized in such a way as to assist the surveyors in the preparation and completion of their daily work. Further, it is of interest to note that with a view to the production of surveys of the most uniform and " perfect " kind, they were provided with a specially compiled model survey, styled " the precedent ", arranged in exactly the same way, which furnished them with every conceivable type or example in regard to these seven special sections, showing that every allowance had been made for difficulties before the actual work of valuation began.[1]

In the newly discovered " instructions for method ", henceforth to be quoted as " the method ", the Surveyor-General urged his men to return all manors " entire ", taking every care not to " break " or

[1] Lincoln Parl. Surv. No. 6, for example, or Middlesex No. 29 (manor of Halliford) are typical surveys of the Commonwealth period.

certify them in parcels unless they found great cause to do so. By way of illustration to accompany the " method ", Colonel Webb prepared for the use of the county surveyors a remarkably humorous " precedent " or specimen survey of premises which he called " the imaginary manor of Sale "—a manor, that is to say, imagined to lie in Surrey and also about to be surveyed and sold. Bounded by the Thames in the north, and with the rivers Clear, Dally, Madewell, and Runwell within its borders, Sale manor was supposed to lie either within or adjacent to the parishes of Bets, Bidmost, Burton, Fairset, Sample, and Sale. Its rents were drawn from many sources some of which were the townships of Beldon, Morton, Parkhall, and Blackley, not omitting the tithings of Crayford, Fyfield, and Hornden,[1] with certain special rents from the Borough of Dale and corn or egg rents from the tithings of Grain and Poultry. A rent resolute of 30s. was annually paid to the neighbouring manor of Holding.

Sale was not only a manor but a parish, possessed of church and vicarage, common and green, the principal seats being Sale Court, Sale Bury, and Sale Park. The impropriate rectory was connected with Burton, and the manor house with Sale Court. The lodge and keeper's house in the park, the almshouses at Burton, and various messuages, tenements, and cottages are not overlooked, nor are the deer and timber in the park forgotten. Bridges of stone cross the rivers, two of them bearing the names of Hallbridge and Partners' bridge. Deep Ditch, Mardike, Great Pond, and Conduit Head find a place in the record along with Tithes Lane and Church Lane, Blatt Causeway, Uxbridge Highway, and the respective roads to Sale and Restwell. Two farms, those of Galter and Bidmost, and two water grist mills under one roof, called Stamp Mills, are also named and valued. There is the usual gravel pit. The crofts include Bell's Croft, King's Croft, and Pye Croft. West field and the common or town fields duly appear in their places. Some of the parcels include Bent and Long furlongs, Disney furlong, and Long Shot, Stack hedge, Low Inges, Broadland, Poor's land, the Riddles, Thistlepiece, and the Hurlers Ground. The various closes include Calves Close, Jump Close, Cow pastures, Oatfield, and Stubblefields, while the meadows, seven in number, bear names such as Bass mead, Gull mead, and the New and Silver meads. The Common is appropriately called Bareheath, and the woods are known as Cramp Wood, Seekwood, and Springwell.

Among the tenants and other persons connected with this imaginary manor of Sale are Francis Ask, Jos. Buy, and Wm. Take, Jn. Lame, and Luke Stile, Thos. Willing, Lionel Tuck, and Thos. Thr've. The chief ranger and master of the game, Sir Jockie Begwell, has fled to Scotland leaving Jn. Cavy in charge. Thos. Lovewell is employed as bailiff, Timothy Stout as underkeeper of the park, and Isaac Trim,

---

[1] The townships and tithings have names selected from Northumberland, Lincoln, Derby, Lancashire, Kent, and Essex.

aged 63, as housekeeper and gardener. Jn. Holdfast, who bears the name of a neighbouring village, is Vicar of Sale, while Thos. Gott, Esq., of London, has a lease of Sale Bury, Solomon Burley, Gent., of "Barnet in Middlesex", being acknowledged as the "mediate tenant" at the time of the survey. Andrew Waiter claims the reversion of the office of chief ranger. The miller is named Jn. Monk, but the doorkeepers, alleykeepers, hayward, and reeve are unnamed. Only one yeoman, Thos. Stukeley, occurs in the "precedent", thus calling attention once again to the probability of this class being over-rated in importance by economic writers. The copyholders, however, are numerous and among them will be found, as students of economic history at once perceive, the prophetic name of Adam Smith. The whole survey indeed is a unique example of ready wit and learning, the perplexities of the law being handled with extra-ordinary skill and judgment by the Surveyor-General.[1]

In the "method" Colonel Webb casually refers to the title of the new surveys, but in his "precedent" he shows how to set this out in triangular fashion, giving the month of September, 1649, as the period when the specimen survey was completed. He shows that the titles were to include all essential facts relating to the name of the manor, its rights, members and appurtenances, the county, the former owner, the date, and the authority for the action now taken. The former possessors of manorial estates are referred to in various ways in the Parliamentary surveys. Sometimes it is "the late king", Charles Stewart, who is recorded, at other times "the late Queen", Henrietta Maria, "in right of her dower", and occasionally both owners are referred to. The Earldom of Chester and the Duchy of York seldom are mentioned, but the Duchy of Lancaster frequently occurs and "the late Prince", Charles, Duke of Cornwall, is duly indicated. In the Surrey surveys there are examples of almost every kind of royal ownership. Thus the Queen's lands are found at Chertsey, Egham, Ham, Nonsuch Park, Petersham, Walton-upon-Thames, and Wimbledon, while the estates of the Prince of Wales, as Duke of Cornwall, are surveyed at Kennington. All the rest of the documents concern the Crown lands of the deceased monarch. In the case of Surrey, too, the various titles refer to surveys which include not only hundreds and manors, but castles, parks, church, and monastic lands of earlier days, rivers, mills and quays, woods and warrens.[2]

---

[1] Analysis of the "Precedent", showing the principal features of the "Imaginary Manor" of Sale, supposed to lie in Surrey. The newly discovered document exhibits a delightful mixture of humour and deep learning. See Appendix III (i), for "Method".

[2] "Method," f. 1, and "Precedent", f. 1. For examples to illustrate the various characteristics referred to, see Essex, Nos. 10–11, 13–20 ; Cambridge, No. 5, f. 1 ; Cornwall, No. 3, f. 1, and other instances in the same county ; Surrey, Nos. 9b, 25, 31, 33, 34, 39–41, 44–5, 71–2, all of which refer to Queen Henrietta or the Prince of Wales. See Madge, Parliamentary Surveys of Surrey, Surr. Arch. Soc. Coll., vol. xxxvii, part ii, pp. 200–210 ; also the titles photographed and the notes attached, Madge, Rural Middlesex, pt. i, pp. 272, 287, 289, and pt. ii, pp. 405–6 ; Lennard, Rural Northants, p. 28.

After the title had been recorded, the surveyors were to clearly indicate not only the rents of assize of the freeholders, copyholders, and customary tenants, but the nature of their tenures and the times when their payments were usually due. In cases where several townships belonged to the same manor the separate rents were to be indicated. Next the surveyors were to turn their attention, as shown in the " method ", to the customary works of the tenants, certifying all the rents in wheat, barley, or other grain, as well as capons and eggs, pannage rents, and profits of fishings, or tolls of markets and fairs ; all these were to be very carefully entered according to the custom of the manor, with the dates when such payments were made. Payments found to be " uncertain " were to be made " certain " by computing the average profits over a term of years. Lastly, it was necessary to particularize the most notable instances of fines connected with descent or alienation, reliefs, heriots, waifs and estrays, and all other profits and perquisites of courts, baron and leet, appertaining to the royalty of the manor. As the values were to be estimated by taking one year with another, the officials were advised to procure accounts for as many years as possible preceding 1641. In this connection the nature of the different tenures required particular care, the fines being regarded as of especial importance. Mr. Lennard, who most unfortunately was not aware of this, omits the fines in his essay and in consequence, as will appear later, came to grief over the question of common rights and tenants' holdings.

These various features find abundant illustration in the Surveyor-General's " precedent ", which records payments of a variety of tenants at Lady Day, Michaelmas, Pentecost, and Martinmas, with special payments at " Christ-tide " and the period of All-hallows. The main tenurial rents range from £2 11s. to £13, not all of the fines paid by the tenants being fixed. The rent hens, to the number of 109, had a value of sixpence each, while the grain rents include 62 quarters of wheat at 44s. per quarter. The rents for works of tenants amounted to nearly £5, the value of harvest, wood, and carriage works being estimated at about one-third of this sum. Pannage rents and profits from driving the commons at certain periods are only about a pound less ; but the profits from fishings exceed £7, and the tolls from markets and fairs are only a little short of £30. Other items make up a total, stated to be £240 1s. 10¾d., but in reality £242 11s. 7¾d. ; and in this connection it may be noted that since some of the entries in the " precedent " are not valued and others include purely nominal values, it is clear that the main purpose of the specimen survey was to establish the form of the entries and to illustrate the types of values, so that the additions composing the totals were of quite secondary importance.

When we turn to the surveys of Sussex we find numerous examples of actual values, first of all in the surveys of hundreds, as shown below,

SPALDING MANOR SURVEY, LINCOLNSHIRE, 1650

(Parts I-VI, ff. 816. Part III destroyed 1834)

[face p. 14.

where the common fines include at times the Alderman's fine (No. 7, 8), and the profits represent frequently the improved values arising from the hundred courts. The totals range from 36*s*. 8*d*. to £54, and the whole amount recorded exceeds £143. No figures occur for survey No. 2, which is said to be missing.[1]

XXXI. LIST OF FINES AND PROFITS IN SUSSEX HUNDREDS

Nos.	Fines.	Profits.	Totals.
1	£1·8	£5·7	£7·5
3	2·6	6·7	9·3
4	—	1·8	1·8
5	6·7	—	6·7
6	0·1	8·3	8·4
7	10·5	39·0	49·5
8	26·3	27·7	54·0
9	0·8	5·3	6·1
Totals	£48·8	£94·5	£143·3

Among the quit rents of Sussex may be mentioned totals which range from 1*s*. to £5 7*s*. 4*d*. but some of them relate to cathedral property which should not be included here. Rents of copyholders in one manor come to £5 8*s*. but in a second instance, where the fines are variable, the total is not recorded. Court baron and other fines ranging from 33*s*. 4*d*. to £10 are recorded, though the full amounts are in some instances not entered. The items for " sheriffs' Turn " include £2 3*s*. 4*d*. and £20, also " Endlewick Rents " total £29 10*s*. 11*d*., and Duchy of Lancaster fines in the rape of Pevensey £14 6*s*. 8*d*. The value of Old Shoreham Ferry is wrongly given in the printed abstract as 15*s*. instead of £15. Three cases occur in which the total values of rents, perquisites, and royalties amount to £24, £39, and £87, so that the annual profits and perquisites recorded for the county of Sussex on no occasion appear to have reached the total given in the " precedent ". At Halliford, Middlesex, the total is less than £14. In Kennington, Surrey, the amount reaches £127 16*s*. 11½*d*. At Raunds, Northamptonshire, the quit rents were only 22*s*. per annum (not £22 as stated by Mr. Lennard), but the rents of the customary tenants whose fines were certain amounted to £45 2*s*. 8*d*.[2]

[1] Table XXXI. This list of fines and profits is compiled from the figures recorded in the first nine surveys of Sussex, as printed in *Sussex Arch. Soc. Collections*, vol. xxiii, pp. 224–42.

[2] " Method," f. 1, and " Precedent ", ff. 1–2 ; Lennard, op. cit., p. 116 ; and analysis of Sussex surveys, Nos. 23, 26–8, 39, 42, 49, 50 ; Surrey, No. 33 ; Middlesex, No. 29 ; and Northants, No. 44. Some additional instances showing the amounts of annual profits may be given from the surveys : Bedford, No. 9, £88 1*s*. 8*d*. ; Berkshire, No. 14, £64 13*s*. ; Bucks, No. 20, £2 15*s*. 4*d*. ; Cambridge, No. 1, £77 0*s*. 9½*d*. ; Cheshire, No. 11, £34 1*s*. 3*d*. ; Cornwall, No. 31, £10 1*s*. 6*d*. ; Cumberland, No. 1, £20 6*s*. 6*d*. ; Derby, No. 25, £9 6*s*. 2¾*d*. ; Devon, No. 8, £11 3*s*. 4½*d*. ; Dorset, No. 5, £175 1*s*. 11*d*. ; Essex, No. 12, £49 10*s*. 8*d*. ; Hereford, No. 16, £33 5*s*. 0¼*d*. ; Herts, No. 22, £107 5*s*. 9*d*. (including £1 for fairs, and £19 for weekly markets) ; Hunts, No. 3, £150 4*s*. 0¾*d*. ; Kent, No. 18, £36 9*s*. 5½*d*. ; Lancashire, No. 7, £175 17*s*. 7¾*d*. ; Leicester, No. 7, £29 1*s*. 3*d*. Lincoln, No. 6, £76 7*s*. 11½*d*. (fairs £1, markets £2 12*s*.) ; Norfolk, No. 8, £2 1*s*. 4*d*. ; Northants, No. 15, £45 17*s*. 11*d*. ; Notts, No. 18, £26 13*s*. 1*d*. ; Oxford, No. 10,

The greater portion of every manorial survey is naturally devoted to the specification of the various component parcels and the statement of their extent and value. First to be considered were the demesnes in possession, and next such lands as were demised or granted for variable terms of years or lives. When the manor house and site were not in possession at the moment of survey, the surveyors were to proceed with other lands in hand, and after finishing these the manor house and appurtenances were to be given first place among the leases. Very precise instructions provided for the cutting out of each separate parcel under its usual name, together with its size and definite abutments. When all the lands lay close together there was no necessity to do more than abut the parcels upon a single field or close, but when they lay interspersed within the common fields, it was advisable to indicate particularly one boundary and one abutment so that the property might not remain obscure. In cases where parcels were numerous and mistakes would most likely occur the most convenient plan was obviously to distinguish the premises by recording all the boundaries and abutments.

Features such as these receive distinctive treatment in the " precedent " where the premises in possession are seen to consist of four parcels, namely, Sale Court, Sale Park with its lodges, certain tenements in the town of Bidmost, and the coney ground. The first of these consisted of a mansion or court house, described in detail, with courts and orchards, together with a close of pasture or meadow divided into four parts, and a piece of meadow ground; the whole, amounted to 45 acres, the value of which was estimated at £133 per annum. The manor house, however, was in such good repair that demolition was inadvisable, but should this be required the materials would be worth £700, clear of all charges, and then the value of the land as a cleared site would be £26 13s. 4d. per annum. Sale Park, consisting of 90 acres with an estimated value of £180, contained a lodge and keeper's house worth about £6. There were 150 deer in the park, worth 18s. 8d. on the average, and 4,500 trees worth altogether £900, while the vesture of coppice, 90 acres in extent, was considered to be worth 25s. per acre, or £112 10s. in all. Details of the dwellings are given and it is suggested that the park might well be divided into three parts, consisting of 450 acres at 3s. per acre, 150 at 4s., and 300 at 5s. 6d., with the trees apportioned accordingly. Timber for the

---

£30 9s. 6¼d.; Somerset, No. 16, £44 4s. 11d.; Suffolk, No. 12, £24 9s. 7¼d.; Surrey, No. 45, £40 7s. 10d.; Warwick, No. 12, £108 17s. 3½d.; Westm., No. 5, £176 13s. 4¾d.; Wilts, No. 23, £357 16s. 6d.; Worcester, No. 7, £62 10s. 0¼d.; Yorks, No. 34, £27 6s. 4d.. Of instances from Wales, the following may be quoted: Brecon, No. 8, £5 6s. 11d.; Cardigan, No. 1, £28 7s. 6d.; Carmarthen, No. 4, £30 18s.; Carnarvon, No. 2, £84 9s. 3½d.; Denbigh, No. 3, £579 11s. 7¾d.; Merioneth, No. 2, £184 3s. 11d.; Monmouth, No. 1, £152 0s. 0¼d.; Montgomery, No. 1, £58 10s.; Pembroke, No. 4, £64 12s. 8d. This gives averages of £52 for Area I, £86 Area II, £61 Area III, and £132 Area IV. For the whole of the thirty-nine counties indicated the average is about £84.

navy is indicated, as well as a small franchise or liberty worth 30s. per annum, while the benefit of commonage and absence of tithe are duly placed on record. The tenements include a shop, 42 by 29 feet, and two stores badly decayed, 26 by 58 feet : no values are given for these. The coney warren covered 10 acres, but the game belonged properly to the king as owner of Sale Court and park, though the ground when enclosed might be worth £12 per annum. Certain reprises are enumerated, but the amounts are not deducted since they are disallowed from the totals which close this section of the " precedent ".[1]

Next to be considered were the demesnes in farm. As the trustees were empowered to let the premises for one year, and sequestrators and others had already let certain of the lands from year to year, the specimen " method " provided that surveyors were to distinguish them as let out for the present, placing the reserved rents and improved values in the left and right margins respectively of their particulars, and stating at the conclusion of each, " This is worth upon improvement over and above the said rent per annum so much." But besides the premises in possession thus let out, there were the lands, messuages, or tenements under demise or grant for various terms to be recorded, in which connection the surveyors were advised to keep strictly to the rule, namely, that where the manor house and site were in lease for one, two, or more lives, all the leases for lives of the whole of the premises in the same township should be finished first, and that where the contrary was the case then all the leases for years should precede those for lives. The work in this important section was to proceed with caution along the following lines. The surveyors were first of all to set out their particulars precisely as they found the premises during their inspection, taking care to record the most modern boundaries ascertainable. Should doubts arise, as well they might, in regard to proper names the uses of an *alias* would be advisable. Every parcel, moreover, should be completely certified before passing on to the next. So with apt words and sufficiently full statements the officials were advised to compose their matter in such a way that, with the evidence running clear from first to last, the trustees might ground their conveyances with safety upon these particulars—a good example of the saying, " he who runs may read."

To assist the surveyors in this difficult portion of their work, Colonel Webb supplied them with a most methodical section of his " precedent ", in which he dealt with particulars of all lands, tenements, and hereditaments belonging to the imaginary Manor of Sale known to be under demise or grant for lives as well as years.[2]

When the particulars had been completed the next step was to

[1] " Method," f. 1 ; and " Precedent," ff. 3–8. See Appendix III, Sect. i.
[2] " Method," ff. 2–3 ; " Precedent," ff. 8–17.

set forth the right or claim of the tenants, and surveyors were advised to proceed by way of memoranda, " as by your precedents," they were told, " is declared." Abstracts, therefore, were needed both for leaseholds and copyholds. As to the leases the main thing was to certify every parcel separately and completely, not forgetting to mention all important covenants, exceptions, and provisos, so that the rights of the lessee and the benefits accruing to the lessor might be correctly established for each. If the leases were for lives, then each life named should be certified as aged so many years or in being, every care being taken not to be deluded by the names of persons properly outside the grant ; and if, on the other hand, leases were for years then the concluding statement should notify the fact that there were so many years to come on a definitely indicated date.

Five special points in regard to leases demanded close attention as well as accurate judgment on the part of the surveyors. There was the case first of all in which antedating or racing of leases or deeds occurred : all these leases had to be examined and their contents certified accordingly. Secondly, there were double leases, and sometimes more, not always dated alike but enjoyed under one entire rent by a single person : in this case it was necessary to certify whether the premises were occupied alone by that person or whether they were rented by others, so that the improved values might be distinctly shown in connection with each of the parcels and the acknowledged rent apportioned to each according to such improvements. Thirdly, there were instances in which the lease of a particular manor, grange, farm, or other premises included also some rectory or parsonage with glebe or tithes, the rent reserved upon the whole being one entire rent : then, as before, it was necessary not only to distinctly set forth the several improvements of the premises in regard to valuation, but to apportion with certainty the entire rent according to these respective improvements. Where the lands or tenements, however, were found to be free of tithe, it was important to certify that " the aforesaid premises we find to be tithe free and so have valued them ". Fourthly, there were recent leases to be considered, namely such as were dated subsequent to 26th March, 1641 : here, unless the lord of the manor had power to grant estates, the surveyors were urged to be most careful to find out and certify exactly what estates were surrendered in favour of the new lease, and the official " method " contained a useful hint that the surrender might sometimes be found recited as a consideration in the latest lease. Lastly, in the event of the whole manor being leased out for a term of lives or years, the lord of the manor during that period having the power by custom of granting estates, the surveyors were ordered to certify the grand lease in full at the end of the survey next to the final abstract of values.

Six of such leases are quoted by way of illustration in the

" precedent ", their dates ranging from 1611 to 1638, the periods being one, two, or three lives, with an exceptional case of " six years or three lives ", whatever that might mean,[1] and a normal one of ninety-nine years or three lives. All these lives are certified as existing at the time of the survey, their ages ranging from twenty-two to sixty-three. Thomas Gott's case is taken first, his lease being dated at Westminster (as a supposition) 3rd May, 1634, the grant being for ninety-nine years or three lives. The capital messuage or manor house, described minutely, occupies 2 acres 3 roods, and is worth per annum £5 10s., while twelve other parcels of various kinds—including pieces of arable and meadow in the common fields—the size of which vary from 5 roods to 17 acres, and the values from 10s. to £8 10s., bring up the apparent total of the premises to 95 acres, supposed to be worth £40 per annum, though the actual figures given are somewhat less. The grant, however, in this case includes the impropriate rectory of Burton, with 8 acres, and the tithes of corn, hay, lamb, and wool derived from five tithings, the whole being estimated at £98 1s. 4d. In this lease, therefore, we have the lessee as occupier, enjoying premises which include rectory and tithes under one entire rent of £30 10s., so that an apportionment of the rent and improved values is necessary, and this is done as follows[2] :—

XXXII. APPORTIONMENT OF RENT AND IMPROVED VALUES

Premises.	Acres.	Yearly Rent.	Improved Values.
Sale Bury . .	95·25	£10 0 0	£22 9 11
Rectory and Tithes	7·75	£20 10 0	£77 11 4
Totals . .	103·00	£30 10 0	£100 1 3

A second instance involving apportionment occurs through the non-residence of the lessee, Solomon Burley of Barnet, Middlesex, whose premises are alleged to be granted by letters patent of 9th April, 1634, for his own life and those of his wife Sibyl and daughter Frances. These premises, however, are rented by four under-tenants, Thos. Gould holding Galters Farm, Jn. Monk occupying the two water-grist mills, and Jn. Lame and Luke Stile the remaining lands and tenements. The entire rent of £15 10s. and the improved value of £75 13s. 4d., making a total of £91 3s. 4d., are accordingly divided among the four parcels in proportions which, had they been more accurately stated, would have been better understood. The covenants of this lease and those of Thos. Thrive are quoted : both are to keep their premises in good repair and relinquish them at the end of their periods in proper condition, all sorts of botes being allowed for the purpose of maintenance and comfort ; the rest of the timber is reserved for the use of the lessor and is valued accordingly. In Burley's case he has to

[1] It was probably intended to be sixty years.
[2] Table XXXII. The method of apportionment of rent and improved values is illustrated by reference to the " Method ", ff. 2–3, and the " Precedent ", ff. 8–13.

properly fence Springwell Coppice and deliver every sixth year a terrier of his estate in lease.

The earliest leases so far discovered among the Parliamentary surveys include two of Edward VI's reign for Sussex, and four of the reign of Henry VIII for Essex, Middlesex, and Surrey—the former being for sixty and ninety years, the latter for ninety-nine years or (in one instance) a single life. Leases for the reigns of Elizabeth and James are common in most of the county surveys. But the most remarkable of the early leases are four in number. One of these, the earliest of them all, was granted by the Abbot of St. Peter's, Chertsey, 2nd January, 33 Henry VI (1454) and of its 200 years four were still unexpired in June, 1650, when the surveyors of Surrey were at work. Three others,[1] granted by the Master of the Savoy Hospital in 1561 or 1562 were even in force in 1787, though the counterpart of the lease relating to the manor of Hallatreholme, Durham, was no longer extant and the date of expiry was not definitely known; but in the case of the manor of Dengy, Essex, where the lease was granted for 600 years, this would not expire before the year 2161, while the lease of certain chantry lands in Chorley, Langworth, Poulton, and Walton, Lancashire, granted for the term of 1,000 years will apparently continue until the year 2562 ![2]

The majority of the leases in the rural surveys of Middlesex have been found to belong to the reign of Charles, but those of Northamptonshire appear to be chiefly of the preceding reign. There is another distinction, moreover, for whereas in Middlesex the tendency is for the leases to increase in number according to lives rather than, for terms of years, in Northamptonshire the reverse process appears to operate. Omitting two of the Commonwealth leases for Middlesex, which were for a single year, and one or two of the reign of Henry VIII for Northamptonshire, we have the following result[3] :—

XXXIII. TUDOR AND STUART LEASES

Leases.		Middlesex.	Northants.	Sussex.	Totals.
Tudor :	Lives	1	34	—	35
	Years	6	27	10	43
Stuart :	Lives	19	9	2	30
	Years	7	155	17	179
	Mixed	—	9	1	10
	Totals	33	234	30	297

[1] See later, under 1787 in Part V, Section iii, p. 281.

[2] As examples of leases of earlier date than the reign of Elizabeth we may note : Essex, No. 19, f. 2 ; Middlesex, No. 14, f. 3 ; Surrey, No. 11, f. 5, No. 14B, f. 6, and No. 29, f. 3 ; Sussex, No. 47. The leases of 1561 in Durham, Essex, and Lancashire are referred to in the printed list of surveys of the year 1787. For the records relating to Crown Leases, see S. Bird's *Guide*, pp. 191-6, and Giuseppi's *Guide*, vol. i, index, p. 385.

[3] Table XXXIII is based on the figures given in Lennard, op. cit., p. 120, and Madge, op. cit., pt. i, p. 277, pt. ii, p. 455 ; the figures for Sussex have been obtained by analysis of the surveys for that county. For Northamptonshire leases, see Lennard, index, p. 134.

It will be seen from the table above that whereas in Middlesex the leases for lives are more than half the total, in Northamptonshire the proportion is less than a quarter; and it is interesting to note that although single lives were altogether preferred in the first of these counties they never occur at all in Northamptonshire, in which county three lives is almost invariably the rule as the following results show[1] :—

	XXXIV. Leases for Lives			
Lives.	*Middlesex.*	*Northants.*	*Sussex.*	*Totals.*
One . .	10	—	2	12
Two . .	7	1	—	8
Three . .	3	42	—	45
Mixed with Years	—	9	1	10
Totals .	20	52	3	75

Again, in reference to terms of years the position in the two counties is reversed, for although in Middlesex short periods up to thirty years were not favoured in Tudor times they form the majority of the leases for years under the Stuarts, whereas in Northampton-shire such leases are never common, the period of thirty-one years being preferred under Elizabeth and Charles, but forty and sixty years under James. As will be seen below the majority of the Northamptonshire leases were for terms of from thirty to forty years[2] :—

	XXXV. Leases for Years			
Years.	*Middlesex.*	*Northants.*	*Sussex.*	*Totals.*
1 to 10	–	—	—	—
11 ,, 20	2	20	—	22
21 ,, 30	5	20	13	38
31 ,, 40	2	102	3	107
41 ,, 60	4	40	10	54
61 ,, 99	–	—	1	1
Totals .	13	182	27	222

Leases for twenty-one years of Elizabethan date have been noticed in Nottingham and Shropshire Surveys; three occur in Sussex, and eight have been found in Northamptonshire and Surrey. Others for thirty-one years are recorded in the surveys of Stafford and Suffolk, but while eleven have been discovered in Northamptonshire, only one has come to light so far in Surrey and none at all in Sussex. Of eighteen leases examined in Surrey surveys only four refer to lives, as against thirty-four out of sixty-one in Northamptonshire; these are for three lives in each case, but in Sussex no leases for lives of this period have been found. Only one lease for fifty years has been seen

[1] Table XXXIV. This also is based on the figures given in Lennard, op. cit., p. 120, and Madge, op. cit., pt. ii, p. 455, with the addition of the analysed results for Sussex surveys.
[2] Table XXXV is compiled from the figures recorded by Lennard, op. cit., p. 120, and Madge, op. cit., pt. ii, p. 455. Periods of ten years are taken, the range extending from eleven to sixty years both for Middlesex and Northants. The figures for Sussex are added for comparison with those of the other counties.

in connection with Surrey, but five occur in Northamptonshire. Of Elizabethan leases for sixty years two have been noticed in Surrey and three in Sussex, but Northamptonshire appears to have none.

Turning next to Stuart leases, of which about sixty have been examined in Surrey and Sussex, we find a marked tendency to shorten their duration in those counties. In Surrey the system of mixed lives and years is introduced during the reign of Charles, the lives being always three in number, and the years either sixty or eighty, but where leases for lives alone occur they do not exceed a single life. In Sussex, too, the single life is preferred. The two counties reveal the following differences, but it should be noted that the figures for Surrey do not embrace the whole of the county as some of the surveys have not yet been completely analysed[1] :—

XXXVI. Leases for Various Terms

Leases.	Surrey. Tudor.	Surrey. Stuart.	Sussex. Tudor.	Sussex. Stuart.	Totals.
Lives . .	4	4	–	2	10
Mixed with Years	–	5	–	1	6
1 to 20 years .	–	–	–	–	—
21 to 30 years .	8	8	4	9	29
31 to 40 years .	2	11	1	2	16
41 to 60 years .	4	8	5	5	22
61 to 99 years .	–	1	–	1	2
Totals . .	18	37	10	20	85

Commonwealth leases occur in several counties of which Middlesex, Northants, Northumberland, Oxford, and Surrey may be mentioned. They are always granted for a single year, the object being not to fetter the sale of the premises. The rents where named vary from £4 to £300. In Sussex fifteen leases of this period are recorded, but although the values range from half a crown to £77 only three definite rents are stated; in one of these the full value of £10 is obtained, through the lease, and in a second case six-sevenths of the estimated value of £21, but in the third instance only £17 could be obtained for premises said to be worth £38. In one Oxfordshire lease, the rent and improved values were £300 and £633 3s. 10½d. respectively, an increase of more than 200 per cent over the annual rent of the premises.[2]

[1] Table XXXVI is made possible by a full analysis of the surveys of Sussex, and a partial analysis of those of Surrey, the Tudor and Stuart leases being distinguished from one another. Elizabethan leases will also be found in Notts No. 14, Oxford No. 10, Shropshire No. 3, Staffs. No. 44, Suffolk No.17.

[2] Commonwealth leases for a single year, authorized by the surveyors, in connection with the sales, will be found among the surveys of Northants No. 19, Northumberland No. 4, Oxford No. 12, Surrey No. 46, Sussex No. 39. See Madge, op. cit., pt. i, p. 277. The calendar of Pipe Office Leases contains seventy-three documents relating to Middlesex for the Commonwealth period; some of these are warrants, particulars, conveyances, and indentures, while others refer to pensions, annuities, or exemplification of fines. Fee farm rents and forfeited lands are included and the terms of the leases are usually for twenty-one years. No. 2287, relating to a messuage in Cateaton Street, let for twenty-one years from 1st April, 1658, had a yearly rent formerly of only 1s., but it was now raised to £5 6s. 8d. per annum.

Abstracts were next required of the claims of all copyholders of manors, excepting those relating to copyholders of inheritance. Only the first of a series of similar tenures need be given in full, but English was to be used instead of Latin, the surveyors being advised to abstract merely those items of interest and utility which concerned the dates and particulars of the premises, the number of lives granted (specifying those now in being with their ages), and the annual rent paid as well as the various considerations connected with fines. In making their returns they were to place the present rent, fines, and heriots in the left margin, and the clear improvement in regard to value in the margin on the right. As the profits of the lord of the manor were comprised in fines upon descent and alienation there was no necessity to abstract the copies of copyholders of inheritance or customary tenants, but their fines were to be valued on the average of a series of years. But as fines were sometimes certain and at other times quite arbitrary the distinction between the types was to be carefully made by the surveyors. Where such fines were arbitrary it was convenient to certify the clear annual improvement over the rents of all copyhold estates of the Manor or one gross sum amongst the memoranda, so that each purchaser of estates might satisfy his own judgment in regard to the valuation set upon the fines by the surveyors. In order to accomplish this part of the work with speed the officials were permitted to calculate this gross value upon inquisition or examination on oath, without spending any time in viewing the particular lands of such tenants. Among the memoranda, too, the surveyors might certify the requisite information as to the method of paying fines when they were certain, showing whether for example, the fine was so much upon the acre, messuage, or tenement, or by the year's rent of assize, or indeed by any other method discoverable.

For the guidance of the individual surveyors eight examples of copyholds for lives are given in the " precedent ". These range from 2nd August, 1619, to the latest copy granted, namely, that of 5th August, 1640. The lives included unusual numbers, namely, four and five, and not in every case are all the persons supposed to be still living. Sometimes the consideration is vaguely stated : it is " good service " in one case, and " a good consideration " in another. One rent and one of the fines cannot be stated, but the improved values are always recorded. Of four heriots, one stipulates definitely that the best beast was required. Three grants in reversion only are indicated. As for the rents they are said to range from 1s. to £1 6s., the improvements over and above the rent from 19s. 6d. to £13 4s., and the fines from £35 to £85. In tabulated form the eight " copies " reveal the following details[1] :—

[1] Table XXXVII. The eight instances are recorded in the " Precedent ", where they are given to illustrate the copyhold system and the method of valuation adopted by the surveyors in connection with the Parliamentary Surveys. " Method " f. 3 ; " Precedent," ff. 16–17.

XXXVII. IMPROVEMENTS OF COPYHOLDS, 1619–50

Dates.	Lives.	Rent.			Improvements.			Fines.
		£	s.	d.	£	s.	d.	£
1619, Aug. 2	2		1	0	1	12	0	—
1624, Apr. 6	3	1	4	0	12	6	0	80
1627, Aug. 3	3		7	6	4	2	6	—
1629, Sept. 7	2	1	6	0	13	4	0	85
1632, Jan. 6	3		13	4	5	13	4	35
1633, July 7	5		6	6	7	0	4	—
1634, Jan. 12	5		—			19	6	—
1640, Aug. 5	4		11	0	11	9	0	60
Totals .	27	£4	9	4	£56	6	8	£260

In one of the Devonshire surveys, where the lord of the manor claimed the power to grant by copy of court roll any of his tenements "when and to whom he pleaseth", grants were made, usually for three lives, and all the twenty-eight persons appear to have been living at the time of the survey aged from two years to sixty. Two grants of 1599 and 1600 were still in force in another instance in Dorsetshire, one survivor being 70 years of age, while the latest copy granted in the same manor was dated 3rd May, 1650, the three lives concerned being entered by the surveyors as aged 40, 16, and 14 years. In Sussex few copies of the tenants are mentioned, but in the case of the Manor of Duddleswell there are surveys eight years apart so that it is possible to compare the extant copies and note the changes that appear to have taken place in the interval. The totals for 1650 and 1658 only differ very slightly, but the number of copies of uncertain date in the two cases increases threefold in the eight years probably owing to increasing laxity, difficulty, and even opposition to the work of the surveyors. The earliest date given is that of 11th October, 1603, and the latest belongs to 6th April, 1658, so that the comparison between the two surveys of the manor of Duddleswell taken 1st June, 1650, and 7th July, 1658, is as follows[1] :—

XXXVIII. STUART COPYHOLDS IN A SUSSEX MANOR, 1603–58

Period.	1650.	1658.
1603–1622 .	6	—
1629–1648 .	44	15
1649–1658 .	2	23
Uncertain dates	11	32
Totals .	63	70

In some parts of the country it was impossible to see the original deeds or other evidences that were necessary for correct calculations to be made or claims of tenants to be tested, recognized, and recorded. The churchwardens and other ancient folk in a Gloucestershire inquiry affirmed that they had " lost many evidences and writings of

[1] Table XXXVIII. The comparative figures are taken from the two surveys of Duddleswell manor, Sussex, dated 1st June, 1650, and 7th July, 1658. In the later survey the copies of James I have apparently expired, but there is a notable rise of Commonwealth copyholds from two in 1650 to two dozen in 1658. (Sussex Nos. 26 and 27.)

their public lands and stocks in the time of the late trouble ". In Kent and Lincolnshire actual opposition was encountered at times and books were not forthcoming so that courts of survey were necessary in order to gain information. Lewis, steward of the Duchy Courts of Farnborough, Kent, carried away the court rolls to Oxford. At Newark and Woodstock the surveyors found it necessary to take the records into their own custody. Occasionally both leases and copies were indecipherable. Robert Emery, for example, of the Cliff near Lewes held certain lands in the parish of South Malling " by pretence of a copy granted about forty years since ", but when the document was produced it was found to be " soe eaten with Myce or Rattes that noe date was left therein ". As he was a poor man with many children and no other means of subsistence than the profits arising out of these premises, the surveyors were inclined to treat the case leniently. In another noteworthy instance two leases of 1630 and 1640 for sixty years or three lives were brought from London to Yorkshire and there " laid in the ground in the time of the war and there consumed so as nothing remaineth save only the seal and 2 or 3 small pieces of rotten parchment wherein appeared to us some ground of some letters yet not legible ".[1]

The covenants of the leases may be illustrated from Sussex examples. Here provision was made for the lessee to pay all taxes to State, Church, and " the poor ", all " water scots and reparations ", and sometimes " all scott and lott ". Next, re-entry might occur if rent had not been paid within twenty-one days or at the most forty days, and definitely in any case where the lessee had committed treason or felony or been outlawed. Again, premises were not to be assigned by will or otherwise to any person other than wife or child without consent of the grantor, though tenants in portreeve service at Pevensey, or others holding in free portreeve and burgage tenures were able to sell or give their lands and tenements at their own free will without licence or payment of fine. Further, not only did the grantor of a lease reserve the right for himself, his sons and servants to "meet with convenient companies" for the purpose of hawking or hunting upon the lands demised, but the tenant was compelled to entertain the manorial steward, surveyor, and other servants during two days yearly, the cost of meat, drink, and provision for man and beast being estimated in one instance at 30s. per annum. There was provision for reparation and maintenance of the premises, and timber was freely allowed to meet this cost. By a wise provision tenants were required to manure their lands with marl, especially after they had ploughed or burnt off the turf where woody bushes or rough ground existed,

---

[1] Devon, No. 14 ; Dorset, No. 9 ; Glos, No. 7 ; Kent, No. 24 ; Lincoln, No. 20 ; Notts, No. 19 ; Oxford, No. 12 ; Surrey, No. 72 ; Sussex, Nos. 26, 27, 39 ; York, No. 50. For copyholds see Jacob, op. cit. ; Hone, *Manor*, pp. 128, 180, 313, 317, 321-2 ; Lennard, op. cit., *Index*, p. 133.

and afterwards they were not to "densher" or burn the lands, particularly in the mead and pasture grounds. Where a clause was inserted for the lessee to "plant or graft six crab stocks or perry stocks" every year, we have some indication of the importance of the cultivation of apples for cider in Sussex at this time.[1]

Nothing is said in the Surveyor-General's official "method" as to the actual procedure to be adopted by surveyors when measuring land, and there is nothing in the "precedent" to indicate how this was to be done. Clearly, it was assumed that the surveyors were fully qualified men, able to make true surveys, as they promised to do in their oath, according to their "best skill and cunning". It is true that in the printed instructions given to the surveyors of Bishops' lands in 1646 it was expressly stated that "nothing in the Instructions, Oath, or in this present Ordinance, shall be construed to compel the Surveyors to make any admeasurement of the Lands, or any particular Survey of the number of Acres, unless they in their discretion shall think fit"—instructions which were applied to later tasks in connection with capitular and royal estates; but as the special intention of Parliament in those early years was to effect the speedy return of surveys and by that means the speedy sale of the premises, it is certain that the resulting "neglects and imperfections" (checked as they were later by the Surveyor-General's appointment), were not regretted simply because the surveys were imperfect, but because they hindered the sale of the property. Mr. Lennard has argued that even in Tudor days the application of intelligence and commercialism to rural economy had developed the art of land surveying, and that the progress made in the theory of the subject had important practical results. Fitzherbert's work on surveying appeared as early as 1523, followed fourteen years later by Sir Richard de Benese's "Boke of the Measurynge of Lande", and other works by Digges and Leigh before the century closed. Especially useful were the treatises written by Norden, Folkingham, and Rathborne between 1607 and 1616, with the aid of which the surveyors of the Commonwealth period were well equipped to undertake their important work. As Mr. Lennard truly says, "the surveys of Crown lands made by order of Parliament at the time of the Great Rebellion are at once the test and the triumph of the contemporary surveyor's art. They are well and carefully made, and that this should be so is an indication that a tough tradition of professional efficiency in surveying had already been established." It is quite possible that the manuscript treatise preserved in the Sloan collection in the British Museum was actually used by the surveyors of Crown lands in Sussex, for it is dated 1649 and was purchased in that county in May, 1691, its title being : "Exact Rules and Directions

---

[1] Sussex, Nos. 18, 21, 22, 31, 39. The covenants of the Halliford lease will be found in Madge, op. cit., pt. ii, pp. 417-19; see also pp. 448 and 453 for those of Islington and Twickenham.

for the compleate mensuration of land collected from the best authors, by an experienced Practitioner. Also something of Dyalling &c. of Practical Use." Two of its elaborate tables illustrate the actual measurement of land. The first consists of nine columns in one of which it is shown how to convert 190,080 " barley cornes ", or 63,360 inches, into " ffeete, yardes, elles, soades, passes (the number being 1,056), perches, scores, ffurlongs " and finally into a mile. The second table, which has no less than fifteen columns, converts, *inter alia*, 16,000 square perches, or 4,000 " daies worke " into quarter and half roods, then into roods, half acres, and lastly 100 acres exactly. By its side is a note of importance showing that " this rate is sett downe y't 40 perches in length and 4 in breadth must make an acre of land ". [1]

Herein lies the solution of a problem which completely baffled Mr. Lennard and consequently affected the correctness of three of his general statistical tables. Dealing with the survey of Chelveston-cum-Caldecott, parcel of the manor of Higham Ferrers, in Northamptonshire, he gives an area " as it seems " of 619 acres 2 roods 27 poles, of which he says that the extent of meadow land " appears to have been " 65 acres 35 poles. He then adds : " The one doubt about these figures concerns the meadow on three holdings, which amounted apparently to 55 acres 32 poles. In the case of these three holdings the meadow is measured in a peculiar way. Instead of giving its area in square measure, the surveyor describes the meadow as being 66 poles long and 6 broad, 148 poles long and 28 broad, and 148 poles long an 29 broad, respectively. The obvious interpretation of these figures, which yields the total given above, becomes doubtful when we notice that the value of these pieces of meadow is on this supposition abnormally low. On the other holdings where the meadow is measured in the ordinary way its average value is nearly £1 an acre ; on the three holdings in question we have apparently 55 acres 32 poles worth only £6 4s., or scarcely more than 2s. 3d. an acre." The extreme lowness of this value should have warned Mr. Lennard that his own method of calculation was at fault. If we take the figures from the survey itself, we shall find them recorded on folios 11, 19, and 24, where the meadow grounds are seen to be appurtenant to the messuage therein specified. Now these lands vary in the number of their " parcels or doles ", the first having five and the second and third ten each. But all these twenty-five parcels have their own measurements, being so many poles long and so many wide, therefore, their individual areas vary greatly in size. The dimensions in poles given by the surveyors are as follows[2] :—

[1] The Sloan MS. at the British Museum is marked " 3932 : 2 ", and the tables referred to will be found on p. 66. See Lennard, op. cit., pp. 23–5, and Firth and Rait, op. cit., vol. i, pp. 902–3 ; vol. ii, pp. 85–6, 172.

[2] Table XXXIX. The measurements are given in poles just as they are recorded in the survey, Northants, No. 19, ff. 11, 19, 24. By the first method, Mr. Lennard multiplied the lengths and widths of the three parcels of meadow ground, viz. 66 poles

XXXIX. Measurement of Meadow Doles

Northants Holdings.	No. 1. Length.	No. 1. Width.	No. 2. Length.	No. 2. Width.	No. 3. Length.	No. 3. Width.
Chelveston	14	1	7	4	7	4
	12	1	6	4	6	4
	20	2	30	4	30	4
	10	1	5	2	5	2
	10	1	8	2	8	2
			40	4	40	4
			12	2	12	2
			10	3	10	3
			20	1	20	2
			10	2	10	2
Totals	66	6	148	28	148	29
Values	10s.		£2 15s.		£2 19s.	

Here two methods of procedure present themselves for the calculation of the areas of the three meadow grounds, viz. :—

(a) Multiplying the separately added lengths and widths of each group, and then adding the three products to give the area in square poles.

(b) Adding the separately multiplied lengths and widths of each group and combining the three results to show the total area in square poles.

There can be no doubt whatever as to which of these two methods is the correct one to follow. Mr. Lennard took the first, the method of error, whereas the surveyors rightly intended the second, so that there is wide discrepancy between the two sets of calculations, for by the second method the areas of the doles barely exceed 1,000 square poles as will be seen below[1] :—

XL. Variation in Computed Areas

Meadow Grounds.	No. of Doles.	Lennard (sq. poles).	True Area (sq. poles).	Valuations. £ s. d.
1st	5	396	86	10 0
2nd	10	4,144	452	2 15 0
3rd	10	4,292	472	2 19 0
Totals .	25	8,832	1,010	£6 4 0

This gives 6·312 acres as a true result instead of 55·2 acres by Mr. Lennard's method, so that the average value of the meadow ground is not 2s. 3d. per acre but 19s. 8d., as one would naturally

and 6 poles in the case of No. 1, 148 and 28 in No. 2, and 148 and 29 in the third instance ; he then added the products so that the area became 8,832 sq. poles. By the second method, the surveyors added together the results of 25 separate multiplications, the areas of the doles of No. 1 being 14, 12, 40, 10, and 10, a total of 86 sq. poles ; those of No. 2 likewise, 28, 24, 120, 10, 16, 160, 24, 30, 20, and 20, a total of 452 sq. poles ; and those of No. 3 similarly, 28, 24, 120, 10, 16, 160, 24, 30, 40, and 20, a total of 472. The result by the second method is only 1,010 sq. poles. Lennard, op. cit., pp. 97-8.

[1] Table XL. The results of the two methods of calculation are here compared, and it will be seen that Mr. Lennard's error raises the area of the three meadow grounds from 1,010 sq. poles to 8,832 sq. poles, a total which is nearly nine times too large. Lennard, op. cit., pp, 97-8, and footnote.

suppose. There is, therefore, no doubt about the extent of the meadow land, nor is the area of the entire survey in the least uncertain. It is true that the measurements are set out in a different way, but that is not at all " peculiar " ; and although the surveyors gave the total of the lengths and widths of each of the three holdings they neither multiplied those figures together themselves nor expected others to do so. The interpretation of the figures is perfectly " obvious ", but not in the sense intended by Mr. Lennard, nor is the value " abnormally low ". He agrees that the average value of the holdings of meadow land, " measured in the ordinary way," is approximately £1 an acre, and it is clear that " the ordinary way " is the one that should be followed here giving as a result 19s. 8d. an acre. Further, the correctness of this view is confirmed by a second instance on folio 15, where a piece of meadow ground consisting of six parcels or doles is measured in terms of " Roods and Poles " in regard to the length and width. As the total area in this case amounts to 7 roods and 4 square Poles the average value is again just under £1 per acre. This error in the calculations of Mr. Lennard causes some confusion, as a consequence, in the statistical tables, which he gives at the close of his essay. " On account of this uncertainty," he says in a footnote, " I have not included any of the Chelveston meadows in the general statistical table at the end of this chapter, which gives the values of the different kinds of land ; but in the tables dealing with the size of holdings and the proportions of the land subjected to different uses I have included them at their apparent area, as the amount of error thus introduced must be insignificant." Yet the amount of error is not so slight after all, for the area he records at Chelveston is approximately nine times larger than it should have been, and the average value is correspondingly nine times too small. When referring to the holdings at Chelveston Mr. Lennard admits that " the doubt about the meadows makes these figures uncertain ", but when he adds that " in any case " six of the nine holdings " must have been " between 60 and 120 acres, two others between 30 and 40, and the one remaining just 7¾ acres, he is still in error as the evidence now supplied reveals. The whole of this section in Chapter IV of his book, indeed, needs to be revised.[1]

---

[1] The whole of section 6 in chapter 4 of Mr. Lennard's book needs revision in the light of the present criticism. It may be observed that Mr. Lennard omits as of no economic importance the surveys numbered 1–14, 22, 31, and 42 ; his references to Nos. 25, 30, 37, 38, 47, and 49, are also very brief, in some cases a mere statement occurs that they are of little value and may be ignored by students. There is a doubt as to the inclusion of some of the figures in the statistical tables, for example, No. 47 ; and certainly one lot of meadow land in No. 46 is definitely excluded on the ground that the value is " not clearly legible"—in the survey, f. 57, however, the value of the 25 acres is shown to be £6 5s. Among his queries are several that need not appear ; in No. 20, for example, " Chall mead ", " Munks wood," and " hanke leyes hedge " are quite correct (pp. 46, 51, 60, or ff. 79, 53, 63). On the other hand " Larason close " and " Nan leyes " should be " Laeasen " and " Nun " (pp. 52, 59, or ff. 75, 57). On page 42 of the same survey 4 acres of pasture appears as 14 acres in the original (f. 95), and the reference on page 28 to a missing folio is incorrect, since f. 100 is merely followed by a folio that is wrongly

But measurements of this character are not the only ones that call for care and watchfulness, for there is yet another source of error that is even less known to students, and that is the variation found from time to time in the standards of measurement used by surveyors. One such example relating to a survey of Grafton Park in 1558 is casually dismissed by Mr. Lennard in a footnote : "We are told that this was measured by a pole of 18 feet." Yet the fact is of importance, for unless we can be certain as to the actual method of measurement employed there will always be doubt as to the proper interpretation of statistical data. In Cornwall most of the surveys have a note referring to the custom of the county in regard to " every acre of land Cornish ", and in one instance there is a special note that " the Lord is to provide overseers of weights and measures within the manor that they may be good according to the custom of the country and that none may be deceived by them ". The legal pole of 16½ feet is expressly indicated in some of the surveys of Lincolnshire, Wiltshire, and Worcestershire. The 18-foot pole, found in Northamptonshire in 1558, occurs also in a number of Common-wealth surveys in Lincolnshire. In Lancashire, where a Decree of Trinity term 1618 is quoted, copyholders in one manor are said to pay 6½d. per acre, measured by the standard of 7 yards to the pole. In some cases the work was admittedly inaccurate. Thus in measuring a certain common fen in Lincolnshire the surveyors declared their inability to " exactly and precisely survey " the marsh, adding very cheerfully " but we guess the same to contain at least 10,000 acres ". In a Norfolk example double reckoning occurred, but correction of 10 acres was made by a subsequent certificate. The term yard-land is met with several times in the Midlands : it is stated in regard to Leicestershire that " in these parts " it measures 26 acres, and it occurs in the " precedent " as equivalent to 13 acres in Surrey, the half yard-land being counted as 9 acres. One particular yard-land sought by surveyors in Yorkshire was eventually declared to be " lost and cannot be found by us, neither can we find that the same was at any time enjoyed either by the lessee or the now tenant ". Some remarkable differences between earlier and later measurements are revealed in the surveys of Sussex. Thus in a lease of 9th February, 1601, the premises were said to comprise 35 acres, for which a rent of £6 13s. 4d. was payable. In the more precise survey of 12th April, 1650, the acreage was returned at 54A. 1. 39, the rent at £20 and the improved value at £22 more. In another survey ten cases occur in connection with

numbered f. 102. In connection with No. 17 the "mysterious sentence" to which he alludes on p. 97 has nothing to do with "souses"; the sentence, properly transcribed, reads : "take downe other coppie hould *houses* without lysence" (f. 13). The lease in No. 16 dated 30th July, 14 Eliz., has no term mentioned, therefore 31 years is a conjecture (p. 37, f. 26). The list of townships recorded in No. 26 is incomplete ; Whittlewood is Whittlebury, and Maidford does not occur, but Duncott, Burcott, and Heathencott should be included (p. 99, ff. 96–8).

EAST DEREHAM MANOR SURVEY, NORFOLK, 1649

[face p. 160

indentures or lease polls where the area is stated to have been collectively 233 acres; but under the more careful work of the Parliamentary Surveyors this was returned at the higher figure of 312A. 3. 19. Sir Thos. Pelham's land was expressly stated to have amounted to " 11 acres more than is granted in any original lease ", and there are at least twelve other instances recorded by the surveyors, the combined results of which show an excess of more than 150 acres over the area of land actually specified in the deeds. These increases indicate that the surveyors had detected cases of " encroachments ", for which they were evidently on the look out in every county they visited.[1]

Many are the examples recorded by the Surveyor-General in his " precedent " to illustrate the instructions relating to the different kinds of land in a manor, as well as their extent and valuation. Foremost among these come premises attached to dwellings, such as Sale Court and the park lodges, regarded as being in possession, or the parsonage and farms, the water grist mill, and the messuages and cottages held by various leaseholders or copyholders. Details are few in regard to size and construction of the actual dwellings, though the description is adequate so far as the Court house, lodges, and certain of the messuage are concerned. But although two tenements in Bidmost are measured with precision, it is rare to find the houses and their associated premises computed apart from each other, so that the size of the gardens and orchards can only be guessed, the crofts alone being indicated with care. So far as can be ascertained with any degree of certainty, the area of the houses and surrounding premises appears to be about 67 acres. The rest of the lands fall into several classes according to their respective agricultural uses, but not all the parcels are separately valued. The areas of arable, meadow, and pasture lands in the manor of Sale are apparently 102 acres, 98, and 1,009 respectively, the last named including a park of 900 acres. The woodlands extend to 23 acres, and the " mixed lands " of meadow or pasture to 31 acres. Lastly the miscellaneous lands include a coney

[1] On the subject of land measures see Seebohm, *Customary Acres*, 1914; the custom of measuring land in Cornwall, *Cambridge MSS.*, vol. iv, p. 361; Rawlinson MSS., B. 392, ff. 55–6; B. 450, f. 380; C. 459, f. 222; Brit. Mus. MSS., Add. 5884, f. 14; Add. ch. 7014, Harl. 54D, 37; 83D, 30; 55G, 30; 54H, 40; *Campb.*, vol. xvi, p. 8; Hist. MSS. Com. Report, 1, pt. i, pp. 65, 97. The subject has been discussed for years in Notes and Queries: see 2 ser. vol. ix, p. 426; vol. xii, p. 136. 4 ser., vol. i, pp. 98, 181, 424, 496; 5 ser., vol. i, p. 260; 6 ser., vol. vi, pp. 41, 189, 229; 8 ser., vol. vii, p. 250; 9 ser., vol. v, 349; vol. vi, pp. 303, 381, 461; 10 ser., vol. x, pp. 326, 373; 11 ser., vol. vi, p. 6. See also *Commissioners' Reports, Woods and Forests*, rep. xiv, app. No. 12, pp. 35–6. For forest measures see *Hist. MSS. Com. Report*, vol. 3, p. 7, and Beverley *MSS.*, p. 161; *Treasury Books*, 1660–7, p. 196; *Commissioners' Reports, Woods and Forests*, index to 1793 volume. Lennard's casual note on land measurement is on p. 75, f. n. 3. The Parliamentary surveyors quoted are Cornwall, No. 36, f. 24; Lancashire, No. 8b, f. 17; Leicester, No. 7, f. 3; Lincoln, No. 14, f. 27, No. 15, ff. 33–5, No. 21, f. 14, No. 26, f. 21; Norfolk, No. 17A, f. 1; Sussex, Nos. 18, 22, 39, 43; Wilts, No. 45, f. 6; Worcester, No. 3, f. 20; York, No. 52, f. 2.

ground of 10 acres, and certain unspecified "lands" (which are probably arable) amounting to 18 acres. The total area, therefore, of the imaginary manor which Colonel Webb calls "Sale in Surrey" is approximately 1,360 acres, and of this the arable portion forms 7·5 per cent, the meadow 7·2 per cent, and the pasture 74·3 per cent. At Halliford manor, where the total did not exceed 195 acres, the house and premises measured 10 acres, the arable 86, meadow 40, and pasture 16, the remainder consisting of mixed lands and waste. At Halliford, therefore, the percentages of definitely arable, meadow, and pasture lands were 44, 21, and 8 respectively.

The total amount of land of different kinds described in the surveys of rural Middlesex and Northants, will be found recorded in the table below, wherein particulars are also given concerning the county of Sussex[1] :—

XLI. Proportions of Utilized Lands

Lands.	Middlesex. Acres.	Northants. Acres.	Sussex. Acres.
Houses and Premises	92·5	548·0	1,513·0
Arable . . .	167·0	3,525·5	273·0
Meadow . . .	217·0	1,042·0	18·5
Pasture . . .	9,366·5	4,075·5	64·0
Wood . . .	589·0	957·0	1·0
Mixed . . .	582·5	2,091·0	609·0
Miscellaneous .	401·5	3,253·0	8,344·5
Totals . .	11,416·0	15,492·0	10,823·0

It should, however, be noticed that whereas Mr. Lennard divides the leys among pasture and arable lands, they are included here (with the parks) among the pastures, those classed as "arable and leys" being entered under the heading "mixed lands". The term "miscellaneous" is intended to include "lands", unspecified in character though probably arable in the main, also moorlands, marshes, wastes, and "ways". The Northamptonshire figures given by Mr. Lennard, useful as they undoubtedly are, do not, however, reveal the true position in that county. The Chelveston error, for example, reduces the area he records of meadow land by nearly 50 acres. Then again, the whole of the figures for lands in Kettering and the manors of Irchester and Kingscliffe are excluded on the ground of incompleteness of the surveys.

Moreover, the perfectly sound method of classifying under "houses and their premises" all lands not measured apart from dwellings is varied from time to time, as in the case of "barns" (even when people are living therein), and a particular tenement with its close in Greens Norton, the last-named being recorded by Mr. Lennard among the pasture instead of being placed, according

---

[1] Table XLI is based on figures given by Lennard, op. cit., pp. 88, 98 n., 100 n., 110 n., 119, 121 ; and Madge, op. cit., pt. ii, pp. 423, 454 ; also the analysis of Sussex surveys.

to rule, under the "houses and premises". The figures in the table above in any case are instructive. They show that pasture lands predominate in two of the counties, the percentage of the total being lowest in the case of Sussex where it is not even 1 per cent, compared with 26 per cent in Northamptonshire and 57 per cent in Middlesex. The area associated with dwellings is least in Middlesex and greatest in Sussex, but the figures given for meadow, pasture, and woodlands, separately measured, are surprisingly low in Sussex, mainly because the Crown lands in that county consisted almost entirely of parks, forest lands, and "waste". Even the "mixed" lands contain very little meadow and pasture, whereas the total given under "miscellaneous lands", includes no less than 7,578 acres of "common waste ground", in addition to 469 acres of marsh and a further 17 acres of "uplands and marsh". The extent of arable land in Northamptonshire is remarkable in that it is seen by the table to be eight times larger than the acreage recorded for the arable of Middlesex and Sussex combined. Considered from the point of view of separately measured portions alone this area of 3,525 acres for Northamptonshire forms 23 per cent of the whole total; but if we add to this the amount of "arable and leys" entered under "mixed lands" the percentage rises to 38 per cent, while the exclusion of the area of the four parks surveyed at Grafton, Higham, Holdenby, and Potterspury would raise the proportion of arable to 44 per cent of the new total. In 1660 the surveys of ten of the Crown manors in Northamptonshire recorded an even greater result, the arable forming 56 per cent of the total cultivated area on that occasion, but that may be due to greater precision in the description of the various parcels. When the three surveys of 1619, 1650, and 1660 are compared for Grafton and Hartwell the percentage of arable remains almost constant at 48 per cent of the total acreage surveyed.

Figures which give the average values of the different sorts of land recorded in the "precedent" are a little difficult to ascertain because the Surveyor-General, content to set out the form of an entry for the guidance of his surveyors, is undecided at times in regard to the value of a particular parcel. But in so far as measurement and value accompany precise descriptions of property, averages can readily be obtained. Now Colonel Webb's illustrations in the specimen survey suggest that the calculations of land values were intended to meet two contingencies, in one of which the premises were not measured apart from dwellings, and in the other where every parcel of land was regarded as a "cleared site" and had its own separate measurement. In the manor of Sale 320 acres are included with dwellings under a combined valuation of £298 11s. 10d., which yields an average of 18s. 8d. per acre. Where building land was concerned, as in the case of Sale Court and a certain much decayed tenement in Bidmost, the alternative value of the ground and soil, considered as a " cleared site " had to be estimated ; but in the former case the building was in too good a condition for demolition to occur, whereas in the latter case it was urgently necessary owing to the cost of keeping the place in proper repair. As the premises stood, Sale Court with its 20 acres 2 roods of ground had an estimated value of £92 5s., but its worth as a cleared site was not more than £26 13s. 4d. or £1 6s. 8d. per acre per annum. The arable lands separately measured ranged in size from 1 to 9 acres, the full total of 24 acres being worth £6 3s., which gives an average of 5s. 2d. per acre. In the same way meadow ground in Sale manor varied from 4 to 11 acres, giving a total of 26 acres valued at £26 13s. 1d., or 14s. 9d. per acre on the average. In one case the value of 5 acres is said to be only 16s. 8d., owing to the fact that the fore-crop of the meadow belonged to the Vicar of Sale. Of separately valued pasture, the size of which ranged from three to seventeen acres, the total was less than forty acres, and as the combined value was apparently £15 7s. 4d., the average value only came to 8s. 4d. per acre per annum. Here again allowance had to be made for the parson's right of pasturing a horse and two cows in a close of thirteen acres ; so the value of this close was reduced to £3 4s.

With one exception all the parcels of pasture consist of close, one of which is subdivided into four others of about four acres each. Sale Park, 900 acres in extent, of the average value of 4s., illustrated the case of land which ought to be subdivided for greater utility, the surveyors suggesting that one part might contain 450 acres worth 3s. on the average, a second 150 acres worth a shilling more, and the third 300 acres at the highest value of all, viz. 5s. 6d. per acre. If the park and the separately valued parcels of pasture be added the average value for the whole of the pasture lands in Sale Manor would become 4s. 2d. per acre. As the entire manor appears to be not less than 1,358 acres in extent, and the value as far as can be clearly established does not exceed £570 6s. 3d. (leaving out of consideration an estimated value of £120 for the vicarage and its rights) the average for the whole manor as it was supposed to exist in the year 1649 works out at 8s. 5d. an acre.

We may next take an actual example from Middlesex instead of the suppositious one from Surrey. Halliford manor, surveyed in 1650, consisted of 195 acres, worth £127 13s. 4d. or 13s. 1d. per acre. The manor house and premises were valued on the average at 16s. The waste lands were naturally worth very little, only 5s. Next in value come 86 acres of arable at 8s. per acre, although 26 acres of arable and meadow have an average value of 8s. 11d. Pasture lands, 16 acres in extent, follow with an average of 17s. 6d. an acre, but four other acres of pasture and ley have a reduced value of 13s. 4d. in consequence of their admixture. Lastly we have the value of the meadow lands, 40 acres of which yield an average of 25s. per acre, but there are in addition 3 acres of "aits", obviously meadow land, that are worth five shillings more than this. With these figures may be compared those given by Mr. Lennard for Grafton, Northants, where the average value of 322 acres of arable is 4*s*. 2*d*. an acre per annum, 165 acres of meadow about 15*s*. 6*d*. and 338 acres of pasture 19*s*.; so that the average values of arable and meadow in the Middlesex manor are considerably in excess of those shown for Grafton, where the pasture alone has a higher average value. This excess value in the case of Middlesex would be due to proximity to London.

When we turn to the figures obtained for the three counties of Middlesex, Northamptonshire, and Sussex, important results emerge, as will be seen from the comparative figures in the following table[1] :—

XLII. Agricultural Values

Counties.	Lands.	Acres.	Annual Values. £	Average Values. s. d.	Range.
Middlesex	Arable	167·0	99·0	11 11	8*s*. to 25*s*.
	Meadow	217·0	239·0	22 0	16*s*. to 48*s*.
	Pasture	9,366·5	5,724·5	12 3	6*s*. 3*d*. to 30*s*.
Northants	Arable	2,986·0	699·2	4 6	2*s*. 8*d*. to 12*s*.
	Meadow	970·0	869·9	18 0	10*s*. to 51*s*. 5*d*.
	Pasture	3,299·5	2,394·0	14 6	4*s*. 11*d*. to 80*s*.
Sussex	Arable	273·0	126·3	9 3	4*s*. 6*d*. to 20*s*. 11*d*.
	Meadow	18·5	14·3	15 5	14*s*. 8*d*. to 25*s*.
	Pasture	64·0	19·7	6 2	5*s*. to 15*s*. 4*d*.

As Mr. Lennard omits the Chelveston meadow grounds, correction is made in this table, the acreage being increased by 6 acres 1 rood 10 poles and the annual value by £6 4*s*., so that the average may now be given as 18*s*. per acre for Northamptonshire meadow lands. The figures for Middlesex exclude all consideration of lands of semi-urban type recorded in a somewhat lengthy series of surveys for this county. In regard to Sussex one survey is omitted in order to avoid double reckoning, namely, Lancaster Great Park (No. 26), its area of 14,000 acres being subsequently re-surveyed and the results incorporated in separate surveys (Nos. 10 to 17 and 27), all of which find inclusion in the table of statistics. The areas separately measured are seen to be very unequal in extent, the smallest recorded being only 18 acres while the largest exceeds 9,000, the annual values corresponding to these areas ranging from £14 to £5,700. The averages likewise vary considerably. In the case of arable lands, the lowest value, namely for lands in Northamptonshire, is barely a third of that shown for Middlesex, which also stands first in the list in connection with average meadow values, doubtless owing to its proximity to the metropolis. Sussex values are lowest of all both for meadow and

---

[1] Table XLII. This incorporates the statistical calculations recorded by Lennard, op. cit., pp. 64–5 ; and Madge, op. cit., pt. ii, pp. 423, 456. To these figures others from Sussex have been added.

pasture. On the other hand Northamptonshire has an average value for pasture which is not only 2s. 3d. more than that ascertained for Middlesex, but more than double that shown in the table for Sussex.

The variation disclosed by the table in regard to the values of an acre of land, differently used in different counties, is remarkable. If we consider first the different sorts of land surveyed, it is clear that the values of arable land fluctuate least in Northamptonshire and those of meadow as well as pasture least in Sussex; whereas the greatest fluctuations occur in Middlesex in the case of arable, and in Northamptonshire in connection with both meadow and pasture. Taking the localities next and testing the range of values shown for each county, we find that in Middlesex arable shows least divergence and meadow most; also that in Northamptonshire the position is similar except that pasture takes the place of meadow; and that in Sussex meadow and pasture are equal in the extent of their range.

The variation disclosed by the table in respect to the values of an acre of land, differently used and differently situated, is even more remarkable. For the different sorts of land the figures show differences in value so great that the range recorded for pasture is more than equal to those of arable and meadow combined[1] :—

XLIII. COMPARATIVE LAND VALUES

Lands.	Lowest Value.	Highest Value.	Differences.
			£ s. d.
Arable	2s. 8d. in Northants	25s. in Middlesex	1 2 4
Meadow	10s. in Northants	51s. 5d. in Northants	2 1 5
Pasture	4s. 10d. in Northants	80s. in Northants	3 15 1

For land differently situated and used in different ways the variations per acre per annum are greater still; in this instance the extreme values for Northamptonshire, exceed those of Middlesex and Sussex put together[2] :—

XLIV. RANGE OF DISTRICT VALUES

Counties.	Lowest Value.	Highest Value.	Differences.
			£ s. d.
Middlesex	6s. 3d. for pasture	48s. for meadow	2 1 9
Northants	2s. 8d. for arable	80s. for pasture	3 11 4
Sussex	4s. 6d. for arable	25s. for meadow	1 0 6

From an examination of the evidence thus supplied we arrive at the conclusion, that however much or little may be the variation in the range of values within each of the counties and for each of the three sorts of land, the divergence between them is least in the case

[1] Table XLIII. The separate values for the different sorts of land utilized for agricultural purposes are worked out on the basis of figures recorded by Lennard for Northants and Madge, for Middlesex; the figures for Sussex are well within the extremes shown. For Lennard's numerous instances of land values in Northamptonshire see the index to his volume, p. 134.

[2] Table XLIV. The ascertained values for the different districts are calculated in a similar manner to Table XLIII (q.v.) from the same sources, with the addition of the analysed figures for the Sussex surveys. Madge, op. cit., pt. ii, pp. 423, 456; Lennard, op. cit., pp. 64–5, 119.

of arable land and most in that of pasture, just as it is greatest in Northamptonshire and smallest in Sussex.[1]

The average values for Northamptonshire, owing to insufficient data being given by Mr. Lennard, cannot be quoted in connection with the item " houses and their premises ", but for Sussex the average per acre per annum for lands not measured and valued apart from dwellings is found to be 10s. 7d., whereas in Middlesex, where values are naturally greater though the acreage is less in extent, the average is nearly £5 10s. The probability in the case of Northants is that the average would be under £1. Even in the matter of woodlands the average for Middlesex is much more than that of Sussex, being 7s. 9d. for the former county and only 5s. for the latter, though in this case there is great disparity between the acreage compared in the two counties, so much of the woody ground being included among the " mixed " lands. When the values are compared in connection with lands described under two or more names, as " arable or meadow ", or " meadow, pasture, and wood ", the average value per acre is again much in favour of Middlesex as against Sussex, the two results being 11s. 7d. and 7s. respectively. Not so great, however, is the difference where " miscellaneous lands ", such as marshes, commons, or wastes, are concerned, for the average of 4s. 11d. per acre obtained from Middlesex surveys is only about a shilling more than that of Sussex. Lastly, to complete the series of comparative averages, it may be added that when account is taken of every sort of land, whether measured and valued separately or in association with dwellings, the average for the entire area described is 5s. 1d. per acre for Sussex, and not less than 12s. 8d. for the Crown lands in the rural parts of Middlesex.

In a third direction differences emerge in connection with land, namely in respect to the size of various parcels measured and valued by the surveyors and held by tenants of the Crown. Some indication of what was expected of these officials may be gleaned from the " precedent " where in the Surrey manor of Sale fifty-three parcels are recorded more or less clearly, ranging in size from less than an acre in two cases to the largest parcel of all, 900 acres in extent ; of these thirty-five are seen to be under 10 acres and only one exceeds 50 acres. Mr. Lennard's method in compiling his statistical table of Northamptonshire holdings is to count distinct farms held by the same person as a single holding,[2] even when partners are found in one or other of the tenancies, but this has the disadvantage of decreasing the number of holdings and increasing their average size. He omits all cases of unrecorded acreage and does not include the troublesome

---

[1] The divergence, closely examined, amounts to 7s. 8d. arable, 64s. 9d. pasture ; also 6s. 1d. Sussex, 65s. 9d. Northants.

[2] The attempt to reckon the holdings in this way is liable to create confusion for errors are almost certain to occur ; some of these may, however, be avoided by utilizing the " Index of Immediate Tenants ", which the writer has prepared from documents relating to Sales of Crown lands. See Appendix II, Sect. iii (YY(b)).

Chelveston meadow grounds or several of the parks. A list of twenty-four somewhat doubtful holdings relating to Hartwell, compiled from a survey of 1605, includes four of less than an acre, fourteen with 10 to 60 acres, and one of larger size though less than 100 acres in extent. In another survey, dated 1619, out of eighty-five holdings in Grafton, twenty-six were smaller than an acre, and only five were above 100 acres; the remainder included twenty-eight which ranged from 10 to 60 acres each. Taking the whole of the Parliamentary surveys analysed by Mr. Lennard, we find that twenty-four out of 160 holdings were less than an acre in size and eighteen exceeded 100 acres, the largest of them all being 1,715 acres in extent. In the table below will be found some comparative figures of holdings in three counties, but as Mr. Lennard divides his results so as to show 60 instead of 50 acres the Northamptonshire figures for the area " 50 to 60 acres " need to be restated. Mr. Lennard's total of 160 appears to be unduly small for a county which had so many " immediate tenants " among the purchasers of Crown lands.[1]

XLV. Comparative Size of Holdings

	Middlesex.	Northants.	Sussex.
Under 1 acre	10	24	12
1 to 10 acres	73	32	62
11 to 50 acres	21	57	55
51 to 100 acres.	4	29	8
101 to 500 acres	9	14	9
Above 500 acres	1	4	6
Totals	118	160	152

The majority of the holdings in Middlesex were quite small, 38 per cent of the total being under 5 acres and 70 per cent under 10 acres. The largest in the list is of course that of Enfield Chase, which consisted of 7,904 acres, but in the later survey of 1658 this was subdivided into more than fifty portions, some as small as a rood but one of them as large as 1,522 acres. In a similar manner and in the same year Lancaster Great Park in Sussex, nearly 14,000 acres in size, was parcelled out and its nine lodges disappeared as component parts of the great forest enclosure. It may be added that the range of holdings in the Sussex surveys extends from three poles to 1,843 acres. For the purposes of comparison we may separate the holdings of these counties into three classes, regarding all areas up to 10 acres as " smallholdings ", those between 10 and 100 acres as " moderate ", and all above 100 acres as " large holdings ".[2]

[1] Table XLV. The comparative size of holdings in Northants and Middlesex are recorded by Lennard, op. cit., pp. 77, 80, 120, 124; and Madge, op. cit., pt. ii, p. 457.
[2] Table XLVI. In this table the percentages are calculated for three counties in connection with smallholdings, those of moderate size and those of the largest kind. See Lennard, op. cit., pp. 77, 80, 120, 124; and Madge, op. cit., pt. ii, p. 457. The Sussex figures are based on analysis of the surveys of that county.

XLVI. Percentages of Various Holdings

Holdings.	No. of Instances.	Middlesex.	Northants.	Sussex.
Small	213	70	35	49
Moderate	174	21	54	41
Large	43	9	11	10
Totals	430	100	100	100

From the calculated percentages it is certain that the small holdings formed a larger proportion of the total in Middlesex than in either of the other two counties, Northamptonshire coming last with a percentage only half as great. At the other extreme we find Northamptonshire, although Sussex is only slightly below. Of moderate size holdings, however, those of Northamptonshire easily stand first, when compared with the figures for the other two counties.

Some evidence, though the amount is inconsiderable, is found in the Parliamentary Surveys in regard to enclosures, but too often the entries are vague—as of "lands lately enclosed", or of others "formerly enclosed"—and not infrequently the character of the lands is unspecified, so that it becomes a matter of some uncertainty when the progress of the movement is under review. In the case of Northamptonshire Mr. Lennard concludes that these surveys throw little light on the "vexed question of the progress of enclosure and conversion in the Midlands" either at this period or in the century before, though the evidence he produces does at any rate show that the movement continued during some centuries. At Grafton enclosure began early and was easily accomplished owing to the proximity of forest land; the principal survey certainly shows thirty-three closes definitely used for pasture and fourteen others that were probably used in the same way, but only in three instances may the existence of closes of arable land be suspected. The least valuable of the pasture closes was one of about 9 acres, worth a little less than 4s. 11d. per acre per annum. At Kettering a small close of one acre of unspecified character was worth 35s., but Mr. Lennard does not include this among his statistical tables, and perhaps it is as well for the close appears to be of a semi-urban character. At Greens Norton the closes of pasture varied considerably in value, some being worth only 8s. an acre, though the highest value of all, namely £4 per acre, is stated to belong to a little "plot" of only 26 poles, and must be viewed with suspicion. At Ashton one entry alone refers to enclosure, but its 8 acres are not valued apart from the cottage to which it belongs. Much of Holdenby Manor is clearly enclosed, for besides the park of 500 acres, there are closes whose area exceed 600 acres more, while at Greens Norton fully 2,235 acres are enclosed. Raundes and Rushden evidently represent real "refuges of medievalism", for not only are leaseholds entirely absent in the former manor, but over 4,700 acres remained to be enclosed later, with 3,500 more at Rushden, in the period of activity between 1778 and 1797. It is certain from the Northamptonshire evidence that very many of the Crown lands were in a decidedly medieval state of agriculture when the surveyors first set to work in 1649, and we might reasonably expect to find that the number of tenants would be large and the average size of their holdings small.[1]

At Halliford, Middlesex, the enclosures are five in number, and these include " Hoe Close " which since 1633 had been divided. Three of the closes are very small, ranging from 4 to 8 acres, being devoted to pasture in 1650 ; their values are stated to be 10s. at the lowest and 23s. 4d. at the highest, the average being 17s. 6d. per acre per annum. A fourth enclosure, 20 acres in extent, consisted of meadow land, worth £1 10s. per acre, nearly four times the value of the arable land, and fully 50 per cent greater than that of the meadow land in the divided " Hoe Close ". The fifth and last of the closes, measuring altogether 26 acres, was divided (under the name already quoted of " Hoe Close ") in the proportion of 24 acres of arable in its upper portion and 2 acres of meadow in the lower part, the values being given separately at 8s. an acre in the first case and £1 in the second ; as a result of the division and consequent conversion of part of this close, values were now more than twice as great as in 1633. Within the same manor, moreover, was an unsuspected close of " pasture or Leazow ground ", one of the few instances indeed in which enclosures of ley are mentioned in the Middlesex surveys. Not only does this parcel agree in area with two out of three of the enclosures of pasture, but its average value of 13s. 4d. per acre is exactly the same as the value assigned to the second close ; and, if confirmation were needed as to its condition, the survey of 1633 would supply the proof since it is there definitely called " a close of Meadowe called Noward ", a name which the surveyors of 1650 convert into " Nowoods ".

Several of the Sussex surveys record the existence of enclosures. Sedgwick Park, 1,033 acres 25 poles, is described as " anciently disparked and now divided into divers several farms ". Lancaster Great Park, 13,991 acres 27 poles in extent, which the surveyors of 1650 call an " unpaled park anciently divided into three wards and since subdivided into six walks ", was subdivided still further in 1658 when much of the land came under the heading of " open common or waste ". Of this enormous area only the lands definitely described as enclosed in the later surveys are considered in the table of acres below[2] :—

---

[1] The transactions of tenants and original creditors in regard to the sales of Crown lands are numerous in the case of Northamptonshire.

[2] Table XLVII. The values are calculated for enclosures, the number of closes and the acreage being recorded in connection with each type of land reviewed. See Sussex surveys Nos. 12, 13, 15–17, 19, 21–2, 26–9, 32, 34, 38, 45, 47, 48. Enclosed courts

XLVII. VALUES OF ENCLOSED LANDS IN SUSSEX

Closes.	No.	Acreage.	Value. $£$
Arable .	49	270·5	137·3
Meadow	5	15·5	11·5
Marsh .	6	28·0	21·0
Pasture.	2	58·0	15·2
Mixed .	28	194·0	94·7
Totals	90	566·0	279·7

In this county the evidence points to enclosure of arable land in the main, unlike Northamptonshire, where pasture appears to be the chief consideration. The " mixed lands " include some that are stated to be cut into two or even four " divisions ", and others again are merely described as " closes " or " enclosed grounds ". A minimum of two in such cases may be assumed for the purpose of calculating the number of closes. The two enclosures entered under pasture are encroachments from the forest of Ashdown, enclosed within Buckhurst and Newnham parks. The area of 566 acres definitely referred to in the table as enclosed lands may well be increased by the items, nine in number, which relate to " Lodges and grounds ", for probably most of the lands connected with these dwellings were in the nature of enclosures; in which case another 531 acres, worth £179 2s. 8d., might be added to the amount mentioned above. Thus the percentage of closes among the Crown lands of Sussex, setting aside the early enclosures of Ashdown and Sedgwick, would not be less than 5 per cent and might very well be placed at even 10 per cent ; but even then it must not be forgotten that there are five further entries relating to mixed " closes and parcels "—the exact amount of the former cannot be calculated with any precision—so that some proportion of an additional 398 acres, valued at £112, belongs to the total area of enclosed lands in Sussex. The closes are for the most part quite small ; the arable lands, for example, are in closes of less than 20 acres, and fourteen of them are not more than 6 or 8 acres in extent, the average of such lands being rather less than six acres.[1]

Of considerable interest and importance are the particulars given by the surveyors in respect to dwellings. In the " precedent " illustrations are given of rents and improvements of cottages, tenements, messuages, and farms, the rents ranging from 1s. for a cottage to

of the Castle at Pevensey (No. 39) extend to 68 A. 2 R. 11 P., valued at £8 10s., or more than £1 per acre on the average. Mr. Lennard found larger closes in Northants, one being 148 acres and a second 217 acres.

[1] For closes of land in Middlesex see Madge, op. cit., pt. ii, pp. 408–414. The following Northamptonshire surveys contain evidence of enclosures of various sizes : No. 15, f. 1 ; No. 17, f. 3 ; No. 19, ff. 2, 6, 13, 17, 21, 26, 30, 31 ; No. 20, f. 2 ; No. 22, f. 5 ; No. 23, f. 5 ; No. 25, f. 1 ; No. 30, f. 1 ; No. 32, f. 82 ; No. 34, f. 1 ; No. 35, ff. 1–4, 12, 14–16, 19, 37 ; No. 38, ff. 3–6 ; No. 40, ff. 11, 25 ; No. 41, f. 2 ; No. 47, ff. 1, 4.   In regard to Sussex, Gonner, " Progress of Inclosure " (English Hist. Review, vol. 23, p. 492) shows that the amount of open road indicated in Ogilby's map of 1677 is on too small a scale for any useful inference to be made.

£4 9s. for a farm. In the Middlesex surveys many details occur which point to adaptation of premises, particularly in London, with corresponding variation in values. Thus nine houses in the parish of St. Katherine Cree have been altered to twelve tenements since 1542. Two houses in Old Fish Street were formerly nothing more than a cottage and storehouse, while a tenement in St. Michael's, Crooked Lane, altered into three small tenements, is described as mean and much out of repair, although the rent had risen from 5s. in 1607 to £10 in 1649, when a lease for one year was granted to the tenant. In this instance the division of the house was so contrived that a cobbler had a small shop in one part, a " meal-man " a little shop in another part, while in the back of the building was the kitchen with its divided chamber and garret above, the entire building being no more than 40 by 28 feet. Divisions even of garrets and kitchens are mentioned in connection with a dwelling in Old Fish Street; and the hall is separately indicated in a house at Whitefriars, while the " Glovers' Arms " at Clerkenwell evidently contained both a " shop and a drinking room ". Tenements appear in quite out of the way places, as for example in the back yard of Somerset House. In London a number of " back-houses " are found to adjoin main structures, some having upper rooms added. " Sheds " are measured, with particular values recorded in some cases, having been added as improvements in courtyards and " backsides ", notably at Westminster, where it is clear that they were being used as private dwellings. Here we have evidence of crowded areas in Stuart days. Many of the buildings are measured with exactness, their length and breadth in feet, with the areas given in " poles ". " The Halfmoon," Stepney, a messuage of 3 poles, is valued at £6 per annum, and another messuage at Whitefriars, 20 poles in area has a value of £40. Cottages of £2 and houses of £3 are found at St. Botolph's without Aldgate. The " Nag's Head " at Clerkenwell is declared to be worth £32, while two tenements at Charing Cross, measuring 55 by 12 to 14 feet, were valued at £34 and £40 per annum. Some interesting cases relating to early grants, and later valuations due to conversion of premises, have come to light, the following being noteworthy [1] :—

XLVIII. Valuation of Buildings, 1542–1650.

Grants.	Premises.	Old Rents.	New Values.
1542	St. Katherine Cree : nine houses converted into twelve tenements.	No account ; £145 2s. 8d. later.	£165
1588	Clerkenwell : " Nag's Head " messuage	3s. 4d.	£32
1606	Old Fish Street : one tenement divided into two.	6s. 8d.	£16 10s.
1607	St. Michael, Crooked Lane : one tenement divided into three.	5s.	£10
1616	King's Printing House : a cottage converted.	£4 6s. 8d.	£2

[1] Table XLVIII. The table illustrates the increased rents of premises in London upon the expiration of grants ; Madge, op. cit., pt. i, pp. 298–303.

The leases of 1606 and 1607 were for forty years and had only recently expired : the former provided for a rent of 6s. 8d. with an additional payment of 6s. 8d. for a lamb by way of increase, the premises in this particular case having frontages to the street of from 15 to 21 feet. In the 1616 instance, subsequent conversion into a dwelling has decreased the value of the premises.

The evidence as to valuation of dwellings in Northamptonshire is almost ignored in Mr. Lennard's essay, although for the benefit of students of rural economy he notes the fact that decay of houses had occurred at Hartwell before 1526, and that in 1619 cottages had been newly erected upon the waste at Grafton, Hartwell, and Roade. It may also be added that decayed cottages and other buildings were noted by the surveyors at Chelveston, Grafton (where a tenement of Sir John Wake was found to be " lately burnt " and not since repaired), Higham Park, and Holdenby. New Lodge at Higham owing to its condition was only worth 10s., and at Grafton the surveyors readily allowed £3 10s. 11d. per annum on account of decayed rents. Cottages on the waste occur in various places : three small ones in Foxcote and three others at Aldrington are valued at 10s. in each case ; one at 2s. 6d. and four at 3s. 4d. are mentioned at Grafton, and two more at King's Cliffe are likewise valued at 2s. 6d. and 3s. 4d. each. Cottages other than those erected upon the waste appear to vary from 3s. 4d., as at Grafton and Hartwell, to £2 at Potters Pury, while the recorded range of values for tenements varies in a corresponding manner from 3s. 4d. at King's Cliffe to 40s. at Potters Pury, one group of seven tenements at King's Cliffe having a value of between 3s. 4d. and £1. Messuages not specifically described, though with a few roods of land attached, are considered to be worth from 10s. to £3 5s. at Chelveston and the values mentioned in other places are approximately £2. In a particular instance at Higham Ferrers, one house with 12 acres of land is rented at 7d. only ; in another case, at Kettering, a house with 9 acres has a value of £6. In Kettering, too, houses or shops are worth from 12s. to £1 4s. and even the " Town Barn " has been converted into a dwelling-house, though the schoolhouse is worth no more than 14s. 11d., even with its adjacent dwelling. Three lodges, at Grafton and Higham Park, had values of £7, £13 6s. 4d., and £240, but the third instance includes a considerable quantity of land. The corn mills of Aldrington, Holdenby, and King's Cliffe are worth from £7 to £20. An inn at Holdenby is valued at £2 per annum. The mansion house in the same manor, with 38 acres of land, had a value placed upon it of £103 10s. 4d., but the surveyors thought that its two acres of building land, considered as a " cleared site ", would not be worth more than £1 per annum.

Values in Sussex differ in some cases considerably. Although nine cottages are stated to be worth from 10s. to £3 each, one which is situated on the waste of the manor has a value of £1. The rent of another cottage (which with its orchard measured 189 by 30 to 55 feet) was only fourpence per annum. Various messuages or houses are enumerated and their values range from £1 10s. to £8. The "George" in Pevensey with its rood of ground was estimated to be worth at least £4. Three tenements, indifferently described, vary from 13s. 4d. to £1 10s. in annual value, but one other "now divided into three" is declared to be worth £8 3s. 4d. in consequence. A lodge and 2 roods of land, a mill and a farmhouse have values recorded of £2, £30, and £60 respectively. Three forges or iron mills vary in their values from £27 to £32 ; one of them is a copyhold held by a tenant who pays no more than 8d. The value of ten shops does not exceed £16 1s. in total value. The walls of the old castle at Pevensey, valued merely as so much building material, are worth £40 clear when the cost of pulling them down is considered.[1]

After the annual profits of the manor and the detailed particulars of the premises had been certified with discernment and care, the surveyors were required to turn their attention to the timber standing and growing upon the various estates. Four considerations were to be kept in mind, as the official "method" shows, when recording the values of the timber. First of all, whenever the timber on the demesnes was found to exceed the quantity provided by the "botes" for the maintenance of all the premises, the excess was to be valued and the gross amount inserted (whether the premises were in lease or otherwise) immediately after the particulars recorded of the premises. Next, in regard to copyholds, inquiry was to be made as to the respective rights of the tenant and his lord, the information thus obtained being certified later in the survey among the customs of the manor. The procedure differed, however, in connection with the timber in the parks and upon the commons ; the best method in the former case, so the decision ran, was to value the timber along with the parks, whereas it appeared to be a wiser course to value the timber on heaths, moors, and waste grounds separately and then insert the estimated value after the entry of all leases and copyhold estates. The directions respecting woods and underwoods depended upon whether the premises were in possession or not. The practice followed where woods were actually in possession was simple enough, for the surveyors merely valued the vesture standing upon the premises at a gross amount, and then estimated the value of the soil at so much per acre per annum ; but where leaseholds were concerned the surveyors were advised to value the vesture in accordance with the covenants of the particular lease, and the soil at an amount per annum over and above the rent reserved by the lease. As a final observation, the officials were warned to place all their gross values in the body of the survey, close up to (but not within) the right hand margin. Examples

[1] Lennard, op. cit., pp. 71, 74, 99, 111, 128 ; Madge, op. cit., pt. i, 298–303. Sussex surveys, Nos. 11, 14, 16, 19, 25, 27, 29, 30, 32–6, 38, 39, 47.

occur in the "precedent" which are intended to illustrate these directions. We learn, therefore, that the timber of Sale manor in Surrey, clear of necessary botes, was not worth more than £15 ; that the timber trees in Sale Park, 4,500 in number, were valued at £900, or 4s. each on the average, and that the navy claimed 1,650 other trees in the park for shipbuilding ; and finally that the vesture of a coppice, 90 acres in extent, was worth 25s. an acre, or £112 10s. in all.

Some Middlesex figures may be quoted in regard to the values assigned to timber. At Halliford, the surveyors found upwards of 500 small elm trees worth £58 11s., but as this was not sufficient to " maintayne ye Bootes " they were left out of the account. At Chelsea there was no timber. At Edmonton the timber on the waste consisted of 217 trees of oak, elm, ash, and walnut ; as these were valued at £140, the average was just under 13s. per tree compared with 2s. 4d. at Halliford. In Enfield Park there were 7,093 trees of oak and hornbeam, many of great age and some of great size, and in addition there was an unspecified number of small trees of hornbeam, whitethorn, and maple ; the entire value is placed at £1,762 2s. 6d., quite apart from 397 timber trees marked for the use of the navy and accordingly not valued in the schedule. The average values were 1s. 6d. for lopped pollards of hornbeam, and 3s. for old oak dotterels ; but as fifty-four trees standing in Hamers Wood Grove were valued at 3s. per tree, the amount recorded of £7 2s. shows an over valuation amounting to £1. Old oak trees are said to be worth 13s. 4d. each, but the survey mentions 225 " great old oaken trees " that possessed an average value of £2. Taking the values of trees as a whole the average does not exceed 4s. 6d. The three lodges of Enfield Chase, moreover, had 1,470 trees worth £284 2s. ; these consisted of oak and beech trees of various sizes, some newly planted ash trees, and with these were a number of maples and thorns. One great oak tree was worth £5, but the average value of the trees appears to be about 4s.

In Enfield Chase, twice valued within eight years, there were in 1650 no less than 2,500 timber trees worth £1 each, with others not here valued because they were reserved for naval needs ; trees of smaller size and value, such as hornbeams, were given a total value of £12,500. Eight years later, when the value of the wood is said to be £2,254 12s., the timber trees were valued as a whole at £6,979 12s. The trees on the waste of the manor in 1650 were small in size and only worth £13. At Hampton Court, likewise surveyed on two occasions, we find 635 trees, chiefly of oak and elm, worth £218 15s. 8d. in 1650, but most of these were discovered to be on the waste lands. Three years later, the combined value of the wood and an unspecified number of trees amounted to £1,203 5s. In the case of Highbury Woods and Little St. John's Wood a note states that the value of the soil is estimated on the basis of improvement " by ploughing and stocking up and converting into tillage ". Here the trees, numbering 371, were worth £148 8*s.* or an average of 8*s.* each. But many more trees, reserved under the terms of the lease, existed at Great St. John's Wood, no less than 2,000 being surveyed at an average price of 4*s.* each; the underwoods, however, in this case had suffered much damage during the raids of Londoners at the time of the great scarcity of coal in 1644 and 1645. Lastly we find 1,446 trees growing in Twickenham manor and 221 more upon an estate later known as Orleans House, but whereas there was sufficient timber in the manor to provide for the necessary botes, and even to give an excess worth about £50, in the smaller estate the whole of the value of £55 was absorbed in making provision for the maintenance of the premises, so that, as at Halliford, the surveyors were unable to add anything to the account from this source. The whole extent of separately measured woodland in the surveys of rural Middlesex does not appear to have exceeded 589 acres, and this was worth on the average 7*s.* 9*d.* per acre, the lowest value recorded being 6*s.* and the highest 16*s.* 8*d.*[1]

In Northamptonshire most of the wood grounds lay very naturally in the manors adjacent to the three forests of Rockingham, Salcey, and Whittlebury. At Grafton the separately measured portion consisted of 88 acres in 1650, and in the survey of 1526 the proportion formed 6 per cent of the total. Mr. Lennard calculates the area of woodland in the surveys of that county at 957 acres; this would form 6 per cent of the whole area surveyed, compared with a little over 5 per cent in the case of Middlesex, but as he does not state the value of this land the average per acre cannot be calculated. With the two exceptions of Higham Park and Holdenby, where he mentions the number of trees but not their values, Mr. Lennard has nothing whatever to say concerning the timber on the various estates. Yet the evidence is plentiful and easily procured. Taking the surveys in which such valuations occur, twenty-one in all, and excluding only the entries relating to waste, the amount recorded for timber and other trees such as ash and willows, also decayed trees, underwoods, and vesture, is found to be as follows [2]:—

XLIX. VALUATION OF NORTHAMPTONSHIRE TIMBER

Values.	No. of Surveys.	No. of Trees.	Total Amount. £
Under £10 .	1	22	5·5
£10–£50 .	5	268	82·0
£51–£100 .	2	280	133·6
£101–£500 .	7	865	1,685·6
£501–£1,000 .	2	3,754	1,490·0
Above £1,000	4	6,964	12,378·5
Totals .	21	12,153	£15,775·2

[1] *Jacob's Law Dictionary*, art. Bote; "Method," f. 4; "Precedent," ff. 4, 6, 7; Madge, op. cit., pt. ii, pp. 416, 428, 433, 455, 435-6, 440, 444, 447-9, 452-3.
[2] Table XLIX is compiled from the following Northamptonshire surveys, Nos. 15-20, 23, 25, 26, 28, 29, 33-5, 39-41, 43, 46, 48, 49. Mr. Lennard is silent on the subject of Forestry, but he has mentioned some of the woodlands; see his index, p. 135.

COLONEL WHALLEY'S REGIMENTAL CONTRACTS :
LETTER OF ATTORNEY, 1649

The entire range of values for these surveys extends from £6 or a little under to more than £4,980. Two special cases of waste committed by tenants occur in the surveys, one of them being at Holdenby, where the damage is assessed at £7, and the other at Brigstock, the amount in that case being £2 less. The trees are not always indicated by name, for although " timber trees " constantly occur, only seventy-nine willows and eighteen ash trees appear to be separately recorded and these are at Chelveston. Nor are the values of the trees always given apart from underwoods and vestures, but of the 12,153 mentioned, 8,359 can be isolated and their value placed at £4,204 19s. 11d. This would give an average value of 10s. for each tree, taking one sort with another throughout the county, but the highest value of all is found at Holdenby where 376 timber trees in the spinneys are declared to be worth £403 12s., whereas 2,817 in the park are only valued at £1,010 5s. At Higham Park 1,134 timber trees are valued in gross at £510 6s., but there are 2,193 others described as " old decayed trees " with a further value of £1,644 15s., making a total for them all of over £2,150.

Of the Sussex valuations of woodland and timber much might be written, but the evidence points unmistakably to the great destruction wrought for years past in Ashdown Forest. If we exclude the area of Lancaster Great Park as surveyed in 1650, only a single acre of woodland separately measured appears in the surveys of this county. Some of the surveys speak of " small store of wood " or of " no timber of any sort " ; many refer to the fact that the timber is of " little worth but for firing " or for making charcoal; others again mention that there has been " much spoil and destruction ". In the survey of the forges or iron mills of the dis-afforested region of St. Leonards reference is made to the very great destruction of wood since the grants of 1601 and 1631 had been made ; but the surveyors add that in their opinion " there is sufficient coppice wood yet remaining to make good the said coals and woods if well preserved ". Their valuations include £8 5s. for thirty cords of wood to be taken out of the forest for the use of the forges, and £202 1s. 8d. in a second case for 250 loads of charcoal for a year's supply under average conditions. If we examine twenty-one of the surveys which contain references to timber we may note over thirty valuations for Sussex which may be classified as follows [1]:—

L. VALUATION OF SUSSEX TIMBER

Values.	Valuations.	No. of Trees.	Total Amount. £
Under £10 .	6	86	30·2
£10–£50 .	15	1,957	325·0
£51–£100 .	8	750	667·5
Above £100	4	800	840·0
Totals .	33	3,593	£1,862·7

[1] Table L. This records the results arrived at from the analysis of twenty-one Sussex surveys, viz. Nos. 10, 12, 13, 15–18, 21, 22, 26, 27, 31, 34–6, 38, 39, 45, 47, 48, 51.

In this county the value of wood ranged from £1 13*s*. 4*d*. to £490, excluding the amount of £600 for Lancaster Great Park in 1650 owing to the re-valuation in the later surveys of 1658. In eighteen instances where the number of trees is given as well as their values, these vary from five to 2,657, though the different sorts are rarely indicated. The averages likewise vary in the different surveys, being as low as 1*s*. 8*d*. per tree at Ashley Mills in Ashdown Forest, 2*s*. 3*d*. in one case at Chesworth House, 3*s*. to 3*s*. 8*d*. at Bexley, Horsham and the so-called Sedgwick Park, 4*s*. in two instances at Chesworth (where 200 trees are worth £40), and at the highest value of all, namely 5*s*. at Pevensey, where on the demesne lands fifteen oaks, four elms, and three ash trees exactly total £5 10*s*. As the total value recorded for 3,593 trees, apart from underwoods, is £620 13*s*. 4*d*. the average, taking one kind of tree with another, is thus seen to be 3*s*. 5*d*. for the timber on the Crown lands in the county of Sussex.

The annual profits of the manor and the valuation both of premises and timber having been certified in accordance with the " method ", supplemented by the instructions recorded in the " precedent ", the surveyors next turned their attention to the question of the reprises associated with the premises. Here they were reminded of the necessity of recording, either in full or by means of complete abstracts, all patents granted to manorial officers, so as to show precisely what their fees were and whether they were charged upon manors, lands, or tenements. Two alternatives were permitted in practice. The surveyors might make their returns of such patents either in conjunction with particular manors or lands, or " in capite or chiefest of those manors ", where several were jointly answerable for the recorded fee ; but in either case they were to take the greatest care not to return the same patent twice. Two other considerations were to be borne in mind : several patents might show fees chargeable upon the same manor, and such fees again might relate to several manors. In the former case all the patents were to be returned with the survey of the manor in question, and in the latter they were to be entered along with all other reprises so that the statements relating to deductions might in every case be complete. It followed, therefore, that the reprises for the patents were to come first, and that all others of a general or particular character relating to the premises were to follow next. The surveyors were urged to be diligent in their inquiries concerning such matters in order to leave nothing uncertified in regard to patents, annuities, boons, rents resolute, or encumbrances of any kind. These directions, clear enough in themselves, find illustration in the " precedent " relating to the manor of Sale. There the chief ranger, " Sir Jockie Begwell, of Holdfast, Knight ", held his office for life by virtue of letters patent supposed to date from 10th September, 1617. He is allowed 40 marks for life, with the disposal of the lodge and rights of pasture in the park for two geldings, a mare, and six cows. Timothy Stout, the under-keeper, holds his position for the lives of himself and his son Thomas by letters patent dated 1st November, 1637. In his case he has a fee of 2*d.* a day with a tenement for habitation and a yearly robe worth 13*s.* 4*d.* ; he also has rights in the park which permit the running of horse or mare and the keeping of two cows. Isaac Trym, house-keeper and gardener, also produces his patent, showing that he holds his office for life as from 30th April, 1611, receiving an annual fee of £4 11*s.* 3*d.* with a couple of robes worth yearly 30*s.* He makes a claim for the profits arising out of the orchard and gardens ; this is acknow-ledged for the years in which the court is not kept there. A further claim he brings, namely, the right to the crop of Silver Mead ; but this is limited to the " after feed ", for the first crop is admitted to have been allowed usually for the " wintering of deer in the park ". Trym is still alive and is aged 63, and so are Stout and his son, the father being 47, but the son 25 years younger. As for Sir Jockie Begwell the surveyors declare that he has fled to Scotland leaving Jn. Cavy to " carry on ". All these claims by way of patent are minutely examined and the various fees and profits are estimated on the basis of a series of years, so that Begwell's office is declared to be worth £46 13*s.* 4*d.*, and the other two £10 and £16 10*s.* respectively. Some alleged reprises, however, are disallowed. No reprise is granted for several indicated offices, because the various doorkeepers, alley-keepers and the like are unable to produce any grant ; the surveyors, therefore, decide that such officials merely hold their posts at the pleasure of the lord, and when the victims plead that their chief livelihood lies therein, the surveyors reply that they leave the matter " to better judgment ". Andrew Wayter believes himself entitled to the reversion of the place and profit belonging to Sir Jockie Begwell, but as he proves nothing in regard to his title, this matter likewise is deferred. Finally the surveyors admit their inability to make any reprise whatsoever for the cost of fencing or keeping up the pale of the park, because they have valued the premises not in relation to their present condition, but in the light of future improvement, and in such case the fences of the park would clearly not be required. Various reprises are mentioned, but without values being given, for the bailiff in one case, six almsmen and four women in another; also, an annuity, a conduit pipe, causeway, and several bridges. Other deductions include 12*s.* for two loads of wood for the use of the bailiff and 16*s.* for the forecrop of an acre of ground for the reeve, 13*s.* 4*d.* for the hayward, £1 10*s.* in connection with a rent reserved, and £2 2*s.* as reprise to the Vicar of Sale on account of his right to run a horse, gelding, or mare in the lord's pasture yearly.

The Parliamentary Surveys of the various counties provide numerous illustrations of the deductions permitted by the surveyors :

their variety may be seen from the examples given in the list recorded below [1]:—

LI. Reprises Allowed by Surveyors

Surveys.	Reprises.	Values. £ s. d.
Bedford, No. 16	Ancient fee of Steward	1 6 8
Berks, No. 11	The Reeve for gathering Rents	2 0 0
Bucks, No. 16 .	A portion of forest lands	20 0 0
Cambridge, No. 1	The Bailiff's fee during pleasure . . .	2 0 0
Cheshire, No. 12	Stipend of the Constable	6 13 4
Cornwall, No. 38	Decay of rents, reparations of passage boats, etc.	20 0 0
Cumberland, No. 5	Four foresters or rangers	6 8
Devon, No. 6B	Court keeper's fee at pleasure	5 0 0
Dorset, No. 5	Reeve's allowance at the audit	13 4
Essex, No. 14	Beadle's fee for collecting rents . . .	11 3
Gloucester, No. 21	Two cottages in the Forest of Dean pulled down	17 6
Hampshire, No. 18	Commonage for 20 cows and a bull . . .	13 6 8
Hertford, No. 24	The Jury's dinner at the Court Baron or 1s. in lieu thereof	12 0
Kent, No. 56 .	The upkeep of Thames Wall	13 13 4
Lancashire, No. 8	Porter or Keeper's fee for the gaol or castle of Clitheroe	3 0 8
Leicester, No. 7	Mowers, haymakers, and carters and the " pollster "	16 0
Lincoln, No. 5	Repair of the Pound	4 0
Middlesex, No. 16	Edmonton bridges and common pound . .	5 3 6
Norfolk, No. 16	Charge of maintaining seawalls distributed among three tenants	209 11 8
Northants, No. 22	Decayed rents	3 10 11
Nottingham, No. 13 .	Repair of Trent Banks	13 4
Oxford, No. 10	Commonage for the Cowgate of 70 cows . .	3 10 0
Stafford, No. 38	Steward's fee at pleasure of Parliament . .	1 4 0
Suffolk, No. 15	Repair of Causeway and five timber bridges .	4 0 0
Surrey, No. 72	Dinner for the Steward and landowners . .	5 0 0
Sussex, No. 18 .	Repair of a wooden bridge near Horsham . .	6 8
Warwick, No. 31	Tenants' dinner at the Court of Killingworth .	4 0
Westmorland, No. 1	The Keeper of the Chase as his fee . . .	2 13 4
Wilts, No. 26 .	Allowance for waste and spoils in four divisions of Clarendon Park	500 0 0
Worcester, No. 7	Schoolmaster of the free school as stipend . .	10 0 0
York, No. 23 .	Repair of wall or bank of River Humber . .	20 0 0

At Halliford, Middlesex, no reprises were found to be necessary. Some of the usual payments at Edmonton were disallowed, namely those relating to the steward's fee of 40s. for keeping the courts every Whit Tuesday, and the expenditure of £5 on the court dinner by the bailiff. At Enfield under a grant of 29th July, 1622, thirty loads of " fee wood " were allowed to various officials, besides payments of £6 1s. 8d. to the Keepers of the three lodges, £9 2s. 6d. to the ranger, £5 to the steward, 5 marks to the bailiff, and a fee in addition to fire-wood of 4d. a day to the woodward. In connection with the park trackway at Marylebone the surveyors were authorized by an order of the Committee for Obstructions to make a deduction of £6 17s. 6d. at the approximate rate of 26s. 8d. per acre.

[1] Table LI gives a list of reprises allowed by the surveyors in different counties of England. In Cumberland, No. 5, the Earl of Northumberland's office of " bowbearer of the park " was considered to be useless and his fee of £3 0s. 10d. was therefore disallowed.

Nothing is stated by Mr. Lennard in regard to the reprises of Northamptonshire. However, at Grafton and Greens Norton, in addition to the allowance for decayed rents three deductions were permitted for the bailiffs' fees, the amounts varying from £1 10s. to £2 13s. 4d. At Grafton, too, there belonged to the lord a small cottage with an acre of meadow which was given according to custom to the town haywards, so that an allowance of £1 4s. per annum was readily made in this case.

In Sussex few reprises are mentioned, and with one exception the amounts are small, but they illustrate the permissibility of deductions being allowed for five kinds of charges, namely, those in connection with (1) charity, as seen in the payment of a rent of 3s. 4d. said to be due to the poor of Cliffe, near Lewes, (2) public premises, as in the case of those charged with the office of headborough every fourth year at Horsham, declared to be worth 13s. 4d. per annum on the average ; (3) communications, as at Newbridge near Horsham, where charges amounting to 6s. 8d. per annum, taking one year with another, were made to cover the cost of repairing " a wooden bridge and some gutter lugges " ; (4) covenants, mentioned in two cases in reference to maintenance of premises, the average value of the house, fire and other botes being calculated in one case at £8 and in a second instance at £2 more ; and (5) official profits, indicated at Duddleswell manor, where the value to six keepers of as many walks in the park and just as many lodges and lands is stated to amount to £54 6s. 4d., but a claim for an allowance for deer is refused in this instance. One special entry at Chesworth indicates the value over a series of years of " convenient entertainment for the steward and his servants for meat drink and lodging, and provision for their horses " during two days every year, so £1 10s. per annum is thought to be quite a reasonable amount to claim for such a recognized custom. But the claim is rejected in the section devoted to reprises, the Surveyor-General observing that this item should not be valued here, but " charged by way of addition to some rent " paid by the lessor.[1]

After the recital of the patents and the decision in regard to reprises, the surveyors were advised by the " Method " to carefully weigh the evidence forthcoming as a result of their inquiries concerning the following special matters :—

(1) What are the customs of the manor now being surveyed ?

(2) What moors, commons, and waste grounds lie within it ?

(3) How is it bounded ?

(4) What are the chief matters that concern the manor in general ?

[1] " Method," f. 4 ; " Precedent," ff. 6–8, 18 ; Madge, op. cit., pt. ii, pp. 429, 439, 449. The surveys quoted are Northants, Nos. 20, 22, 26 ; and Sussex, Nos. 18, 24, 26 36, 48B.

The results of these inquiries were to be set down in the order shown, the surveyors taking care to certify as many of the customs as were of chief concern, then the names and situation of the common lands and the boundaries of the manor if they were " clearly and notoriously known " but not otherwise, for " if dubiously given you, it were better be silent therein ". As to the memoranda concerning the manor in general a variety of matters might be recorded as a result of inquiries, but these were left to the discretion of the surveyors. In one important direction guidance was definite and deliberate, namely in connection with the heriots and benefit of commonage, or common of pasture. When these were included in the values of premises belonging to copyhold tenants for lives, the surveyors were to certify to that effect among the memoranda at the end of the survey ; on the other hand, when they were not so included their values were to be separately certified among the perquisites and royalties at the beginning of the survey. It is therefore clear that Mr. Lennard is in error when he writes : " another doubt envelops the statistics because it is impossible to know whether the manors surveyed included large common pastures in addition to the lands which are measured and described. In some cases, as for example in the principal survey of Grafton, we are definitely told that the value of common rights was included in the value of the several holdings, so that this uncertainty really attaches to the values of the various kinds of land as well as to the proportion obtaining between them. It is therefore far from easy to use the figures as a basis for comparison." But at Grafton, as else-where, the surveyors were acting upon their instructions, and when they wrote their note among the memoranda at the end of the survey, certifying that " The Benefit of Common, Common of Pasture and sheep walks to each of their several tenements belonging are compre-hended within the values of their Respective Holds ", they put in practice their first rule. This procedure was of course unknown to Mr. Lennard who therefore missed its significance, and moreover he failed to notice the operation of the second rule through ignoring most persistently the fines, perquisites and royalties recorded in the early part of the manorial surveys. Mr. Lennard's doubts in this direction may now be dispersed, because after all we do definitely know whether rights of common are included or not, and with the removal of this uncertainty it is less difficult to use his figures as a basis for comparison.

In the survey of one manor in Lancashire the surveyors confessed that they were unable to " certify anything by way of memorandum " concerning the commons and waste lands as well as the " benefits of commonage " or common of pasture " and such like " because all these things had passed away from the premises by a grant made in 1640. In another instance, this time in Lincolnshire, the surveyors certified that " benefit of commons and common of pasture " had been included in the improved values of the leasehold and copyhold tenants. In

Norfolk it is stated that "the Lord of the Manor as Lord of the Manor of West Walton" had the commonage of 200 sheep and twenty-four great beasts upon the fens and droves, and that this right of common was "valued in the Lord's" estate. In Surrey a long list of moors and commons is recorded in one of the surveys, two of the commons measuring 100 acres each. Sussex surveys have a number of references to common and waste ground : one called Prestridge is most precisely butted and bounded, its 417 acres being valued at £73. Sheepwalks, feedings for cows and pannage of hogs are valued at from £1 to £40 in this county, while the proportions of common allowed for cattle of tenants in Ashdown Forest are worked out in a most remarkable manner in the survey of Lancaster Great Park in 1650. In this survey the cattle belonging to nine parishes are apportioned at the rate of 1 acre 2 roods 20 poles for each animal, the entire area of 4,522 acres being divided up for the use of 2,783 cattle belonging to the various proprietors. The largest share belongs to John, Earl of Thanet who is allowed 162 acres for his total of 100 cattle.[1]

Upon the subject of manorial customs a separate book might be written, so great is the wealth of information disclosed by the Parliamentary Surveyors. In the "Precedent" the Surveyor-General considers only three cases for the guidance of the officials. One of these relates to the payment by freeholders of the manor of Sale of 4d. by way of "relief upon descent" ; the second concerns the fine paid by copyholders, one year's rent of assize being demanded for alienation or descent ; and the third deals with the issues connected with alienation or descent of copyholders, a uniform rate being recorded of 1s. for every acre of arable, 1s. 8d. for meadow land, 2s. for a tenement, and 3s. 4d. for each messuage. Many instances of customs relating to Middlesex have been published and some for Northamptonshire have been noticed by Mr. Lennard. At Kingscliffe, for example, copyholders held by fine certain, paying 2d. an acre for all kinds of lands, and half a year's rent for their cottages ; they possessed the right to cut down trees, and their estates descended from the father to the eldest son, with the possibility of equal division among the daughters. At Brigstock 4s. was paid as fine for every house alienated, and provision was made in this manor for the inheritance of youngest sons. The customs of Edmonton and Enfield manors are set out at length ;

---

[1] "Method," ff. 4–5 ; "Precedent," f. 20, but f. 19 appears to be missing, and this may have contained the manorial customs and other memoranda ; also ff. 14–15, now missing, may have referred to timber and some of the leases. Lennard, op. cit., p. 125. Middlesex customs and memoranda will be found in Madge, op. cit., pt. ii, pp. 428–9, 436–7, 451. The surveys quoted are : Northants, No. 16, f. 37 ; No. 20, f. 98 ; No. 29, f. 47 ; No. 40, f. 18. Lancashire, No. 7, f. 8. Lincoln, No. 5, f. 74. Norfolk, No. 18, ff. 8–9. Surrey, No. 38, ff. 13–14. Sussex, Nos. 10–17, 20, 26, 27, 30, 39, 47. The cattle belonging to 219 proprietors mentioned in Sussex, No. 26, were methodically apportioned in Ashdown Forest : although 75 owners possessed less than five cattle, 54 had from six to ten each, 86 from eleven to fifty, and the remaining four proprietors had from fifty-one to a hundred.

in the former case when copyholders die intestate the lands and tenements descend to the youngest sons, according to ancient usage, whereas in the neighbouring manor of Enfield as well as at Twickenham the alternative practice of succession in the line of eldest sons prevails.

In Sussex the Courts were variously named. There is the Court of the hundred of Aldwick for instance, where fines and amerciaments of defaulters are collected and felons' goods seized. The Court Baron of Chesworth could only be held yearly at the will of the lord, and in actual fact no court had been kept since 1623, to the detriment of the lord in respect to royalties, privileges, profits and the perquisites of courts. Courts leet for Younsmere and Old Shoreham are mentioned, the constable presiding over the former and the bailiff acting as reeve in the latter when his second year of office came round. In the Duchy of Lancaster lands Aveshold, Swainmote and Woodmote courts were yearly held, the tenants at the first of these courts paying a halfpenny for a bullock and a penny for each horse grazing in Ashdown forest. The Three Weeks Court held for the various hundreds as well as the Duchy lands was continued at the periodic intervals indicated for the trial of actions under 40s.; that belonging to the hundred of Manhood was usually held at the Bishop of Chichester's palace, but the jurisdiction of the court at Endlewick had of late been greatly infringed by the sheriff and his officers. Two claims by tenants of manors may be noticed. At Duddleswell the copyholders held by the custom of succession of eldest sons or eldest daughters. At Old Shoreham the tenants claimed the privilege of being free not only from service at assizes or sessions, but from all tolls at fairs and markets in the county.

Among the customary services mentioned in one of the surveys of Westmorland it was stated that every tenant from the age of 16 to 60 ought to be " in their just defensible array for the warrs ready to serve their Prince upon horseback and foot at the West borders of England " adjacent to Scotland, entirely at their own cost, always being ready " night and day at the Commandment of the Lord Warden of the said West marshes ". Warning was to be given by " Beacon fire, Post or Proclamation ", and tenants were to continue in this service as long as the Warden should desire.[1]

Next in succession to the memoranda relating to manors comes the rental of freeholders, copyholders, and customary tenants, although the " Method " permitted the surveyors to use their discretion as to whether they were to be inserted in the survey or not; but it was a necessary condition that whenever such lists did appear the total value should correspond with the several sums certified earlier in the

[1] " Method," f. 5 ; " Precedent," f. 20 ; Lennard, op. cit., pp. 96–7, 110, 111, 113–14 116–17, 119 ; Madge, op. cit., pt. ii, pp. 428–9, 436–7, 451. See the surveys of Sussex, Nos. 1, 3, 6, 23, 26–8, 39, 42, 50 ; and Westm., No. 5, f. 6.

survey. Rentals therefore are somewhat exceptional, and sometimes they are followed by the certification of leases, especially where the entire manor is leased to a subsidiary lord for a term of years or lives. But the " Precedent " does not illustrate either of these features, so it can hardly be said that they were essential, though the wording of the " Method " in regard to the leases was certainly of a less permissive character.

When rentals are given the individual amounts are generally seen to be very small. Thus in five surveys of Berkshire, the combined rentals of which amount to £138 8s. 6¼d., there are no less than 337 items recorded, only fifty-one of which relate to copyholders. Of this total ninety-nine freehold and eight copyhold rents are less than 1s. in amount, and only fifteen rents exceed £2. Of the rents in Northamptonshire unfortunately little can be gleaned from Mr. Lennard's account. The survey of Grafton, however, shows that out of thirty-five items twenty-one are less than a shilling, and the entire rental does not exceed £2 6s. 3d. The free-rents of Hanslope are only 7s. 6d., the lowest being 4d. and the highest 2s. 2d. Similarly the free rents of Hartwell range from 2d. to 3s., and one of the nine items is " a redd rose ". The quit rents of Greens Norton number sixty-five, and of these twenty-eight are less than 1s. and the largest amount paid is only £5. At Higham Ferrers the range of seventeen freehold rents is from 4d. to £2 4s. 1d., while seven copyhold rents are recorded between a halfpenny and 13s. 4½d. A red rose also occurs at Potterspury and a needle at Pury. The rental of copyholders of Little Weldon manor is elaborately set out in five columns of figures, yet the items only range from 6d. to £1 6s. with a total of £14 17s. 8d., and of the thirty-six rents recorded one-third are less than 2s. in amount.

In Middlesex the tenants of the Manor of Halliford are entirely freeholders. The rents were mostly small varying from 4d. to £2 13s. 4d., the average being 8s. 9d. in Lower Halliford and 5s. 6d. in Upper Halliford. In the Edmonton survey the rental is arranged according to wards, the total amount involved being £84 14s. 6d. of which £7 13s. represents the freeholders' portion. The total number of items is 165, of which the copyholders claim ninety-one, but the range of the rents recorded is most remarkable for there are fifty-nine separate amounts, no two being alike in the majority of cases, extending from a minimum of 1d. to a maximum of 18s. 4d. The rental which accompanies the survey of Enfield manor contains only four items less, and of these fifty refer to freeholds, while sixty-seven and thirty-five others concern old and new copyholds respectively. In this manor the range extends from a halfpenny to 37s. 7d. Here again there are no less than sixty different amounts, but the majority are less than 1s., and indeed only thirty-one items in the rental exceed half a crown. The rental attached to Hampton Court mentions only eight freeholds and fifty-six copyholds, making sixty-four holdings distributed among fifty-four families, the variation in this manor being greater, namely, from 1*d.* to £3 0*s.* 6*d.* At Twickenham the surveyors discovered thirteen freehold and thirty-six copyhold rents, held by forty-four families ; the total is £10 0*s.* 6*d.*, made up of thirty-two distinct amounts which range from 1*d.* to £2 15*s.* 2*d.* There were six payments of 6*d.* each and five at 2*s.* 6*d.*, although twenty-one payments were for smaller amounts than a shilling.

In Sussex the rentals are few but they are complicated, for those of Lancaster Great Park and Duddleswell are in part duplicated, and others relating to Pevensey involve portreeve service and tallages, while two further rentals concerning Sharenden and Combe concern Church lands and are out of place here. The following particulars emerge, however, from a comparison of these lists [1]:—

LII. RENTS IN SUSSEX

Survey.	Rents.	Items.	Amount. £ s. d.	Range.
No. 23	Tenants . .	64	5 7 6	1*d.* to 6*s.* 8*d.*
,, 27	Freehold . .	6	6 4½	4*d.* to 2*s.* 4*d.*
,, 27	Copyhold . .	69	2 19 6	1*d.* to 10*s.*
,, 28	Free suitors .	6	13 6	1*s.* to 2*s.* 6*d.*
,, 39	Portreeve service	108	19 6 11¾	¾*d.* to 19*s.* 9½*d.*
	Totals . .	253	£28 13 10¼	¾*d.* to 19*s.* 9½*d.*

In No. 39 there are additional entries relating to burgage tenures. Of the sixty-two tenants distinctly described at Pevensey, eighteen are recorded as gentlemen, eleven as yeomen and seven as esquires. Once again we find the yeomen relatively unimportant.[2] The total payments made in that manor are for premises which include 2,657 acres of land and forty-two messuages with their orchards, gardens, crofts and tofts.

An examination of the rentals recorded for twenty-three counties, taking one survey from each at random, reveals results that are incorporated in the table below—from which it appears that out of 3,135 rents examined the proportion of freehold rents is almost exactly a quarter ; but on the other hand their average rent, which comes to 5*s.* 1*d.*, is as much as 2*s.* 10*d.* below that of the copyholders. Moreover, 29 per cent of the total rents are less than 1*s.* and only 9 per cent exceed £1.[3]

[1] Table LII. The rents contained in this table have been collected from Sussex, Nos. 23, 27, 28, 39. The rentals of Sussex are very few in number, and the amounts are usually very small.

[2] They form about 17 per cent in this instance.

[3] Table LIII. "Method," f. 5. The "Precedent" rental is missing. See the surveys referred to, viz. Berks, Nos. 11, 14, 17, 23, 29 ; Northants, Nos. 20, 26, 32, 40, 43, 46, 48. Sussex, Nos. 23, 26–8, 39, 49 ; also the various surveys included in this table, and numbered as follows : Berks, P.S., No. 14 ; Bucks, 12 ; Camb., 7 ; Corn., 25 ; Derby, 28 ; Dors., 5 ; Ex., 14 ; Herts, 21 ; Hunts, 4 ; Lancs., 18 ; Leic., 7 ; Linc., 6 ; Mx., 16 ; Northants, 32 ; Notts, 19 ; Som., 16 ; Surr., 33 ; Sx., 27 ; Warw., 1 ; Westm., 5 ; Wilts, 40 ; York, 17 ; Monm., No. 1. See also for Middlesex, Madge, op. cit., pt. ii, pp. 421–2, 430–1, 440–1, 445, 451. The rents of Freeholders and Copyholders are distinguished in the table.

LIII. Manorial Rentals Classified

Areas	Counties	Freehold Rents		Copyhold Rents		Below 1s.	Above £1
		No.	Amount	No.	Amount		
(i) Metropolitan	7	325	£ 86·6	888	£ 346·9	453	91
(ii) Extra-Metropolitan	11	211	62·7	666	307·6	225	96
(iii) Borderlands	4	224	48·6	715	252·5	193	83
(iv) Wales	1	22	2·4	84	22·5	39	5
Totals	23	782	200·3	2,353	929·5	910	275

The details of these various rents, recorded in the selected surveys, can be examined more closely when arranged under counties. Freeholders are absent in one case and copyholders in another. In every instance, save one, the majority of rents are below £1.

LIIIA. Manorial Rentals in Counties

Surveys.	No. of Rents.		Amounts.		Below 1s.	Above £1
	F.	C.	F. £	C. £		
Berks, No. 14	132	11	51·4	1·8	41	15
Bucks, No. 12	13	—	4·0	—	3	1
Camb., No. 7	—	117	—	44·2	32	3
Cornwall, No. 25	30	101	3·4	3·3	20	—
Derby, No. 28	33	71	4·9	13·3	47	2
Dorset, No. 5	9	77	15·4	49·7	11	22
Essex, No. 14	74	361	10·0	77·6	180	11
Hertford, No. 21	24	293	13·2	176·7	96	63
Hunts, No. 4	6	89	1·9	36·4	37	13
Lancs., No. 18	50	324	4·6	95·8	96	19
Leics., No. 7	6	46	0·7	22·9	6	8
Lincoln, No. 6	91	58	18·2	41·7	39	17
Middx, No. 16	74	91	7·6	77·1	63	—
Northants, No. 32	22	7	7·8	1·2	8	2
Notts, No. 19	18	14	6·6	4·3	8	4
Somers., No. 16	1	59	0·1	40·6	3	11
Surrey, No. 33	2	63	0·1	10·7	20	1
Sussex, No. 27	6	69	0·3	3·0	50	—
Warwick, No. 12A	16	33	3·2	17·3	2	4
Westm., No. 5	46	255	12·3	130·6	56	50
Wilts, No. 40	9	95	3·9	36·0	32	10
Yorks, No. 17	98	35	28·3	22·8	21	14
Monmouth No. 1	22	84	2·4	22·5	39	5
Totals	782	2,353	200·3	929·5	910	275

Lastly come the summary statements or " abstracts " recorded at the end of each survey, the surveyors being directed by the " Method " to show in their return " an abstract of the whole survey in the point of values ", taking all possible care to make the statement plain, usually in a single sheet, and avoiding all mixing of rents and confounding of improvements. This abstract is illustrated, so far as its form is concerned (though without any values being given), in the official " Precedent " where it is set out in three parts, the first showing the total of present profits per annum—derived from rents of assize and royalties, the demesnes in possession, the reserved rents upon the leaseholds, and the rents of copyholders for lives—the second giving the total of future improvements arising from premises in the hands of leaseholders and copyholders, and the third section stating not only the amount of the materials of the manor house and other things in gross, but the value in " present money " of the wood, underwoods and timber in present possession of the lord of the manor, and the value also of the timber upon the demesne lands not granted by virtue of any lease. In Sussex no less than twenty-one of the surveys record the total area surveyed as well as the computed values, so that a complete record is available for the Crown lands of that county within the short compass provided by means of these abstracts. One example, taken from the survey of the manor of Old Shoreham, will suffice to show the nature of these short statements :—

LIII*B*. Abstract of Old Shoreham Manor

	£	s.	d.
(1) The present rent of the Manor per ann.	5	9	0
(2) The improvement per ann. . . .	1	16	8
(3) The value of the ferry per ann. . .	15	0	0
(4) Total of annual values . . .	£22	5	8

The premises, which were discovered by John Urlin, are stated to be in the possession of the trustees. Signatures of five of the surveyors then follow with a note that this survey was " perfected ye 11th of November 1651 ", and the Surveyor-General's endorsement then brings the record to a close.[1]

---

[1] " Method," f. 5, which is illustrated in the " Precedent " but without any values being assigned to the items. Sussex surveys include twenty-one with areas recorded in the abstracts. Old Shoreham survey is recorded in Sussex, No. 50.

PART IV

THE PARLIAMENTARY SALES OF CROWN LANDS

CHAPTER I

THE RECORDS OF LAND SALES

We have now considered the policy of the Commonwealth Government in regard to sequestration and sale of the various types of estates acquired in the moment of victory. In the course of our inquiry concerning the fate of the Crown lands we have traced their origin, discussed their development, examined at some length their specialized characteristics, as well as the early Exchequer methods of accountancy and the Parliamentary legislation of later days. As a result of this investigation we have discovered that, instead of confiscation taking place, national ownership of Crown lands and rents became more pronounced under the new phase, until at last the rigid control of Parliament over the State lands ceased and the royal estates were surveyed, valued, offered for sale, and dispersed. The doctrine of political necessity had triumphed.

Under the special legislation of this period, due to the extreme urgency of the financial situation of the new government, surveys of an elaborate and accurate character were necessary before the Crown lands could be exposed to sale, and, as we have already seen, the county surveyors were greatly aided in their task of valuation by the " Instructions for Method " and the " Precedent Survey ", both specially prepared for their guidance, so that they were able to forward their returns almost daily during the next three years to the government officials presiding over the different departments at Worcester House in the Strand. In this way the first of the great offices connected with the sale of the Crown lands, the department of surveys, was organized by the able administrator, Colonel Wm. Webb, formerly Surveyor-General under the Acts relating to the sale of Church lands. Upon these remarkable surveys, the analysis of which has now for the first time been accomplished, the official Particulars were grounded in order that negotiations for the sale of the premises might begin. These Particulars, upon request, were prepared, issued, examined and signed, under the orders of the Contractors for sale of the Crown lands, in the department of registration, presided over by Hy. Colbron and his deputy, John Wheatley. Then there was the department of claims and accounts, jointly controlled by the trustees, through their special officials, Hy. Robinson and Hy. Sefton, the Comptroller and his deputy, assisted by Wm. Potter, the Registrar of Debentures. As there was a separate department for the sale of fee-farm rents, it will be seen that Worcester House, the town residence of the late Marquis of

Worcester, was the scene of extraordinary activity on the part of government officials during the stirring days of the Commonwealth sales.[1]

In order to illustrate the procedure adopted in reference to the sale of Crown lands it will now be necessary to trace the records belonging to the various officials of the departments above mentioned in Worcester House. It is reasonable to suppose that with the advent of the Restoration many republican officials who were concerned in these sales became anxious, not only for the security of the records in their custody, but for their own personal safety as well. Their official duties, however, enabled them eventually to plead the " general issue " and to quote the Act of 16th July, 1649 in evidence, so that Parliament did all that it could in the meantime to protect the trustees, treasurers, contractors, and other officials against charges that might subsequently arise. The records of Worcester House appear to have been sufficiently secured, for we have already seen how large is the number of surveys preserved and how satisfactory is their general condition. Cole, Deputy Keeper of the Public Records, in 1846, was greatly puzzled in regard to the period when these records were first placed in the late Augmentation Office, and was obliged to confess that the date " is at present uncertain " ; but as the Clerk of the Pipe, in the Act for selling the fee-farm rents, was appointed to issue certain certificates relating to the value of the property, Cole suggested that it was " likely that these Surveys may have formed part of the Records of the Pipe (of which the Records of the Augmentation Court were made part by Statute) ". We have an indication of attempted concealment of records in a petition of Anthony Cogan about September, 1660, and if we follow up this clue we shall discover the answer to the question which Cole had in mind. Cogan had declared his knowledge of frauds on the part of trustees for the sale of Crown and Church lands, asserting that they had tried " to embezzle their writings and papers by conveying them to secret places ". Wm. Ryley, always active where records were concerned, also presented lists at this time to Sir Edw. Nicholas, remarking of the Committees for Crown and Chapter lands, sitting between 1642 and 1659, " their registrar Baker lived at Thistlewood," Isleworth, though whether he was dead or alive was unknown. A treasury warrant of 17th July, 1660, directed to Sir Gervase Lucas, had already authorized him to deliver all the surveys of manors, parks, lands, and tenements " lately remaining at Worcester House ", then in his custody for safe keeping, to the Surveyor-General and Auditors of the revenue. In consequence of Cogan's petition the Earl of Southampton thus addressed Colonel

---

[1] See Part iii, Section ii, for the " Instructions " and " Precedent Survey ", and the various officials employed at Worcester House. For the Restoration Accounts, see Exch. L.T.R., Pipe Office, Declared Accounts, Nos. 602–4, given in Appendix VI, Sections i–iii.

WASHINGTON BILLS, WHALLEY'S REGIMENT:
HAVERING PARK, ESSEX, 1650

Wm. Webb, Ralph Hall, and twenty-two others who had been intimately connected with the Commonwealth surveys : " I understand that in your hands are many books, papers, writings, etc., which concern His Majesty's Crown Lands and Revenue, all which ought to be brought into some place of record for His Majesty's service. And it hath lately been in the care of the two Houses that they should be disposed accordingly. And now having ordered Mr. Cogan and Mr. Reeve my messengers to go to you to demand all such books, papers, writings, etc., I require you for His Majesty's service and as you'll answer the contrary, to cause to be delivered unto them all such books, papers, writings, etc., whom I have commanded to carry them into the office of Sir Thomas Fanshaw, His Majesty's Remembrancer in the Exchequer, and leave them with Mr. Payne an attorney there. And as I expect your obedience, so in case of disobedience I require a seizure of them." It was through this avenue of the King's Remembrancer, therefore, that these important records entered the Exchequer and found their way with the aid of the Clerk of the Pipe into the Augmentation Office.

The Duchy of Cornwall surveys in the custody of Surveyor-General Prideaux, and other records about to be transferred from the Clerk of the Pipe, are referred to in February, 1660, by Treasurer Southampton, who shrewdly observed that " we cannot have too much light on what concerns his Majesty's revenues ". In the same year, on 15th February, the Treasury ordered all surveys of the lands and revenues of the Duchy of Lancaster, " taken by order of the late Trustees at Worcester House," to be removed at once from the office of the Clerk of the Pipe to that of the Duchy of Lancaster. And finally, 14th June, 1662, we come to a money warrant for £40, made out to Sir Rob. Croke, Clerk of the Pipe, " for services in removing the Records, Surveys, etc., which concerned the state of his Majesty's lands, from Worcester House into the Augmentation Office." [1]

Apart from the four great collections of Parliamentary Surveys already described, many separate documents and books relating to the sales have been discovered and analysed for the purposes of the present investigation. One choice work, a folio volume in vellum entitled " A General Index of Crown Lands ", is mentioned among the manuscripts of the Marquis of Lansdowne in the fifth report of the Historical Manuscripts Commission ; it was immediately acquired by the British Museum, and is now marked Add. MS. 30208. The volume contains an alphabetical account, arranged in Counties, of the Land Revenues of the Crown as they appeared in the Parliamentary Surveys and Books of Entry in the Surveyor General's

[1] For the references which concern this section see D.K.P.R., rep. 7., p. 224 ; S.P. Dom., Chas. II, 1660–1, p. 392, vol. 22, No. 139 ; ibid., 1670, addenda, p. 656 ; Treasury Books, vol. i, pp. 6, 64, 91, 125, 398. The Warrant, printed in D.K.P.R., rep. 7, vol. ii, p. 67, is recorded in full.

Office since 1649, the transactions of three generations being recorded up to the year 1752. The contents of the Index are arranged in ten columns, every page showing (1) the county, (2) the names and situations of the estates, (3) the grantees, (4) the terms—in the case of the Commonwealth entries it is " for ever ", (5) the yearly rents, (6) the improved values, (7) dates of the transactions, (8) references to surveys and entry books, (9) fines—in the Commonwealth entries the rates of purchase mentioned in the Particulars are given, and (10) occasional notes, some of which refer to groups of sales in combined counties. An important reference in column 8 gives the authority for the statements made, but although the four volumes there referred to were in use between 1713 and 1770 they have not since been traced. According to the inventories of 1713 and 1726, preserved in the British Museum, they consisted of four large books of parchment marked A. B. C. and D., with four similarly marked indexes, containing Particulars grounded on surveys taken between 1649 and 1653 and " Rated in Order to the Sale of several Crown Lands " ; the first two contained 1,109 folios of the years 1649–1650, the last two 1,069 folios of the period 1650–1653. They were last referred to in 1770 when Chambers lent Dr. Burrell one volume of original Parliamentary Surveys and four volumes of Particulars marked as above ; can it be therefore that they have since been converted into rolls ? [1] The British Museum has also acquired a few separate documents relating to Particulars for sale of Crown lands and fee-farm rents, a number of transcripts of documents (as, for example, those made by Burrell for his Sussex collections), a calendar of Particulars and Conveyances similar to the one in use in the Public Record Office, and notes and correspondence relating to army and other purchases in bound volumes preserved in the Harleian, Stowe, and other collections.[2]

Many important records concerned in the Parliamentary sales have been discovered since Deputy Keeper Cole referred to the fact that the Particulars for sale of Crown lands and fee-farm rents were in existence among the national archives ; but in spite of the hint thus given little attention has been paid to this source of information,

---

[1] I think not. The volumes appear to have been lost after 1770.

[2] See Hist. MSS. Com. Rep. 5, p. 259, which was acquired by the British Museum, 9th December, 1876 (" General Index of Crown Lands ", Add. MS.3 0208). The four entry books referred to are also recorded in Add. MS. 30206–7 ; there were also four corresponding indexes to these books. In Add. MS. 5705, ff. 8, 55–8, is the following note among Dr. Burrell's Collections on Sussex : " Mr. Chambers sends Dr. Burrell one volume containing all the original Parliamentary Surveys in the (Surveyor-General's) Office and Dr. Burrell may have the following Books of Parliament Particulars one at a time when convenient to him." It is not probable that these books of Particulars were afterwards converted into rolls. Also see Add. MS. 21327 (a copy of the Calendar of Particulars and Conveyances at the P.R.O.), and the references to Fee Farm Rents in Harl. 5013, Stowe, 184–5, and Baynes Papers, Add. MSS. 21417–27. In Harl. 5013, ff. 202, will be found material relating to fee farms of lands in Derby, Gloucester, Hereford, Leicester, Lincoln, Northants, Rutland, and Worcester ; it is dated 1650 and is provided with an alphabetical index.

and in consequence a wide field for exploration now lies open to the student of land finance in Commonwealth times. First of all, taking the Crown lands alone for clearness of reference, the minute book of the Trustees, 1649–1659, and the Journals of the contractors in two volumes, 1649–1653, may be mentioned. These are preserved among the Exchequer records of the Augmentation Office, along with a volume of miscellaneous accounts and orders of the trustees and various Commonwealth Committees during the period of 1642–1652, which contains amongst other things, bills for the quartering of soldiers; also the Particulars for sale of the royal estates, in twenty-two bundles, and the Counterparts of the Deeds of Sale (Conveyances) in eight bundles more, a single list serving as index to both classes of documents. Moreover, in the King's Remembrancer of the Exchequer are five additional bundles, containing the Certificates of the Treasurers in regard to the rates of the Particulars and the moieties paid by the purchasers upon their contracts. As to the enrolment in the Chancery of the Bargains and Sales of Crown lands, the entries on the Close Rolls from 1650 to 1659 are very numerous so that the search is of the most laborious kind, but with the aid of Palmer's Indexes (avoiding the lands of delinquents as one proceeds) the items may be tested with comparative ease.[1] The documents relating to the Sales of Fee-farm Rents, preserved at the Public Record Office, form another extensive series which will be considered later.[2]

From the account just given of the records accessible to students in London it would appear that very few documents of importance escaped the vigilance of officials at the Restoration in 1660; for not only have we found the "Instructions for Method" still preserved, along with the "Precedent Survey" which the Surveyor-General prepared for the guidance of his surveyors, but over two thousand of the surveys and certificates by the county surveyors to Worcester House have been traced, together with large numbers of Particulars grounded upon those surveys—all prepared within the government office in the Strand for the purpose of selling the Crown lands and fee-farm rents with the least possible delay. Then, too, the Minute Books and Journals of the trustees and contractors have been discovered[3]; and although the bundles of Certificates and Counterparts of Deeds of Sale are not very numerous, the enrolments of the conveyances upon the Close Rolls in the Chancery fill up some of the

---

[1] See D.K.P.R., rep. 7, p. 224; Augm. Off., Misc. Bks, 173–4, and 314; twenty-two bundles and index volume, with eight other bundles of Augm. Office records relating to certificates and Counterparts of Deeds of Sale; Palmer's Indexes 78 and 79 for enrolments upon the Close Rolls. Other volumes include Exch. L.T.R. Miscellanea, vol. 121; Exch. K.R. Misc. Bks, ser. i, vol. 53; Augm. Off., Misc. Bks., 135–7, 139–144, 175. The Particulars for Sale are in forty-seven files, with a calendar in three volumes. See Scargill Bird's *Guide*, pp. 70–1, 72–3, and Giuseppi's *Guide*, references as in the index.
[2] For the Fee-farm Rents, see S. Bird's *Guide*, pp. 72–3, Giuseppi's *Guide*, vol. i, p. 376, and Appendix II (YO–YZ).
[3] They have been indexed by the author for the future use of students.

gaps and make the investigation of the subject more complete. Presently we shall find that other documents exist, by means of which we may test our estimate of the proceeds arising from these various sales, but at the moment they need no further reference.

Certainly we miss several documents that we might reasonably expect to find in connection with the registration of these various transactions. Where, for example, are the accounts showing the rents received from Crown lands in the intervals between the sales, especially in connection with the leases allowed from year to year by the surveyors ? [1] Is it possible that the conveyances of the premises were so few that the rolls preserved in the Public Record Office represent the whole of the work accomplished by officials in that direction ? Did the tenants avail themselves of their right to preferential treatment in purchasing estates, and if so are there no documents to show the extent to which this was done ? How did the original creditors fare in their own period of ten days when they decided to buy what the immediate tenants declined to purchase ? Did buyers organize to control the bids and thus restrict competition ? Were Assigned Bills used to any great extent, and if so who used them, and what amount was produced by this means ? Such questions as these puzzle the minds of students, and as none of them can be directly answered from the documents preserved in London, we have to search elsewhere for the necessary evidence. This will be found in a remarkable series of records, now in the University Library at Cambridge. The wonder grows with the perusal of these documents how they came to be so successfully secreted in order to avoid seizure, and also, for the thought intrudes, how students in the past could have so completely overlooked them.

Three of the most important of these records at Cambridge relate to immediate tenants, original creditors, and persons in possession of assigned bills. Arranged in columns, the information collectively presented by them gives particulars of the premises sold in the various counties, the times when these were contracted for, the persons to whom they were sold, the amount of the purchase money and reprises, the payments of the first and second moieties and the dates when the conveyances were perfected. There is another document of the greatest value at Cambridge relating to conveyances of Crown lands, 653 of such transactions being indicated, compared with the few Counterparts of Deeds of Sale preserved in the Public Record Office. Here the information given is concisely arranged in nine columns, which collectively and very carefully record the dates of the contractors' warrants, the treasurers' certificates, and the conveyance, the amount of purchase money, the situation and description of the premises, together with the purchasers' names and the names

---

[1] One volume of rents and revenues between 1649 and 1653 is in the Cambridge University Library, marked " Dd 13. 20."

of the trustees who sealed the conveyances. Farther on in the book is an insertion which records the amount of money received from tenants and others for lands held by them or leased to them by the surveyors, between 8th October, 1649 and 22nd December, 1653. There are a number of other documents relating to Crown lands and fee-farm rents at Cambridge, but as the records are dealt with very fully in the Bibliography, they need not here be more particularly named.[1]

[1] The documents preserved in the Cambridge University Library are important. The press-marks are Dd. 8, 30 (Nos. 4–6); Dd. 13, 20 (1 and 2). Other documents of interest are those marked Dd. 13, 21 (1, 2); Ee, 3, 11, with 3, 18 (1, 2), and 3, 42 (5, 8–11); Ll., 2, 1; and Oo., 7, 29.

CHAPTER II

THE METHOD OF PROCEDURE

With the discovery and examination of these various records we are now in a position to ascertain the method of procedure adopted by persons who desired to acquire for themselves or for others the manors, parks, and minor premises of the late monarch and his family. To make the general outline clear it will only be necessary at this stage to trace the successive operations, each in their turn, from the commencement of the surveyors' work to the completion of the conveyance and the enrolment of the whole transaction in the Chancery.[1]

The survey of the premises had first of all to be undertaken, and when this was accomplished the surveyors returned their valuation with a duplicate copy of the survey to Worcester House, where their returns were numbered and dated, one copy being forwarded to the Surveyor-General for his approval to be certified. Then the survey was announced in a list posted on the walls of the registrar's department for the benefit of purchasers, the date being important because the immediate tenants had the right of pre-emption for the first thirty days and the original creditors for the next ten, so that while members of the general public might early send in their names with a view to purchasing particular premises, it was not until forty days had passed that they could make a definite agreement with the contractors and purchase the lands themselves.

If the immediate tenants, certified as such in the surveys, secured their own estates then the original creditors had to wait until other premises were free; hence the practice of asking the trustees to order Particulars of several premises, so that one estate at least might be secured. Should the immediate tenant exercise his right then the other persons withdrew at once, only to return in cases where the tenants failed to complete their purchases. Under these circumstances we might expect the rate of purchase to show a tendency to rise, and the tenant might be unable to secure his premises after all. In actual fact, however, as we shall presently see, there is very little evidence of intensely competitive prices being paid, and in any case it was to the interest of the State to sell the property quickly.[2]

[1] There were seven stages recognized in every person's agreement with the Contractors and Trustees, after the survey of the property, viz.: (1) Valuation, (2) requisition, (3) agreement, (4) authorization, (5) registration, (6) certification, and (7) enrolment of the Conveyance.

[2] For the Parliamentary Surveys reference may be made to the old Calendar in P.R.O. Press 5, No. 25, and the Madge Calendar in 11 vols. in Press 14, No. 82. A second Calendar of rents, sales, and purchases, indexed, in 12 vols., has been presented in January, 1937.

The survey having been returned, approved, and posted, "requests" were next made for Particulars of the premises, and these the trustees ordered the registrar's department to prepare, examine, date, and sign, and then deliver to the contractors with an intimation that they might now proceed with the sale of the property. The requests and orders are combined in entries which largely fill the "Trustees' Journal", in the margin of which are notes stating the order in which they would be considered on specified days, in accordance with rules laid down for that purpose.

Reference to the existing calendars in the British Museum or the Public Record Office will enable one to ascertain whether the Particulars granted by the trustees are still in existence, in which case they may be compared with the original surveys and the subsequent conveyances. As the Particulars were grounded upon the surveys in question, the dates of both are recorded in the final statement, which is generally signed by John Wheatley, the deputy registrar. At this point the Particular ended, but the subsequent proceedings connected with the contract and conveyance are usually found stitched to the parchment roll, with two further signatures of Wheatley (the last of which indicates that the proceedings are now closed), the entry and registration of the sale having been completed by the clerks in the registrar's department.[1]

LIV.[2] TRUSTEES' JOURNAL, 1649–1659
The column of Requests (1233) includes renewals.

Areas.	Counties.	Requests.[3]	Particulars.	Years.	Orders.[3]
(i) Metropolitan	10	450	452	1649	105
(ii) Extra-Metropolitan	16	456	512	1650	846
(iii) Border-Lands	13	290	436	1651–3	103
(iv) Wales	13	37	121	1654–9	16
Totals .	52	1,233	1,521	Totals	1,070

The next stage in the proceedings was reached in the office of the contractors at Worcester House. Here the agreement with the officials was signed, the entry in the Contractors' Journals indicating the name and location of the premises, whether the estates were in present possession of the State or otherwise, and the rates of purchase of the various portions now to be sold. Beyond the poundage required by the Acts of Parliament, the payments were to be made, one-half in ready money and the other half in debentures, and it was expressly stated in the agreement that no review or reconsideration was to be expected which would result in lessening the value of the premises.

[1] The Trustees' Journal is preserved in the Augm. Off. Series of Miscellaneous Books, No. 314. The Calendar of Particulars and Conveyances will be found at the P.R.O. in Press 5, No. 5, or in the British Museum, Add. MS. 21327. The roll of Particulars had its membranes numbered and stitched together, subsequent additions being made during the progress of the sale.

[2] Tables LIV–LVIII each contain two sections which relate to (a) areas and (b) years.

[3] Including renewals; but the orders of the Trustees relating thereto number 1,070.

The signature of the purchaser will be found at the foot of each entry in the Contractors' Journals, in the margins of which may be seen the values of the premises and the total agreed upon by the purchaser. A copy of the contract and agreement with the contractors was thereupon added to the roll of particulars, the signature of the deputy registrar being recorded for the second time as an attestation of accuracy.

If now we wish to test the claims of the purchaser, as declared in his request to the trustees for a Particular, three of the Cambridge documents are available; these will show whether the purchaser exercised his right as immediate tenant or as original creditor, or whether his contract was made by means of assigned bills. Each of the three lists in question gives the name of the purchaser of the property, the date of the contract, and the amount agreed upon; also (for the names sometimes differ) the names of the persons for whom the premises have been rated and to whom they will be conveyed, with an indication of importance as to whether the instalments have been fully or partially paid.[1]

LV. Contractors' Journals, 1649–1653.

(A) Agreements. (B) Immediate Tenants. (C) Original Creditors. (D) Assigned Bills.[2]

Areas.	A.	B.	C.	D.	Years.	A.	B².	C².	D².
(i) Metropolitan	330	95	125	48	1649	42	23	–	–
(ii) Extra-Metropolitan	362	183	126	40	1650	680	124	272	69
(iii) Border-Lands	224	20	94	41	1651	153	20	25	49
(iv) Wales	46	2	14	7	1652–3	87	–	2	20
Totals .	962	300	359	136	Totals	962	167	299	138

The next step was taken by the contractors who, having attested the contract and agreement with their signatures, immediately issued their warrant authorizing the trustees to draw up and seal a conveyance of the premises either to the purchaser himself or to those persons who, with his consent, were named in the actual rating of the particulars. This attestation, with the Contractors' Warrant was then added by the deputy registrar to the roll of particulars already mentioned.

At this point we can apply a further test by means of the " General Index of Crown Lands " preserved in the British Museum, a volume which is based on the Contractors' Warrants and certain books of particulars that were available before 1770. Here the purchaser's name alone appears, but the yearly rents and the improved values of the premises are also given as a rule, and in most cases the amounts agreed upon for rating the various premises are recorded as well. The work, in spite of duplicate and misplaced entries hitherto

---

[1] See the Contractors' Journals, Augm. Off., Misc. Bks., 173–4; also Camb. Univ. Lib., Dd. 8, 30 (No. 4, Original Creditors, No. 5, Immediate Tenants, No. 6, Assigned Bills).

[2] The Cambridge lists of Tenants, Creditors, and Bills are in columns B², C², D². See note to Table LIV.

unrecognized (and of course the usual casual errors which necessarily must occur in so vast an array of figures), is distinctly well performed and merits high praise for its general accuracy.[1]

LVI. Contractors' Agreements and Warrants, 1649–1655.[2]
(A) Agreements. (B) Index of Crown Lands (B. Mus.). (C) Warrants.

Areas.	Counties.	A.	B.	Years.	A.	C.
(i) Metropolitan	10	330	361	1649	42	2
(ii) Extra-Metropolitan	16	362	369	1650	680	387
(iii) Border-Lands	13	224	254	1651–3	240	226
(iv) Wales	13	46	82	1654–5	–	31
Totals	52	962	1,066	Totals	962	646

Thus far have we traced the negotiations for sale which, commencing with the return of the survey and the posting of the list at Worcester House, have been followed by the granting of a Particular at the request of a bidder, the agreement with the contractors to purchase particular premises, the attestation of the contract and the issue of the Contractors' Warrant authorizing the trustees to convey the property to the purchaser. In the majority of cases all this work was accomplished in less than two months. Now it was the turn of the registrar, who, receiving this authorization from the trustees, was instructed to prepare a certificate of the premises sold to the purchaser. These certificates, showing the rating of the particulars, were based on the terms of the contract, and they therefore record the name of the purchaser (and when different, the names also of the persons to whom the property was to be rated and conveyed), the amount of the purchase, and the times when the moieties were to be paid, with the method of payment involved. In order to secure the premises until the payment of the second moiety, a lease for ninety-nine years was issued by the treasurers.

The Certificate of Rates, signed by the deputy registrar, John Wheatley, was then forwarded by him to the treasurers. In it the declaration was made that the premises were to be sold with all their indicated appurtenances, including customary lands, tenements, commons, waste grounds and ways, but excluding of necessity all things not expressly mentioned, more especially those that were excepted and reserved for the use of the State in the Acts of Parliament associated with the sale of Crown lands and rents. To-day these Certificates of Rates may be consulted in their bundles. But as the terms of the contract had already been added to the roll of particulars, there was nothing further to place on record in connection with the contract, except the final certificate or declaration to the trustees, namely, that " this Particular with all proceedings thereupon as it is

[1] For the attestation of the Contractors and the Contractors' Warrant see the note recorded on the Particulars in the third section of the roll, where the names of the officials concerned are recorded in both cases. See the General Index of Crown Lands, a fine folio volume of 1752 (Add. MS. 30208).
[2] See note to Table LIV.

thus finished is entered and registered by me " ; and with the date and signature of John Wheatley added for the last time the work of the registrar's deputy in this direction came to an end.[1]

Not that the transactions connected with the sale of Crown lands were as yet complete, for the Registrar's Certificate of Rates merely set in motion the quills of other men who, in the new department of debentures, awaited the signal to work. Whereupon the registrar and his clerks prepared a Certificate of Debentures, in which the treasurers were notified that so many bills or debentures (already signed by the trustees and now forwarded) were due to the persons named in the Rate and Conveyance, from the particular regiments or individuals specified, to whom assignments had been made in proportions stated and for the total amounts shown. These Certificates of Debentures, signed by the registrar, Wm. Potter, and entered by the deputy comptroller, Hy. Sefton, may easily be overlooked as they are hidden away inside the Registrar's Certificates, while the books in which they were originally entered have not been found. The Certificates of Debentures are officially referred to as Treasurers' Certificates in contradistinction to those of the registrar previously referred to. These debentures were drawn up in the following form [2]:—

" ALL lawful deductions made, there remaineth due from the Commonwealth to . . . his Executors, administrators and assigns, until the day of the date hereof, the sum of . . . which said sum of . . . is to be paid to the said . . . his Executors, administrators or assigns, upon the . . . day of . . . which shall be in the year of our Lord . . . BUT if the said . . . his Executors, administrators or assigns, do before that time become a purchaser of any (of) the lands or particulars enacted to be sold for security of the said debt, that in such case allowance shall be then made thereof, according to the said Act, if the same be required, and the Commonwealth to be thenceforth discharged of the said debt, or so much thereof as shall be defalked upon such purchase."

When a year or two later the treasurers returned these bills and debentures to the registrar for cancellation, it was usual for Potter to record a note to that effect upon the certificate, with the date when this took effect. This done, the work of his department at Worcester House was completed, just as the final note upon the Particulars brought the work of the registrar of contracts to a close. By 1653 the surveyors also had practically finished their tasks.[3]

[1] Certificates of Rates will be found in five bundles in Exch., King's Remembrancer, E. 121. The entry and registration of the rates for the various sales are recorded in the fourth section of the roll of Particulars.
[2] Act for further Instructions concerning the Sale of Crown Lands, 23rd November, 1649, Firth and Rait, *Acts and Ordinances,* vol. ii, p. 282.
[3] The Certificates of Debentures are inserted within the Certificates of Rates, Exch. 121, in five bundles. Potter's books marked A to E (and perhaps others) appear to have been supplemented by those of the Comptroller, but they have not been found. The note as to cancellation of the debentures is entered on the Certificate of the Debentures, as an endorsement.

LVII. Treasurers' Certificates and Receivers' Rents, 1649–1655 [1]

(A) Particulars. (B) Receivers' Rents. (C) Warrants. (D) Certificates

Areas.		Counties.	A.	B.	Years.	B.	C.	D.
(i) Metropolitan	.	10	452	55	1649	27	2	2
(ii) Extra-Metropolitan		16	512	56	1650	50	387	391
(iii) Border-Lands	.	13	436	31	1651–3	65	226	320
(iv) Wales	. .	13	121	–	1654–5	–	31	39
Totals	. .	52	1521	142	Totals	142	646	752

We come now to the final stage in connection with land transactions, for the Contractors' Warrant had authorized the trustees
to make the sale effective, and the treasurers were satisfied in the matter
of security by the receipt of the two certificates from the registrars
of contracts and debentures. The trustees therefore proceeded to
seal their indenture conveying the premises to the persons named in
the Contractors' Warrant. This part of the work was done at considerable length and with very great care, as may be seen from the
surviving counterparts of the Deeds of Sale in the bundles at the
Public Record Office.

It is here that we meet with a little difficulty because the counterparts of the Deeds of Sale that remain in the Public Record Office are
only a few in number. This is betrayed at a glance by the calendar
prepared for " Particulars and Conveyances ", where the same letter
and number is used for both types of records whenever the same
property is referred to. The eight bundles of conveyances fail to
conceal their scanty store. Fortunately other sources are available, for
two indications of the great activity of the Commonwealth trustees
in this direction survive. One of these is to be found in the University
Library at Cambridge, where a large folio volume records the completion of about 650 conveyances, the names of the trustees who
sealed the indentures being recorded in almost every instance. The
second source is revealed by one of Palmer's Indexes at the Public
Record Office, but although this is useful so far as it indicates the
enrolment of the Bargains and Sales of Crown lands on the Close
Rolls, the volume nevertheless errs by excess for our present purpose
since the forfeited lands of delinquents are also included, and the
references in any case are difficult to follow in the old notation of
Palmer's time. Yet with the aid of Palmer's index one may estimate
the care with which the indentures relating to the sales of Crown
lands were enrolled in the Chancery, for each entry records the names
of the trustees who sealed the conveyance, the purchaser of the premises,
and the total amount paid, the terms of the contract in regard to rates
and moieties, and the three dates when the indenture itself was made,
acknowledged, and enrolled.[2]

[1] See note to Table LIV.
[2] See Conveyances at P.R.O. (Counterparts of Deeds of Sale), in eight bundles ;
they are lettered and numbered to correspond with the Particulars. See also the list
of Conveyances, 653 in number, in Camb. Univ. Lib., Dd. 13, 20. The Calendar of

LVIII. Enrolment of Conveyances, 1649–1659 [1]

(*A*) Conveyances (P.R.O.). (*B*) Conveyances (Cambridge List). (*C*) Bargains and Sales (Palmer's Index, P.R.O.). (*D*) General Index of Crown Lands (Brit. Mus).

Areas.	*Counties.*	*A.*	*B.*	*C.*	*Years.*	*B.*	*C.*
(i) Metropolitan	10	135	240	516	1649	2	–
(ii) Extra-Metropolitan	16	181	232	676	1650	281	296
(iii) Border-Lands	13	104	150	772	1651–3	314	1,175
(iv) Wales	13	31	31	96	1654–9	56	589
Totals	52	451	653	2,060	Totals	653	2,060

From the description given above it will be seen that the task of future historians and topographers is greatly simplified since it is now possible to trace almost all the property of the late monarch in this way. By way of illustration, fully documented in the Appendix, the case of Halliford manor in Middlesex may be taken. This small estate was surveyed in September, 1650, by Ralph Baldwin, Rowland Brasbridge, John Brudenall, and Richard Heiwood, who certified that the manor contained 195 acres, the present rent being £18 6s. 8d. per annum, the future improvement £122 11s. 3½d., and the total valuation £140 17s. 11½d. per annum. Of this total £3 13s. 4d. represented the value of the royalties of the manor. The timber was negligible in amount. These are the basic facts upon which the rates of purchase subsequently turned. There remained one important point to be considered, and that was the discovery of the ¦" immediate tenant " of the manor, for he was allowed preferential treatment in the first month after the posting of the list of surveys at Worcester House. Quoting successive grants of 12th July, 1599,[2] and 26th January, 1637—the latter to Robert Sharpe for eighteen years, which would not take effect until 1654 and therefore not expire until 29th September, 1672—the surveyors decide that Wm. Westbrooke's claim to be the immediate tenant is proved by the fact that he is the son of Joan, who in her second marriage was the wife of Robert Sharpe, and whose first husband was Thos. Harrison, the preceding tenant of the manor house in the time of Christopher's lease. The survey is accompanied by a useful rental of freeholders holding lands in Upper and Lower Halliford, but no manorial customs or memoranda are quoted. Completed in September, 1650, the survey was then signed by the county surveyors and forwarded in duplicate to Worcester House, where the trustees' copy was marked No. 543 with the date of receipt, 7th October, 1650, and forwarded the same day to Colonel Wm. Webb. Two days later the Surveyor-General returned it with

Particulars serves as a Calendar for the Conveyances as well; both are combined in a single volume. Palmer's Indexes 78 and 79 assist in tracing the enrolments on the Close Rolls, but Delinquents' lands are also included with the Crown lands. The references now need to be " keyed up " with the modern numeration. Thus " Close Roll, 1650, pars. 65, No. 16 " is now simplified as No. 3556, mm. 23–5. The companion volumes of Indexes, Nos. 80–1, relate to the enrolments of Church lands.

[1] See note to Table LIV.
[2] To George Christopher, for the term of thirty years.

his approval and signature, and thus the first stage of the proceedings closed.[1]

If now we turn to the Journal of the trustees, we shall find three entries dated 14th and 16th October, 1650 relating to the manor of Halliford. The first two, dated 14th October, are requests from Edw. Moore and Captain Jn. Nelthorpe, both of whom require Particulars of the manors of Halliford and Twickenham—the latter seeking to include the manor of Berkhampstead, lands in Shaftesbury, and the office of Escheator in Lancashire as well. The entries are as follows :—

(*i*) Request for Particulars and Orders to the Registrar : *Trustees Journal*,[2] f. 87, dated 14th October, 1650 :—

Att the request of Ed. Moore It is this day ordered That the Regist'r (do forthwith make and fairly engross in parchment a) Pert'r of the Mannor of Twickenham with the rights members & app'ten'nc's Com' Midd' p'cell of the Hon'r of Hampton Court, and of the Mannor of Halford. Com' pr'd in possession. Late p'cell of the possessions of the late Kinge whereupon &c. (the Contractors may proceed to make Sale thereof. And that hee—the Register—doe deliver the said Particular Examined and signed under his hand, unto the said Contractors or any five or more of them, according to the Acts of Parliament in that behalfe).

(*ii*) Second request for Particulars : Ibid., f. 87 *b*, dated 14th October, 1650 :—

Att the request of Captaine John Nelthorpe It is this day ordered &c. (as above) Pert'rs of certen Landes in Shaftsbury in Com' Dorsett, the Mannor of Wickenham in the County of Midd', the Mannor of Halford in the County of Midd' the Office of Escheats in the County of Lancaster and the Mannor of Barkhamsted in Com' Hertford in p'nte possession Late p'cell of the possessions of the Late Kinge, whereupon &c.

(*iii*) But on the 16th comes a request from Wm. Westbrooke, who styles himself " immediate tenant ", and he asks that the trustees shall order the registrar to furnish him with a Particular of his own manor and nothing more. Hence the third request for Particulars, " The Immediate Tenant " : *Trustees Journal*,[3] f. 88, dated 16th October, 1650 :—

" Att the request of Will'm Westbrooke imed' Ten't It is this day ordered a Pert'r of the Mannor of Halford Com' Midd' Late p'cell of the possessions of the late Kinge, whereupon &c."

---

[1] The operations connected with Halliford manor can be followed very closely from the documents given in the appendix. This may be taken as a model for tracing the estates of the Crown in all the remaining counties of England or Wales. For Halliford, see the Survey, Middlesex, No. 29, in Madge, op. cit., pt. ii, 404-423.

[2] Augm. Off., Misc. Books, vol. 314, ff. 87-8. Both requests bear the same date. In the margin of the premises indicated in No. (i) is " Manor of Twickenham et al. No. 3 p' Monday " ; in the second case the marginal reference is " Lands in Com. Dorset p' Monday ".

[3] Augm. Off., Misc. Books, vol. 314, f. 88, Mercredi, 16th October, 1650. Margin : " Mannor of Halford." Present this day : Sir Ric Saltonstall, Cols. Humfry and White, Messrs. Ayres, Bond, Cressett, Searle, Stoccall, and Sydenham. The requests of Moore and Nelthorpe were set aside in favour of Westbrooke, who proceeded to sign the contract.

All these Particulars were doubtless provided, that of West-brooke being preserved to-day in the Public Record Office, with the subsequent proceedings connected with the sale stitched to the roll of membranes. Thereafter we can follow with ease the smooth course taken by the transactions. On the 21st October, Westbrooke signed the agreement with the Contractors, when the terms arranged for the rates of purchase were these :—

(*a*) Four years for the clear improved yearly value of £118 17*s*. 11½*d*. in reversion.

(*b*) Fifteen years' purchase for the yearly rent of £18 6*s*. 8*d*., for the manor.

(*c*) Twenty years for the yearly value of £3 13*s*. 4*d*. for the royalties of the manor.

The agreement made by Wm. Westbrooke with the contractors is entered in the Contractor's Journals,[1] die Lunae, 21st October, 1650, as follows :—

Agreed with the Contractors for the purchase of the Mannour of Hallford al's. Hallowford lying and being in the parish of Shupardton in the County of Midd' menc'oned in the p'ticular to be in the p'nt possession of the State being Three poundes Thirteen shillinges and foure pence in possession, (inserted above : att Twenty yeeres purchase). And for the purchase of the Mannour house of Halford als. Hallowford w'th the Scite and app'rten'nces thereof and the demeasnes of the said Mannour together with the quitt rents to the said Mannour belonging all heretofore demised to Robert Sharp gent for eighteene yeeres to com'ence at Mich'as 1654 after the expirac'on of a former gr'nt Att the rate of ffifteene yeeres purchase for the present yeerely Rent of the premisses being eighteene pounds six shillings and eight pence in possession.

And att the Rate of foure yeeres purchase for the Improved yeerely value thereof being one hundred and eighteene pounds Seaventeene shillinges and Eleaven pence half penny in Rev'con. The purchase (over and above the eight pence p' pound) to be satisfied the one half in ready money and the other half in debentures And noe Review to be expected for lessening the value of the premisses I say agreed by me.

(Signed) Will Westbrooke.[1]

On this basis the amount to be paid worked out at £823 18*s*. 6*d*., of which sum Westbrooke was to pay as poundage to the contractors, trustees, and treasurers £27 9*s*. 3¼*d*. upon signing the contract, leaving the remainder to be disposed of in two payments, one half in two month's time and the rest six months later. The arrangements included a plan whereby Westbrooke might pay half the money in cash and the other half in bills or debentures ; and so that there should be adequate

---

[1] Augm. Off., Misc. Bks., vol. 174, ff. 27*b*–28. The marginal entries are : " Midd' £823. 18. 6 : p. £20. 11. 11½ : £6.17.3¾ : Total £27. 9. 3¼."

security for the payment of the second moiety the premises were to be held in the meantime by a lease for ninety-nine years.[1] After this, on 6th November, the contractors made their attestation in regard to the contract, and on the same day the Contractors' Warrant was issued to the trustees authorizing them to draw up and seal a conveyance of Halliford manor. The Registrar's Certificate of Rates, is dated 14th November, 1650, and is signed by Wheatley, whose signature appears also on the roll of Particulars. This certificate gives the terms of the contract of 21st October, 1650, and mentions that the premises are sold to Wm. Westbrooke, but rated at his desire in fee simple for Thomas Stroud and Richard Hill. Inserted within this document and foliated with it is the interesting Certificate of Debentures, usually termed the Treasurers' Certificate, dated 18th December, 1650, which is signed by Wm. Potter, registrar of debentures, examined by " J. H." (i.e. John Humphreys), and entered by Hy. Sefton, the deputy Comptroller. This certificate to the treasurers shows that four bills or debentures, already signed by the trustees, are being forwarded because they are due to Stroud and Hill in connection with the rating of the Particulars. The total amount involved is £398 8s. 9d., but there are four bills for this amount and these are apportioned by three assignments [2] as follows :—

(a) To Major Edm. Rolph, assignee of Geo. Gregson, as captain of a company, and captain and major to Col. Pride's Regiment of foot (in 2 equal bills). . . . £374 11 0
(b) To Major Edm. Rolph, assignee of Thos. Chapman, as soldier and corporal in the troop of Capt. Winthrop in Col. Harrison's Regiment of Horse (1 bill) . . . £14 3 9
(c) To Major Edm. Rolph, assignee of Nich. Saunders, as soldier in Capt. Anthony Morgan's troop in Commissary Gen. Ireton's Regiment of Horse (1 bill) . . . £9 14 0

These certificates are not referred to in the proceedings incorporated with the roll of Particulars (whereon Wheatley had entered his final observation, by way of certificate to the trustees, showing that the record had been completed and registered on 9th December), probably because the first moiety permitted by the contract had been paid before the expiration of the eight weeks, the limit of which was 16th December.[3]

---

[1] See Trustees' Journal, Augm. Off., Misc. Bks., 314, ff. 87, 87b, 88 (three Requests for Particulars and Orders in reference to the same); Add. MS. 21327, f. 79, or P.R.O. copy, p. 60, with Particulars and Conveyance, both marked L. 16 ; Agreement with the Contractors, 21st October, 1650, in the Contractors' Journal, Augm. Off., Misc. Bks., 174, ff. 27–28 ; Contracts made by Immediate Tenants, Camb. Univ. Lib., Dd. 8, 30 (5), f. 11. The date of the Contract is quoted in all subsequent transactions.
[2] For regimental contracts, see Table No. LXIII in the next section.
[3] Attestation of Contractors, 6th November, 1650, on the roll of Particulars, L. 16, m. 6 ; Contractors' Warrant, 6th November, 1650, recorded likewise, L. 16, m. 6 ; Camb. Univ. Lib., Dd. 13, 20, p. 60, No. 245 ; General Index of Crown Lands, Add. MS. 30208, f. 122, Nos. 144–5, recorded as 6th November, 1651, by an error, with reference to Book

As the second moiety was not due before 16th June, 1651, the final proceedings were conducted in a more leisurely manner, so that it was not until 10th March, 1650–51 that the indenture of the trustees was prepared and sealed. Then were the premises conveyed to Thomas Stroud, of Westminster, Gent., and Richard Hill of Wimbledon, yeoman, as expressed in the terms of the contract, the Contractors' Warrant, and the Treasurers' Certificate. On the following day the conveyance was brought into the Chancery by Silvanus Taylor and Jn. Hunt, the enrolment on the Close Rolls taking place ten days later, 21st March, 1650–51. Only once after this is reference made to the sale, and that occurs when Wm. Potter, registrar of debentures, received back the four bills from the treasurers, and after acknowledging their receipt he notifies their cancellation, 15th September, 1652, thus bringing the long series of transactions connected with the sale of Halliford manor completely to an end. In this way the negotiations were conducted for the whole of the estates that were purchased throughout England and Wales, so that by following the stages illustrated above in the case of Halliford, it is quite easy to trace the procedure (through similar documents) for any other manor in the kingdom.[1]

of Particulars, C., ff. 167–8. By a curious mistake this entry is recorded under Somerset, instead of Middlesex, just as the manor of Widcombe, Somerset, is given as Partic. N. 16 for Northants, but P. 5 for Somerset in the Calendar, Add. MS. 21327, ff. 86b, 91. The Treasurers' Certificate, dated 14th November, 1650, is preserved in E. 121, bun. 3, No. 4, f. 1. The Certificate of Debentures, 18th December, 1650, is within the last-named document.

[1] The Conveyance, dated 10th March, 1650, is marked L. 16 to agree with the roll of Particulars. See Calendar, Add. MS. 21327, f. 79b, P.R.O. copy, p. 60; Camb. Univ. Lib., Dd. 13, 20, p. 60, No. 245, with the names of the trustees who sealed the Conveyance; Palmer's Index, vol. 78, p. 10, which refers to Close Roll, 1650, part 65, No. 16 (No. 3556, mm. 23–5). The cancelled debentures are referred to in the endorsement upon the Treasurers' Certificate of 18th December, 1650 (E. 121, bun. 3, No. 4, f. 2).

OFFICIAL REGULATIONS CONCERNING COMPETITION, 1649

(Damaged 1834)

[face p. 209

CHAPTER III

THE CONTROL OF THE MARKET

As we see from their Journal, the trustees first met on 22nd
February, 1649–1650, when Sir Wm. Roberts, Sir Ric. Saltenstall,
and eight others were present. Between that date and the final entry of
2nd March, 1658, over 150 meetings were held, the great majority
taking place in 1650. The average attendance was never greater than
eleven during any month of the period; often it was as low as six,
and the record as we might expect shows a steady drop in attendances
from the first year to the last two or three, after which the attendances
of members began to be uncertain. They even sat on Christmas Day,
1650, when nine trustees were present, four requests for Particulars
were received, and orders to supply these were given to the registrar.
Meetings were held at first on Fridays, then every Monday and Wednesday until 25th December, 1650, but occasionally Thursdays and
Saturdays were included; afterwards the meetings appear to have
been fixed for Wednesdays, though the intervals range from a week
to a month at times, until at length the dates become altogether
irregular in the years that follow 1652.[1]

Business was naturally very brisk in the first year, no less than
ninety-three requests being considered at four of the meetings in
1650; but later the work became more leisurely, for on thirty-five
occasions after 1654 only a single item is recorded in the Journal.
The whole number of requests made to the trustees for Particulars
of premises, including some cases where repeated applications were
made, appears to have exceeded one thousand, as we see from the
table below [2]:—

LIX. REQUESTS FOR PARTICULARS, 1649–1658

Years.	Meetings.	Average Atten- dance.	Requests[3] and Orders.
1649	8	11	105
1650	95	9	846
1651	24	7	84
1652–53	16	6	19
1654–58	15	6	16
Totals	158	8	1,070

[1] Analysis of the Trustees' Journal, 1649–1658, which now has its folio numbers
recorded, the whole contents being indexed for the present study.
[2] Table LIX is compiled from the results of an analysis of the Trustees' Journal,
Aug. Off. Misc. Bks., vol. 134. Cf. the second section of Tables LIV–LVIII (years).
[3] Including renewals of applications there are 1,233 " requests " and orders number
1,070 as shown.

From the record of meetings, attendance, and transactions it becomes clear that the busiest months were March, April, and July, in the order named, and a calculation shows that over 40 per cent of all the requests made for Particulars were presented to the trustees during those three months of the year.

The orders recorded in the Trustees' Journal are in the main of three kinds. A few relate to their own internal organization, as for example the appointments of Tayleur as clerk and Miller as messenger, while others deal with altered dates of meetings. The majority, however, concern the work of the registrar's department, the object being to provide a constant supply of " Particulars " to meet the needs of persons who had expressed a desire to purchase Crown property. These orders have already been illustrated in the case of Halliford manor, and their extent is shown in the preceding table. The remainder refer to decisions affecting the conduct of contractors and purchasers.[1]

The contractors first of all call for attention, for on the very first page of the Journal are rules which relate to their work. They were to meet every Monday and Wednesday from 4th March, 1649–1650, between the hours of 9 and 12 a.m., and members were to take the chair in succession month by month. A penalty of 1s. was provided for defaulting contractors who, without leave of the chairman, failed to appear before 9.15 a.m., or who left the meeting before midday ; this penalty was increased to 2s. if they were absent without permission for an entire sitting, or if their excuse at the next meeting was not considered reasonable. Fines of this character might be returned, but in any case the money had to be " deposited before the excuse propounded ", the penalties being " kept as a stock to be disposed of as the majority of the Committee think fit ".[2]

Dr. Savine has shown as a result of his inquiries in connection with sixteenth century sales, that different types of buyers, more or less connected with the court of Henry VIII, procured monastic property in varying proportions, while Liljegren, with remarkable industry and shrewdness, has proved the existence of land-jobbers among his various categories of conspicuous buyers. The Commonwealth sales carry the story still further, for operations of an extensive character were conducted by persons who, when not acting alone, were engaged in pairs or in companies with the obvious intention of making a profit on their transactions ; and it is of particular interest to the historian to know that the regulations approved by the trustees at their first meeting on 22nd February, 1649, are the first of their kind yet discovered. The official rules prepared for the assistance of purchasers were of a strict, yet sensible

---

[1] Trustees' Journal, ff. 9, 24, 104, 105. See Halliford manor on p. 205, and also Table LIX.

[2] See the Trustees' Journal, f. 9.

and methodical character ; but, as we shall presently see, there were other rules of an unofficial kind made by the buyers themselves for their own particular guidance, with the intention of restricting competition.[1]

From the outset the trustees made one rule quite clear, namely, that abstracts of surveys must in every case be posted at Worcester House before sales could begin, and that when orders were issued they must be attested by the clerk for the sake of authenticity. Similarly, attestation of memoranda was necessary, this time by the deputy registrar as well as the clerk, to guard against interlineation of Particulars, for the prospect of fraud was ever present and instances were bound to occur. Although Particulars so altered might be admitted for the purpose of effecting a contract, yet the Contractors' Warrant for the preparation and sealing of a conveyance was not permitted " except for Particulars fairly engrossed without inter-lineation ". With this in view the next chairman was ordered to sign " Presse " of every Particular presented at the time the contract was made, and it was expressly ordered that upon subsequent re-writing of the Particular " the new and old portions shall be compared ". Once the contract had been signed, the valuation mentioned in the Particular was not to be varied to the detriment of the State, the only corrections allowed being those of a verbal character associated with differences in the survey upon which it was grounded. Contractors were on no account to issue an order permitting valuations to be reviewed in a downward direction ; indeed the fixed amount was regarded as of such importance that a special clause was inserted in every contract debarring purchasers from the expectation of a review in their favour.

The rule concerning requests for Particulars provided that purchasers must express their desires in writing with the date attached, after which the request would be read in the presence of five or more contractors, " the Chairman giving his *Fiat* and numbering the desires in such order as granted, and according to which number the Clerk shall place them in the paper for the day from time to time."[2] It was ruled also that the survey must not only be certified by the registrar before the contractor could give his order, but produced as well at the time when the Particular was read, to permit of com-parisons being made—an eminently fair decision. Another rule provided that although no one might " treat " for either an immediate tenant or an original creditor within the forty days collectively allowed to these classes of purchasers, yet if letters of attorney were forth-coming for this purpose and then left with the contractors, permission would be readily granted. But in this connection it is significant to

---

[1] Savine, quoted by Fisher, *Polit. Hist. of Eng.*, vol. v, app. ii, pp. 497–9, " The disposition of the monastic lands " ; Liljegren, *Fall of the Monasteries*, pp. 31–109. See also Trustees' Journal, ff. 9–11, and next section (iv) on " Frauds ".

[2] As already shown in the case of Halliford, p. 205.

notice that, at the desire of the General Council of the Army, " treaty for anything in possession of the State " might at once be suspended for the space of thirty days.

There were six rules governing competition and these are of particular interest. The first decided that the method to be adopted was " Sale by the Box ", which was to be opened at the end of " that day sevennight ", though without prejudice to the original creditors concerned, but in the meantime publication was to be made by posting up the papers connected with the sale. The second rule decided what competition there should be : " No competition to be adjudged in any case except where, after a Particular is desired by one person, a second shall desire an order for a Particular of the same thing on some sitting day before the day appointed for the first person to treat for it." The contractors, however, were warned to take notice of the Particulars in their books before adopting this method of exposing things to sale by the box. The third rule stipulated that all " offers at the Box " were to be made certain without reference to what another person would give, as for example, such a statement as " I will give £5 more than any other offers ". If any such reference should be made then, according to the rule, " only that which is certain shall be taken as the offer, and that which is more (in reference to the other offers) shall be taken as *null*, to advance the certain offer." The fourth rule debarred " receders from competition " from taking part in the " treaty " until others refused to buy the premises. The fifth rule stated that papers put into the box were to be sealed and subscribed with competitors' names, and that the number of years' purchase they were prepared to give should be written down, so that when the time came for opening the box " he to have the purchase who offers most to the advantage of the State and not under the proportion appointed by Act of Parliament ". The sixth and last rule required the name and address of the competitor to be given, together with the assurance that he would be present (or at any rate would be represented) at the time when the box was opened so as to acknowledge his paper and sign the contract when called upon. The papers of absent competitors were to be ignored. " If there is only one paper in the box (or several papers of one person only) the papers shall not be opened but the party shall be admitted to treat verbally for the purchase." Very wisely the trustees ordered that " the Contractors and their Officers are not to discover any competitors' names. In case of competition it is not to be in the power of competitors to prevent the thing being exposed to Sale by the State ". As an example, it may be mentioned that Windsor Great Park was exposed to sale by the box in accordance with these rules, on the Saturday following 3rd April, 1650.[1]

[1] Trustees' Journal, f. 29. On 20th March, 1649, Edw. Scotton requested a Particular of the property on behalf of Col. Desborough's Regiment (f. 19).

To estimate the extent to which competition entered into the sales is a task by no means easy, for it requires a thorough examination of the Trustees Journal and a complete analysis of its thousand or more unindexed entries.[1] On a limited scale it may be attempted in order to test the frequency of entries relating to " Sale by the Box ". Taking three counties widely separately, one in each of the regions into which we have divided England for the purpose of this study—Bedford in the Battle Area, and Cambridge and Cumberland in the Protected Areas of the Parliamentary or Royalist forces in the east and north— and analysing the entries that refer to them in this volume we obtain some rather curious results [2]:—

LX. INDIVIDUAL AND COMPETITIVE PURCHASES

	Bedford.	Cambridge.	Cumberland.	Totals.
(i) *Premises.*				
Baronies, Honors, and Manors	6	1	8	15
Farms, Granges, and Lands .	4	2	3	9
Houses and Tenements . .	5	2	1	8
Parks, Warrens, and Woods .	5	1	–	6
Rents and Royalties . .	–	2	–	2
Totals	20	8	12	40
(ii) *Requests.*				
Immediate Tenants. . .	9	–	2	11
Original Creditors . . .	4	2	1	7
Assignees	–	1	1	2
Regiments	8	4	2	14
Other Individuals . . .	4	4	10	18
Totals	25	11	16	52
(iii) *Papers.*				
One only	15	7	9	31
Two sets	4	–	2	6
Three sets	1	–	1	2
Four sets	–	1	–	1
Totals	20	8	12	40
(iv) No competition . . .	18	8	12	38
Box ordered . . .	2	–	–	2
Totals	20	8	12	40

In connection with these three counties there are fifty-four entries scattered throughout the Journal, one half of them relating to Bedfordshire. Three-quarters of the property consist of Honors, Manors, parks, warrens, and woods, but about 20 per cent includes messuages large or small, with tenements, cottages, and little plots of ground. In Bedfordshire the immediate tenants were active,[3]

[1] Nevertheless, this has at length been done in connection with the present study.
[2] Table LX. The table is based on the analysis of Augm. Off., Misc. Bks., vol. 314. For Bedford, see ff. 15, 16, 18, 20–5, 29, 31, 32, 54, 55, 168 ; Cambridge, ff. 17, 22, 29, 47, 55, 89, 98, 105 ; Cumberland, ff. 20, 34, 60, 62, 63, 68, 85, 86, 118. See the appendix for Abstracts from this volume (III. Sec. ii).
[3] They were more active still in Northamptonshire.

but in Cambridge few were prepared to buy their lands. Various regiments were represented by attorneys who made requests on their behalf. In all three counties individual purchases predominate, for only in about a quarter of the instances do we find two or more sets of buyers prepared to negotiate for the same property. If these instances are in any way typical of the country as a whole then competition was completely ruled out in 75 per cent of the sales. And since there are but two instances recorded of " sale by the box ", both occurring in the battle area, it is clear that even in the remaining instances competitive action disappeared before the date of the sale, leaving only 5 per cent as an average for the three counties combined to represent the cases where competitive prices appear to have prevailed. " Ordered," says the Bedfordshire note of 6th April, 1650, in reference to Brockborough and Beckerings Parks, " that the several parks in Bedford (for which competitors have appeared), be exposed to sale by the box." It is clear from the infrequency of such orders that purchasers made their own arrangements to defeat the government plans, and by combining in their own defence utilized the market for their own advantage.

During the first week in April, 1650, not only were the parks of Windsor, Beckerings, and Brockborough, in Bedford and Berkshire, " exposed for sale by the box," but the Castle Park in Stafford and the fourth part of St. John's Wood, Middlesex, as well.[1]   On 6th April the trustees made the following order concerning agents or attorneys [2]:—

" Ordered That all such persons who as attorneys on the behalf of Original Creditors offer at the box, and upon their offer Carry the purchase, do forthwith upon determination made by the Contractors that the purchase is carried by them produce their letters of Attorney from such original creditors on whose behalf they act other wise their papers to be taken as null."

A little later in the month, owing to the practice of withdrawal of papers or requests, somewhat drastic steps were taken by the trustees to check a growing scandal, as the following order shows [3]:—

Whereas upon the 22th of February last It was ordered by this Committee That in case of any Competition it should not be in the power of any or all the Competitors to take off the Lands for which such competition should be from being exposed to sale by the box which order is now hereby published And whereas notwithstanding that order divers persons out of Corrupt and sinister ends (for their own private lucre) tending

[1] Other references to such sales during the years 1650–3 concern the counties of Berks (f. 29), Cornwall (f. 33), Essex (f. 32*b*), Kent (f. 29), Lancs (f. 89), Mx. (f. 94*b*), Northants (ff. 32*b*, 94*b*), Oxford (f. 33), Staffs (ff. 32*b*, 33), Surr. (ff. 29, 33), Sussex (f. 33), Wilts (f. 94*b*).
[2] Trustees' Journal, Augm. Off., Misc. Bks., vol. 314, f. 31*b*, ' Order for producing r'les of Attorney ", 6th April, 1650.
[3] Ibid., f. 39, dated 29th April, 1650.

both to the abuse of the State, as also to the interruption of this Committee in their proceedings by unnecessary deceits have and do use to withdraw their papers of desires for Particulars after they have sent in the same It is now this day further ordered That in case any person desiring an order for a Particular of any Lands to be made forth shall after withdraw his paper, such person shall never be treated with for those lands or any other nor (in case of any sale by the box) shall his paper be owned by or admitted by this Committee as of any effect in Relation to such sale.

Two months later, when notices concerning the expiration of terms of pre-emption for tenants and creditors were being torn down by unruly competitors, a fresh order was made by the trustees [1]:—

Whereas (notwithstanding the exposing to sale of the Lands of the late King Queen and Prince and publication thereof by the Contractors be by the act made essential as to the limitation of the beginning and ending of the respective times of pre-emption as well of Original Creditors as of Immediate Tenants yet) divers persons out of a sinister resort to their own private Interest have after such exposing to sale and publication thereof torn down the papers that have been posted to notify the same, on purpose to keep others from taking notice thereof both to the great disadvantage of the State and prejudice of such others standing in an equal capacity with themselves as to the pre-emption thereof, It is this day ordered That in case of any such irregularities committed for the future by any person or persons The Actors and accessories therein shall be looked upon by this Committee as persons unworthy to be treated with for any Lands or tenements so exposed to sale and be dealt with all accordingly And further That upon tearing down of any such papers by any person whatsoever before the day or days appointed for treaty for any particular therein contained, The papers shall be posted again and no particular for which any order was formerly granted shall be treated on till the second sitting after such second posting, any former (order) of this Committee to the Contrary notwithstanding.

Three years later we find evidence that sales of Crown lands were slackening and that purchase money was in arrears in connection with existing contracts [2]:—

Ordered That all such persons as have Contracted for any of the Honors &c. of the late King Queen or Prince and not yet paid in any purchase moneys do by this day fortnight the 17th instant pay in such purchase moneys as are by them respectively due and in arrears, or on that day show good cause to the contrary, And in default thereof that the premises by them respectively contracted for be exposed to sale again.[3]

[1] Trustees' Journal, vol. 314, f. 49, dated 3rd June, 1650.
[2] Ibid., vol. 314, f. 161b, dated 3rd May, 1653.
[3] Other references to sales of special interest between 1650–8 may be noted in connection with the following counties : Berks, f. 29 ; Bucks, f. 166 ; Ches., f. 101 ; Corn., ff. 159, 160b ; Derby, ff. 153b, 179b ; Essex, ff. 32b, 79, 168b ; Hants, f. 89 ; Heref., f. 82 ; Herts, ff. 82b, 179 ; Kent, f. 29 ; Lancs, ff. 89, 112b, 176b ; Linc., ff. 123, 164 ; Mx., ff. 48b, 94b, 166b, 167, 168 ; Norf., f. 178 ; Northants, ff. 75, 112b, 118, 160b ; Som. f. 114b ; Surr., f. 28 ; Sx., ff. 26b, 33, 168b ; Wilts, ff. 91b, 94b, 130, 160b–165, 177, 179b ; Yorks, ff. 24, 111b, 125b, 179b ; Carmarthen, f. 85. The references to Clarendon Park, Wilts, reveal a triangular contest between Colonel Dove, Colonel Joyce, and Mr. Wilcox, with Dove as eventual purchaser of Hunt's division for £7,000.

This view is confirmed by the evidence of earlier sales, of which a number had occurred in every reign since the death of Henry VIII. It has already been shown that during the sales of Crown lands which had been ordered by Charles in 1626, a "society or combination of land-buyers" sprang into existence, of whose members it was said that they put their purses together, and when they had discovered suitable estates, bought them in gross and then retailed the lands in small parcels of a few acres each. Charges were made against them in consequence of this wastage of manorial lands. Such action was considered to lead to the destruction of the ancestral homes of the gentry, the severing of lands and tillage from the manor houses contrary to the statutes relating to enclosures and depopulations, and above all to " the enhauncinge of the prices of lands and thereby of Rents fermes corne and other commodityes ", and the very seriously regarded social evil of " making of a parity between Gentlemen and Yeomen and them w'ch before were laboringe men," with the consequence that pride and stubbornness were born in such men so that they became more and more refractory to the government of the country. Two members of this land buyers' society, Cooper and Shapdam, were specially mentioned as notorious buyers. A list of lands, houses, and manors purchased in Norfolk accompanies these charges. In one case the purchasers sold the stone and timber, and in a second they felled the wood, while at Holme £400 profit was made by the sale of a house and land.[1]

The extensive arrangements made by the Society of Land Buyers in the late reign doubtless recalled when the Commonwealth sales began. Cooper and Shapdam, pilloried in connection with the Norfolk plans, do not appear among the purchasers in the later sales, nor do the three prominent buyers Sir Henry Bedingfield, Sir Hamon le Strange and the Rev. Thomas Thorowgood; but that may be because they were discredited or disinclined to buy, or perhaps some of them were dead, although the last three purchasers were certainly alive in 1653. Thomas Bedingfield, of Gray's Inn, was one of the many lawyers who purchased delinquents' lands, and he may have been a son of Sir Henry Bedingfield.

Arrangements such as these would be something more than a mere memory in 1650, for well might they serve as a pattern for bolder schemes in the great confusion of those times. One of the most remarkable indications that organized buyers were actively operating in the market for Crown lands is revealed in a document preserved in the collection of Baynes Papers in the British Museum. It is endorsed " A way to Induce all originall Creditors mutually to

---

[1] Hist. MSS. Com. Rep. 12, pt. ix, app., p. 134 (Gurney MSS., vol. xxii, misc. ff. 82–3). This is quoted by Rye, *Norfolk Archæology*, vol. xv, 1904, pp. 1–3 (" The Land Buyers' Society "). The sales referred to were probably those of 1626, which were authorized by Charles I. See Table XV.

agree to prevent Compettitors in purchasing The King's lands, &c." [1] The method disclosed is so ingenious and the wording so very quaint that no paraphrase of its contents would do full justice to the intentions of those who compiled it. There are nine rules recorded, as follows :—

" First.[2] Mutually to engage to assist each other for the procurem^t of such further securety as the Parliament shall thinke fitt for satisfying all the Origginall Creddittors that shall ioyne in the Ingagement, in case the present securety shall not be sufficient.[3]

2^{ly}. That one man may be appoynted to keepe a booke for the uses following, and have a sallary for his paynes from every purchaser for every Purchase that shall be made.[4]

3^{ly}. That theis p'ticulers agreed upon shall be Ingrossed into the said booke, and that every one that shall expect to reape any benefitt thereby shall Ingage to be bound upp by them by subscribing thereto, or otherwise as shall be thought fitt.[5]

4^{ly}. That noe man soe agreeing shall desire an order for a Perticuler (nor any for him) of the Contractors appoynted to sell the said lands, til first he have entered his name & the thing he desires to purchase in the said booke.[6]

5^{ly}. Hee that first entreth his name in the said booke, shall take out the Perticulers of the lands he desireth to buy, and shall Contract for the same.[7]

6^{ly}. All others whoe shall go to the said booke and shall find that a Perticuler is already desired of the lands he or they shall desire to purchase, shall onely enter himselfe or themselves as Compettitors for the said lands (which shall be before the day of Contract), but shall proceed noe further, til the first man hath contracted." [8]

---

[1] Another set of rules (Add. MS. 21427, f. 91) is headed : " A way for an agreement amongst Contractors or Attorneys in purchasing of the King's lands, &c., so as to prevent Competitorshipp."

[2] Rules 1–3 are shortened in the version recorded in Add. MS. 21427, f. 91. Rules 4–8 become 5–9 in that copy, owing to Rule 3 being recorded in two parts (Nos. 3–4). " Lastly " varies in both versions. See the following notes.

[3] Add. MS. 21427, f. 91. "*Imprimis.* That all may engage jointly to move for further security till all arrears be satisfied in case the present security hold not out to satisfy all that doth so engage as well as such as shall be satisfied as those that shall not be satisfied before the security be spent."

[4] Ibid., " 2^{ly}. That one man may be appointed to keep a book for the uses following and have a salary from every purchaser for the same."

[5] Ibid. In two parts, viz., " 3^{ly}. That the agreement shall be written in the said book." Also " 4^{ly}. That all men that shall purchase for themselves or others (that shall join in this agreement) shall engage himself to perform the Contents thereof by subscribing the said agreement so writ in the said book or otherwise as you shall think fit."—

[6] Ibid., f. 91, where the above fourth rule now becomes No. 5, as follows :— " 5^{ly}. That no man so agreeing shall desire an order for a particular (nor any for him) of the Contractors appointed for sale of the said lands, before he enter his name in the said book as purchaser of such a manor park or parcel of lands as he shall so desire a particular of."

[7] Ibid., " 6^{ly}. That he that first entreth his name in the said booke shall purchase or contract for the said lands he contracteth himselfe to be purchaser of."

[8] Ibid. " 7^{ly}. All others whoe shall goe to the said booke to enter their names for the said lands soe put in for as aforesaid before the day of treaty shall onely enter their names as Competitors to show that first put in for it but shall not moove the Contractors for a particular or doe anything to preiudice him that first put in for it."

The seventh and eighth rules refer to the contract and the subsequent procedure connected with the casting of lots :—

" 7ly. He that first entred his name, and shall goe on to Contract, shall upon notice of any Compettitor or Compettitors enter bond to the Maior gen' or whoe shall be thought fit to be Contented to take his lott with the said Compettitors for the lands he shall soe Contract for.[1]

8ly. The said lotts shall be Cast or drawne before the Maior gen' or who shall be thought fit, And he on whome the lott falls shall have the purchase assigned over unto him by him that did soe Contract for it as aforesaid, he paying to him that did soe Contract what money he had disbursed in or about the same." [2]

Evidently the eighth rule gave trouble, as those who framed it foresaw, so an alternative plan was suggested to obviate the impracticability or inconvenience of the rule [3]:—

" If theis things prove not Practicable, or shall not be thought Convenient, It is further humbly offered,—That the said lotts may be cast or drawne the day before the day of Contract, and he on whome the lott falle shall Contract for the said lands himselfe, and he who tooke out the Perticuler shall give him the best Assistance he can therein, recieving his Charges as aforesaid.

Also, it is humbly offered that he that keeps the Booke shall take out a p'ticuler of all the Surveyes as they come in, to give an account to the Orriginall Credittors of the Vallues, Conditions, and which is in lease and which not, and the date of the returne of every survey and Publication thereof."

The last rule of all made provision for avoiding competition whenever Original Creditors who were outside the Agreement permitted lands to be sold by the " method of the box ", for the object in view throughout was to keep the rate of purchase as low as possible within the limits assigned by the Council of Officers :—

" 9ly. If any others of the Orriginall Credditors whoe shall not Joyne in this agreement shall bring any of the said lands to the box, that then any that are within this agreement shall have liberty to bidd for the said lands soe sett to sale."

And the reason for such rules being drawn up and obeyed is very frankly stated :—

[1] Ibid. " 8ly. That he that first entres his name and that shall goe on to contract as aforesaid, shall enter bond to the maior genl. or whome you shall thinke fit to stande to his lot for the said lands, he shall soe contract for with those whoe have soe entered themselves as his compettitors before the day of treaty."

[2] Ibid. The eighth rule is recorded as " Lastly ", and is combined with an alternative proposal, for which, see below.

[3] Ibid., f. 91, where the last recorded rule is also included as follows : " Lastly the said lotts shall be drawne or cast before the maior genl. or whome you shall thinke fit and he on whome the lott falls shall have the purchase paying him that did soe contract what money he shall have disbursed for or about the same And if this shall not prove practicable or thought convenient it is further humbly offered that the said lotts may be drawne or cast as aforesaid the day before the day of contract and he on whom the lott falleth shall Contract for the said lands himself, and he whoe desireth the particular shall give him the best assistance he can for that purpose."

" That all men shall ingage not to give a greater rate for any lands they shall purchase then shall be determyned by the Councell of Officers, provided that noe man so Ingaging shall buy the said lands from them." [1]

With a system of this character in operation, one reason for so little competition being found in the counties we selected becomes quite clear ; indeed, after reading the rules it is difficult to avoid the inference, that had the rest of the counties been examined as closely the result would have been much the same. Certain it is that for the first seven counties of England, taken in alphabetical order, no sales by the box are recorded save in connection with the parks already mentioned in Bedfordshire and Berkshire, and the Manor of Bonalva in Cornwall. We may, therefore, conclude that competition for Crown lands was vigorously restricted in all parts of England and Wales ; that when it occurred it was largely ineffective ; and that the proportion of cases concerned was, at the very outside, not more than 5 per cent of the whole.

But the subject deserves closer investigation, for although the efforts of Dr. Savine and Dr. Chesney have resulted in the classification of groups of purchasers of monastic and sequestered property between 1540 and 1660, no such attempt has hitherto been made in connection with the confiscated Crown lands of the period 1649 to 1660. An attempt was made at the Restoration to classify the buyers in six divisions, namely, as tenants, members of the army and of Parliament, adventurers, " covetous men," and men of ill-fortune who " cannot restore the purchases " they have made. That is a very different classification to those adopted by Chesney and Liljegren who carefully make a distinction between purchasers acting in a private or public capacity—a distinction which is applicable in the case of Crown lands (a large proportion of which was secured by agents in order to pay off arrears due to officers and men in the army), except that Contractors, Trustees, and Surveyors were debarred from acquiring such property, unless they were tenants or their salaries were hopelessly in arrears. This may be the reason why the Webb family procured lands and messuages in Northants, Wiltshire, and Yorkshire, for which they appear to have paid £3,050. Even the notorious Commissioner for Somerset, Colonel John Gorges, of whom Chesney complains secured in conjunction with Thomas Saunders several manors in Cornwall and Devon at a cost of £20,800. Military officers, Parliamentarians, lawyers, and London Capitalists— such as Captain Alured, President Bradshaw, John Nelthorpe, and Sir Thomas Allen—will be found in the lists relating to Crown lands

[1] For the agreement in another form, see Baynes Papers, Add. MS. 21427, ff. 90–1 (old f. 230). See f. 90, which is endorsed : " Relative to purchasing King's Lands." The service rendered to the study of these records by the Society of Antiquaries of London should be widely acknowledged, for various papers have appeared since 1779 in the *Proceedings*, or in *Archæologia*, or the early volumes of *Vetusta Monumenta*. This particular agreement was printed in the *Proceedings of the Society*, vol. iv, pp. 42–4 (1859).

as well as delinquents' estates. Dr. Chesney's list of 140 private purchasers includes eighty-four merchants, four goldsmiths, and three scriveners. Palmer's Index to the Bargains and Sales enrolled on the Close Rolls shows a varied collection of buyers of Crown lands. In 100 of these recorded conveyances the descriptions include a yeoman and a knight, two peers, three widows, four merchants, twenty-eight gentlemen, thirty-six esquires, and a number of citizens and traders of various kinds. These last-named citizens of London are particularized in a lengthy list which includes the baker, chirurgeon, clothworker, cutler, draper, embroiderer, fishmonger, gardener, girdler, merchant taylor, sadler, stationer, tallow-chandler, and turner. The conveyances themselves record four instances of small purchases made by husband and wife,[1] of lands in Northants, Shropshire, Yorkshire, and Brecon: one of these concerned the Surveyor-General, Wm. Webb, and his wife Anna, who bought certain premises in Yorkshire valued at £142 10s. The total amount of these four sets only came to £732 3s. 4d. In three cases corporate purchases [2] were made amounting to £583 2s. 10d. for premises situate in the counties of Devon, Lincoln, and Norfolk :—

LXI. CORPORATE PURCHASES

Authorities.				Amounts.		
				£	s.	d.
(1) Mayor and burgesses of King's Lynn	.	.	.	104	0	0
(2) Governors, Assistants, etc., of the Hospital, Plymouth				230	0	0
(3) Aldermen and burgesses of Grantham	.	.	.	249	2	10
Total	.	.	.	583	2	10

In two other cases[3] the contracts were made by and the conveyances granted to Dame Jane Evington and Anne Goldesborough; the property consisted of a meadow and messuages in Surrey, which cost £108 16s. 11d.

There is considerable evidence that purchases of Crown lands were made by groups of buyers, alternating in membership and varying in size. Thomas Baker purchases in company with Noah Banckes messuages and lands in Northants worth £832 7s. 6d.; but he joins Anthony Wilmer when buying some very small and scattered estates in Kent, Northants, Stafford, Surrey, Sussex, and Warwickshire, for which only £164 11s. 8d. is required. Then George, Noah, and Thomas Banckes are engaged in other transactions, either among themselves or with John Menheire, whereby they procure manorial lands in Essex and Northants of a cost which exceeds £1,400. Godfrey Ellis is another instance, but he is a man more adventurous than the

---

[1] The earliest warrant was 14th August, 1650, and the latest conveyance 7th June, 1653.

[2] The purchases included tolls of Grantham and Lynn, and " the water and poole of Sutton ", Plymouth.

[3] Nos. 326 and 327 in the Cambridge list of conveyances. The full names and details of purchases of the various groups yet to be indicated in the pages which follow are made accessible by the writer's indexes (Brit. Mus. Collection, vols. I-XV).

last, for he not only paid £8,005 for three contracts in his own name, but £9,101 for five other conveyances (working with a second partner) and £5,404 for two additional purchases which he made in conjunction with ten other persons : by which means Crown lands were secured in no less than eleven counties. We see, therefore, that the extremes in the matter of sales lie between the individual purchases of men like Captain Walter Blith, who buy for their own needs in a a single county, and the collective operations of attorneys who act as agents for the army, in groups of varying size, and who buy estates of exceptional value throughout England and Wales. Thus while Blith [1] bought messuages and lands in Northamptonshire for £659, and Cornet Joyce, with or without the aid of Edward Sexbey, secured premises in Dorset and Hampshire for £3,679, Thomas Lilburne and Samuel Saunderson, working with partners in groups of six, nine, and seventeen persons, contributed close on £50,000 for manors, parks, leaseholds, and royalties in the counties of Cumberland, Hampshire, Lincoln, Surrey, Wiltshire, and York.[2]

Taking all the transactions into account, individual and collective, and exercising every care in the analysis to avoid duplication of entries, we find that the purchasers of Crown lands group themselves very definitely into the following categories, so far as number and receipts are concerned. Most of the items refer to sales within single counties, for which receipts amount to £1,114,888, so that the

LXII. INDIVIDUAL AND COMBINED PURCHASES [3]

Divisions.	Counties.	Persons.	Items.	Range of Purchases.		Amounts.
				£	£	£
Corporations	3	—	3	104–	249	583.1
Individuals .	45	341	451	10–	22,299	633,761.3
Pairs . .	37	108	123	23–	19,517	254,362.5
Threes . .	14	56	26	117–	13,562	80,594.6
Fours . .	11	34	11	95–	17,215	57,051.0
Fives . .	4	15	4	332–	12,858	27,944.1
Sixes . .	16	48	24	946–	35,873	173,985.9
Sevens . .	7	28	9	752–	18,775	51,132.9
Nines . .	1	9	1		3770	3,770.6
Tens . .	7	20	5	830–	6,610	15,915.1
Elevens .	4	11	2	1,336–	4,067	5,403.9
Seventeens .	1	17	1		10,320	10,320.9
	—	—	—			
Totals .	52	687	660	£10–	£35,873	£1,314,825.9

[1] Walter Blith was the author of *The English Improver, or a new survey of husbandry.* The British Museum contains two editions of 1649, two copies of the third impression of 1652, and another edition, enlarged, of the third impression, dated 1653.

[2] These conveyances of Blith, Joyce, Lilburne, and Saunderson are recorded in the Cambridge list, Nos. 320–1 (£659 9s. 4d.); 340 and 397 (£3,679 2s. 7d.); 40, 74, 85, 87, 91, 97, 99 (£35,426 7s. 2d.); 406 (£3,770 11s. 8d.); 451 (£10,320 18s. 5½d.)— £49,517 in all for the groups of six, nine, and seventeen associates, or army agents.

[3] This table is based on the Cambridge list of Conveyances. The individual persons, working singly or in groups, number 687. The items (660) are contained in 648 conveyances, five duplicates being excluded. The Counties (52) are all represented. The lowest entry of " £0,000 : 1 : 0 " is apparently an error for £12 1s. It occurs in Northants.

interests of immediate tenants would be the main factor here in deciding the prices paid for the various estates. The residue, £199,938 altogether, came from purchasers who procured lands in several counties, and as these were the original creditors—mostly army agents —prices would be largely determined by the subtle agreements made between the various groups not to compete against each other. On the whole prices would tend to rise during the first thirty days of recognized " tenant's option ", fall during the next ten days when the " original creditor's option " became effective, and fall still further subsequently when the " land market ", under compulsion of financial stringency, became glutted with wares.

As an example of the practice followed by the Council of Officers when proceeding to purchase Crown lands in accordance with the rules of their non-competitive scheme already mentioned, one of the orders issued by Major Gen. Lambert may be referred to. This order, which is dated 27th March, 1650, gave " liberty and directions " to Captain Baynes, Major Saunderson, Captain Goodrick, and Captain Shepperson, as attorneys for the Northern Brigade,[1] to " treat and contract with the Contractors of Parliament for sale of the late King's lands ". With two other captains named in the order, these attorneys were empowered to send in their requests, " either jointly or severally ", in order to obtain the official " Particulars " of specified premises in various counties, and then proceed to contract for the manors of Steppingley, Wirksworth, and Rosedale, in the counties of Bedford, Derby, and York, also the parsonage and rectory of Wimbledon in Surrey, " as they the said attorneys shall agree among themselves, what and for how much each of them shall contract." The Baynes Papers and other bound volumes in the British Museum contain further and even more considerable evidence of the activity of the army agents.[2]

The agreements between the Contractors and the army officers have not hitherto been examined by historians so the amount of their contracts, as original creditors, may now be recorded for the first time. Ranging from £814 to £105,000, the total amount of the regimental contracts came to close upon half a million sterling out of a total of £1,424,892 received in connection with tenants, original creditors, and assigned bills. The largest amount is that of the Northern

---

[1] See Table LXIII, Regimental Contracts, and Appendix, p. 357.

[2] See Trustees' Journal, ff. 29, 31, 33 ; *Proceedings of Society of Antiquaries,* vol. iii, p. 52 (1854). Debentures or bills connected with army purchases are to be seen in Add. MS. 21427, ff. 12, 15, 16, 62–5, also Harl. 427, which is of great interest in this connection. See also S.P. Dom. 1650, p. 164 ; 1652–3, p. 452 ; 1654, pp. 49, 87–8, 99, 262 ; 1655, p. 231 ; 1656–7, pp. 97, 133–4, 197, 212, 215, 268–9, 298–9 ; 1657–8, pp. 147–8 ; 1658–9, pp. 54, 196–7, 225, 250–1 ; 1659–60, pp. 334, 408–9. For the " Soldiers' Claims " made in 1661 see Add. MS. 30206, f. 45. The total annual value of the lands claimed by soldiers, 20th September, 1660, was said to be £12,012 5s. 2d. (Cal. S.P. Dom., 1660–1, p. 271). See also T.A. Larcom, *The Down Survey,* 1851, index, pp. 404–5, 408, for the army agents and Irish Crown Lands, 1655–6, and Goblet's work on the same survey, 2v., 1930.

LXIII. Regimental Contracts

Brigade : No. 23. Garrisons : Nos. 24, 26, 27, 30. Un-named : No. 33. Regiments :
Nos. 1–35, named after their Colonels.

Regiments.	Locality of Crown Lands Purchased.	Contracts. £
1. Barksted	Kent	12,583.3
2. Bennett [1]	Cornwall	1,376.3
3. Constable	Cardigan, Monmouth	1,896.8
4. Cox	Bedf., Berks, Camb., Wilts	3,771.6
5. Cromwell (Hy)	Bedford	8,311.0
6. Desborough	Berkshire	22,755.0
7. Duckingfield	Staff., Denbigh	13,171.1
8. Fairfax (Horse)	Herts, Mx.	35,873.6
9. Fairfax (Foot)	Hertford	10,594.9
10. Fenwick [2]	Cumb., Kent, Northants, Northumb., York	15,724.8
11. Fleetwood	Mx., Norf., Oxford	25,415.0
12. Hackert	Cumberland	12,903.5
13. Harrison	Middlesex	13,215.3
14. Haslerigge	Durham, York	2,866.1
15. Haynes [3]	Dorset	2,722.0
16. Hewson	Derby, Lanc., Suff., Sx.	20,599.1
17. Horton	Berks, Surrey	1,721.3
18. Ingoldsby	Lincoln	6,610.5
19. Ireton	Norfolk	2,064.2
20. Jones [4]	Monmouth	2,411.3
21. Lilbourne [2]	York	2,812.1
22. Morgan	Stafford	1,709.4
23. *Northern.*	Bedf., Hants, Lanc., Leics., Linc., Northants, Surrey, York	104,909.0
24. *Nottingham*	Derby, Nottingham	5,414.9
25. Okey	Bedford, Cambridge	14,971.4
26. *Plymouth.*	Cornwall	814.0
27. *Portsmouth*	Hampshire	3,200.0
28. Rich	Hereford, Kent	34,527.8
29. Saunders [5]	Stafford, Warwick	46,065.8
30. *Southampton*	(Included in No. 27, Portsmouth)	
31. Tomlinson	Lincoln	1,148.7
32. Twisledon	Lincoln, Nottingham	19,864.5
33. *Un-named* [6]	Cornwall	1,743.8
34. Waller	Cornwall	6,210.4
35. Whaley [7]	Ex., Herts, Mx., Norf., Notts	37,264.1
	Total	£497,242.6

[1] Another entry in Orig. Cred. List, f. 15, under Thos. Hearne may refer to this regiment. See also No. 33 below.

[2] Includes three contracts, of which the Cumberland Manor, £10,320 18s. 5½d. is jointly shared by Colonel Fenwick and Colonel Lilbourne's regiments. The attorney is Cornet Sam. Saunderson.

[3] Two other entries in Orig. Cred. List, f. 27, are marked " Jn. Warr for Col. Jas. Haynes ".

[4] An entry on f. 16, Orig. Cred. List, in the name of " Roger Humphreys for Col. Jones ", may perhaps refer to this regiment.

[5] Includes five contracts by Captain Zanchey or Sankey, and " Coronet Combey ", ranging from £3,245 to £18,775.

[6] May be associated with the purchases of Crown lands in Cornwall in connection with the Plymouth Garrison, or the regiments of Col. Rob. Bennett or Sir Hardres Waller.

[7] Includes seven contracts by Captain Jn. Grove, ranging from £1,120 to £12,108. The transaction connected with the Northern Brigade includes twenty-two contracts (£71 to £22,299), the work of a group of twelve attorneys, of whom Adam Baynes, Jn. Saunderson, Adam Sheppardson, Geo. Smithson, Ric. Sykes, and Thos. Talbot were the most active. For Col. Whaley's Regiment, see Harl. MS. 427 (732 names).

Brigade at York, which is nearly a quarter of the whole. The four garrisons of Nottingham, Plymouth, Portsmouth, and Southampton, with an unnamed regiment which appears to be associated with Plymouth, share contracts between them amounting to £12,173. Thirty-two other regiments include Lord Fairfax's Regiment of Horse, General Fairfax's Regiment of Foot, Major-General Ireton's Regiment, those of Sir Wm. Constable, Sir Arthur Hazlerigge, Sir Hardres Waller, Col. Hy. Cromwell, and the rest of the regiments in the list[1], the largest individual share of the contracts, £46,066, being awarded to Colonel Saunders' regiment. The entire transactions were accomplished by a non-competitive body of forty-eight attorneys who acted on behalf of the various regiments. The list includes Majors Barber, Bridge and Saunderson; Lieut.-Colonel Goffe, Lieut. Allen, and Thos. Talbot, Esquire; Ensigns Hancock and Mortlock; Cornets Combey and Sam. Saunderson. The remainder appear to have held the rank of Captain, viz. Adam Baynes, Braddon, Buckner, Burges, Crooke, Disher, Ellis, Eyton, Farrer, French, Goodrick, Grove, Hearne, Hemsdall, Henchman, Holmes, Humphreys, Lilbourne, Lloyd, Mandowson, Margery, Margetts, Menheire, Nelthrop, Orpin, Richardson, Rookeby, Scotton, Sheppardson, Smithson, Spencer, Styles, Sykes, Thomson, Tracie, Wagstaff, Warr, Zanchie.[2] The calculations are worked out with such precision that Colonel Twisledon's regimental account includes $8\frac{1}{2}d.$ plus one-quarter of a halfpenny; and that of the Northern Brigade is recorded as $10\frac{3}{4}d.$ plus two half farthings plus one-quarter of a farthing.

[1] See Table LXIII, p. 223.

[2] These army " land jobbers " may be compared with the " Society of Land-Buyers " under Charles I, and the purchasers of Monastic Lands recorded by Savine and Liljegren. The Commonwealth agents are recorded in the writer's index to Original Creditors in the British Museum. (Collections relating to Crown Lands, vols. vi–vii; also in Madge Collection on Crown Lands, at the London School of Economics, vol. cx. Col. Whaley's Regimental book of contracts, with its letter of attorney (dated 4th February, 1649–50), and several acquittances and lists of bills, has been preserved (Harl. MS. 427). The name of John Washington occurs eleventh in the list attached to the letter of attorney : his claims for arrears due in respect to service in Capt. Chillenden's troop of Whaley's regiment are recorded, viz. (1) Service under Lord Manchester, £48 3s. (of which £34 13s. $8\frac{1}{2}d.$ was allowed), and (2) service in the " New Moddell " under Lord Fairfax, £24 15s., for which he received two bills of £12 7s. 6d. each in the set of bills assigned to Capt. Cannon's troop, in connection with the purchase of Havering Park, Essex. See Harl. MS. 427, ff. 33, 45, 53, 132; also E. Peacock, Army Lists of Roundheads and Cavaliers, (1642), 2nd ed., 1874, who records Lt.-Col. Washington, Capt. Henry Washington (son of Sir William), and Ensign John Washington (pp. 18, 73, 75). Col. Adam Washington, as " immediate tenant ", purchased Bowser's tenement or farm, Chertsey, Surrey, 14 Oct.– 9 Dec. 1650, the rent being £2 17s. 6d., improved value £25 2s. 6d. more, and sale price £354 3s. 9d., for 25 acres of land. (Surrey Survey No. 10; Add. MS. 21327, f. 94b; Add. MS. 30208, f. 114; and two Cambridge lists.)

GRANGER'S CONFESSION : SHORTHAND NOTES, 9th January, 1654

[face p. 22

CHAPTER IV

THE DISCOVERY OF FRAUDS

It will be necessary to refer, though very briefly, to the question of fraud in connection with the sales of Crown lands, for it soon became clear that the precautions taken by the trustees in the matter of inter-lineation and alteration of parliamentary surveys were fully justified. In February, 1649–50 a long story of fraud opens with the discovery of forged warrants and Bills of Exchange— a discovery which had important consequences the moment it was decided to commit Wm. Broome and Abraham and John Granger to Newgate prison. The charge preferred against them on 9th February was the simple one of " misdemeanours against the peace "—a charge on which Nicholas Greenway, John Bond, and Captain Stephens were also arrested and sent to the Gatehouse prison, Westminster. But behind that charge were others which, when judicially examined outlined an extraordinary story of deceit.[1] During the next few weeks the prisoners were examined, but it was not until a fortnight before Easter that Parliament showed its displeasure and concern when the confessions of the confederates were read and considered by the House. In the words of Henry Scobell, recording the decisions on Monday, 1st April, 1650, we get the first glimpse of an approaching financial crisis caused by a lowering of national credit through bribery and corruption. " Col. Ven'e [2] reportes from the Com'ittee of ye Army," he writes, " a paper contayning the further voluntary confession of Abraham Granger.[3] And also another paper entituled the voluntary discovery of matters of consequence, acted against the High Court of Parliament, knowne to William Broome,[4] Captaine Nicholas Greenway,[5] John Stephens,[6] John Cotten,[7] John Granger [8] : the Examinac'ons and Con-fessions of Captaine Nicholas Greenway, John Stephens, John Cotten, John Granger and John Bond, w'ch being read and the Howse having taken considerac'on of the seuerall Examinac'ons and Confessions did proceed to give Judgment vpon each of them.

" Resolued by the Parliament That Abraham Granger be adjudged

---

[1] Cal. S.P. Dom., Council, Day's Proceedings, 9th February, 1649–50, p. 510 (vol. iv, No. 11).
[2] Col. Jno. Venn or Fenn, treasurer of petty emptions, Cal. S.P. Dom., 1649–50, index, p. 693.
[3] Ibid., 636.   [4] Ibid., 611.   [5] Ibid., 637.
[6] Ibid., p. 510 (Capt. Stevens).   [7] Ibid., 618 (Cotten, or Cotton).
[8] Ibid., 636. See the reference in the Calendar, 1649–1650, page 510 (and vol. " i ", pp. 615–17, in the records) to the arrest of the prisoners, which was ordered by the Council of State at their meeting on 9th February, 1649–1650.

to be set on the Pillory on Wednesday next in the new Pallace Yard at Westminster during the space of two whole howres, Videl't from eleven of the clock in the forenoon vntill one of the clock w'th a paper set vpon the Pillory contayning in Capitall L'res his Offence (Videl't) for forging Warrantes and Counterfeiting hands to Bills of Exchange, whereby he w'th others hath procured three thousand pounds to be paid to them out of the Publique Treasuries in the Citie of London and severall Counties, And that there he shall loose his right Eare, And that on ffryday next the saide Abraham Granger bee sett on the Pillory at the Ould Exchange London for the like space from Eleven of the clocke vntill one w'th the same pap'r sett on the Pillory and there to loose his left eare, And from thence to be Com'itted to the Howse of Correcc'on there to remayne and bee kept to hard labour dueing the space of one whole yeere."

Sentences in identical terms follow, as resolutions of Parliament, in regard to Abraham Granger's fellow-conspirators, Wm. Broome, Captain Nicholas Greenway, John Stephens, John Cotton, and John Granger, all of whom were to stand together in the pillories at New Palace Yard and the Old Exchange, on Wednesday and Friday, 3rd to 5th April, 1650, losing the right ear in the City of Westminster and the left ear in the City of London. After which resolutions Parliament proceeds to give the following orders, John Bond alone being discharged :—

"Ordered by the Parliam't. That the Sheriffs of London and Midd's bee Injoyned and required to see the seuerall Judgments aforesaid to be Executed vppon the severall Persons aforesaid.

"Resolved &c., That John Bond,[1] servant to Nicholas Greenway bee discharged.

"Ordered, That it bee referred to the Com'ittee of the Army to pay vnto Captayne John Vernon [2] the sume of one hundred pownds for his Charges and paynes in discouering the Offenders aforesaid.

"Ordered, That it bee referred to the Com'ittee of the Army to pay such Sum'es of money as hath bin disbursed in Charges by the Persons Imployed in this discouery And likewise to give some recompence to the Marshall and Souldiers not exceeding the sum'e of Thirty pownds.

"Ordered &c., That the Com'ittee bee alsoe required and Authorised to pay the sum'e of ffive pownds vnto (—) [3] whoe was a meanes to discover the Offendors aforesaid.

"Ordered, That the Com'ittee of the Army bee Authorized and Required to take into their possession all such Jwells, Rings and other

---

[1] Cal. S.P. Dom., 9th February, 1649–50, p. 510. He had been committed to the Gatehouse with Greenway.
[2] Cal. S.P. Dom., 1649–50, p. 262.
[3] Space unfilled, as if the name were uncertain, or the person concerned had no wish to be named in this discreditable business.

goods of the said Abraham Granger, Will'm Broome, Nicholas Greenway, John Stephens, John Cotton, and John Granger w'ch were taken with them and to dispose of them for the purposes aforesaid. And that all such Persons as haue any of the said Jewells Rings or other Goods in their Custodie bee required to deliuer the same vnto the said Com'ittee or such Person or Persons as they shall appoint.

" Ordered &c., That it bee referred to the Com'ittee of the Army to examine the matter touching any Sum'es of money appearing to haue bin paid or receiued as Bribes or rewards for payment of any of the Sum'es of money vppon the said Counterfeit Warrants or Bills of Exchange and to report their oppinions to the Howse.

" Ordered &c., That all and every the Persons whoe haue in their hands any Sum'e or Sum'es of money receiued from Abraham Granger or any of his Confederates and by them receiued out of the Publique Treasuries vppon fforged Warrantts or Counterfeite hands to Bills of Exchange shall forthw'th pay the same to the Trea'rs at Warre at Guildhall London to be by them disposed of to the vse of the Army by Warrant of the Committee of the Army." [1]

Although these men lost their ears by way of punishment their activities did not cease, for Greenway assumed an alias, was henceforth known as " Freeman " and was arrested again in 1652. So too were Abraham Granger, and John Stephens, with new confederates— Bayley, Daniell, Fugill, Ladd, Philpot, and Quick.[2] In May, 1652, the concern of the Government is deepened by the revelation of an extensive series of frauds, and particularly by the discovery of forged debentures, in consequence of which Joshua Fugill and others were committed to the Gatehouse prison in order to be examined. As a result of the disclosures then made twelve persons were in custody three months later for forging debentures and public faith bills, fifteen others were named in warrants already issued for their arrest, and twenty-two more were viewed with such suspicion that similar action was contemplated in their case as well; for which reason Abraham Granger and his friends had already fled either to Gravesend or Dover, where officers waited for them in order to seize and search their trunks, books, and papers.[3]

In a report of June, 1653, Fugill, Quick, and Bayley are said to have confessed to no less than seventeen months of very profitable forgery, at which time the opinion was expressed that " four-sixths

[1] From a manuscript which came into the writer's possession by purchase, 19th December, 1935. It is headed " Die Lune j° April 1650 ", endorsed " Proceedings of ye howse contra Granger j° April 1650 ", and signed on f. 4. " Hen. Scobell, Clerk of ye Parliament." Presented to the British Museum, 5th February, 1937. (Add. MS. 44937.)
[2] Cal. S.P. Dom., 28th–29th May, 1652, p. 565.
[3] There are many entries in S.P. Dom., Commonwealth, concerning fraudulent transactions. See, for example, Calendar, 1651-2, pp. 263, 272, 275, 299, 300, 358, 365, 366, 368, 376, 401, 405, 408-9.

of the bills put off at Worcester House on fee-farms were counterfeit, and sold at from 6*d.* to 1*s.* 2*d.* in the pound ". It was said of these men and their friends that " they were so expert in those forgeries that they counterfeit a man's hand, so that he would not know it himself; that scriveners, citizens, and brokers were of their number and some of the Drury House clerks ". A search which lasted for forty days led to the discovery that bills worth £115,000 had been counterfeited. " Some way," says the report, " should be thought on to discover how the State has been cheated in hundreds of thousands, for after this rate not all the lands in England, Scotland, and Ireland will satisfy public faith bills and debentures ".[1]

With the progress of the inquiry prominent officials become implicated—Colonel Jn. White of the High Court of Justice in February, 1653, Colonel Rob. Thorpe in the following May, Colonel Jn. Jackson, the Agent-General of the new forces, in October, 1654, Matthew Siddall of the Prize Office, Greene and Tandy of Drury House, and Richard Nonelly of the Army Committee, in succeeding months. The depositions of Fugill and Granger, notwithstanding that the official reports are written in shorthand, make lively reading, especially after Granger is released on bail for £5,000 in November, when no one is safe from his wild charges. Four-fifths of the Public Faith Bills are said to be forged, and two-thirds of the claims to receive payments are believed to be false. Granger admits under repeated examination that he had been in the pillory, having lost his ears for forgery,[2] and Siddall agrees that his wages as assistant cashier are but 15*s.* a week. Bateson is said to have sold false bills valued at £15,000, and Hill £20,000 ; while Quick and Fugill stand charged with forging and vending bills for £70,000 and £80,000 respectively. The wives of Colonel Keys and Colonel Farrington are declared to have jointly vended £30,000 more in similar bills. Wilmore first obtained printed bills or debentures signed by Hodges and other Army Commissioners and these also were forged and sold with considerable profit. Officials in the Prize Office, Customs House, and the Treasury become involved. Berners and Steed are even accused of plotting to have the Council's seal cut in Holland. Colonel White's examination is of particular interest for, after a time, he admits that he knows Granger and goes on to describe their meetings and transactions at Drury House. " When Parliament first exposed the estates of Delinquents to sale," says the report, " White was employed by several persons to buy some of the lands, and purchased to the value of £40,000 or £50,000, at which time there were a company of people called Bill Brokers that frequented Drury House, and had their design upon all purchasers, to take off their bills for them to double upon the said lands."

[1] See Cal. S.P. Dom., 1652–3, pp. 63, 378–9 ; ibid., 1653–4, p. 414 ; and the published volumes for 1654 and 1655.
[2] See Scobell's record of the pillory punishment, already quoted.

It is affirmed that Granger received 1*s*. 6*d*. in the pound for what he bought, but he says that Colonel White only gave him 6*d*. for debentures. Manley admits that his bills for £3,000 were false and that some remain in Drury House still, though others have been burnt. Captain Cannon, with seven or eight others of " higher note whom I dare not name ", attended a daily dinner, " and they told me," says Granger, " that they never passed a bill without 1*d*. or 2*d*. in the pound, for their word was ' Come, come, you some, and I some '." On 28th December, 1654, Granger " begins to hope that the Almighty has heard his prayers "; but by 6th March, 1655–56, that seems improbable for Fugill has signed articles of forgery and high treason against him, and even Colonel White's friends now mock him and say, " What have you gotten by serving the State ? " [1]

This and a great deal more is contained in a deplorable story of tangled Commonwealth finance, for the adequate telling of which much space would be required. Propositions for discovering false debentures are at length made, and the registrar's accountants in Drury House, Gurney, and Worcester House are required to keep distinct registers, watching all entries closely ; " for if they who have so grossly cheated the State can so far insinuate with the State's officers as to cheat them, such officers, without great circumspection, will be deluded, and rather made the executioners of these villains' malice, and revenge upon innocent persons, than instruments of righting the soldiery, whose blood has been a mere prey for these vermin ".[2]

In 1655 curious articles of agreement between Granger and his associates are discovered and his doom is sealed. The promises which Granger made to his confederate Greenway are recorded in a paper preserved by Colonel Clarke. In this document it is agreed (1) not to reveal by word, sign, or token, their joint design ; (2) not to proceed in any transaction secretly ; (3) not to conceal anything, particularly in cases where Greenway has been " an instrument for procuring any paper or writing conduciary to any design ", but Granger will allow the full proportion of any benefit arising therefrom ; (4) not to seduce his agents from pursuing their joint undertaking ; (5) not to discourage friendship of third parties. Granger further agrees that if any profit should arise from an enterprise in which he was engaged, he would employ Greenway in preference to any other, " if I can do so without prejudice to myself, provided you only meddle with your own share and accept such share as I allot you, and the matter is kept secret, even if I should not again use you in it." As a final proviso, Granger stipulates that what he finds unaided he is at liberty to carry out alone in which case all the profit would be his own ; and he concludes

---

[1] The agreement between Granger and Greenway will be found in S.P. Dom., 1655, p. 11. For Granger's evidence, in shorthand, see S.P. Dom., vol. 94, no. 15.
[2] See Cal. S.P. Dom., 1655, p. 576.

with the warning: "If I reveal in any way what has passed between us, I hope that I may have no prosperity in this world, and that it may come against me at the last judgment." It certainly came against him in the day of judgment of which these records speak.[1]

Fugill, too, writes about the same time from the Press Yard, Newgate, though he thinks he may yet be " spared at the pit's brink of hell ". To Colonel Clarke he specially writes : " If you appoint some men of trust to seize all the books in Gurney and Worcester House, by comparing them you may find out the fraud," and as he knows herrings from pilchards he offers to " sort out of all sorts ". He declares that Richard Hill told him " there was a trade going on to renew leases relating to Crown, Dean and Chapter, and delinquents' lands, and make them of a longer date ", and he adds that he knows " Granger can take two or ten lines out of any lease, and put in what he pleases, so as the witnesses or any one else would believe it all to be in one hand and ink." [2]

In November, 1655, a commission is advised to call to account all treasurers and receivers of State money since 1642, so as to examine and audit their books. In the following April another commission is advised, this time for the purpose of examining fraudulent debentures which have been used in purchasing the lands of the late monarch, fee-farm rents, delinquent estates, and various other lands which have been exposed for sale by the State. Eventually, the date being 20th August, 1657, important instructions were drawn up to enable Commissioners to examine Public Faith bills, and further guidance followed for a committee to whom the returns of the Public Faith were to be made ; but by this time Granger and his friends had been executed, and it may be doubted whether public opinion ever completely regained its confidence in the debentures and bills of the Commonwealth, or its belief that government officials might be relied on for disinterested service. It was calculated after the Restoration by Dr. Warner, that 60,000 persons had paid for the various Church, Crown, and Delinquents' estates by means of forged debentures, the price of which ranged from 10d. to 1s. 4d. in the pound, and it is known that the Commission of 1655 actually discovered not less than £70,000 of these counterfeited bonds in the possession of sixty persons alone.[3]

---

[1] S.P. Dom., 1655, pp. 7–13, where the details concerning frauds are of great interest.
[2] Cal. S.P. Dom., 1655, p. 12.
[3] The subject of fraudulent transactions and the remedies applied is referred to in subsequent volumes of S.P. Dom., notably 1656–7, pp. 6, 15, 38, 46, 50, 64, 77 ; 1657–8, pp. 32, 43, 73–6, 107 ; also S.P. Dom., Chas. II, 1676–7, pp. 494–6.

CHAPTER V

THE SALE OF FEE-FARM RENTS

Turning from the Crown lands for a moment we may now
consider the important series of documents relating to the Commonwealth sales of fee-farm rents, and as they are mainly preserved in
three of the Exchequer departments, this side of the land transactions
may also be studied with comparative ease. In the first of these
departments, that of the Augmentation Office, are preserved the
Minute Book of the Trustees,[1] 1650 ; three volumes of Particulars
and Certificates, 1649–1653, with forty-seven files of Particulars,
and a Calendar in three volumes ; four volumes of Contracts, 1650–58 ;
a volume of Accounts, 1650, and another of the same year containing
an imperfect statement of the stipends and rents of church officials.
In addition, the Public Record Office contains a large number of
Counterparts of Deeds of Sales, arranged in twenty-three boxes,
with a very complete calendar in two volumes. The files of the
Particulars are thus arranged : the first forty refer to the counties of
England, the next five to the Duchy of Lancaster, and the last two
concern the stipends and pensions of Vicars, Curates, and School-
masters, the Certificates of which were prepared for the use of the
trustees in order that a proportion of the fee-farm rents might be
reserved for such payments. Besides these there are two boxes containing twenty-four rolls of Particulars for Denbigh, and a portfolio
of certificates and contracts for the sale of fee-farm rents. In the
second department, that of the Lord Treasurer's Remembrancer, other
records relating to these sales will be found : one is a volume of
423 pages containing Certificates and accounts of payments of fee-
farm rents from 1650 to 1652, while among the portfolios of Warrants
and Particulars for Leases will also be found a number of Particulars
for the sale of these rents in several counties during the Commonwealth. A further volume, containing copies of orders made by the
trustees for the sale of fee-farm rents between 1650 and 1654, exists
in the department of the King's Remembrancer of the Exchequer.
Particulars for the sale of the various rents of the Duchy of Lancaster
are also contained in two bundles in the Duchy series of records, the
Calendar of which contains references to the Augmentation Office
Particulars as well. The Duchy of Cornwall Office likewise contains
two volumes of Particulars relating to its own series of surveys.[2]

[1] Augm. Off., Misc. Bks., vol. 139. "The chairman's Books of Contracts" and
the "Reprize Book" are contained in portions of vols. 143-4. See Appendix II for
records of fee-farm rents and their sales (YO–YZ).
[2] Documents preserved in the Cambridge University Library are included among
the references in Appendix II (YO–YZ).

The Minute Book of the Trustees [1] contains considerable evidence as to the activity of buyers in the first year of the sales of fee-farm rents. The officials do not appear to have had their salaries [2] fixed until the sales had progressed for at least nine months; but at length the two " Counsells " were allowed £150 each, the solicitor £100, and the messenger and two doorkeepers [3] £30 apiece. The orders to the Clerk of the Pipe and the Auditors are numerous : they appear to be somewhat slow in their response, and renewed orders insist on the production of their books of fee-farm rents for each county before 1st April, 1650, as well as the insertion of the names of tenants in Certificates. Sir Henry Croke and the Auditors were brought before the Trustees at their meeting in the afternoon of 1st April (Monday, the first day of the sales) " to show cause why they have not brought their Certificates "—a reprimand being given four days later to Sir Henry for not having " returned ye Certificate for Wales ".[4] Meanwhile the publication of the impending sales was ordered, Colonel Webb being instructed to subscribe the letters to surveyors and other officials, and the Committee for removing Obstructions informed that the Trustees desired the Clerk of the Pipe and the Auditors " to deliver in their Certificates under Oath ".[5]

The imposition of this oath may have impeded the preparation and presentation of the certificates, and may perhaps account for the delay in fixing the salaries of the officials. On 5th April the Trustees took the step of appointing Clement Baker " to make Certificates of the Contracts to ye Treasurers ",[6] and his methodical statements occur weekly in the Minute Book. Not only was this appointment notified to the Committee of Obstructions but various difficulties in connection with the sales, with suggested remedies for their removal by that Committee.[7] In May the Trustees ordered their " two Counsells ", Graves and Darnall, " to advise with Mr. Halls and Mr. Jenckes about Drawing up a Supplementary Act," at the same time expressing a desire for apportioning the poundage charges of 3d. in the pound.[8] The most noteworthy orders in the interval between the first and second Acts for selling the fee-farms relate to the certification

[1] " The Books of Orders, Warrants, etc., issued by the Trustees for Sale of the fee-farm rents, etc., lately belonging to the late King, Queen, and Prince," 1649-1650 (Augm. Off., Misc. Bks., vol. 139, ff. 1-55).
[2] Augm. Off., Misc. Bks., vol. 139, under date 7th January, 1650-1.
[3] The last entry in S.P. Dom., Interreg., K. 8 (Council of State), 8th February, 1659-60, refers to the payment of arrears of Wm. Bellamy, late porter of Worcester House, whose widow was permitted to continue in residence there.
[4] Ibid., 9th February, 1649-50, March 13th, 14th, 16th, 20th, also April 1st and April 5th, 1650. Auditor Powell attended the Committee on April 2nd.
[5] Ibid., March 14th, 16th, 20th, 1649-50.
[6] Ibid., 5th April, 1650, with notification of his appointment to the Committee for Removal of Obstructions three days later.
[7] Ibid., 8th April, 4th May, 11th July, 1650.
[8] Ibid., May 13, 15th, 30th, 1650. For the Act of 13th August, 1650, see Appendix II (YO a (2)).

of the poundage apportionment, the treasurers' receipts, and the County Lists of Hundreds—the last-named being certified in a special list by Mr. Broughton instead of Clement Baker.[1]

The Act of 11th March, 1649, supplemented by the explanatory Act of 13th August, 1650, and the additional Acts of 6th February, 1650, and 3rd June, 1652, eventually led to an order by the Trustees for the production of accurate rentals, an order which is entered in the Minute Book as follows [2]:—" By the Trustees for Sale of the Fee Farm Rents. By vertue of the last Additional Act [3] for sale of the said Rents : These are to require you to bring in to us, sitting at Worcester House in the Strand, London, full and true Rentals of all such Fee Farm Rents, Tenths, or Rents reserved, Dry Rents, Hundreds, Liberties, Bailywicks, Franchises and Pentions, that are or lately were within your . . . . upon . . . . Tuesday the . . . . next :

" In which Rentals you are to certifie the Premises out of which the Fee Farms Rents &c., issue, with the Names of the person or persons that are the Tenants of the same ; And certifying the Fee Farm Rents by themselves, the Tenths by themselves, and so of the rest :

" Which said Rentals you are then to deliver in upon Oath, according as is appointed in the said Act ; whereof, you are not to fail. R. Harison, Corn. Cooke, M. Stocall, Ri. Sydenham, Edw. Cressett, N. Lempriere, Tho. Ayres." [4]

It is quite impossible, even after close study of these records, to state how many thousands of little rents of tenants and fee-farmers were exposed to sale between 1649 and 1659. The Particulars for London in Portfolio 3 File 20 alone number 386, and it is very likely that the total exceeded 20,000 for the whole kingdom. The annual value of the rents was certainly not less than £70,000. An attempt on this basis to analyse 1,100 entries, a tested sample of perhaps 5 per cent, scattered among the Particulars or Counterparts of Deeds of Sale for forty-three counties, throws some light on the range of these rents in the various divisions of the royal estates.

LXIIIA. ANALYSIS OF FEE-FARM RENTS, 1649–1659

Areas.	Under 10s.	10s. to £2.	£2 to £10.	£10 to £50.	Over £50.	Total Number.	Amounts.	Range.
(i) Metropolitan .	388	265	104	16	6	779	£2389·1	½d.-£500.
(ii) Extra-Metropolitan	128	71	47	16	2	264	£843·5	1d.-£135·8
(iii) Border-Lands .	22	19	18	13	1	73	£550·1	1s.-£116·4
(iv) Wales . .	10	5	2	4	—	21	£102·5	1s.-£34·3
Totals . .	548	360	171	49	9	1,137	£3,885·2	½d. to £500.

[1] Ibid., 30th May, 9th July, 8th September, 1650.
[2] Printed with blanks ; in Aug. Off., Misc. Bks., vol. 143, f. 101, under date 11th August, 1652.
[3] Act of 3rd June, 1652. See Appendix II (YO a (4).)
[4] The signatures have been added to the printed form.

The items included in the above analysis comprise a great variety of scattered fee-farm rents, annual tenths, rents reserved upon grants, dry rents and the like. " A fee-farm rent," says John St. John,[1] " is defined by some writers to be a rentcharge issuing out of an estate in fee, of at least a quarter of the annual value of the lands at the time of its preservation. But the true meaning of fee-farm is a perpetual farm or rent, the name being founded on the perpetuity of the rent or service, not on the quantum." [2] In the present instance examples have been selected from almost every county in England and Wales to illustrate the varied nature of the transactions registered at Worcester House after 11th March, 1649-50. The order books show that these rents issued out of, and the tithes were payable upon, premises of great variety—all of which amounts were advertised, " desired," rated, exposed to sale, and purchased :—

LXIII*B*. THE VARIETY OF FEE-FARM RENTS, ETC.

Description.	Counties.	Amounts. £	s.	d.
Advowson of Vicarage	Leicester	10	0	0
Assize rents	Cheshire	1	4	2
Barn rent	Herts		1	0
Borough rents	Berks	102	16	7
Brass House rent [3]	Herts			0½
Burgage rents	Northumberland		3	4
Capital messuage rent	Northants	9	17	4
Castleward rents	Surrey		3	4
Cellar rents	Monmouth		3	4
Chase rents [4]	Wilts	135	15	0½
Chamber rents [5]	Monmouth		13	4
Chantry rents [6]	Gloucester	3	4	0
Chapel tithes	Northumberland	3	6	8
Church Acre rent	Hants		1	0
Close rent	Middlesex	2	13	4
College rents	Warwick	5	0	0
Common fines	Leicester	10	0	0
Convent rents	Warwick		9	4
Coppice rents	Wilts	7	0	0
Corn mill rents	Lancashire		7	0
Cottage rents	Durham		9	4
Croft rent	Staffs		2	6
Customary tenement rents	Oxford	1	4	0
Fair dues [7]	Middlesex	1	0	0
Farm rent	Herts		13	4
Fishing rents [8]	Yorks		7	8
Free rent [9]	Warwick			8
Freehold rents	Derby		3	0
Friary rents	Bucks	12		3
Fulling mill rents [10]	Northumberland	4	0	0

[1] John St. John, *Observations on the Land Revenues*, 109-110.
[2] Spelman says one-third of the annual value. Coke confines the denomination to rents of at least a quarter the value of land.
[3] St. Albans.   [4] With grange, etc.   [5] With Shop.
[6] Brocklebury's Chantry ; the Master, etc., of Emanuel College, Cambridge.
[7] With Market tolls.   [8] In "Ayre Water".
[9] A discovery.   [10] With a corn mill.

Description.	Counties.	Amounts. £ s. d.		
Gardens	Herts . .			3¾
Glebe land rents . . .	Yorks . .	20	0	0
Grain tenths	Warwick . .	1	0	0
Grange rents	Warwick . .		6	8
Grove rent [1]	Warwick . .		4	0
Guild rents [2]	Warwick . .	7	13	9
Hall rent [3]	Suffolk . .		1	0
Hay tithes [4]	Yorks . .	2	6	8
House rents [5]	Dorset . .	1	0	4
Hundred rents [6] . . .	Bucks . .	16	9	5
Inn rent [7]	Herts . .		2	0
Lamb tithes [8]	Gloucester .		9	8
Land rent	Bucks . .			8
Lordship rents . . .	Herts . .	28	0	0
Manor rents	Bedford . .	3	11	4½
Mansion House rents [9] . .	Middlesex . .	10	0	0
Market tolls	Middlesex . .	1	0	0
Marsh rents	Essex . .		7	7
Meadow rent	Herts . .			2½
Messuage rent [10] . . .	Essex . .		4	0
Mill rent	Yorks . .	1	0	0
Monastery (site) rent . .	Northumberland	1	12	0
New River profits, etc. (moiety) [11]	Herts . .	500	0	0
Park rents	Middlesex . .	8	18	0
Pasture rents [12] . . .	Warwick . .		18	0
Pension from a Rectory . .	Devon . .		13	4
Prebend rents and tithes [13] . .	Durham . .	8	8	0
Priest's land rents . . .	Lancashire .	5	6	8
Priory rents	Northumberland		3	4
Quit rents	Essex . .	2	10	0
Rectory tithes . . .	Lincs . .	28	7	6
Shop rent	Monmouth .		3	4
Spiritualities	Lancs . .	6	13	4
Sundry premises . . .	Herts . .		7	6
Temporal lands . . .	Warwick . .	2	15	11½
Tenement rent . . .	Herts . .		2	8
Tenths of grain . . .	Warwick . .	1	0	0
Tithes (various) . . .	Durham . .	7	16	0
Town rents [14]	Carmarthen .	34	6	8
Township tithes . . .	Northumberland	28	13	4
Vicarage pension . . .	Oxford . .		5	0
Wapentake tithes [15] . . .	Lancashire .	23	19	8
Waste land rents . . .	Kent . .	3	0	0
Water mill rent . . .	Leicester . .	2	0	0
Windmill rent . . .	Middlesex . .	1	0	0
Woodland rents . . .	Wilts . .	7	0	0
Wool tithes [16]	Gloucester .		9	8

[1] With a meadow.   [2] Birmingham.   [3] Euston Hall.
[4] Grain and hay.   [5] Crouch House.
[6] Aylesbury (3 hundreds) ; see the separate list of Hundreds, App. V (iv), pp. 384-5.
[7] Swan Inn, St. Albans.
[8] Wool and Lamb.
[9] Chelsea Place ; " Manor Place," Oxfordshire, 5s. 4d.
[10] Messuage, garden, and 6 oxgangs of land, Yorkshire, £1 13s. 4d.
[11] City of London, £100.
[12] Pasture ground (¼ acre), Monmouth, 1s. 4d.
[13] For the President and Society for Propagating the Gospel in New England.
[14] St. Albans, £10. Northampton, borough £120, and improved value, £31 6s. 8d.
[15] See List of Hundreds (or Wapentakes), in Appendix V (iv).
[16] Wool and Lamb.

The Certificates signed by Clement Baker in 1650, as recorded in the Minute Book of the Trustees, were issued weekly and at first were forwarded to the Council of State alone, but from the beginning of July these certificates appear in two series, one of which was sent as usual to the Council of State while the second was forwarded to the Committee for the Army.

In the first ten days, according to " A state of the Fee Farm Proceedings presented to the Council of State " on 11th April, 1650,[1] " from 1st April (the first day of Tenants' pre-emption) the Trustees have sat every day morning and afternoon to dispatch the immediate tenants coming to purchase. Within the said time thirty-six desires of Tenants to purchase " were sent in, with the following result :—

	£	s.	d.
7 tenants with yearly values (unrecorded) .	—		
29 tenants with yearly rents amount to . .	1,302	19	11½
12 tenants with yearly rents contracted . .	300	8	3½
Treasury Account from these twelve Contracts	2,914	8	5¼

By the end of the month the " desires " had risen to 126 and the Contracts to sixty-six, while the summary of the preceding five weeks' sales made on 7th May, 1650, recorded a total of £59,199 17s. 6¾d. paid into the Treasury. At the close of the first quarter, 29th June, 1650, the contracts numbered 339 and the available fund

LXIIIC. Trustees' Weekly Certificates of Sales, 1650

(A) Treasury Account for Council of State.

(B) Ditto, for Council of State and Committee for the Army.

A

Dates. 1650.	Statements. £	Dates. 1650.	Statements. £
April 6	1,786·2	May 25	84,182·7
,, 13	3,233·4	June 1	90,978·0
,, 20	3,674·4	,, 8	97,124·5
,, 27	13,172·8	,, 15	101,935·2
May 4	59,199·9	,, 22	106,745·8
,, 11	68,886·7	,, 29	113,871·6
,, 18	71,647·9		

B

Dates.[2] 1650.	State Certificate. £	Dates. 1650.	Army Certificate. £
July 6 .	120,355·6	July 11 .	42,144·8
August 5 .	129,083·6	August 5 .	66,275·1
September 7	152,497·3	September 2	75,720·9
October 5 .	183,625·9	October 7 .	117,904·7
November 2	192,966·2	November 4	126,316·2
December 7	218,235·8	December 9	144,598·9
January 4 .	233,157·3	January 6 .	163,000·7
February 1 .	257,864·8	February 3	178,432·5
February 24	273,282·1		—

[1] Aug. Off., Misc. Bks., vol. 139, f. 4. References to the sales of £12,071 in April and £92,058 gross (£90,978 net) in May will also be found in vol. 140, ff. 8, 9. Receipts from sales in 1650 are referred to in S.P. Dom., 1650, p. 92, and see index ; with casual references to Contractors, Trustees, Registrar, and Sales, 1651–9, in the later volumes of the Calendar.

[2] In the Statement of 12th October, 1650, an allowance of £4,744 odd reduced the gross sum from £187,509 to £182,765 5s. 6¼d. " clear money " (Aug. Off., Misc. Bks., vol. 139, f. 116).

£113,871 12s. 9d. This gives an average of twenty-six contracts per week, with average sales of £8,759 7s. 2d.

The Certificates forwarded to the Committee of Parliament for the Army portion appear on record for the fortnight ending 16th September, 1650. In the above table the growth of the funds is shown month by month, instead of weekly. The contracts for the entire period shown number 783, ranging from two per week to 104 ; the smallest number (in August, 1650) produced only £38, but the largest number increased the account by over £46,027.[1]

The statement in the Minute Book under 12th September, 1650, towards the close of the second quarter of the Account is headed : " To the Committee of Parliament for ye Advance of present money." The Certificate then refers to the " Clear yearly Revenue we are to sell (as returned to us) as near as we can compute ", namely £77,000 per annum in fee-farms. Three summaries between 12th September, and 14th December, 1650, show how one-third of this revenue was disposed of in the next few months [2]:—

LXIIID. Annual Revenue from Fee-farm Rents, 1650

Statement, 1650.	September 12.	November 23.	December 14.
	£	£	£
Already contracted for . .	17,000	22,965	25,300
Sale whereof producing [3] .	153,000	212,593	225,650
Remaining to be sold . .	60,000	54,035	51,700
Original clear yearly Revenue	77,000	77,000	77,000

This discloses the fact that originally £77,000 was the estimated clear annual revenue of the fee-farms now exposed for sale, and further that more than £50,000 remained in December, 1650, as yet unsold. In September it was believed that by selling these residual rents " at 12 years' purchase upon doubling public debt " an amount equal to £720,000 would eventually be obtained. " But we conceive," adds the statement, " that if convenient freedom be given for doubling Public debts upon the aforesaid £60,000 per annum, there will be advanced in present money to ye State £400,000." Three months later, 14th December, this rate of purchase was regarded as the mean of five rates, so that the residue of £51,700, if sold upon doubling public debts, would produce varying amounts according to the following rates, viz. :—

At 8 years' purchase			£413,600
At 10	,,	,,	517,000
At 12	,,	,,	620,400
At 14	,,	,,	723,800
At 16	,,	,,	827,200

[1] On 4th May, 1650, Council of State. During the period 11th May to 13th July, 1650, the Trustees usually sat thrice a week, instead of daily, so that purchasers might prepare for their contracts on alternate days. The final statement in the Minute Book is dated 24th February, 1650, showing the net result after deducting the charge of 3d. in the pound.

[2] Aug. Off., Misc. Bks., vol. 139, ff. 61, 128b, 135.

[3] Cf. Table LXIIIC.

One further statement, dated " tertio Feb. 1650," [1] but showing the position of the Treasury account up to 6th February, throws some light upon the deductions that were made from gross receipts. The clear amount of " What hath been contracted for " is stated to be £276,776 9s. 1d., whereof the poundage is as follows :—

	£	s.	d.
(a) The 3 pences come to	3,459	14	1¼
The 3 pences that have been paid into the Treasury upon Contracts afterwards forfeited and ye things resealed [2]	63	7	0¼
Total of all the 3d.	3,523	1	1½
(b) Which being divided into ye 30 parts, each part is .	117	8	8
Whereof received by each person	80	9	1
Remaining due to each	£36	19	7

The total recorded on 24th February, 1650–51, " of all that hath been contracted ffor upon ye Sale of Fee Farms for clear money " from the first day of sale, 1st April, to the last day shown, 6th February —a period of ten months—reduces the amount given above to £273,282 2s. 9¼d., when all the charges based on 3d. in the pound are deducted.[3]

[1] Aug. Off., Misc. Books, vol. 139, f. 157 (and compare f. 162 under date 24th February, 1650–1).

[2] Five cases of forfeitures are named, 24th–26th September, 1650.

[3] Two Order Books covering the period 13th March, 1649, to 12th November, 1659, are marked : " Council of State, K. 7 and K. 8 " (P.R.O. List 43, p. 42). The fee-farm side of the sales of Crown Lands is referred to by Colonel Webb, the Surveyors and Auditors, in notes on various folios of Cheshire Parl. Survey, No. 8, Cornwall, No. 38, Derby, No. 27b, Essex, No. 2b, Gloucester, Nos. 14b, 17, Lancashire, No. 6, Leicester, No. 4, Northants, No. 28, Warwick, No. 19, Brecon, No. 2, Monmouth, No. 6. In the British Museum are indentures of sales of fee-farm rents in Suffolk, 30th July, 1650, and Yorkshire, 15th February, 1652–3, for £360 12s. 10½d. and £325 0s. 3d. respectively (Add. Ch. 15168, 27328). The five seals of Trustees are missing in the first conveyance, but they are attached to the second and also to the conveyance for Eckington, Derby, 1652, which is in the possession of Mr. B. R. Leftwich, F.S.A. The Suffolk indenture was purchased of J. W. Thorn, 15th July, 1859. An important survey of rents in Derby, Glouc., Heref., Leic., Linc., Northants, Rutland, and Worcester, dated 1650, is in Harl. 5013. Many notes relating to fee farms in Northants and other counties will also be found in Stowe MS. No. 184, ff. 262–7. Northampton rents, part of Col. Whaley's regimental contracts, recorded in Harl. MS. 5013, ff. 150–1, 192–3. A reference to Moulton, Northants, will be found in P.R.O., Sweetman's Slips (obs. 836, No. 229) under the dates 13–20 Charles II (1661–68). Earlier sales of 10 James I in Middlesex are entered in Ex. K.R. Misc. Bks., Ser. i, No. 52, where (on f. 134) some of the late possessions of Sir Wm. Cavendishe are included : e.g. " Firm' Maner' de Haringgay, cu' terr' de d'mical de ffermfeld in Haringay " —an elusive manor of the Bishop of Exeter in Hornsey—the rate of purchase being 18 years at the clear annual value of £10, or £180 in all, on 16th Feb., 1612. Hornsey, Highgate, and Muswell Hill records of the Commonwealth period will be found at the Bodleian, Lambeth, and P.R.O. See, for example, P.R.O., Lists 6, p. 249, and 39, p. 82, also D.K.P.R. rep. 20, p. 113 ; Rawl. MSS. Cat. 715 (113) ; Palmer's Index to Bargains and Sales, 1654 ; Home Cos. Mag., i, 57–8. The conveyance of the premises at Muswell Hill, 1654, is enrolled on Close Roll 3808 mm. 25–6.

Chapter VI

THE SALE OF FOREST LANDS, 1650–59

The special legislation of the Commonwealth government for the Survey and Sale of "the four forests or chaces" in Gloucestershire, Nottingham, Stafford, and Sussex, has already been recorded, but the results of the protracted parliamentary action in regard to these forest lands have not hitherto been collected and compared. Some notes on the special valuations made by the officials may therefore be recorded here.

First, there are records to be considered wherein the progress of the work may be traced. The instructions to surveyors and the petitions of Commissioners are referred to in pamphlets in the Guildhall and in Add. MS. 21427.[1] Collections and notes on "the business of the forests", the orders, particulars, rents and values, will be found in S.P. Dom. 1649–59; also in Add. MSS. 21427, ff. 253–9, 21437, f. 129, 34668, ff. 51–80, and Stowe MSS. 879–880, ff. 36b and 74; with further notes in Bagot and Webb MSS. collections in the Historical MSS. Commission reports.[2]

Next, there are the actual surveys[3] themselves, preserved among the records of the Augmentation Office in the Public Record Office. Thus, the series includes Gloucs. Parl. Surv., No. 12, dated 26th May, 1652, where Kingswood is styled "Forest, Chace and Wood"; Notts., Nos. 11–25, dated September, 1654, to March, 1658; Staffs., Nos. 8–37, surveyed between May, 1650 and April, 1659; and Sussex, Nos. 10–27, called "Ashdown Forest or chace als. Lancaster Great Park", with dates ranging from September, 1656 to July, 1658. The only duplicates are in the Land Revenue Office Series for Gloucestershire and Sussex.[4] We have a glimpse of the cost of making these surveys in a warrant of 27th November, 1656, for £250, by means of which Walter Frost, treasurer for contingencies of Council, was authorized to pay John March "towards the charge of surveying our fowre forests and chase called Enfeild Chase".[5]

---

[1] Catalogue, p. 213, and MS., f. 259. The legislation has already been dealt with in Part II, Sect. vii–viii above (q.v.); see also Firth and Rait, *Acts and Ordinances*, vol. iii, index.

[2] Reports, 4, p. 339, and 7, p. 688, in vol. i, Rudder's *Gloucestershire*, 1779, pp. 458–9, gives details concerning Kingswood Chase, acreage 3,432 a. 2 r.

[3] Seals accompany the signatures of surveyors in Notts P.S., 11, 15, 22b, 23, 25, Staff. P.S., 10–32, Suss. P.S., 10–17, and 27. Berks P.S., 13, likewise has its seal.

[4] L.R.O., vols. 280, ff. 243–316, and 299, ff. 235–264, with a late copy of 1770 in Add. MS. 5707, ff. 60–5. These surveys were kept in the Surveyor-General's Office, 1714–26, as shown in Add. MS. 30206–7.

[5] S.P. Dom., 1656, p. 175 : Privy Seal Book of Pell Office, No. 13, p. 89, 17th December, enrolled 27th December; D.K.P.R., rep. 5 (1844), app. ii, No. 4a, p. 258.

Then we come to the sales of these surveyed forestal lands. Needwood and Sherwood appear not to have been sold; and in any case not a single conveyance, or its counterpart, has been preserved in connection with the four forests, strange to say. Yet we know from the Baynes Papers [1] at the British Museum that Captain Baynes purchased Kingswood Chase, Gloucestershire, and this is confirmed by the " Original Creditors' List " at Cambridge,[2] which shows that Captain Adam Baynes on 21st July, 1652 paid £21,938 15s. 4d. for this property. The same list also records the contract of John Sanderson, amounting to £41,299 17s. 4d., for the purchase of Ashdown Forest on 26th June, 1650.

Of great importance to the Contractors and Trustees were the valuations of the premises, annual and gross, with the measurement of areas and enumeration of the trees. These are details that are best set out in tabular form, for there they are seen more clearly and in perspective whenever comparisons are made with other properties surveyed and sold. In the following summary of the tables [3] Enfield Chase is added to " the four forests " in order to make the valuations more complete. The shrinkage in area and annual values in eight years becomes obvious when these figures are compared with earlier surveys of Ashdown,[4] Needwood,[5] and Enfield.[6]

LXIII*E*. THE VALUATION OF THE FIVE FORESTS AND CHASES, 1652–8

Forests or Chases.	Counties.	Dates.	Divisions.	Acres.	Ann. Values.	Gross Values.
1. Ashdown .	Sussex	1657–8	9	7,860·6	1,205·4	647·0
2. Kingswood .	Gloucs	1652	8	3,432·3	1,241·0	2,052·5
3. Needwood .	Staffs	1658	21	4,533·7	1,228·6	7,254·6
4. Sherwood .	Notts	1658	5	3,221·8	484·2	24,170·1
5. Enfield .	Midds	1658	55	7,544·2	2,254·3	6,979·6
Totals			98	26,592·6	£6,413·5	£41,103·8

The addition of Enfield Chase to " the four forests " which, after considerable hesitation, the Council of State at length consented to sell, was due in large measure to the influence of the Army Committee, for the Old Park of Enfield and the three Lodges of the Chase had already been surveyed and sold—and a share of the spoils had already been seized by officers and men of one of the regiments.[7] The pressure of the Committee for the Army was therefore strong

---

[1] Add. MS. 21427, ff. 172, 174.
[2] Cambridge MS., Dd. viii, 30 (4), Gloucs, and Sussex.
[3] See the tables in Appendix V, Section (ii), pages 379–383.
[4] Ashdown, 1650, acreage 14,000, ann. value £2,507, gross values £620.
[5] Needwood, 1650, area 6,500 a., ann. value £2,761 1s., gross values £13,251 18s.
[6] Enfield, 1650, area 7,904 a., ann. value, £4,742 8s., gross values £15,163.
[7] Griffith Lloyd, by his contract signed 18th September, 1650, purchased Enfield Old Park " on behalf of Col. Chas. Fleetwood and the officers and soldiers of his regiment. Certificates were then issued for 134 bills, recorded in the name of the regiment, which were finally cancelled 20th February, 1651–2. See Firth, *Clarke Papers*, iii, p. 72, for army purchases of 9th September, 1656, and the audit of 10th July, 1662 (appendix VI (iii)) covering the years 1653–6.

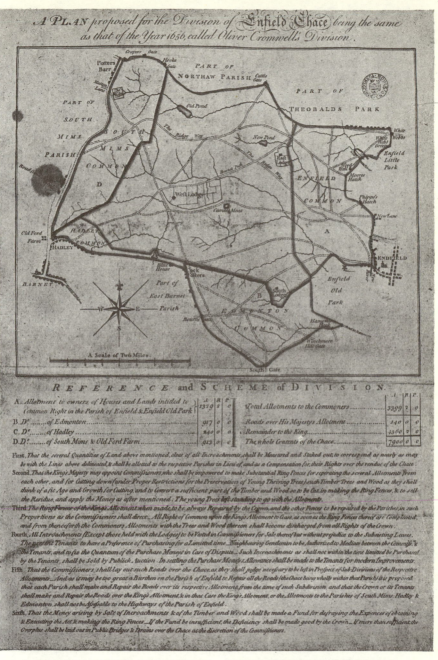

ENFIELD CHASE, MIDDLESEX : CROMWELL'S DIVISION, 1656

[face p. 240

enough to insist on the inclusion of the entire chase when the sale of the forestal lands was decided upon in Parliament. By reason of its accessibility to the metropolis and the close scrutiny of its records the proceedings taken in the case of Enfield Chase possess features of special interest that are well worth careful study.

In the first place, the available records are more numerous and detailed than in the case of the more distant lands of Ashdown, Kingswood, Needwood, and Sherwood, and they have been well preserved both in the Duchy of Lancaster Office and the Public Record Office. Besides the instructions and petitions already mentioned there are the Thomason Tracts, Harleian MSS., and papers in the Cambridge University Library, such as Ee. iii 18 (1) f. 3, with a unique document and map to supplement the numerous surveys relating to the Chase in the years 1650 to 1658.[1] By means of these records it is possible to reconstruct the work of the Parliamentary officials in the various stages of department activity which marked the progress of the Government scheme of land transference. Below we can trace the seven stages through which these republican transactions passed— the valuation, requisition, agreement, authorization, registration, certification, and enrolment—and to which attention has been drawn in the section dealing with " method of procedure ".[2] From first to last—from survey to Close Roll enrolment—a period of nine months sufficed in the case of Norris' Lodge, but Dighton's Lodge required a full year, Enfield Old Park, through interruption, two years, and Potter's Lodge almost three years to complete the transaction and fully secure the title to the estate. Payments were made partly in ready money but partly by means of bonds or bills, the first moiety being due eight weeks after the date of the contract or agreement, and the second moiety six months later. As security for payment of the purchase money the premises were held in the meantime by lease for ninety-nine years, in accordance with the terms of the Act of 16th July, 1649.

The whole of the proceedings connected with the purchase of Enfield Park and the three lodges in the Chase in the occupation of William Dighton, Samuel Norris, and Mr. Potter may be traced with great facility owing to the methodical arrangement of the records in connection with the present study. The surveyors who accomplished the initial work were Ralph Baldwin, Rowland Brasbridge, John Brudenell, Richard Heiwood, with the Surveyor-General, Colonel William Webb as supervisor and referee ; and their surveys

---

[1] See Madge, *Rural Mx.,* pt. i, p. 312, for classification of the surveys of the Augm. Off. series, pp. 17–20, April, 1650–November, 1650. Other surveys will be found in Land Rev. Off., Misc. Bks., vol. 288, ff. 179–189, Dy. of Lanc. Off. series, P.S. 44–5, Bodl. Lib. MSS. No. 18016, and Camb. Univ. MSS. Dd. ix, 27, No. 514. See also Lysons, *Environs of London,* vol. ii, pp. 186–9, Cox, *Royal Forests,* pp. 78–81, and Hone, *Manor Records,* p. 340.

[2] See ante, Part II, sect. ii, and Table LXIII*F.*

LXIII*F*. THE SEVEN STAGES OF LAND TRANSFERENCE.

	Enfield Chase Lodges.			*Enfield Park.*
P. Surv. Nos. 18 and 20.	*Dighton.*	*Norris.*	*Potter.*	*Park.*
I. Surveys received[1]	1650, Sept. 16	1650, Sept. 16	1650, Sept. 16	1650, Apr. 4
„ returned	„ „ 18	„ „ 18	„ „ 18	„ „ 5
II. Particulars ordered[2]	„ „ 16	„ „ 16	„ „ 16	„ „ 6
„ made	„ „ 16	„ „ 16	„ „ 16	„ „ 8
III. Contract signed[3]	„ „ 18	„ „ 18	„ „ 18	„ „ 8
Sale authorized[4]	„ „ 23	„ „ 23	„ „ 23	„ „ 12
Attestation recorded	1651, Apr. 30	1651, Apr. 30	„ Nov. 11	„ May 27
IV. Contractors' Warrant[5]	„ „ 30	„ „ 30	„ „ 11	1651, *Jan.* 14
V. Registrar's Rates[6]	„ „ 30	„ „ 30	„ Dec. 5	1650, May 31
VI. Treasurer's Certificate				
No. 1[7]	„ May 16	„ May 14	1651, Nov. 29	„ June 10
„ acceptance	„ „ 17	„ „ 15	„ Dec. 9	„ „ 19
Bills, etc., cancelled,				
No. 1[7]	„ Sept. 15	„ Aug. 8	1652, Feb. 20	„ Aug. 8
Particulars entered	„ May 3	„ May 3	„ Nov. 30	1651, Jan. 23
Treasurers' Certificate,				
No. 2	—	—	„ Dec. 8	„ Feb. 2
„ acceptance[8]	—	—	„ „ 11	„ „ 7
Bills, etc., cancelled,				
No. 2	—	—	1653, *Aug. 12*	„ „ 20
VII. Indenture made[9]	„ June 26	„ June 11	1652, Mar. 15	„ „ 18
„ acknowledged	„ July 2	„ „ 11	„ „ 16	„ „ 18
„ enrolled	„ Sept. 30	„ „ 12	„ „ 16	1652, Apr. 8

are preserved to-day in the Augmentation Office Series [10] at the Public Record Office. Journals of Contractors and Trustees record the requests for Particulars of the premises and orders to the Registrar to supply them.[11] The Particulars thus supplied are still preserved.[12] Certificates of rates of purchase, with other certificates of bills or debentures enclosed, are in accessible bundles that are easily found.[13]

Although the various contracts are found duly entered and signed in the Contractors' Journals, and even affixed in due course to the lengthening roll of Particulars, only one conveyance or counter-

---

[1] Transmitted the same day.
[2] Requests for Particulars and Orders to Registrar (vol. 314).
[3] Record of agreement based on Particulars (vols. 173-4).
[4] Vol. 314, with Orders : "No 4 on Apr. 12," and "No. 3 on Monday next" (23rd September) ; not "by the box".
[5] Add. MS. 30208, f. 76, No. 14, records 11th November, 1651, for Potter's Lodge. The date for Enfield Park is late, 14th January, 1651-2, revealing interruption in the proceedings. Warrants authorizing Conveyances.
[6] Jn. Wheatley's Certificate of Rates of Particulars of Sale.
[7] Certificates of Wm. Potter, Registrar for Debentures, for 1st moiety, afterwards returned and cancelled.
[8] Acceptance of Certificates and Contractors' Warrants authorizing Conveyances.
[9] Sealed by five Trustees.
[10] Mx. P.S., 18, and 20 ; referred to in Calendars and indexes at the British Museum, Add. MSS. 21327, f. 79, and 30208, f. 76.
[11] Aug. Off., Misc. Bks., vol. 173, f. 29, vol. 174, f. 10, vol. 314, ff. 31, 79*b*.
[12] P.R.O. Particulars marked L. 29, 32, 42, and 45.
[13] P.R.O. Bundles marked E. 121, Bun. 3, No. 4, items 9, 70, 71, and 87, enfolding six sets of bills, etc. (marked L. Bu. Bv. Cl.), containing 185 items. These rates are also summarized on the Particulars and form part of the Contract or agreement.

part of deeds of sales has been preserved at the Public Record Office.[1] But if we consult the Cambridge series of documents no less than four conveyances may be traced.[2] In the same series the list of Original Creditors [3] records quite correctly the names of the purchasers and the amounts they paid for the park and lodges of Enfield. It is, therefore, by reference to the Trustees' Book in Cambridge University Library that we can prove the former existence of conveyances that were signed and sealed by Wm. Bosseville, Thos. Coke, Cornelius Cooke, Ralph Harrison, Thos. Hubbert, Jn. Hunt, Jn. Sparrow, and Wm. Steele between 11th June, 1651 and 15th March, 1652-3. To confirm this inference, in the absence of counterparts of deeds at the Public Record Office, we need only consult the Close Rolls [4] where all four purchasers are duly and fully recorded. Besides all these accessible records there are others to which many references point but which are no longer available. Such, for example, are the books of Particulars and discoveries, registrations and entries formerly in the departments of the Surveyor-General, Registrar, and Comptroller.[5]

From the Particulars preserved in the Public Record Office we learn that the Enfield premises were rated in fee simple for Griffith Lloyd, of St. Ives, Hunts., Arthur Evelyn of Wallingford, Berks., Chas. Whitehead, of Abingdon, Berks., and Jn. Nelthorpe, of Gray's Inn, London, and " Utterby Grange, Yorkshire ".[6] The actual conveyances were, however, made out differently. The indenture of " Old Enfeild Parke " was between Wm. Steele (and other Trustees of the King's lands) and Griffith Lloyd, Stephen White of Wellingborough, Thos. Else of West Haddon, and Richard Ashby of Bugbrooke, Northants.[7] Evelyn and Nelthorpe purchased the lodges ", as attorneys " on behalf of themselves and the Original Creditors ", but Dighton's Lodge is recorded in the Close Rolls as being conveyed to Charles Whitehead.[8] With the exception of Ashby and Whitehead, styled " Gentlemen," all the other persons named are referred to as " Esquires ". The details of valuation and purchase are as follows :—

---

[1] P.R.O. Conveyances, L. 42, No. 534, dated 15th March, 1652-3. Caley's index, p. 59.

[2] Camb. Univ. MSS., Dd. xiii, 20, Nos. 319, 334, 423, 534, each conveyance sealed by five named Trustees.

[3] Ibid., Dd. viii, 30 (4), ff. 3, 22.

[4] Close Rolls, enrolments, 1651-2, Nos. 3573, mm. 40-1, 3,580 mm. 39-40, 3,676 mm. 8-9, and 3,686, mm. 40-41. Palmer's *Index*, vol. 78, pp. 15, 17, 68, 72.

[5] Referred to as Books marked A to G in entries made by Potter, Wheatley, and others in Certificates, Surveys, and the Index of Crown Lands (Add. MS. 30208).

[6] Qy. Lincoln ; Utterby, Yorks., in Close Roll enrolment.

[7] The Certificate of Sale states that Lloyd purchased " on behalf of Col. Chas. Fleetwood and the officers and soldiers of his regiment " (134 bills).

[8] The Contracts for the three lodges were revised (Aug. Off., Misc. Bks., vol. 174, f. 10). Nelthorpe was also attorney for Wm. Arscott in his purchase of Potter's Lodge (Certificates, E. 121, Bun. 3, No. 4, item 87).

LXIII*G*. The Rating of the Enfield Estates

Rates and Bills.	Enfield Park. £	Dighton's Lodge. £	Norris' Lodge. £	Potter's Lodge. £
1. Pres. yearly value	343·5	45·2	40·1	79·6
2. Coneys : Gross value	15·0	6·7	6·0	10·0
Deer : Gross value	45·0	—	—	—
Wood : Gross value	1,964·0	128·4	24·6	131·0
3. Total Purchase Money	7,520·0	904·4	712·3	1,493·9
4. Reprises allowed	60·0	—	—	—
5. 1st Moiety : Amount due	3,760·0	904·4	712·3	747·0
„ Bills or Debs.	3,760·3	904·0	711·5	747·8
6. 2nd Moiety : Amount due	3,700·0	—	—	746·9
„ Bills or Debs.	3,700·0	—	—	747·8
7. Payment in ready money	—	0·4	0·8	
8. No. of years' purchase	16 years	17 years	17 years	17 years
9. No. of bills or debs.	134 bills, etc.	40 bills, etc.	2 bills, etc.	9 bills, etc.

The classification of the later Parliamentary Surveys of Enfield Chase in the Official Calendar at the Public Record Office is very confusing. Within the surveys are " Plot letters " (A to WW) in agreement with a plan preserved at the Bodleian Library, Oxford,[1] and these are quoted to indicate the boundaries of each division of the Chase. But on the surveys are endorsements of later date (marked with the letters A to RR), so that the classifications of these documents is further complicated—the more so since there is entire disagreement throughout the series between the letters marked within and without the individual surveys. Thus A in the plan is D (*b*) for the survey, and AA in the case of the survey corresponds to TT on the plan. The survey marked " O " contains not one, but eight surveys, each with its own internal " Plot letter ". It seems better, therefore, to quote the original lettering of the plan, and this has been done in arranging the surveys here.[2] The original certificate of the Surveyors of Enfield Chase to the Committee of Appeal, forwarded upon the completion of their task, in November, 1658, has been discovered among the Cambridge University Library Collections (Dd. ix, 27, No. 514). It is a well-preserved folio document of twenty-seven leaves, undated, and is quite unique in form and substance, no copy having been preserved at the Public Record Office or elsewhere.

As there is no other copy of the Cambridge document in existence a summary of its contents may be given here.[3] The title (f. 1) runs thus : " For the Right Honorable the Lo[rd] Lambert, Generall Desborough, Colonell Sidenham, S[r.] Gilbert Gerard, John Trevor

[1] Gough Prints and Drawings, Mx., p. 12B, contains a coloured " Plan proposed for the Division of Enfield Chase, being the same as that of the year 1658 called Oliver Cromwell's Division ". The copy dates from *c.* 1776 and is reproduced in a sketch in Robinson's *Enfield*, 1823, vol. i, 194-5. Divisions A–D contain 3399 A. 2 r. out of the entire area of 7,900 A. in the copy. At the P.R.O. the Enfield Surveys are recorded as Augm. Off., P.S. 17, 17A to RR, 18–20. (Bodleian shelfmark : Gough Maps 17, f. 12 *b*.)
[2] See Madge, *Rural Mx.*, pt. i, p. 312, pt. ii, p. 442. The duplicates are P.S. 17, O (*b*, *d*), 17 X, Z, 17 DD, GG, LL, MM. See Appendix, pages 382–383.
[3] Certificate of Jn. Boynton, Hugh Webbe, Edm. Rolfe, and Nich. Gunton, Surveyors of Enfield Chase, to the Committee of Appeal. Date about November, 1658. The original paper cover is endorsed : " Endfield first Certific't, Commonwealth, to the Committee of Appeale." The word " Needwood " is erased.

and Josias Bernards, Esq^rs., the Committee of Appeale appointed
by Parliament to heare and determine matters concerning the Sale
of ffower fforrests and Enfeild Chace, May it please yor· Honn^rs.,
In obedience unto two severall Commissions with Instructions thereunto annexed from his Highness the Lord Protector . . . for surveying
of Enfeild Chase . . . and in pursuance of two Ordinances . . .
Parliament begun at Westminster 17th September, 1656, we have
repaired to the said Chase and have surveyed the same in all things
according to the several powers, and instructions given us for that
purpose." Then follow (f. 1) the names of the divisions of the Chase,
with references to records in the Tower, 18 Edward II to 9 Henry V,
a decree in the Duchy of Lancaster dated 27 Henry VIII, and a
description of the Chase made by Hexam in the reign of Elizabeth
and said to be in the possession of " Mr. Pecke, of Mount Pleasant " ;
the bounds of the Chase (f. 2), the quantity and ownership (f. 3),
the quality, and the wood and timber (f. 4) ; [1] the erections (f. 4),
allowances for highways, with customs and privileges associated with
the Chase (f. 6). Folios 10 to 20 are occupied with details concerning
the number of houses and acres of land in " Enfeild ", the interests
of the manor of " Edlemonton als. Edmonton ", Hadley, South
Mimms, the valuation of " Old ffold " and the survey of " Old
Enfeild Parke ". Marginal notes refer to a decree in the Duchy
Court, 7th December, 3 James I, and other points of agreement or
disagreement in connection with Edmonton. Claims next are dealt
with (ff. 21–25), especially those of Wm. Alston, Franc. Atkinson,
Allen Bryant, Rob. Cordell, Wm. Hall, Edm. Kidderminster, Jas.
Meggs, Eliz. Sanders, Stephen Venables, and Mr. Wakefield.

The remainder of the survey (ff. 26–7) contains a tabulated
statement of the claims and allowances. The whole Chase is shown
to contain 7,900 acres, and Enfield Old Park, entirely pasture ground,
553 acres. As the total claims allowed amount to 3,362 A. 3 r. 14 p.,
" for the State remains 4,537 A. 0 r. 26 p." Houses number 348 in
Enfield, 313 in Edmonton, 220 in South Mimms, 72 in Hadley and
one in Oldfold, making a total of 955. The acreage is as follows, but
the total exceeds the reputed total for the Chase itself :—

LXIII*H*. Claims and Allowances in Enfield Chase, 1658

	Arable. Acres.	Meadow. Acres.	Pasture. Acres.	Woodland. Acres.	Totals. Acres.	Claims Allowed. Acres.
Enfield . .	2,090·0	789·5	1,382·0	—	4,261·5	1,260·0
Edmonton .	1,200·0	600·0	1,000·0	1,300·0	4,100·0	824·5
Hadley [2] . .	—	—	335·7	—	335·7	220·0
South Mimms [3]	1,456·5	1,279·0	1,279·0	—	4,014·5	820·0
Oldfold . .	65·5	70·0	70·0	—	205·5	65·0
Old Park .	—	—	553·0	—	553·0	33·5
Highways .	—	—	—	—	—	140·0
Totals .	4,812·0	2,738·5	4,619·7	1,300·0	13,470·2	3,363·0

[1] With the note : " They know nothing to the contrary."
[2] The acreage is recorded for " Pasture and meadow " combined.
[3] A note in the left margin (f. 26) reads : " If yor Hono^rs thinke fitt to allow the
same."

The yearly values per acre are of interest, especially as they disclose the values of lands of various kinds after ten years of Commonwealth government, only a few months before the restoration of monarchy in May, 1660. Woodlands are not separately indicated, as the timber alone was needed. Arable land was 6s. 8d. per acre at Enfield and Edmonton and 8s. for Oldfold and in South Mimms. Pasture was worth £1 an acre.[1] Meadow in Oldfold and at South Mimms is valued at £1, but it was worth £1 6s. 8d. per acre in Enfield and Edmonton. The highest value, however, is recorded for the mixed " pasture and meadow " of Hadley, not otherwise distinguished, for in this instance the surveyors assess the land at £2 per acre per annum.

[1] The order for Old Park is : " Purchase their rights of common at xxs. p. ann."

Chapter VII

THE DISPERSION OF THE CROWN LANDS

We have now studied in considerable detail the political and financial aspects of the Commonwealth land policy, especially in connection with the disposal of the royal estates to keen but cautious buyers. With a wealth of evidence before us it is at last possible to pronounce judgment in definite form as to the success or failure of the republican policy. We may agree at once with Mr. Lennard when he says that " whatever may be thought of the political aspects of the policy of sale, there can be no doubt that it was really moulded by financial needs, and it is primarily on financial grounds that it must be judged. And, in the first place, there is no denying the fact that the sales did relieve the pressing necessities of the Government ". How great was that relief Dr. Shaw has shown, for although the figures which he gives are by admission " very roughly reckoned ", there can be no doubt that " the extraordinary sources of income "—such as the sales from year to year of Church, Crown, and Royalist possessions —fully made up the annual deficit of £450,000 and " kept the Commonwealth fairly solvent " until about the year 1654. This view finds support in the figures given for the sale of Crown lands in the present study—figures which are not " roughly " but very carefully reckoned from all available sources of information, tested in the last resort by the calculations of the Treasury officials in the early days of the Restoration period. Mr. Lennard quotes the instructive speech made by Cromwell on 4th September, 1654, to the first Parliament of the Protectorate. " All your treasure was exhausted and spent," he said, " when this government was undertaken : all *accidental* ways of bringing in treasure were, to a very inconsiderable sum, consumed —That is to say, the ' forfeited ' lands are sold, the sums on hand spent ; rents, fee-farms, King's, Queen's, Prince's, Bishops', Dean-and-Chapters', Delinquents' lands sold. These were *spent* when this Government was undertaken. I think it's my duty to let you know so much. And that's the reason why the taxes do yet lie so heavily upon the people ; of which we have abated £30,000 a month for the next three months." [1]

That the Crown lands had been largely sold and the money spent by 1654 is undoubtedly true. The Contractors' Journals do not contain a single entry relating to agreements after 1653, and it may be

---

[1] See Lennard, *Rural Northants*, pp. 22–3, and his quotation of Carlyle's letters and speeches, ed. S.C. Lomas (1904), vol. ii, pp. 357–8.

noted that of the total of 962 entries recorded in their books, less than 25 per cent refer to the years that follow 1650. Wherever we look the evidence is the same. By the end of 1651 the immediate tenants cease to buy, the last score of entries in the Cambridge list appearing in that year. The lists of original creditors and assigned bills likewise show that the last two of the former and the last two dozen of the latter were disposed of either in 1652 or 1653, while the list of rents and revenues received by officials in the interval between the sales also comes to an end in 1653. After that year only sixteen requests for Particulars, thirty-one warrants of contractors, and thirty-nine certificates of treasurers are included among their records. Of 653 conveyances referred to in the Cambridge collections less than sixty belong to the period 1654–9. The enrolments of Bargains and Sales, for royal as well as delinquents' lands, were almost the only transactions that occurred after 1653, and even then less than 30 per cent remained to be recorded. It has been shown in the tables of statistics which illustrate the procedure adopted for selling Crown lands, that there is a remarkable uniformity throughout the series of records in this respect, for with the single exception of the enrolments, which necessarily came last in the scheme of operations, all the entries reach their maxima in the same year, namely 1650, after which they drop sharply and then gradually cease. Even in the case of the Bargains and Sales enrolled in the Chancery the maximum number is reached in 1652–3, by which time registration had been completed for earlier sales and the debentures of purchasers had been cancelled.[1]

The great activity of the various officials at Worcester House during the period of the government sales is revealed by the statistics just recorded. But it may be considered also from another point of view, for the territorial transactions based upon Colonel Webb's surveys concerned not only a variety of premises, but several classes of tenants scattered throughout the counties of England and Wales. Their estates had ·suffered unequally during the recent struggle, so that values were often difficult to assess. From the table below we can see that both the Parliamentary region in the centre and east of England, and the Royalist region in the north and west, were areas of almost equal size, but it should be remembered that the former embraced more than a dozen counties that lay in the " battle zone ".[2]

The extremes were thus entirely within the backward, feudal region of the Royalist strongholds ; but the Extra-Metropolitan division contained the largest group of counties, and sent more members to Parliament in 1653 than any other division. Under these

---

[1] The statements here made are based on analyses of the various documents quoted, especially those in the Cambridge University Library Collection already referred to.

[2] Table LXIV. The sources have already been indicated. See the Cambridge and P.R.O. documents and Table I. " Areas of Land Valuations." In Edward I's reign this group sent 166 members to Parliament ; in 1653 the number was ten less, while the Borderlands dropped from 152 to 110.

LXIV. Territorial Transactions, 1649–1659

Regions.	Counties.	Area. sq. miles.	Requests.	Particulars.	Conveyances.[1]	Bargains and Sales.
(a) Parliamentary.						
(i) Metropolitan	10	9,020·9	450	452	238	516
(ii) Extra-Metropolitan	16	19,006·8	456	512	232	676
Totals . .	26	28,027·7	906	964	470	1,192
(b) Royalist.						
(iii) Border-lands	13	22,319·1	290	436	148	772
(iv) Wales . .	13	7,973·3	37	121	30	96
Totals . .	26	30,292·4	327	557	178	868
Totals . .	52	58,320·1	1,233	1,521	648	2,060

circumstances we should expect to find the centres of greatest activity in connection with republican sales in the two areas constituting the Parliamentary region, and this, as the table clearly indicates, is actually the case. In the whole table only once do we find the Royalist region with the highest total,[2] and that, naturally enough, occurs in the case of the enrolments of Bargains and Sales, where the lands forfeited by royalists are included by Palmer. The Parliamentary region in all the other cases stands highest, the percentage of entries hardly ever dropping below 70 per cent. As to the payments made by the tenants for their properties, these are seen to be quite small, usually under £100, whereas the values of premises conveyed to original creditors ranged as a rule from £1,000 upwards.

LXVA. Payments by Tenants and Agents

(A) Immediate Tenants. (B) Original Creditors. (C) Assigned Bills. (D) Regiments.
(E) Conveyances.[3]

Range.	A.	B.	C.	D.	E.
Under £100 .	143	13	7	—	56
,, £500 .	100	56	53	—	181
,, £1,000 .	25	68	29	1	117
Above £1,000 .	31	195	47	17	271
,, £10,000	—	26	—	16	23
Totals .	299	358	136	34	648

From the General Index of Crown lands it is possible to ascertain the annual value of the royal estates. Of 1,003 rents recorded in that volume, sixty-five were under £1 and only eleven exceeded £500. The total amounted to £48,573 per annum. Not all of these show the improved value given by the surveyors, the record of which needs to be sought in the surveys themselves; but 560 rents, amounting annually to £16,248, are seen to be worth £75,148 under the new valuation, thus revealing clear improved values of nearly £60,000 per annum. The average rent of royal property was about £48 per annum; and the average improved value £105, which is more than double the yearly rent.

[1] Not including five later re-sales of the same property, 1654–5.
[2] Table LXIV. Borderlands area.
[3] Five later re-sales of the same property, 1654–5, are excluded.

Improved values of premises equal in amount to the existing rents are seldom recorded by the surveyors, but seventy-four have been noted where the amounts are less than the old rents, so that in their case the surveyors record the new Commonwealth values as showing increases of less than 100 per cent. On the smallest of these rents, £3 18s. 5d. in Lancashire, the clear improved value is £2 12s. 6d., making £6 10s. 11d. per annum altogether. The largest rent, £953 6s. 4½d. in Kent, shows an increase of less than £5 10s. as the improved annual value. Such valuations from 7s. upwards are to be found in thirty counties of England and Wales. But by far the greater number of improved values exhibit increases that exceed the " ancient rents " very considerably. Thus, if we take the most noteworthy instances, one from each of forty-one counties, we may classify these exceptional improvements as follows :—

LXVB. Exceptional Increases of Rental Values

Numbers.	Range.	Rents.	Improvements.	
9 Rents under £1,	total £4 3s. 4d.,	show £151 17s. 2d.	increase.
17 others „ £5,	„ £49 12s. 4d.,	„ £1,517 1s. 11d.	„
7 „ „ £10,	„ £47 0s. 8d.,	„ £2,425 19s. 3d.	„
5 „ „ £20,	„ £55 7s. 5d.,	„ £1,035 4s. 3d.	„
3 „ „ £50,	„ £93 6s. 8d.,	„ £848 4s. 9d.	„

So that in these forty-one counties, upon rents ranging from 1s. to £43 6s. 8d. with a total of less than £250, the clear improved annual values were close upon £6,000.[1] In other words, whereas Charles I was unable to obtain a greater rent-roll in these instances than £249 10s. 5d., the Commonwealth government succeeded not only in raising the amount to £6,227 17s. 9d. but made the new valuation the basis of its rates for sale of the premises to purchasers. And this improved value of £24 for every £1 of " ancient rent " was very largely retained by the Surveyor-General and Lord Treasurer in their new surveys and grants after 1660.[2]

LXVI. Yearly Rents and Improved Values [3]

(A) Clear improved value over present rent. (B) Full annual value.

Division.	No.	Yearly Rents. £	No.	Improved Values. A. £	B. £
Under £100 .	891	19,129·9	396	11,133·8	19,672·1
„ £500 .	101	20,593·0	144	30,017·4	35,252·0
„ £1,000.	9	5,930·1	17	12,687·6	14,893·8
Above £1,000.	2	2,920·3	3	5,062·0	5,330·6
„ £10,000	—	—	—	—	—
Totals .	1,003	48,573·3	560	58,900·8	75,148·5

[1] A Norfolk example shows rent 8s., improved value £19 12s. Other notable examples are : Dorset, 13s. 4d. and £46 12s. 8d. ; Devon, 18s. and £34 11s. 6d. ; Lincoln, £1 16s. and £177 12s. ; Northants, £2 13s. 4d. and £361 4s. 2d. ; Berkshire, £3 3s. 4d. and £71 3s. 4d. ; Lancashire, £4 2s. 4d. and £230 ; Middlesex, £5 6s. 8d. and £1,610 8s. 4d. ; Kent, £6 13s. 4d. and £382 2s. ; York, £11 4s. and £318 10s. ; Cambridge, £20 and £283 7s. 3s. ; Herts, £30 and £449 17s. 6d. ; Brecon, £43 6s. 8d. and £115. But, of course, all these instances are exceptional.

[2] See Part V, Sec. ii.

[3] Table LXVI. Analysis of Add. MS. 30208.

The General Index already referred to has a number of entries dealing with the rates quoted in the certificates for the purchase of royal property. Thus 373 are found to represent a total of £789,047, giving an average rate of £2,115. The yearly rent involved in this instance exceeded £24,697, and as the clear improved value was a little over £35,100, the total valuation placed upon the premises by the surveyors was nearly £60,000. We are able, therefore, to establish the connection between the yearly rent, the new value per annum, and the amount forthcoming by way of payment for purchasing the estates. Few of these rates were below £100, only thirty-one being found in that class ; but on the other hand 164 ranged from £1,000 to £10,000 and thirteen others were for even larger sums.

LXVII. Rates of Particulars for Purchasers

Division.	No.	Yearly Rents.	Clear Improved Value.	Total Annual Value.	Rates.
		£	£	£	£
Under £100 .	31	36·3	302·1	338·4	1,899·2
,, £500 .	97	684·1	2,440·7	3,124·8	25,708·6
,, £1,000 .	68	1,538·3	3,856·4	5,394·7	49,780·1
Above £1,000 .	164	14,000·9	24,355·7	38,356·6	481,274·6
,, £10,000	13	8,437·6	4,146·5	12,584·1	230,384·4
Totals .	373	24,697·2	35,101·4	59,798·6	789,046·9

The various payments made by the purchasers can be discovered by a careful search among the Cambridge papers. Thus the Immediate Tenants paid £114,275, an average of £382. The Original Creditors made 358 payments, the total reaching £1,152,166, an average of £3,218, or eight times as much. Assigned Bills amounted in 136 cases to £158,451, giving an average of £1,165. It is worthy of note, that if we except the Northern Brigade, thirty-three regiments are credited with an average of £11,919, their total being £393,334, an amount which the Northern Brigade increased to £498,243. The distribution of these payments is of particular interest, for in every case the Parliamentary region stands first, and in two cases out of three the metropolitan area is at the top of the list. In the following table the totals include amounts from combined areas.[1]

LXVIII. Divisional Payments of Tenants and Creditors

Areas.	Immediate Tenants.	Original Creditors.	Assigned Bills.
	£	£	£
(i) Metropolitan .	53,028·3	467,749·4	50,833·9
(ii) Extra-Metropolitan	52,055·7	340,032·4	53,460·6
(iii) Border-lands .	7,940·1	219,464·3	40,796·4
(iv) Wales . .	1,000·6	26,375·6	10,506·8
(v) Combined . .	250·0	98,544·1	2,853·9
Totals . . .	114,274·7	1,152,165·8	158,451·6

[1] Tables LXVIII and LXIX. These figures are taken from the analysis of the Cambridge documents.

The total payments received from these three sources amounts to slightly less than £1,500,000, which is about £100,000 more than the total shown in the Cambridge list of conveyances. The scale on which these payments were made by tenants or allowed to creditors may be judged from the analysis of the statistics in the next table.

LXIX. PROPORTIONATE PAYMENTS OF TENANTS AND CREDITORS

Division.	Immediate Tenants. £	Original Creditors. £	Assigned Bills. £	Totals. £
Under £100	6,251·4	729·5	527·8	7,508·7
,, £500	24,879·3	15,348·3	13,934·3	54,161·9
,, £1,000	17,697·6	48,032·9	21,422·6	87,153·1
Over £1,000	65,446·4	626,758·6	122,566·9	814,771·9
,, £10,000	—	461,296·5	—	461,296·5
Totals .	114,274·7	1,152,165·8	158,451·6	1,424,892·1

The average values of many of the items may now be given. First of all the yearly rent of all kinds of royal property in England and Wales is found to be £48 8s. Then the clear improved value of property, on the average, is a little over £105 ; also for the total annual value under the Commonwealth calculations the average is £134. The average rate of £2,115 in the case of purchasers has already been mentioned, and it may be added that this exceeds the average for the known conveyances by as much as £86. The average, moreover, of all kinds of property conveyed in the Metropolitan area is £1,829, which is £121 more than that of the Extra-Metropolitan area. In the Border-land division the average does not exceed £1,471, but even this amount is £126 more than the average for Wales. Finally, the average value of lands of every kind in all the four areas, excluding only those in which the areas are combined, is £1,783. This is less than the averages for all the manors and parks, but it exceeds the rest of the property named in the table. The highest rents, improved values, and contract prices, as well as the range of yearly rents and sales, for each of the counties of England and Wales may be more clearly and concisely stated in the following form :—

LXX. COUNTY VALUATIONS AND PURCHASES

Counties.	Range of Rents. £	Highest Improved Values. £	Range of Purchases.[1] £
ENGLAND.			
Bedford . .	0·2– 420	92	11·6–11,208·1
Berkshire .	0·9– 1,371	250	46·3– 6,739·1
Buckingham .	0·7– 210	818	9·9– 4,796·1 [1]
Cambridge .	1·2– 123	283	240·0– 1,722·0
Cheshire .	0·4– 59	163	46·8– 1,195·6 [1]
Cornwall .	1·3– 157	923	113·3– 6,823·0 [1]
Cumberland .	2·0– 357	175	504·0–10,320·9 [1]

[1] The highest values thus marked are recorded in the conveyances of " Manors and their appurtenances " (Cambridge list), but the sums do not include separate conveyances of manorial " lands and houses ", parks, and woodlands. The yearly rents are based on Add. MS. 30208, also the " Improved values ", which represent clear gains over the yearly rents. The new Commonwealth valuation is expressed in the total of yearly rents with their associated " Improvements ".

Counties.	Range of Rents. £	Highest Improved Values. £	Range of Purchases.[1] £
Derby . .	0·4– 93	233	122·7– 1,496·2
Devon . .	0·7– 203	1,673	97·8–19,517·6 [1]
Dorset . .	0·7– 76	813	132·3– 5,900·0 [1]
Durham . .	8·0– 20	50	128·0– 404·9
Essex . .	0·7– 104	117	17·3– 4,733·8
Gloucester .	3·8– 22	69	311·3– 795·2
Hampshire .	10·9– 225	49	946·5– 3,878·0
Hereford . .	2·7– 93	192	113·2– 2,956·4
Hertford . .	1·0–1,549	479	83·4–10,594·9 [1]
Huntingdon .	6·0– 810	345	1,406·2–19,885·7 [1]
Kent . .	0·2– 953	382	96·0–16,615·7 [1]
Lancashire .	0·1– 445	408	33·5– 6,853·8
Leicester . .	0·2– 37	31	27·4– 720·9 [1]
Lincoln . .	0·2– 425	584	62·4–12,857·8 [1]
Middlesex . .	0·3– 628	1,778	40·0–13,215·3
Norfolk . .	0·4– 349	919	104·0–12,107·7 [1]
Northampton .	0·3– 552	749	34·9–22,299·3 [2]
Northumberland	0·2– 9	114	10·5– 463·8
Nottingham .	1·0– 457	413	230·0– 6,953·4
Oxford . .	4·5– 754	41	70·0–17,215·0 [1]
Rutland . .	—	—	—
Shropshire .	6·7– 8	20	140·6
Somerset . .	2·0– 59	871	252·0– 7,151·4 [1]
Stafford . .	0·8– 461	70	577·1– 7,697·6
Suffolk . .	1·0– 162	165	332·7– 4,106·6 [1]
Surrey . .	0·1– 550	286	16·0–16,825·9 [1]
Sussex . .	0·9– 132	234	117·6– 2,573·2
Warwick . .	6·0– 100	943	173·7–18,775·2 [1]
Westmorland .	3·0– 218	16	—
Wiltshire . .	2·0– 219	449	30·0– 8,393·0 [1]
Worcester .	3·1– 62	145	110·5– 5,915·7
Yorkshire .	0·1– 363	408	90·2– 6,967·4 [1]
WALES [3]			
Anglesey . .	104– 614	40	—
Brecon . .	4·5– 65	115	72·0– 917·9
Cardigan . .	7·4– 42	—	514·1– 9,898·5 [1]
Carmarthen .	2·2– 40	8	136·0– 2,138·8 [1]
Carnarvon .	104– 109	—	1,662·7 [1]
Denbigh . .	0·1– 561	39	7,672·3 [1]
Flint . .	20·0– 143	—	270·0
Glamorgan .	52	25	959·5 [1]
Merioneth. .	104– 193	20	2,049·0 [1]
Monmouth .	11·1– 110	50	161·0– 2,411·3 [1]
Montgomery .	—	—	—
Pembroke . .	2·0– 34	—	42·0– 689·2 [1]
Radnor . .	0·1– 74	34	41·1– 3,452·5 [1]
COMBINED AREAS [4]			
England .	0·3–1,549	342	22·9–35,873·6
Wales . .	2·7– 43	115	1,776·5– 2,238·0 [1]
Mixed . .	0·3– 561	446	223·6–13,171·1 [1]

[1] See note 1, page 252.
[2] The lowest amount of a conveyance is recorded as " ooo : oi : o ", by mistake perhaps for £12 1s., in the Cambridge List. It is omitted here.
[3] In several counties of Wales, as in Shropshire also, only one conveyance can be quoted, and for Rutland, Anglesey, and Montgomery there appear to be none preserved.
[4] Many of the Conveyances include premises scattered over several counties of England, and there are some which include estates in both England and Wales. These are separately recorded in the above table under the heading " Combined Areas ". The highest rents, improvements, and purchases in the case of the Borderlands area combinations are found to be £445, £175, and £6,909 respectively.

From the Cambridge documents we can not only discover the amounts recorded in the conveyances, but at the same time we may divide the property into manors, lands, houses and so on, although there may be cases of over-lapping here and there. Only a long continued search among the conveyances themselves—checked by the enrolments on the Close Rolls so as to include conveyances now missing from the collection in the Public Record Office, and then separation of the items where several appear in the same conveyance or enrolment—would entirely prevent the inclusion of border line cases within each class. Even so, we see again that it is the Parliamentary region which takes first place, for, only on a single occasion, and then among the miscellaneous items, does the Royalist area hold the premier portion. The metropolitan area takes first place for the values of houses and parks, as we should expect, and the extra-metropolitan area for the remaining categories in the list. In numbers, the metropolitan area stands first for houses and woodlands, the extra-metropolitan for lands and parks, and the border-lands for manors and miscellaneous items. Only fifty of the entries out of 653 concern mixed areas and these are omitted in the calculations of averages for the separate divisions. But again it must be confessed that only the most searching examination of the details of each conveyance separately will ever disclose the exact number of manors, houses, woodlands, warrens, mines, fisheries, parcels of land, and miscellaneous premises that were actually sold and conveyed to purchasers; and even then caution compels one to add that the enrolments on the Close Rolls should be examined with equal care and the two results [1] critically compared with the analytical summary given below in connection with the Parliamentary surveys.

LXXI. Different Kinds of Crown Property Surveyed for Sale [2]
(A) Hundreds.   (B) Honours and Manors.   (C) Lands.   (D) Houses.
(E) Parks.   (F) Woodlands.   (G) Miscellaneous.

Areas.	Cos.	A.	B.	C.	D.	E.	F.	G.	Totals.
(i) Metropolitan	10	65	110	112	159	38	83	13	580
(ii) Extra-Metropolitan	16	114	154	74	80	46	68	34	570
(iii) Border-lands	13	47	133	42	49	9	16	40	336
(iv) Wales	13	1	69	12	13	—	1	5	101
Totals .	52	227	466	240	301	93	168	92	1,587

All that may be said with confidence concerning the conveyances included in the Cambridge list is that 603 out of 653 relating to single counties or single areas in the Parliamentary and Royalist regions sufficiently indicate the types of property conveyed to the purchaser. Thus we can say that 200 of the conveyances relate to manors, 123 to separated lands, 158 to houses and lands, and forty-eight to parks, while thirty-five concern woodlands, six refer to warrens, and thirty-

---

[1] It is because these two results should largely agree that Table LXXI is offered as a guide, showing what such a suggested search would reveal.
[2] Analysis of the Parliamentary Surveys.

three others relate to mills, mines, quarries, and other miscellaneous premises. The remaining fifty conveyances, about 8 per cent of the whole, overlap the territorial divisions and slightly confuse the classification, since the purchase price does occasionally include manors, parks, and miscellaneous property; still, exercising every care, it is possible to estimate the amounts paid for the respective types surveyed by the parliamentary surveyors and subsequently sold by the contractors as follows [1]:—

LXXII*A*. VALUES OF THE DIFFERENT KINDS OF PROPERTY CONVEYED

Areas.	Manors.	Lands.	Houses.	Parks.	Wood-lands.	War-rens.	Mis-cell.
	£	£	£	£	£	£	£
(i) Metropolitan	167,435·7	33,268·1	88,292·9	171,653·6	15,561·8	809·9	6,826·0
(ii) Extra-Metropol.	214,268·6	67,703·5	42,806·6	97,878·9	20,961·5	1,699·5	5,728·6
(iii) Border-lands	182,533·9	15,372·3	5,681·8	19,867·2	5,985·7	—	14,893·5
(iv) Wales	45,260·8	1,211·8	411·6	—	—	—	270·0
(v) Combined	69,342·1	608·1	2,560·9	7,899·0	7,417·7	—	614·3
Totals .	678,841·1	118,163·8	139,753·8	297,298·7	49,926·7	2,509·4	28,332·4

If we add the various totals in the 653 conveyances recorded among the Cambridge documents, and at the same time combine the totals given in the lists of Immediate Tenants, Original Creditors, and assigned Bills, and then compare the results, we may expect to ascertain the probable amount realized by the sales of Crown lands. In the case of the conveyances the amount is £1,314,826, but this falls short of the total we obtain from the lists of tenants and other purchasers by about £110,000, so that our calculations lead to the supposition that the sum realized by the sales was approximately £1,424,000.

LXXII*B*. TOTAL VALUE OF PROPERTY CONVEYED IN PARLIAMENTARY AND ROYALIST AREAS.

Areas.	Totals.
	£
(i) Metropolitan	483,847.9
(ii) Extra-Metropolitan.	451,047.2
(iii) Border-lands	244,334.5
(iv) Wales	47,154.3
(v) Combined	88,442.0
Amount of Conveyances [2]	1,314,825.9
Residual Amount [3]	110,066.2
Total of Sales [4]	£1,424,892.1

How very close our calculations have led us to the actual truth will be realized by turning to the Audited Accounts of the

[1] Table LXXII*A*. Analysis of the Conveyances, Cambridge University Library Dd. 13, 20. The five re-sales of the same property, 1654–5 are excluded. The amounts are identical (except in the case of Nos. 586 and 601, Wilts, viz. £3,834 10*s*. 10*d*. and, £3,384 10*s*. 10*d*., a clerical error obviously).

[2] As in Table LXXII*A* above. See also Table LXXVII.

[3] Derived from Cambridge lists. See page 246, note 2.

[4] As in Table LXXIII below, page 256.

Restoration period given in the Appendix (App. VI (i)), where it is recorded that John Wheatley's book of Certificates shows the payment to the King's Remembrancer of £1,423,710 18s. 4d.; to which other sums were added by Receivers General, farmers, and tenants, making a total of £1,434,278 15s. 5d. derived from the sales under the Act of 16th July, 1649. Two further sums realized by sales under Acts of 1652 and 1654 bring the final total up to £1,464,409 5s. 8d.

LXXIII. AMOUNT REALIZED BY SALES OF CROWN LANDS

(A) Regiments, Garrisons, and Northern Brigade.
(B) Other Creditors, Tenants, and Assigned Bills.

Divisions.	Conveyances.[1]	A.	B.	Totals.[2]
	£	£	£	£
Under £100 .	3,251·4	—	7,508·7	7,508·7
„ £500 .	47,596·9	—	54,161·9	54,161·9
„ £1,000.	84,032·7	814·0	86,339·1	87,153·1
Above £1,000	809,355·2	55,990·7	758,781·2	814,771·9
„ £10,000	370,589·9	440,438·3	20,858·2	461,296·5
Totals .	1,314,825·9	497,243·0	927,649·1	1,424,892·1

Our examination of the existing records, therefore, has shown how well they have been preserved, and how little has been omitted during the present search. For if we add to the sum just ascertained two further amounts from other audited accounts of the Restoration period (Appendix No. VI (ii–iii)) we obtain a total sum of close on two million pounds received by the Government[3] as a result of its policy in transferring the Crown lands and rents from the control of the State to the custody of its citizens.[4]

LXXIV. SALES OF CROWN LANDS, FEE-FARM RENTS, AND FOREST LANDS

Audited Accounts of Sales.   *Total Receipts.*
                                                    £   s.   d.
(1) Crown Lands, 1649-56   1,464,409   5   8
(2) Fee-farm rents, 1649-57.   .   .   .   528,809 13   0½
(3) Forest lands, 1653-56 .   .   .   .   733 18   4

                                                £1,993,952 17   0½

[1] For 648 conveyances, excluding five resales of 1654-5, for £11,069 11s. 3d., which may after all be only deferred (completed) Sales and therefore duplicate entries.

[2] The total of A, B exceeds that of the Conveyances by £110,066. See Table LXXII B.

[3] See the documents in Appendix VI (i–iii).

[4] This applies to England. In addition, the forfeiture of Crown Lands in Ireland and Scotland (Acts of 26th Sept., 1653 and 12th Apr., 1654) produced amounts which are unknown. The references in Firth and Rait, *Acts and Ordinances of the Interregnum*, under "Adventurers in Ireland" (ii, 744-5), and "Pardon to Scotland" (ii, 875-6), are very slight. For the Down Surveys in Ireland, in comparison with English surveys, see L. Treguiz (*pseud.* Y. M. Goblet), *La Transformation de la géographie politique de l'Irlande au XVIIe siècle dans les cartes et essais anthropogéographiques de Sir William Petty*, 2 tom., 1930.

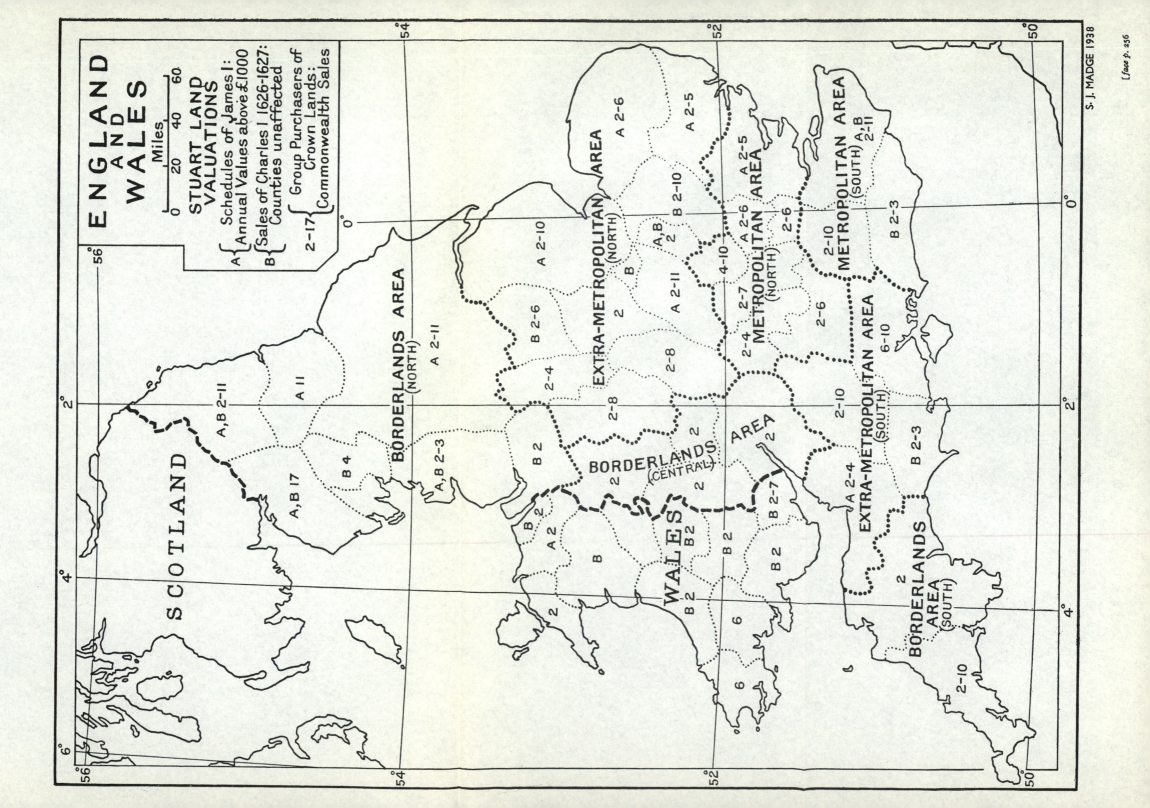

ENGLAND
AND
WALES

Miles
0   20   40   60

STUART LAND
VALUATIONS

A { Schedules of James I:
Annual Values above £1000

B { Sales of Charles I 1626-1627:
Counties unaffected

2-17 } Group Purchasers of
Crown Lands:
Commonwealth Sales

SCOTLAND

A,B 2-11

A 11

B 4

A,B 17

BORDERLANDS AREA (NORTH)

A 2-11

A,B 2-3

B 2-6

2-4

2-8

B 2

B 2

A 2

B

B 2

B 2

2

6

A 2-10

EXTRA-METROPOLITAN AREA (NORTH)

A 2-10

A 2-6

A 2-5

B 2-10

A 2-11

2

B

A,B
2

A 2-5

B 2-10

A 2-6

4-10

2-7

2-4

2-6

METROPOLITAN AREA (NORTH)

2-6

2-10

B 2-3

METROPOLITAN AREA (SOUTH) A,B 2-11

EXTRA-METROPOLITAN AREA (SOUTH) 6-10

A 2-4

2-10

2

BORDERLANDS AREA (SOUTH)

B 2-3

2-10

BORDERLANDS AREA (CENTRAL)

WALES AREA

2

B 2-7

B 2

B 2

2

6

2

2

2-8

S. J. MADGE 1938

[face p. 256]

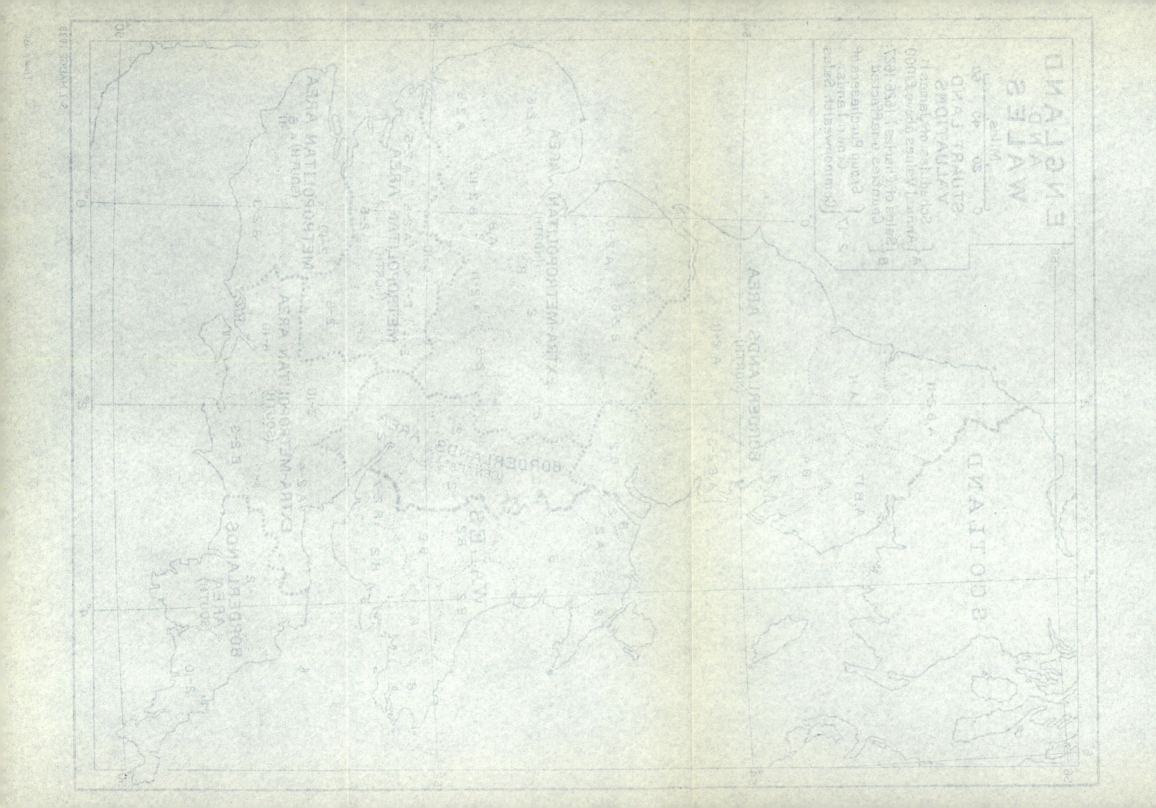

PART V

THE RESTORATION OF THE CROWN LANDS

CHAPTER I

THE PARLIAMENTARY SETTLEMENT

The story of the republican transactions in connection with the royal lands has now for the first time been told, and the sequel must be left to those who, with youth and leisure, can make of it a separate and a special study. It remains but to add that difficulties lay in the way of restoring the lands of the Crown thus widely scattered. Some of these difficulties are seen in the paper which has been preserved among the Egerton collection, endorsed : " Considerations touching the Sale of his Maties Lands and Rents." After pointing out that the property consisted of three kinds—(1) forests, parks, and chases, etc.,[1] (2) manors and lands let by lease,[2] and (3) fee-farm rents and the like [3]—the purchasers are referred to. These our anonymous writer very precisely specifies, for he believes them to be " of six sorts " :—

" 1. Parliament men who enrich themselves and gayne a party to them bought themselves and caused sale to be made to other ffarr under the values and these are very happy if the lands they have purchased cary not back some parte of their owne with them.

" 2. Souldiers now under the commands of the Lord Generall Monck who in respect of their returne to their obedience and reall service to His Majesty deserve their money with interest after six per centum, merritt may receive other recompence of His Majesty and it is beleived few of them will desire to settell themselves upon His Majesty's inheretance.

" 3. Souldiers of fortune (late without fortune) who to inrich themselves, have prolonged the warr and kept His Majesty from his Crowne and the kingdome in slavery they may be objects of mercy but if they be rewarded by satisfaction it will be an incourigement to others, to doe the like hereafter.

" 4. Men of covitus desire suddenly to inrich themselves and to testyfie their adherance to the party thereby to gett imployment and preferment : if these men goe away with what they have gotten, they are very happie.

" 5. There are some which cannot restore their purchasess haveing pulled downe His Majesty's houses of accesse and cutt downe tymber. If theis be stripped to their shurtts [4] it will not give satisfaction, and therefore inqussission would be made who bought the materyalls, who were

---

[1] Including " houses of accesse and some lands keept for provision of His Majesty's household ".

[2] " At the ould rents for termes the most parte yett indureing."

[3] Said to be " more than the other two sortts ".

[4] Even as Charles I, who " offered he would sell himself to his shirt ". S.P. Dom. 1st October, 1640, p. 128.

as ill affected as the others which sould them and ought to give satisfaction for the same.

"6. There are some which were tenants by lease, and to preserve the tymber upon their farmes bought the same which if they have really done, they may deserve some favor by addition of terme to their estates in being." [1]

There appeared to be very little doubt about the purchasers of fee-farm rents. They had bought these rents in batches and it ought not to be difficult to recover them. Thus Blomeley bought 173 such rents in the City of London, ranging from 8*d.* to a little over £4, the total rental in his two bundles [2] amounting to £81 9*s.* 1*d.* Similarly, Thomas Lane purchased 185 rents in Warwickshire, the lowest being 1*d.* and the highest just over £16 15*s.*, the total being £225 6*s.* 4*d.*[3] For Middlesex there were 385 such rents, ranging from 8*d.* to £100, the whole amount of the rental being £674 7*s.* 5*d.*[4] The entire sum received from the sales of fee-farms during the Commonwealth had been over £528,000—about one-third of the produce of the sales of Crown lands. In the case of these buyers it was the opinion of the writer of the Egerton manuscript that "all the purchasers of the King's and Queen's fee farme rents have received their money as againe and most of them their interest soe that they are fitt presently to be received to their Majesty's uses." [5]

There remained only the purchasers of Queen Henrietta's lands to consider, a new factor being involved in this case. "For the lands in the Queen's Majesty's Joynter it is to be considered whether or noe any satisfaction is fitt to be given to the purchasers, Her Majesty being but Tenant for terme of life." There is no indication of any special ruling in these matters beyond the warning recalled by the words, "The ould rule is caveat emptor." [6]

The fee-farm rents of Coventry appear to have been the first to be returned to the King, in May, 1660, when an address of welcome was forwarded together with the plea of "self-preservation" by way of excuse for purchasing the rents. During the following months

---

[1] Egerton MS. 2542. ff. 518-9. See also S.P. Dom. Charles II (1660-1) p. 81, vol. v, No. 14, ff. 195-6.
[2] Counterparts of Deeds of Sales, Fee-farm rents, Cal., vol. i, 267-278, and bundles W. 2, Nos. 11, 12.
[3] As printed in the *Midland Antiquary*, vol. iii, pp. 1-7 (1884), the amount totals £225 9*s.* 5½*d.*
[4] Particulars for Sales and fee-farm rents, Portf. 3, File 20. No less than 116 of Blomeley and Lane's rents, with 79 of those in Middlesex, were less than 5*s.* a year.
[5] A note, endorsed by Auditor Lowell, 25th July, 1651, on the final membrane of the City of London Particulars (Portf. 3, file 20, No. 56, items 230-350), refers to the Act of 22 Hen. VIII, by which all such rents and tenths, dry rents, and the like, if unpaid for three months forfeit a quarter of the rent more, if nine months then one half: "and so for every six months one whole year's rent more as by the said Act more fully appeareth." By applying the provisions of this Act to the new holders official pressure would bring about the return of such rents.
[6] See Table LXXV.

there were other returns and newer excuses from the Mayors and burgesses of Oxford, Lyme Regis, Lancaster, Abingdon, Gloucester, and Doncaster. St. John's College, Oxford, followed suit in December, but there appears to be no great haste on the part of the late purchasers to return the title-deeds. Lincoln has to search for its deeds, which are eventually sent 26th June, 1660. Oxford had expended £400 on purchases, while Abingdon's expression of " infinite joy " at the Restoration of the monarch cost that little borough £295 9s. 3d. —the loss of its purchase money.

The jointure lands of Queen Henrietta were under consideration of the House on 23rd June, 1660, when it was ordered that the Queen should be restored to the unsold estates of Somerset House and Greenwich Palace, and it is from the schedule of Sales then exhibited and read that we learn the names of the most important purchasers of her various manors and lands—persons whose estates were now in danger of forfeiture. The list includes the following estates with their purchasers :—

LXXV. Restoration of the Queen's Lands, 1660

Counties.		Premises.	Purchasers.
Bedford	.	Ampthill and Millbrooke Manors . .	Col. Jn. Okey
Essex .	.	Westham Manor	Humph. Edwards
Huntingdon		Somersham (five Manors), Parks, and Chase	Val. Walton.
Kent .	.	Old Court Manor	Rob. Titchborne
Lincoln	.	Crowland Manor	Val. Walton
,,	.	Spalding Manor	Adrian Scrope
Norfolk	.	West Walton and Terrington Manors	Edw. Whalley
Suffolk	.	Eye Honor and Manor	Edw. Dendy.
Surrey	.	Nonsuch House and Park . . .	Maj. Gen. Lambert.
,,	.	Nonsuch Great Park	Col. Thos. Pride
,,	.	Richmond House and Manor . . .	Sir Greg. Norton
,,	.	Egham Manor	Capt. Jn. Blackwell

These purchases included the materials of Nonsuch House and Richmond, but only part of Spalding Manor and a parcel of Westham. A later order, 27th June, withdrew Terrington Manor from the list for the time being. It is therefore evident that the Queen's estates were recovered with comparative ease. We may discover the probable extent of the various recoveries of royal manors and rents throughout the reign of Charles II by considering the figures recorded in the following table, which gives also some indication of the fee-farm rents in the king's possession after 1660, but which were subsequently sold [1]:—

---

[1] The figures in this table are obtained from analyses of (1) General Index of Crown Lands, Add. MS. 30208 ; (2) P.R.O., List 25 ; (3) Index to Treasury Books ; and (4) the Fee Farm Rents sold between 1672-80, Treasury Book IV (based on Add. MS. 28073). The voluntary restitutions, arrears of assessments, decimations, sequestrations, sales of bishops' and other lands, and of Crown lands, etc., are summed up in the Cal. of Treasury Books, vol. i, p. xxviii for the period 1660 to 1667. The amounts vary from £160 to £5,060 in a single year, the total being £8,550. Of this sum £693 was received in 1660, £479 in 1661, £5,060 in 1662, and £1,634 in 1663, after which the amounts became smaller and then disappear.

LXXVI. The Restoration Settlement, 1660–1685

Areas.	Lists of Royal Manors.	Index to Crown Lands.	Rentals and Surveys.	Fee-farms sold. £
(i) Metropolitan	97	217	24	13,127·4
(ii) Extra-Metropolitan	154	157	51	12,858·8
(iii) Border-lands	143	200	34	26,654·1
(iv) Wales	50	41	2	—
Totals . . .	444	615	111	52,640·3

The difficulties in the way of recovering some of the Crown lands were great indeed, especially in connection with the soldiery, and from the figures given in the above table it is clear that they were not fully overcome, for whereas the entries relating to Commonwealth estates in the General Index of Crown lands number 1,066, the items subsequently added for the recovered leases and re-leases of Charles II number only 615 for the whole period of his reign ; and after the sales of that monarch the entries fall to fifty-two under James II, though they rise again to 253 under William III, only to sink finally to less than 140 under Anne. Most of these entries for the reign of Charles II relate to the Metropolitan and Border-land areas. So too in the Public Record Office List of Rentals and Surveys,[1] we see that instead of 3,322 Tudor documents, with 1,485 others for the period of James I and Charles I, these records drop to 171 for the entire period between 1660 and 1702. And lastly, there is the confession very clearly made in the record of the sales of fee-farm rents by Charles II. Of the £52,640 realized by this means during the years 1672–5, a quarter comes from the Metropolitan area, but the greatest amount comes from the Border-lands where the royal troops had always been able to hold their own.

LXXVII. Territorial Complications, 1660

Divisions.	Single Counties. £	Combined Counties. £	Total Receipts. £
Corporations .	583·1	—	583·1
Individuals .	583,232·0	50,529·3	633,761·3
Pairs . .	213,670·8	40,691·7	254,362·5
Partners (3–5) .	131,264·1	34,325·6	165,589·7
„ (6) .	113,119·3	60,866·6	173,985·9
„ (7–17) .	73,018·5	13,524·9	86,543·4
Totals .	£1,114,887·8	£199,938·1	£1,314,825·9

The record of the Commonwealth sales, moreover, shows the difficulty of restoration, for there were not less than 443 individual purchasers, whose payments totalled £633,761, besides two hundred or more who in groups of from two to seventeen bought lands for speculative purposes in so many cases. Thus the group-purchasers

---

[1] The computation of documents here given is subject to official confirmation. It is probably an under-estimate. In Table LXXVI the " Royal Manors " are taken from the indexes of Treasury Books ; but not all manors were restored, or even retained when restored.

complicated the question of restoration, for their purchases were not only numerous, but they were scattered over as many as six or eight counties at a time.[1]

During the Civil War Parliament resolved upon the virtual abolition of the notorious Court of Wards and Liveries, and in 1645, the decision was taken to convert the tenures to which wards were incident into free and common socage. The final step was accomplished by a statute entitled " An Act taking away the Court of Wards and Liveries and Tenures *in capite*, and by Knights' Service and Purveyance, and settling a Revenue upon his Majesty in lieu thereof." Then was the decision reached that the tenures in question as well as the court itself had been " more burthensome, grievous, and prejudicial to the kingdom than beneficial to the King ", and in the place of the feudal revenue Parliament substituted excise duties on spirits and beer.

Although immediately after the Restoration the sales made during the preceding period were declared void, forbearance on the one hand and " concealments " on the other, resulted in a greatly modified resumption of the King's honours, lands, houses, rents, and hereditaments. But the Crown lands so recovered proved to be " but a shadow of their ancient bulk ", and in consequence the revenue from this source was gravely impaired. Parliament, in a most generous mood at the Restoration, settled a permanent revenue of £1,200,000 a year on the king of which the royal demesnes formed a very small part. By 1663, when values were rising a little, the land revenues were estimated to produce £100,000 annually, or about 8 per cent of the whole yearly revenue settled on the monarch ; but even though the values of the forests,[2] parks, and chases were not included in the estimate of 1663 the income derived from Crown lands seems never to have reached that figure during the whole reign of Charles II. For the Commons having consented,[3] to the alienation of fee-farm rents, and the king being disposed to regard his meagre demesne as a source of private emolument, the power to alienate was exercised so thoroughly after the Restoration that even to-day it is quite impossible to state the full extent to which it was utilized or to trace the unprofitable directions in which these revenues were squandered. In any case, as Scargill Bird has said, "We cannot doubt that the power of alienation was unequal to the will," [4] and after all the

---

[1] Analysis of the Conveyances, Cambridge University Library, Dd. 13, 20. See also Add. MS. 30208 for the statistics of the Commonwealth period and Charles II ; and Public Record Office List 25, Rentals and Surveys, for documents of the reigns from Charles II to Anne.

[2] The Forest of Dean alone was valued at £5,000 per annum.

[3] Act of 22–3 Chas. II, 1670-1. In 1660 the revenue of farms and rents is said to have amounted to £218,000 per annum at least (*Commons Journal*, vol. viii, p. 150), but this appears to be mere conjecture since it is at variance with known facts.

[4] Notes on Crown Lands in the *Antiquary*, 1886. Dowell, *Taxation*, vol. ii, p. 29, says that the income from the demesne in 1663 was £120,000. But this amount is open to doubt. See the reference to " Casual or Lost Revenue ", which follows, p. 264.

profligate pleasures of the king form an idle excuse for the loss of national revenue and honour.

From the report of the Committee of Enquiry into the King's revenue in 1660 we see that the estimate of £217,900 excluded a further sum of £45,700 on the ground that it was "casual and for the most part lost". A similar report three years later boldly cut this estimate of revenue down to less than one-half, it being conceived to be possible, if the farms and rents were "well managed" by the officials of the Exchequer and the Duchies of Lancaster and Cornwall, that the income of the Crown from this source might amount to £100,000 a year. If these two statements represent the true position of affairs, then very great alienation of Crown lands must have occurred in that short period. "It would be endless to enumerate the many instances of large grants of Crown lands made in the beginning of this reign. What might in some cases be justified by the necessity of the times, and considered as a liberal reward for services (such as the grants to the Duke of Albemarle, the Earl of Sandwich, and others who had been principally instrumental in the King's restoration) in other cases proceeded from mere heedlessness, wonted extravagance, and profusion. This was the opinion of the Committee in 1660 and 1663, as may be inferred from the resolutions which followed their reports." [1] But none of the regulations then proposed or later [2] were utilized to preserve the land revenue, and as even the ordinary forms of office were ignored, the income from this source seriously dwindled.

How did the Commons arrive at the generous figure of £1,200,000 as the future permanent income of Charles II? It would appear that the Committee of Enquiry set up by the House in 1660 considered that the approximate income of his father had been £900,000 a year, so they probably suggested an addition of one-third to meet the new conditions; whereupon they proceeded to set out the different heads on which their estimate was grounded, showing by what means the total sum might be annually obtained. But in this estimate they failed to reach the full amount as the following summary shows [3]:—

LXXVIII. REVENUE OF CHARLES II, 1660-3

Departments.	Estimates.
	£
1. Customs	400,000·0
2. Hereditary Excise . . .	274,950·0
3. Hearth Money [4]	170,603·6
4. First Fruits and tenths, coinage, etc.	105,156·7
5. Post Office	26,000·0
	£976,710·3

[1] St. John, *Observations on the Land Revenue*, pp. 91–2.
[2] In 1660, 1663, and 1667.
[3] Sinclair, *Public Revenue*, vol. i, p. 298, and *Commons Journal*, vol. iii, p. 498 (1663).
[4] "Chimneys" provided the greatest surprise to the Committee. See Hist. MSS. Com., Bagot MSS., rep. 4, p. 329, dated 12th May, 1663. The amount for London was only £18,000.

This amount, which merely represented the supposed yearly income of Charles I before 1649, still left £223,290 to be found, and it may be inferred from the Commons' Statement of Account that it was originally intended to make up this deficiency from the land revenue. Now if the estimate of 1660 had been correctly made, it must have been assumed that the revenues from Crown lands, with the "casual receipts" included, would completely wipe out this deficit and make the total annual income of the king, as voted, fully £1,200,000. But the Committee of 1663 discovered that this was not the case, owing to the extensive alienations that had taken place in the last three years. They reported to the House that £100,000, with £5,000 extra for Dean Forest, was the most reasonable estimate that could be made in connection with the land revenues of the Crown at that time, thus raising the total annual income to £1,081,710 only. Charles II therefore was partly to blame for the annual deficiencies which followed.

Dr. Shaw's view is that the estimate of £100,000 per annum for Crown lands was "such a wild estimate" that it becomes "an inscrutable mystery" why it should have been made at all.[1] But the reason he offers in connection with the deficiency shown in the Customs receipts is probably the right one to offer here : either the Parliamentary Committee of Ways and Means was actually misled in its estimate at the outset of the reign or else the estimate it gave simply stated the gross yield instead of the net revenue. "The Crown lands had all been sold during the Civil War and Commonwealth, their recovery and reassumption to the Crown was a question of time and it was problematical whether they would be recovered to the Crown in anything like their entirety."[2] Even so, it is difficult to believe that the Parliamentary Committee of Ways and Means was deliberately misled in making its estimate. The fee-farms of the Crown, it is admitted, were worth over £52,000 per annum.

With the aid of Dr. Shaw's statistics we may discover the average annual receipts in connection with the land revenues during the reign of Charles II. How far the heading "Crown lands and rents" in the Parliamentary estimate of £100,000 per annum proved to be deceptive, may be realized by considering the average receipts from the five main sources[3] which composed this section of national revenues recorded in the following survey of the reign :—

[1] In Lord Bagot's MSS., Hist. MSS. Com., 4th Report, p. 329, under date 12th May, 1663, Wm. Chetwynd states that the Crown Lands' total of £100,000 has been given in at £68,000. Does this not seem to point to "gross receipts" for the total, and "nett yield" for the lesser amount ?

[2] Shaw, *Treasury Books*, vol. vii (pt. i), p. xix.

[3] These five items total £256,428, and give an average of £14,410 per annum during a period of seventeen years (items 1, 3, 4, 9, 11 in Table LXXIX, p. 266).

LXXIX. Land Revenues of Charles II,[1] 1660–1685

Receipts.	No. of Years.	Total Amount. £	Average p.a. £
1. Receivers-General of the King	17	190,240·3	11,190·6
2. Sale of Fee farms [2]	8	52,640·3	6,580·0
3. Fines of Leases .	21	28,965·3	1,379·3
4. Sheriffs of Counties	21	26,024·2	1,239·3
5. Fines on Alienations	17	22,793·8	1,340·8
6. Farmers of Timber	5	18,275·0	3,655·0
7. Duchy of Cornwall	4	10,896·1	2,724·0
8. Voluntary Restitution, etc.	7	8,550·7	1,221·5
9. Rents of land .	18	8,477·2	471·0
10. Assarts, Wastes, etc.	5	3,550·1	710·0
11. Bailiffs and Cities	21	2,721·5	129·6
12. Sale of Woods .	5	2,694·7	538·9
13. Rents reserved on Grants	1	1,587·7	1,587·7
14. Seizures of Lands	20	589·5	29·5
15. Redemption of lands	2	101·0	50·5
Total	1–21	£378,107·4	£32,847·7

Dr. Shaw states that the average annual yield, represented by the payments into the Exchequer, from the Crown lands branch of the revenue for the first eleven years after the Restoration was less than £12,000. The table shows this to be largely true, although if the five items which mainly compose the " Crown lands and rents " section are added the average annual yield over a period of seventeen years exceeds £14,400. " In this connexion," he says, " it must be borne in mind that the fee-farms of the Crown were worth over £52,000 per ann. But more than half of this yield was arrested before it came into the Exchequer and always had been, even in pre-Commonwealth times. The sum was absorbed by the so-called fixed county charges, being local charges for upkeep of roads, harbours, schools and so on. These deductions had been a standing charge on the fee-farms since the days of Edward VI, of course in varying amounts." He concludes by stating that up to 1672 there was an annual shortage of over £88,000 on the Crown lands branch of the revenue alone. Then, in the crash caused by the Exchequer stoppage, the king sold his own private estate, consisting of fee-farms of the Crown, in order to reduce the total of national indebtedness—an action, permitted by Parliament, which " completely extinguished this branch of Charles's revenue and for the rest of his reign the Crown lands produced practically nothing. On this branch of the revenue alone there was a total shortage over the whole of the reign of over two millions ".[3]

[1] This table is based on the figures given by Dr. Shaw in his *Treasury Books,* but the averages are now added.
[2] I assume eight years, from 1672–1680, as Dr. Shaw is uncertain about the period. He records £23,099 for the years 1676–1680 alone. The larger sum is derived from Add. MS. 28073, " with much trepidation." The number of years of each account varies from 1 to 21, and allowance must be made for this.
[3] Shaw, *Treasury Books,* vol. vii, p. xx. In vol. iii, p. xi, he shows that the item " Receivers-General ", accounts for payments made to the Exchequer of £12,000 in 1670 and 1671, but that from 1673 onwards this item yields only between £1,000 and £1,500 a year.

CHAPTER II

THE ADOPTION OF THE PARLIAMENTARY SURVEYS

The restoration of Charles II to the throne of his ancestors, like the return of Louis XVIII to the ancient line of Princes in France in later days, marked the end of the era of political warfare and the dawn of conciliation and personal liberty. But the revolutions in England and France differed greatly in their effects by reason of differences in point of time and racial temperaments. In France the violence of twenty years had done the work of twenty generations, and in consequence a new body of proprietors with a new tenure possessed the soil.[1] But in England, where the Peasants' Revolt had long passed into history, ten years of republican government did not materially alter the existing laws in regard to land tenures, for Littleton and Coke still remained the source of legal knowledge on the subject of the soil. Indeed Englishmen, with their incurable propensity to reach decisions by compromise, saw to it that the bulk of ecclesiastical property still remained, colleges still possessed their estates, and even clergy their tithes.[2] Little wonder then that the Crown lands and fee-farm rents, recently dispersed, began slowly to return again to the son of the slain monarch—to the grandson of the Scottish king who had founded the new dynasty and accentuated the spirit of unrest and strife.

This truly English trait of reasonableness with its inevitable termination in compromise finds its illustration in connection with the parliamentary surveys and valuations; for not only were steps taken to secure the records of the trustees and contractors for sale of the Crown lands, but they were carefully calendared and preserved by Exchequer and Duchy officials who evidently recognized their great value for administrative purposes. Much of this work was done before 14th June, 1662, on which date Sir Robert Croke, Clerk of the Pipe, received £40 for his " Services in rendering the Records, Surveys, etc. which concerned the State of his Late Majesty's lands, from Worcester House into the Augmentation Office."[3] Moreover, they were not merely preserved but they were utilized by the new Surveyors General of the Exchequer and the Duchy of Cornwall for the purpose of issuing new leases and grants almost as soon as the Restoration had placed the monarch on the throne. John Collins, the tenant of St. John's Wood, was one of the first purchasers to have his statement

---

[1] Macaulay's Essays (Sir James Mackintosh, *History of the Revenue*), popular edit., pp. 327–8.
[2] Not until 1936, three hundred years later, was the end of tithes in sight.
[3] Cal. Treas. Books, vol. i, p. 398. Early Entry Bk., vol. iii, p. 319.

tested, namely, that he had redeemed one of the three-quarters he had purchased in that wood for £1,791 18s. in 1650, and that he had " tried in vain to delay paying the purchase money, till he could pay it to his rightful sovereign "; and John Tracey, a merchant, was another early example of the same apologetic kind since he admitted the purchase of Hyde Park, but pleaded that he had done his best to preserve the timber.   Collins asked for a lease of his property for ninety-nine years, and Tracey begged a grant for the two houses he had built on the Knightsbridge Road.[1]

Many such apologists [2] offered their regrets, especially after 13th October, 1660, when Pepys watched Major-General Harrison hanged, drawn, and quartered, at Charing Cross, the victim " looking as cheerful as any man could do in that circumstance ".   He himself made merry with a London goldsmith whom he met a year later when on his way by coach to the Lord Privy Seal's house at Chelsea, for " having taken up Mr. Pargiter, the goldsmith (who is the man of the world that I do most know and believe to be a cheating rogue) we drank our morning draft there together of cake and ale, and did make much good sport of his losing so much by the King's coming in, he having bought much of Crown lands, of which, God forbide me ! I am very glad." [3]

Many references to the Parliamentary Surveys are to be found in the Crown Lease Book of 1660–61,[4] and the " Warrants nòt relating to Money " during the reign of Charles II.   Sometimes the values are compared with those in Norden's Surveys, made about 1600– 1625, and at other times with the latest surveys of Sir Richard Prideaux or Sir Charles Harboard.   The Surveys of the Commonwealth were often questioned by petitioners, but the decisions are fair, since the " over-valued " premises are reduced when proved to be so, and the " under-valued " are increased with reasonable fines.   This is particularly true in cases where the holders suffered for their loyalty in the Civil War.   Indeed, at a time when the auditors' books showed some confusion these Parliamentary Surveys must have been of great service to officials charged with the duty of recovering the Crown lands and rents ; for, as John Bowring says in his proposal to re-erect the Courts of Augmentation and Survey,[5] the king may then have " a full view of his revenue, as now restored, the auditors' books being no longer such certain marks to understand as previously ".   His suggestion is that by having " a full survey of all lands " to guide the Lord Treasurer in granting leases it would be possible to avoid " the difficulties arising from the disorder of the older books of

¹ S.P. Dom., 1660–1, pp. 290–5, about September, 1660.
² Sir Rob. Reynolds, M.P., says he was " over persuaded " in his Contracts (S.P. Dom., 1660–1, p. 106).
³ *Pepys Diary*, Wheatley's edit., vol. ii, p. 123, under 21st October, 1661.
⁴ Stowe MS. 498, summarized by Dr. Shaw in his *Treasury Books*, vol. vii.
⁵ S.P. Dom., 1660–1, p. 462, vol. xxvi, No. 101.

Survey ". By depositing the majority of the Parliamentary Surveys in the Augmentation Office in 1660 the issue of fresh leases, based on the advice of the Surveyor-General, became a comparatively easy task.

When Sir Hugh Bethel, a troubled purchaser of the Manor of Hempholme, Yorkshire, applied for a lease of his lately acquired lands, not only was the Parliamentary Survey quoted, but an earlier survey by Aaron Rathborne,[1] dated 1608, was compared with it to show the injustice under which Bethel suffered. Originally, by an exchange of lands with Queen Elizabeth, Sir Thomas Heneage had acquired the Manor, the value of which in 1608 was raised from £35 13s. 4d. to £105 13s. 4d. per annum. Bethel purchased at the higher value of £146 10s. recorded in the Parliamentary Survey, out of which £16 was deducted owing to the cost of repairing banks and common rivers on the Estate. " I am credibly informed," is the official comment, " that this year's profit has been destroyed by the great fall of rain and waters which have made great breaches in the banks and surrounded most part of the premises and may require £100 to repair them again." The Surveyor-General recommended in this case a lease for thirty-one years at a small rent as Bethel was " very instrumental in His Majesty's happy restoration " through his correspondence with General Monk.[2]

Norden's Surveys in the reign of James I are frequently compared with those of the Commonwealth in connection with Cornwall and Dorset. Usually the former show a smaller acreage than the latter, the Parliamentary Surveyors recording an area of 218 acres for four tenements in the place of 164 acres stated by Norden—an increase of one-third which may be due to " intakes " quietly made in the intervening years. In two other instances the Commonwealth valuations are £2 lower than those of Norden ; in two more the later valuations of Sir Richard Prideaux are from £2 to £12 higher than the Parliamentary Surveyors thought fit to assign to the premises. In another case Prideaux gave a first estimate of £53 12s. 8d. followed by a second which showed an increase of £4 10s., but even then the Surveyor-General advised the Lord Treasurer that he " dare not rate this particular under the value of Norden's survey ", which made the value £72 in the reign of James I, an amount which the Parliamentary Surveyors increased to £98. Prideaux, however, consciously dropped " Cranowe Downe " out of the proposed lease, leaving only an acreage of 119, against Norden's 137, and the Commonwealth Surveyors, who had found the whole extent to be not less than 176

---

[1] Rathborne was the author of *The Surveyor in Four Books*, 1616. His corrections on the final page follow his reflection : " Mens workes have faults, since Adam first offended, And those in these, are thus to be amended."

[2] *Treasury Books*, vol. vii, p. 1617, dated 7th August, 1661. There was a fresh lease to Bethel, 7th March, 1686-7, for 99 years or three lives at a rent of £5 with fine £240.

acres in 1650. In this group of compared surveys [1] in Cornwall and Dorset, the grants of new leases were thirty-one years or three lives (one or two fresh lives being substituted in some cases), and the conditions attached involved the payments of " ancient rents " of from 6s. 4d. to £2 12s., increased rents ranging from £3 15s. to £28, and fines which rose from £8 16s. to £100. This was the first result in the year 1661 of using the Parliamentary Surveys and comparing their values with Norden's earlier and Prideaux's later surveys. John Strode, of Ryme, Dorset, expressed his willingness to " relinquish his new purchase made under the late usurped powers " in return for a lease ; and Edward Phillips asked that a deduction might be made for one of the three lives in his lease as the person indicated had been " slain in the King's service ".

During 1661 the Parliamentary Surveys of Berkshire, Cheshire, Cornwall, Derby, Devon, Dorset, Lincoln, Surrey, Warwick, Wiltshire, and Yorkshire,[2] were under consideration by the Surveyor-General, whose advice was usually accepted by the Lord Treasurer when making new grants to tenants. Roger Whitley, of Iveley, Cheshire, is recommended because " he has deserved well of his Majesty ", so his fine is only £10. Thomas Gewen, of Bradridge, Devon, for the same reason pays a reduced fine of £300 " as of the King's special grace and favour to him ". On behalf of John Frecheville, who seeks a reversionary lease of Eckington Manor, Derby, the Treasurer writes : " As there have been many pretenders to the tenancy of the said Manor, I leave it to your Majesty whom to choose, needing to put no character upon this petitioner, to your Majesty, whose merit and service is so well known to yourself." In this case, the Parliamentary Survey of 1650 records a clear yearly value of £222 8s. 8d. over the rent of £83 7s. 2d.; and as it was part of the lands chosen by the agents of Lord General Monk to make up the value of his estates, the Duke of Albemarle declared his willingness to put this portion aside in favour of Frecheville. In the case of John Lyne, of Potters Park, Chertsey, it was made a condition of his fine of £10 and yearly rent of £1 16s., that he should " relinquish all pretences as a purchaser under the late pretended powers ". Joan Franke, whose fine for premises in Barton, Yorkshire, is only £5, is informed that her new lease for thirty-one years under a rent of £5 per annum carries with it the obligation that " the King's title must be defended against the pretended purchaser from the Crown " : the Parliamentary Survey value in this case is £11 2s. per annum.

Complaints about the valuations of the Commonwealth Surveyors are met with in 1661, but these were always considered in the light

---

[1] *Treasury Books*, vol. vii, 26th March, to 22nd August, 1661 ; Stowe MS. 498, pp. 60, 89, 90, 180–2, 193, 222, 246.
[2] *Treasury Books*, vol. vii, 4th March, 1660–1, to 19th September, 1661 ; Stowe MS. 498, pp. 11, 18, 31, 53, 89, 94, 102, 110, 115, 137–9, 142, 149, 180–2, 184, 185, 187, 218, 220–2, 228, 240, 252–3.

of earlier surveys made by Norden or recent reviews by Prideaux and other men. Lady Moore, of Maydencote Manor, Berkshire, says that the alleged improved value of £4 14*s*. 4*d*. over the rent is " more than the true value thereof ", so she pays the old rent of £6 11*s*. 8*d*. with £1 4*s*. for a coppice, and suffers a fine of £10 for a lease of thirty-one years. Roger Whitley, of Cheshire, likewise escapes, the Surveyor-General being informed that an improvement of £13 15*s*. is too high, as the premises are " not worth double the old rent " of £5 18*s*. 6*d*. William Farrington, of Macclesfield in the same county urges that the Parliamentary Survey value of £7 would be more reasonable if reduced by £2 per annum : but his reversionary lease for twenty-six years costs him not only the old rent of 8*s*. but an increased rent of £2 with a fine of £10. The Mayor of Dartmouth complains in 1661, and does so again in 1674, that the improved value of £6 2*s*. 8*d*. over the recognized rent of £14 13*s*. 4*d*. is much too high for the needs of the port ; but the judgment is affected by the advice of the Surveyor-General, who says, " I cannot conceive the premises to be worth less than £20 per annum above the rent," so a fine of £80 (as in 1625) accompanies the new rent of £20. Upon renewed complaints in 1674, the case was reviewed, Treasurer Danby agreeing then with the Surveyor-General's report which stated that since the Commonwealth Survey had been made, the profits of the water bailiwick " are much abated by the decay of Newfoundland fishing and of the trade of that place (Dartmouth) in General by reason of the late wars ". The lease therefore was renewed for three lives under a fine of £20.[1] Nathaniel Fiennes receives a lease of Princes Wood and the Warren, Bromby, Lincolnshire, for the term of thirty-one years, but as the Parliamentary Survey values are checked by a later survey on a basis of 30*s*. per acre for vesture and 2*s*. per acre for the soil, he has to pay a new rent of £25 and a fine of £100. William Dover, of Kennington, Surrey, and Captain Benjamin Phipps, of Kenilworth, complain that they were forced by circumstances to purchase Crown lands or take forced leases. Dover's complaint is that he had to take 10 acres at a rent of £94 per annum from Captain John Arundell, and in 1656 a lease from " the pretended purchaser " of ground which cost him £100 per annum in rent, and subsequently £1,500 in improvements, whereas such land had never before been let for more than £16 8*s*. 9*d*., nor had the King's lessee received at any time more than £40 for Prince's Meadows. Phipps declares that the Parliamentary values for a lodge and timber in Kenilworth Chase are excessive, the lodge not being worth £80, and the timber " only old trees and firewood " which had since been cut up.[2] So £60 is allowed to him as

---

[1] *Treasury Books*, vol. iv, p. 686, under date 26th February, 1674–5, Warrants not relating to Money, vol. v, pp. 260–1.

[2] The values on which the purchase was arranged were £120, and £27 for timber. A late survey agreed that the acreage was 240 and the premises were worth £120.

a discharge for the lodge in which his brother had lived, his loyal services to the monarch being thus recognized. Sir Orlando Bridgman, of Bowood Park, Wiltshire, received a lease for three lives at a rent of £30 per annum for the King's Park. This decision rested on the following evidence [1]:—

1607. Forest land before imparking.
1640. Constats for sale : 968 acres, value £310, and timber £4,000.
1653. Parl. Survey; 960A. 1r. 16p., value £457 11s., with timber £4,512 10s. 2d.
1660. Woodward's View : 963 acres, value £321 10s., timber only £248.

This appears to be a clear case of over-valuation, and other instances are acknowledged in Cornwall and Yorkshire. In Cornwall, where great care was exercised in preparing new leases, the Surveyor-General says that the Parliamentary Survey of Bradridge in the Manor of Boyton was "certified at much more than the true value", which is less than £140 per annum, whereas the petitioner, Thomas Gewen, was compelled to repurchase his inheritance (held since the reign of Edward VI) for £1,200, and still owes much of the money he borrowed for that purpose. George Glyn, of Boyton, bought his premises in 1655 from William Combey for £550 and had since spent £250 on improvements which the Parliamentary Survey showed were much needed. The Surveyor-General advised a fine of £210 as the premises covered 130 acres and were worth £42 a year; but the new lease, which was granted for three lives, made the fine £50 less, and the old rent of £48 was raised to £66 a year. John Kneebone's complaint, which was renewed by his son Edward in 1686, was that, not only did the Parliamentary Survey over-value his tenement of 37 acres at £27 per annum, but that the surveyors added £10 of this amount "out of prejudice to his father, being an officer in the King's Army". A survey made in 1661 reduced the value to £15 10s., whereupon the Surveyor-General advised the Treasurer that he "dare not rate this fine according to £15 10s. without the Lord Treasurer's express order". For the addition of a new life in reversion of two others (aged 70 and 40 years) the old rent was increased by £6 10s., and the fine to £18 10s., as a compromise. In 1686 the over-valuation was admitted as "purposely" done and the suggestion was made that even the son's life was shortened by his fidelity to the throne. Still, the fresh lease of the same tenement of Upton in Carnedon Prior, was only granted by the infliction of a fine of £60, with the old rent, and heriots worth £1 0s. 4d.[2]

These are illustrations showing the use made of the work of the

[1] *Treasury Books*, vol. vii, 4th March, 1660-1 ; Stowe MS. 498, pp. 11-12.
[2] *Treasury Books*, vol. vii, p. 1,611, dated 29th July, 1661, and Warrants not Relating to Money, vol. xi, pp. 331-2, under date 28th July, 1686.

HOLDENBY HOUSE, NORTHAMPTONSHIRE : CONVEYANCE, 1650

[face p. 272

Commonwealth Surveyors in the first year after the Restoration.[1] They embrace valuations that relate to the manorial lands of nine counties in England. The new leases for thirty-one years or the addition of lives (one to three) showing the following range of rents and fines, are based largely on the Parliamentary Surveys :—

LXXX. RANGE OF LEASES, RENTS, AND FINES, 1660-1

	Terms.	Lowest.	Highest.
(a)	Lives	1	3
	Years	31	99
		£	£
(b)	Ancient Rents	0·2	48
	Increased Rents	1	18
	Fines	5	300

That the surveys of the Commonwealth period continued to be in use among officials for at least three generations is quite certain from the indications that come to us from three sources. In the first place, the Crown Lease Book of 1660-1 has already shown this to be true for the early years of the reign of Charles II, and the early warrants and later lease books provide similar evidence for the close of that reign,[2] as well as the subsequent reigns of James II,[3] and other sovereigns to 1760.[4] Secondly, the Index to Crown lands contains full references to the fluctuating values of the period 1649 to 1752, each new grant being added under the values and rents of the parliamentary surveyors. And thirdly, it became the practice in the Duchy of Cornwall to attach to the office copies of the Commonwealth period the new terms of successive leases after 1660. By 1760 there existed a reorganized mass of statistical evidence stretching back to the days of Charles I—the basis of decisions in regard to leases of Crown lands throughout the reign of George III, until the changes of 1810 brought the Commissioners of the Land Revenues into office. As an example of the ease with which, in spite of the Revolution, the historical continuity of English manors may be traced by means of these records we may take the case of Halliford Manor, Middlesex, the old rent of which between 1534 and 1800 remained at £18 6s. 8d. The intervening leases remain in existence, and the documents relating to the sale of

[1] In the instructions to the Commissioners for Kingswood Chase, Gloucestershire, 17th July, 1671, the first item states that they are to compare their work "with the Commonwealth Survey" (*Treas. Bk.*, vol. iii, p. 911).

[2] For the period 1672-1684 see Early Warrants, vol. xliii, p. 320-2 ; Warrants not relating to Money, vol. iv, p. 106 ; vol. v, p. 260 ; vol. vii, pp. 24, 44, 210, 258, 264 ; vol. ix, pp. 36, 86, 106, 172, 206, 207, 212, 214, 321-2 ; Reference Book, vol. i, pp. 22-5, 176, 410 ; Out Letters (General), vol. vii, p. 416. These relate to the counties of Berkshire, Cheshire, Cornwall, Devon, Kent, Surrey, York, and Radnor.

[3] For the use of Parliamentary Surveys during the reign of James II, see Warrants not relating to money, vol. xi, p. 37, 58-60, 104, 181, 186, 331-2 ; vol. xii, pp. 167, 194, 205, 226, 249-250, with reference to estates in Berkshire, Cornwall, Dorset, Northumberland, Surrey, and Radnor.

[4] For example, Launceston, 1690, Exmoor, 1737 ; Millbank, Westminster, 1739 ; and Romford, 1741, in Treasury Papers, vol. xiii, No. 21 ; and Crown Lease Books, vol. iv, pp. 249-250 ; vol. v, pp. 204-6 ; vol. vi, pp. 40-1.

the Manor in 1650.[1] The Improved value,[2] clear of the rent, was £122 11s. 3½d. when purchased. In 1723, it amounted to £141 10s., which was promptly taken in the form of "increased rent" when Matthew Johnson received a grant for fourteen years and a half (after the expiration of the previous lease in 1739). In 1739 the increased rent of £140 17s. 11½d. was accompanied by a fine of £470, which was paid by Jeffrey Johnson for his lease of sixteen years (after 1754). And once again, in 1769, with the same ancient rent, but an increased rent of £160 in addition, the same fine of £470 procured for John Rayner a lease of sufficient years after the expiration of the last grant to make up the customary thirty-one years from the actual date in order that it might expire in 1800.

[1] The subsequent history can be traced at the Middlesex Deeds Registry, commencing with Book No. 2 for 1800 (Item No. 577, Christie of Pall Mall, Grantor, Moorland, Hosier, and Hall, Grantees). The earlier history of Halliford is connected with Westminster Abbey, to which it was presented by King Edgar, in 962, and from which it was finally separated by the Abbots' Lease to Gabriel Pawlyn in 1537 and subsequent acquisition by the Crown. The feet of fines commence in 1207, Ministers' Accounts in 1340, and the Court Rolls in 1356. There is also an Extent of c. 1380 at the Public Record Office, and a Rental of 1445 at the British Museum (Harl. Ch. A. 14). See also Appendix IV.

[2] See Appendix V, Valuation of Crown Lands. The increase in value of urban land since the Commonwealth period is astonishing. A square foot of freehold land in any part of the City of London after the fire of 1666 cost only five shillings. In 1866 a square foot of such land in the neighbourhood of the Bank of England was valued at £15. In 1901 the value had risen to £70 a foot for freehold land in the same district. Sir Alfred Bower, Lord Mayor, in his speech of 4th November, 1925, declared that the rateable value of the City in six centuries had increased six hundred-fold, as follows :—

1339.	Edward III.	£12,000
1771.	George III.	£457,701
1871.	Victoria.	£2,186,487
1925.	George V.	£7,000,000

CHAPTER III

THE NEW CONTROL OF PARLIAMENT

With the restoration of Charles II, and the partial restoration of his royal estates the question of mismanagement of the Crown lands enters on its latest and most active phase, for the King almost immediately proceeded to disperse them afresh. The commissioners of 1792, who attempted to estimate the revenue obtained by Charles through his reckless sales of fee-farm rents referred very pointedly to the irregularities practised at that date. " What sum was passed by means of those sales cannot now be easily discovered, owing partly to the careless and lavish character of the King ; for many rents were granted away without any valuable consideration, and without any deeds being recorded in the office of the proper auditor of the Land Revenue, before whom the rents were in charge ; and it appears from a report of Lord Hawley, Sir Charles Harbord, Sir Wm. Heywood, and Sir Jn. Talbot, who were themselves Trustees appointed by these Acts, that no exact account of the alienations was ever kept, or could even have been made out by them." [1]

However great the national disquietude might be on the subject of the squandered revenue from land, the parliamentary settlement of a revenue fixed at £1,200,000 made Charles independent of legislative control throughout his reign. His brother James II was equally fortunate in this respect, for his revenue was raised by Parliament to £1,850,000 [2] an amount which was increased to two millions sterling by the addition of his income as Duke of York. His reign, however, was too short and his opportunities too few to alienate the Crown lands further or to make any changes in their administration. His successor William III, the recipient of the first Civil List, continued the alienations to favourites and courtiers to such an extent that Parliament, thoroughly alarmed at last, proposed the resumption of all grants and other revenues made since 1684—a measure which even the King's death did not restrain until a compromise had been reached over grants in fee. This was the last attempt to bring about the resumption of Crown lands, no act of this nature having met with success since the sixteenth century ; but by this time only " a miserable remnant of these formerly vast possessions was left ", the rents of

[1] Commissioners' Reports, vol. xii, 1792, pt. i, p. 9, and App. No. 1, p. 49. The Duke of Leeds MSS. (Add. MS. 28073) deals with these sales. Dr. Shaw's Summary of Annual Values and purchase prices records a total for rents that were sold, partly sold, or reserved of £789,917 3s. 10d.
[2] Hume, *Hist. of England,* vol. iii, ch. 71, quoting *Commons Journal,* 1st March, 1689.

estates in possession in England being no more than £482 16s. 7½d. a year.[1] The finances of the kingdom at this time were in such a deplorable state that John Philips, one of the auditors of the revenue, had received no salary for over fifteen years, while Wm. Story received only £200 instead of £511 at the end of seven years—during which time he had lived without salary, and fed the birds and beasts of St. James's Park without receiving the usual money for their food. After such a discreditable state of affairs among Government officials it is not surprising that the surveyors of land revenue residing in Bristol were eventually charged with " not being at their office an hour in a month ".[2]

By this time, too, the rents and values of lands were falling. In the Isle of Thanet, for example, the value of land in 1693 had fallen 20 per cent, and was now but 16s. an acre.[3] It was difficult to let the woods in Calstock Manor, as eight and a half years' purchase were required in 1685 to pay off the increased rent of £35 10s. which the Parliamentary Survey recorded as " clear improved value " over the old rent of £8 10s. in 1650. Sir Hugh Piper declared that the Parliamentary Surveyors' estimate for Launceston Park, namely, 30 acres, valued at £20 12s. 4d., was nearer the mark than Prideaux's later survey, 34 acres, valued at £34, because he " could never make above £20 a year of it ". Thos. Howell, went further, for applying for the office of Constable of Launceston Castle—described by the Commonwealth Survey as " much in decay and only two rooms standing "— he offered to keep the place in repair at a cost of £120, provided the fee of £13 6s. 8d. might be retained by him. The inhabitants of Bray petitioned that whereas in the reigns of Henry VIII and Elizabeth grants of pasture ground had been made under a rent of £50, with the addition of a fine of £55 in 1610, the present lease was not worth above £30 in wet years or £20 in years that were dry. Newcastle-on-Tyne was prepared to take a grant of its castle, valued by the Parliamentary Survey at £116 15s. 6d., but only by striking a bargain over the supply of coal to London. The complicated case of the tolls of Radnor market took ten years to settle. No rent had been paid for 130 years, when they were offered to the Earl of Worcester in 1683 at a rent of 13s. 4d., with a fine of £133 6s. 8d., and even next year at a rent of £10 without a fine, the treasurer adding on the second occasion, " My Lords desire to know what rent you will give for these tolls without a fine." In the end Ald. Haynes, of Worcester, appears to have been willing to pay a rent of £13 6s. 8d., instead of the Parliamentary estimate of £20. " This fall is occasioned," said the Surveyor-

---

[1] Notes from the *Antiquary*, vol. xiii, 1886, quoting the Commissioners' Report No. 12 (1792). The net produce of the entire revenue from Wales in this reign barely reached £1,900 per annum.

[2] *Treasury Papers*, Wm. III, introd., pp. xxxii–xxxv, and vol. 1697–1702, No. lvi (60).

[3] *Treasury Papers*, 1556–1696, p. xlix.

General, "by making some graziers freemen of that borough (Knighton), who bring in multitudes of sheep and other cattle into the market and are exempt from toll." [1]

The Civil List Act of 1 Anne (1702) brought about a new development in the management of the Crown lands department and the preservation of its records, for now it was possible not only to restrain the monarch from further alienations of residual property, but to prevent the passing of new leases of lands beyond thirty-one years (alternatively three lives) or of houses for a longer period than fifty years. Moreover, a committee of the House of Lords, sitting every year from 1703 to 1719 reported to the house the results of its consideration of " the method of keeping Records in Offices, and of Ways to remedy what shall be found to be amiss ".[2]

One of the first things accomplished early in the eighteenth century was the completion of a " General Index of Crown Lands ", commencing with the valuations of the Parliamentary Surveyors and adding the leases granted after 1660, all references being under county headings. The entries in this work end with the year 1752,[3] so that the manorial values in each county for a hundred years are visible at a glance. It is a very choice folio volume in vellum,[4] the entries being arranged under the ten heads, namely, (1) County, (2) Names and situations of the estates, (3) to whom granted, (4) for what term—" forever " in the case of the items dated 1649–1660, (5) yearly rents, (6) improvements, (7) dates, (8) in what surveys and entries to be found, (9) fines—" purchase price " for the Commonwealth entries, and (10) occasional remarks and references.

This orderly arrangement of Crown leases and sales for a period of more than "ninety-nine years or three lives" is a most commendable piece of work. The eighth column shows that it is based on two sets of records, namely, " Particulars grounded on surveys 1649–1653, and rated in Order to the Sale of several Crown lands," [5] and the

[1] Leases 1678 to 1690: *Treasury Books*, vol. v, p. 1144; vol. vii, pp. 809, 1300; Warrants not relating to Money, vol. xi, pp. 37, 59, 186–7; vol. xii, pp. 194, 205; and *Treasury Papers*, vol. xiii, No. 21. The case of the inhabitants of Bray, is recorded in *Treasury Books*, 1686–7, p. 1245.

[2] It reported, 17th January, 1718-19, that the great weight of records in the room over the Prince's Chamber had caused the floor to sink. *House of Lords Journ.*, Cal. i, pp. 215, 278.

[3] In the counties of Lancashire, Middlesex, Westmorland, and Carmarthen only. Monmouth entries end in 1667, London 1696, Montgomery 1701, Glamorgan 1702, and Cornwall 1714. The entries of other counties end between 1730 and 1752. There are no references to Crown Lands under Rutland between 1649 and 1752. It is possible, that this volume is the work of Owen Davies, who has left some notes, marked " O. D." 21st May, 1739, in Parl. Surveys, Sx., No. 48B, Wilts. Nos. 27B, 28, 31.

[4] See Hist. MSS. Com., 5th report (1876), p. 259, MSS. of Marquis of Lansdowne, Div. 6, No. 173. In 1924 a letter from the Earl of Kerry to Mr. A. I. Ellis, located this volume in the British Museum (Add. MS. 30208), where it was acquired 9th December, 1876.

[5] Add. MSS. 30206, 30207, 30208, show that these books of " Particulars and Rates " were in existence in 1714, 1726, and 1752. They consisted of four folio books of parchment (with four paper indexes), marked with the letters A, B, C, D, the first two dated

various " Books of entries of peticicions, Reports, Warrants, etc."
covering the period 1660–1752.[1] Its importance is increased by the
fact that the Commonwealth books and their indexes have disappeared
since 1752; so that the present analysis of the contents of Add.
MS. 30208 indirectly reveals the extent of the loss :—

LXXXI. CROWN LANDS, 1649–1752

Periods.	Volumes.	England.	Wales.	Total.
Commonwealth	A–D	984	82	1,066
Charles II .	A–Q	574	41	615
James II . .	Q–R	49	3	52
William III .	R–Y	233	20	253
Anne . .	Y–D2	125	11	136
George I .	D2–N2	304	2	306
George II .	O2–D3	569	27	596
Totals .	56 vols.	2,838	186	3,024

The increases shown during the reign of George I and George II
are due to the sub-divisions of premises in the Westminster area and
the greater frequency of leases consequent upon the Act of 1702 with
its limits of thirty-one and fifty years for lands and buildings
respectively.

Such a loss of records [2] is not surprising in view of the Commissioners' report in 1792 concerning the management of Crown
lands at the beginning of the eighteenth century. " It appears from
the Journals of the House of Commons [3] that on the 9th April, 1701,
and on the 13th February following, the Surveyor-General was
ordered to lay before the House " An Account of all lands belonging
to the Crown, both in Possession and Reversion, undisposed of ".
No such account, however, is to be found ; and on reference to the
Office of the Surveyor-General [4] we are informed " that such an
account dated 16th March, 1701–2 was prepared but that no perfect
copy of it was preserved in that office ". A draft copy when perused
showed that leaves were missing, that there were defects in the
information given to Parliament since (1) no accounts for Cambridge
and Suffolk had been kept since 1674, (2) no particulars or rentals
had been delivered to the Auditors in connection with Derby, Essex,
Hertford, Lincoln, Middlesex, and Nottingham, and (3) the account

1649–1650, and the last two 1650–1, and 1650–3. Their importance may be judged
from the fact that they contained 2,178 folios. Earlier books still, relating to the lands
of King Henry VIII and the period 1630–5, are referred to in the lists of 1714–1726. A
continuous search for five years has failed to find this group of records.
    [1] The same Add. MSS. record the existence of books marked A to Z, 1660–1706
(24 vols.), A2 to Z2, 1706–1742 (24 vols.), A3 to D3, 1742–1752 (4 vols.). The Crown
Lands of Charles II are referred to in vols. 1 to 16, those of James II in vols. 16–17,
Wm. III, vols. 17–23, Anne, vols. 23–8, George I, vols. 28–37, and George II, vols. 38–52.
    [2] " One of the problems of historical research is to account for documents dispersed
in divers custodies."—Hall, Repertory of British Archives, vol. i, p. 145 n., with notes on
destruction of records, pp. 87 and 265.
    [3] Commons Journals, vol. xiii, pp. 478, 742.
    [4] App. to Report of Commissioners, vol. xii, No. 3, and Report, p. 11.

dealing with the Jointure Estates of Queen Henrietta and Catherine, Queen Dowager, omitted to mention premises in Buckingham, Cambridge, Essex, Middlesex, Nottingham, Suffolk, and Warwick.

Reporting on the mismanagement of the forest lands, the same Commissioners discovered a lamentable state of affairs during the eighteenth century.[1] The forests had been placed under the sole management of a Surveyor-General without the slightest effective check or control over his department. Officers had become neglectful owing to the unwise and improvident mode of payment by fees, perquisites, and poundages instead of by regular salaries. Timber had been wasted on an alarming sale, and unprofitable expenditure on work done in the forests tended to increase. In consequence of this lack of control, limitations of common rights in every forest were forgotten or obscured; numerous encroachments and ill-founded claims gained strength from long or uninterrupted possession; and the rights of the Crown were now so much endangered that their value had almost disappeared. When the Navy Board, acting on the instructions of the Committee on Timber,[2] attempted in 1771 to make a general survey of all timber growing on private estates in England they were interrupted in their work by the proprietors before the second county had been completed; and the Commissioners of 1792, " seeing no reason to expect that what was then objected to would now be allowed," were compelled to gain information in other ways. Yet they discovered that, taking the same ground, the amount of timber recorded in surveys of 1603–1625 was nearly six times greater than at the close of the eighteenth century. From 1730 to 1787 the whole of the forests, parks, and chases of the Crown furnished only 77,256 loads of oak timber, an average of 1,356 loads per annum. As the average yearly consumption of oak timber for the Navy amounted to 50,542 loads, and the existing opinion of experienced surveyors inclined to the view that, with forty trees per acre and a growth of 100 years, two loads of timber might be secured, the Commissioners believed that the needs of the Navy could be met by the provision of thirty-four trees, each containing one load, per acre.[3]

An admirable " Account of all the Manors, messuages, lands, tenements, and hereditaments, in the different counties of England and Wales, held by lease from the Crown "[4] was prepared by G. A. Selwyn, Surveyor-General, 17th November, 1786, and published in the following year. It contains a description of all Crown

---

[1] Commissioners' Reports, vol. xi (1792), pp. 8, 15, 22.
[2] Commons Journ., vol. 33, pp. 246–357; Commons' Reports, vol. 3, p. 15; Commissioners' Reports, vol. xi, p. 8.
[3] Thus, thirty-four loads of timber girt measure, equal to fifty loads square measure, would require only 1,000 acres to supply the Navy for one year in 1792.
[4] As contained in the " Report of the Commissioners appointed to inquire into the State and Condition of the Royal Forests, Woods, and Land Revenues ".

property, as entered in the books of the Surveyor-General's office, distinguishing between premises granted for long terms prior to the passing of the Civil List Act (1 Anne) and as yet unexpired, and those granted since 1702 for terms not exceeding thirty-one years or three lives in the case of lands, or fifty years or three lives in the case of messuages and tenements. These two classes, however distinguished, did not exhaust the Crown property of that period, for it was vaguely known that there were other estates—not included in this list, because " not entered in the Surveyor-General's Office " —which had been granted for long terms prior to the reign of Anne, and these were dismissed with the remark that they " will become the objects of future attention ". From this account it appears that the " old rents " amounted to £10,563 12s. 1d. and the " new and increased rents " to £6,221 0s. 2¾d., the annual value of the estates in lease being £102,626 14s. 1d. and one-eighth.[1] Arranged according to areas, with the addition of the leases granted since the Restoration, so far as known, the valuation of Crown lands in 1787 may be thus recorded :—

LXXXII. LEASES OF CROWN LANDS, 1660–1787 [2]

Areas.[3]	Leases.		Valuation of Leases, 1787.		
	1660–1702.	1702–1752.	Old Rents. £	New Rents.[3] £	Annual Value.[4] £
(i) Metropolitan	349	698	6,857·1	4,985·0	79,791·9
(ii) Extra-Metropolitan	207	142	1,574·3	575·5	10,349·5
(iii) Borderlands .	300	158	1,681·1	538·1	10,962·5
(iv) Wales [5] . .	64	40	450·4	122·3	1,422·3
Totals . .	920	1,038	10,562·9	6,220·9	102,526·2

The leases for the period 1702 to 1752 include 136 for the reign of Anne (compared with 253 for William III), 306 for George I's reign and 596 for a portion of the reign of George II.[6] Four-fifths of the leases for the period 1727 to 1752 belong to the Metropolitan area by reason of the sub-division of premises in Westminster and neighbouring parishes, the other areas having only seventy-five, eighty-six and twenty-seven leases respectively. The percentage of the " old rents " to the total rents (adding the old and new rents together)

---

[1] The additions, tested in the printed copy, give £6,220 19s. 6¼d. for new rents and £102,643 1s. 2¾d. for annual values. The amounts for Wales are £1,346 16s. 0½d. annual value, and £417 11s. 11d., plus £122 5s. 7½d. for old and new rents. Monmouth in addition shows £32 15s. 7d. old rents, and £75 10s. 4½d. annual value.

[2] This table is based on the values shown in the 1787 Account of Manors, and the Leases recorded in Add. MS. 30208 (from the entry books of 1660–1752).

[3] The number of counties in the 1787 valuation is forty-six. The " New Rents " include " Increased Rents ".

[4] Adding £116·9 for the Channel Isles (Alderney), the total becomes £102,643·1.

[5] Including Monmouth. Some of the Welsh rents are " uncertain ".

[6] The number of royal manors recorded in the indexes of Treasury Books for the reign of George II is eighty-nine.

is 32 per cent in the Metropolitan area, 11 per cent in the Extra-Metropolitan, and 51 per cent in the Border Lands. The percentage in the case in Wales is obscured by the existence of " Uncertain rents ".

Three examples of leases granted for terms that were shortened, and three others where the terms were so long that they had not expired in 1787 and are even now in being, may be considered in connection with the Act of 1702. The long term leases [1] were granted by the Master and Chaplains of the Savoy Hospital in 1561 or 1562 at rents then considered to be adequate, viz. :—

(1) Durham: Hallatreholme Manor, £6 13s. 4d. rents, but term unknown.[2]

(2) Essex: Dengie Manor and Church, three rents of £14 6s. 8d. each, term of 600 years.

(3) Lancashire: Poulton Chantry lands, peppercorn rent, term of 1,000 years.

The expiration of the first of these cannot even now be ascertained as the counterpart of the lease is not extant.[2] The second will not expire before 23rd January, 2161, and the third will run until 29th September, 2562! Their yearly values could not be estimated by the Surveyor-General in 1787.

On the other hand, we may take three cases that occurred in the reign of George II, where the leases were granted for terms which expired before Selwyn prepared his report in November, 1786. Here we can trace the effect of the new Civil List Act of 1702 quite clearly.[3]

(1) Devon and Somerset: Exmore Forest (18,927 acres, 2 r. 24 p.). This forest was granted to Robert, Lord Walpole, 6th July, 1737. It was valued in the Parliamentary Survey at £483 3s. 5d., including rents and profits, but £46 13s. 4d. was allowed as a rent payable out of the Manor and forest to the Crown. Leases for two lives and for two periods of thirty-one years between 1660 and 1678, preceded the present reversionary lease of sixteen years, expiring 21st July, 1766. The only rent charged was the Crown rent of £46 13s. 4d., and no fine was paid. The terms were distinctly easy.

(2) Essex: Romford market tolls. These were granted to Mark Frost, 30th September, 1741. They were valued by the Parliamentary Surveyors at £100 per annum, and were leased twice at £70 between 1694 and 1706. In 1725 the lease was only for 15¾ years from 1738, and in 1741 for 18¼ years, thus expiring at Ladyday 1772 ; but the old rents of £2 were charged in both instances, with a fine of £184 14s. in 1725, increased to £200 in the present lease. These terms were far from easy.

[1] Recorded in the 1787 Account of Manors, pp. 11, 13, 19. None of these are recorded in the Crown Lands Index of 1752 (Add. MS. 30208).

[2] So in 1787 when the Lessee could not be named, though Hugh Bethel (pp. 11, 72) was in possession of the Manor.

[3] Add. MS. 30208, and Treasury Books and Papers, 1737, No. 103, 1739, No. 161, and 1741, No. 149 (Crown Lease Books, vol. iv, pp. 249–50 ; vol. v, pp. 204–6 ; vol. vi, pp. 40–1).

(3) Middlesex: King's Slaughter House, Millbank, Westminster. This lease was granted to Jos. Emms, 25th September, 1739. The premises consisted of a strip of ground 105½ feet by 100 feet, with a passage 20 feet wide to the street: with the old brick building and shed this was worth about £40 per annum. A special report [1] from the Surveyor-General is given in this case because although the title was indisputably the king's it "never produced any benefit or advantage to the land revenue". As an estate held in right of his office it had been enjoyed for forty years by Henry Powell, one of the clerks, under the protection of the Lord Steward, but without any registered warrant; for which reason the Surveyor-General invokes the powers of the Act of 1702, adding that "if the Treasury decide to grant a Lease of the premises it may be a means to discover other parcels held thereabouts without legal authority."

As for the fee-farm rents, which had been exposed for sale almost continuously since 1660, the Commissioners decided to expedite the process, but as the annual payments had been for the most part very small, the net annual amount, after payment of land tax, had not exceeded £1,370 a year. The new proprietors, 1,200 in number, paid £41,000 for these rents, an amount which was immediately used by the Commissioners in the purchase of £55,000 in 3 per cent Consols.

Very great difficulty was experienced by the Commissioners in their efforts to give a distinct account of the land Revenue of the Crown, particularly during the eighteenth century. The lapse of time in itself created one difficulty, but there were circumstances of a special kind which created the utmost confusion in the management of the lands and rents. To begin with, there were ten separate offices or departments involved in their acquisition, preservation, or dispersion—the Surveyor-General of Crown lands, the Auditors of the Exchequer (seven in number), the Clerk of the Pipe, and the lingering body of trustees for sale of fee-farm rents. And, as if that absurd system were not bad enough, there were also distinct officials who managed the Queen Dowager's Jointure Lands, to the extent of £30,000 per annum—the actual possession and control of which, with all the associated surveys, rentals, and other documents, were transferred to the Queen and her trustees, and "remained out of view and control of the officers of the Exchequer for upwards of thirty years".[2] Still further confusion was caused by the practice of issuing reversionary grants of portions of the Queen's estate to commence with the date of her death, and therefore extending the period of divided control, or lack of control, considerably. Moreover,

---

[1] He shows that it had not been used as a slaughter-house for the king's household since (or even before) the royal purveyances were disallowed by Parliament; and that the premises had been converted into warehouses for the sale of coal and wood, the rents and profits of leases being diverted from the Crown by the officers in possession (Treasury Books and Papers, 1739, pp. 55–6).

[2] Commissioners' Reports, vol. xii, 1792, pp. 11–12.

many of the grants between 1660 and 1702 had passed without any reference to the Surveyor-General, who could not account for them even as late as 1787. Nor were the enrolments of these grants complete, for some of them were either not received by the Auditors or their enrolment was overlooked, whether by design or accident, with consequent loss in some cases of both lands and rents.

As a sequel to these various changes in land administration after the Commonwealth period it may be added that in 1706, the auditors were again reduced in number, this time to three, but under the statute 2 William IV cap. 1 (1830) their offices were abolished altogether, such duties as were entrusted to them by way of audit being then transferred to the Commissioners of Audit, while a new department known as the office of " Land Revenue Records and Enrolments " was established to provide for the duties they had hitherto performed in connection with the registration and enrolment of covenants, deeds, leases, and other documents relating to the land revenue of the Crown. When it is remembered that, quite apart from this important series of documents, there is an extensive and most valuable series of " Ministers' and Receivers' Accounts " dating from the reign of Henry VIII; and that in addition to the entries upon the early Pipe and Chancellors' Rolls and the various rolls of special importance already indicated, large numbers of original accounts have accumulated in the Treasury of the Exchequer—owing to the apparently general practice of Sheriffs, bailiffs, reeves, and other accountants bringing them to the yearly audit and leaving them there—one cannot fail to acknowledge the wonderful manner in which the student of manorial economy and land tenures is furnished with even the minutest details concerning the possessions of the Crown, not only for the whole of the counties, but for all the reigns since Henry III.[1]

Two surviving offices connected with the administration of the Crown lands were finally abolished by Statute 50 George III cap. 65 (1810). These were offices which had been established after the abolition of the Court of the Augmentations, when Surveyors-General of Crown lands and of Woods and Forests received appointments with definite duties of control. To the first of these officials was entrusted the entire superintendence and management of the royal estates, since it was his duty not only to make surveys and write out particulars for leases of houses and lands from time to time, but to suggest covenants and agreements for insertion in the leases, and to record and preserve all memorials, reports, warrants, surveys, leases, and other documents connected with the extensive work of his office. The duties of the second official were confined to the management of the forests and woodlands of the Crown; but in general the two

---

[1] With appreciation and gratitude research students must acknowledge the admirable work accomplished by the officials of the Public Record Office, who have made the vast mass of materials so easily accessible, especially since 1896.

surveyors worked together in a corporate capacity, until their offices were abolished and their functions transferred, in 1810, to the newly created Board of Commissioners henceforth known as Commissioners of His Majesty's Woods, Forests, and Land Revenue. Under the Forestry (Transfer of Woods) Act of 1923, the greater part of the Forestal Land, including New Forest and the Forest of Dean, was transferred to the Forestry Commissioners, and the Commissioners of Woods have been known since 8th December, 1924, as the Commissioners of Crown lands.[1]

If we compare the extent and value of the Crown land revenues in the later years of the reigns of Queen Victoria and George V [2] with the state of the revenue in the eighteenth century we can realize how very greatly improved the management of the Crown lands has become since the Commissioners of 1787–1792 issued their reports. Exclusive of copyholds held of the Crown, foreshores, and areas in which the Crown owns the minerals but not the surface, the property is now of considerable extent and value, as we see from the following statement :—

LXXXIII. CROWN LANDS AND REVENUES, 1890–1936

Property.	Victoria. 1890.	George V. 1928.	Edward VIII. 1936.
	Acres.	Acres.	Acres.
(i) Agricultural land [3]	69,617	108,000	135,000
Woodland and Wastes [4]	115,293	88,300	94,500
Total acreage	206,720	226,000	259,500
	£	£	£
(ii) Agricultural land [3]	82,081	120,241	242,999
House Property [5]	252,188	1,237,909	1,431,426
Mines and Quarries	30,656	95,349	126,988
Fee-farm rents, tithes, etc.	43,891	20,244	18,060
Total gross Revenues [6]	529,862	1,595,843	1,918,095

[1] In a communication dated 27th April, 1929, the Commissioners inform me that " the greater part of the Forestal Land, including New Forest and Dean Forest, and certain estate lands adjoining the woodlands, which was formerly under the management of the Commissioners, was transferred to the Forestry Commissioners as from 31st March, 1924, pursuant to the Forestry (Transfer of Woods) Act, 1923. As regards Ireland, the Land Revenues of the Crown in the Irish Free State were transferred to the Irish Free State from 31st March, 1923." See pages 287n, 332–3.

[2] Report of Select Committee on Woods and Forests and Land Revenues, 1890, and 106th report of the Commissioners of Crown Lands, 28th June, 1928. The property consists largely of the Hereditary Estates of the Crown in England, Wales, Scotland, (Northern) Ireland, and the Isles of Alderney and Man. Report 114 is for the year ending 22nd June, 1936.

[3] In England (where their value was £82,081, in 1890), the acreage was 76,400 in 1928, and 110,275 in 1936, in addition to 2,800 acres of unenclosed commonable waste within certain manors. The number of farms of from 50 to 1,000 acres in England increased from 224 in 1928 to 353 in 1936. Five others to-day contain 8,830 acres of woodlands.

[4] Of which 81,000 consist of unenclosed wastes subject to common rights in 1928, and 80,000 in 1936.

[5] Including ground rents in London £237,008, in 1890.

[6] England, £442,852 ; Wales, £14,284 ; Man and Alderney, £10,263 ; Irish fee-farms, £38,261 ; Scotland, £24,202. These values were recorded in 1890.

During centuries of Tudor and Stuart rule, though the fate of Charles I provided an unusual warning, the control of Parliament over the Crown lands could not entirely prevent the monarch from selling the hereditary estates or even squandering the proceeds in unexpected ways. All the sovereigns from Henry VIII to William III exercised their freedom in this respect and none of them were seriously checked by threatened Acts of Resumption.[1] It was fatally easy to try the expedient of exposing Crown lands to sale, and since the Commonwealth government had used the plea of necessity, Charles II was not hindered by conscientious scruples in dispersing the lands and rents a second time. Dr. Shaw seems to think that Parliament badly let him down. "When the crash came, Parliament condescendingly permitted Charles to sell fee-farms (i.e. his private estate to discharge national debt). The sale completely extinguished this branch of Charles's revenue, and for the rest of his reign the Crown lands produced practically nothing." That may be true, but Charles needed no encouragement to do what his father and grandfather had so often and so extensively done before.

The Act of Queen Anne, at the beginning of her reign, certainly did prevent future alienations, at least on a large scale, but the plea of necessity was always in reserve. John St. John, writing in 1787,[2] argues against the objection often urged, namely, that the sale of Crown forests and wastes would bring so much land into the market as to lower the price of that species of property. He says : " Supposing this to be true, why are we to consider such an effect as a public evil ? That it might be prejudicial to individuals who at this time want to sell their lands, may be true to a certain degree. But the nation is no loser by the sinking of the money price of land, when the fall in the price of the commodity proceeds only from there being an extraordinary plenty of it." He agrees that if the value of land fell because of exhaustion, lack of people or stock, or inability to dispose of produce, a public calamity would be apparent. " But if land were to be purchased cheaper, or if in consequence of a greater quantity being brought to market, I am at a loss to see how this could be a public grievance."

Nor did the plea of necessity for the sale of Crown lands in the seventeenth century stand alone, for at the very beginning of the reign of George III an anonymous writer in the *Gentleman's Magazine*,[3] in proposing a scheme for raising money to carry on the Seven Years War, which was to cost England £60,000,000 before it was finished, reminded his readers that " there is a very obvious, easy, and cheap method of raising a considerable sum of money towards carrying on the war, without any new fund, which I am amazed has not been hit

---

[1] The last effective Act of this nature belongs to the reign of the earliest Tudor king.
[2] *Observations on the Land Revenues*, pp. 161-2.
[3] *Gentleman's Magazine*, 1762, vol. 32, p. 135.

upon, and might be done immediately. What I mean is, the sale of all the Crown lands and estates now let upon lease ; these are now vested in the publick by the Civil List Act at his Majesty's accession, who has a neat income in lieu of them, consequently would be no way prejudicial to his Majesty's rights, as no forests, demesnes, parks, or indeed anything but what is actually in lease, now paying quit-rent to the publick, is meant to be sold ; all of which together, would produce a considerable sum by sale, though the rents and fines are small, and the parcels are so scattered all over the kingdom, that it is a most unprofitable kind of estate to the public, a troublesome one to the tenants, and a great bar to all improvements." He then elaborates his proposals, suggesting fresh valuation and limited periods for payment from tenants, with compensation for officials displaced or discharged in the process of selling the lands. "What sum this would raise cannot be known without examining the proper offices, but it must be a very considerable one," and in any case the writer thought that it would bring in a class of persons whose subscriptions to the public loans were few and far between, and thus open fresh resources in times of need.

A later proposal, made during the war with France, was suggested by Mr. Biddulph and put forward in Parliament during the year 1808. His resolutions for selling the Crown lands provided for the transference of the amount thus raised " to the hereditary revenue of the Crown ". This was not acceded to, we are told,[1] and, " requiring the concurrence of the Crown, of course fell to the ground." But in little parcels and at various times, as the reports of the Commissioners assure us, sales of Crown lands and rents, purchases of new lands and exchanges of old ones have frequently taken place since 1760, and even in the reports of our own time [2] examples are to be found to illustrate the same tendencies, though now subject to the control and approval which Parliament failed to obtain before the republican experiment of 1649.

We who within a single year have witnessed, not only the passing of the late King George V, but the abdication of Edward VIII and the accession of his brother George VI, can now realize how decisive were the actions of the men who first of all attacked the Crown lands during the Commonwealth, and later inspired the passing of the Civil List Act of Queen Anne. Gone are the Crown lands from the control of the king. Challenged and overthrown, tenure by " Grand Sergeantry " alone survives to show what the feudal system was in earlier days. The theory of the constitution has changed since 1649,

---

[1] *Gentleman's Magazine,* vol. 78, pt. i, p. 535, dated 13th April, 1808.
[2] Sales of estates in 1927-8, £68,608 19s. 11d., and in 1930, £76,008 3s. 10d. In 1935-6 the sales included £85,410 18s. 1d. for estates, £2,013 16s. 6d. unimprovable rents, and £50 for encroachments in Wales ; but on the other hand the purchases of estates amounted to £25,115 12s. 6d.

for the functions of reigning and governing are now divided. So, too, are the costs connected with these functions : the Civil List provides the one, and parliamentary grants the other. But the Civil List, adjusted with unusual care in 1937, is much less than the profits derived from the Crown lands. In the year ending 22nd June, 1936,[1] the Commissioners of Crown lands were able to report that the excess of gross revenue over expenditure was £1,367,773. It is therefore " quite simple truth ", as Lord Hugh Cecil points out in *The Times* (17th May, 1937), " that the profits of the Crown lands more than defray the cost of maintaining the dignity of the Crown, and that therefore the taxpayers gain by an exchange which gives them the profits of the Crown lands in exchange for annuities of considerably smaller value. The King would be richer if the Civil List Bill did not pass. But doubtless it is a convenient arrangement for him, as for the taxpayers, that the Crown lands should be under public management."

[1] Although the 115th Report, for the year 1937, is not yet ready for publication, the Commissioners of Crown Lands have very courteously furnished in advance the following information, in their letter to me of 16th August, 1937 :—

(i) *Area of Crown Lands, as at 31st March*, 1937.

	Acres.
Agricultural land	138,000
Woodland and Wastes . . .	88,000
Total area of Crown Lands .	261,500

(ii) *Rents of Crown Lands, as at 31st March*, 1937.

Agricultural land	£147,387
House Property . . .	£1,413,572
Mines and Quarries . .	£137,540
Fee-farm rents, tithes, etc. . .	£17,027
Total Gross Revenues . .	£1,866,389

APPENDIX

APPENDIX I

THE AVENUES AND INSTRUMENTS OF RESEARCH [1]

NOTE.—To facilitate cross-reference, this Bibliography is arranged on the following plan, the entries being recorded under a system of consecutive letters extending from A to Z and AA to ZZ. (Appendix I–II) :—(1) Short titles are used, with first and last editions indicated. (2) One initial for Author's Christian name shown, and only the first author among collaborators. (3) Subjects are referred to in notes under special authors. (4) Volumes are distinguished by roman figures, and page references immediately follow. (5) MSS. are named or numbered, and the folio indicated. (6) As a rule not more than three references from the same volume are given. In case of doubt, consult the fuller titles given by works in Section (i), or the Catalogues of the British Museum ; and in every case, refer to the indexes of indicated works for more numerous references than space will permit to be given here.

I. BIBLIOGRAPHICAL STUDIES

A   Anon. Bibliotheca regia. 1659.
B   Barwick, G. Aslib directory. 1928.
C   Bird, S. Public Record Office documents. 1891–1908.
D   Davenport, F. English Manorial History. 1894. (Radcliffe Coll.)
E   Davies, G. Bibliography of Stuart History. 1928.
F   Giuseppi, M. Public Record Office Manuscripts. 2 v. 1923–4.
G   Gross, C. Sources of English History. 1900–1921.
H   Hall, H. Repertory of British Archives. I. 1920.
I   Humphreys, A. County Bibliography. 1917.
J   Marvin, J. Legal Bibliography. 1847. (See E., No. 452.)
K   McCulloch, J. Literature of Political Economy. 1845. (See E., 1847.)
L   McDonald, D. Agricultural Writers. 1908.
M   McKerrow, R. Introduction to Bibliography. 1927.
N   Moore, M. Select Bibliographies. 2 pt. 1912.
O   Pollard, A. Short Title Catalogue. 1926. (Bibl. Soc.)
P   Power, E. History for Teachers. 1921.
Q   Roberts, R. Historical MSS. Commission Reports. 2 v. 1914–1935. (See AI.)
R   Rye, R. Libraries of London. 1910–1927.
S   Steele, R. Bibliotheca Lindesiana. 3 v. 1910.
T   Various Studies : Cambridge Studies in Legal history. 6 v.
U   —— Columbia Studies in History.
V   —— Harvard Studies in Economics and History. 35 v.
W   —— Helps for Students in History. 38 v.
X   —— London School of Economics Studies.
Y   —— Oxford Studies in Social and legal history. 9 v. 1909–1927.
Z   —— Yale Studies in History.

[1] The manuscript sources are specially dealt with in Appendix II.

II. Departmental Collections

AA Agriculture Ministry—Reports on Crown Lands. 1906–1924.
AB Cornwall Duchy. List of extents and surveys. 1920.
AC Crown Lands Office. Reports. 1924–1936.
AD Exchequer: Aug. Off. Records. 1922 (AP. 46).
AE —— Aug. Off. Class List. 1924.
AF —— E.O.R., K.R., L.T.R., T.R. Class Lists.
AG —— L.R., L.R.R.O. Class Lists.
AH Forestry Commission—Reports on Crown Lands. 1917–1930.
AI Historical MSS. Commission. Reports. 1870–1930.
AJ Home Office. Records. 1914 (AP. 43).
AK Lancaster Duchy. Records. 1901. (AP. 14; Pal. Courts and Wales, AP. 40.)
AL Land Registry. Office Indexes. (H. 164.)
AM Parliament Office. Indexes to Journals: (a) H. of Com. 13 v.; (b) H. of Lords, 12 v. (Cal. 2 v.)
AN Public Record Office: Chronicles and Memorials. 1858–1930. (Rolls Ser.)
AO —— D.K.P.R. Reports. 1840–1930.
AP —— Lists and Indexes. 50 v. 1892–1924. (Obs. lists, Cat. 1923.)
AQ Record Committees: Reports (a) Lords, 1719; (b) Select, 3 v. 1732–1836; (c) Local records, 1902.
AR —— Royal Commissions: (a) Ser. i. 4 v. 1800–1837; (b) Ser. ii. 3 v. 1912–1919.
AS —— Works published. 1771–1856. (F. i. 353, Transcripts.)
AT Requests Court. Records. 1906. (AP. 21.)
AU Star Chamber Court. Records. 1901. (AP. 13; and 7 v. MSS.)
AV State Paper Office: (a) Cal. 200 v. 1858–1930; (b) Lists, 2 v. 1894–1914. (AP. 19, 43.)
AW Stationery Office. Record works. Lists, 1917–1936.
AX Treasury. Records. 1922. (AP. 46.)
AY Woods Office: Commissioners' Reports—(a) Ser. i, 17 v., 1787–1793; (b) Ser. ii, 6 v., 1812–1829; (c) Ser. iii, 95 v., 1830–1937; (d) Ser. iv, Special Reports, 8 v., 1847–1894.
AZ —— Surveyor-General's Reports, 4 v., 1787–1809. Index, 1812.

III. Library Lists

BA Antiquaries of London. 2 v. 1887–1899. Card Index. 1930–6.
BB Bodleian, Oxford: Early books. F. Madan. 2 v. 1895–1912.
BC —— Charters and Rolls. H. Coxe. 1878.
BD —— General Cat.: (a) Old, 1697; (b) Quarto, 14 pt. 1848–1918.
BE British Museum: Early Books. 3 v. 1884.
BF —— Charters and rolls. H. Ellis. 2 v. 1882–1912.
BG —— General Cat.: (a) Additions, 1787–1937; (b) Subject Index 9 v. 1881–1930.
BH —— Manuscripts: (a) Early, S. Ayscough, 2 v. 1782; (b) Class Cat. 100 v. 1782–1937.
BI Cambridge University: Early books. C. Sayle. 4 v. 1900–1907.
BJ —— Manuscripts. 6 v. 1856–1864.
BK —— Pamphlets. Card Index. 1928.

BL Gray's Inn. Legal Works, 1906.
BM Guildhall, London. 1889. Card Index, 1928.
BN Historical Research. Institute bulletins. 1923–1930.
BO House of Lords. E. Gosse. 1908.
BP Lambeth Palace. H. Todd. 1812. M. James, I. 1930.
BQ Law Society. 2 v. 1891.
BR Lincoln's Inn. Pamphlets. 1908.
BS London Library. Subjects. C. Wright. 1909–1920.
BT London Sch. of Economics. 4 v. 1931–2. Card Index. 1937.
BU Public Record Office : Books, (*a*) T. Craib, 1902–9 ; (*b*) Reference,
       1937.
BV —— Manuscripts : (*a*) General, 1923 ; (*b*) Printed, card index, 1937.
BW —— Museum. Sir H. M. Lyte. 9th ed. 1922.
BX Signet, Edinburgh. Legal works. 2 Supp. 1891.
BY Temple, Inner. F. Inderwick. 3 v. 1896–1901.
BZ —— Middle. 3 v. 1914.

IV. Periodical Publications

CA Antiquaries Journal. 17 v. 1920–1937. (DA.)
CB Antiquary. 40 v. 1880–1900.
CC Archæologia Aeliana. 20 v. 1822–1894.
CD —— Cambrensis. 5 ser. 1846–1900.
CE —— Cantiana. 18 v. 1858–1889.
CF Cambridge Historical Journal. 3 v. 1923–6.
CG Clare Market Review. 1904–1920. (BT.)
CH Economica. 1922–1930. (BT.)
CI Economic Journal. 40 v. 1891–1930.
CJ Edinburgh Magazine. 18 v. 1834–1851.
CK English Historical Review. 45 v. 1886–1930.
CL Gentleman's Magazine. 103 v. 1731–1833.
CM Gloucestershire Notes and Queries. 9 v. 1882–1902.
CN History. 2 Ser. 1912–1930.
CO Home Counties Magazine. 1899–1904.
CP Law Magazine. 55 v. 1829–1856.
CQ —— Review. 32 v. 1845–1856.
CR Middlesex Notes and Queries. 4 v. 1895–8.
CS Midland Antiquary. 1882–7.
CT Norfolk Archæology. 1847–1930.
CU Northants Notes and Queries. 1884–1905.
CV Notes and Queries. 13 Ser., 159 v. 1856–1930.
CW Periodicals : Subject Index. Library Assoc. 1915–1928.
CX —— Poole's Index. 1882–1904.
CY Quarterly Journal of Economics. 1896–1907.
CZ Vetusta Monumenta. 7 v. 1747–1810. (DA.)

V. Society Transactions

DA Antiquaries of London : Archæologia. 80 v. 1770–1930. (CA.)
DB —— Proceedings. 2 ser., 24 v. 1843–1905. (CZ.)
DC Archæological Societies' Congress. Papers, 1665–1908.

DD   Bristol and Glouc. Arch. Soc.   30 v.   1876–1907.
DE   British Academy.   Records of econ. history.   6 v.   1914–1927.
DF   —— Record Soc.   Index Library.   54 v.   1888–1928.   (DO.)
DG   Camden Soc. Publications.   1840–1897.   (DN.)
DH   Chetham Soc.   114 v.   Indexes.   1863–1893.
DI   Cornwall, R. Inst. Journal.   1818–1906.
DJ   Cumberland and Westm. Arch. Soc.   7 v.   Index.   1885.
DK   Derby Arch. Soc. Journal.   1879–1912.
DL   Devon Assoc.   30 v.   1862–1909.
DM   Historical Assoc. (*a*) Bulletins, 10 nos.; (*b*) Leaflets, 50 nos. 1907–
      1921. (CN.)
DN   —— Soc. (Roy.) 4 ser.   1871–1930.   (DG.)
DO   Index Soc.   Index Library.   17 v.   1878–1888.   (DF.)
DP   London and Mx. Arch. Soc.   1855–1930.
DQ   Manorial Soc. Publications.   1907–1915.
DR   Pipe Roll Soc.   45 v.   1884–1930.
DS   Royal Soc. Classified Papers.   Index.   1907.
DT   Selden Soc. Publications.   44 v.   1888–1927.
DU   Somerset Arch. Soc. Proceedings.   40 v.   1849–1898.
DV   Suffolk Inst. of Arch. Proceedings.   9 v.   1848–1898.
DW   Surrey Arch. Soc. Collections.   38 v.   1858–1928.
DX   Sussex Arch. Soc. Collections.   50 v.   1848–1906.
DY   Wiltshire Arch. Soc. Magazine.   32 v.   1853–1902.
DZ   Worcester Hist. Soc. Publications.   1894–1928.

VI. Special Collections

EA   Additional MSS. Cat.   1783–1930.   (BH.)
EB   Agarde.   Indexes.   60 v.   (F. i., 356.)
EC   Ashmole.   Cat. W. Black.   2 v.   1845–1866.   (BD.)
ED   Ayloffe.   Calendars.   10 v.   (F. i., 359.)
EE   Burney.   Cat. 2 v.   1840.   (BH.)
EF   Clarendon.   Cal. O. Ogle.   3 v.   1869–1876.   (BD.)
EG   Cotton.   Cat.   1802.   (BH.)
EH   Crace.   Cat.   1878.   (BH.)
EI   Dodsworth.   Cat. J. Hunter.   1838–1879.   (BD.)
EJ   Douce.   Cat.   1840.   (BD.)
EK   Egerton.   Cat. Additions to 1930.   (BH., see JM.)
EL   Gough.   Cat. B. Bandinel.   1814; (*a*) MS. Cat. F. Garlick.   (BD.)
EM   Hargrave.   Cat. 1818.   (BH.)
EN   Harley.   Cat. T. Horne.   4 v.   1812.   (BH., see FT.)
EO   King's MSS. Cat.   1841.   (BH.)
EP   Lansdowne.   Cat.   2 v.   1819.   (BH., see FO.)
EQ   Madge.   Crown Lands.   152 v.   1920–1937.   (BG. 15 v.; BH. 2 v.;
      BT. 111 v.; BU. 23 v.; QA. 1 v.)
ER   Palmer.   Indexes.   152 v.   1720–1730.   (F. i, 392.)
ES   Rawlinson.   Cat. W. Macray.   1862–1900.   (BD.)
ET   Sloane.   Index.   E. Scott.   1904.   (BH.)
EU   Stowe.   Cat. 2 v.   1895–6.   (BH.)
EV   Tanner.   Cat. A. Hackman.   1859.   (BD.)
EW   Thomason.   Cat. 2 v.   1908.   (BH.)

EX   Western MSS.   Cat. F. Madan.   6 v.   1895–1905.   (BD.)
EY   —— Cat. Sir G. Warner.   4 v.   1921.   (BH.)
EZ   Williamson.   Transcripts.   70 bun.   (F. i., 354.)

VII.   Subsidiary Papers [1]

FA   Ancaster MSS.   1 v.   1907.   (Q. 66.)
FB   Bath MSS.   3 v.   1904–8.   (Q. 58.)
FC   Beverley MSS.   1 v.   1900.   (Q. 54.)
FD   Buccleugh MSS.   2 v.   1899–1903.   (Q. 45.)
FE   Carlisle MSS.   1 v.   1897.   (Q. 42.)
FF   Cecil MSS.   14 pt.   1883–1923.   (Q. 9.)
FG   Cowper MSS.   3 v.   1888–9.   (Q. 23.)
FH   Dartmouth MSS.   3 v.   1887–1896.   (Q. 20.)
FI   Egmont MSS.   3 v.   1905–1920.   (Q. 63.)
FJ   Foljambe MSS.   1 v.   1897.   (Q. 41.)
FK   Gawdy MSS. 1 v.   1885.   (Q. 11.)
FL   Hodgkin MSS.   1 v.   1897.   (Q. 39.)
FM   House of Lords MSS.   n.s. 8 v.   1870–1922.   (Q. 17, AI 1–14.)
FN   Kenyon MSS.   1 v.   1894.   (Q. 35.)
FO   Lansdowne MSS.   4 v.   1872–7.   (AI. 3–6, see EP.)
FP   Le Fleming MSS.   1 v.   1890.   (Q. 25.)
FQ   Malet MSS.   2 v.   1876–9.   (AI. 5, 7.)
FR   Middleton MSS.   1 v.   1911.   (Q. 69.)
FS   Ormonde MSS.   n.s. 8 v.   1895–1920.   (Q. 36, AI. 14, app. 7.)
FT   Portland MSS.   8 v.   1891–1907.   (Q. 29, see EN.)
FU   Rutland MSS. 4 v.   1888–1905.   (Q. 24.)
FV   Sackville MSS.   2 v.   1904–1920.   (Q. 49.)
FW   Various Coll.   8 v.   1901–1913.   (Q. 55.)
FX   Verulam MSS.   1 v.   1906.   (Q. 64.)
FY   Webb MSS.   1 v.   1879.   (AI 7 app. 1.)
FZ   Wells MSS. n.s. 2 v.   1885–1914.   (Q. 12, AI. 10, app. 3.)

VIII.   Treatises and Record Works

GA   Adair, E.   Sources for history of the Privy Council.   1924.   See
     also (a) Dasent, Acts of Privy Council, n.s. 37 v., 1890–1931;
     (b) Nicolas, Proceedings, 7 v., 1834–7; and CK. v. 30, 38.
GB   Adames, J.   Treastise on Manorial Law.   1593.
GC   Adams, G.   Constitutional documents.   1911.   Other collections
     are edited by (a) Gardiner, 1887–1906; (b) Prothero, 1894;
     (c) Robertson, 1919; (d) Stubbs, 1913; (e) Tanner, 1922.
     See works in E. (i), J., P., and BG.
GD   Adams, J.   Index villaris.   1680–1690.   (FP. 398.) This may be
     supplemented by (a) Spelman, Villare Anglicanum, 1678; (b)
     Bartholomew, Gazetteer, 1914; (c) Cassells, Gazetteer, 6 v.,
     1898; (d) County court index, 1897–1907 (AW.); (e) Kelly's
     County Directories, 1895–1937.
GE   Addy, S.   Church and Manor.   1913.   Consult: (a) Charity
     lands (AP. 10, 1899); (b) Nonarum inquisitiones, 1807; (c)

[1] See also the Parl. papers of J. Robinson, Surv. General of Woods, 1774–84 (1922).

Papal bulls (AP. 49, 1923); (*d*) Papal registers, 13 v., 1894–1925; (*e*) Taxatio ecclesiastica, 1802; (*f*) Valor ecclesiasticus, 6 v., 1825–1834. See also (*g*) History of eccles. revenues, 1685; (*h*) Selden, Tithes, 1618; (*i*) Snape, English monastic finances, 1926; (*j*) Lunt, Papal Revenues, 2 v., 1934; and C., E. iv, F., G., N., TK., TZ.

GF   Adkin, B. Copyhold and other land tenures. 1907–1911. Consult: (*a*) Feudal aids, 6 v., 1899–1921; (*b*) Hall, Red Book of the Exchequer, 3 pt., 1897 (AN. 99); (*c*) Testa de Nevill, 3 pt., 1921–31. See also (*d*) Effect of primogeniture on land (CI. xv., 619, xix. 431); (*e*) Liber tenur', Lanc., 3 v. (AO. xxx, 12); (*f*) Legeancia legens, 1661 (BR. 197); (*g*) Moore, Frank pledge system, 1910 (V. hist.); (*h*) Old tenures, 1515–1532, 1575; and B. 240, C., F., G., H., J., N.; AI. vi, 232; ix, 391; xiii, 81. AY. (*a*) index; BH. i, 249; BH. (*b*) xlvi, 637; BZ. iii, 178; CV. ser. 1–3, 5, 7–11; EA. 5760 (4), 5837 (95); EC. 158; EN. iv; EP. ii; RU. (*e*).

GG   Adolphus, J. General view of Crown possessions. 4 v. 1818. (CL., lxxxiii (i), 232.)

GH   Agas, R. Preparative to plotting for surveys. 1596.

GI   Akermann, J. Baynes papers, 1853–6. (DB. ii, 30; iii, 144, 243, 256.)

GJ   —— Competitors for King's lands. 1857. (DB. iv, 42.)

GK   —— Contract of Northern Brigade. 1854. (DB. iii, 52.)

GL   —— Conveyance of Holdenby House. 1865. (DB. iii, 251.)

GM   Andrews, C. The old English Manor. 1892. (Hopkins Univ.)

GN   Andrews, J. Precedents of leases. 1897. See (*a*) Account of Crown manors held by lease, 1787; (*b*) Leases of 999 to 3,000 years (CV. ser. 1, 5, 7, 9, 10); (*c*) Missing entry books, 1629–1775 (AP. obs. 837–842; AY. (*a*) iii, 17, 25, app. 11–13; EA. 30206–8. Writers on leases are referred to in BG. and BZ. iii. Records will be found in C., F., H., BH. (*b*).

GO   Arkwright, C. Parl. Survey. of Wirksworth. 1912. (DK. xxxiv, 13.)

GP   Ashley, W. Surveys,[1] historic and economic. 1900.

GQ   Atkinson, A. Frauds and abuses in Crown revenues. 1603. (EO. 1734; 267.)

GR   Attwell, G. The faithful surveyor. 1662.

GS   Bacon, F. Discourse on alienation office. (AI. ii, 2; iii, 214.)

GT   —— The King's Revenue. (BP. 215.)

GU   Bacon, M. Leases. 1798.

GV   Bacon, Sir N. State and reformation of the revenue. (EA. 32379: 34.)

GW   Baldwin, J. The King's Council during the middle ages. 1913.

---

[1] On the subject of surveys, see also (*a*) Exact rules for mensuration of land, 1649 (ET. 3932 (2)); (*b*) Form of a field book, 1812 (AY. (*b*) i, 130); (*c*) Hall, List of Agrarian Surveys, 1922 (CH. 4); (*d*) Instructions for surveying Crown estates, 1812 (AY. (*b*). i, 133); (*e*) Leybourn, complete surveyor, 1679. Catalogues, indexes, lists, schedules and other works are to be found in B., C., D., F., G., H., N.; AI. v, 259; AO. iv, app. 8; AP. 25, 1908; AP. obs. 836–842; AQ. (*b*), 1800, p. 12; AR., 1812, app. 54 (1819 repr. 56); AY. (*a*) index 43; BG.; BH. (*b*) 62; BS.; EA. 21350, 23749, 30206–8; MC.; MK.; RP.; TZ.; VC.; XA. See also Fordham's "Notable Surveyors," 1929.

GX Ballard, A. British Borough charters. 2 v. 1913–1923.
GY —— Castle guard and barons' houses. (CK. v. 25.) References to boroughs occur in (*a*) Commissioners' Reports on Corporations and markets, 1835–9, 1876–1880; (*b*) Gomme, Lit. of munic. institutions, 1886; (*c*) Gross, Bibl. of munic. history, 1897 (V. hist.); (*d*) Hemmeon, Burgage tenure. in med. Eng. (V. hist. 20); (*e*) Madox, Firma burgi, 1726; (*f*) Sheppard, Corporations, 1659; also C., D., F., H., I., Q., R., BH. (*b*).
GZ Baring, F. Making of the New Forest. (CK. xvi, 427.)

HA Barker, A. Parl. Survey of Crane Wharf, Richmond. (DW. xxvii, 144.)
HB Barlee, W. Concordance of laws concerning manors. 1578–1917. (DQ. 6, 10.)
HC Barry, J. Tenures and defective titles. 1637.
HD Barthelet, T. Book of surveying. *c*. 1545.
HE Bates, F. Graves' Memoirs of the Civil War. 1928. For the literature of the period see E. ii. (Esp. sec. vi.)
HF Bax, A. Parl. Survey of Guildford Castle. 1903. (DW. xviii, 9.)
HG Bayldon, J. Art of valuing rents [1] and tillages, 1824–1876. See also (*a*) Curtis, Valuation of lands, 1912–20; (*b*) Emmett, notes on perusing titles, 1927; (*c*) MacSwinney, land values, 1917; (*d*) literature in D., G., N. and BG.; (*e*) records of fee-farm and other rents in C.
HH Bayley, J. Proceedings in Chancery. 3 v. 1832. Consult: (*a*) Early proceedings (AP. 12, 16–20, 29, 38, 48, 1901–1922); (*b*) Later series, i (AP. 47, 1922); (*c*) ser. ii, (AP. 7, 24, 30, 1896–1909); (*d*) ser. iii, (AP. 3, 9, 42, 44, 45, 1913–17); (*e*) Indexes (DF. 2, 5, 6, 14, 29, 32); (*f*) Chancery rolls (AP. 27, 1908); (*g*) Various rolls, 1921; (*h*) Warrants, 1927.
HI Baynes, A. Papers, 12 v. (AB. orig. FY.; EA. 21417–21427).
HJ Bazeley, M. Extent of English forest in the 13th cent., 1921. (DN. 4 ser. iv, 140.)
HK Behan, J. Use of land affected by covenants. 1924.
HL Beighton, H. New plotting table for surveying. (DS.)
HM Beldam, J. Parl. Survey of Royston. 1866. (DA. xl, 123.)
HN Benese, Sir R. de. Book of the measuring of land. 1537–1564, 1577.
HO Bennett, F. Historical sketch of English land system. 1893. See (*a*) Adeane, The land retort, 1914; (*b*) Remarks on the history of land, 2 v. 1785; (*c*) Reports of Roy. Commission on land, 5 v. 1894–6; (*d*) Land Enquiry Committee Report, 2 v. 1913–1914; also works in D., L., BG.
HP Bentley, J. Woods felled and sold in forests. 1648. (EW. i, 652.)
HQ Bingher, Sir J. Report on Crown revenues. 1614. (FG. i, 85.)
HR Bird, S. Notes on the history of Crown lands.[2] 1886. (CB. xiii, 89, 159, 194.)

[1] For rents see C., F., H., AI., AP. 25, BH. (*b*) lxii, 1953, EA. 30207 (5), EN. iii, 538, FD. ii, 37.
[2] See AY., ML., PM. and TG., and the records in C. 66, F., H., Q., AY., AZ., BH. (*b*) 59, 62, EA. 3844 32469. Returns to parliament in 1640 and 1701 are referred to in AG. misc. bks. 56–7; and for restrictions under the Acts of 1701 and 1782, see AI. v, AI. (Fortescue) viii, EA. 30215.

HS   Bisschop, W. Rise of the London money market. 1913. See (*a*) Foxwell collection (R.) ; (*b*) Scroggs, (Eng. Finance under the Long Parl.). (CY. 21) ; (*c*) Shaw, Select tracts and documents, 1896 ; (*d*) Dietz, Eng. Public Finance, 1558–1641 (1932) ; also E. v. (ii), K., BG., UE. iii, app.

HT   Blackstone, Sir W. Charter of the forest. 1759.

HU   —— Considerations on copyholders. 1762–1771.

HV   Bland, A. Economic history documents. 1914. See also (*a*) Hall, Bibl. of med. econ. hist., 1914 (E. 1846) ; (*b*) Tawney, Tudor econ. documents, 3 v., 1924 ; and records and works in E. ii, vi, K., N., BG.

HW   Blount, T. Fragmenta antiquitatis. 1679–1909.

HX   Bonner, Sir G. The office of the King's Remembrancer. 1930. (AF.)

HY   Boothe, N. Rights of Windsor Forest. 1719.

HZ   Bowles, C. Parl. Survey of Edmonton. 1897. (CR.iii, 20, 88.).

IA   Brewer, J. Henry VIII. Letters and Papers.[1] 21 v., 1862–1920.

IB   —— For the State Papers, Dom. Series, see Lomas, State Papers of the Stuarts (DN. n.s. cvi, 91) ; and records in C., F., H., AV., AW., edit. by R. Lemon and others, arranged as under :—

      (IB.) Edward VI, vol. i, add vi, 1856–1870 ;

      (IC.) Mary, vol. i, add. vi, 1856–1870 ;

      (ID.) Elizabeth, 6 v. add. vii, xii, 1856–1872 ;

      (IE.) James I, vol. viii–xii, 1857–1872 ;

      (IF.) Charles I, 23 v., 1858–1897 ;

      (IG.) Commonwealth, 13 v., 1875–1886 ;

      (IH.) Charles II, 22 v., 1860–1921 ;

      (II.) William III, 8 v., 1896–1925 ;

      (IJ.) Anne, 2 v., 1916–1925 ;

      (IK.) George III, 4 v., 1878–1899.

IL   Brickdale, Sir C. Land transfer in various countries. 1894.

IM   —— Methods of land transfer. 1914.

IN   Bridgman, Sir O. Conveyances. 1682–1725.

IO   Brown, J. Forests of England. 1883.

IP   Brown, T. King's property in sea-lands. (BS. 272.) Refer also to (*a*) Moore, Hist. and law of the foreshore, 1888 ; and (*b*) records and works in C., F., H., AG., HM. iii.

IQ   Brown, W. Compendious treatise on recoveries. 1678–1704.

IR   Brush, T. Making of ground plots. (BH. ii, 680.).

IS   Brydall, J. Ars transferendi dominium. 2 v. 1697.

IT   Burgh, J. Book of Crown revenues. 1619. (EA. 11598.).

IU   Burrell, P. Transcripts of parl. surveys of Crown lands. *c.* 1780. (EA. 5705.)

IV   C——, A. Timber cutting to make iron. *c.* 1610. (ET. 665.)

IW   Cæsar, Sir J. Crown revenues and forests. *c.* 1610. (EA. 10038.)

IX   Caley, J. Parl. Survey of Wimbledon. 1791. (DA. x, 399.)

IY   —— Post mortem inquisitions. 4 v. 1806–1828. Consult : (*a*)

---

[1] Compare the early edit. of Hen. VIII's papers. 11 v. 1830–1852 (AS.).

Abstracts for Gloucs., London, and Wilts., 1893–1920 (DF. 9, 13, 15, 21, 23, 26, 30, 37, 40, 47, 48 ; PH.) ; (*b*) Calendar, ser. i, 10 v., 1904–21 ; (*c*) Ser. ii, 2 v., 1898–1915 ; (*d*) Duchy of Lancaster, 3 v., 1823–1834 ; (*e*) Index, 1907–9 (AP. 23, 26, 31, 33) ; (*f*) Inquis, ad quod damnum (AP. 17, 22, 1904–6) ; (*g*) Misc. inquis, 2 v., 1916 ; (*h*) Roberts, Cal. genealogicum, 2 v., 1865.

IZ Calthrope, C. Relation between the Lord and copyholder. 1635–1917. (DQ. 10.).

JA Cam H. Studies in the Hundred Rolls. 1921. (Y. 6.)
JB —— The Hundred. 1930. Records : (*a*) Rot. hundredorum, 2 v., 1812–1818 ; (*b*) unpublished material at P.R.O. (C. 158, F. i, 380.)
JC Carew, Lord. Retrospect into the King's revenue. 1661. (BX. Supp. ii, 493.)
JD Carlyle, T. Cromwell's letters and speeches. 2–3 v. 1845–1904. See (*a*) Ramsey, Studies in Cromwell's family circle, 1930 ; and (*b*) biographies, E. vii (iv) and NS. (*e*.)
JE Carter, M. Honor redivivus. 1655.
JF Carter, S. Lex custumaria. 1696–1796.
JG Charnock, J. History of Marine Architecture. 3 v. 1802–1803. Also see (*a*) Bushnell, Complete shipwright, 1664–1688 ; and (*b*) records in C., E. iii, F., H., AP. 18, AY., AZ.
JH Clay, T. Tables of rents and leases. 3rd. ed. 1624.
JI Clowes, R. Indexes and transcripts of parl. surveys of Crown lands. (AB.)
JJ Coate, M. Duchy of Cornwall. 1927. (DN., 4 ser. x, 135.)
JK Coke, Sir E. Complete copyholder. 1641–1764.
JL —— Les reports. 1600–1659. (E. 458 ; FG. i, 291, 295.)
JM Collier, J. Egerton papers. 1840. (DG., EK.)
JN Collins, W. Duchy of Lancaster, computus. 1631–1640. (BJ. ii, 40.).
JO Concanen, G. Parl. survey of Tewington, Cornwall. 1830. (Rowe *v*. Brenton.).
JP Cooper, C. Papers : Record Commission. 53 v. (F. i, 348 ; AR.)
JQ Copinger, W. Rents and the sales of lands. 1886. For land sales see F., BG., BZ. iii, 427, HG., PK., TE.
JR Corbett, W. Elizabethan village surveys. 1897. (DN., n.s. 11.)
JS Cotton, Sir R. Cotton posthuma. 1679.
JT Coventry, Sir W. Essay concerning decay of rents. (BH. ii, 681.)
JU Cowell, J. The interpreter. 1607–1637.
JV Cox, J. Royal forests of England.[1] 1905. (Antiq. books.)
JW Cradocke, F. Expedient for raising a revenue. 1660. (EW. ii, 331.)
JX Crisp, F. Papers relating to Henrietta Maria. 9 v. (F. i, 352.)
JY Crotall, J. Proposal for increasing the King's revenue. (BP. 207.)
JZ Cuddon, J. Treatise on copyhold acts. 1865.

[1] For the literature and records relating to forests refer to C., D., F., H., I., L., N., AA., AH., AP. 25, AW.–AZ., BG., BH., BZ. iii, EA. 30206, 38444, 38579, 38760, WV., WZ. The special reports of Commissioners, 1787–1793, relate to the forests of Essex (AY. ser. i, No. 15), Gloucester (No. 3), Hants (No. 5, 6, 13), Northants (No. 7–9), Notts (No. 14), and Oxford (No. 10).

KA　Dalrymple, J.　Essay on the history of feudal property.　1758.

KB　Dalton, M.　Officium vice-comitum.　1623.　Refer to (a) Morris, medieval sheriff, 1927 ; (b) list of Sheriffs (AP. 9, 1898).

KC　Davenant, C.　Discourse on public revenues.　1698.

KD　——　Discourse on grants and resumptions.　1700–4.　See (a) Ancient deeds, 6 v., 1890–1915 ;　(b) Charter rolls, 6 v., 1903–1927 ; (c) Charters, edit. by Birch, Earle, Hardy, Kemble, Round, Stevenson, Stubbs, Thorpe ; (d) Grants certified, 1640–1667 (EA. 30206 : 39–41) ; (e) Hales, Treatise on validity of grants 1657–1703 ; and records in C., F., H., AP. 25, BC., BF., BH., HR., ML., RU. (d), SH.

KE　Day, R.　Decay of wood and timber.　1652.　(EW. i, 874.)

KF　Devon, F.　Issues of the Exchequer.　3 v.　1835–7.　(AD.–AG.)[1]

KG　Digges, L.　Pantometria.[2]　1571–1591.

KH　Doddridge, Sir J.　History of Wales, Cornwall, and Chester.　1630–1714.　For Wales see also (a) Land Revenues of N. Wales (AI. v, 259) ; (b) Records of Crown lordships or manors (AR. (b) ii, pt. 2 : 259) ; (c) Report on Crown lands, 1783 (AI. iii, 145 ; AP. xlvi, 47) ; (d) Stephens, Official Report on land in Wales (CI. vii, 137) ; (e) Works on land tenure, 1896 (D. Thomas in R. Com. on land in Wales, app. B.) ; and references in C., E. xiv, F., H., I., Q., AP., 40, BG., BH. (b).

KI　Doubleday, H.　Victoria County History.　1900–1936.　Completed Counties.　See also (a) Guide to Collections, 1912.　The only completed counties are Beds, Berks, Bucks, Hants, Herts, Surr., Worc., and Yorks.

KJ　Dove, P.　Domesday Studies.[3]　1888–1891.

KK　Dowell, S.　History of taxation.　2 v.　1884–8.

KL　Duff, A.　Treatise on deeds used for feudal rights.　1838.

KM　Dugdale, Sir W.　Baronage of England.　3 v.　1675–7.

KN　——　History of imbanking fens.[4]　1662–1772.

KO　Elton, C.　Early forms of landholding.　(CK. i, 427.)

KP　——　Law of copyholds and customary tenures.　2 v.　1874–1898.

KQ　——　Law of gavelkind.　5th ed.　1897.

KR　Evans, F.　The Principal Secretary of State.　1923.　(AV.)

KS　Evelyn, J.　Sylva.　1664–1706.

---

[1] The records include : (a) Accounts Declared (AP. 2, 1893) ; (b) Exchequer (AP. 35, 1912) ; (c) Foreign (AP. 11, 1900) ; (d) Ministers (AP. 5, 8, 34, 1894–1910) ; (e) Hughes, Dialogus de Scaccario, 1902 ; (f) Pipe Rolls (DR., with 1 v. ed. by Cannon, 1918 and 4 v. by Hunter, 1833–1844) ; (g) Playford, Rot. Originalium, 2 v., 1805–1810 ; (h) Special Commissions (AP. 37, 1912) ; and records in C., F., H., AO. ii–iv., AY (a) index 9, BH. (b) xiii, 1033, SH. (ch. on Exchequer). A book of entries, Chas. II lies hidden in Vol. 293 of parl. surveys. (AG.)

[2] Other works by the same author are (a) Stratioticos, 1579–1590 ; (b) Tectonicon, 1556–1656.

[3] The literature relating to this subject includes (a) Ballard, Domesday boroughs, 1904 ; (b) Ballard, Domesday inquest, 1906 ; (c) Baring, Domesday tables, 1909 ; (d) Ellis, Introd. to Domesday, 2 v., 1933 ; (e) Inman, Domesday statistics, 1900 ; (f) Maitland, Dom., and beyond 1897. See also (g) Domesday Book, ed. Farley, 4 v., 1783–1816 ; the later photozincographic copy, 2 v. ; and the references in C., D., F., G., H.

[4] Works on drainage will be found in EV. vii, see also AI. vi, 451 (Dugdale) ; BZ. iii, 443 ; and AI. iii, 215 (Callis) ; CK. xxxiv, 385 (Richardson).

KT   Fanshaw, Sir T.   Practice of the Exchequer Court.   1658.   (EW. ii, 208.)
KU   Farrer, W.   Honours and knights fees.[1]   3 v.   1923–5.
KV   Field, C.   Landholding in various countries.   1885.
KW   Finlayson, W.   History of the law of tenures.[2]   1870.
KX   Firth, Sir C.   Acts and Ordinances of the Commonwealth.   3 v. 1911.
KY   —— Clarke Papers.   4 v.   1888–1901.   (DG.)
KZ   —— Study of 17th cent. history.   1913.   (DN. 3 ser. vii.).   See works in E. 408, and Bibliography, 1928.

LA   Fisher, J.   Landholding in England.   1876.
LB   Fisher, —.   Treatise on copyhold tenure.   1794.
LC   Fitzherbert, Sir A.   Book of surveying and improvements.   1523–1587.
LD   Fleetwood, W.   Treatise on forest laws.   1592.   (AI. ii, 20 ; EA. 26047, EU. 850 : 339.)
LE   Flower, C.   Public works in medieval law.   2 v.   1915–1923.   (DT. xxxii, 40.)
LF   Folkingham, W.   Feudigraphia.   1610.
LG   Foster, W.   Plea for preservation of court rolls.   (Arch. Assoc., n.s. v. 171.)
LH   Fowler, W.   Ancient terms for measurements of land.   1884.   (Surv. Inst. Trans.)
LI   Fuller, E.   Tenure of land by customary tenants.   (DD. ii, 285.)
LJ   Fustel de Coulonges, N.   Origin of property in land.   1891.   (CI. i, 63, 754 ; v. 584.)
LK   Gardiner, R.   England's grievance (coal-trade).   1655–1796.
LL   Gardiner, S.   History of Commonwealth.   3–4 vol.   1894–1903.
LM   —— History of England, 1603–1642.   10 v.   1863–1884.
LN   Garnier, R.   History of English landed interest.   2 v.   1892–1908.
LO   George, E.   Origin of the declared account.   (CK. xxxi, 41.)
LP   Gibson, S.   The Escheatries.   (CK. xxxvi, 218.)
LQ   Gilbert, Sir G.   Forest laws.   (EM. 340.)
LR   —— Law of tenures.   5th ed.   1824.
LS   —— Treatise on Court of Exchequer.   1758–1796.
LT   —— Treatise on rents.   1758.
LU   Gilbert, N.   Papers : Transcripts of parl. surveys of Crown lands. c. 1780.
LV   Giuseppi, M.   Parl. Surveys of Southwark.   1898–9.   (DW. xiv, 42.)
LW   Godwin, W.   History of the Commonwealth.   4 v.   1824–8.   Pamphlets of this period are included in E. vii, and EW.
LX   Golding, T.   Book of the use of the cross-staff.   1660.

[1] See also H. Chew, Eng. Eccles. Tenants in Chief, 1933.
[2] See also E. Kimball, Serjeanty Tenure in Med. Eng., 1936. Feudal socage was extinguished under Lord Birkenhead's legislation, 1926.

LY   Goldsmith, H.   Timber felling on copyhold estates.   1619.   (EV. 91 : 176.)
LZ   Gonner, E.   Common land and enclosure.[1]   1912.

MA   Green, M.   Committee for advance of money.   3 pt.   1888.
MB   —— Committee for compounding.[2]   5 pt.   1889–1893.
MC   —— Letters of Henrietta Maria.   1857.
MD   Greenwood, W.   Authority and method of keeping courts.   1668–1730.
ME   Gurton, T.   History of courts baron and leet.   2 v.   1731.
MF   Guybert, —   French treatise on surveying.   1619.   (BZ. iii, 462.)
MG   H——, H.   Royal revenues.   1909.
MH   Hale, Sir M.   Treatise on conveyances of land.   1710.
MI   —— Treatise on sheriff's accounts.   1683.
MJ   Hall, H.   Antiquities of the Exchequer, 1891.
MK   —— Formula book of historical documents.   2 v.   1908–9.
ML   —— History of Crown lands.   1886.   (CB. xiii, 1 ; HR.)
MM   —— Studies in historical documents.   1908.
MN   Hardres, Sir T.   Exchequer reports, 1655–9.   Other reports, including (a) Jenkins, 1220–1623 ; and (b) Lane, 1605–1612, will be found in BZ. iii, 172.
MO   Hardy, Sir T.   Rotuli de liberate.   1844.
MP   —— Rotuli de oblatis et finibus.   1835.
MQ   —— Rotuli litterarum clausarum.   2 v.   1833–1844.
MR   —— Rotuli litterarum patentium.   1833.   See the later P.R.O. calendars (AW.), viz. (a) Close rolls, 37 v., 1892–1929 ; (b) Liberate rolls, 1917 ; (c) Patent rolls, 60 v., 1891–1929 ; also (d) Phillimore, signet bills (DF. 4).
MS   Harrington, J.   Commonwealth of Oceana.   1656–1924.   Political science is referred to in E. v. ii.
MT   Harrison, Sir G.   Memoir respecting hereditary revenues of the Crown.   1838.
MU   —— Observations on the King's right to escheats.   1832.
MV   Harrison, J.   The accomplished practiser in Chancery.   5th ed.   2 v.   1767.
MW   Hart, W.   Parl. surveys of Nonsuch, Richmond and Wimbledon.   1871.   (DW. v, 75.)
MX   Hatton, Sir C.   Papers on Crown revenues.   (EA. 21898.)
MY   Haward, L.   Charges issuing forth of the Crown revenues.   1660.   (EW. ii, 318.)
MZ   Hazeltine, H.   Gage of land in medieval England.   1904.

[1] See (a) Gay, Domesday of Inclosures, 1904 (DN., n.s. 18) ; (b) Gras, Evolution of Corn Market, 1915 ; (c) Gray, Eng. field systems, 1915 ; (d) Leadam, Domesday of Inclosures, 2 v., 1897 (EM., n.s. vi, viii, xiv) ; (e) Lists of Enclosure awards (F., AW.) (f) Report of Select Com. on Commons 1844 ; and literature and records in C., D., E.–I., L., N., BG., BH. (b), VA.
[2] For the parliamentary sequestrations, surveys and sales of delinquents' estates, see (a) Cat. of persons compounding, 1655 ; (b) Clay, Royalist comp. papers, 3 v., 1895–6 ; (c) Peacock, Index of royalists' names, 1878 (DO. 2) ; (d) Phillimore, Index of names, 1889 (DF. 3) ; (e) Stanning, Comp. papers, 4 v., 1891–8 ; (f) Welford, Records of Com. for Compounding, 1905 ; and works referred to in C., E., F. (esp. ii, 10–12), H., I., AI. (e.g. iv, 338), AP. xliii, 34, BG., BH. (b), IG., KX.

NA Hazlitt, W. Tenures of land and customs of manors. 1874.

NB Hearnshaw, F. Leet jurisdiction in England. 1908.

NC Heckford, B. Discourse on book-land and folk-land. 1775. (BZ. iii, 279.)

ND Herne, J. Law of conveyances. 1656. (EW. ii, 158.)

NE Hewlett, —. Papers dealing with land revenues. 354 bun. 1832–1903. (P.R.O.)

NF Hobart, Sir H. Records concerning royal revenues. 17th cent. (EA. 25262.)

NG Hobhouse, Bp. Somerset forest bounds. (DU. 37, pt. ii.)

NH Hone, N. Manor and court baron. 1909. (DQ. 3.)

NI —— Manor and manorial records. 1905–1912. (Antiq. books).[1]

NJ Horsman, G. Precedents in conveyancing. 2nd. ed. 2 v. 1757. Other works on conveyancing are recorded in BG. and BZ. iii, 94.

NK Horwood, A. Year Books. 20 v. 1863–1911. See also the volumes edit. by (a) Deiser, (b) Pike, and (c) Vinogradoff; also (d) Geldart (CK. xxvi), and references in BG.

NL Hoskold, H. Notes on ancient and modern surveying. 1900.

NM Hunter, J. Fines, sine pedes finium. 2 v. 1835–1844. Also see (a) Fine rolls, 9 v. 1911–1927; (b) Hardy, Mx. feet of fines, 2 v. 1892; (c) Roberts, Excerpta e rotulis finium. 2 v., 1835–6; (d) Salzmann, Early fines (CK. xxv).

NN Ibbetson, J. Dissertation on folkland and bocland. 2nd ed. 1782.

NO Isham, Sir C. Estimate of Holdenby in 1650. 1886. (CU. i, 182.)

NP Jackson, W. Survey of controversies touching late purchased titles. 1660. (EW. ii, 332.)

NQ Jacob, G. Complete court keeper. 1713–1819.

NR —— Court keeper's companion. 1717.

NS —— Law dictionary. 1729–1744. Other useful dictionaries or encyclopædia articles are those of (a) Blount, 1670–1717; (b) Century Cyclopædia of names; (c) Cowell, 1727; (d) Dict. of Eng. history; (e) Dict. of Nat. Biog.; (f) Dict. of polit. econ. 3 v., 1891–1926; (g) Ency. Brit. ed., 9–14; (h) New Oxford dictionary; (i) Spelman, 1664–1687.

NT Jenkins, D. Lex terrae. 1647.

NU —— Pacis consultum (court leet). 1657.

NV Jenkinson, H. Exchequer tallies. (DA. lxii, 367.)

NW —— Numerals in Eng. archives. 1926. (CA. vi, 263.)

NX Jenks, E. Land tenure and legal execution. (CK. viii, 47; xxii.)

NY Jeudwine, J. Foundations of society and the land. 1918.

NZ Johnson, A. Disappearance of the small landowner. 1909.

OA Kennedy, —. Tenancy of land in Great Britain. 1827–8.

---

[1] On the subject of manors see (a) Cheyney, Eng. manorial documents, 1896 (Univ. Penn. iii, 5); (b) Court rolls, 1896 (AP. 6); (c) Form of a steward's charge at a court of survey (AI. ii, app. 89); (d) Hardy, List of Manor court rolls, 3 pt., 1907–1910 (DQ.); (e) Modus tenendi cur' baron, 1511–1915 (DQ. 9); (f) Order of keeping a court leet, 1650–1914 (DQ. 8); (g) Return of Crown manors, 1845 (RU (b), 1801–1852, index 252); and references in C., D., F., G., H., N., AI., AY., AZ., BH., CI., CV., GN. (a), and "Advice to stewards", 1731. (HV. 526.)

OB   Kennedy, W. English taxation. 1913.
OC   Kerry, Earl of. Parl. survey of King's Bowood park. 1922. (DY. xli.)
OD   Kitchin, J. Jurisdictions. 3rd ed. 1656–1675.
OE   Knowles, J. Law and incidents of tenure. 1912.
OF   Lambard, W. Notes on the forest law. (AI. iv, 411 ; EA. 32097 : 166.)
OG   Lany, A. Opinion concerning fines on non-manorial land. (EV. 91 : 177.)
OH   Lapsley, G. County palatine of Durham. 1900. (V : hist., 8.) See also the records (a) Hardy, Regis. Pal. Dunelmense, 4 v., 1873–8 ; (b) Longstaff, Durham halmote rolls, 1889 (Surtees Soc.) ; (c) Raine, Northern Registers, 1873 (AN. 61) ; and AP. 40.
OI   Larson, L. The King's household in England. 1904.
OJ   Lasalles, T. Wastes of forests and chases. c. 1608. (EA. 38444 : 4.)
OK   Laurence, E. Duty of a steward to his lord. 1727.
OL   Lauterbach, W. De alienatione rerum. 1652–1671. See J.L. and other works on alienations in BG. and BZ. iii.
OM   Leadam, I. Security of copyholders in 15–16th cent. (CK. viii, 684.)
ON   Lee, W. Order of keeping courts leet and baron. 1650.
OO   Lee, W. Essay on the value of leases. 1737.
OP   Lefevre, C. (Baron Eversley). English commons and forests. 1894–1910.
OQ   Legg, —. Account of the revenue of the Crown. 1788. (FO. iii, 145.)
OR   Leigh, V. Science of surveying of lands. 1577–96.
OS   Lennard, R. Parl. surveys of Crown lands. 1916. (Rural Northants under the Commonwealth : Y. 10.)
OT   Lewis, G. The Stannaries.[1] 1908.
OU   Liljegren, S. Fall of the monasteries. 1924. (Tawney in CK. xl, 130.)
OV   Lilly, J. The practical conveyancer. 3rd ed. 1742.
OW   Lily, J. Precedents of leases for years. 1889.
OX   Lindsay, J. Proposals to advance the Queen's revenue. 1707. (EU. 322 : 99.)
OY   Littleton, Sir T. Tenant en fee simple. 1481–1903.
OZ   Lloyd, G. Enfranchisements under the copyhold acts. 1913.

PA   Lloyd, J. Forest of Brecknock. 1905.
PB   Lowndes, —. Crown revenues at several periods. (TX. ii, 364.)
PC   Lyndon, J. The Crown lands. 1871.
PD   Lyte, Sir H. Historical notes on the Great Seal of England. 1928.
PE   Macdonald, J. Systems of land tenure. 1906.
PF   Maclean, Sir J. Forms of land tenure. (DI. 12.)
PG   Madge, S. England under Stuart rule. 1898.
PH   —— Inquisitiones post mortem. 2 v. 1901–3. (DF. 26, 30.)

---

[1] Refer also to (a) Moller (DN. 4 ser. viii, 79) ; (b) Pearce, Laws and customs of Stannaries, 1725 ; and literature and records dealing with mining in C., E. v. i, F., K., BG., BH., LK.

PI   Madge, S. Parliamentary Surveys: descriptive list. 11 v. 1927. (BU. ref. Press 14, No. 82, 1–11 ; EQ.) [1]

PJ   —— Ibid. Cornwall and Lancaster Duchies. 2 lists. 1927. (AB., BK., 4 (92), 761.) [2]

PK   —— Ibid. Index of purchasers. 1927. (BK. 4 (92), 771.)

PL   —— Ibid. King's printing house, London. 1922. (CV. 12, ser. x, 269.)

PM   —— Ibid. Middlesex. 2 pt. 1922–3. (Rural Mx. under the Commonwealth : DP. n.s., iv, 273, 403.)

PN   —— Ibid. Surrey. 1927. (DW. xxxvii, 201.)

PO   Madox, T. History and antiquities of the Exchequer. 2 v. 2nd. ed. 1769.

PP   Maitland, F. Court baron. 1889. (DT.)

PQ   —— Select pleas in manorial courts. 1889. (DT.)

PR   Manwood, J. Treatise on forest laws. 1598–1665. (TG app. i, 1.)

PS   Marks, T. The land and the Commonwealth. 1913.

PT   Marriott, Sir J. The English land system. 1914.

PU   Maxwell, W. Customs of abbey manors. (DY. xxxii, 311.)

PV   Meriton, G. Landlord and tenant. 1681. (BZ. iii, 278.)

PW   Middilton, W. Manner of keeping courts baron and leet. 1544.

PX   Milbourn, T. Parl. survey of Royston. 1874. (DP. proc., 193.)

PY   Mills, M. Reforms at the Exchequer. 1927. (DN. 4 ser. x, 111.)

PZ   Milton, J. Project for increasing the revenue. 1621. (AI. iv, 305.)

QA   Morell, T. Collections relating to customs and land tenures. c. 1763. (EQ.) [3]

QB   Morris, J. Introduction to the study of local history. 2 v. 1910. See also (a) Gill, Studies in Midland history, 1930 ; and the references in E. ii, (vi) and xi, H., I., R., BG.

QC   Munger, J. Land tenure. 1884.

QD   Munro, J. Crown lands. 1915. (Dict. Polit. Econ. i, 468.)

QE   Neale, E. Copyhold tenure and enfranchisement. 1885.

QF   Neilson, N. Customary rents. 1910. (Y. ii, no. 4.)

QG   Nelson, W. Lex maneriorum. 1728.

QH   Newman, W. The complete conveyancer. 3 v. 1788.

QI   Newton, A. The treasurer of the Chamber. (CK. xxxii, 348.)

QJ   Nicholls, J. Collectanea topog. et genealogica. 1834–1843.

QK   Nisbet, J. History of the Forest of Dean. (CK. xxi, 445.)

QL   —— Our forests and woodlands. 1900.

QM   Nordau, M. Interpretation of history. 1910.

QN   Norden, J. The surveyor's dialogue. 1607–1738.

QO   —— Touching the improving of forests. 1612. (EA. 38444 (5) ; TG. app. ii, 3.)

QP   Norfolk, Duke of. Doctrine of perpetuities. 1688.

QQ   North, R. Arguments for a register of estates. 1698.

QR   Northey, Sir E. Opinion on the Queen's jointure. 1714. (EA. 17019 : 133.)

[1] Also Parliamentary Sales : indexes. 12 v. 1937 (BU.).
[2] Also Crown Lands, 1649–1660 : lists and indexes. 15 v. 1937 (BG., ref. 10349, r. 16).
[3] Madge MSS. Presented to the Society of Antiquaries, 23rd February, 1937. (MS. Soc. Antiq. Lond., 671.) Dr. Morell was Secretary of the Society.

QS Gwen, E. Ancient tenures of land in N. Wales. (CK. 26.
QT Palgrave, Sir F. Ancient Kalendars and inventories. 3 v. 1836.
QU —— Rotuli curiae regis. 2 v. 1835. Reference may also be made
    to (a) Ancient correspondence and Petitions (AP. 1, 15, 1892–
    1902) ; (b) Curia regis rolls, 6 v., 1923–33 ; (c) Hale, Historia
    placitorum coronae, 1–2 v., 1678–1800 ; (d) Maitland, Pleas of
    the Crown, 1884 ; (e) Phillimore, Coram rege roll., 1897 (DF. 19) ;
    (f) Placita de banco (AP. 32, 2 pt., 1910) ; (g) Placita de quo
    warranto, 1818 ; (h) Plea rolls (AP. 4, 1910) ; (i) Rose, Abbrev.
    placitorum, 1811.
QV Palmer, A. Parl. survey of Bromfield and Yale. (Transcript, Wrex-
    ham Lib.)
QW Parker, F. Forest laws. (CK. xxvii, 26.)
QX Parry, R. Valuation tables for the use of surveyors. 1913.
QY Pearson, C. History of England. 2 v. 1865.
QZ Percy, Lord E. The Privy Council under the Tudors. 1907.

RA Petrie, H. Monumenta Historica Britannica, I. 1848. (AS.)
    See also documents edit. by (a) Cole, 1844 ; (b) Ellis, 3 ser. 11 v,
    1824–1846 ; (c) Hardy, 3 v., 1862–1871 ; (d) Henderson, 1892 ;
    (e) Thomas, 3 v., 1856 ; also (f) Petrie transcripts, 15 bun.
    (F. i, 348, 352) ; (g) Rymer's Foedera (Clarke, 4 v., 1816–1869,
    and Hardy, 3 v., 1869–1885 ; AS., AV.) ; and the treatises
    referred to in G., N., BG.
RB —— The Chronicles and Memorials Series includes records relating
    to the following reigns by H. Luard and others (AN.) :—

    (RB.) Edward Confessor. No. 3. 1858.
    (RC.) Stephen. No. 82. 1884.
    (RD.) Henry II. Nos. 49, 82. 1867–1884.
    (RE.) Ric. I. Nos. 38, 49, 82. 1864–1890.
    (RF.) Hen. III. No. 27. 1862–6.
    (RG.) Edw. I. No. 76. i. 1882.
    (RH.) Edw. II. No. 76. ii. 1883.
    (RI.) Hen. IV. No. 18. 1860.
    (RJ.) Hen. V. No. 11. 1858.
    (RK.) Hen. VI. Nos. 7, 56, 1858–1872.
    (RL)   Ric. III. No. 24. 1861.
    (RM.) Hen. VII. Nos. 10, 24, 60. 1858–1877.

RN Pett, P. Autobiography. Ed. W. Perrin. 1918. (Navy Records Soc.)
RO Pettus, Sir J. Fodinae regales. 1670.
RP Petty, Sir W. History of the Down Survey. 1861. (Irish Arch. Soc.)[1]
RQ Philipps, S. Necessity of preserving tenures in capite. (BX. ii, 540.)
RR Pitt, J. Papers on Woods. (AY (a), index 43.)
RS Plott, R. Discourse on felling timber. 1687.
RT Pollock, Sir F. Early English freeholders. (DL. xxvi, 25.)

[1] For the Parl. surveys of Irish estates see (a) Headfort Papers (Rep. on records of
Ireland, 1818, viii, 21, app. A., B, and 1902, xxxiv, app. 1) ; and references in E. xiii, KX.
iii, WL. A contract of 1658 occurs in Sotheby's Cat., May, 1910, 13. See above,
p. 256, n.4.

RU Pollock, Sir F. History of English law.[1] 2 v. 1895.
RV Poole, R. The Exchequer in the 12th Century. 1912.
RW Posthlewayt, J. History of the public revenue. 1759.
RX Powell, B. Forest law. 1893.
RY Powell, J. Essay on the nature and effect of leasing powers. 1787.
RZ Powell, R. Antiquity of the Ancient courts of leet. 1642-1688.

SA Probyn, J. Systems of land tenure in various countries. 1881.
SB Proctor, S. Orders which may advance the casual revenue. c. 1612.
      (EN. iii, 206.)
SC Prynne, W. Account of the King's late revenue. 1647. (EW. i, 510.)
SD —— Aurum reginae. 1668. (BR. 220.)
SE Purves, Sir W. Revenue of the Scottish Crown, 1897. The records
      and special works relating to Scotland are indicated in E. xii,
      F., AW., BG.
SF Raleigh, Sir W. Discourse on tenures. (Works, 1829, viii.)
SG Ramsay, Sir J. Accounts of Edw. V. and Ric. III. 1888. (CB. 18.)
SH —— History of the revenues of the Kings of England.[2] 2 v. 1925.
SI Rastell, J. Les termes de la ley. 1629-1641.
SJ Rathborne, A. The surveyor in four books. 1616.
SK Reid, R. Barony and thanage. (CK. xxxv, 161.)
SL —— King's Council in the North. 1921.
SM —— Warden of the Marches. (CK. xxxii, 479.)
SN Reynold, J. Case of severance of joint tenancy. 1720. (EV. 91 : 178.)
SO Richardson, H. British forest history. (R. Scot. Arbor. Soc.
      Trans. 36.)
SP Ritson, J. Jurisdiction of the court leet. 2nd. ed. 1809-1811.
SQ —— The office of bailiff of a liberty. 1811.
SR Robinson, T. The common law of Rent. 1741-1897.
SS Rogers, J. Domesday drawing nigh. 1653. (EW. ii, 43.)
ST Rogers, J. T. Hist. of agric. and prices in England. 7 v. 1866-1902.
      See also (a). Economic interpretation of history. 1888.
SU Ross, W. Discourse upon the removing of tenants. 1782.
SV Round, J. Crown lands.[3] 1886. (CB. xiii, 85.)
SW —— Domesday measures of land. (Arch. Rev. i.)
SX —— Family origins. 1930.
SY —— Feudal England. 1895-1909.
SZ —— King's serjeants and officers of state. 1911.

[1] On the subject of law see (a) Parl. accounts 1801-1930 (AW.) ; (b) Parl. Papers,
1731-1930 ; (c) Parl. reports, 1696-1930 ; (d) Parl. rolls, 8 v., 1771-1832 ; (e) Stat. of
Realm, 22 v., 1885-1909 (earlier ed. Ruffhead, 9 v., 1763-5 ; Tomlins, 11 v., 1810-1822).
Also (f) Holdsworth Hist. of Eng. law, 3-9 v., 1903-1927 ; (g) Husband, Collection of
Acts, 2 v., 1649-1653 ; (h) Plucknett, Statutes and their interpretation, 1922 ; (i) Pollock,
Land laws, 1896 ; (j) Pound, Interpretations of legal history, 1923 (T.) ; (k) Robertson,
Laws of the Kings of Eng., 1925 ; (l) Scobell, Collection of Acts, 1658 ; (m) Thorpe,
Ancient laws, 2 v., 1840 ; (n) Twiss, Bracton's Legibus, 6 v., 1878-1883 (AN. 70) ; and
the references in E. i (iii, iv), J., AM.
[2] In connection with Revenues, see (a) Auditors' certificates (EA. 30206 (39),
30207 (24)) ; (b) Commissioners for land revenues, 1786-1794 (AP. ii, 162) ; (c) Profits of
land revenue for 10 years, 1816 (RU. (a) index, 1801-1852, 1069) ; and the references in
C., F., H., BH. (b).
[3] A later paper on " Crown Lands " by A. S. Gaye, was read at the Chartered Surveyors' Institution, 9th January, 1933 (Times, 10th January, 1933).

TA Rouse, R. Copyhold and court keeping practice. 1837.
TB —— Copyhold commutation. 1841.
TC —— Copyhold enfranchisement. 1852–8.
TD Russell, F. Report on Crown revenues. 1783. (FO. iii, 145.)
TE Rye, W. The land buyers' society. 1904. (AI. xii (ix), 135 ; CT. xv. 1.)
TF Ryley, W. Papers on forest lands. 1653. (IG.)
TG St. John, J. Observations on the land revenue of the Crown. 1787.
TH Sanders, F. Surrenders of copyhold property. 1819.
TI Sandys, C. Consuetudines Kanciae. 1851.
TJ Savine, A. Copyhold cases in early Chancery proceedings. (CK. xvii, 296.)
TK —— English monasteries [1] on the eve of the Dissolution. 1909. (Y. i, No. 1.)
TL Sawyer, T. Teutonic settlements and land tenure. 1884.
TM Scofield, C. Study of The Council of Star Chamber.[2] 1900.
TN Scriven, T. Law of copyholds. 3rd. ed. 1833–1896.
TO Scroggs, Sir W. Practice of courts leet and baron. 1702–1728.
TP Seebohm, F. Customary acres. 1914.
TQ —— The English village community. 1883–1896.
TR —— Feudal tenures in England. (Fort. Rev. n.s. 7.)
TS Selby, P. History of British forest trees. 1842.
TT Selden, J. Ad Fletam dissertatio. 1647–1925. (T.)
TU —— Titles of honour. 1614–1672.
TV Seymour, Sir J. Perpetuities, certified to Parliament. 1667. (EA. 30206 : 40.)
TW Shaw, W. Cal. of Treasury Books. 9 v. 1904–1930.
TX —— Ibid. Books and papers : (a) Reddington, 6 v. ; (b) Shaw, 5 v., 1868–1903.
TY —— Commonwealth and Protectorate. 1906. (Cam. Mod. Hist., iv, ch. 15.)
TZ —— History of the English church,[3] 1640–1660. 2 v. 1900.

UA Sheppard, W. Court keeper's guide. 1641–1791.
UB —— Precedent of predecents. 1655–1825.
UC —— Touchstone of common assurances. 1641–1820.
UD Sinclair, E. Land values. 1910.

[1] See also Liljegren ; and for revenues see Snape's *Eng. Monastic Finances*, 1926.
[2] For records of this Court see C., E. i (ii, 30), F., H., AU., BH. (b).
[3] The literature and records relating to parliamentary surveys and sales of ecclesiastical property are scattered. See (a) Burgess, No sacrilege to alienate or purchase lands, 1660 ; (b) Cox, Hist. of a parish, 112 ; (c) Ducarel, Index of Lambeth surveys, dated 1760 (BP.) ; (d) Giuseppi, Surr. Rec. Soc. xxiv (Sect. " Aa. 14-77 ") ; (e) Johnson, assurance of church lands, 1687 ; (f.) West Wales Hist. Records, xiv, 1930 ; and the references in C., F., H., S. i, No. 3131, AI. i, 53, xiv, p. viii. ; AO. i, app. iii, 22 ; AR. (a) 1812, p. 7 (app. S. 183) ; AR. (a) 1837 (app. R. 395) ; BH. (b) ; BP. ; ER. 80 ; ES. (ref. " D. 715 ") ; EW. ii, 332 ; FZ. ii, 514 ; KX. ; MM. 306 ; OS. ; TZ. app. iv–xi ; UE. iii, app. 98. Certificates of rates of sales of Bishops lands, 1643–1659, are indicated in AV. (F. ii, 13, Commonwealth Exch. Papers, 289). Many published parl. surveys in this series are the work of Bax, Boddington, Browne, Cave, Hall, and Kershaw ; these relate to the counties of Glouc., Mx., Surrey, Wilts, and Worcs (CM. ii, 214 ; CO. i–iii ; DW., vii. 51, xvii, 83 ; DY. xix, 182, xl, xli ; DZ., 1924). To these may be added Ely, 1933, by T. D. Atkinson (app. ix).

UE   Sinclair, Sir J.   History of the public revenue. 3 v. 1785–1804.
UF   Skeel, C.   The Council in the Marches of Wales. 1904. (Girton Coll. Studies, 2.)
UG   —— The Council in the west. 1921. (DN. 4 ser. iv.)
UH   Skrimshire, S.   Valuations. 1915.
UI   Slater, G.   Historical outline of land ownership.[1] 1913. (Land Enquiry, I.)
UJ   Smith, A.   Nature and causes of the Wealth of Nations. 1776–1904.
UK   Snell, F.   Customs of old England. 1911.
UL   Sneyd, C.   Relation of the island of England, 1500. 1847. (DG. 37.)
UM   Solly, E.   Hereditary titles of honour. 1880. (DO. 5.)
UN   Somers, Lord.   Collection of tracts. 16 v. 1748–1815.
UO   Somner, W.   Treatise on gavelkind. 1617–1660.
UP   Spelman, H.   Tenure by knight service. (Works, 1727.)
UQ   Steele, Sir R.   Crisis of property. 1720.
UR   Stenton, F.   Types of manorial structure. 1910. (Y. ii, No. 3.)
US   Stevens, C.   Fluctuations of prices and land-rent. 1882.
UT   Stevens, F.   The New Forest. 1925.
UU   Stevens, J.   The royal treasury of England. 1725–1733.
UV   Stokes, E.   Surrey Crown lands during the Commonwealth. (DW. xxii, 192.)
UW   Straton, C.   An English manor, temp. Elizabeth. (DY. xxxii, 288.)
UX   Tapping, W.   The copyholder's enfranchisement manual. 1852.
UY   Taprell, A.   Parl. survey of Glouc., Aug. Off. Ser. No. 2. '(BD. iii, 354.)
UZ   Taverner, J.   List of the Queen's forests. 1585. (EP. i, 83.)

VA   Tawney, R.   The Agrarian problem in the 16th century.[2] 1912.
VB   Tayleur, W.   Instructions for sale of forests. 1653. (S. i, 364.)
VC   Thomas, F.   Handbook to the public records. 1853.
VD   —— History of public departments.[3] 1846.
VE   Tout, T.   Administrative history of Medieval England. 4 v. 1920-8.
VF   Treherne, G.   Laws of the forest. (EA. 25254, EN. i, 20, 37.)
VG   Trevelyan, G.   England under the Stuarts. 1904–1910.
VH   Turnbull, P.   Ancient and present state of tenures. (BX. ii, 540.)
VI   Turner, G.   Select pleas of the forest. 1901. (DT. 13.)

[1] On the subject of " The Transference of Lands in England, 1640–1660," see the paper by the Rev. H. E. Chesney (R. Hist. Soc., 4th ser., xv, pp. 181–210, read 10th March, 1932). The Parliamentary Surveys are only referred to in a footnote, p. 210, suggested by Dr. H. Hall. The break up of estates in this country since 1917 has been astonishing. One firm of estate agents alone sold in four years ending December, 1921, no less than 1,776,728 acres, equivalent to the counties of Bedford, Berks, Bucks, Herts, and Middlesex, and in eight years (1914–1921) one-twelfth of the entire acreage of Scotland (*Daily Telegraph*, " The Land Monopoly," leading article, 21st August, 1923).
[2] For the literature and records relating to Agriculture see (*a*) Prothero, Eng. farming, 1912, app. I ; and the references in C., E. v (iv), F., H., L., N., AA., BG., BH. (*b*).
[3] See also (*a*) Bond, Handy book for verifying dates, 1866–1889 ; (*b*) Cotton, Exact abridgement of records, 1657 ; (*c*) Index and directions for records, 1739 ; (*d*) Martin, Record interpreter, 2nd. ed., 1910 ; (*e*) Powell, Directions for search, 1622 ; and references to Records in C., F., H., I., Q., BG.

VJ   Turner, R.   Arrears of the revenue.   1659.   (EV. 51 : 95.)
VK   Tyssen, J.   Parl. surveys of Sussex.   1871–3.   (DX. xxiii–xxv.)
VL   Usher, R.   Rise and fall of the High Commission.   1913.
VM   Vernon, C.   Considerations for regulating the Exchequer.   1642.
         (BR. 104.)
VN   Vinogradoff, Sir P.   Growth of the Manor.   1905–1911.
VO   —— Villainage in England.   1892.
VP   W——, S.   The practical surveyor.   1725.
VQ   Wallace, G.   Origins of feudal tenures.   1783.   (BX. ii, 540.)
VR   Wallinby, O.   Planometrie.   1650.
VS   Watkins, C.   Treatise on copyholds.   2 v.   1797–1825.
VT   Webb, S. (Lord Passfield).   The manor and the borough.   2 v.   1908.
VU   Whitaker, Sir T.   Ownership, tenure, and taxation of land.   1914.
VV   Wight, T.   Order of keeping courts leet and baron.   1603–1625.
VW   Wilkinson, J.   Treatise on Courts.   1618–1638.
VX   Worsop, E.   Sundry errors committed by land-meters.   1582.
VY   Wright, Sir M.   Introduction to the law of tenures.   2nd. ed.   1734–
         1792.
VZ   Yeatman, J.   Law of ancient demesne.   1884.

IX. Various Maps, Plans, and References

WA   Agriculture Ministry.   Enclosure maps.   (See Bramwell's Anal. table
         of private statutes.   2 v.   1813–1835.   Index of local Acts, 1801–
         1899.   Returns to H. of Com., viz. Nos. 455 of 1893, 50 of
         1904, 399 of 1914.   For maps at P.R.O., see AO. ·xxvi, app. 1, 7.)
WB   —— Tithe maps.   (Return to H. of Com.   1887.)
WC   Bartholomew, J.   Royal Atlas and Index.   1899.
WD   —— Survey atlas.   1903.
WE   Bodleian Library.   Gough maps.   MS. Cat.   (EL.)
WF   British Museum.   King's Library Maps and prints.   Cat. 1829.
WG   —— MS. maps and plans.   3 v.   1844–1861.
WH   —— Printed maps and plans.   2 v. (additions).   1885–1937.
WI   Cornwall Duchy.   MS. List.   1920.   (AB.)
WJ   Ellis, G.   County atlas.   1819.
WK   Fordham, Sir H.   Studies in carto-bibliography.   1914.
WL   Headfort Coll.   Parl. surveys of Irish estates :   Down Survey (A.O,
         Ireland, xxxiv. app. 1 ;   AR. (a), 1812, 191, app. 304 ;   RP.)
         Other Irish maps are referred to in F. ii, 5, 18.
WM   Lancaster Duchy.   List.   (F. i, 329 ;   AO. xxx, app. 1 ;   AP. 14.)
WN   Land Registry.   Plans annexed to deeds.   Indexes.
WO   Land Revenue Office.   Maps.   (AG. 94, AP. obs. 841 : 63 ;   formerly
         L. R. Misc. bk. 366 : 63.)
WP   Ordnance Survey.   Parish and County maps (6 in., 25 in.).   Cat.
         1915.
WQ   —— Indexes, and summary of publications.   Cat. 1915.
WR   Parliamentary Surveys.   Only five plans have been discovered
         among the surveys of Crown lands (AE.), Viz. Derby, No. 19 f.,
         28 ;   Mx. No. 25 f., 8 ;   Norf. No. 10 f.9. No. 14 f., 5 ;   Notts.
         No. 10A f., 10 with dup. No. 10 B.   In Robinson's Hist. of
         Enfield, i, 193, is a plan of Enfield Chase (from WE.).   Nothing

is known as to plans[1] of Church lands and delinquents' estates. (MB., TZ.) For the Down Survey, see RP., WL.

WS   Pearson, C. Historical maps. 1869.

WT   Philips, G. Junior historical atlas. 1923. (DM.)

WU   Public Record Office. Various departments. (F. i, 388 ; ii, 237., AG., AO. xxvi, app. 1, 7 ; xxx, app. 1 ; AP. 14. AP. 25, AV. AX., AY. (*a*), index 43.)

WV   Speed, J. List of forests, parks, and chases. (AP. xxv, 415.)

WW Surveyor-General's Office. List. 1726. (EA. 30207 : 26.)

WX   Various References :[2] B. 176; C. 349; F. ii, 117, 237; I. 457; AI. iv, 363 ; BF. ii, 291 ; BH. (*b*) 93 ; EA. 12541 ; EH. ; EN. iii, 529; EU. 821 ; FF. xiv, 303 ; FX. 186 ; IF. x, 149, 258 ; LZ (*c*) ; TW. iii, 531 ; VA.

WY   Wales. Maps and plans. (F. i, 324 ; I. 457 ; AP. 14 ; AP. 25.)

WZ   Woods Office. (AY. (*a*) index 43.)

[1] Some plans, mostly coloured, of Parliamentary Surveys of Crown Lands in Derby, Dorset, Essex, Surrey, and Sussex have been discovered in Land Rev. Off. Misc. Books, vols. 279, f. 281, 280 ff., 33*b*, 227 ; 366, f. 63 (obs. 841, p. 63, obs. 842, p. 57 ; No. 112, T. Lane, 1654) ; and Duchy of Lanc., Map No. 47 (dated 1653). A missing " Plott ", Augm. Off. Survey, is referred to on f. 25 of Linc. No. 14. A " Plott of Enfield Chase, 1658 " is said to be among the vestry records at Enfield : at the Bodleian Library the Shelf-mark of the same Plan is " Gough Maps 17, f. 12*b* ". Surveyors of Forest Lands were ordered to " return maps " with their surveys (S.P. Dom., 1654, vol. lxix, No. 53, Cal. pp. 97–8).

[2] Prints of Crown property may be seen in topographical works, and drawings also in collections at the British Museum, Cambridge, and Oxford (EH., WF., XL., and p. 5, 293–4, above). Worcester House, Strand, is shown in Hollar's drawing in the Pepysian Library, Magdalene College, Cambridge (No. 327,*c*). There are prints from this drawing in the Crace and Guildhall Collections (BM., Vaughan-Pennant, 1805, ii, pp. 122–3 ; EH., Views, Portf. v, No. 168). These prints may be traced to Wilkinson's *Londina Illustrata*, 1808, pl. 8, and 1819, same pl., i, pl. 99. The stairs of " Woster House " west of Savoy Stairs, on the river-front, are shown in a map of 1682 (EH., Maps, Portf. ii, No. 58). Rocque's map of London, 1746, shows " Beaufort Buildings " on the site. Prints or drawings of the surveyors are difficult to discover, and the only print of Col. Wm. Webb, the Surveyor-General, that I have found is at the Bodleian (Shelf-mark : Sutherland 81, No. 408). The *Dictionary of National Biography* ignores Col. Webb.

APPENDIX II

ADMINISTRATION, SURVEYS, AND SALES OF CROWN LANDS

I. Parliamentary Surveys, 1649–1660.

XA *Augmentation Office Series (P.R.O. ref. " E. 317 ")* [1] : These documents, prepared at Worcester House in the Strand during the Commonwealth, were placed at the Restoration in the custody of the Clerk of the Pipe ; they were sent before 1739 [2] to the Aug. Off., where they were calendared in 1764, and after narrowly escaping destruction in the fire of October, 1834 at the Houses of Parliament were transferred to Carlton Ride in 1842, and subsequently to the P.R.O. (*a*) The Parl. surveys in this series are arranged in order of counties, every one of which in England and Wales is represented, in fifty-six portfolios. (AV. vii, 224 ; viii, 52.) (*b*) There are calendars, indexes, inventories and lists by Ducarel, 1764 ; Fordyce, 1787 ; Caley, 1790–1801 ; Cole, 1846–7 ; and Madge, 1927. For references see F. i, 160 ; AE. ; AO. ii ; iv. 9 ; vii, 20, 224 ; viii, 52 ; ix, xx, 91 ; xxiv, 39 (" incomplete ") ; xxv, xxvii, xxx, 260 ; xxxii ; AO. index, i, 240 ; ii, 103. AP. xxv (" revised ") ; AP. No. 692 (now Obs. 791) ; AS. (Rec. Com., specimen list, *c*. 1800) ; EA. 21327, 21328 (purchased by Brit. Mus. of C. Devon, 12th Apr., 1856) ; EQ. ; GN. (*a*) app. iii, 81 ; PI. ; VD. (*c*), 85.

XB *Bodleian MSS.* : Two Parl. surveys only are preserved at Oxford and these relate to Edmonton and Enfield Manors, Mx. ; they are in the Gough collection. See EL. 175 ; EX. iv, 236 (No. 18016 : 1–5) ; WR.

XC *British Museum Series* : A scattered series of Parl. surveys and sales relating to the counties of Berks, Derby, Devon, Glouc., Heref., Hunt., Kent, Leic., Linc., Mx., Norf., Northants, Notts, Rut., Som., Staff., Surr., Sx., Worc., It includes MSS. from the Baynes, Burrell, Lansdowne, and Webb collections in the Hist. MSS. Com. Reports. There are catalogues, indexes and lists referring to this series, for which see the references BF. i, ii ; BH. (*b*) (ref. Topog. v, 2175–2185) ; EA. 5700, 6669, 6682, 6687, 6693, 15664, 21348, 22060–1 ; EN. 5013 ; EN. (roll Y. 32) ; EQ. ; EU. 322.

XD *Cambridge MSS.* : Apart from the important series of papers relating to Parl. sales of Crown lands and rents, only one Parl. Survey, has been found in the Univ. Library ; this is a survey of Enfield Chase, Mx. For references see BJ. i, 351, 385, ii, 78 ; EQ. ; PJ. (Lanc. Duchy).

XE *Cornwall Duchy Series* [3] : This is a very extensive but little known collection of Parl. surveys which appears to have been preserved in the Surveyor-General's office from 1660 to about 1725, since which date the books, bundles, and rolls have been kept in the Duchy Office. The documents

---

[1] See Table XXIV.
[2] Some notes dated 1739, signed " O. D." (for Owen Davies), are recorded on certain Parliamentary Surveys that were under examination that year. He may have prepared the " General Index of Crown Lands " (EA. 30208). See XW, ZM.
[3] See Table XXVII.

relate to lands and rents in Berks, Buck., Corn., Dev., Dors, Hants, Herts, Leics, Lincs, Northants, Som., Surr., Sx., Warw., Wilts, and Card., Mer. and Pembroke in Wales. A Cornish survey (No. 6 in Aug. Off. series) was missing before 1915, but many new documents were discovered in 1926–7. The arrangement suggested for this collection (PJ : Cornwall Duchy, 16th June, 1927) refers to : (*a*) Paper books, 9 bun. ; (*b*) Paper books, abstracts, *c*. 1750, a parcel with 3 bun. ; (*c*) Parchment Roll, Liskeard ; (*d*) Transcripts, *c*. 1698, in 2 vol. (No. xix, xx) ; (*e*) Transcripts, *c*. 1753, in 18 vol. (No. 1–xviii) ; (*f*) Various papers, in 3 vol. (viz. " Baynes Papers ", " Old Shoreham accounts," and " Surveys of non-Duchy lands "). The Baynes Papers were originally in the Webb Collection of the Hist. MSS. Reports. There are Lists and Indexes by the Surveyor-General, 1713–1726 ; also Gardiner, 1847 ; Clowes, 1920 ; and Madge, 1927. For references see AB. ; AK. ; AO. vii, 224 ; viii, 81 ; EA. 30206 (32), 30207 (20) ; EQ. ; HI. ; PI. ; PJ (Cornwall Duchy) ; XS.

XF *Historical MSS. Commission* : The reports of the Hist. MSS. Com. contain several references to Parl. surveys in collections that are now dispersed ; these are indicated below under " Various MSS.". For the Baynes, Lansdowne, Webb, and Williams collections see XR.–XY.

XG *King's Remembrancer Records* (*P.R.O. ref.* " *E. 163* ") : Among the documents transferred in 1842 were several Parl. surveys discovered by Mr. Hunter among the " Misc. Records " of this Department. Between 1843 and 1850 others were discovered and added to the Aug. Off. series, viz., Ches. No. 6, 10, 13, 14, 16, 18, 21, 23 (present references) ; Derby, 14, 27, 29 ; Herts, 30 ; Linc., 7, 10, 13, 22, 31, 37, 38, 41, 44 ; Notts, 10 ; Sx., 25 ; Carnar., No. 1.   References will be found in AF. ; AO. iii, 5 ; vii, 224, 228, 231 ; viii, 54 ; AP., xxv ; AP., obs. 791 (notes added) ; EQ. ; PI.

XH *Lambeth Library MSS.* : The Parl. surveys of Church and Crown lands, at Lambeth and the P.R.O. respectively, are found at times to supplement each other. For example, the Crown manor of Halliford, Mx., is referred to in the Church survey of Shepperton, and the prebendal manor of Tottenham Court is likewise recorded among the particulars for sales of Crown lands.   The two series need to be carefully compared ; for although the separate calendars prepared by Dr. Ducarel between 1760 and 1764 exhibit clarity of judgment in the matter of classification (so that Lambeth is said to possess no Parl. surveys of Crown lands among its records), it is nevertheless true that at least three of the Parl. surveys of Church lands for Bedford and Sussex are included among the P.R.O. Crown lands series. For the ecclesiastical series at the P.R.O. see F. i, 68, and for other references AE. (Sx., No. 49 ; two surveys) ; AG. (ref. " L.R. 2 ", vol. 276 ; 126, Bedford) ; BP. xii, 173 ; EA. 21327 p. 81 (or p. 64 in P.R.O. copy).

XI *Lancaster Duchy Series* (*P.R.O. ref.* " *D.L. 32* ") [1] : This series of Parl. surveys was transferred from the Duchy Office to the P.R.O. in 1868. It consists of 87 documents arranged in counties in 3 bundles. In the transfer list these records are styled " Oliver Cromwell's Surveys ", But some of them are Particulars for Sales. The counties comprised in this collection are Berk., Camb., Ches, Derby., Ex., Hants, Hunt., Lanc., Leic., Linc., Mdx., Norf., Northants, Notts, Oxf., Staff., Surr., Sx., Warw., York,

[1] See Table XXVIII.

314

and Glam., and Monmouth in Wales. The earliest list is that of Hardy, 1847. For references see F. i, 332 ; AO. vii, 224 ; viii, 80 ; xiv, 90 ; xxx, app. No. 1 (2, 40) ; xxxii, p. xxv ; AP. xiv ; EQ. ; PI. ; PJ.

XJ *Land Revenue Office Series (P.R.O. ref. " L.R. 2 ")*[1] : This is the second largest collection of Parl. surveys, 763 in number, and although mainly consisting of duplicates of those in the Aug. Office there are many important documents whose existence had been unsuspected before 1927. Transferred from Worcester House to the custody of the Auditors of the Land Revenues and the Surveyor-General in 1660, this series was subsequently placed in charge of the keeper of the Office of Land Revenue Records and Enrolments in 1832, and after being separately housed these records were removed in April, 1903 to the P.R.O. (*a*) The Parl. surveys in the series are arranged in order of counties (Rutland alone being unrepresented), in 19 vols. of " Miscellaneous Books " (AG. 39, ref. " L.R. 2. Misc. bks.", Eng. 276–302, Wales 303–304, and odd surveys v. 255). (*b*) There are calendars, indexes, and lists by the Surveyors-General, 1713–1775 ; West, 1793 ; and Madge, 1927. For references see F. i, 169, 172 ; ii, 114. AI. v, 259 ; AO. ii, 23 ; iv, 9 ; vii, 6, 224 ; viii, 80 ; xxv (p. xxii) ; xxvii (p. vii) ; lxv, 5 ; AP. xxv (few refs.) ; AP. obs., 835, 837–842 ; AQ. (*b*), rep. 1800 (12) ; AR. (*a*), rep. 1812 (54) ; 1819 (358) ; EA. 23749 (purchased at Bryant's sale, 15th June, 1860) ; EA. 30206 (12), 30207 (11)—both originally in West's possession, and purchased by the Brit. Mus. of the Marquis of Lansdowne, 9th Dec., 1876—EQ. ; FO. ; PI.

XK *Local Collections* : Some of the Local History and Topographical collections in public or private ownership contain copies of Parl. surveys, but the leisure of a lifetime might be spent in so wide a field of research. A transcript has been found at Wrexham Library, and an Original Survey at Bowood, Wilts. For references see E. xi ; H. pt. iii ; I. ; QV. ; XW.

XL *Printed Series* : Since references to the Parl. surveys first appeared in the calendars and indexes of 1739–1764, many notable papers have been printed by the Soc. of Antiquaries between 1765 and 1866, and many surveys have been wholly or partially printed in County or Society publications. The present list contains references to surveys of Camb., Corn., Derby, Glouc., Mx., Northants, Som., Surr., Sx., Wilts., and Worc. See the references AP. obs. 791 ; BP. ; BV. (*b*) ; CZ. ii (pl. 23, Richmond, pl. 25, Placentia, East Greenwich) ; DA. v, 429 (Nonsuch, Surr.), x, xl ; DB. ii–iv ; DU. xxx, 78 (Frome and Kilverdon Hundreds, Som.) ; DX. xiv, 48 (Ashdown For., Sx.) ; DY. xli, 413 ; EQ. ; GO. ; HA. ; HM. ; HZ. ; IX. ; JO. ; LV. ; MW. ; OC. ; OS. 121 ; PL.–PN. ; PX. ; UX. ; VD. (*c*) ; VK. ; and Evesham Jour., 17th Nov., 1906. See also Canon Manley's account of " Parliamentary Surveys of the Crown Lands in Braden forest ", in *Wilts Arch. Mag.*, June, 1933.

XM *Rentals and Surveys Series (P.R.O.)* : The general inventory of 1908, incorporating an " entirely revised " list of Aug. Off. Parl. surveys, includes nothing from the Duchy of Lancaster series, little from the Land Rev. Off. series, but much additional matter collected from the " Miscellaneous books " of the Aug. Off., Ex. K.R., L.R.O., Treas. of Receipt, and the Special Commissions and State Papers. The counties concerned in these certificates, rents and surveys of the Commonwealth period are

---

[1] See Table XXV.

Bed., Buck., Camb., Ches, Corn., Dev., Ex., Glouc., Herts, Lincs, Mx., Norf., Northants, Notts, Staff., Sx., Warw., Westm., Wilts, York, and Denb., Flint and Monm. in Wales. See the references in AF. ; AP. xxv, 179, 201, 215, 238, 240, 339, 363 ; EQ. ; PI. ; XA. ; XG. ; XJ. ; XN. ; XO.

XN *Special Commissions (P.R.O.)* : In this series are some certificates and surveys referring mainly to the counties of Glouc., Hants, Lincs, and York. The Special Commissions of the Duchy of Lancaster also include drafts, surveys, warrants, and other papers relating thereto. See AO. xxxviii, 130 ; AP. xiv, 100 ; xxv, xxxvii, 31, 34, 57, 120 ; EQ. ; PI.

XO *State Papers, Dom. Series (P.R.O.)* : A number of certificates and surveys are preserved in this collection. In the main they relate to forests and woodlands, and to the marking, felling, and selling of timber reserved for the navy or otherwise disposed of chiefly in the counties of Berk., Corn., Ex., Glouc., Hants, Kent, Northants, and Surrey. For references see AP. xxv, 21, 49, 110, 119, 154 ; AV. ; EQ. ; IF. (ref. vol. 520, No. 31) ; IG. (ref. vols. 3, 16, 25, 26, 32, 54, 67, 81, 126) ; PI.

XP *Surveyors-General Office Series* : This series of Parl. surveys was transferred from Worcester House at the Restoration. Its subsequent history in connection with the auditors of the Land Revenues, the keeper of the Office of Land Revenue Records and Enrolments, and the Deputy Keeper of the P.R.O. has already been recorded (XJ.). The loss of records, is referred to in H. 86 ; AY. (*a*) iii, 25 ; and below under YW. (*e*) and ZM. See also AO. vii, 67, where the order of 17th July, 1660, for removal of records is quoted.

XQ *Valuations from Parl. Surveys, 1660–1760* : After the Restoration a Commission of Enquiry examined the methods and proceedure of the Commonwealth surveys and sales. The importance of the Parl. surveys being realized, they were henceforth quoted in the constats and particulars for leases and grants of the Auditors and Surveyors-General. See Leases and Grants of the period in F. i, 379, 385 ; ii, 221 ; and for other references see TW. iii, 911, 1215 ; iv, 397, 433, 686 ; v, 505, 576, 1016, 1144, 1167 ; vi, 536, 798 ; vii (32 refs.) ; viii (11 refs.) ; TX. (*a*) 163 ; TX. (*b*) iii, 326 ; iv, 55, 498.

XR–XY *Various Parl. Surveys* : Lists, transcriptions, and dispersed collections arranged as under:—

XR Several lists and transcripts of Parl. surveys by Burrell, Clowes, Gilbert, Palmer and others are at the British Museum, Duchy of Corn- wall, and elsewhere. Other collections reported upon by the Hist. MSS. Commission and now dispersed are referred to below. See references in EQ., IU., JI., LU., PI., PJ., QV., XF.

XS *Baynes MSS.* : Several volumes were originally in the Webb Collection, but the Brit. Mus. now possesses 11 vols. and the Duchy of Cornwall office has the 12th. ("Baynes Papers," purchased 25th June, 1913.) See AB., EA. 21417–21427, EQ., FY., GI.–GL., HI., XE., XX.

XT *Ibid* : (*a*) Imaginary Manor of Sale, Surrey, 19 ff., 1649, Sept. This apparently was the "precedent survey" of a manor proposed for sale, as a guide for the parliamentary surveyors to adopt. See AB., FY. 688, HI., XE. A certified copy is in EQ., and has since been presented to the British Museum. (Add. MS. 44937.)

XU *Ibid* : (*b*) Method of drawing up and engrossing surveys.

5 ff., 1649. This is the companion to XT. (*a*) issued for the guidance of surveyors. Both are in the "Baynes Papers" at the Duchy of Cornwall office. See AB., FY. 688, HI., XE.; also a certified copy in EQ., which is now in the British Museum, 5th Feb., 1937. (Add. MS. 44937.)

XV *Burrell MSS.*: These contain transcripts of Parl. surveys and Particulars for Sales of Crown lands in Sussex, made in 1770. The original Particulars of the Surveyor-General's office are now missing. See EA. 5705, EQ.

XW *Lansdowne MSS.*: The schedules of Parl. surveys, dated 1713–1726, and the "General Index of Crown lands", *c.* 1752, were acquired in 1876 by the Brit. Mus. Copies of Parl. surveys still remain at Bowood, Wilts, one of them being utilized by the Earl of Kerry recently. See DY, xli, 413; EA. 30206–30208; FO.

XX *Webb MSS.*: These papers have now been dispersed, the "Baynes Papers" being acquired by the Brit. Mus. and the Duchy of Cornwall. Several items quoted in the Report of Hist. MSS. Com. (FY. 681, 688) have not been traced, amongst them being the following :—

(*a*) Breviate of instructions sent to Parl. surveyors, 2 pp., 1649.
(*b*) Divisions of surveyed manors, 1650, 14th Oct.
(*c*) Index to a book of precedents, 5 ll., 1649.
(*d*) Instructions from surveyors, 1649. (See HI.; KX. iii, 132.)
(*e*) Letters from trustees to surveyors, 1649–1653. (See EA. 21417–21427.)
(*f*) Order to stewards to continue in office. 4 copies, 1649.
(*g*) Warrants to surveyors, 1st Oct., 1649.

XY *Williams MSS.*: A reference to Parl. surveys, with the date 2nd Nov., 1586, in the Report of the Hist. MSS. Com. in connection with Dr. Williams' Library has been ascertained (July, 1927) to be erroneous. (AI. iii, 367; EQ.)

XZ *Various References*: Acts, castles and forts surveyed, Exchequer surveys, maps and plans, mines and quarries surveyed, operations on MSS., origin of Parl. surveys, State lands, transfers of surveys, 1660–1903, Valuations, Warrants. See the references in C. 201; F. i, 168, 393; H. 52; AO. iii, 5; iv, 9; vii, 67; ix, 15, 26; xxii (p. xxv); xxx, 2, 40; lxv, 5; AP. obs. 791 (f. 35 "Linc., No. 7A."); CV. 2, ser. xii, 309; 4 ser. viii, 167, 255, 269, 486; EA. 30208; EQ.; EW. ii, 78; FY. 688; IG. i, 586; iv, 600; ix, 181; xii, 106, 372; KX. ii, 744; iii, 42, 131; MM. 306; OS. ch. i,; PM. pt. i; RU. (*g*); RU. (*l*); TG. 88, 138; VC. 239, 475; VD. 145, 187; WR.

II. LAND ADMINISTRATION, 1625–1660

YA *Crown Lands (King's Lands), 1625–1660*: The land revenues of King Charles I were largely derived from estates which he held (1) as King of England; (2) as Duke of Lancaster; and (3) temporarily, as Duke of York. The Duchy lands of Lancaster and York are mentioned below (YF., YG.), and the royal estates in Scotland and Ireland are referred to by Hume (Hist. of Eng., ch. liii), with other references in IF. i–xxiii, IG. i–xiii, RP., SE., WL. The estates designated "King's Lands" in the Parliamentary surveys of the Commonwealth period are distributed throughout all the counties of England and Wales. For general references to these lands see S. i ; F. i, 355, 369 ; AG. 110 ; AI. v, 423 ; vii, 593 ; AI. (Lonsdale), 20, 56 ; AM. (*a*) index 618, 623 ; AM. (*b*), index I (i), 104, 315, (ii), 62 ; AO. xx, 124 ; xl, 471 ; AP. ii ; xxv ; AY. (*a*) index 15 ; BE. i, 109 ; BH. (*b*) ; BJ. ii, 75, 78, 81 ; iv, 537 ; EA. 24721 ; FI. i, 79, 81 ; IF. i–xxiii ; IG. i–xiii ; KF. (*d*), No. 1661–1672 ; KX. iii ; MA. ; MB. ; YH.

YB *Queen's Lands, 1625–1672*: The jointure lands of Queen Henrietta Maria were surveyed with precision by the Parl. surveyors of 28 counties, viz., Beds, Berks, Camb., Ches, Corn., Cumb., Ex., Glouc., Heref., Herts, Hunt., Kent, Lanc., Linc., Mx., Norf., Notts, Suff., Surr., Warw., Wilts, Worc., York, and Anglesey, Carnar., Denbigh, Merion., and Montgomery in Wales. For references to these lands during the three periods of ownership as (1) Queen Consort ; (2) Widow of the late King Charles I ; and (3) Queen Dowager in the reign of Charles II, see the following : F. i, 380 ; S. i, No. 3231 ; AF. (ref. " Ex. K.R. 20 : 5 ") ; AG. (ref. " L.R. 1, 6, 7, 9 ") ; AI. iii, 145, 226 ; iv, 36, 62 ; v, vii ; x (vi), 179 ; xi (i), 10 ; AI. (Finch) ii, 5 ; AI (Heathcote), 53, 256 ; AO. ix, 17 ; xx, 146 ; xxxviii, 136 ; xliii, 29, 166 ; AP. xxv, 417 ; xliii, 20 ; xlvi, 38 ; AP. obs. 842 (75–78) with schedules of 23 Parl. surveys in 15 counties ; BF. ii, 300 ; BJ. ii, 83 ; ES. 116 (17) ; EW. i, 286, 652 ; ii, 319 ; FT. iii, 170 ; FM. xii, app. 6 (442) ; FW. ii, 363 ; IF. i–xxiii ; IG. v, 421, 663 ; vi, 627 ; vii, viii, xiii, 677 ; xvii, 196 ; IH. i–xxi ; KF (*d*), No. 1661–1672 ; KX. iii ; MA. 1600 ; MB. 99, 511, 3038 ; TW. i, 828 ; iii, iv, v, 1625 ; vi, 998.

YC *Prince's Lands, 1630–1660*: The lands in the possession of Prince Charles, afterwards Charles II, are separately distinguished from those of the King and Queen in the Parl. surveys, where they are distributed among 17 counties, viz., Berks, Bucks, Ches, Corn., Dev., Dors, Herts, Leics, Lincs, Norf., Northants, Som., Surr., Sx., Warw., Wilts, and Denbigh in Wales. These estates fall into two classes—(1) lands held in right of his Principality, and (2) Lands belonging to the Duchy of Cornwall and Earldom of Chester. For references to the second class see YD., YE. For general references to the lands of Prince Charles see the following : F. i, 407 ; AI. vii, 76 ; iv, 52 ; v, vii, 76, 595 ; AM. (*a*) index, 161 ; AM. (*b*) index, I. (i), 484, 637 ; AP. xxv ; BJ. ii, 83 ; ES. 116 (17) ; FT. i, 286 ; iii, 170 ; IF. iii–xxiii ; IG. v, 636 ; vi, 12, 600 ; KF. (*d*), No. 1661–1672 ; KX. iii ; TW. iii, vii, 1301, 1544, 1611.

YD *Duchy Lands and Other Royal Estates, 1625–1660*: Besides the Crown lands of the King, Queen, and Prince, there were estates belonging to the duchies of Cornwall, Lancaster, and York, the earldom of Chester, the Elector Palatine, and Princess Mary of Nassau. The claims of Prince James and Princess Mary, children of Charles I, were not recognized between 1643–1660, but the parliamentary commissioners adjusted the revenue of the Prince Elector, and apportioned the ownership of the duchy lands to Charles I, Henrietta Maria, and Prince Charles, under whose titles they appear in the Parl. surveys.

    (*a*) Earldom of Chester : These lands are styled " Prince's lands " in the Parl. surveys. See the surveys of Ches. No. 13A, 17, and 20. (XA.)

    (*b*) Lands of Princess Mary, wife of Wm. of Nassau and mother of Wm. III : See the references in IF. xvii, 500 ; KX. i, 784.

(c) Revenues of Prince Chas. Lodowicke, Prince Elector, Count Palatine of the Rhine : By the ordinance of 8th Oct., 1645, his revenue was fixed at £8,000 p.a. (KX. iii.)

YE *Duchy of Cornwall, 1630–1685* : The lands of Prince Charles, as Duke of Cornwall, are incorporated in the Parl. surveys of 15 counties. (See YC., omitting Ches and Denbigh.) After 1660 they were the possessions of Prince James, Duke of York. For Parl. Particulars of Sale see YW. (b). For general references to the lands of the duchy in the three periods of (1) Charles I, (2) Commonwealth, and (3) Charles II, see the following :— F. i, 367 ; AB. ; AI. iii, 286 ; AM. (a), index, 318 ; AM. (b), index, I, (i), 144, 315 ; (ii), 83 ; AP. xxv, ; AY. ; AZ. ; BJ. ii, 76 ; EA. 30206–30209 ; EU. 322 (57) ; IF. iv-xxiii ; IG. i–xiii ; IH. i ; JJ. ; KH. ; KX. iii ; MA. ; MB. ; TW. i–vii ; TX. (a), i ; WI. ; XE.

YF *Duchy of Lancaster, 1625–1685* : The lands of Charles I, as Duke of Lancaster, are separately distinguished in the Parl. surveys, where under the title of " King's lands in right of the duchy " they are distributed over twenty-five counties, viz : Berk., Buck., Camb., Ches, Derby, Ex., Hants, Hunt., Kent, Lanc., Leic., Linc., Mx., Norf., Northants, Nott., Oxf., Staff., Suff., Sx., Warw., Wilt., York, and Glam. and Monm. in Wales. From 1660 these estates became the (restored) property of Charles II. In AP. obs. 825 there is an account of how certain lands came to the duchy at an earlier period. For Parl. Particulars of Sale see YW. (c). For general references to Duchy lands during the three periods of (1) Charles I, (2) Commonwealth and (3) Charles II, see the following :—F. i, 385 ; ii, 234 ; AM. (a) ; AM. (b), index I. (i), 181, 325 ; AO. xxx, i, 3, 5, 8, 10, 12, 41 ; xxv, 1 ; xxxvi, 161 ; xli, 7 ; AP. xiv, 70, 74, 81, 87, 89, 99, 101, 129, 142 ; xxv, 369 (and ref. " DL. 7 : 11," f. 17) ; AP. obs. 519 ; AP. obs. 826 ; BJ. ii, 76 ; EA. 30206–30208 ; EN. iv, 489 ; EU. 319 ; EW. i, 866 ; ii, 1, 101 ; IF. i–xxiii ; IG. i–xiii ; IH. i ; KH. ; KX. iii ; MA. ; MB. ; TW. i–vii ; TX. (a) i ; WM. ; XI.

YG *Duchy of York, 1625–1685* : The lands of Prince James, Duke of York (1643) and subsequently James II, were not recognized by the Parliamentary Commissioners as being in his possession, but were recorded as " King's lands " in the Parl. surveys. See the surveys of Yorks, No. 19 and 24 (XA.). For his share in the confiscated lands of the Regicides after 1660, see AI. v, 158 ; EA. 30206 (42) ; EK. 2551 (134, 143). For other references to Duchy lands before his accession see EA. 15896 (54) ; ES. (ref. " A. 245 : 11 ") ; IH. v, 185 ; vi, 209 ; vii, 367, 462 ; viii, 162, 322, 370 ; xv, 258, 424 ; TW. viii, 516, 2291, 2680 ; TX. (a), iv, No. clxxix (3).

YH *Miscellaneous References, 1625–1660* : Concealed lands, courts and court rolls, defective titles, derelict lands, discoveries, drowned lands, encroachments, eroded lands, fen drainage, fines, foreshores, freeholds and copyholds, grants, leases, mines and quarries, reclaimed lands, rentals and surveys, salt marshes, sewers, tenants, tenures and services, tidal lands : The Parl. surveys contain a mass of information relative to these and other subjects. The " Ditchfield Grants " made to Edw. Ditchfield and other trustees of the City of London in 1628, in repayment of a loan of £320,000 occupy three complete Patent Rolls, each consisting of three parts ; the conveyances of these Crown lands, enrolled upon the Close Rolls, extend over a long period of the King's reign. (F. i, 22, 31, 168 ; ER. xxiv.)

The increasing difficulty of administration of Crown lands under Charles I, especially after 1640, and the state of utter confusion during the Commonwealth period, are clearly exhibited in the records, the references to which are so numerous that only the sources and volumes can be indicated here, viz.: C.; F. i, ii; H.; S. i; AB.; AD. (ref. "Partic. of Grants ", 1 v.); AE. (ref. "misc. bks.", 143 : 10); AF. (ref. "E. 104, 105 ", and "misc. bks.", 19 : 4); AF. (ref. "L.T.R.", f. 1); AG. (ref. "L. R.", 1, 2, 10, 13); AG. (ref. "L. R. R. O.", 94); AI, i–xv; AI. (Exeter, Fortescue, Laing, and Montagu MSS.); AM.; AO. ii, iv, v, xx, xxiv, xxviii, xxx, xxxii, xxxv, xxxviii, xli, xliii, lxx; AP. ii, vi, x, xiv, xxv, xxvii, xxxv, xxxvii, xliii; BE. i; BF. i, ii; BG. (b); BH. (b), xlvi, lix, lxii; BJ. i, ii, iv, v (ref. "Dd. 13, 20 : 2 "; "Dd. 13, 21 : 2 "; "Ee. 3, 42 : 8, 9 "; "Ll. 2, 1 "); BR.; BZ.; CS. iii; DW. xiii; EA. 11764, 30206–30208, 33902, 37482; EA. (chart), 26377; EK. 2553; EM. 292 (6 f. 84), 418 (4 f. 10, 14); EN. iii; ER. lxix; ES.; ET. 3243, 3299 (158); EU. 326; EV.; EW. i, ii; FA.; FB. ii; FF. xiv; FG. ii; FI. i; FM. i, vi; FS. i; FT. i; FW. v; GF.; GN.; HG.; HR.; HV.; IF. i–xxiii; IG. i–xiii; IH.–i, ii; II. vii; IP.; IZ.; JK.; JV.; KD.; KN.; KX. iii; LZ. (e); MA.; MB.; ML.; OS.; OT.; TW. iv; TX. (a); TX. (b); VA.

YI   *Revenues of the Crown, 1625–1660* : The inadequacy of the revenue under Charles I, and the intensity of the financial strain during the Commonwealth, can be realized by means of the following references :—F. i, 355, 399; S. i; AF. (ref. "E. 163 : 19–21 "); AG. ("L.R."), 110, 113; AI. i, 31; ii, 90; iii (xii), 45, 81; iv, 35, 292, 304, 306; v, vii, 31, 594; viii (i), 98, (ii) 63, (iii) 12, xi, (i); AI. (Lonsdale); AM. (a) index 194, 196, 198, 208, 963; AM. (b) index I (i) 484; (ii) 77; AO. ii, 209; xxxviii, 136; xliii, 34, 36, 41; AP. ii, 19, 69; xxxvii, 66, 104; xliii, 30; BF. i, 786; BH (a) i, 200; BH. (b) xii, xiii, 877; lxxxii, 293; BJ. i, 512; ii, 75, 78, 83; iv, 19, 537; v, 77; BM. 778; BS. 272; BX. (ii), 493; CV. i, ser. xii, 337, 358, 390; CV. 2. ser. vii, 161, 192; EA. 5497, 5501, 11597, 21427 (265), 25271–2, 28854, 32471, 34324 (268), 36452 (175), 38854 (23); EM. 321; EN. i, 49; iii, 80, 82; EP. ii, 85; ES. (ref. "C. 358 : 28 ", "C. 389 : 18, 21 "); ET. 2251 (63); EU. 185 (186), 313, 322 (69), 325 (117); EW. i, 132, 286, 573, 578; ii, 235, 562; FG. i, iii; FH. iii, 96, 104; FT. i; IF. i–xxiii; HS. (b, d); IG. i–xiii; IH, x, 645, 650; KF. (d) No. 1661–1672; KX. iii; MA.; MB.; OS. 7; SH.; TW. vii, 1560; UE. iii, app. ii, 98.

III. SALES OF CROWN LANDS, 1625–1660

YJ   *Sales of Crown Lands by Charles I* : Accounts, bargains and sales, Commissions, compositions, contracts, declarations, deeds and papers, enrolments, land jobbers, memoranda, particulars, proposals, purchases, registry, reports, trustees :—C. 67; F. i, 359; ii, 7; AE. 135 ("misc. bks."); AG. (ref. "L.R. 2 : 56, 75 "); AI. v, 396; vii, 77; viii (ii), 66; xi (i), 83, 143; AO. ii, 23, 44; xliii, 41, 46, 98, 136; AP. xxv, 2; xliii, 18 (Minute book, 1626–7); AY (a). iii, 13, index 37; BF. i, 18, 231, 346, 412, 615, 635; ii, 296; EA. 30206 (38); EM. 418 (4), f. 9; EN. iii, 82 (No. 3796); ES. (ref. "D. 399 : 121 "); FG. i, 341; GE. 261; HR. 162, 195; HS. (d) index, 465; IF. i, ii, v (" Particular Man," 300); xvi, xvii, 338; xxiii, 731 (MS. vol. xlii, 52); ML. 6; OS. 10; OU. 129 (9 refs.); TE.

YK *Fee-farm Rents*: F. i, 376; AO. xliii, 41, 98, 136; AP. xiv, 108, 130; xxv, 114, 329; BJ. i, 512, 518; ii, 76; HG.; IF. i, 502; ii, 239; v, 32

YL *Forests, Chases, Parks, and Wood Sales*: F. i, 196, 377; ii, 226; S. i, 348; AE. 29; AG. (ref. " L.R. 2 : 26 "); AI. iii, iv, 38, 41; v. 22, 47, 106, 109, 111, 388; vii. 77, 593; xi (i) 31, 80, 160; xiv (ix) 487; AI. (Denbigh), 68; AI. (Lonsdale) 51; Am (*a*) index 339, 800, 1109, 1137; AM. (*b*) I (i), 161, 213, 253, 320, 399, 615, 640; AO. ii, 221; xx, 184; xxxviii, 130; xliii, 6, 8, 13, 25, 28, 41, 46, 50, 88, 111, 117, 133, 160; AP. xxv, 8, 93, 135, 239, 294, 376, 417; xxxv, 108; xxxvii, 120; xliii, 22; BF. i, 205, 737; ii, 83, 296; BH. (*b*); BJ. iii, 407; BM. 231; DN. n.s. xvi, 108; EA. 20078 (45, 54), 34712 (207), 34729 (3, 89); EK. 2648 (72); EM. 321 (5); ES. (ref. " A. 297 " : 65); EU. 821; EW. i, 109, 652; FA. 403; FF. xii, 384; FT. i, 517; FU. iv, 534; FW. iv, 174; HP.; IF. ii, 113, 202; iii, 422; V. 154; xvii, 285; xviii–xxiii; JV.; MA.; MB.; TG. app. iii, 5; TX. (*a*) i, 3.

YM *Sales of Crown Lands by Parliament, 1649–1660*: Attorneys, auditors, bargains and sales, claims, competition, debentures, deeds and papers, doubling, frauds, mines and quarries, officers, petitions, policy, proclamations, public faith bills, registrar, rentals, research (AO.; AP. obs. 672–684, fees) salaries, speculation, State lands, tenures, treasurer, treatment of royal estates, trustees, warrants, Worcester House. In addition to notes of sales inscribed upon the covers of Parl. surveys of several counties, the following references contain much information upon the subject of Commonwealth land Sales :—C. 70; F. i, 359, 368; ii, 10, 12; S. i, No. 2890, 2975, 2999, 3000; AE. (" misc. bks.", 481: 38, 88); AF. (" K.R. misc.", 20 : 1); AI. iii, 192; v, 180; vii, 14, 76, 595; AI. (Exeter), 326; AI. (Finch), i, 73; AI. (Popham), 208, 239; AM. (*a*); AM. (*b*) index I (i), 670; (ii), 376; AO. iv, 9; v, 249; xxx, 16, 22, 41; AP. xxxvii, 125; AY (*a*) index 15, 37, 46; BF. i, 4, 12, 22, 173, 231, 254, 263, 295, 298, 306, 366, 373, 499, 554, 588, 603, 645, 755, 758, 773, 780, 824, 843, 853, 935; ii, 298; CV. 1 ser. i, 277, 339, 389, 421, 458; ii, 127, 141; DB. iv, 42; EA. 21417–21427, 22060–1; EA. (chart), 12628–12630, 27327–8; EN. iii, 440; EQ.; ER. 78; EU. 184 (54) f. 232; EV. 58 (88); EW. i, 286, 652, 787; ii, 78, 95; FL. 46; FT. i, 517, 683; iii, 170; FW. iv, 2; GJ.; IG. i–xiii; IH. xviii, 494; KX. iii, 62; MA. 43, 532, 534, 538; MB.; OS.; TW. i, 6, 125, 398, 727; vii, 1544, 1584; TY. iv, 457.

(*a*) *Acts and Ordinances.* Resolutions of 21st February and 10th March, 1653, 10th August, 1654, 18th April, 29th July, and 17th September, 1656 (referred to in YQ. (*a*) 1, " Decl. Acc., Crown Lands, 1662) are missing in AM. (*a*). Other Acts are given below under " Forests " (YP.). For references see AI. vii, 76; AM. (*a*) vi, 261, 325, 367; vii, 239, index 618; IG. vi, x; KX. iii; RU. (*g*); RU. (*l*) ii, 51, 97.

(1) 1649, 16th July. Act for the sale of honours, manors, etc., of the late king, queen and prince: EN. (ref. " Roll DD. 5 "); KX. ii, 168.

(2) 1649, 23rd November. Act with further instructions to treasurers, etc., and the stating of accounts : KX. ii, 282.

(3) 1649, 18th February. Act for removing of obstructions in the sale of Crown lands : KX. ii, 338.

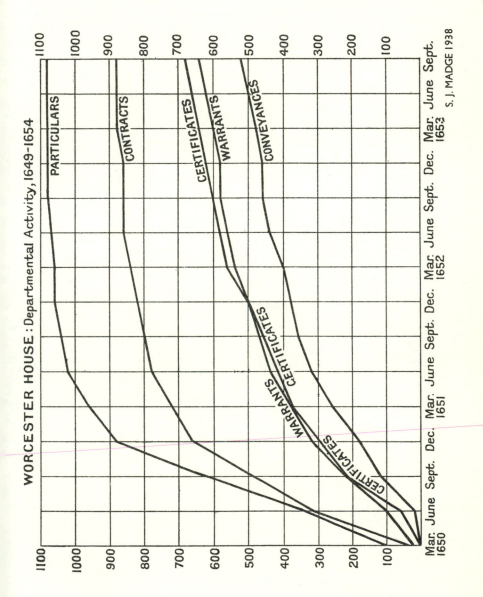

WORCESTER HOUSE: Departmental Activity, 1649–1654

PARTICULARS

CONTRACTS

CERTIFICATES

WARRANTS

CONVEYANCES

CERTIFICATES

WARRANTS

CERTIFICATES

Mar. June Sept. Dec. Mar. June Sept. Dec. Mar. June Sept. Dec. Mar. June Sept.
1650   1651   1652   1652

S. J. MADGE 1938

[face p. 320

(4) 1652. 12th October. Act for further improving the commissioners for removing obstructions to determine claims : Proclamation, S. i, 359; EW. i, 886.

(5) 1652, 31st December. Act for exposing to sale castles, houses, parks, lands, etc., exempted from sale : AI. vii, 76 ; KX. ii, 691.

(6) 1653, 16th July to 4th November. Act concerning the determination of claims now depending before the Commissioners : Proclamations, S. i, 362 ; EW. ii, 42.

YN Parl. *Sales of Crown Mansions, Castles, and Goods* : F. ii, 13 (ref. " Commonw. Exch. Papers ", bun. 282–5) ; AG. (ref. " L.R. 2 " : 124) ; AI, iii, 291 ; vii, 76 ; EA. (chart), 13341 ; EN. 4898 ; IG. i–xiii ; IH. i, 458 ; also Hume, Hist. of Eng., ch. lxii, and Law, Hist. of Hampton Court, ii, 165.

(a) *Acts and Ordinances.* 1649, 4th July ; 1651, 17th July ; 1652, 31st December. See KX. ii, 160, 546, 691.

YO Parl. *Sales of Fee-farm Rents* : Arrears, bailiwicks, charges, commissioners, deeds and papers, Duchy rents, fees, hundreds, petitions, proclamations, registrar, treasurers, trustees, warrants : Numerous bailiwicks and hundreds are among the Parl. surveys, while notes relating to " Sales on the fee-farm side " are often found written in the margins or upon the covers of manorial surveys in the same series. For other references see C. 70 ; F. i, 143, 148, 376 ; ii, 10, 12, 225 ; S. i ; AE. 3 (ref. " misc. bks.", 135–143, 481) ; AF. (ref. " Ex. K.R.", 1 ser. 53 : 2) ; AG. (ref. " L.R., 1 : 308 ", " L.R. 2 : 83, 102–3," " LR. 13 ") ; AO. iv, 9 (10 boxes quoted) ; xxxviii, 130 ; xli, 9 ; AP. xxxvii ; 37 ; xliii, 33, 42 (ref. " G. 18 ") ; AY. (a) index 46 ; BF. i, 27, 67, 261, 535, 827, 853 ; ii, 298 ; BJ. ii, 77, 81, 83 ; iv, 542 (ref. " Ee. 3, 11 ; Ee. 3, 42 : 5 ; Oo. 7, 29 ") ; DV. xv. 298 ; EA. (chart) 15168, 27328 ; EU. 184 ; IF. xvi, 101, 605 ; IG. i–xiii ; KX. ii, 358, 417, 588 ; iii, MA. ; MB.

(a) *Acts and Ordinances.* AM. (a) vi, 380, 454, 531 ; vii, 138, 175, 316, 562, 577 and index 169 ; AO. xx, 81 (No. 10) ; KX. iii, 58 ; RU. (l) ii, 106, 126, 151, 188, 207, 238, 389. The Act referred to in AO. xxiv, app. 35 cannot be found at the P.R.O.

(1) 1649, 11th March. Act for selling the fee-farm rents belonging to the Commonwealth of England and heretofore payable to the Crown of England, Duchy of Lancaster, and Duchy of Cornwall : KX. ii, 358. There is a draft of this Act, dated 16th February, 1649, in AE. (" Misc. bks., 136 : 2," after f. 35).

(2) 1650, 13th August. Act for the further explanation of the preceding Act : IG. ii, 250, KX. ii, 412.

(3) 1650, 6th February. Additional Act for sale of fee-farm rents and for doubling of monies : KX. ii, 498.

(4) 1652, 3rd June. Additional Act for sale of fee-farm rents : KX. ii, 583.

(5) 1652, 9th September. Additional Act for sale of fee-farm rents : KX. ii, 614.

(6) 1653, 8th September (confirmed 26th June, 1657). Explanatory additional Act for sale of the remaining fee-farm rents and the finishing of that whole affair : EW. ii, 35 ; KX. ii, 720, 1137.

YP Parl. *Sales of Forests and Woodlands* : Abuses, agents, assarts, carriage, chases, claims, commissions, committees, control, deeds and papers, embezzlements, felling, improved lands, lists, merchants, naval timber, preservation, purveyors, registrar, spoil, surveys and surveyors, timber, treasures, trustees, utilization, warrants, warrens, waste lands. For a tract by S. Taylor, 1652, see EW. i, 87; UE. iii, app. ii, 98. Other references are as follows :—F. i, 94, 97, 216, 328, 332; ii, 115; S. i, No. 3016; AE. 29 (ref. " E. 325 "); AI. iv, 339; AK.; AO. iv, 194; v. 249, 258; xliii, 137; AP. xxxvii, 31; BF. i, 205, 729, 737; BJ. ii, 84 (ref. " Ee. 3, 42 : 10 "); EN. iii, 440; EU. 185 (77); IF. xvii, 296; IG. i-xiii (MS. vol. xl, No. 31-9); KX. ii, 1422; iii, 28, 60, 104, 140; MA.; MB.; OS.

(a) Acts and Ordinances. AM. (1) vii, 240, 354, 503, 552, 563 and index, 1137; IG. vi, vii, ix; RU (l) ii, 322, 324, 348, 396, 514. A resolution of 18th April, 1656, missing in AM. (a) vii, 421, is referred to in " Decl. Acc., Forests, 1662 ". (YQ. (a), 3.)

(1) 1653, 22nd November. Act for the de-afforestation, sale and improvement of the forests and of the honours, manors, tenements, etc., within the usual limits and perambulations, belonging to the late king, queen and prince : EW. ii, 46; KX. ii, 783.

(2) 1654, 21st August. Ordinance for appointing Commissioners to survey the forests, honours, manors, lands, etc. (amending the preceding Act): EW. ii, 78; KX. ii, 946.

(3) 1654, 30th August. Ordinance for sale of the four forests or chases (viz. Ashdown, Enfield, Kingswood and Needwood) for collateral security to soldiers : EW. ii, 78; KX. ii, 993. Also Sherwood Forest.

(4) 1657, 9th June. Act for the mitigation of the rigour of the forest laws, and for the preservation of wood and timber in the Forest of Dean : KX. ii, 1114.

(5) 1657, 19th June (partially confirmed 26th June, 1657). Instructions agreed upon in Parliament for Commissioners for surveying the four forests : BM. 231; EW. ii, 187; KX. ii, 1116.

YQ Special Procedure of the Parliamentary Land Sales, 1649–1660 : (a) Accounts. These appear to be imperfect. See the references F. i, 81, 124, 128, 148, 161; ii, 226; AE. 29 (ref. " Misc. bks.", 140 and 175 : 2 f. 25); AF. (ref. " Ex. L.T.R. misc. bks.", 121); AO. xx, 81; xxiv, 35; AP. ii, 20 (also Roll 569); AP. obs. 842 (75 : No. 7, 23–24); BJ. i, 513; FT. i, 626; IG. ii, 92; iv, 523, 532; KX. ii, 282, iii. Also the following special rolls :—

(1) Decl. Acc. (ordered 23rd March, 1660, decl. 20th December, 1662),
     " Exch. L.T.R., Pipe Off. Crown Lands " : AP. ii, 20, roll 603.
(2) Ibid, Fee-farm rents : AP. ii, 20, roll 602.
(3) Ibid, Forests : AP. ii, 20, roll 604.

(b) Army Transactions. See the Certificates, Contracts, Conveyances and Particulars below (YR.-YT, YW.), the " Commonw. Exch. Papers " (bun. 1–119, 126–147), Restoration Enquiry, abstracts of claims of " Coldstreamers " and other troops, and the following references : S. i, No. 3155; AE. ("misc. bks.", 5, 6); AI. v, 180; AP. xxv, 419 (ref. " L.R. misc. bks.", 266 : 26–100); AP. obs. 842 (76 : No. 33–35); EN. index 427; FL. 46; IG. vii-x; IH. i, 171, 247, 271, 608; KX. iii, 11; KY. 72, 270; iv, 269; MB. 310, 711; TW. iv, 778, 803; vii, 1546, 1573, 1618, 1621, 1732.

YR Certificates of Sales (Crown Lands): These documents are arranged at the P.R.O. in the order of counties of England and Wales, in five bundles, of which the fifth contains also " Divers Counties ". (AF., ref. " E. 121 : 1–5 ".) Other references to certificates will be bound in F. i, 89 ; AF. (" Ex. K.R."), ii, 159 ; AO. xx, 33 ; BJ. i, 351 ; ii, 78 (ref. " Ee. 3, 18 : 1 ") ; MB. 681 ; TW. ii.

(*a*) *Fee-farm Rents, 1649–1653.* These certificates are entered in seven vols. among the Aug. Off., L.T.R., and S.P. Office records (AE., ref. " misc. bks.", 135–7, 143 ; AF. ref. " Ex. L.T.R. misc. bks.", 121 ; AV. ref. " Council of State : K. 5, 6 "). For other references to these certificates see F. i, 128, 143, 148 ; ii, 10 ; AE. 3 (ref. " E. 308 " : portf. 6–7, files 46–7) ; AO. iv, 9 ; xx, 81 ; xxiv, 35 ; AP. xliii, 42 ; FT. i, 546.

YS *Contracts for Purchase (Crown Lands)* : Agreements with contractors are contained in the " Journals " (below), and special classes of contracts are referred to under " Purchasers " (YY.) See references in F. i, 149 ; AO. xx, 80 ; BG. (*a*) notice (ref. " 669, f. 15 : 17 ") ; EA. 21427 (15, 90) ; EW. i, 787 ; IG. iv, 300 ; ix, 505, x.

(*a*) " *Contractors' Journals* " : 2 v., 1649–1652. (AE. ref. " Misc. bks.", 173–4.)

(*b*) *Fee-farm Rents, 1650–9.* These agreements with Contractors are recorded in seven vols. among the Aug. Off. and S.P. Office records (AE. ref. " misc. bks.", 141, 142, 144 ; AV. ref. " Council of State : K. 1–4 "). The reversed end of AE. " misc. bks. 144 " is called " The Chairman's Book of Contracts ". For other references see F. i, 148 ; ii, 10 ; AE. 3 (ref. " E. 308," portf. 7) ; AO. xx, 81 ; xxiv, 35 ; AP. xliii, 42 ; EA. 21427 (112) ; IG. ii, iii, ix ; MB. 1141.

YT *Conveyances, or Counterparts of Deeds of Sale (Crown Lands) 1650–5* : The Counterparts of these deeds are arranged at the P.R.O. in the order of Counties, in eight boxes, each document being lettered and numbered within the series " A.–Y, XX., and ZZ ". (AE. ref. " E. 304 " with list of individual letters and numbers.)

(*a*) *Calendars,* 1764–1801, are in the Brit. Mus. and P.R.O. (F. i, 141 ; AE. 37 ; EA. 21327 and the imperfect copy EA. 24717).

(*b*) *S.P. Office* documents include some conveyances, 1650–1654, in three boxes. (AP. xliii, 42, boxes " C.D.E.").

(*c*) " *Trustees' Book,*" *1649–1655.* This valuable record is at Cambridge. (BJ. i, 512, ref. " Dd. 13, 20 ".)

(*d*) *Conveyances (Fee-farm Rents).* F. i, 143 ; ii, 10 ; AE. 40 ; AO. iv, 9 ; xx, 81 ; xxiv, 35 ; xli, 9 ; AP. xliii, 42 ; BF. i, 27, 67, 261, 535, 827, 853 ; ii, 298 ; EA. (chart), 15168 (purchased by the Brit. Mus. of J. W. Thorn, 15th July, 1859). The Aug. Off., Pipe Off., and S.P. Office series are as follows :—

(*e*) *Aug. Off. Counterparts.* These documents are arranged at the P.R.O. in twenty-three boxes, the bundles bearing letters and numbers in the scheme " A. 1–Z. 1 ". Some of the counterparts are missing, viz. " F. 1 (14)," " M. 2 (3)," " P. 1 (2)," and " T. 2 (14)." The Calendar is in 2 vols. (AE. ref. " E. 307.")

(*f*) *Pipe Off. Crown Leases.* This series contains some counterparts intermixed. (See list in BU. (*b*).)

(*g*) *S.P. Domestic.* These records include counterparts which are kept in five boxes. (AV. ref. " Council of State : K. 9, 10, and boxes 1–3 ".)

YU *Discoveries and Enrolments* : (*a*) The "Registrar's Book of Discoveries" is now missing, but many of its entries may be noted in the references given in the "Certificates", in the margins or at the foot, as well as in the Parl. surveys, where the names of upwards of 140 "discoverers" and their claims are recorded. See Appendix III, sect. ii–iii.

(*b*) *Enrolment of Sales.* See the reference in F. i, 22, 24 ; AO. ii, 44 ; AP. xxvii ; ER. lxxviii, and index locorum lxxix; EQ. ; also "Chancery List ", 74 (ref. " C. 54 ") for the numbers of Close Rolls, 1649–1660, upon which the various sales are enrolled. Thus the sales of the Crown lands and rents in Middlesex will be found in " C. 54, No. 3533–4033 ". Palmer's index (ER. 78) contains " Forfeited lands " as well.

YV *Obstructions and Orders* : (*a*) References to the Committee for Removing Obstructions to Sales will frequently be found in the Parl. surveys, where special sheets signed by Col. Webb, the Surveyor-General, are sometimes found attached, recording decisions and orders of the committee, 48 of whose members are named in the Surveys. See also F. i, 158 ; AE. (ref. "misc. bks.", 314 : 24, 26, 28, 114, 118, 123, 164); AF. xx, 424 ; AI. v, 403 ; AI. (Finch), i, 73 ; EW. ii, 42 ; HR. 195; IG. ii, 27, 195 ; iv, 300, 522 ; v–xii ; KX. iii ; MA. ; MB. ; ML.

(*b*) *Orders.* Numerous inquiries, orders and reports of the various Committees for Crown lands, Fee-farm Rents, Obstructions and Revenues, are referred to in F. i, 153 ; S. i, No. 3000; AE. (ref. " Misc. bks.", 143 : 101); AF. (ref. " Ex. K.R.", 1 ser. 53 : 2); AG. 221 (ref. "L.R. 1 : 308 ", " L.R. 2 : 83," and " Misc. bks.", 336); AI. iv, 339 ; vii, 166, 168 ; AM. (*a*), vii, 689 ; AM. (*b*) index I (ii), 181 ; AO. xx, 88, 145 ; AP. xliii, 42 ; DV. xv, 298 ; EW. ii, 21, 311 ; FT. i, 683 ; iii, 170; IG. ; v, 282, 298 ; vii, 105 ; viii, 65, 146 ; x, 97, 133 ; KY. iv, 269 ; MB. 449, 2952, 3509. See also the following important volumes among the Aug. Off. and S. P. Office records :—

(*c*) "*Day Book of Orders*," 1653–9 : AV. (ref. " Council of State : K. 7, 8.")

(*d*) "*Minute Book of Proceedings* " (Crown Lands), 1649–1659. Contains requests for Particulars, and Orders to the Registrar to supply them : AE. (ref. " misc. bks.", 314).

(*e*) "*Minute Book of Proceedings (Fee-farm Rents)* " : AE. (ref. " misc. bks.", 139).

YW *Particulars for Sales* (*Crown Lands*) : These documents are arranged at the P.R.O. in 22 bundles, the method of using letters and numbers being similar to that of the Conveyances. (AE. ref. " E. 320.")

(*a*) *Calendars*, 1764–1801, include the Conveyances (YT.), but " N. 16 " under Northants ought to be placed with " P. 5 " under Somerset, and it may be noted that " S. 8 " under Cambridge has been printed. (AE. 37 ; EA. 21327 and EA. 24717, which the Brit. Mus. purchased of C. Devon, 12th April, 1862.)

(*b*) *Duchy of Cornwall Office.* The collection is said to contain two vols. of Particulars, but they have not been inspected. (XE.)

(*c*) *Duchy of Lancaster Series.* The Parl. surveys include several Particulars relating to the counties of Derby, Lanc., Leic., Linc., Northants, Staff, and York. (XI. ref. "D.L. 32 " : No. 10, 25, 33, 53.)

(*d*) *Land Revenue Office.* The series of Parl. surveys likewise contains some Particulars relating to Berk., Corn., Linc., Northants, Staff., and York. (XJ. ref. "L.R. 2 " : 277, 291, 292, 295, 298.)

(e) *Surveyor-General's Office.* There were in this office between 1713 and 1793 " Particulars grounded on Parl. surveys, 1649–1653, and rated in order to the sale of the several Crown lands," consisting of four large parchment vols. with 2178 folios or pages, and four paper paper vols. of indexes (the references being " A. 1, 2 ; B. 1, 2 ; C. 1, 2 ; D. 1, 2 "). These volumes cannot now, after a long search at the P.R.O. and elsewhere, be found, but transcripts or extracts are among the Burrell MSS. for Sussex at the Brit. Mus. (AP. obs. 837–842 ; EA. 5005, 30206 (37), 30207 (5), 30208 ; FO. v, 259 ; XP. ; XV.)

(f) *Surveys.* A number of fragmentary or mutilated copies of Particulars form the parchment covers of several Parl. surveys in the Aug. Off. and Duchy of Cornwall series for the counties of Cumb., Hants, Linc., Mx., Northants, Oxf., Som., Surr., Sx., Warw., Wilts., and York. (XA., XE. (a), bun. 1, 4, 5, 7–9.) For other references to Particulars for Crown lands see F. i, 141, 161 ; AO. ii, 23 ; iv, 9 ; xx, 90 ; xxx, xli, 29 ; AP. obs. 842 (76 : No. 44, 75) ; YV. (d).

(g) *Particulars for Sales (Fee-farm Rents).* F. i, 143 ; ii, 13 ; AE. 1–3 (and " Misc. bks.", 135–7, with two boxes containing twenty-four rolls) ; AO. iv, 9 ; xx, 81 ; xxiv, 35 ; xxx, 41 ; xli, 9 ; BJ. iv, 542 (ref. " Oo. 7, 29 "). There are particulars among the Aug. Off., Land Rev. Off. and S.P. Office records, and some are included also among the Crown leases of the Pipe Office. (AG. ref. " LR. 2, misc. bks.", 102, 103, List for Pipe Off. in BU. (b) ; and S.P. Dom. ref. " Commonw. Exch. Papers," bun. 288.)

(h) *Aug. Off. Series.* These Particulars of Fee-farm Rents are arranged in order of counties, in seven portfolios or forty-seven files, of which pf. 6 (41–5) relate to the Duchy of Lancaster. The calendar, 1769, is in three vols. (AE. ref. " E. 308.")

YX *Petitions and Reprises :* (a) *Petitions.* F. ii, 12 ; AI. (Finch), i, 73 ; IG. ii, 195 ; vi, 326 ; vii, ix, 105 ; MB. 164, 3509. For papers of the Com. of Petitions, 1649–1652, see " Commonw. Exch. Papers ", 265–9. There is also a loose document of four pages, concerning almshouses at Westminster, 1656, in " S.P. Dom. Interreg. : K. 8 " (between pp. 140–141).

(b) *Reprises.* Numerous instances of these valuations are recorded in the Parl. surveys for almost every county. There is a volume of Reprises among the Aug. Off. records, covering the years 1650–1. (AE. ref. " misc. bks.", 144 : a vol. of 70 ff. in two sections.)

YY *Purchasers of Crown Lands and Rents, 1649–1660 :* F. i, 149, 200 ; S. i, No. 2999, 3131 ; AE. (ref. " E. 320 : A. 2 ") ; AI. v, 259 ; vii, 14 ; AM. (b) index I (ii), 181 ; AO. xxiv, 41 ; AP. obs. 842 (75 : No. 13) ; AY. (a) index 15 ; BJ. i, 351 ; CV. I, ser. i, ii ; EA. 21327 ; EN. 427 ; EQ. ; EU. 821 (18) ; EV. 58 (88) ; IG ; ii, 503 ; v, 282, 298 ; vii, viii, 96 ; xi, 280 ; KY. iii, 72 ; MA. ; MB. 310, 1619, 2643 ; PK. ; TX. (a) i, No. 1 ; UE. iii, app. 98, 107. State purchases for Cromwell's establishments are included in the above. Indexes of the following are in EQ. :—

(a) *Assigned Bills.* There is an important list of these contracts at Cambridge (BJ. i, 351, ref. " Dd. 8, 30 "). For forms and other references see EA. 21427 (62) ; EQ. ; KX. iii.

(b) *Immediate Tenants.* Also at Cambridge (BJ. i, 351, ref. " Dd.

8, 30 : 5 "). The immediate tenants are carefully recorded in the Parl. surveys. For an important list of receipts from tenants' rents and other revenues, preserved at Cambridge (BJ. i, ref. " Dd. 13, 20 : 2 "), and other references to tenants, see S. i, 350; EQ.; EW. i, 787.

(*c*) *Original Creditors.* Also at Cambridge (BJ. i, 351, ref. "Dd. 8, 30 : 4 "). See also DB. iv, 42; EA. 21427 (90); EQ.; IG. i–xiii.

(*d*) *Various.* For the Army purchases see EQ.; YQ. (*b*) and for other lists of names see EA. 21327 and 30208. There are fifty names of purchasers, some being army officers, recorded in marginal notes or on the covers of Parl. surveys. Inside the covers of " S.P. Dom., Interreg. : K. 8 " will also be found a loose document (No. 175) giving forty pages of names, with parishes or other references, from Sec. T. 22 of a volume not yet traced. Venetian purchases are referred to in Cal. S.P. (Venice) xxviii, 92, 95, 115, 175, 278, 318.

YZ *State Commission of Enquiry into Commonwealth Sales, 1660–3* : Abuses, accounts (YQ.), Acts, Annexation, Army transactions (YQ.), arrears, audit, casual revenues, certificates (YR.), commissioners, committees, compositions, concealments, confirmations, confiscations, considerations, constats, contracts (YS.), conveyances (YT.), discoveries (YU.), enrolments (YU.), fixed charges, grants, houses (YN.), informers, jointure lands (YB.) and revenue, leases, lists, obstructions (YV.), orders (YV.), Particulars (YW.), perpetuities, purchasers (YY.), receipts, records, registrars, regulations, reservations, restoration, returns, royalties, treasurers, trustees, waste :— F. i, 111, 168; S. i, No. 3131, 3155, 3173, 3195, 3203, 3248; AG. (ref. " L.R. 2 : 56 "); AI. v, 204, 206; AM. (*a*), index, sec. vi, 25; AM. (*b*) xi, 170, index I (ii), 181; AO. ii, 23, 44; xx, 49; xxx, 214, 245; xxxviii, 132, 134, 136; AP. ii, 20; xxv, 419; xxxvii, 104; AP. obs. 842 (44, 75); AY. (*a*) iii, 14; xii, 8; BX. ii, 266; EA. 30206 (40); EW. ii, 319, 332, 342; FT. i, 697; IH. i–xiv; IJ. i, 418; KY, iv, 269; TG. app. 28; TW. i–vii, viii, 2016; TX. (*a*) 1–15; TX. (*b*) ii, 526; also Pepys Diary (Wheatley, 1903), 11, 123, and the following :—

(*a*) *Catalogue* of sums of money and lands divided among members of the late Long Parl., 1660 : UE. iii, app. ii, 107.

(*b*) *Considerations* as to purchasers of public lands, 1660 : EK. 2542 (518); EW. ii, 322; IH. i, 81; UE. ii, app. ii, 98.

(*c*) *Fee-farm Rents.* AP. ii, 20; xxv, 419; AP. obs. 842 (75, No. 13); EA. 30206 (40); FW. ii, 363; TW. iv, 447, 609, 778, 803; vii, 1544, 1761.

IV. ALIENATIONS, RESUMPTIONS, AND SALES BEFORE 1625

(i) *Early Period, 1000–1485*

ZA *Alienations of Crown Lands at Various Periods* : Accounts, acts, Alienation Office, assignments, certificates, commissions, compositions, considerations, conveyances, farms, fines, frauds, grants, inquiries, instructions, licences, loans, mortmain, observations, pardons, petitions, proclamations, receivers, recoveries, restraints, revenues, tallies, warrants :— *Terræ datæ* of the period 1066–1485 will be found in AY. (*a*) ii, 4; v, 24; xii, 6, 49; HR. 89, 160; ML. 2; QD. i, 468; RU. (*d*) i–v; SH. 1, ii. For other references, chiefly relating to the Tudor and Stuart periods see F. i, ii; S. i, No. 1066, 1074, 2915; AF. 129 (ref. " E.O.R.", 6 : 80); AF. (ref.

" Ex. K.R.", i, 1) ; AI. i, 33 ; iii, 25 ; iv, 353, 464 ; v, 416 ; vii, 39 ;
viii, 11 ; AI (Coventry), i, 34 ; AM. (*a*) index 56 ; AM. (*b*) index I (i),
11 ; AO. ii, 24 ; xx, 112 ; xxx, 32 ; xl, 468 ; xli, 5, 33 ; xliii, 179 ; AP. ii,
2 ; xvii, xxv, 88, 92 ; xxxv, 1 ; xlvi, 38 ; AY. (*a*) index 10 ; BC. 649 ; BF. i,
338, 600, 724, ii ; BH. (*b*), xiii, 697 ; EA. 12498, 30206 (40), 32091 (147) ;
EN. iii, 206 ; EP. ii ; ES. (ref. " B. 102 : 36," " D. 1012 ") ; EU. 322 (2),
323 (3), 822 (117) ; EV. No. 79 (36) ; FA. 416 ; FG. i, 291, 295 ; FH. iii,
101 ; xii, 331 ; FM. i, 70 ; ii, 222 ; xiii, 34, 377, 395 ; xiv, 40 ; FN. 276 ;
FZ. ii, 267, 273 ; GA. (*a*), xi, 93 ; IC. i, 506, 535, 702 ; ID. iii, 169, 414 ;
iv, 4 ; v, 224, 518 ; vi, 244 ; IE. viii–xii ; IF. i, 513 ; v, 590 ; xiii, 624 ;
xv, xvii, 447, 478 ; xxii, 408 ; IG. ix, 252 ; IH. i–x ; II. i–vi ; KX. i, 833,
iii ; MA. 170 ; MB. 1302 ; RU. (*d*) ; RU. (*e*), i, 234 ; TG. 103 ; TW.
i–viii ; TX. (*a*), 1–vi ; TX. (*b*) i–v ; UE. iii, app. 120.

ZB   *Resumptions of Crown Lands at Various Periods* :   For the proposed
resumption of Royal Estates by Charles I, and the partial resumption at
the Restoration see Hume, Hist. of Eng., ch. liii, lxii, and the references
below (ZM.). Resumptions of Crown lands in earlier reigns, particularly
in the Plantagenet period, are referred to as follows :—F. i, 259 ; AI. iii,
183 ; AI. (Devonshire), 901 ; AI. (Lonsdale), 56 ; AO. xl, 476 ; AP.
xxxv, 206 ; AY. (*a*), index 45 ; CV. 5, ser. iv, 187, 395 ; EG. 7 ; FW. ii,
190 ; GA. (*b*), vi, p. xxv, lxxv ; HH. (*f*), 98 ; HR. ; IF. xiv, 30 ; xxii,
408 ; ML. ; RM. (No. lx), ii, 215 ; RU. (*d*) index 761 ; RU. (*e*) index 125.

ZC   *Sales of Crown Lands before the Tudor Period* :   Sales of Royal
property between 1000 and 1300, and wood sales from 1150 to 1500 are
recorded in AI. v, 437 ; AO. xx, 126 ; xl, 472 ; AP. xxxv, 108, 351 ; BF. i ;
EG. viii, 37 ; FC. 44 ; RU. (*e*). See also the following :—

(*a*) Stat. of 1 Edw. III st. 2, c. 13 for land purchase : RU. (*e*).

(*b*) Cautions in buying estates, Hen. VI : CV. 4 ser. v, 61 ; vi, 103 ;
      EC. 107 (No. 61 : 10) ; EP. ii, 130 (Nos. 470, 762, art. 2).

(*c*) Precedents for Wood Sales : EP. ii (No. 171 : 175).

(ii) *Tudor Period*, 1485–1603

ZD   *Sales of Crown Lands in the Tudor Period : Henry VIII* :   Accounts,
acts, bargains and sales, breviate of dealings, commissions, deeds and
papers, enrolments, lists, particulars, purchasers, receipts, rentals and
surveys :—C. 66, 70 ; F. i, 359 ; ii, 221, 250 ; AI. (Exeter), 20 ; AO. ii,
23 ; xx, 14, 82, 90 ; xli, 14, 29 ; AP. xxv ; BF. i, 51, 492, 579, 652, 657 ;
ii, 284 ; EA. 32311 (81) ; EN. ii, 301 ; EP. i (ref. " 16 : 55 ") ; ES. (ref.
" C. 254 " : 32) ; HR. 194 ; IA. v–xxi ; JM. 285 ; OU. 19, 32 (numerous
refs.) ; RU. (*e*) index 27 ; TK. ; and Savine's appendix in Fisher's Polit.
Hist., v. app. ii, 497.

(*a*) *Wood Sales*. AE. 29 (ref. " E. 325 ") ; AI. xii (ix), 440 ; AO. xx,
92, 127 ; xl, 472 ; AP. ii, 20 ; xxxv, 118, 120 ; BF. ii, 285 ; EA. 21310 (58) ;
FC. 172 ; IA. xx, (ii), app. 7 ; TK. 52, 144, 201.

ZE   *Edward VI* :   Accounts, bargains and sales, deeds and papers,
enrolments, particulars, registers, rentals and surveys :—C. 66 ; F. i, 359 ;
AI. (Exeter) 6 ; AG. (ref. " L.R. 2 " : 65) ; AO. ii, 23 ; xx, 79, 90 ; xxx,
260 ; xli, 14 ; AP. xiv, 31, xxv ; EP. ii, 292, No. 1216 ; GA. (*a*) ii, 289 ;
vii, 373 ; HR. 194 ; IC. i, 5, 51, 53 ; ML. 5 ; OU. 126 (8 refs.) ; TG. 73 ;
and Cal. Pat. Rolls, Edw. VI, i, p. iii, and index.

(a) *Wood Sales.* AE. 29; AO. xx, 92, 127; xl, 472; AP. xxxv, 122; IC. i, 34, 40.

ZF *Mary*: Commissions, memoranda, purchasers, rentals and surveys, security: AP. xxv; IC. i, 55, 74, 100, 102, 108; OU. 127 (13 refs., 4 relating to Sales).

(a) *Wood Sales.* AO. xx, 127; AP. xxxv, 117, 122; FU. i, 63; GA. (a), iv, 6, 29; v, 104; IC. i, 64, 70, 80, 113.

ZG *Elizabeth*: Accounts, acts, assignments, bargains and sales, commissions, deeds and papers, frauds, instructions, leases, limitations, memoranda, particulars, petitions, purchasers, rentals and surveys, values :— C. 66; F. i, 359; AF. (ref. "Ex. K.R. misc. 23": 17–18); AG. (ref. "L.R. 2": 66–74); AI. iii, 10, 198; vi, 251; vii, 195; xi (vii), 133; AM. (b) index I (i), 471 (Act of 23 Eliz.); AO. ii, 23; AP. ii, 20, 144 (bun. 593: roll 600); xxv. 320 (bun. 522–3); BF. i, 110, 763; EG. 499; EP. i, 83 (67), 114 (45); ii, 151 (146, 149), 169 (51); FB. i, 162; iii, 310, 377; vi, 251, ix–xiii; FF. i, 162; iii, 311; x. 11,424; xi, 194, 340, 538; xiii, 423; FU. i, 277; GA. (a), xiv, 255; xviii, 239; xix, 297; HR. 195; HS. (d), index, 465; ID. i–vii; ML. 5; OU. 128 (276 refs.).

(a) *Fee-farm Rents.* AG. (ref. "L.R. 2": 101); BF. i, 780; ii, 289.

(b) *Wood Sales.* AE. 29; AO. xx, 127; xl, 472; AP. xxxv, 115, 119, 122; xxxvii, 122; EN. i, 216; FF. v, 530; xiii, 122, 209, 211; GA. (a) xvi, 363; ID. i, iii, 216; v, 117, 431.

(iii) *Stuart Period: James I,* 1603–1625

ZH *Sales of Crown Lands in the Stuart Period: James I*: Accounts, bargains and sales, commissions, contractors, covenants, deeds and papers, instructions, lists, particulars, purchasers, registrars, rentals and surveys, royalties, warrants :—C. 66; F. i, 359; ii, 7; AG. (ref. "L.R. 2": 74–5); AI. iii, 11, 14, 18, 22, 25, 27, 29; AO. ii, 23; AP. ii, 20; xxv, 149, 373, 375, 415; AY. (a) xi, 6; BE. ii, 1153; BF. i, 346; BJ. iv, 441; EA. 29975 (19); EP. i, 92 (5); ii, 151 (27), 171 (175), 292 (No. 1217); ES. (ref. "B. 253," "D. 908 : 7"); FB. iii, 192; FW. viii, 8; HR. 195; HS. (d), index, 465; IE. viii–xii; MB. 2763; ML. 6; OU. 129 (3 refs.); QN.

(a) *Fee-farm Rents.* S. i, No. 1013; AP. xxv, 415; GA. (a), 1613 and 1614, p. 138; IE. xii, 440.

(b) *Forests, assarts, and Wood Sales.* S. i, No. 1013, 1081; AE. 29 (ref. "E. 325"); AI. iv, 334; AO. xx, 92, 127; xl, 472; AP. ii, 20 (Roll 601; "Ex. L.T.R.", Pipe Off., decl. acc., bun. 308); xiv, 45; xxv, 375; xxxv, 114, 116, 119, 123, 129; AY. (a) index 46; EG. 530; EK. 808; EP. ii, 161 (142), 171 (175); IE. viii–xi.

ZI *Charles I*: Crown Lands, Fee-farm Rents, forests, chases, parks, and wood sales. See "Land Administration and Sales", 1625–1660. (YJ.–YL.)

ZJ *Commonwealth*: Parl. Sales of Crown lands, Crown mansions, castles and goods, Fee-farm Rents, forests, and woodlands, and special procedure of the Parl. Sales. See "Land Administration and Sales", 1625–1660. (YM.–YZ.); also the following section (ZK.–ZO.).

V. RECOVERIES AND SALES OF CROWN LANDS, 1660–1702

ZK *Restoration, Recoveries, and Settlement*: Commission of Enquiry into Commonwealth Sales. See YZ., ZJ.

ZL   *Confiscation (Lands of Cromwell and the Regicides)*:   For the trial of the Regicides see BG. (*a*) under " Charles " (ref. " Vol. 24, C." ff. 134–5, consisting of 23 items, 1660–1) ; and for other references see F. i, 223 (" King's Bench : Indictments : Baga de secretis ") ; AI. iv, 279, 563 ; v. 150, 153, 158, 184, 200, 205 ; AM. (*a*) index (sec. ii, 22) ; AO. xxxviii, 132, 134, 141 ; AP. xxv, 419 ; xlvi, 34 (ref. " T. 48 " : 1) ; AP. obs. 842 (75, 77) ; EA. 6694 (1), 30206 (42, 44), 37719 (196) ; EK. 2551 (134, 143) ; EW. ii, 312, 703 ; FS. i, 32 ; iii, 15 ; IH. 1–xix ; TG. 90 ; TW. i–vii.

ZM   *Recoveries and Administration of Crown Lands, 1660–1685*:   For Crown lands restored, resumed or re-purchased, see S. i, 3131, 3203, 3173 ; AI. v, 204, 206 ; AI. (Finch), ii, 58 ; AM. (*b*) xi, 170 ; IH. i, 4, 291, 458 ; iii, 262 ; xix, 68 ; TW. ii, 288 ; vii, 1573 and Pepys Diary under date 29th March, 1663. There are lists of Royal Manors in the indexes of TW. i–vii (624 names, some repeated).   In the schedule of Entry Books in AP. obs. 842 (1–3, 86), are 4 vols. for 1660, 8 others for the years 1661–1678 (making 12 vols. for the period preceding the financial failure, and the institution of the sales of Fee-farm Rents.   This schedule enumerates 77 vols., covering the years 1660 to 1783, marked in a series extending from " A. to E. 4 ", and containing 26,096 folios or pages ; yet the whole of these records, compiled by fourteen Surveyors-General, in spite of a reference in the Commissioners' Reports of 1788 (AY. (*a*) iii, 17), cannot now be found at the P.R.O. References to these records and valuable information from them concerning Royal Manors will be found in EA. 30208 [1] (613 items for Charles II, 441 for Jas. II to Anne, and 902 for the years 1714– 1752). Surveys taken since the Restoration are referred to in AP. obs. 842 (38–41). Surveys of 20 counties (8 of those in Mx. dating from 1660 to 1666) were contained in a volume which was lost when Lord Galway was Surveyor-General, 1747–1751 (AP. obs. 842 : 38).   For other references of a general character concerning administration of Crown lands in the period 1660–1685 see the following :—F. ; H. ; S. ; AF. (ref. " E. 163 ", and " L.T.R.") ; AG. (ref. " L.R."), 27, 31, 68 ; AI. i, 32 ; iii, 96, 124, 145 ; 414 ; iv, 329, 481 ; v, 144, 204, 206, 396 ; vi, 685 ; vii, 817 ; viii, ix (ii) 4 ; x (iv), 148, (vi) 122 ; xi, 119 ; xiv (viii), 23, 103 ; xv (x), 6, 127 ; AI. (Astley) 48, 58 ; AI. (Finch) ii, 58 ; AI. (Fortescue) i, 509 ; AM. (*a*) index, 169, 193, 476, 479, 489, 618, 621, 623, 634, 728, 1110, 1137 ; AM. (*b*) index I (ii), 44, 63, 137, 147, 168, 176, 193, 221, 257, 289, 312, 338, 342, 359 ; AO. ii, 22, 24, 209 ; vii, 15, 44, 68 ; xx, 41, 61, 89, 184, 186 ; xxiv, 36 ; xxx, 22 ; xxxviii, 132, 134, 136 ; xli, 7, 29, 33, 346 ; AP. ii, 2, 40, 160, 162 ; xiv, 70 ; xxv, xxxv, 111 ; xxxvii, 66, 74 ; xliii, 33, 43 ; xlvi, 34, 38, 41, 47 ; AP. obs. 842 (75, and No. 28 on p. 76) ; BF. i, ii, 299 ; BH. (*b*) topog. v, 2187–2193 ; BR. 221, 250, 252 ; BZ. iii, 184 ; CV. 7 ser. xii, 126, 257, 334 ; CV. 10 ser. vii, 189 ; EA. 10122, 17018 (47), 25460 (335, 338), 27448 (219), 28073, 28081, 30206–30208, 32518 (221), 32519 (225), 34195 (69), 34258, 35103, 35117, 35906 (15) ; EA. (chart) 25564–25748 ; EK. 2542 (408, 425, 443), 2882 (245) ; ER. lxxiii, cxxiii ; ES. (ref. " A. 248 ", " C. 502 : 1," " D. 790," " D. 888 : 31," " D. 918 : 193 ") ; EU. 498 ; EW. ii, 311 ; FB. i, 40 ; FD. i, 184 ; FI. 2551 (134, 143) ; FM. ii, 63, 168 ; FN. 85 ; FP. 169, 193, 384, 398 ; FS. iii, 55, 59, 373 ; v, 430 ; vi, 119 ; vii, 1 ; FT. i, 697 ; ii, 145, 199 ; iii, 315 ; viii, 8, 120, 276, 346, 359 ; FU.

---

[1] See XA. *note* on Owen Davies.

ii, 7; HV. 363, 670; IH. i–xxii; OS. 125; RU. (*e*); TW. i–vii; TX. (*a*) i–vi; UE. iii, app. ii, 98, 104.

ZN *Revenue Settlement, 1660–1685*: For the Civil List Act of 1660, the Parl. Enquiry into Crown Revenues, 1660–1664, the settlement and subsequent financial collapse, see Coxe, Cat. Cod. MSS. ii, 25,[1] Hume, Hist. of Eng., ch. lxiii, and the following references :—F. i, 399; ii, 249; S. i, No. 3354, 3743, 3775; AF. (ref. " E. 163 " : 20); AG. (ref. " L.R. "), 41; AI. i, 58; iii, 90, 96, 217, 316; iv, 329, 373; v, 156, 158, 174, 195, 206, 208, 259,651; vii, 149, 182, 799, 817; viii, 98; ix (ii), 397; xiv (viii), 23, 190; AI. (Finch) i, 153, 161, 255, 414; ii, 101; AI. (Heathcote), 83; AM. (*a*) index, 198, 205, 618, 621, 623, 963, 997; AM. (*b*) index I (ii), 67; AO. ii, 209; AP. obs. 842 (76); BF. ii, 300; BX. ii, 266; EA. 15896, 18046–18058, 30206–8, 30218, 34217 (78); EK. 2542 (299, 524); EN. i, 423, 611, 621; ES. (ref. " A. 112 : 70," " A. 245 : 12," " B. 340 : 18 "); EV. 49 (55); EW. ii, 310, 354; FS. iii, 69, iv, vi; FT. iii, 242, 273, 360; IH. i–xxii; TG. app. vi, 28; TW. i–vii, viii, 2025.

Charles II, 1660–1685

ZO *Sales of Crown Lands and Fee-farm Rents since the Restoration : Charles II* : Bills, certificates, exemptions, King's rights, liabilities, loans, mortgages, particulars, registrar, trial :—BF. i, 346, 635, 843; EA. 30206 (40); ET. 647 (122), 3299 (182); IH. x, 656; xx, 220; TW. iii, 559; iv, 346; v, 757; vii, 966.

(*a*) *Fee-farm Rents*. Accounts (" L.R.R.O. 3," and Rolls, 1484–1519), Acts (ER. lxxiii), bargains and sales, bills of sale (polit. squib), books of sales (TW. iii, 417, 472), certificates, chantries, commissioners, complications, confusion, considerations, contracts, Duchy rents (TW. iii–v), county payments, debt settlements, deeds and papers, directions, enquiries, enrolments (" L.R.1."), entry books (EA. 30208), estimates, exemptions, fixed payments, improvements (TW. iii, iv), jointure lands (TW. iii), lists (25 Eng., 8 Welsh counties), loans on Crown lands (TW. ii–vii, beginning of the sales), losses, management, mortgages, office, orders (" Ex. K.R. 20 " : 4), particulars, pension books (" L.R.R.O. 8 "), procedure, purchases, receipts, receivers, registration, reprisals, reservations, rules and regulations, schedules, town rents (TW. iii, 1055, 1075), trust deeds. (TW. iii, iv, referred to confusedly as " first and second books "), trustees, unsaleable, sold, or unsold rents (EW. ii, 311; TW. ii–v; described as " all sold ", v, 54, " doubly sold," v, 131, vi, vii, " doubtful," v, 131, " encouraged," vii, 686, " quickened," iii, v, " slow," iii, " stopped," iii, v), warrants :— See the references in F. i, 376; ii, 114, 117; S. i, No. 3535, 3540; AF. (" K.R."); AG. 13, 219; AI. viii, 142; AO. ii, 44; xx, 186; AP. ii, 23, 40; xxv, 365, 369, 419; AP. obs. 842 (1, 38, 44, 77, 86); AY. (*a*) ii, 4; xii, 9, 49, app. 1; BF. i, 346, 635, 843; ii, 299; EA. 30206 (40); EA. (chart) 44843–6; ES. (ref. " D. 790 "); ET. 647 (122), 3299 (182); FT. ix, 409; IH. xi–xx; TW. ii–vii.

(*b*) *Forests, and Wood Sales*. AI. v, 150; AP. xxxv, 121, 323; AP. obs. 842 (77); IH. i–x; TW. i, 481, 533, 853; iii, 1031; iv, 562; v, 1659; vi, 269, 311, 738, 746; vii, 966, 1186, 1633, 1968.

---

[1] The index gives the reference " Omn. An. cclii. 72 ".

James II, 1685–1689

ZP *James II* : Accounts, commissioners, county charges, deeds and papers, double sales, enrolments, Exchequer items, lists, particulars, purchases, rentals and surveys, trustees :—F. ii, 114 ("L.R.R.O. 3"); AG. ("L.R. 1"); AO. ii, 23 ; AP. xxv; BF. i, 635 ; ES. (ref. "D. 790"); TW. viii ; TX. (*a*) i, 21.

(*a*) *Fee-farm Rents.* AG. 219 ("L.R. 1").
(*b*) *Wood Sales.* AP. xxxv, 121 ; TW. viii.

William III, 1689–1702

ZQ *William III* : Accounts, enrolments, Exchequer items, exorbitant grants, particulars, purchasers, rents and surveys, reports, trustees :— F. ii, 114 ("L.R.R.O. 3"); S. i, No. 4278 ; AG. ("L.R. 1"); AI. xiv, 144 ; AO. ii, 23 ; AP. xxv ; AP. obs. 842 (76) ; AY. (*a*) xii, app. 6, 16 ; BS. 272 ; EA. 21339 ; FM. ii, 144 ; TX (*a*) i, 344.

(*a*) *Fee-farm Rents.* AG. 219 (ref. "L.R. 1") ; ES. (ref. "D. 790") ; FT. ix, 409.

(*b*) *Wood Sales.* AI. xiii (v) 366 ; xiv (vi) 64 ; AY. (*a*) viii, app. 22 ; ix, app. 21 ; x, app. 13 ; xiii, app. 14, 15 ; xiv, app. 28 ; FM. ii, 168 ; TX. (*a*) i, 207.

VI. SALES OF CROWN LANDS SINCE THE CIVIL LIST ACT, 1702–1936

Anne, 1702–1714

ZR *Anne* : Accounts, bargains and sales, enrolments, index of grants (EA. 21340), particulars, rentals and surveys, trustees :—F. ii, 114 ("L.R.R.O. 3"); AG. ("L.R. 1"); AM. (*b*) index I, (ii), 290 ; AO. ii, 23 ; AP. xxv ; FW. viii, 248 ; HR.

(*a*) *Civil List Act.* AM. (*b*) index I (ii), 67 ; AY. (*a*) index 13 ; EN. iii, 365 ; iv, 332 ; TX. (*a*) iii, No. xcv, 83.

(*b*) *Fee-farm Rents.* AG. ("L.R. 1") ; AY. (*a*) xii, 9 ; TX. (*a*) No. xciv, 117.

(*c*) *Wood Sales.* AY. (*a*) vii, app. 16 ; viii, app. 18, 19 ; xiv, app. 26 ; TX. (*a*) i–iv.

George I, 1714–1727

ZS *George I* : Accounts, enrolments, particulars, rentals, and surveys :—F. ii, 114 ("L.R.R.O. 3"); AG. ("L.R. 1"); AI. (Stuart), ii, 373 ; AO. ii, 23 ; xiii, 24 ; AP. xxv, 151 ; xlvi, 34 ; TX. (*a*) v, 435.

(*a*) *Fee-farm Rents.* AG. 219 (ref. "L.R. 1").
(*b*) *Wood Sales.* AY. (*a*) vi, app. 9 ; xiv, app. 29 ; TX. (*a*) v, vi.

George II, 1727–1760

ZT *George II* : Accounts, enrolments, particulars, rentals and surveys, trustees : As under George I.

(*a*) *Fee-farm Rents.* AG. 219 (ref. "L.R. 1") ; TX. (*b*) iii, 236, 364.
(*b*) *Wood Sales.* AY. (*a*) vi, app. 16 ; xiv, app. 30 ; TX. (*b*) i, 26, 341, 365 ; ii, iii, 15, 80.

George III, 1760–1820

ZU *George III* : Accounts, enrolments, particulars, rentals, and surveys. As under George I—with AY. (*b*), i, 151, app. 9 and indexes ; AZ. indexes, and the triennial reports of Com. of Woods and Forests under the

Act of 50 George III, 1812–1819 (AY. i–iii). For the proposals to sell Crown lands in 1763, after the Seven Years' War, see CL. xxxii, 135 ; UE. ii, app. ii, 102.

(*a*) *Fee-farm Rents.* AY. (*a*) ii, 4 ; iv, xi, app. 6, 12 ; xii, 9, app. 26 ; xvi ; AY. (*b*) i, app. ii.

(*b*) *Wood Sales.* AY. (*a*) ii, app. 32–5 ; v, app. 37–41 ; vi, app. 9, 10, 14, 16, 32, 35 ; vii, app. 17 ; viii, app. 20 ; ix, app. 21, 22 ; x, app. 13, 14 ; xiii, app. 14 ; xiv, app. 28 ; xvii, app. 2, 4 ; AZ. i, app. 12, 13 ; ii, app. 7, 8 ; iii, app. 7 ; iv, app. 8 and index 13, 54.

George IV, 1820–1830

ZV *George IV* : Accounts, enrolments, fee-farm rents :—F. ii, 114 ("L.R.R.O. 3 ") ; AG. 219 ("L.R. 1 ").

(*a*) *Forests and Woods.* Triennial reports of Com. of Woods and Forests under Act of 50 George III, 1823–9 (AY. (*b*) iv–vi).

William IV, 1830–1837

ZW *William IV* : Accounts, enrolments (by books), fee-farm rents :—F. ii, 114, 115 ("L.R.R.O." 3, 15) ; AY. (*c*).

(*a*) *Forests and Woods.* F. ii, 114, and Ann. reports of Com. of Woods and Forests under Act of 10 George IV, 1830–6 (AY. (*c*) No. vii–xiii).

Victoria, 1837–1901

ZX *Victoria* : Accounts, enrolments (by books and deposit), fee-farm rents :—F. ii, 114–117 ("L.R.R.O." 3, 13–17, viz. Office of Woods, 1837–1901, Office of Works, 1852–1901, Board of Trade, 1866–1901) ; AY. (*c*).

(*a*) *Forests and Woods.* F. ii, 114, and Ann. reports of Com. of Woods and Forests under Acts of 10 George IV and 14–15 Vict., 1837–1900 (AY. (*c*) and (*d*) No. xiv–lxxviii).

Edward VII, 1901–1910

ZY *Edward VII* : Accounts, enrolments (by books and deposit), fee-farm rents :—F. ii, 114–116 ("L.R.R.O.", 3, 13–17).

(*a*) *Forests and Woods.* Ann. reports of Com. of Woods and Forests under Act of 14–15 Vict., 1901–1909 (AY. (*c*) No. lxxix–lxxxvii).

George V, 1910–1936

ZZ *George V* : Accounts, enrolments (by books and deposit), fee-farm rents :—F. ii, 114–117 ("L.R.R.O. ", 3, 13–17). Since 1st July, 1914, a single chronological arrangement of enrolments has been adopted.

(*a*) *Forests and Woods.* Ann. reports of Com. of Woods and Forests under Act of 14–15 Vict., 1910–1935 (AY. (*c*), collective reports, No. lxxxviii–cxiii). In Report 106 for 1928 various sales of Crown lands in England, Wales, Scotland, Ireland, and the Isles of Alderney and Man are recorded (pp. 2, 4–6, app. 1, 2, 4, 5, 8, 11, 13, 15, 17). See also " Abstract Accounts for 1929 " (January, 1931) for various items of sales, and the same Accounts for the years 1930–5 (published Jan., 1932–7).

Edward VIII, 1936

ZZ (*b*) *Edward VIII* : Annual report of Commissioners of Crown Lands, under the Acts of 10 Geo. IV. c. 50, 2 Will. IV. c. 1, 11–12 Vict. c. 102, and 14–15 Vict. c. 42 : Report No. 114, dated 22nd June, 1936. For sales of property in England, Wales, Scotland, Isle of Man, and Isle of Alderney, see appendices No. 3, 7, 10, 12, 13. Exchanges, leases, purchases, and rents, are referred to in appendices No. 2, 4–6, 8, 9, 11, 14. " Abstract Accounts, 1936," for the year ending 31st March, 1937, as " Ordered, by the House of Commons, to be printed ", will be published in January, 1938.

George VI, 1936

ZZ (c) George VI : Annual report of Commissioners of Crown Lands, as under Edward VIII. (ZZ. (b)): Report No. 115, issued in Sept., 1937. " Abstract Accounts, 1937," for the year ending 31st March, 1938, will not appear before January, 1939. For particulars as to area and rents, 31st March, 1937, furnished in advance by the Commissioners, see page 287, *note.*

THE PARLIAMENTARY SURVEYS OF CROWN LANDS

I. SURVEYORS' INSTRUCTIONS FOR METHOD OF MAKING SURVEYS [1]

Duchy of Cornwall Office: Baynes Papers, 5 ff., 1649. British Museum: Certified Copy (Add. MS. 44937), 9 ff., 1926.

(folio 1) .

INSTRUC'ONS for a method in Drawing up & Ingrossing Surveyes

After the title

To begyn' wth ye Rentes of Assize of ye free Coppiehold & Customary Ten^{a}nts of Inheritance & to certifie them wth their sev'^{r}all tenures & times wherein they are payable.

Quit Rents & of Assise

If there be sev'^{r}all Townshipps belonging to one Manor lett ye Rents be distinguished by Townshipps

And soe alsoe ye dem^{a}esnes (in their due place) both Leased & unleased

Customary rents & royaltyes

To certifie all ye Customary workes of ye Tenn^{a}antes in money extended or not extended All rent Wheat, Rent Barly or other graine Rent Capons Chureletts, Rent Eggs Rent for Pannage p'fitt of Fishinges & of Games Tolls of faires & m'kettes & all other p'fittes of ye like nature wch shall come to yor knowledge According to ye Custome of ye place upon wch you are, wth ye sev'all times of their paym^{te} & soe many of them as you find unc'taine you are to make c'taine, by Computing ye p'fittes of them as they may bee worth to ye Lord Coi'bz Annis

Courtes & p'quisites

To certifie all Court Barrons & Leetes all fines upon discent or Alenac'on Reliefes Herriottes Waiefes estraies fellons goodes Wreckes of Sea (if bordering upon ye Sea coast) & all other p'quisittes & Royalties not forgetting to p'ticuler those wch are most eminent, in ye Manor or place by you retorned And to value them by estimac'on Coi'bz Annis—wherein Cheefe Regard must be had to ye natures of ye sev'all tenures And to ye fines usually p^d at ye taking up of ye ten^{a}ntes landes.

note /.

If you can gett Accomptes to help you in yor Computac'on of p'quisittes Lett it bee (if to bee had) by accompting of ye yeares together backwards from 1641

When you have incerted all Annuall p'fittes more especially belonging to a Royalty,

---

[1] This document was discovered among the Baynes Papers in the Duchy of Cornwall Office in 1926.

demesnes in possession
Then fall upon ye demesnes in poss'ion & therein first wth ye Manor house & Scite thereof wth the Appurtenªnces & soe Consequently, all Lands groundes & woodes therewth all used occupied or enioyed, Let each p'cell bee sett forth p'ticulerly wth the Contentes by estimac'on their usuall names & abuttmtes in Case of obscurity

Butting
You neede not abutt yor Landes or groundes when they ly together more then upon one feild or Close, but if they ly in ye Com'on feildes amongst other mens landes then one boundary & one abuttmt wilbee necessary & some-times where there may bee mistakes (by reason of sev'all p'cells) there it wilbee convenient to butt & bound either Round, or soe farr as may make a plaine distinguishmt of p'cells.

landes in possession first entered:
If ye Manor house & Scite be not in poss'ion & there are other Landes tentes or hereditamtes wthin ye same Manor in prsent poss'on let ye p'ticulers (so in poss'on wth their values be first Certified And ye Scite wth thappurtenªnces in the first place among ye Leases.

(folio 2) demesnes in farme
In yor setting forth of demªesnes in poss'ion if you either lett them yorselves for one yeare (if you have power soe to doe) or find them sett by the Sequestratrs or others from yeare to yeare to sev'all p'sons Lett them be distinguished by p'cells, as they are so lett or sett for ye p'snte & lett ye p'snte Rent res'ved thereon (as all other res'ved Rents be placed in ye m'gent next yor left hand, And if you find them to be of further ymprovement place ye same in ye m'gent next yor right hand, & incert theise or ye like wordes in ye Conclusion of each p'ticuler: But is worth upon imp'vemt ov' & above ye sd Rent p' Ann' soe much)

Leases together ot Towneshipes.
If ye Manor house & scite thereof wth thappurtenªnces bee in lease for lives then finish all Leases for lives wthin the same Townshipp before you fall upon Leases for yeares

And so E. contra

messuages &c.
In c'tifiing of landes mess's or tentes under demise first sett forth yor p'ticulers exactly as you find them upon yor p'snte view & according to ye most modern boundings wth Apt wordes sufficiently full to ground a Conveyance upon If you do'bt any p'per names or other names of p'sons or things in regard of various denominac'ons make use of an Al's And soe Compose yor matter yt it may run Cleere from ye first entry thereupon to ye Close thereof

memorand'
And when you have finished yor p'ticulers then sett out the ten'tes Right or Claime by way [of] memorandu' as by yor p'sidentes [1] is declared

---

[1] Here we have a reference to the " Precedent " or model Parliamentary Survey, which is preserved in the same volume of Baynes Papers (or Webb Surveys). This docu-ment deserves to be printed in full. Like the Instructions, it dates from September, 1649 ; but it is incomplete, as folios 14–15 and 19 are missing. The certified copy, dated 18th

abstracting
leases

When you begyn' to Certifie any p'cell Comp'hend' wthin one Lease passe not away from that p'cell to any other, till you have fully finished all thinges Concerned & conteyned in ye s^d Lease forgett not in abstracting yor Leases to mention all Considerable Coven^antes Excepc'ons & provisoes therein conteyned & agreed betweene ye Lessor & ye Leassee & accordingly take care to sett forth ye lesso^{rs} benefitt, by any such Excepc'on Covenant or p'visoe, by way of p'sent or future Improvem^t & the Lessees right in the same by way of Reprizall

yeares

Lives

If Lease by [or] for lives then Certifie all, or such & such lifes soe aged or in being, & being very Carefull, you bee not deluded by any lives not intended by the gr^aunte

m^d

If for yeares then in ye Conclusion of ye p'misses Certifie to this effect There was . . . . . ye^r to Come on ye . . . . . of ye last . . . . .

leases doble

If two or more Leases alike dated or of sev'all dates bee enioyed by one & the same p'son & by himself occupied, or Rented to any other Under one Intire Rent Let them bee distinctly Certified wth their sev'all improvem^t And ye Rent according to ye sd Improvemts apporc'oned

(folio 3)
improvem^{ts}
of Leases

If there be leased together wth any Manor Grang' farme or other Lands tenem^{tes} hereditam^{tes}, any Rectory Parsonage Gleab tithes or Porc'ons of tithes & ye Rent res'ved upon ye whole be an Intire Rent Be sure in your valuac'on of ye p'misses to sett forth ye sev'all ymprovem^{tes} distinctly And apporc'on ye s^d Intire Rent according to ye respective improvem^{tes}

Tythfree

What other landes or tenem^{tes} you find to have enioyed or letten tithe free Certifie to this effect : The fores^d p'misses wee find to be Tithe free & soe have valued them

Coppyholds
abstracted

When you have finished yor Lease holdes Proceede to yor Coppie holdes for lives (if you find any wthin ye same Manor abstract soe much of their Coppies, as you find most usefull viz't ye dates p'ticulers, ye lives gr^aunted ye Annual Rent p^d & ye Considerac'ons for fines (if therein menc'oned) only lett yor first Coppie bee retorned verbatim & ye rest (if of ye same tenure) abstract as befores^d. Sett ye p'snte Rent Fines & Herriottes in ye Margent next yor left hand & ye Cleere ymprovem^t next yor Right hand And lastly Certifie what Lyves, wth their ages are in being

June, 1927, consists of 32 folios, instead of 21. No names of surveyors are recorded, but the triangular title runs as follows :—" A Survey of ye Imaginary Man'or of Sale wth ye Rights | members & appurten^ances thereof lying & being in ye County | of Surrey late p'cell of ye poss'ions of Charles Stewart | late King of Eng^{ld} made & taken by us whose names | are hereunto subscribed in ye moneth of September | 1649, by virtue of a Com'ission granted | upon an Acte of Com'ons assembled | in Pa^rliament for Sale of the | Hon^{rs} Mann^{rs} & Landes here | tofore belonging to the late | King Queene & Prince | under the handes & | Seales of five or | more of the | Trustees in y^e | s^d Act named | & appoint- | ed | ."

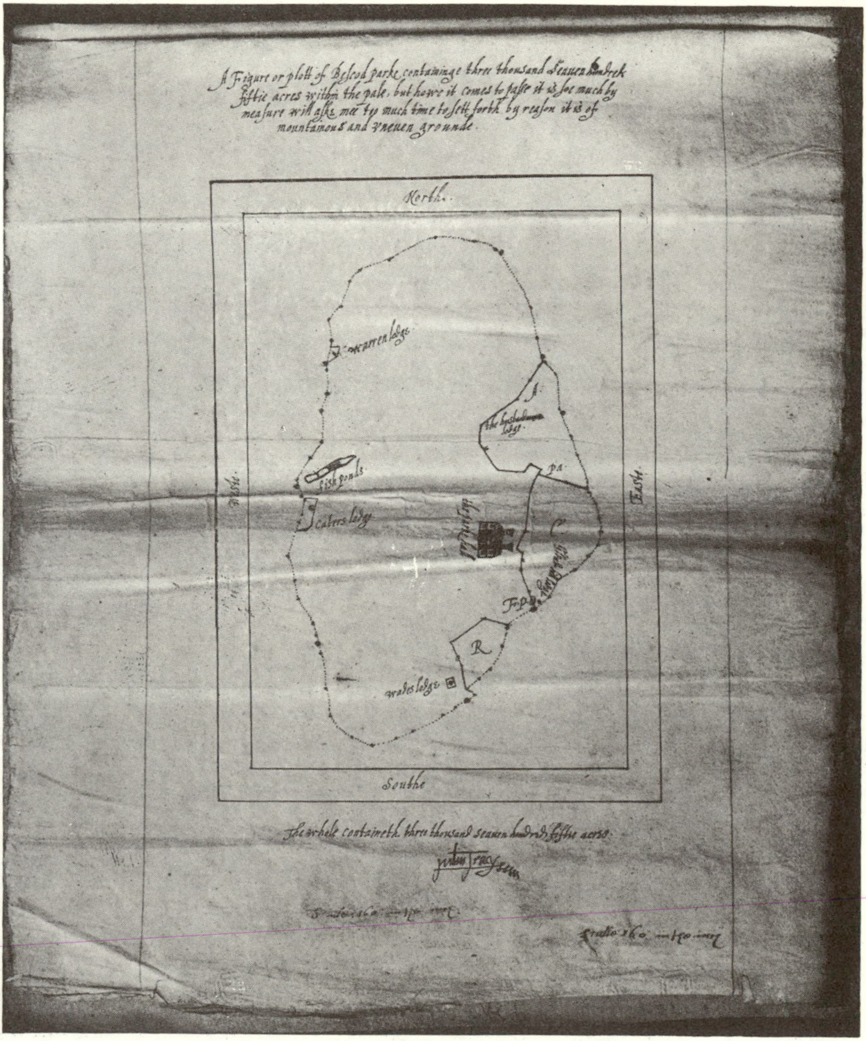

BESTWOOD PARK, NOTTINGHAMSHIRE: PLAN, 1650

Fines

Lett y^r Retornes bee in English If y^r Coppieholders bee Coppieholders of inheritance or Customary ten^{a}ntes there wilbe noe need of abstracting their Coppies, ye p'fitts of ye Lords by such Lands being comprized in ye fines upon discent & Alienac'on, wch is Appointed to bee valued (as before Coi'bz Annis) only where such fines are Arbitrary it wilbe Convenient to Certifie ye Cleere Annuall ymprovem^t of all ye Coppiehold estates, belonging to ye s^d Manor in one grosse sum'e amongst ye memorand^s that soe ye Purchasor may satisfie his owne Judgm^t in y^r valuac'on of ye fores^d fines wch grosse value you may Calculate or gaine upon Inquisic'on exam'ac'on on oath, wthout spending time in viewing the p'ticuler Landes of such Tenem^{ts} And where ye fines are Certaine, it wilbee requisitt alsoe that you certifie (among y^r Memorand^s how they are p^d whether by soe much upon the Acre messuage or tenem^t or by the yeares Rent of Assize or any other way.

leases since 26th March: 1641:

If you find any Lease gr^{a}unted since 26° Maij 1641 unlesse where ye lord for ye time being hath a power to gr^{a}unte such a Lease Bee carefull to find out & certifie what estates were surrendered att the taking of ye s^d Lease or Leases & Retorne them accordingly

You may find some times ye surrender recited as a Considerac'on in ye new Lease.

(folio 4) Timber on leases.

If you find more Tymber or Wood upon any Deme^{a}sne Land (In Lease or otherwise) then will satisfie for ye maintenance of necessary Bootes allowed, or fitt to be allowed to ye p'misses you are to value it in grosse, after ye p'ticulers of ye afores^d p'misses

or Coppeholds.

And if you find ye like upon any ye Coppiehold Landes you are to enquire into ye Customes of ye s^d Manor conc'ning ye Right of ye Lord or Tenen'c therein and certifie ye same among ye s^d Customes

woods & underwoods & vesture

In all woodes & underwoodes in poss'ion you are to value ye vesture there standing & growing in Grosse & ye soile at soe much each Acre p' Ann' But they bee in Lease you are to value ye vesture there growing According to ye Coven^{a}nts of ye s^d Lease And ye soile at soe much p' Ann' ov' & above ye rent res'ved thereon

Timber on Com'ones

Tymber in Parkes wilbee best valued wth ye same Parks.

Timber upon Com'ons, Heathes Moores & Wastes by themselves after ye entry of all Leases & Coppiehold estates

nota

Lett not grosse value bee brought into any of yor m'gent but let it be c'tified in ye body of yor Sheete short of yor m'gent next yor Right hand

Patents

abstracted

If there be any Patent gr^{a}unted to an officer or officers wth a c'taine fee chargable upon divers Manno^{rs} Lands tenem^{tes} or hereditam^{tes} or upon any p'ticuler Manor or p'cell of Landes lett ye s^d Pattent be retorned, either wth ye s^d

p'ticuler Mano^{rs} or p'cell of Land or in Capite or Chiefest of those Mano^{rs}, wch are Jointly & sev'ally answerable for ye same. If there bee many Pattentes Charged upon one Manor then Retorne them all wth ye survey of that Manno^r if Charged upon sev'all Mano^{rs} Retorne same wth others that they may bee Reprized accordingly.

Reprised
First retorne ye Pattents or abstract thereof & make yor Reprizall for them amongst yor other Reprizes & nev^r Retorne any Patent twice vizt upon no Manno^r then one

Reprises
Next will p'perly follow a Retorne of all Gen'all or p'ticuler Reprises belonging to ye Mano^r or p'misses, wch you have surveyed

About wch diligent inquiry must be made That no Pattents Boones Annuities, or Rentes Resolutes Issuing out of ye p'misses, or any p'te thereof or any Incumbrances thereon be first unc'tified

Customes
Then ye Customes of y^e Manor at Least wise soe many of them as are of Cheefe conc^{r}niment are to be Certified

Com'ons & wasts
The Moores Com'ons & wast grounds

Bounder^s
The boundaries of y^e Manors (if cleerely & notoriously knowne but if dubiously given you, it were better bee silent therein

(folio 5) [1] **Mem$^{ds'}$**
The memorandums wch Concerne y^e Manor in gen'all of wch there be divers as upon inquiries 'twill be found

nota
If heriottes & benefitt of Com'onage or Com'on of pasture be included in y^e value of y^e Coppiehold tennantes for lives it must bee soe certified amongst y^e Memorandu^s if not it must bee valued & incerted amongst ye p'quisites & Royalties in ye beginning of ye Survey

Rentalls
Then may follow exact Rentalls of ye sev'all rents of ye free & Coppiehold & Customary tenem^{tes} of ye Manor wch must Correspond in ye value with the sev'all sum'es first Certified in gen'all

Antedateing or Raceinge
Care must be taken to examine or enquire into Antedating raceing of Leases or deedes & what is therein found must be certified accordingly

Surveyes faire writt.
The surveyes & Duplicates must bee fairely ingrossed wthout bloting or scraping

The(y) must be exactly su'med Compared & exa'ied & (as neere as may bee) made Agreeable in ye folio & Contents in each follio

Returnes intire
Retorne yor Mano^{rs} entire breake them not by certifying in p'cells unlesse you find great Cause soe to doe If ye whole Manor be leased out for lives or yeares & ye Lord for ye time hath ye power to gr^{a}unte estates, according to y^e

Leases certified
Custome of ye Manor att any time during ye terme of his Lease Lett ye Grand Lease by wch ye meane Lord holdeth

---

[1] Folio 5 is endorsed as shown below.

be largly Certified att ye ende of ye Survey next before the abstract of ye values of ye whole Manor

Abstract of the whole

And lastly in one Page if it will Comp'hend it An Abstract of ye whole survey in ye point of values & lett that Abstract bee plaine & not confounded wth Mixture of different Rents & improvem^{ts}

Keepe close to yor p'sident [1] where they will answere yor work before you, & to this method where they come short.

Endorsed :

Further Instrucc'ons f^r ingrossinge and drawing up Surveyes. (folio 5.) [2]

II. CONCEALED CROWN LANDS, 1650–1656

The Trustees' Journal : Exch., Augm. Off., Misc. Bks., Vol. 314

(*a*) *f. 52. Dated 12th June, 1650.*[3]

Upon Information given to this Committee by a member thereof That (Col. Ro. Lisburn) was ready to discover certain of the Crown Lands concealed from the surveyors, to the value of one hundred pounds p. ann' or thereabouts in case he might be admitted as an original Creditor to the pre-emption thereof without Competition, Ordered That the said (–) [4] upon such discovery and return of the Survey have the pre-emption accordingly.

(*b*) *f. 108. Dated 22nd January, 1650.*

Whereas divers discoveries are offered to be made by several persons of sundry of the late King Queen and Princes Lands in such places where the surveyors have done their work ; in case such persons might have convenient encouragement thereunto ; The Contractors doe declare that all such persons as shall make any such discoveries shall have the pre-emption of the Lands by them discovered at 20 years purchase in assigned bills, they tendering themselves to purchase the premises in some convenient time after the Return of the Survey : Provided such discoverers be neither Tenants to the premises, nor have been formerly surveyors or auditors of the counties or places where the lands so to be discovered shall lie, nor come in to purchase in the behalf of such Tenants Auditors or surveyors either directly or indirectly which (being afterwards proved) shall be taken sufficient matter to avoyd the Contract.

---

[1] Another reference to the accompanying " Precedent " or model survey. The certified copy, presented to the British Museum, 5th February, 1937 (Add. MS. 44937), is inscribed as follows (f. 32) : " I certify that the foregoing is a true and authentic copy. Walter Peacock, Secretary and Keeper of the Records, Duchy of Cornwall Office, 18th June, 1927."

[2] The certified copy, now placed in the British Museum, concludes thus : " I hereby certify that the within written Instructions have been examined with the contemporary copy of the original document bound up in a volume labelled ' Parliamentary Surveys—Baynes Papers ' preserved in the Duchy of Cornwall Office and is a true copy of such contemporary copy. Dated this twenty-sixth day of March 1926, Walter Peacock, Keeper of the Records of the Duchy of Cornwall."

[3] There are other references to Discoveries and Concealments between 1650 and 1652 in Berks (f. 164), Cheshire (f. 101), Derby (f. 153 *b*), Hants (f. 89), Hereford (f. 82), Lancs (f. 112 *b*), Middlesex (f. 48 *b*), Northants (f. 112 *b*), York (f. 111 *b*).

[4] Blank in fol. 52.

(c) f. 164. Dated 26th July, 1653.

Ordered, that the party pretending a discovery to a parcel of Clewer farme (Berks), and the former purchaser of the residue of the said farm be both heard before there be a sale made to either.

(d) f. 178b. Dated 14th May, 1656.

Upon a discovery of certain lands now propounded by Capt. Miller, Capt. Bolt and Capt. Thomson, we do order That the said discoverers (paying for the Survey of the said Lands) shall not upon their Contract for the same or any of them be demanded above fourteen years purchase, Provided that upon passing Conveyance by the Trustees of the premises, the parties to whom Conveyances shall be made do give such assurance to such as have purchased the present rents of any of the said lands as fee farme Rents, as by the Counsel of the Trustees shall be advised for such purchasers enjoying the said Rents accordingly.

III. List of Discoverers of Concealed Lands

The " Book of Discoveries " has not been found ; but many names have been recovered from the Parliamentary Surveys in the Augmentation Office and Land Revenue Office series. The references are given as " PS ", followed by a number, or as " L.R. 2 ", followed by the folio number of the volume quoted.

Bedford : Capt. Thos. Margaretts (Land Rev. Off., vol. 276 f. 67).
Berkshire : Major Jn. Browne, Wm. Cooke, Capt. Jn. Hemsdall, Ric. Heywood, Jn. Hoare, Rog. Humphries, Major Jn. Joanes, Capt. Jas. Keys, Capt. Hy. Thornton, Thos. Webb (PS. 12, 13, 15, 21, 25, 30–2, 34, 44).
Buckingham : Wm. Hayle, Mich. Lea, Lewis Rye, Jn. Urlin, Capt. Wheatley (PS. 1, 4, 5, 7, 13, 15, 16, 18 and LR. 2, vol. 278 f., 68).
Cambridge : Ric. Fulcher (PS. 6).
Cheshire : Anth. Booth of Macclesfield, Lord Jn. Bradshaw, Hercules Comander, Major Eaton, Humph. Kelsall, Thos. Morrice of West-minster, Hy. Rolin of Liscott, Wm. Steele, Capt. Wm. Tracey (PS. 7, 9, 10A., 15, 16B.).
Cornwall : Anth. Rowse (PS. 13).
Cumberland : No name (PS. 6).
Derbyshire : Ric. Boucher, Edw. Bradshaw, Capt. Jn. Hemsdell, Major Knight, Jn. Taylor (PS. 12A, 13, 14A, 17, 27B).
Devon : Rob. Fisher, Wm. Maye (PS. 8 and L.R. 2, vol. 280 f., 18).
Dorset : Ezekias Lambe, Jer. Whitworth (PS. 3, 4, 21).
Durham : Sir Hy. Vane, Senr. (PS. 4).
Essex : Jn. Singleton (PS. 20).
Gloucester : Thos. Cary, Ralph Gardiner,[1] Wm. Thorpe (PS. 15, 17, 18A).
Hampshire : Capt. Jn. Urlyn, Jer. Whitworth (PS. 14).
Hereford : Wm. Phillips, Major Jn. Wildman (PS. 13, 14, 17).
Hertford : Nic. Elton, Rog. Humphryes (PS. 6 (b), 12, 17).
Kent : Thos. Bavington, — Bradshaw, Major Jn. Browne, Jn. Clarke, Walt. Coules, Col. Rob. Gibbons, Capt. Dan. Goldsmith, Jn. Hill, Geo. Hooper, Capt. Rob. Joseph of Dartford, Major Ralph Knight,

---

[1] Citizen of London.

Wm. Manning, Wm. Mar, Wm. Moyes, — Skinner, Wm. Weaver, Hugh Webb (PS. 11, 12, 13, 18, 24, 27, 32, 34, 40, 46–8, 53, 59, and L.R. 2, vol. 282 f., 4).

Lancashire : Col. Thos. Birch, Ric. Cottham, Humph. Kelsall, Col. Ric. Shuttleworth, Capt. Jerem. Whitworth, Jn. Winstanley, Lieut.-Col. Chas. Worsley, and another *unnamed* (PS. 9–12, 16, 17, 19, 20, 22–7).

Leicester : Ric. Dann, Jn. Houghton, Isaac Hunt, Matt. Scarborough (PS. 6, 8–11, 13).

Lincoln : Capt. Adam Baynes, Ric. Fulcher, Jn. Houghton, Matt. Jacques, Major R. Knight, Mich. Lea,[1] Jegon Mandeville, Wm. May, Matt. Scarborough, Nath. Waters (7A, 8, 11, 12, 24, 25, 28, 35, 37A, 38B).

Middlesex : Wm. Bell, Jn. Dennis,[2] Capt. Geo. Harbert, Capt. Jn. Hemsdell, Wm. Hobby, Jn. Johns of London,[3] Thos Lawton,[4] Elia Palmer, Mrs. Hugh Peters, Jn. Phelpes, Mr. Robinson, Wm. Savile, Matt. Scarborough of London, Capt. Edw. Strutton, Hy. Thornton of Westminster, Capt. Steph. White, Jn. Williams, Nic. Willis (PS. 11, 13, 15, 23, 30, 35, 43, 44, 49, 61, 63, 64, 70, 73, 74, 76, 78, 80, 94 ; also L.R. 2, vol. 288 ff., 29, 162).

Norfolk : Sir Wm. Paston, Jn. Yonge (PS. 12, 15).

Northants : Lieut. Jas. Horton of Alderton, Thos. Tibbs, Jn. Urlyn (PS. 24, 33, 42, 48, and L.R. 2, vol. 290 f., 159).

Nottingham : Capt. Jn. Boundly, Wm. Walker (PS. 16, 24 (*b*), and L.R. 2, vol. 293 f., 150).

Oxford : Capt. Jn. Buttler, Geo. Hearne, Mich. Lea (PS. 8, 9, 11).

Shropshire : Wm. Kelton (PS. 6).

Somerset : Dr. Geo. Powell, Hy. Seeley, Geo. Vaux (PS. 14, 15, 34–6A, 41).

Stafford : Ric. Bourchier, Jn. Hemsdall, Capt. Jeremie Jordan, Capt. Blunt Sadler, Matt. Scarborough (PS. 7, 40, 42, 44 (*l*), also L.R. 2, vol. 295 ff., 9, 68).

Suffolk : Jn. Houghton (PS. 10).

Surrey : Edw. Bushell, Capt. Cleer, Wm. Hart, Wm. Hobby, Thos. Smith, Nic. Willis, Major Geo. Wither, and another *unnamed* (PS. 12, 35–7, 42, 48–50, 54).

Sussex : Edw. Badby, Capt. Christ. Bodly, Capt. Ric. Mortlock,[5] Major Jas. Pittsone, Jn. Urlin (PS. 20, 25, 28 (*b*), 30, 33–5, 45, 50, 51, and L.R. 2, vol. 299 f., 295).

Warwick : Wm. Dawgs, Edw. Harrison (PS. 6, 11).

Westmorland : Jer. Baynes, Capt. Thos. Browne,[6] Arth. Otway, Jn. Singleton [7] (PS. 2, 4, 5, 6 (*a*)).

Wiltshire : Patrick Boyle, Thos. Cromwell, Nic. Fountaine, Mich. Lea, Wm. Murford of Easton, Som., Mathias Nicholls (PS. 19, 24, 36, 37, 39, 45).

Worcester : Major Salloway (PS. 4, 6).

Yorkshire : Ric. Clapham, Jas. Conyers, Francis Dickinson, Bernard

---

[1] On behalf of — Skepper.
[2] Entered in Surveyor-General's " Book of Discoveries " (LRO., Misc. Books, vol. 288, Mx., f. 29).   [3] Merchant.
[4] Citizen and Haberdasher of London.   [5] " For Coronet Wm. Combey."
[6] PS. 2 reference dated 7th January, 1652 (entered at Surv. Gen. Off., Lib. B., f. 174).
[7] " On behalf of Jn. Houghton, Wm. Zanchy and Col. Thorpe."

Emott,[1] Capt. Adam Eyre (or Ayre), Jn. Harrison, Ralph Hassell, Thos. Hutchinson, Jas. Ibesonn, Mich. Moyses, Capt. Jn. Northen,[2] Sam Richardson, Capt. Blunt Sadler, Matt. Scarborough,[3] Jn. Singleton, Clement Tomlinson, Jn. Tomlinson (PS. 14, 17, 18, 29, 30, 32, 33, 36, 37, 40, 42–4, 61, and L.R. 2, vol. 302 ff., 314, 352–5, 407, 433).
Brecon : Dav. Morgan, Wm. Phillipps (PS. 3, 4, 7, 9).
Cardigan : Dav. Morgan (PS. 4, 5).
Carmarthen : Dav. Morgan, Wm. Rowe of Westminster (PS. 2, 6, 8–11, 15, 17, 19).
Denbigh : *Unnamed* (PS. 2).
Monmouth : Reynold Rowse of Monmouth, and another *unnamed* (PS. 4, 5 (*b*)).
Pembroke : Capt. Castle, Sir Jn. Lenthall, and another *unnamed* (PS. 2, 3, 5–7).

IV. LIST OF REGICIDES, REPUBLICANS, AND OFFICIALS ASSOCIATED WITH CROWN LANDS SALES, 1649–1659

Notes : (A) Act of 16th July, 1649 : Committee members (23rd February, 18th April, 9–11th May, 29–30th June, 7–13th July).
  (C) Contractors for Sale of Crown Lands.
  (O) Committee for removing Obstructions : Orders in Parl. Surveys.
  (R) Regicides : Members of Committees.
  (T) Trustees for Crown lands.
   * Purchasers of Crown lands, actual or prospective.[4]

Aldworth, Rob. (A, O). Allanson, Sir Wm. (A, O). Allen, Ald. Fran. (A, T)*. Andrews, Ald. Thos., Treasurer. Anlaby, Mr. (A). Atkins, Ald. Thos. (A, O). Attorney-General (A). Ayers or Eyres, Thos. (C). Ayloffe, Receiver.

Barkham, Sir Edw. (T). Berners, Jo. (O). Blackiston, Jn. (A, R). Blunt,[5] Col. Thos. (T)*. Bond, Nic. (A, C). Boone, Mr. (A). Bossevile, Col. Wm. (A, T).[6] Bourchier, Sir Jn. (A, O, R). Bradshaw, Ric. (Ches. P. S., No. 8). Brewster, Ro. (O). Brough, Thos. E., Clerk to Surveyor-General. Browne, Jn. (O). Browne, Ric.[7]

Carey (Carew), Jn. (A, O, R). Caser, Jn., Examiner. Challenor, Jas. (O). Challenor, Thos. (A, R). Claidon, Wm. (Mx. PS. No. 37B). Cleypool, Jn. (T).[5] Coke, Thos, (T).[8] Colbron, Hy., Registrar. Collins, Jn., Examiner. Cooke, Cornel. (T).[9] Corbet, Jn. (O). Corbet, Miles (A, R). Cowper, Jas. (Mx. PS. No. 37B). Crachley, Thos., Deputy Receiver. Cressett, Edw. (C). Cromwell, Lieut.-Gen. Oliver (A, R).

[1] A note states that he " assigned over the same to Scarborough ".
[2] He assigned his discovered lands to Richardson.
[3] See Northen ; also the order of the Com. of Obstructions as to his Petition, 26th January, 1653. (L.R. 2, vol. 302 ff., 352–5.)
[4] The identification of the ultimate purchaser is obscured at times by Agents or attorneys. Different names frequently occur in the Particulars, Rating Certificates and Enrolments.
[5] Excused.
[6] Sealed 297 conveyances. See Camb. Univ. MSS. : Dd. xiii, 20.
[7] Flint, PS. No. 1 was addressed to " his house at the Crowne in ffleetstreete ".
[8] Sealed 226 conveyances.
[9] Sealed 389 conveyances.

Danvers, Sir Jn. (A, O, R). Darley, Mr. (A). Darnall, Ralph, Counsel for Sale and Conveyancing.* Dethick, Ald. Jn., Treasurer. Dormer, Jn. (O). Dove, Jn. (A, O).*

Edwards, Hy. (O). Edwards, Humph. (A).*

Fenwick, Col. Rob. (A, C). Fibberley, Jn. (O). Fielder, Col. Jn. (A, O). Fleetwood, Col. Geo. (A. R).

Garland, Aug. (A, O, R). Gay, Wm. (O). Gerard, Sir G., Receiver (?). Goodwin, Jn. (A, O). Gould, Nic. (A). Gray, Thos. (O). Grey, Lord Wm. (A). Graves, Ric., Counsel for Sale and Conveyancing. Gurdon, Jn. (A).

Hallowes, Nath. (A, O). Hall, Ralph, Registrar. Hall, Wm., Auditor. Harrington, Sir Jas. (A).* Harrison, Jn. (O). Harrison, Ralph [1] (T).* Harrison, Col. Thos. (A, R).* Harvey, Col. Edm. (A). Hay, Wm. (O). Hill, Ric. (A).* Hippesley, Sir Jn. (A, O).* Holcroft, Sir Hy. (T).[2] Holland, Cornel (A, O).* Holliday, Mr. (Mx. PS. No. 16 rental). Hubbert (Hubbard), Dr. Thos. (T).[3] Humphreys, Jn. (C).[4] Hunt, Jn.[5] (T).* Husey, Thos. (O).

Ireton, Commissary Gen. Jn. (A, R). Ireton, Jn. (T).[6]

Jessop, Wm., Examiner. Jones, Col. Jn. (A, R).* Jugh, Wm., Auditor.

Kenwrick, Wm. (T).[7] Kighte, Hy. (Berks. P.S. No. 33).

Lascelles, Col. Fra. (A, O). Lea, Mich., Secretary to the Trustees. Lechmere, B. (O). Leman, Wm. (A). Lempriere, Nic. (C). Light, Jn., Examiner. Lister, Thos. (O). Loue, Nic. (O). Lovibond, Hy. (L.R. 2, vols. 285–6, Lincs. : signs " H.L. " at the foot of every folio). Lucy, Ric. (O). Ludwell, Jn. (Glouc. PS. No. 14 (a)).

Mallet, Mic. (L.R. 2, vol. 276, Bedf., f. 154).[8] Mandeville, Jegon, Examiner.[9] Martin, Col. Hy. (A, R). Masham, Wm. (O). Mildmay, Sir Hy. (A).* Millington, Gilb. (A, R.). Monson, Lord Wm. (A, O). Mussenden, Fra. (O).

Nevill, Hy. (O).

Oldsworth, Mr. (A). Oxenbridge, Jn. (Sx. PS. No. 49 (a), f. 8b).

Palmen, Jn. (O). Parker, Jn. (O). Pennington, Ald. Isaac (A, O). Pierpoint, Mr. (A). Pitt, Hy. (O). Potter, Wm., Registrar for Debentures. Powell, Mr., Auditor (Mx. PS. No. 37B).[10] Pratt, Ralph, Registrar (?).[11] Purefoy, Col. Wm. (A, R). Pury, Thos. (A, O).

Ragge, Jacob, Clerk. Ralegh, Carew (O). Reynolds, Rob. (A). Rich., Col. Nath. (A).* Rigby, Col. (A). Roberts, Sir Wm. (C, O). Robinson, Hy. (A), Comptroller.* Ryley, Wm., Record Clerk (?) (Wilts PS. No. 34).

Saltenstall, Sir Ric. (C). Salwey, Maj. Ric. (A, O). Say, Wm. (A, O, R). Scott, Thos. (A, R).* Scott, Wm. [12] (T).* Searle, Dan. (C). Sefton, Hy., Deputy Comptroller. Skinner, Aug. (O). Skippon, Maj.-Gen. Phil (A).* Smith, Hy. (A), Comptroller. Smith, Jas., Clerk to Obstruction Committee.

[1] Sealed 460 conveyances.
[2] Trustee until the Act of 31st December, 1652 ; sealed 14 conveyances.
[3] Sealed 152 conveyances.
[4] Resigned when Act of 31st December, 1652, was passed.
[5] Sealed 445 conveyances.
[6] Excused.
[7] Sealed 124 conveyances.
[8] Signs with Wm. Ayloffe, but the lands are Deans' and Chapters'.
[9] Qy, Clerk of the Pipe.
[10] Addressed to " his office in Aldersgate Street."
[11] Occurs in Parl. Surveys of Derby, Notts, and Wilts.
[12] Sealed 88 conveyances.

Sparrow, Jn.[1] (T).* Stapley, Col. (A). Steele, Wm. (T).[2] Stephens, Wm. (O). Stockall, Jas. (C). Sydenham, Ric. (C).
Taylor, Silvanus (T).[3] Taylor or Tayleur, Wm., Clerk. Thorpe, Serj. Rob. (A).* Toll, Mr. (A). Tracey, W. (Derby PS. No. 19, plan signed).[4] Trenchard, Jn. (A).* Trevor, Sir Jn. (A).
Valentine, Matt. (O). Vane, Sir Hy., senr. (A).* Vane, Sir Hy., junr. (A). Venn, Col. Jn. (A, R).
Wauton (Vaughton, ? Wharton). Col. Val. (A, R). Weaver, Wm. (A).* Webb, Col. Wm.,[4] Surveyor-General.* Wentworth, Sir Pet. (A). Wheatley, Jn., Deputy Registrar to Hy. Colbron. White, Jn. (C). Whittaker, Mr. (A). Wilson, Ald. Row. (A). Wollaston, Ald. Sir Jn., Treasurer.

V. List of Parliamentary Surveyors of Crown Lands

* Seals of Surveyors and Commissioners occur in some surveys after 1652. Numbers within brackets show the totals of surveys and certificates in which the names occur.

(1) *Surveyors in Single Counties.*
Ayloffe, Jos. (5).[5] Ayres (or Eyres), Sam. (27). Ayres, Thos. (5).* Barber, Jos. (34). Baynard, Thos. (42).[6] Beesley, Jn. (17). Bodley, Arth. (8). Boynton, Jno. (49). Clarke, Thos. (27). Cokayne, J. (14). Dober, Jn. (14). Duckett, C. (15). Erbery, Wm. (2). Ford, Thos. (1).[7] Frank, Ro. (25).* Glover, Rob. (5). Gunton, Nic. (49). Hall, Ezek. (2).[8] Hindley, Hugh (54). Inwood, Jn. (76). Ivory, Wm. (42). Johnson, Ric. (9).* Jones, Ayliffe (13). Kaynes, B. (15). Kinsey, J. (25).* Kirby, Rob. (13). Langrishe, Hercules (6). Manning, Wm. (6). Marr, J. (1). Roberts, Wm. (1). Robinson, Jas. (2).* Rolfe, Edm. (49). Royse, Thos. (21). Sargent, Geo. (25).* Sheppard, T. (12). Stokes, Ric. (1).[8] Strowd, Jn. (1).[8] Taylor, Sylvanus (1). Wale, Jn. (75). Walker, Jo. (14). Wharton, Hy. (30).—The counties concerned are Berks, Herts, Hunts, Kent, Lancs, Lincs, Mx., Northants, Notts, Staffs, Surr., Sx., Wilts, York.

(2) *Surveyors in Two Counties.*
Bocton, Rob. (7). Bridge, Thos. (31). Cholmly, Jn. (26). Cokayne, Thos. (5). Colberne, Thos. (28). Croke, Wm. (9). Crompton, Geo. (56). Dewell, Hy. (26).* Gamage, Jos. (10).* Gentleman, Geo. (63). Goodman, Geo. (62). Hook, Edw. (33). Hore, Edw. (63). Hutchinson, Ric. (33). Jackson, Thos. (15). Lobb, Jo. (27). Norcliffe, B. (6). Peglord, Wm. (11). Randall, Giles (8). Richardson, Abel (22). Richardson, Sam. (17). Thornton, Wm. (6). Uslett, Jn. (7). Webb, Jn. (76).—Counties : Ches, Corn., Cumb., Derby, Dev., Dur., Ex., Hants, Heref., Lanc., Norf., Northumb., Notts, Oxf., Staffs, Suff., Surr., Sx., Warw., Westm., Worc.

---

[1] Sealed 290 conveyances.
[2] Sealed 71 conveyances.
[3] Trustee, sealing 302 conveyances, until Act of 31st December, 1652, when he became Asst. Surv. General. The remaining 83 conveyances are recorded without Trustees' names in Camb. Univ. MS. Dd. 13, 20.
[4] See Surveyor's List, Sect. v.
[5] " Sir Jos. Ayloffe " in margin of Suff. No. 17 f. 3. Wm. Ayloffe's name occurs in Land Rev. Off., vol. 276 f. 154, as Surveyor of Deans' lands in Bedford.
[6] Surveys dated at Stoke Bruern in June and August, 1650.
[7] Qy, Thos. Fowle, as in L.R.O., vol. 281 f. 224.
[8] Surveyor of Navy Timber.

(3) *Surveyors in Three Counties.*
Careless, Wm. (11). Charlton, Sam. (25). Collin, Phil. (6). Ferrers, Thos. (9). Gray, Wm. (23). Halsey, Jn. (25). Hart, Jas. (11). Lloyd, Lodowick (5). Marsh, Thos. (33). Southcote, Geo. (22). Tracey, Wm. (22).[1] Counties : Berks, Cumb., Derby., Dur., Ex., Glouc., Herefs, Herts, Leic., Lincs, Norf., Notts, Oxf., Suff., Westm., Worc., Carnar., Denb., Flint.

(4) *Surveyors in Four Counties.*
Baldwin, Ralph (80). Blith, Walt. (27).[2] Carter, Hy. (41). Hill, Wm. (42). Jones, Benj. (18). Smith, Jn. (26). Stafford, Rob. E. (19). Tine, Sam. (23). Ward, Jn. (43).*—Counties : Beds, Bucks, Camb., Ches, Cumb., Derby, Dur., Glouc., Heref., Herts, Hunts, Mx., Norf., Northumb., Staffs, Warw., Westm., Worc.

(5) *Surveyors in Five Counties.*
Brudenell, Jn. (87). Fowle, Thos. (44).*—Counties : Beds, Bucks, Camb., Derby, Herts, Hunts, Mx., Norf., Warw.

(6) *Surveyors in Six Counties.*[3]
Andrews, Benj. (14). Blomfield, Thos. (14). Lloyd, Jn. (34). Speed, Dav. (15).—Counties : Wales (five counties) and Monmouth.

(7) *Surveyors in Seven Counties.*[3]
Makepeace, Hy. (48). Marriott, Jn. (38). Price, Peter (48).—Counties : Wales (five counties) and Monmouth.[3]

(8) *Surveyors in Eight Counties.*
Birchensha, Jn. (75).—Counties : Ches., Dur., Lanc., Mx.,ª Nott., Shrop., Westm., York.

(9) *Surveyor in Eleven Counties.*
Heywood, Ric. (124).—Counties : Bed., Buck., Derby., Ex., Herts, Linc., Mx., Norf., Northants, Rut., Sx.

(10) *Surveyors in Twelve Counties.*
Rowley, Alex. (103). Thorne, Jn. (107).—Counties : Beds, Berks, Camb., Ches, Derby., Dur., Ex., Herts, Hunts, Lancs, Leics, Lincs, Mx., Norf., Northants, Notts, Rut., Shrop., Suff., Westm., York.

(11) *Surveyors in Thirteen Counties.*
Dawgs, Wm. (152).* Fiske, Jn. (149).[4] Tanner, Thos. (136).— Counties : Beds, Berks, Camb., Corn., Dev., Dors., Ex., Glouc., Hants, Heref., Herts, Hunts, Linc., Mx., Norf., Northants, Rut., Som., Suff., Sx., Warw., Wilts, Worc., Wales (five counties).

(12) *Surveyor in Fourteen Counties.*
Taylor, Gabriel (147).[5]—Counties : Beds, Ches, Corn., Derby., Dev., Dur., Lanc., Leic., Mx., Northants, Notts, Shrop., Westm., York.

---

[1] Unusual signature in Notts. No. 10A., and he signs the Plan in Derby No. 19.
[2] The author of the *English Improver,* 1649-1653 ; he surveyed lands in Beds, Camb., Hunt., and Norfolk.
[3] All Welsh Counties collectively surveyed, but each surveyor worked in a group of six counties. The name of Speed is noteworthy.
[4] Including five Welsh counties.
[5] He signs with the year attached to the signature, just as Col. Wm. Webb does. In Lanc. PS. 23 a tenement near Castleton Moor is in " the occupation of Gabriel Taylor ".

(13) *Surveyors in Fifteen Counties.*
Baynes, Jerem. (183).[1] Cottman, Sam. (190).[2] Haddock, Jn. (195).[2]
Counties : Corn., Dev., Dors, Glouc., Hants, Heref., Lanc., Som., Sx.,
Wilts, Wales (six counties).

(14) *Surveyor in Eighteen Counties.*
Sadler, Ric. (203).—Counties : Berk., Buck., Ches, Derby., Herts,
Kent., Leic., Linc., Mx., Norf., Northants, Oxf., Staff., Suff., Surr., Sx.,
Warw., York.

(15) *Surveyor in Twenty-two Counties.*
Conigrave, Frank (180).—Counties : Bed., Berk., Buck., Ches, Derby.,
Dors, Dur., Kent., Lanc., Leic., Northants, Notts, Oxf., Shrop., Som.,
Staff., Surr., Sx., Warw., Westm., Wilts, York.

(16) *Surveyors in Twenty-four Counties.*[3]
Brasbridge, Row. (157) and Marr, Wm. (240)*.—Counties : Berk.,
Buck., Ches, Corn., Derby., Dev., Glouc., Hert., Kent, Lanc., Leic.,
Linc., Mx., Northants, Notts, Oxf., Shrop., Staff., Surr., Sx., Warw.,
Wilts, York and Carmarthen.

(17) *Surveyor in Twenty-five Counties.*[3]
Webb, Hugh (309)[4] : In the same counties as Brasbridge and Marr
(except Herts), but with Dorset and Somerset in addition.

(18) *Surveyor in Fifty-two Counties.*
Webb, Col. Wm., Surveyor-General (951), signs surveys in all English
counties except Rutland, and all Welsh counties, including Monmouth.

VI. REVISED REQUESTS AND DELAYED WARRANTS,[5] 1654–1658

Trustees' Journal : Augm. Off., Misc. Bks., vol. 314, ff. as shown.

Norfolk. f. 178. Dated 7 May 1656.
Whereas Erasmus Spilman of East Dereham (Norf), Gent. hath now
presented his desire to us to have a new particular made forth of
seven Inclosures of Land in Est Dereham aforesaid as the Survey
thereof is now amended, the Reversion whereof was formerly
purchased by him and conveyed by the Trustees.to him the said
Erasmus Spilman and one Ric. Browne (being only trusted by and
for the said Erasmus Spilman) hath since released all his Interest
to him the said Spilman and his heirs, And the said Spilman hath
further desired that we would give warrant to the Trustees for
Sale of the said Honors &c. for passing an additional conveyance
upon the said new Particular for Confirmation of the Premises to

---

[1] See Baynes Papers in Brit. Mus., and Baynes Surveys in Duchy of Cornwall Office.
Six of the counties are in Wales. Westm. PS. 4 has a note : " To acquainte Lt. Col. Baines
before this be ex'd."
[2] Including six Welsh counties.
[3] One Welsh county included.
[4] He adds a note to Kent PS. No. 53 (which should be in Surrey) : " The Moated
place was hereunto added."
[5] Particulars applied for and ordered after 1653 include the following :—1654 :
Middlesex, ff. 166*b*–167*b*. 1655 : Lancs, f. 176*b* ; Wilts., ff. 177, 177*b*. 1656 : Herts,
f. 179 ; Norf., f. 178. 1657 : Essex, f. 168*b*. ; Middlesex, f. 168 ; Sussex, f. 168*b*. 1658 :
Derby, f. 179*b* ; Wilts, f. 179*b*. ; York, f. 179*b*.

the said Erasmus Spilman only and his heirs. We the said Contractors having taken the premises into our serious consideration do hereby order that the Register do forthwith make out a new particular and prepare a warrant to the said Trustees thereupon for our signing according as is desired. And for so doing this shall be unto him a sufficient warrant. Signed W. T. &c.[1]

Middlesex. f. 168. Dated 15 April 1657.

Upon the desire of Jn. Rushworth and Edw. Green Esqrs. Trustees appointed by Col. Thorpe for carrying on and disposing of all the Contracts made by him with the Committee It is this day ordered that the Register do prepare a new warrant for the Contractors signing for passing the Conveyance of the Manor of Newnham, the Rents of Bowland, a parcel of ground called Scalamore and several tenements at Charing Crosse to Geo. Dewg (?) of Symonds Inn gent., Amos Stoddard of Moorefeilds Esq. Benj. Andrewes of Londo' Esq. and Rob. Cowley of London gent and their heires and that in order thereto the particular be remanded from the Trustees, and the former warrant signed by the Contractors to pass the Conveyance to the said Jn. Rushworth and Edw. Greene to be expunged. W. T. &c.

[1] The signature of William Tayleur, Clerk attending the Contractors.

APPENDIX IV
DOCUMENTS RELATING TO THE SURVEY AND SALE OF HALLIFORD MANOR, 1633-52

I. Survey of Halliford Manor, September, 1650

(*a*) Survey of Halliford Manor. Augm. Office, Parliamentary Surveys. Dated September, 1650. (Middlesex No. 29.) [1]

(*b*) There is a duplicate of this survey in the Land Revenue Office Series, Misc. Books, vol. 288, folios 15-27. It has no endorsement.

(*c*) The Augmentation Office copy [2] of this survey, which has been transcribed in full, is printed in the Transactions of the London and Middlesex Archæological Society, n.s., vol. iv, part v, pp. 404-423 with divisions added as follows : (i) The endorsement, folio 13 ; (ii) The title, folio 1 ; (iii) The Customary Rents, folios 1-2 ; (iv) The Manor House, folio 3 ; (v) The Fields, folios 3-7 ; (vi) The Arable lands, folios 3-4 ; (vii) The Mixed Inclosure of Arable and Meadow, folios 4-5 ; (viii) The Inclosure of Meadow, folio 6 ; (ix) The Inclosures of Pasture, folios 5-6 ; (x) The Inclosure of " Pasture or Leazow Ground ", folio 7 ; (xi) The Common Meadow, folio 6 ; (xii) The Aits in the Thames, folio 7 ; (xiii) The Waste, folio 7 ; (xiv) The Total Acreage, folio 7 ; (xv) The Timber on the Estate, folio 8 ; (xvi) The Leases, 1599-1650, folio 8 ; (xvii) The Covenants of the Lease, folio 9 ; (xviii) Abstract of the Survey Valuation, folio 10 ; (xix) Rental of the Manor, folios 11-12 ; (xx) List of Freeholders of Lower Halliford, folio 11 ; (xxi) List of Freeholders of Upper Halliford, folios 11-12 ; (xxii) The Total of the Manorial Rental, folio 12.

II. Particulars for Sale of Halliford Manor, 1650

(1) *Requests for Particulars and Orders to the Registrar.*
   Trustees' Journal : Augm. Off., Misc. Bks., vol. 314, ff. 87-8.
   (*a*) Fol. 87, Capt. Jn. Nelthorpe, 14th October, 1650.
   (*b*) Fol. 87*b*, Edw. Moore, 14th October, 1650.
   (*c*) Fol. 88, Wm. Westbrooke, " Immediate Tenant," 16th October, 1650.

(2) *Particulars for Sale of Halliford Manor supplied by the Registrar.*
   Roll L. 16. This roll (q.v.) consists of :—
   (*a*) mm. 1-5. The Particulars,[3] 16th October, 1650.

---

[1] Received 7th Oct. Transmitted 7th Oct. Returned 9th Oct., 1650.

[2] Calendar of Parl. Surveys, D.K.P.R., 8th Report, II, p. 56 ; P.R.O. List, 25, p. 211 ; Madge Cal., vol. vi under Middlesex, No. 29. Earlier references in Add. MS. 21327 f. 21 ; Add. MS. 21328 f. 42 (both No. 29) ; and 1787 list, sec. iii, col. i. " *Premises* : Halford als. Hallowford : the Manor of, with the rights, members and appurtenances, in the Parish of Sheppardton. *Date* : September, 1650, ff. 12." The survey made by Jn. Hynde, Deputy Surveyor to Sir Thos. Hatton, Surveyor-General, and dated at Denmark House, 9th November, 1633, will be found in Aug. Off. Surveys and Rentals, vol. 419, ff. 50-2.

[3] Entries occur in the Calendar of Particulars, Add. MS. 21327 f. 79*b* (P.R.O. copy, p. 60), with reference to Roll L. 16, Wm. Westbrook's purchase, 16th October, 1650.

(b) m. 6.   The Contract,[1] 21st October, 1650.

(c) m. 6.   Attestation of the Contractors, 6th November, 1650.

(d) m. 6.   Authorization of the Contractors,[2] 6th November, 1650.

(e) m. 6.   Certificate of Entry and Registration, 9th December, 1650.

(3) *The Roll of Particulars for Sale of Halliford Manor.*
(Roll L. 16.)

Note : This Roll, which is in five sections as shown below, consists of six membranes stitched end to end with the signature " Jo. Humfrey " repeatedly written across the joined sheets in the left margin. The handwriting of alternate membranes differs, the second and fourth being neater than the rest.

(a) *The Particulars* (mm. 1–5 of the Roll), *16th October, 1650.*
m. 1

Margins[3] (1) The Mannor of Halford als' Hallowford in the County of Midds' wth ye appurten'ncs is vallued in

(2) xviii^{li} vi^s viii^d.

Com' Midds'   Parcell of the possessions of Charles Stuart, & Henrietta Marie late King & Queene of England. ALL THAT the Mannor of Halford als' Hallowford wth all & singular the Rightes members & appurten'ncs thereof lyeing & being in the County of Midds'. And all Quit Rents, Rents of Assize, ffree Rents, Coppyhold & Customary Rents & other Rents whatsoever to the said Mannor in any wise belonging or apperteyning. AND ALL that Messuage Tenement of Mannor howse, Togeather wth the scite thereof commonly called or knowne by the name of Halford als' Hallowford wth their & every of their appurten'nces lyeing & being in the parrish of Shuperton in the said County of Midds' Wth all Howses Outhowses Ediffices Buildings Barnes Stables Orchards Gardens Yards Backsides & Curtilages therevnto belonging or apperteyning, conteyning in the wholl by estimac'on Tenn Acres be the same more or lesse. AND ALL that peece or parcell of arrable Land wth thappurten'ncs commonly called or knowne by the name of the fforty six Acres peece lyeing & being in the Northffeild bounded on the South East, & North parts thereof, wth a certayne Lane called Hoe Lane, & on the West

---

[1] Entries relating to " Immediate Tenants " will be found in Camb. Univ. MS., Dd. viii, 30 (5) f. 11 : Wm. Westbrook, 21 October, 1650 ; £823 18s. 6d, " full paid."
[2] The Contract of Wm. Westbrook, as authorized 6th November, 1650, is entered in Camb. Univ. MS. Dd. xiii, 20, p. 60, No. 245, and in the General Index of Crown Lands, Add. MS. 30208, f. 122, Nos. 14 and 15. These entries record rents of £18 6s. 8d. and £3 13s. 4d. ; Improvements, £118 17s. 11½d., and Purchase money, £823 18s. 6d. The Cambridge document also records the dates of the Contractor's Warrant, 6th November, the Treasurers' Certificate, 18th December, and the Trustees' Conveyance, 10th March, 1650–51, with the names of the five trustees who sealed the conveyance. The General Index wrongly records the year 1651 for the contract, and records Somerset instead of Middlesex. The names of Thos. Strowd and Ric. Hill are entered in Add. MS. 21327, f. 79b. and Camb. MS. Dd. viii, 30 (5) and Dd. xiii, 20.
[3] Divided in left and right margins.

wth the Land of (blank) Townley gent conteyning by estimac'on forty & six acres be the same more or lesse. AND ALL that peece or p'cell of arrable land wth thappurten'ncs commonly called or knowne by the name of the Hoe Close abutting vppon a peece of ground there called the Tenn Acres lyeing in Sunberry ffeild there on the North, vppon Hoebridge on the East & vppon Hoe Lane on the West, conteyning by estimac'on twenty & foure Acres be ye same more or lesse. AND ALL that peece or parcell of Land wth thappurten'ncs commonly called or knowne by the name of the Twenty Acres peece abutting vppon Sunberry Mead there on the East, & vppon the Lower End of a certayne p'cell of Land or Ground called Deane Close on the North, conteyning by estimac'on Twenty Acres more or lesse. AND ALL that other peece or p'cell of arrable land wth thappurten'ncs com'only called or knowne by the name of Part Eastfeild, abutting vppon the River of Thames there on the East, vppon a p'cell of land called Vpper Deane on the North, & vppon a certayne howse therevnto neare adioyning on the West conteyning by estimac'on Twenty Acres be the same more or lesse. AND ALL that peece or p'cell of Meadow ground wth thappurten'ncs commonly called or knowne by the name of Hoe Close lyeing & being at the lower end of the said ffoure & twenty acres peece & heretofore p'cell thereof abutting vppon a p'cell of land called the Tenn Acres lyeing in the said Sunberry feild on the North & vppon the said Hoebridge on the East conteyning by estimac'on Two Acres be the same more or lesse. AND ALL that Close of Pasture Ground wth thappurten'ncs commonly called or knowne by the name of the Vpper Deane Close abutting vppon a certayne howse there on the South West & vppon a p'cell of Land called Lower

m. 2   Deane on the North East[1] lyinge and beinge betweene Hoe Lane and the East field conteyning by estimac'on fower Acres more or lesse, AND ALL that Close of pasture With the appurtinannces Com'only called or knowne by the name of Lower Deane abuttinge East on Hoe Bridge and West on Vpper Deane Close lyinge between the highwaie and the Twentie Acres peece aforesaid conteyninge by estimac'on ffower Acres more or lesse, AND ALL that close of Pasture ground with the Appurtinannces Com'onlie called or knowne by the name of Creame Close abuttinge on Windmyll Hill on the East And a Close called Thames Close on the West, and the Lane there called by the name of Windmill Lane on the North conteyninge by estimac'on Eight Acres more or lesse. AND ALL that peece or parcell of Inclosed Meadowe ground Com'onlie called or knowne by the name of Thames Close adioyninge to the Thames on the West and South And a Close there called by the name of Creame Close on the North and East conteyninge by estimac'on Twentie Acres more or lesse, AND ALL that peece or parcell of Meadowe ground With the appurtinannces lyinge and beinge in the Com'on Meade called and knowne by the name of Stadbury Meade abutting South East and West on the Ryver Thames And North on a piece

---

[1] At the junction of the membranes, here stitched together, the signature " Jo : Humfrey " is written across as a protection against fraud.

of Ground there called the Westerne fferris conteyninge by estimac'on Twentie Acres more or lesse. AND ALL that Eight[1] lyinge and beinge in the Ryver Thames Com'onlie called or knowne by the name of Stodbury Eight abuttinge on the East vppon the Eight of Thomas Harte,[2] and on the North West and South encompassed about with the River Thames conteyninge by Estimac'on One Acre more or lesse, AND ALSOE one other Eight lyinge and beinge on the south East side of the abovesaid Eight in the Ryver of Thames incompassed about as abovesaid conteyninge by estimac'on Two Acres more or lesse, AND ALL that peece or parcell of pasture or Leazow[3] ground Com'only called or knowne by the name of Nowoodes abuttinge on the Ryver of Thames on the South, And on Eastfield on the North and a place there called Wind Mill field o.. the West conteyninge by estimac'on fflower Acres more or lesse. AND ALL that peece or parcell of Course ground com'only called or knowne by the name of Wind Mill ffield adioyninge to the Ryver of Thames on the South, and a place called Creame Close on the West and the aforesaid ground called Nowoodes Close, conteyninge by estimac'on Tenn Acres more[4] or lesse AND ALL waies passages liberties priviledges waters watercourses woods vnderwoods proffittes Comodityes advanntages and appu'ten'nces whatsoever to the said Messuage Lands and premisses belonging or in any wise apperteyning ALL wch said Messuage or Manno^r house and premisses are scituate lyeing and being in the parish of Shuperdton[5] in the County of Midd' and now or late were in the tenure or occupac'on of William Westbrooke his assignee or assignes p' ann'[6]

xviiili vis viiid

THE improved yearly value of the p^rmisses over & above the rent reserved p' ann'

Cxviiili xviis xid : ob.

MEMORANDUM it is certified by the Survey That the late Queene by Ind're dated the xxvith of January in the 13th yeare of the raigne of the late king Did demise and graunt vnto Robert Sharpe of Hallowford in the County of Midd' Gent ALL that the Scite and Manc'on house of the Manno^r of Hallowford wth the appurten'nces and all and singuler the afore menc'oned parcells of land before particularly menc'oned (Except all great Trees Woods Vnderwoods Mynes & Quarries of the p^remisses) ffor[7] the terme of eighteene yeares to commence from Michaelmas 1654 : being the determinac'on of a former lease thereof made & graunted by Queen Elizabeth to one George Christopher for Thirty Yeares at the yearely rent of xviiili vis viiid vizt.[8]   The freeholders of Hether Halford

m. 3

---

1 Eyot, a small island in the Thames.
2 See the Survey of 1633, which follows.
3 Altered from " Learow ".
4 Again, the signature of " Jo: Humfrey ".
5 A line here is marked with a cross (x) in both margins.
6 The amount is placed in the left margin of m. 1.
7 The whole line, " ffor the . . . graunted by ", has been altered and re-written.
8 The three amounts total ½d. less.

iiij^{li} xvi^s iiij^d ob. The Tenantes of Vpper Halford iiij^{li} xiiij^s vij^d and the ffarmor of the Scyte & lands viij^{li} xv^s & viij^d at Mich'as and o^r Lady Day be equall porc'ons the aforesaid Robert Sharpe died & left his wife Adm'stratrix whoe sould her interest to William Westbrooke her sonne whoe is now the Imeditate Tenant[1] whoe hath Twoe & twenty yeares to come at Mich'as last.

Memorandum it is Certified That there are vppon the p^{r}misses five hundred and odd Elme trees wch are valued to be worth Lviij^{li}, xi^s, but they are not brought to Accompt because there is not sufficient to maneteyne the Bootes.

The Leasee Coven'ntes wth the Queene well and sufficently to repaire support maineteyne and keepe in repaire the premisses & soe to leave them.

The Leassee is to be allowed all Competent houseboote hedgeboote ffireboote Ploughboote & Cartboote to be expended vppon the premisses & not elsewhere.

The Leassee is alsoe to have Timber groweing on the woods & lands of the premisses and not elsewhere for and towards the repairac'on of the houses and edifices by the appointm^t of the Queenes : Steward.

The Leassee Covenantes to collect & Deliver a true and perfect accompt of the rentes and proffittes of the said Manno^r at a certeyne Day by him limitted betweene the feast of the Translac'on of king Edward and All Saintes every yeare during the said terme.[2]

m. 4 The Lessee is to fynde and provide for the Steward of the said Manno^r And for others comeinge to the Courte And to survey the said Manno^r at ffower tymes of the yeare duringe the said Terme of Eighteene yeares Meate drincke sufficient lodginge, hay, Oates, and strawe for their horses for and duringe the space of Two Daies and Three Nightes every time and turne ∴ ∴

ALSO the Lessee his Executors and Assignes to gather and leavie all ffynes yssues and Amerciamentes Viewes of ffranck Pledge And all other Courtes there helde Yearelie at his and their owne Costes and Charges accordinge to the Estreates to him delyvered, And thereofe give an Accompt, and delyver a newe Rentall conteyninge all Rentes and Services therevnto belonginge every Three Yeares duringe the said terme ∴

AND in case the Rent happen to bee behinde or anie parte or parcell thereofe by the space of ffortie Daies after anie of the aforesaid Daies of payment The Lessees Lease to be vtterlie voide[3] ∴ ∴

m. 5

Margins[4] : (1) The Royalltyes of ye Mannor of Halford als' Hallow-
        ford in the County of Midds' are vallued in
        (2) iiij^{li} xiij^s iiij^d.

ALL COURTS BARRON COURTS LEETE Lawdayes & other Courts whatsoever, Services ffranchises Customes Custome Workes, fforfeytures

---

[1] Inserted above.
[2] The signature of "Jo: Humfrey" written across Mm. 3–4.
[3] The signature of "Jo: Humfrey" occurs for the last time.
[4] Divided as before, with the amount in the right margin.

Escheats Releifs Herriotts ffynes Postffynes ffynes vppon Discent or alienac'on Issues Amerciaments Perquisitts[1] & Proffitts of Courts & Lawdayes and every of them And all Wayfes Estrayes Deodands, Goods & Chattells of ffelons & ffugitives ffellons of themselves Condemned Persons Clerks Convicted Out Lawed persons & of Persons put in Exigent wth all Woods Underwoodes Tymber trees & other Trees, Rivers Streames Waters Watercourses, hawking hunting ffishing ffowling & all other Rights Royalltyes Jurisdictions Libertyes Priviledges Immunityes proffitts Commodityes advantages emoluments hereditaments & appurten'nces whatsoever to the Mannor of Halford als' Hallowford in the County of Midds' belonging or in any wise apperteyning. Vallued at the present yearly Rent or some of

iii[li] xiii[s] iiii[d].

MEMORANDUM that all & every the aforesaid premisses are in the present possession of the State.

THIS PARTICULER is grounded vppon a Survey taken by Ralph Baldwyn Esquire[1] & others in the Moneth of September last, And is made forth examined & signed by Order of the Contracto[rs] dated the sixteenth day of October, One thousand six hundred & ffifty.

John Wheatley, Dep[t]. Reg[r].[2]

(*b*) *The Contract.*[3] *Dated 21st October, 1650.*

m. 6 (Attached to the Roll of Particulars: L. 16.)

Contracted for y[e] 21 Octob[r] 1650.

The p[r]misses above mentioned are Contracted for and agreed to be sold vnto William Westbrooke.[4]

This particular at y[e] desire & by and w[th] the Consent of y[e] said Wm. Westbrooke is rated in ffee symple for Tho: Stroud of y[e] City of Westm'st[r] gent & Rich: Hill of Wimbleton County Surr': yeoman at Twenty yeeres purchase for ye p[r]sent yeerely value of y[e] Manno[r] of Halford als' Hallowford lying and being in y[e] parish of Shipardton in y[e] County of Midds' mentioned in y[e] p'ticular to be in y[e] p[r]sent possession of the State being Three pounds thirteene shillings and foure pence in possession and at ffifteene yeeres purchase for y[e] present yeerely rent of the Manno[r] house, w[th] the Scite and app'rts thereof and demeasnes & quitt rentes of the Manno[r] aforesaid all heretofore graunted to Robert Sharpe for eighteene yeeres to Commence at Mich'mas sixteene hundred ffifty foure after the expiration of A former graunt being Eighteene pounds six shillings & eight pence in possession and at foure

---

[1] Written over an erasure.

[2] Signatures no longer cross the junction of membranes; but a new style of writing marks the addition of the Contract (m. 6) to the Particulars.

[3] For the agreement, see *Contractors' Journals*, Augm. Off., Misc. Bks., vol. 174, ff. 27-8; also Camb. Univ. MS. Dd. viii, 30 (5), f. 11, Manor of Halliford: date of agreement, 21st October, 1650. Wm. Westbrook, £823 18s. 6d., "full paid."

[4] His farm at Halliford and tithes (£20) are referred to in the Church Surveys at Lambeth: Shepperton, 22nd Oct., 1650 (vol. xii, ff. 173-5). See Madge, *Rural Mx.*, pt. ii, p. 408.

yeeres purchase for ye improved yeerely value of the p^rmisses being one hundred & eighteene pounds seaventeene shillings eleaven pence halfe penny in reversion, According to wch rates and values ye purchase money payable and to be paid for the p^rmisses amounts vnto ye sum'e of eight hundred Twenty three pounds eighteene shillings and six pence WHEREOF The sum'e of Twenty pounds nyne shillings & threepence farthing is payable to ye Contractors Trustees and Trea'rs viz. Twenty pounds eleaven shillings and eleaven pence halfe penny to ye Contract^s & Trustees and six pounds seaventeene shillings three pence three farthings to ye Trea'rs for eight pence p' pound as is directed by act of P'liam^t entituled an act of P'liam^t for ye removeing of obstruc^s in ye sale of the Hon^rs Manno^rs and Lands of ye late King Queene and Prince to be paid by the Purchaser vpon signeing his Contract for ye vses therein expressed wch being deducted out of ye above mentioned sum'e there remaines further payable ye sum'e of seaven hundred nynety six pounds nyne shillings and two pence three farthings of which the one full Moity being Three hundred nynety eight pounds foure shillings seaven pence farthing halfe farthing is to be paid & defalked w^thin eight weekes now next ensueing in manner following That is to say ye one Moity thereof being one hundred ninety nyne pounds two shillings & three pence halfe penny three quarters of A farthing is to be paid in ready money & ye residue of ye said first moity is to be paid by severall debentures or bills Alsoe ye other moity of the said purchase money is to be paid and defalked after ye same manner w^thin six moneths next after ye first paym^t and defalkac'on afores^d for paym^t and satisfactioh of wch latter moity security is to be given to ye Trea'rs by A Lease for ffourescore & nyneteene yeeres of ye p^rmisses hereby Contracted for.

OUT of wch Contract neverthelesse all Messuages Cottages and Lands in possession or reversion parcell of the Manno^r aforesaid not p'ticularly mentioned in the aforesaid p'ticular (other then Customary Lands or Tenem^ts Commons and grounds vsed for Common waies and waste grounds) And alsoe all impropriac'ons parsonages appropriate Advowsons Rights of patronage or presentation vnto any p'sonage or viccaredge or Church donative or p^rsentative & all other things saued or excepted as not to be sold by any ye acts of P'liam^t are excepted.

John Wheatley, Dep^t. Reg^r.

(c) *Attestation of the Contractors. Dated 6th November 1650.*
m. 6 (Entered upon the Roll of Particulars : L. 16.)

IN ATTESTATION of the Contract and agreem^t above mentioned wee the Contractors whose names are subscribed have herevnto put o^r hands ye 6th of November 1650.

Ri: Sydenham
Robt ffenwicke
Ric: Saltonstall
Edw. Cressett
James Stocall

(d) Authorization of the Contractors. Dated 6th November 1650.[1]

m. 6   (Entered upon the Roll of Particulars : L. 16.)

THEISE are to desire and Authorize ye Trustees named and appointed in & by severall Acts of P'liam^t for ye sale of the Hono^rs Manno^rs and Lands heretofore belonging to ye late King Queene & Prince any fiue or more of them to draw vp and seale A Conveyance of the p^rmisses above mentioned hereby Contracted for vnto the said Tho: Stroud & Richard Hill[2] their heires and assignes according to ye Contract & agreem^t above mentioned To have and to hold vnto the said Thomas Stroud & Rich: Hill[2] their heires and Assignes for ever, as amply as ye said Trustees or any of them by the said Acts or any of them are enabled to Convey to ye same, discharged of all demands paym^ts Trusts Accomp^ts and incombrannces as amply as is enacted and p'vided by any the Acts of P'liam^t afores^d in y^t behalfe. DATED ye 6th day of NOVEMB^R : 1650.

> Ri: Sydenham
> Robt ffenwicke
> Edw. Cressett
> James Stocall

(e) Certificate of Entry and Registration. Dated 9th December 1650.

m. 6   (Entered upon the Roll of Particulars : L. 16.)

THEISE are to certifie ye said Trustees y^t this P'ticular wth all p'ceedings therevpon as it is thus finished is entered and Reg^d by me. DATED ye 9 decemb^r 1650.

> John Wheatley, Dep^t. Reg^r.

III. CERTIFICATE OF THE REGISTRAR OF CONTRACTS

E. 121, Bun. 3, No. 4. Dated 14th November, 1650.

> *Note.*—This document consists of four folios, the third and fourth of which are blank. It is marked No. 53 in the top right corner and has other markings in the centre and on the left at the foot.[3]

f. 1

Margin :   Contracted for ye 21th of October 1650.

A Certificate of ye Rate of A Particular of all the Manno^r of Halford als' Hallowford, The Manno^r house & Demeasnes, wth the Rights, Members and Appurt's, sold vnto William Westbrooke.

MANNO^R, Mannor house & Demeasnes of ye Manno^r of Halford. Com' Midd'.

THIS Particular at the desire and by & wth the consent of the said William Westbrooke is Rated in ffee Simple for Thomas Stroud of the Citie of Westminster Gent, & Richard Hill of Wimbleton in

---

[1] Camb. Univ. MS. Dd xiii, 20, p. 60, No. 245, Contractors' Warrant, 6th November, 1650. The General Index of Crown Lands, Add. MS. 30208, f. 122, Nos. 14–15, records the date 6th November, 1651, but misplaces the reference under Somerset instead of Middlesex, and by a similar error records Widcombe Manor, Somerset, under Northants.

[2] Both names written over an erasure.

[3] In the centre at the foot the Greek letter α always appears as an indication that this is the " first certificate ". On the left is a later pencil marking (B. d.).

the Countie of Surrey yeoman, at Twenty yeares Purchase for ye p^rsent yearely value of the Manno^r of Halford als' Hallowford lying & being in ye Parish of Shippardton in ye Countie of Midd', menconed in ye Particular to be in the p^rsent Poss'ion of the State, being Three Pounds thirteene shillings & foure pence in Possession, And at ffifteene yeares Purchase for ye pr'nt yearely Rent of the Manno^r house wth the Scite & app'rts thereof, and Demeasnes & Quit rents of the Manno^r aforesaid, All heretofore granted to Robert Sharpe for Eighteene yeares, to Com'ence at Mich'as Sixteene hundred fiftie foure after the expirac'on of a form^r Grant, being Eighteene pounds six shillings & eight pence in Possession And at foure yeares Purchase for ye Improved yearely value of the premisses, being One hundred & eighteene pounds, seventeene shillings Eleven pence halfe peny in Reverc'on, According to wch Rates & values.

The Purchase money payable and to be pay^d) for the premisses, Amounts vnto the sum'e | *li.   s.   d.* of Eight hundred Twentie three pounds | 823. 18.   6. Eighteene Shillings and six pence.)

Whereof,

the summe of Twentie seven pounds Nyne shillings & three pence farthing is payable to the Contractors Trustees & Trea'rs, vizt,

Twentie poundes Eleven shillings & Eleven pence halfe peny to the Contractors & Trustees and six poundes seventeene shillings three pence three farthings to the Trea'rs, for eight pence p' pound as is directed by Act of Parliament Entituled, An Act of Par'iament for ye Removeing of Obstrucc'ons in the Sale of the Hono^{rs}, Manno^{rs} & lands of the late King, Queene & Prince, to be payd by the

f. 1b   Purchaser vpon Signeing his Contract, for ye vses therein expressed, W^{ch} being deducted out of the above menc'oned sum'e, there remaynes further payable the summe of Seven hundred Nynetie Sixe pounds Nyne shillings & two pence three farthings, of wch the one full Moyetie being Three hundred Nynetie eight pounds foure shillings seven pence farthing halfe farthing is to be paid & defalked wth(in) eight weeks now next ensueing, in maner following, That is to say, The one Moyetie thereof, being One hundred Nynetie Nyne pounds two shillings & Three pence halfe peny three quarters of a farthing is to be payd in ready money And the Residue of the sayd fi(r)st Moyetie is to be payd by severall Debentures or Bills,[1] And the other Moyetie of the sayd Purchase money is to be payd & defalked after ye same maner, w^{thin} Sixe Moneths next after the first payment & defalkac'on aforesayd, ffor payment & satisfacc'on of wch said Latter Moyetie Security is to be given to the Trea'rs by A Lease for fourescore & Nyneteene yeares of the Praemisses hereby contracted for.

Out of wch Contract, neverthelesse, All Messuages, Cottages, & lands in Possession or Reversion, parcell of the Mannor aforesayd,

---

[1] The calculations are very exact: they include one-half, as well as three-quarters, of one farthing. See pages 399, 405.

not p'ticularly menc'oned in ye aforesayd Particular (other then Customary lands or Tenements, Commons, & grounds vsed for com'on Wayes & Wast grounds) And all Impropriac'ons, parsonages appropriate, Advowsons, Rights of P'ronage or p^rsentac'on vnto any Parsonage or Vicarage, or Church Donative or p^rsentative, And all other things saved or excepted as not to be sold by any the Acts of Parliament, are excepted.

John Wheatley, Dep^t. Reg^r.

ffor the Right worPP
ye Trea'rs ye 14° No^r
1650.

IV. CERTIFICATE OF THE REGISTRAR OF DEBENTURES [1]

E. 121. Bun. 3, No. 4. Dated 18th December, 1650.

Note : This paper[2] is inserted in the preceding document, and marked in continuation as folio 2.

(a) *The Certificate. Dated 18th December, 1650.*

f. 2 *Margin* : Int^r. Libr. C. ffoll: 54.

BY vertue of an Act of Parliament Entituled an Act of ye Commons in Parliament Assembled for Sale of the Honors, Mannors and Lands heretofore belonging to the late King, Queene and Prince ; I doe hereby Certifye vnto the Right Wor^ll. S^r. John Wollaston Knight, Thomas Andrews, John Dethick, and ffrancis Allen Aldermen of the Citty of London appointed Tre'rs by the said Act, that there is due by four seu'all Bills, or Debenters herewith sent all of them Signed, and Sealed by two of the Trustees in the said Act named, and by (three : inserted) seu'all Assignements concerning the same to Tho: Strond of the Citty of Westm^r. gent, and Richard Hill of Wimbleton in the County of Surrey yeoman from the seu'all persons hereafter nominated the seu'all sum'es hereafter specifyed (Vizt)

	l.	*s.*	*d.*
(1) Col: Prides Regiment of ffoote. Maio^r Edmund Rolph the assignee of Geo: Gregson as Captaine of a Company and Captaine and Maio^r to the Regim^t two bills each 187^l 5^s 6^d	374	11	00
(2) Col: Harrisons Regim^t: of Horse. Maio^r Edmund Rolph the assignee of Tho: Chapman as souldier and Corpor^ll in the Troope of Capt: Winthroop in the said Reg^t.	014	03	09
(3) Commissary Gen^ll. Iretons Regim^t of Horse. Maio^r Edmund Rolph the assignee of Nicholas Saunders souldier in Captaine Anthony Morgans Troope in the said Reg^t.	009	14	00
Totall	£398	08	09

f. 2b

AMOUNTING in all to the sum'e of Three hundred ninty eight pounds eight shillings and nine pence, whereof the sum'e of three hundred

---

[1] Camb. MS. Dd. xiii, 20, p. 60, No. 245. Treasurers' Certificate recorded 18th December, 1650.
[2] The size is slightly larger, and its presence may thus be detected in each bundle.

ninty eight pounds four shillings and seven pence $\frac{3}{8}$ is to be allowed by way of Defalcac'on for and in discharge of the whole proporc'on of the purchase mony payable in Debenters for the Manno^r of Halford als' Hallowford, the Mannor house and Demeasnes wth the rights Members and appurten'ces in the County of Midd'. Certifyed by the Deputy Reg^{tr} to be sold vnto Wm. Westbrooke the 21th. day of October 1650 and at the desire, and by and with the consent of the said W^m. Westbrooke is rated in fee Simple for the said Tho: Strond and Rich: Hill.

W^m. Potter Reg^{tr}. of Debent^{rs}.
Ex^r. p' J.H.[1]

December the 18th: 1650.
Int^r. p' Hen: Sefton, [2]
Deput' Comptroll^r.

(b) *Cancellation of the Debentures. Dated 15th September, 1652.*

Rec^d. of S^r. John Wollaston Knight and the rest of the Trea'rs w^{thin} named the seu'all bills or Debent^{rs} w^{thin} specified to bee Cancelled as by the said Act is directed and have Cancelled the same Accordingly I say R'c this 15th. of Sept. 1652.

W^m. Potter Rgt^r. of Debent^{rs}.

V. THE TRUSTEES' CONVEYANCE OF THE MANOR OF HALLIFORD[3]
Counterparts of Deeds of Sale : L. 16. Dated 10th March, 1650-1.

m. 1

THIS INDENTURE made the Tenth day of March in the year of our Lord God according to the Computacon of the Church of England One Thousand six hundred and ffifty   BETWEENE William Steele Esquire Recorder of the Citty of London Thomas Coke, William Bosvile John Sparrow, William Kenricke, Ralph Harrison William Scot, Silvanus Taylor, Thomas Hubbard, Cornelius Coke Esquires, John Hunt Gentleman and Sr Edwardd Barkham[4] Barronett being persons trusted by an act of this present Parliament intituled an Act of the Com'ons in Parliament assembled for sale of the Honours, Manno^{rs} and Lands heretofore belonging to the late King Queene and Prince for the conveying of such of the Lands Tenements and hereditaments of the said King Queene and Prince as by the said Act are vested and settled in the said Trustees and their heires in such sort as in the said act is menc'oned of the one part AND Thomas Stroud of the Citty of Westminster Gentleman and Richard Hill of Wimbleton in the County of Surrey yeoman of the other parte   WITNESSETH That the said William Steele, Thomas Coke, William Bosvile John Sparrowe, William Kenricke, Ralph Harrison

---

[1] Apparently John Humphreys, one of the Contractors, whose signature appears across the joined membranes, previously indicated.
[2] The signature is followed by the reference " C. 94 ", but the book has not been found.
[3] This document consists of two membranes and is folded. It contains a number of erasures and alterations. Cal. of Conveyances, Add. MS. 21327, f. 79b, and P.R.O. copy, p. 60. See Note under Particulars : Thos. Stroud and Ric. Hill. Conveyance : L. 16. Fuller details are given in Camb. Univ. MS. Dd. xiii, 20, p. 60, No. 245.
[4] The spelling of the name has been altered.

William Scott, Sylvanus Taylor Thomas Hubbard Cornelius Coke,
John Hunt, and S^r. Edward Barkeham   IN OBEDIENCE to the said
Act, and by vertue thereof and in Execuc'on of the power and trust
thereby Com'itted to them, And att the desire and by the Warrant
of Sr Richard Saltonstall Knight James Stocall, Robert ffenwicke
Richard Sydenham Esquires, and Edward Cressett Gentleman who
together with others named in the said Act or any ffive or more of
them are by the said Act authorized to treat Contract and agree
for the sale of the said Lands, Tenements and hereditaments in
such sort as in the said Act is menc'oned   AND in Considerac'on of
the sum'e of Eight hundred Twenty three Pounds Eighteene
shillings and sixpence of Lawfull monie of England whereof the
sum'e of Twenty and^1 seaven pounds Nine shillings and Three
pence one farthing is menc'oned in the Contract in this behalfe made
to have been already paid by the said Thomas Stroud and Richard
Hill and the residue thereof being seaven hundred ffoure score and
sixteene Pounds Nine shillings and Two pence three ffarthings
Sir John Wollaston Knight and John Dethicke Esquire Aldermen
of the said Cittie of London Two of the Treasur^{ers} in that behalfe
appointed by the said Act HAVE by writeing vnder their hands
beareing date the Eighteenth day of December last past now
p'duced by the said Thomas Stroud and Richard Hill and remaineing
with them certified to have been by them paid and satisfied in such
man'er as by the said writeing appears   HAVE graunted, aliened,
bargained and sold and by these p'ntes doe grant, alien, bargaine
and sell vnto the said Thomas Stroud and Richard Hill their Heires
and Assignes   ALL that the Mannour of Halford al's Hollowford
with all and singuler the rights members and apperten'nces thereof
lyeing and being in the County of Midd'   AND all Quitt rents, rents
of Assize, free Rents Coppiehold and Customary Rents and other
Rents whatsoever to the said Mannour in any wise belonging or
appertaineing   AND ALL that Messuage, Tenement or Manno^r house
together with the scyte thereof Com'only Called or knowne by the
name of Halford al's Hallowford with their and every of their
apperten'ncs lyeing and being in the parish of Shupperton in the
said County of Middlesex with all howses, Outhowses, Edifices,
buildings, barnes, stables, Orchards, Gardens, Yards Backsides,
and Curtilages therevnto belonging, or appertaineing Containeing
in the whole by Estimac'on tenne Acres bee the same more or lesse
AND ALL that peece or parcell of arrable Land with the apperten'ncs
com'only called or knowne by the name of the ffourty six acres
peece lyeing and being in the Northfeild bounded on the south
East and North partes thereof with a certaine Lane called Hoe Lane
and on the West with the land of Towney^2 Gentleman Containeing by Estimac'on ffourty and six acres be the same more or lesse
AND ALL that peece or parcell of arrable Land with the apperten'ncs
Com'only Called or knowne by the name of the Hoe Close abutting
vppon a peece of ground there Called the tenne acres lyeing in

---

^{1} Inserted above.
^{2} A space has been left for his Christian name.

Sunbuerie ffeild there on the North vppon Hoebridge on the East, and vpon Hoe-lane on the West Containeing by Estimac'on Twenty and ffoure acres bee the same more or lesse AND all that peece or parcell of Lands with the apperten'ncs com'only Called or knowne by the name of the Twenty Acres peece abutting vpon Sunburie Mead[1] there on the East, and vpon the lower end of a certaine parcell of Land or ground Called Deane Close on the North Containeing by Estimac'on Twenty acres more or lesse. AND ALL that other peece or parcell of arrable Land with th'apperten'ncs Com'only Called or knowne by the name of Pte East ffeild abutting vpon the river of Theames there on the East vppon a parcell of Land called vpper Deane on the North and vpon a certaine howse therevnto neere[2] adioyneing on the West Containeing by Estimac'on Twenty acres be the same more or lesse AND ALL that peece or parcell of Meadow ground with th'apperten'ncs com'only Called or knowne by the name of Hoe Close lyeing and being att the lower end of the said[3] ffoure and Twenty acres peece and heretofore p'cell thereof abutting vppon a parcell of Land Called the Tenne acres lyeing in the said Sunburie feild on the North and vpon the said Hoe Bridge on the East Containeing by Estimac'on Two acres bee the same more or lesse AND ALL that Close of Pasture ground with the apperten'ncs Com'only Called or knowne by the name of the Vpper Deane Close abuttinge vpon a certaine howse there vpon the South West and vpon a parcell of Land called lower Deane on the North East lyeing and being betweene Hoelane and the East ffeild Containeing by Estimac'on foure acres more or lesse AND ALL that Close of Pasture with th'apperten'ncs Com'only Called or knowne by the name of Lower Deane abutting East on Hoe bridge and West on vpper Deane Close lyeing betweene the high way and the Twenty acres peece aforesaid Containeing by Estimac'on foure acres more or lesse AND ALL that Close of pasture ground with the apperten'ncs Com'only Called or knowne by the name of Creame Close abutteing on Windmill Hill on the East and a Close Called Thames[4] Close on the West and the Lane there called by the name of Windmill Lane on the North Containeing by Estimac'on Eight acres more or lesse AND ALL that peece or p'cell of inclosed Meadow ground Com'only Called or knowne by the name of Thames[4] Close adioyning to the Theames on the West and South and a Close there Called by the name of Creame Close on the North and East Containeing by Estimac'on Twenty acres, more or lesse AND ALL that peece or parcell of Meadow ground with the apperten'ncs lyeing and being in the Com'on Mead Called and knowne by the name of Stadbury Mead abutting South, East and West on the River of Thames[4] and North vpon a peece of ground there Called the Westerne fferris

m. 2 Containeing by Estimac'on Twenty acres more or lesse AND ALL that Eyott[5] lyeing and being in the River of Theames Com'only

1 Written over an erasure.
2 Inserted above.
3 " In the said," written over an erasure.
4 Altered from " Theames " in one case, and " Themes " in another.
5 All these spellings are altered.

Called or knowne by the name of Stodbury Eyott[1] abutting on the
East vpon the Eyott[1] of Thomas Harte and on the North West
and South encompassed above with the River of Theames Containeing by Estimac'on one acre more or lesse AND ALLSOE one other
Eyott lyeing and being on the South East side of the abovesaid
Eyott in the said River of Theames encompassed about as abovesaid Containeing by Estimac'on two acres more or lesse AND ALL
that peece or parcell of Pasture or Leasowe ground Com'only
Called or knowne by the name of Nowoods[2] abutting on the River
of Theames on the South and on East ffeild on the North and a
place there Called Windmill ffeild on the West Containeing by
Estimac'on ffoure acres more or lesse AND ALL that peece or parcell
of Course ground Com'only Called or knowne by the name of
Windmill ffe ld adioyneing to the River of Theames on the South
and a place Called Creame Close on the West and the aforesaid
ground Called Nowoods Close Containeing by Estimac'on Tenne
acres more or lesse AND ALL waies Passages, Liberties, Priviledges
waters Watercourses, Woods Underwoods, proffitts Com'odities
Advantages and apperten'ncs whatsoever to the said Messuage
Lands and premisses belonging, or in anywise appertaineing ALL
which said messuage or Manno[r] howse and premisses are scituate
lyeing and being in the parish of Shuperdton in the County of
Middlesex, and now are or late were in the tenure or occupac'on
of William Westbrooke his Assignee or Assignes ALL which said
premisses are menc'oned in the perticuler thereof to have been by
Indenture beareing date the six and Twentieth day of January in
the Thirteenth veere of the Raigne of the late King Charles Except
all great trees wᴊods[3] vnderwoods mines and Quarries of the said
premisses granted by the late Queene vnto Robert Sharpe of
Hallowford in the said County of Middlesex Gentleman for the
tearme of eighteene[4] yeares from the ffeast of Saint Michaell th'
archangell which shall bee in the yeere of our Lord God One
Thousand six Hundred ffifty and foure vnder the yearely rent of
Eighteene Pounds six shillings and Eight pence payable att the
ffeast of Saint·Michaell the Archangell and the Anunciac'on[5] of the
blessed Virgin Mary by equall porc'ons and to bee vpon improvem[t]
of the yearely value of one Hundred and Eighteene Pounds seaventeene[5] shillings and Eleaven pence halfe pennie over and above the
said yearely rent reserved AND ALL Courts Baron, Courts Leets
Lawdaies and other Courts whatsoever services, ffranchises, Customes[5] Custome workes fforfeitures, Escheates Reliefes, Herriotts,
ffines, post ffines, ffines vpon discent or alienac'on issues, Amerciaments Perquisites and Proffitts of Courts and Lawdaies and every
of them, And all Waifes, Estrayes, Deodanes, Goods and Chattells
of ffelons and ffugitives, ffelons of themselves, Condemned persons,
Clerkes convicted Outlawed persons, and of persons put in Exigent
with all woods, vnderwoods Timber trees, and other trees, Rivers,

[1] See note 5, p. 360.
[2] An alteration: it is "Noward" in the 1633 survey, f. 50b.
[3] Inserted above. [4] Written over an erasure.
[5] All altered spellings.

Streames, waters, watercourses Hawkeing Hunting, ffishing, ffowleing and all other rights, royalties Jurisdicc'ons, Liberties, Priveledges Immunities Proffitts Commodities, Advantages Emoluments, Hereditaments, and apperten'ncs whatsoever to the Mano^r of Halford al's Hallowford in the said County of Middlesex belonging or in any wise appertaineing WHICH said premisses last menc'oned are in the said perticuler menc'oned to bee of the present yearely value of Three Pounds Thirteene shillings and ffoure pence AND the Reverc'on and Reverc'ons, Remainder and Remainders[1] of the said Mano^r Messuage or Mano^r howse, Lands and premisses and of every part and parcell thereof, WHICH said Man'o^r and premisses are menc'oned in the said perticuler to have beene late parcell of the possessions of Charles Stuart and Henrietta Maria late King and Queene of England EXCEPT and allwaies reserved out of this present bargaine, sale, and Conveyance All Messuages, Cottages and Lands in possession or Reverc'on parcell of the Mannour aforesaid hereinbefore not perticulerly menc'oned other then[2] Customary Lands or Tenements holden by Coppie of Courtrolle Commons and ground vsed for Common waies and wast grounds AND allsoe except all impropriac'ons parsonages appropriated, Advowsons, Rights of Patronage or Presentac'on[3] vnto any Parsonage or Viccarage, or Church Donative, or Presentative And all such other things as in and by the said Act are saved or Excepted or appointed to be saved or excepted or not to be sold, TO HAVE AND TO HOLD the said Mannour Messuage or Manno^r howse, Lands, Tenements and Hereditaments and all and singuler other the premisses hereby granted, aliened, bargained & sold or herein before menc'oned to bee hereby granted, aliened bargained or sold with their and every of their Rights, Members and apperten'ncs (Except before excepted) vnto the said Thomas Stroud and Richard Hill their heires and Assignes for ever TO THE onely vse and behoofe of the said Thomas Stroud and Richard Hill their heires and Assignes for ever AS AMPLYE as the said Trustees or any of them by the said Act are enabled to Convey the same DISCHARGED of all trusts Accompts, Demands, payments and Incumbrances As amplye as by the said Act it is enacted or provided in that behalfe. IN WITNESS whereof to the one part of this Indenture remaineing with the said Thomas Stroud and Richard Hill the said Trustees have put their hands and seales And to the other part thereof remaineing with the said Trustees the said Thomas Stroud and Richard Hill have putt their hands and Seales Dated the day and yeare first above written :

The marke of the said   Richard Hill.[4]
Thomas (T. S) Stroud.
Ex^d. Jo. Menheire.

m. 2d   *Endorsed :* Sealed and delivered in the presence of Michaell Lea, and William Andrewes, Secretary to the Trustees. 10 March, 1650. Also marked with the number 246.

---

[1] Further alterations.
[2] Read " *than* ".   [3] The plural form has been erased.
[4] Stroud's seal is missing ; but Hill's is intact, with the representation of a rose.

VI. Enrolment of the Conveyance

Close Roll No. 3556, mm. 23–25. (Old reference: 1650 Pars. 65, No. 16.)
Date: 21 March 1650.

m. 23

Margin: Steele Ar' et al'
et
Stroud.

THIS INDENTURE made the tenth day of March in the yeare of our Lord God one thousand six hundred and fifty BETWEENE William Steele Esquire Recorder of the Citty of London Thomas Coke William Bosevile John Sparrow William Kenrick Ralph Harrison William Scott William Taylor Thomas Hubbard Cornelius Coke Esquires, John Hunt gent and Sir Edward Barkham Baronett being p'sons trusted by an Act of this p'sent Parliam^t Intituled an Act of the Com'ons in Parliam^t assembled for sale of the Honors mannors and lands heretofore belonging to the late king Queene and Prince for the conveying of such of the landes ten'tes and hereditam^tes of the said late king Queene and Prince as by the said Act are vested and setled in the said Trustees and their heires in such sort as in the said Act is menc'oned of the one p'te and Thomas Stroud of the Citty of Westm' gent and Richard Hill of Wimbleton in the County of Surr' yeoman of the other p'te WITNESSETH that the said William Steele Thomas Coke William Bosevile John Sparrow William Kenricke Ralph Harrison William Scott William Taylor Thomas Hubbard Cornelius Coke John Hunt and Edward Barkham in obedience to the said Act & by vertue thereof and in execuc'on of the power and trust thereby com'itted to them And at the desire and by the Warrant of Sir Richard Saltonstall kn^t. James Stocall Robert ffenwicke Richard Sydenham Esquires and Edward Cressett gent Who together with others named in the said Act or any five or more of them are by the said Act authorized to treate contract and agree for the sale of the said landes ten'tes and hereditam'tes in such such (sic) sort as in the said Act is menc'oned . . . [1]

. . . .

m. 25 . . . TO HAVE AND TO HOLD the said Mannor messuage or mannor house landes ten'tes and hereditam'tes and all and singuler other the p'misses hereby graunted aliened bargained and sold or hereinbefore menc'oned to be graunted aliened bargained or sold with their and eu'y of their app'ten'nces except before excepted vnto the said Thomas Stroud and Richard Hill their heires and assignes for eu' to the only vse and behoofe of the said Thomas Stroud and Richard Hill their heires & assignes foreu' as amply as the said Trustees or any of them by the said Act are enabled to convey the same discharged of all trustes accomptes demaundes paym'tes and incumbrances as amply as by the said Act it is enacted or p'vided in that behalfe IN WITNES whereof to the one p'te of this Indenture remayning with the said Thomas Stroud and Richard Hill the said Trustees have put their handes and seales and to the other p'te

[1] As in the Conveyance, but with some variations in spelling. There is therefore no need to give this enrolment in full.

thereof remayning with the said Trustees the said Thomas Stroud
and Richard Hill have put their handes and seales dated the day
& yeare first above written

Margin :   Rich.[1]
Et memorand' q'd un-decimo die martij Anno sup'sir p'fat Silvanus
Taylor et Joh'es Hunt vener' coram Custod' lib'tat Angl' authoritate
Parliament in Canc' ei recogn' Indent' p'dictam ac om'ia et Singula
in eadem content' et sp'fic' in forma sup'd'ca.
Inr' vicesimo primo die Martij Anno p'dto.
Ex^{ur}.

VII. The Survey of Halliford Manor, taken November, 1633,

This document[2] is transcribed from Augmentation Office, Surveys
and Rentals, vol. 419, fos. 50–2.

f. 50   A Suruay taken by order from her Ma^{ts} Comissiono^{rs} bearing
date at Denmarke house Satterday the 9th of this instant November
1633 by John Hynde gent deputie Survayo^r to Sr Thomas Hatton
knight her Mat^s Survayo^r gen'all as followeth vizt :
Imprimis I finde by the Audito^{rs} p'ticuler That the Manno^r of
Hallowford wth the Scite and Lands here after menconed were
grannted by the late Abbot of Westm. to one Gabraell Pawlyn in
Revercon in the eight & Twentieth yeare of the late kinge Henry
the eight for forty six yeares to Com'enc from the yeare of our
Lord God 1548 in the second yeare of the late kinge Edward the
sixte & afterwards graunted in revercon to John Crane by L'rs
pattents from the said late kinge Edward the sixt dated the xijth
of March in the vth yeare of his Ma^{tes} Raigne for xxx^{ty} yeares
And afterwards in revercon by L'res pattentes From the late Queene
Elizabeth Dated the xijth of July in the xljth yeare of her Ma^{tes}
late Raigne for xxx^{ty} yeares at the yearely Rent of xviij^{li}. vj^s. viij^d.
And soe there is yet to come in the said Leases xxj yeares at Mich'as
nexte.
The Scite and Manno^r house of Hawford als. Hallowford wth
Garden Barnes Stable and yardes wth A little Douehouse lately
builte Contayning
OI Ac : O ro : OO 'pches.[3]
Sometymes in the tenure of Thomas Harris or his assignes nowe in
the tenure of Robt Sharpe as Vnder Tennant to Mr. Barker.
A peece of Arrable land lyeing in the East ffeild adioyning to the
house nowe p'te thereof inclosed at 10^s the Acre Contayning
30 Ac: o ro: oo pches.
Value 15^{li} oo^s oo^d

---

[1] Enrolments of later date end as follows :—" And be it remembered that the said
... (*Trustees*) came the ... day of ... in the year above-written before the Keeper of the
Libertie of England by authority of Parliament in Chancery and acknowledged the Indenture aforesaid and all and every thing therein contained and specified in form abovesaid. Inrolled the ... day of ... in the year aforesaid."
[2] The four columns on the right of each folio are headed : (1) Ac: ro: p'ches ; (2)
Value ; (3) Olde Rente ; (4) Clear Value.
[3] No separate value is recorded for this acre of ground.

Another peece of Arrable land lyeing in the same ffeild Eastmeade lyeing south thereof worth 10^s the Acre Contayning 20Ac: 0 ro: 00 pches.

Value 10^{ll} 00^s 00^d

Margin : All the Arrable land belonging to Hallowford Demeasnes is Tyth free.

Alsoe A close of Arrable land Called Howclose being Lam'as grounds Wannow (?)[1] lane lyeing West thereof at 10^s the Acre Contayning 30 Ac: 0 ro: 00 pches.

Value 15^{ll} 00^s 00^d

Alsoe A peece of Arrable land lyeing in a Com'on ffeild Called Steepestilepeece Wannow lane lying towards the North & East at 10^s the acre Con' 10 Ac: 0 ro: 00 pches.

Value 05^{ll} 00^s 00^d

Another peece in the same ffeild adioyning to the foresaid North A little Markeway lying West thereof worth 10^s the Acre Contayning 40 Ac: 00 ro: 00 pches.

Value 20^{ll} 00^s 00^d

f. 50b Alsoe A Close of pasture and Meadowe Called Thamesclose the river of Thames adioyning south worth 1^{ll} 6^s 8^d the Acre Contayning 18 Ac: 0 ro: 00 pches.

Value 24^{ll} 00^s 00^d

Alsoe A Close anciently pasture now Arrable land Called Creame close Thames Close lyeing south and West and the Windemill lane towardes the North and East at 13^s 4^d p'Acre Contayning 08 Ac: 0 ro: 00 pches.

Value 05^{ll} 06^s 08^d

Alsoe a Close of Meadowe Called Noward wherein there is one acre and halfe of freeland it lyes North of the Thames and much worne away by the Thames it lyes for 5 ac' worth 1^{ll} p' acre but Con' 04 Ac: 0 ro: 00 pches.

Value 04^{ll} 00^s 00^d

Alsoe A peece of Meadowe in Stadbury mead the Thames lyeing south and the fferry ditch East at 1^{ll} 6^s 8^d p' Acre Con' 12 Ac: 0 ro: 00 pches.

Value 16^{ll} 00^s 00^d

Another peece in the said Meadowe Ham ffarme lyeing south and East thereof at 1^{ll} 6^s 8^d p' Acre Contayning 08 Ac: 00 ro: 00 pches.

Value 10^{ll} 13^s 04^d

Alsoe Twoe eightes[2] nowe in the tenure of Clem'ent and Richard Coomes one of them lyeing in the Thames neare Stadbury hartes of Shepperton adioyning East con' 01 Ac: 0 ro: 00 pches.

Value 02^{ll} 00^s 00^d

The other adioyning to the Thames Close towards the North the river of Thames running south thereof at 2^{ll} p' acre Con' 02 Ac: 0 ro: 00 pches.

Value 04^{ll} 00^s 00^d

---

[1] Wannow or Wancow.
[2] Eyots, or small islands in the Thames.

Alsoe A peece of barren pasture lyeing in the East ffeild Called
Windmill hill at 2^s 6^d p' acre in the tennure of the said Robt Sharpe
Contayning 04 Ac: o ro: oo pches.

Value oo^{ll} 10^s o^d

The said Robt Sharpe as farmer to the Demeasnes hath A sheepe-
walke in the Comon of Sundbury for 3 seu^{r}all dayes in A weeke
from sunne riseing till the sunne be set & not lodging there all
night this is worth very little in regards the Common lyes about
twoe myles distance from Hallowford.

The ffreehold of Vpper Hallowford   04^{ll} 14s. 07d.
The ffreehold Refite of Nether Hallowford   04^{ll} 16s. 04½d.

Margin :   Olde Rente 08^{ll} 15s. 8½d.
       Cleare Value 122^{ll} 14s. 03½d.[1]

f. 51   A p'cell of Meadow Called by the name of Rochiells peece lyeing
in A Com'on[2] Meadowe Called Ham Meadowe in the p'ish of
Sheperton in the County of Middlesex adioyning to one of the
peeces of meadowe in Stadbury wch belongs to the Demeasnes of
Hallowford grannted by the Lord Gorge to Thomas Bartholmewe
of Sheperton by Indenture beareing date the 23th day of November
in the 10th yeare of the Raigne of kinge James for the Tearme of
one & twenty yeares wch expired at Mich'as last: now in the tenure
of the Widdowe Bartholmewe Contayning at 1^{ll} 6s. 8d. p' Acre.
10 Ac: o ro: oo pches.

Value 13^{ll} 06s. 08d.
Old Rente 04^{ll} oos. ood.
Cleare Value 09^{ll} 06s. 08d.

Richard Wigmore Esqre held by l'res Pattentes graunted the 28 day
of ffebruary in the 38 yeare of the Raigne of Queene Elizabeth for
31 yeares from the feaste of St. Michaell Tharke Angell wch was
in Anno 1602 expired Mich'aes last it Came by Assignement to
Christopher Smyth gent whoe last felled or Cut theise Coppices
in manner following vizt : Beachhill & Leatherlake lyeing in the
p'ish & Manno^r of Egham[3] in the County of Surry & in the fforrest
of Winsor wthin 3 myles of Winsor fallen or Cut six yeares since
and it will be ready to fell againe about 8 yeares hence at wch tyme
it wilbe worth 3^{ll} 10^s p' acre con' 31 Ac: o ro: oo pches wch is
about 5^s p' acre p' Ann' if it mightbe grubbed & turned to arrable
it would be worth 10^s the acre p' Ann'

Value 07^{ll} 15s. ood.
Olde Rente 01^{ll} 07s. ood.
Cleare Value 06^{ll} 08s. ood.

Margin : All the Coppices measured by the 18 foote pole or p'rch.

Margin : Timber & great Trees cut downe 2 yeares since worth 30^{ll} by
     the sayd Smyth.

Stonyryde & Rowick lyeing as aforesaid felled or Cut 2 yeares
since worth 3^{ll} 12s. (altered from £3 10s.) p' acre at 24 yeares groth

[1] The total of the 13 preceding items comes to £131 10s., which is also the amount of
those two items of " Old Rent " and " Clear Value ".
[2] Inserted above.
[3] " Manno^r ", inserted above.

wch is 3^s the Acre p' Ann' worth 6^s the Acre if it were grubbed 30^li worth of Timber & greate trees felled by Smyth 2 yeares since. 15 Ac: 0 ro: 00 pches.

Value 02^li 05s. 00d.
Olde Rente 00^li 14s. 00d.
Cleare Value 01^li 11s. 00d.

Margin : Timber & greate Trees Cut downe worth 20^li.

Ryde Grove al's Runnygroue lyeing as aforesaid neare Egham Towne the wood much stollen by the poore 5^s p' Acre if it were grubbed worth 1^li 5^s the Acre 6 yeares groth con' 08 Ac: 0 ro: 00 pches.

Value 02^li 00s. 00d.
Olde Rente 00^li 07s. 02d.
Cleare Value 01^li 12s. 10d.

APPENDIX V

VALUATION OF CROWN LANDS, 1649–1659

I. THE IMPROVED VALUES IN ENGLISH AND WELSH COUNTIES

Note.—These entries are arranged in order showing (1) the Clear Improved Value, over and above (2) the Yearly Rent of the premises, as recorded in the " General Index of Crown Lands ", Add. MS. 30208, which is based upon the Particulars and Parliamentary Surveys. The total value of the premises under the new valuation will be ascertained by adding together the amounts in the two columns. The Index contains some duplicate entries, also a number of items showing the Yearly Rents but without the Improved Values : these are excluded from this list. For Sale Values of classified premises see Section V below. The unmarked residue of premises named in this list consists of miscellaneous lands and tenements. A number of old forms of spellings of place-names are retained. The following signs are used :—

* Manors.	*Purchasers* [1] :—
† Honors.	
‡ Duchies.	(I) Immediate Tenants.
§ Farms.	(O) Original Creditors.
‖ Houses.	(A) Assigned Bills.

(a) IMPROVED VALUES IN ENGLAND

Premises.	Purchasers.	Clear Improved Values. £ s. d.	The Old Yearly Rents. £ s. d.
Bedford.			
Stepingley.	I	1 15 0	5 0
Biggleswade	—	3 4 5	11 12 0
*Milbrooke	I	4 10 4	1 17 4
Shefford	I	5 10 0	1 1 0
‖Ampthill	I	9 14 8	3 12 0
Bedford	O	15 1 0	1 1 4
*Stepingley.	I	18 7 10	12 2
Milbroke	I	23 0 0	7 0 0
Ampthill	O	24 5 0	63 11 0
*Camelton and Shefford . ..	O	45 0 0	26 4 9
Camelton	I	56 10 4	5 9 8
†Ampthill	O	92 0 0	14 0 0
Berkshire.			
‖Windsor	I	1 11 4	1 8 8
East Garston	—	4 14 4	7 15 8
Wallingford	A	6 9 0	2 1 0
Windsor	O	9 13 4	4 11 4
‖Wallingford	A	9 15 0	1 10 0
Shippon	A	19 13 4	5 6 8
,, ...	I	27 0 0	4 6 8
Windsor	O	28 0 0	—
‖ ,, ...	I	29 3 4	4 5 4
‡Berkshire and Oxford . . .	O	30 17 4½	4 10 0
Clewer	O	31 2 6	4 2 6
§Windsor	O	39 1 1	14 1 7
†Wallingford	A	52 18 0	7 2 0
§Windsor	O	59 19 3	14 15 5
Shippon	O	71 3 4	3 3 4

[1] Extracted from the three lists in the University Library at Cambridge. The Sale Values are recorded in a fourth list, which records the Conveyances. These values are arranged under the names of the manors and lands of each county in the Madge Collection, where they may be easily found by means of the indexes. See above, p. 294, EQ.

EAST DEREHAM MANOR, TOFT WOOD, NORFOLK : PLAN, 1649

[face p. 368

Premises.	Purchasers.	Clear Improved Values.			The Old Yearly Rents.		
		£	s.	d.	£	s.	d.
Berkshire (continued).							
§Windsor	A	107	13	5	13	15	4
Moate Park	O	194	10	0	80	0	0
Reading	—	218	0	0	14	4	0
§Clewer	I	237	6	8	23	0	0
*Cookham	O	250	12	4	84	5	6
Buckinghamshire.							
Chipping Wycombe . . .	O	10	0	0	40	0	0
Eton	I	35	10	11	4	5	0
Burnham	A	69	8	10½	6	0	0
*Eton	A	118	14	8	24	5	0½
Burnham	O	202	6	11	11	18	1
*Creslow	I	818	10	0	210	0	0
Cambridge.							
Cambridge, Norfolk, and Suffolk .	O	45	0	0	25	0	0
*Burwell	O	80	0	0	57	0	9½
,, ...	I	283	7	3	20	0	0
Cheshire.							
*Halton	O	2	16	2	3	4	10
,, ...	O	5	10	8	9	4	
Macclesfield	O	6	12	0	8	0	
Budworth	I	7	8	11	11	1	
Chester	O	8	14	0	23	7	6
*Ively	A	13	15	0½	5	18	6½
‖Northwich	A	16	0	0	3	8	0
*Macclesfield	O	21	0	0	6	13	4
Davenham	I	23	8	5	2	1	7
*Middlewich	O	46	8	4	21	1	0
Dracklowe and Rudlowe . .	O	143	2	6	13	2	10
*Handbridge	O	163	1	8	30	4	6
‡*Cornwall.*							
Lostwithiel	A	5	0	0	2	0	0
Crofthole	A	7	1	8	1	16	2½
*Carnanton	O	7	12	4	52	8	4
Highwood	O	15	2	7	4	13	0
*Trevogie	O	16	0	0	6	8	2
*Gridioe	O	16	8	0	21	2	2
*Anstell Prior	O	17	15	0	4	14	11
,, ...	O	17	15	0	4	0	8
*Northpill	O	18	17	0	1	8	9
Trematon Castle . . .	O	20	0	0	1	6	8
Helston and Taywornale . .	—	20	0	0	20	6	8
*Bucklawren	I	23	0	0	2	5	0
*Trelowya	A	26	6	9	1	6	8
,, ...	A	26	11	9	1	7	0
*Porthea Prior	O	29	0	0	30	6	11
†Launceston Castle . . .	O	30	10	4	38	2	2
*Treverbyn	O	32	9	0	1	10	1
*Calstock	I	53	11	0	8	10	0
*Tregamew	O	54	14	0	4	2	9
Landulph	I	60	4	0	3	1	10
*Trelowya	A	68	6	0	4	13	5
*Fentrigan	A	73	8	6	3	13	9
*Landreyne	A	77	5	7	73	14	0
Clymsland Prior . . .	I	78	16	4	2	13	0
*Rillaton and Stoke Clymsland .	O {	80	0	0	} 57	3	1
Kirribullock	O				8	0	0
*Stratton Sanctuary . . .	O	82	2	0	7	17	0
*Bucklawren	I	82	13	6	6	17	9½

Premises.	Purchasers.	Clear Improved Values.			The Old Yearly Rents.		
		£	s.	d.	£	s.	d.
Cornwall (continued).							
*Eastway	O	86	11	10	5	17	2
Cornwall (County)	A	88	7	0	4	4	7
Liskerrett	O	90	0	0	20	0	0
*Trevennen	O	107	18	0	9	14	9
Trewargie	O	110	14	6	2	12	0
*Bonalva	O	112	5	0	7	16	7
*Treverbyn Courtney	O	122	12	3	12	14	2
*Trelugan	A	126	6	6	6	12	4
*Helston	O	126	8	8	16	13	4
*Landulph	A	170	8	0	12	12	11
*Bucklawren Buck	A	174	7	6	22	8	6½
*Leighdurant	A	215	3	5	22	13	6
Restormell	I	228	13	6	28	7	0
*Carnedon Prior	O	243	19	0	44	19	1½
*Pengelley	O	260	13	4	26	16	4½
*Portlooe	O	296	7	0	20	1	4½
*Boyton	O	370	4	4	47	15	2
*West Anthony	O	447	17	8½	18	18	10½
*Tinten	O	567	9	8	87	11	8½
*Ryalton and Reterth	O	923	16	4¾	60	0	0
Cumberland.							
Cathwaite	O	11	18	4	4	8	4
Haskett	A	57	15	0	3	13	4
*Carlisle	O	58	0	0	2	0	0
„	O	61	7	9	50	0	0
Holme Cultram, etc.	O	89	0	6	42	10	3
Lezonby	O	142	15	4	18	13	4
†Penreth	O	172	13	0	14	1	0
Haskett	O	175	13	8	93	19	8
Derby.							
*Castleton	O	4	7	7	38	15	5
Appletree	O	5	3	6	25	13	0
*High Peak	O	36	2	0	23	11	4
*Wirksworth	O	37	5	0	46	15	9½
*Eckington	O	222	8	2	83	7	2
High Peak	—	230	3	4	11	6	8
Wirksworth	O	233	8	4	73	6	8
Devon.							
Dartmouth	I	6	6	8		—	
Plymouth	I	6	13	0	13	6	8
Pinkworthy	O	15	0	0		16	0
„	O	19	10	0	1	16	1½
*Bradford	O	21	4	0		18	0
†Oakhampton	O	21	19	6	6	13	4
||Pyeworthy	O	34	11	6		18	0
Sidmouth	A	45	6	8	4	13	4
Clawton	O	66	13	0	2	0	0
*W. Ashton	I	110	1	9	11	13	8
†Bradninch	O	1,673	8	8	203	5	10¼
Dorset.							
Fordington	I	18	5	8	2	3	4
Hamoone	O	21	13	4	1	6	8
‡Dorset, Hampshire, Somerset, and Wiltshire	O	22	4	0	10	18	8
Hermitage	O	22	17	4	35	7	5
||Eversholt	O	46	12	8		13	4
Dorchester	O	47	10	0	5	0	0
*Langton Herring	O	84	15	10	6	19	2
*Portland	O	154	18	0	10	0	0

Premises.	Purchasers.	Clear Improved Values. £ s. d.			The Old Yearly Rents. £ s. d.		
Dorset (continued).							
*Ryme Intrinsica	A	297	7	8	55	1	7
Gillingham	I	334	10	0	32	10	0
*Longbridge	O	386	2	4	9	17	8
*Fordington	O	813	0	6	76	6	7
Durham.							
*Softlye	O	8	0	0	20	0	0
*Copwell	A	50	9	1	8	0	0
Essex.							
Westham	I		10	8		16	0
Westham and Barking . .	I	5	4	0		14	0
Westham	I	13	0	0		18	0
,, ...	A	13	10	4		19	8
,, ...	I	13	10	8		19	8
,, ...	I	21	3	4	3	16	8
,, ...	A	21	16	0	6	11	4
,, ...	A	25	15	0	2	15	0
||Havering	I	37	9	6	7	6	0
Stapleford Abbots . .	I	51	10	0	8	10	0
*Westham	I	64	19	6	4	13	2
*Stapleford	A	71	8	5	39	4	4
Westham	O	73	14	10½	6	15	1½
Rumford	O	98	0	0	2	0	0
*Havering Park . . .	O	117	19	2	100	13	4
,, ...	O	117	19	2	104	18	10
,, ...	O	117	19	2	100	13	4
Gloucester.							
Dean Forest	A	58	14	2	22	5	0
Frethern Sauls . . .	—	69	3	0	3	17	0
Hampshire.							
Alice Holt Forest . . .	—		—		60	0	0
Buckolt	O	49	10	0	40	10	0
Hereford.							
||Marden	I	13	17	1	2	13	4
Ledbury Chase . . .	O	18	14	0	31	18	5
*Kingsland	—	18	14	0	36	11	4
*Marden	O	192	2	6	93	4	1½
Hertford.							
Waltham Cross . . .	I	2	15	8	1	13	4
||Hemelhempsted . . .	I	7	0	0	1	0	0
Cheshunt	O	7	16	0	8	6	8
*Theobalds	I	8	0	8	9	13	8
Waltham Cross . . .	I	8	8	8	14	12	8
Flamsted	I	10	6	9	10	0	0
§Waltham Cross . . .	I	15	19	6	7	7	4
,, ...	O	17	15	2	15	19	2
||Cheshunt	I	18	7	0	11	17	8
*Theobalds	I	20	7	2	50	8	0
*Beamonds Hall . . .	O	25	11	10	26	14	7
Waltham Cross . . .	O	32	17	2	20	0	0
Cheshunt	O	33	18	6	32	3	0
*Tring	I	40	4	8	3	5	4
Cheshunt and Waltham Cross .	I	41	18	4	45	16	0
*Hitchin	O	53	12	6	102	8	3
Berkhamsted . . .	I	479	13	6	45	0	6
Huntingdon.							
*Brampton[1] . . .	I : O	40	0	0	6	0	0

[1] Afterwards re-sold to Major Eyton. See p. 378, n.

Premises.	Purchasers.	Clear Improved Values.			The Old Yearly Rents.		
		£	s.	d.	£	s.	d.
Huntingdon (continued).							
*Pidley	O	99	16	8	7	6	8
*Brampton	I	145	18	10	18	10	2
„	O	345	8	5	124	4	10
Kent.							
Newington	—	1	6	5½		9	6½
‖E. Greenwich ...	O	2	10	0	2	10	0
*Eltham	O	5	9	2	953	6	4½
Maidstone	I	9	10	0		3	4
Minster (Isle of Sheppey) ..	—	15	13	5	3	0	10
‖Kingsland	I	16	14	0	5	0	0
Milton	A	16	15	0	16	15	0
‖E. Greenwich ...	O	22	0	0	22	0	0
Sayes Court	I	24	0	0		—	
E. Greenwich	O	25	6	8	5	8	4
Gillingham	O	56	7	4	6	16	2
Dover	A	126	16	6	13	0	6
Gillingham	O	132	6	2	10	13	4
§E. Greenwich ...	O	159	13	0	109	10	0
§Neats Court	I	309	2	10½	70	0	1½
*Old Court	A	382	2	0	6	13	4
Lancashire.							
†Clitherow	O		7	0	10	0	0
Burnley and Colne ...	—	1	13	4		6	8
Colne	—	2	12	6	3	18	5
Clitherow	—	4	10	0		2	4
Hecliffe	O	10	16	2	2	13	4
*Furness	O	12	18	4	445	4	11
*Muchland	O	133	13	2	186	19	5½
Myerscough	O	186	4	9	37	10	0
Lancashire (County) ..	O	230	0	0	4	2	4
§Bowland	O	408	16	11	82	13	6
Leicester.							
†Leicester	—	4	15	8		4	4
Garthorpe	A	8	0	0	10	0	0
Leicester	O	31	1	4	37	3	7½
Lincoln.							
Whapload and Moulton ..	A	1	2	8½		19	0
Smitherby	O	1	16	3	3	0	0
*Croyland	I	2	0	0	8	13	4
*Edlington	O	2	4	0	1	16	0
*Wainfleet	O	2	9	4	12	6	10
*Croyland	I	3	0	0	10	0	0
„	A	3	0	0	24	13	4
Pinchbeck	I	4	8	0	1	2	0
*Whapload	O	5	6	2		3	10
Bromby	I	5	18	6½	1	0	0
Cleythorpe	O	8	15	0		13	4
*Barton upon Humber ..	O	10	7	10	80	12	4
*Spalding	I	11	13	4	1	0	0
Pinchbeck	I	11	19	0	1	2	0
§Yadlethorpe	O	12	13	1½	1	4	8
West Fenn	—	15	0	0	345	0	0
Lands Forfeited (County) ..	O	15	13	9½	3	8	4
Spalding	—	15	19	0	83	6	3
„	—	16	4	0	80	9	9
Barton	O	18	0	0	22	0	0
Sutton St. James's ...	O	18	9	5	3	7	9
Grantham	I	25	8	10	8	17	9

Premises.	Purchasers.	Clear Improved Values. £ s. d.	The Old Yearly Rents. £ s. d.
Lincoln (continued).			
Epworth and Westwood	I	37 15 0	11 0 0
*Spalding	O	41 10 4	39 5 8
Grantham .	A	42 17 4	14 12 8
*Holbeach .	I	44 6 2	1 13 10
„	O	47 2 10½	36 2 11¼
Bromby and Redburn.	O	49 12 1½	3 19 10½
*Loughton	O	52 15 8½	44 6 11¼
Spalding and Pinchbeck	I	58 13 5	6 6 3
Croft	A	61 17 6	66 16 6
*Gouxhill .	O	65 14 8	5 12 10
*Barrow	O	66 5 2½	70 3 3
*Wilberton	O	69 12 10	68 10 5½
*Whapload Abbots	O	75 7 4	81 15 2½
Spalding, etc. .	I	77 2 9½	30 19 7
*Spalding .	I	99 11 6	7 16 4
„	—	104 17 0½	17 15 9
*Hogthorpe	O	112 19 6½	124 5 2½
Kirton in Lindsey	O	119 9 10½	19 16 8
Moulton .	I	127 12 11	2 13 4
§Pinchbeck .	I	159 6 7	15 19 11
Moulton	I	177 12 0	1 16 0
Bollingbrook	I	180 1 5	29 13 9
*Spalding	O	201 19 0	70 3 2
*Epworth .	O	207 13 9	93 2 0
*Inglehy .	O	227 0 9	99 0 0
*Moulton Dominorum .	A	259 9 1½	14 3 2
„ „ .	O	282 10 4½	59 18 3½
*East and West Deeping	I	352 6 4	94 1 3½
§Spalding, etc. .	I	514 0 9	113 15 2
*Spalding	O	584 3 6½	425 2 11¼
Middlesex.			
Tower Dock	I	2 6	—
†Hampton	O	5 19 0	25 8 7
St. James's	A	8 12 6	7 6
St. Michael's, London	A	9 15 0	5 0
Westminster	A	14 3 4	16 8
|| „ .	A	20 0 0	1 6 0
St. Mary le Strand	I	23 3 4	1 16 8
||St. James's	A	23 17 10	1 0 0
||Strand .	I	29 1 8	18 4
||Westminster	O	30 0 0	3 0 0
||Strand .	O	33 6 8	13 4
|| „ .	I	39 6 8	13 4
||Somerset House	I	42 0 0	
Westminster	A	44 10 0	5 10 0
||Strand .	I	54 0 0	1 0 0
||Westminster	I	54 1 8	5 18 4
Islington .	I	55 1 8	4 11 8
||Westminster	O	57 0 0	3 0 0
||Charing Cross	A	58 0 0	2 0 0
St. James's	I	70 0 0	184 5 7
St. Giles's	O	80 0 10	3 0 0
Westminster	O	85 0 0	5 0 0
Twickenham	I	94 17 0	8 13 0
Great St. John's Wood	I	102 9 2	20 6 8
Tower	I	113 0 0	—
„	O	118 0 0	—
*Halliford .	I	118 17 11½	18 6 8
Tottenham Court, etc.	O	120 11 2	24 5 2

Premises.	Purchasers.	Clear Improved Values. £ s. d.	The Old Yearly Rents. £ s. d.
Middlesex (continued).			
*Twickenham	I	138 9 0	3 0 0
Charing Cross	O	150 12 4	2 7 8
„	I	157 0 0	4 0 0
Tower Hill	O	201 16 4	37 13 8
St. James's	A	224 4 10	3 18 6
*Tottenham Court . . .	A	330 18 11	46 0 0
Somerset House . . .	O	723 15 0	62 15 4
St. James's	I	787 4 9	12 16 10
Tower Wharf	O	914 3 0	37 13 8
St. Giles's	O	1,610 8 4	5 6 8
Tower Liberty	—	1,778 3 4	60 0 0
Norfolk.			
Ellingham.	A	6 4 6	15 6
†Bonon Hagnett and Peveril .	O	8 1 1½	2 0 0
*Stockton Socon	I	9 2 0½	51 15 0
East Dereham	I	19 12 0	8 0
†Clare : in Norfolk and Suffolk .	O	29 10 3	35 9 11½
*East Dereham, etc. . . .	O	69 6 1	88 11 1
Methwold	O	70 0 0	30 0 0
West Walton, etc. . . .	O	163 11 7	22 5 5
*Methwold	I	342 10 0	52 0 0
Terrington	O	919 3 1	118 3 11
Northampton.			
Higham Ferrers . . .	O	3 9 0	11 0
Byfield	O	3 18 4	6 8
Alderton	A	4 8 4	6 8
East Cotten End . . .	I	5 5 4	13 0
Paulerspury	I	6 0 0	8 8
Higham Ferrers . . .	O	6 8 6	18 0
Ashton	I	7 5 2	11 6
Higham Ferrers . . .	O	7 18 6	12 0
§Alderton	A	8 8 2	2 5 4
St. James's, Northampton .	O	11 8 0	1 7 0
Greens Norton . . .	I	11 18 0	14 0
‖Grafton	I	12 6 8	1 6 8
Roade	—	12 9 4	1 17 6
Potterspury	I	12 15 4	1 14 8
„	I	13 3 4	1 1 4
Grafton Regis . . .	I	16 0 8	1 10 4
Paulerspury	A	17 1 4	1 13 6
Chacombe. . . .	—	17 1 4	1 13 6
§Alderton	A	17 3 0	1 0 0
Aldrington	O	18 8 3	1 4 1
Greens Norton . . .	I	19 6 8	1 13 4
Grafton	I	21 10 0	1 11 0
*Kings Cliffe	O	22 13 4	62 0 0
Cold Higham and Darlescott .	—	24 9 2	2 6 2
*Blisworth	I	25 1 10	3 8 0
Chelveston cum Chaldecott .	I	26 0 2½	2 19 9½
Higham Ferrers . . .	O	26 3 5	3 16 7
*Blisworth	O	29 5 8	4 8 4
Grafton	A	29 7 4	2 8 8
Potterspury	A	30 2 0½	3 1 5½
Ashton	I	31 14 0	2 3 0
§Roade	A	31 15 1	1 7 6
Stoke Bruerne . . .	A	36 12 0	2 14 8
Chelveston cum Caldecott .	I	38 19 8½	4 7 5
Blisworth	I	40 8 4	9 6 8
Higham Ferrers . . .	I	41 2 4½	4 18 1½

Premises.	Purchasers.	Clear Improved Values.			The Old Yearly Rents.		
		£	s.	d.	£	s.	d.
Northampton (continued).							
Stoke Bruerne	I	41	19	6	2	14	6
Paulerspury	A	42	12	2	3	9	2
Potterspury	O	48	1	4	4	2	6
Chelveston cum Caldecott	A	51	15	4	48	2	0
Pattishall	I	53	9	10½	3	16	7
Greens Norton	A	54	10	0	5	14	7
Higham Ferrers	I	55	18	11	5	13	7
Stoke Bruerne	O	56	1	2	10	12	0
Potterspury	I	56	1	11½	4	6	0½
Grafton	A	58	17	7	13	13	9
„	A	74	16	9	13	9	10
Alderton	A	92	9	4	6	0	2
Blisworth	I	96	11	10	20	2	8
§Hartwell	I	96	19	10	12	18	5
Aldrington	O	106	16	0	16	6	11
Cold Higham	A	108	15	3	8	4	1
*Brigstock	I	115	4	6	66	13	4
§Paulerspury	A	134	15	2	75	3	4
Blisworth	I	148	13	8	15	7	6
*Ashton	I	163	17	8	12	7	0
§Higham Ferrers	I	183	19	11	38	14	2
Greens Norton	A	202	15	1	28	5	2
Ashton, etc.	I	206	13	6	18	5	5
Aldrington, etc.	I	266	9	0	19	13	9
Blisworth	I	304	14	5	28	2	5
Greens Norton	A	332	6	5½	38	5	3
§Stoke Bruerne	I	334	9	2	26	12	7
Higham Park	O	361	4	2	2	13	4
*Grafton	A	533	6	9	42	12	11
‖Holdenby	O	683	17	2	552	18	0
Greens Norton	A	749	7	8	166	18	0
Northumberland.							
Aylmouth	O	—			2	0	0
Newcastle-upon-Tyne	I	114	10	6	2	0	0
Nottingham.							
Barneby	O	8	0	0	1	0	0
*Lound	I	21	5	0	6	0	0
*Newark	O	413	10	0	103	18	4
Oxford.							
†Woodstock	O	—			754	10	7
*Ewelme	O	41	16	1	13	0	0
Rutland.							
No Entries.							
Shropshire.							
Shrewsbury	—	—			8	1	8
Ludlow	—	20	12	8	6	13	4
Somerset.							
Chantry Lands (County)	—	48	0	0	6	6	4
§Chewton	I	62	10	0	4	0	0
Milverton	—	67	12	8	19	3	5
§Midsomer Norton	I	117	3	9	9	15	1
Curry Mallet	I	121	3	4	6	13	4
§Inglescombe	O	130	8	8	12	0	0
*Widcombe	O	187	19	1	7	18	11½
*Inglescombe	O	201	19	6	21	5	0
*Westharptree	I	207	17	4	6	13	4
*Stratton upon Fosse	I	247	16	10½	32	6	2

Premises.	Purchasers.	Clear Improved Values. £ s. d.			The Old Yearly Rents. £ s. d.		
Somerset (coutinued).							
*Laverton	I	271	3	10	27	10	2
*Midsomer Norton . .	O	302	3	8	36	4	8
*Farington Gurney . . .	A	365	12	6	20	15	2
*Milton Falconbridge . . .	O	407	16	8	23	7	3
Exmore Chase	O	446	10	1	46	13	4
*Curry Mallet	I	557	5	2½	39	2	0½
*Stoke under Hampden . .	O	783	6	6	59	13	0½
*Shipton Mallet	O	871	14	0	40	13	9
Stafford.							
Stafford and Warwick (Counties).	O	32	0	9	27	2	0
Tattenhill	A	36	18	4	114	11	8
Hanbury	I	55	15	4	4	6	8
Tutbury	O	70	14	7	61	3	6
Suffolk.							
Goswold	O	13	6	8	1	13	4
Bosmere, etc.	—	25	0	0	17	16	1
Layston	O	48	0	0	20	0	0
§Shimpling	O	85	6	0	80	0	0
*St. Edmund's Bury . . .	O	99	9	4	66	1	3
*Eye Hall	O	165	2	1½	42	14	1½
Surrey.							
Chertsey and Egham . . .	I	7	2		7	2	
Egham	I	19	0		19	0	
Long Ditton	—	1	0	0	1	0	0
Chertsey	I	2	4	0	1	16	0
Egham	O	3	7	0	2	6	
,, ...	I	3	9	6	4	6	
Byfleet and Weybridge . .	I	3	19	0	1	0	
Egham	O	4	16	0	4	4	0
St. Anne's Hill	I	6	0	0	6	8	
‖Chertsey	I	7	16	8	3	4	
*East Moulsey	O	8	10	10	2	19	2
Chertsey	I	8	13	8	5	6	4
Walton upon Thames . .	A	9	6	8	13	6	
Egham	I	9	18	2	6	10	
Byfleet and Weybridge . .	I	11	0	0	1	0	0
Chertsey	I	12	7	0	1	1	8
*Richmond	O	15	6	8	167	13	4
‖Chertsey	A	16	14	0	1	4	4
‖Egham	I	18	2	11	12	1	
,, ...	O	19	13	0	1	7	0
‖Weybridge	O	23	13	4	1	6	8
Egham	O	24	1	4	13	8	
,, ...	O	24	1	11½	14	4½	
‖Chertsey	I	25	2	6	2	17	6
Egham	I	26	11	6	1	2	9
,, ...	O	28	14	5	3	5	2
Walton	I	30	7	2	2	19	6
Chertsey	I	30	17	6	1	13	6
§ ,, ...	A	32	13	8	12	13	4
§Esher	O	33	5	11	3	13	4
§Egham	I	33	19	9	2	4	0
§Walton upon Thames . .	O	35	1	9	3	19	5
‖Chertsey	I	35	17	8	4	7	4
‖ ,, ...	I	36	8	4	3	6	8
*Egham	O	37	16	4	2	8	4
Chertsey and Egham . . .	I	38	3	6	9	7	0
Chertsey	I	40	13	9	3	2	9
§Panshill	I	41	8	2	6	16	4

Premises.	Purchasers.	Clear Improved Values. £ s. d.			The Old Yearly Rents. £ s. d.		
Surrey (continued).							
Weybridge	I	42	5	4½	2	11	5½
§Chertsey	I	47	8	0	2	19	4
§ ,,	I	47	13	4	2	6	8
Weybridge	O	47	16	10	5	3	2
Walton, etc.	A	58	16	9	3	13	0¼
*Petersham	I	82	15	2	8	9	0
‖Weybridge	O	83	4	1	10	10	3
*Hardwich	I	84	8	0	14	19	4
*Walton Leigh	A	98	0	1	19	10	8½
*Byfleet and Weybridge	O	102	7	0½	15	3	8
Egham	A	106	17	2½	4	9	1
Southwark	I	109	7	8	6	0	0
*Ham	I	117	3	1	8	0	0
§Weybridge	I	128	0	0	10	0	0
*East Moulsey	I	147	19	9½	15	3	4
Richmond	I	205	18	4	3	6	8
Egham	O	252	16	8	42	11	8
Kennington	I	281	16	9	6	10	9
*Chertsey Beaumonds	O	286	1	4	54	6	8
Sussex.							
Horsham	I	5	0	0	—		
East Grinstead	A	5	10	0	2	0	0
,, ,,	I	6	0	0	2	0	0
,, ,,	I	7	0	0	2	0	0
Ridgwick	A	8	7	8		17	4
Horsham	I	12	0	0	—		
,,	I	15	6	8	6	13	4
Bexhill and Helsham	—	17	6	8	11	6	8
§Colstable	I	35	10	0	10	10	0
§Bexhill and Westham	—	37	15	0	132	0	2
*Pevensey	O	51	3	9	86	12	6¼
§Bosgrave, etc.	A	54	6	8	20	8	4
Chesworth	I	80	7	10	54	12	2
Westham	I	113	11	8	33	8	4
Helsham	I	118	0	0	18	17	4
Sedgwick Park	I	234	5	0	55	5	0
Warwickshire.							
*Shittington	O	12	19	8	16	0	0
*Hampden in Arden	I	20	1	11	40	4	8
Anstrey	—	31	7	4	18	0	0
§Rowington	O	54	2	8	6	7	4
Kenilworth	O	108	4	1	27	3	4
*Hampton	O	173	9	5½	68	12	8½
Alvescott	O	203	4	0	80	3	8
*Rudfin	O	294	14	4	100	5	0
†Kenilworth	O	943	8	3	100	0	0
Westmorland.							
*Kendall	O	—			176	13	1½
,,	O	—			218	7	0½
,,	O	16	17	6	44	13	4
Wiltshire.							
*Meare	O	13	17	6½	34	6	11
,,	O	31	5	0	4	15	0
,,	O	242	17	4	35	10	0
,,	O	262	0	0	10	0	0
§Cricklade	O	309	5	2	52	11	4
Braddon Forest	O	401	12	0	78	18	0
Creekland Forest	O	449	16	4	78	17	0

Premises.	Purchasers.	Clear Improved Values. £ s. d.	The Old Yearly Rents. £ s. d.
Worcester.			
*Bewdley	I	14 15 1½	7 3 0¼
„	O	61 0 0	3 2 0
‖Ribbesford	O	131 12 8	7 7 4
Bewdley	O	145 13 4½	34 0 0
Yorkshire.			
Kellington	A	6 10 0	1 3 4
Cowick cum Snaithe . . .	O	7 7 4	1 5 0
Barton	A	11 2 0	1 10 0
*Thwing	O	13 5 8	70 11 0
Kippax Ings.	I	18 10 0	6 16 0
Melsa	O	38 18 0	46 12 0
„	O	50 11 4	13 10 8
Snaithe	O	61 6 8	9 14 4
Barnsley cum Dodsworth . .	O	66 1 2	4 6 8
§Rosedale	O	67 2 6	17 12 0
Pickering	O	72 16 6	5 0 0
*Bristoll	O	80 11 5	20 5 6
*Hornsea	O	92 2 9	143 18 5
§Pickering	I	107 3 10	15 8 6¼
Barnsley cum Dodsworth . .	O	125 14 8	21 0 9
Radholme	O	146 2 6	17 6 8
Dalby	A	157 19 0	11 13 4
Pattrington	O	161 13 4	26 0 0
Leaven	A	180 17 8	30 0 0
*Northstead	O	185 4 8	27 6 8
§Rosedale	O	192 12 1	102 11 1
Melsa	O	223 15 6	20 19 6
*Tickhill	O	243 0 8	89 1 10½
Pickering	A	318 10 0	11 4 0
†Pickering and Scalby . . .	O	387 12 6	163 5 6
(b) IMPROVED VALUES IN WALES			
Anglesey.			
*Dindathway	—	40 0 0	104 7 7
Brecknock.			
Brecknock	—	—	4 10 0
„	A	115 0 0	43 6 8
Cardigan.			
*Tallafarne	O	—	7 8 2
*Carwidross	O	—	42 0 5
Carmarthen.			
Eggleskimin	—	4 18 0	4 2 0
*Oysterlowe	O	8 17 0	—
Carnarvon.			
*Pullhey	O	—	103 18 4½
*Carnarvon[1]	I : O	—	109 17 2½
Denbigh.			
*Bromfield and Yale . . .	O	13 0 0	450 0 4½
Seagroat	O	39 0 0	4 1 0
Flint.			
Prestatin	O	—	20 0 0
*Flint	O	—	143 4 0
Glamorgan.			
*Ogmore	I	25 3 7	52 3 3½

[1] Re-sold to Major Eyton.

Premises.	Purchasers.	Clear Improved Values. £ s. d.	The Old Yearly Rents. £ s. d.
Merioneth.			
*Penlyn	—	10 0 0	103 16 7½
,,	A	20 0 0	193 10 2
Monmouth.			
Caldecott	O	8 0 0	22 0 0
*Wondy	O	10 0 0	16 0 0
*White Castle	O	15 19 0	51 12 2
Monmouth	O	50 16 0	54 16 1½
Montgomery.			
No Entries.			
Pembroke.			
Haverford West	—	—	2 0 0
*Florence	O	—	34 9 3
Radnor.			
*Royader	A	1 0 0	16 15 8
*Ischoyd	A	1 10 0	12 2 1½
*Southnethian	A	1 10 0	18 19 6
*Knocklas	A	6 0 0	24 6 2½
*Southagree	A	8 10 0	28 4 2½
Radnor	I	8 18 10	1 2
,,	O	10 0 0	9 12 0
*Glandestry	A	22 12 8	11 14 10
*Presteigne	O	34 0 0	37 2 6

II. VALUATION OF THE FIVE FORESTS OR CHASES

(i) Ashdown Forest, Sussex, 1650–8 [1]

P. Surv. Nos.	Date.	Divisions.	Acres.	Ann. Values. £	Gross Values. £
10	1658	Prestridge Bank	417·0	73·0	120·0
11	,,	Come Deane Lodge	1,055·0	102·7	—
12	,,	Warren Lodge [2]	834·3	157·6	100·0
13	1657	Hindleap Lodge	361·3	63·9	70·0
14	,,	White Deane Lodge	1,856·0	150·0	—
15	1658	Old Lodge	165·0	20·7	4·0
16	,,	Broadstone Lodge	1,145·5	249·7	80·0
17	,,	Pippingford Lodge	725·5	108·0	40·0
27	,,	Duddleswell Lodge [3]	1,301·0	279·8	233·0
		Totals	7860·6	£1,205·4	£647·0

[1] Sx. P.S. No. 26, dated 1650, gives acreage 14,000, annual value £2,507, and gross values £620. The details include rents and royalties £87 1s., reprises £54 6s. 4d., reserved rents on Lord Dorset's lease £29 8s. 4d.; also White House, partly destroyed, £30, its fishpond £50, gross values of deer, woods and underwoods, £120 and £620.
[2] Totals of P.S. 12, 26, and 27 are incorrectly recorded in *Sx. Arch. Coll.*, vol. xxiii.
[3] Rents, perquisites, and royalties, £13 0s. 5½d.

(ii) Kingswood Chase, Gloucestershire, 1652

P. Surv. No.	Date.	Divisions.[1]	Acres.	Ann. Values. £	Gross Values. £
12	1652	Chester Liberty . .	880·7	278·1	1,100·0
	,,	Stableton Liberty .	720·5	155·7	342·5
	,,	Mangersfeild Liberty .	571·0	210·2	115·0
	,,	Stafford's Liberty .	17·5	7·0	—
	,,	Weston's Liberty .	63·5	55·4	—
	,,	Wickham's Liberty .	60·3	48·1	—
	,,	Hanham's Liberty .	604·3	268·0	145·0
	,,	Mallett's Liberty .	514·5	218·5	350·0
		Totals [2] .	3,432·3	£1,241·0	£2,052·5

(iii) Needwood Forest, Staffordshire, 1649–1659 [3]

P. Surv. Nos.	Dates.	Divisions.[4]	Acres.	Ann. Values. £	Gross Values. £
11	1658	Broad Leech . .	251·0	69·0	379·0
12	,,	Mosey Meare . .	110·0	36·7	72·0
13	,,	Leasing Hill . .	204·5	68·2	189·5
14	,,	Brakenhurst . .	184·5	41·5	165·0
15	,,	Brick Kilnes . .	227·5	56·9	331·0
16	,,	Yoxhall Lodge . .	40·7	14·9	18·0
17	,,	Linthurst Banks .	436·0	109·0	925·8
18	,,	Little King's Standing	80·0	24·0	69·5
19	,,	Blakeley Roughs .	436·0	119·9	860·8
20	,,	Rangemore Dimbles .	436·0	130·8	921·2
21	,,	Long Back Stye .	402·0	80·4	540·0
22	,,	Burnt Marles .	196·5	49·1	305·0
23	,,	Island Lodge :			
		New Park	63·0	18·3	10·0
24	,,	New Poole . .	93·7	28·1	112·4
25	,,	Barton Lodge . .	24·0	8·8	25·0
26	,,	Birkley Lodge . .	35·5	15·5	10·0
27	,,	Brankeley . .	425·0	106·2	590·5
28	,,	Blakeley Myers .	185·0	55·5	282·0
29	,,	Lodge Holes . .	153·3	30·7	242·0
30	,,	Mabberley's Frame .	363·5	100·0	1,063·0
36	,,	King's Standing .	186·0	65·1	142·9
		Totals . .	4,533·7	£1,228·6	£7,254·6

[1] Hanham's Liberty and Mallett's Liberty, each with three divisions, and Wickham's Liberty combined with Criswick's Liberty.

[2] The Abstract of P.S. 12 f. 65 records acreage of 3,432 A. 2 r. and total improved value £1,241 0s. 4d. per ann., but the individual sums amount to £1,240 19s. 8d.

[3] Staff. P.S. 9, dated May, 1650, records acreage 6,500; ann. values, £2,761 1s. (of which present profits, £996 3s., and future improvements, £1,764 18s.); gross values, £13,251 18s. Staff. P.S. 37, April, 1652, contains Duchy of Lancaster rents, £52 8s. Staff. P.S. 10 and 34, April, 1659, record rents, £11 7s. 11d. and £125 for game and deer. Staff. P.S. 35 does not concern Needwood Forest, but belongs to Wiltshire surveys.

[4] Staff. P.S. 8, November, 1654, P.S. 31–3, Oct. to February, 1658, P.S. 45, April, 1652, are certificates or surveys dealing with claims, allotments, and fee-farms (the last, being Yoxhall Wardmill). In the Land Rev. Series (L.R. 2 : vol. 278, f. 257), January 1649, is a certificate of "common" in the chase.

The following abstracts of Staff. P.S. 31-3, dated October, 1658, to February, 1658-9, record the allotments of wood and timber " set out ready for sale " in Needwood Forest.[1]

P. Surv. Nos.	Dates.	Allotments.	Trees.	Gross Values. £	Under-wood. £
31	1658	Newborough, etc. .	1,215	288·5	5·0
	,,	Draycot . . .	536	120·0	20·0
	,,	Coton . . .	340	104·0	—
	,,	Hanbury . . .	308	60·0	—
	,,	Hanbury Wood End .	166	25·5	—
	,,	Stubby Lane . .	62	12·0	2·0
32	1658	Rolston . . .	2,590	998·0	5·0
	:,	Tutbury . .	1,750	374·0	5·0
	,,	Challingewood . .	702	231·0	2·0
	,,	Aynslow . . .	523	145·0	10·0
	,,	Tatenhill . . .	503	183·2	—
33	1658	Hamstall Ridware .	639	251·0	4·0
	,,	Barton . . .	616	108·2	2·0
	,,	Hore Cross . .	287	105·0	1·0
	,,	Yoxhall, etc. . .	100	29·5	1·0
	,,	Dunstall . . .	20	5·0	—
		Totals . .	10,357	£3,039·9	£57·0

(iv) Sherwood Forest, Nottingham and Derby, 1650-8 [2]

P. Surv. Nos.	Dates.	The King's Hays.	Acres.	Ann. Values. £	Gross Values. £
11	1658	Birkland . .	899·3	134·9	11,249·0
15	,,	Lyndhurst [3] .	—	29·8	2,516·1
22b	,,	Rufford [4] .	1,410·0	176·2	—
23	,,	Billhay [5] . .	840·5	136·1	9,450·0
24a	,,	Noeman's Wood [6]	72·0	7·2	955·0
		Totals .	3,221·8	£484·2	£24,170·1

[1] In Staff. P.S. 9, May, 1650, the trees number 38,608, and their value is placed at £13,191 18s.—an average of only 6s. 10d. each. In the five divisions of Clarendon Park, Wilts, were 14,000 trees worth nearly £1 apiece. The deer in Needwood Chase, 120 in number, were worth £60 in 1650 (P.S. 9). In April, 1659, the " game and deer yet left upon the deafforested forest or chace " were valued at £125 (P.S. 34).

[2] The earliest survey (Notts P.S. 14), June, 1650, records assarts in Hucknall, £9 ann. value.

[3] Notts P.S. 16, Lindhurst Park, is a " discovery " of September, 1654, giving annual value £85 15s. (of which £2 present profits, £83 15s. future improvements), and gross values £1,830 15s. 6d.

[4] Notts P.S. 22a is a certificate relating to Rufford Waste.

[5] Notts P.S. 23, White Lodge in Billhay had a rent of 6d. per annum, but the future improved value now raised the total annual value to £10. Notts P.S. 25, February, 1658, relates to the timber of Billhay, the value of which is computed at £1,243 8s.

[6] Another discovery of September, 1654, is Notts P.S. 24b, which records the acreage as 60 A., with annual value £6 and gross values £1,400.

(v) Enfield Chase, Middlesex, 1650–8 [1]

Plan.	P. Surv. No. 17.	Divisions.	Acres.	Ann. Values. £	Gross Values. £
A	D*b*	Greene Oake Plane .	126·0	113·4	—
B	H*a*	Fayre Feedings . .	131·3	114·8	10·0
C	H*b*	Great Monky Mead .	101·5	86·3	1·0
D	C	Long Hill .	95·3	76·2	29·0
E	FF	Great Broad Slade .	99·7	72·3	39·0
F	B	Little Broad Slade .	24·5	17·8	1·6
G	D*a*	Little Monky Meade .	34·5	29·3	—
H	M	High Beaches . .	43·5	34·8	6·6
I	L	Hunts Bottom [2]	18·0	16·0	9·0
K	N	Blew howse hill [3]	138·7	111·0	11·0
L	O*b*	Ffennyslade . .	80·5	54·3	45·0
[4] M	—				
N	O*e*	Fairethorne . .	131·0	85·1	89·0
O	KK	North Camelott .	80·0	40·0	52·0
P	JJ	West Camelott . .	110·7	55·4	72·0
Q	II	Camelott Hill .	115·7	70·9	169·0
[4] R	—				
[4] S	—				
T	OO	East Camelott . .	86·3	53·9	243·0
V	QQ	Noddinswell Hill [5] .	88·7	44·4	86·0
W	PP	Leezing Beech . .	103·5	66·0	190·0
X	RR	Horsey Plane . .	149·0	96·8	231·0
Y	HH	Marke Plane . .	138·7	76·3	180·0
[4] Z	—				
AA	G	Merry hill . .	67·5	40·5	120·0
BB	F	Redd Clay . .	65·5	36·0	64·0
CC	A*a*	Mathew Plane [6] .	95·7	52·7	112·0
DD	E	Mathew Brake . .	71·5	39·3	155·0
EE	O*g*	South Cunnyborough [7]	62·0	34·1	44·0
FF	CC	Great Hooke hill .	117·0	58·5	221·0
GG	O*c*	Little Hook Hill[6]	70·0	38·5	150·0
HH	P	Old Pound hill [8] .	109·5	58·8	113·0
II	O*a*	Hartgreene[6] . .	58·3	32·0	29·0
KK	O*f*	West Barvin [9] .	61·7	38·6	109·0
LL	W	South Barvin . .	97·5	56·1	53·0
MM	V	East Barvin .	69·3	46·7	112·0
NN	U	Pond's Course [10] .	102·5	69·2	152·0
OO	R	Cowface . . .	105·0	68·2	121·0
PP	EE	Stroud Head . .	114·0	59·8	112·0
QQ	Y	North Cunnyborough .	74·0	44·4	74·0
RR	Q	Deepeslade . .	115·3	72·0	70·0

[1] Mx., P.S. 17, dated October, 1650, acreage 7,904, ann. value £4,742 8*s.*, gross values £15,163. In these surveys of 1658 the area is 7,544 a., with 360 a. added by Robinson in his *History of Enfield,* 1823, to make up the original total of 7,904 A. For little differences in Robinson's figures or names see his work, vol. i, 194–5.

[2] Robinson, " situated on South Mimms Common ".

[3] Robinson, " New Pond Plane."

[4] In Robinson's list, see below under M, R, S, Z. Missing at P.R.O.

[5] Robinson, " Nodden's Well Hill, perhaps Newton Well Hill."

[6] Robinson's figures for CC, GG, II, TT, WW differ considerably from the above areas.

[7] The Augm. Off. Series contains duplicates of surveys marked in the Plan with the letters L, N, EE, GG, II, KK, LL, TT, WW (the last named in the Duchy of Lanc. Series, No. 44).

[8] Robinson has " Mote Platte " (cf. P.S. No. 17A, *b*, f. 7).

[9] Robinson records KK to MM as " Baroin " and WW as " Dens Larona " (6 A. 3 r.).

[10] Cf. " Pond's End " in P.S. No. 17A, *b*, f. 8.

Plan.	P. Surv. No. 17.	Divisions.	Acres.	Ann. Values. £	Gross Values. £
SS	T	Great Lodge Hill .	86·7	49·9	63·0
TT	AA	Old Lawne [1] . .	34·7	26·1	1·8
VV	S	Little Lodge hill .	16·5	8·2	1·8
WW	BB	Denns Lawne [1] . .	4·7	3·1	0·8
—	I	Mahews peece [2] . .	0·3	0·2	—
—	J	New pond [3] . .	2·7⎫		—
—	J	Camlet Moat . .	2·0⎬ 6·0		—
—	K	Pagetts peece . .	0·5	0·4	—
—	NNa	Enfield Common [4] .	1,522·5	—	1,740·0
—	NNb	Old Parke Common .	31·5	—	42·0
—	NNc	Edmonton Common .	1,224·5	—	1,120·0
—	NNd	South Mimms Common	1,077·7	—	730·0
—	NNe	Hadley Common .	186·5	—	5·0
M	—	Little Plumridge Hill [5]	172·0	—	—
R	—	Great Scootes . .	109·3	—	—
S	—	Little Scoots . .	26·7	—	—
Z	—	Coville's Land [6] .	6·7	—	—
—	—	Allen's Land [7] . .	45·3	—	—
		Totals [8] .	7,904·2	£2,254·3	£6,979·6

III. VALUATION OF HONOURS, 1649–1659

The Clear Improved Values are associated at times with several Manors in combined Counties, and these separate amounts need to be tested in the Parliamentary Surveys.

Counties.	Honours.	Rents. £	Improve- ments. £	Rates of Purchase. £
Bedford	Ampthill [9] . .	63·5	24·4	2,041·3
Cambs [10]	Clare and Richmond	39·6	—	1,683·1
Ches .	Halton . . .	59·2	—	1,195·6
Cornw.	Okehampton [11] .	6·9	22·0	346·1
,,	Launceston [11] .	38·1	30·5	1,376·0
,,	Trematon . .	63·8	—	1,499·2
Devon .	Bradninch [12] . .	203·3	1,673·4	19,517·6
Herts .	Berkhampstead [13] .	51·3	—	1,496·4
Kent .	Otford [14] . .	6·3	—	228·0
Leics .	Leicester . .	37·2	31·1	720·9

[1] Robinson's figures for CC, GG, II, TT, WW differ considerably from the above areas.
[2] Robinson omits the surveys marked P.S. 17 I, J, K above. Cf. P.S. 17A, b, f. 10, for "Fishpond and Camlett Moate".
[3] The annual value includes present rent, £1 5s., and future improvement, £4 15s.
[4] The area of the Surveys marked P.S. 17 NN (a–e) is recorded by Robinson, who gives a total of 4,042 A. 3 r. 5 p.
[5] For Surveys marked in the Plan with the letters M and R, see P.S. 17, Ob, f. 21 and 17, JJ, f. 1.
[6] Robinson, "situated at the north extremity of Enfield Common" (6 A. 3 r.).
[7] Ibid., "Sir F. Allen's" (4 A. 1 r.).
[8] The total recorded in the Surveys of 1658 is only 7,544 A. 1 r., the last five items being added in Robinson's list in accordance with the Plan (360 A. severed since 1650?).
[9] With two manors.
[10] Cambs and Hunts.
[11] Cornwall and Devon.
[12] With the borough.
[13] Bucks, Herts, and Northants.
[14] Tenements and Court Leet.

Counties.	Honours.	Rents.	Improvements.	Rates of Purchase.
		£	£	£
Lincs .	Bolingbroke [1] .	30·4	—	887·8
Mx. .	Hampton Court .	25·4	6·0	558·9
Oxf. .	Ewelme. . .	44·6	—	692·7
,,	Woodstock [2] . .	754·5	—	17,215·0
Staffs .	Tutbury . .	167·4	—	3,245·4
Suff. .	Eye [3] . . .	162·2	—	4,106·6
Warw. .	Kenilworth . .	127·2	1,051·6	18,775·2
Yorks .	Tickhill . . .	89·1	243·0	1,906·1
,,	Knaresborough [4] .	92·5	—	4,669·8
,,	Pickering . .	163·3	387·6	6,730·7
	Totals [5]	£2,225·8	£3,469·6	£88,892·4

IV. VALUATION OF THE HUNDREDS, 1649–1659

Note.—Signed by Ric. Graves and Ralph Darnall, 14th December, 1650: " As we did before, so we do again, certify that the said Hundreds being not appendant to any Honor or Manor are not settled in the Trustees for Sale of the Honors, etc., of the late King, etc.," but in the Trustees for the sale of the Fee-farm rents.

Counties.	Parl. Surveys.	Annual Values. Lowest.	Highest.
		£	£
Bedford [6] . .	Nos. 1–8.	3·0	29·3
Berkshire [7] .	Nos. 2–10.	3·4	23·9
Buckingham .	Nos. 1–6.	14·3	37·1
Cambridge [8] .	*Nil.*	1·5	9·8
Cheshire [9] .	Nos. 1–5, 17.	7·0	27·7
Cornwall [10] .	Nos. 1–2	4·0	17·8
Cumberland .	*Nil.*	—	—
Derby [11] .	Nos. 1–9, 21.	6·5	76·0
Devon .	Nos. 1–5.	13·6	21·8
Dorset [12] .	No. 1.	—	15·8
Durham .	*Nil.*	—	—
Essex .	Nos. 1–9.	1·7	13·8
Gloucester .	No. 1.	5·4	8·0
Hants .	Nos. 1–13.	1·1	10·8
Hereford [13] .	Nos. 1–8.	8·1	25·5
Herts . .	Nos. 1–2.	3·0	10·7
Huntingdon .	Nos. 1–2.	13·8	16·0
Kent [14] .	Nos. 1–10.	7·3	14·4

[1] A second item, with rents, £110, not traced in Conveyance List, occurs in the Orig. Creditors' List.   [2] With Hundred of Wootton.

[3] In Orig. Creditors' List given as £4,016.

[4] With lands in Lancs.

[5] The Improved Values are not all included in this list, but the average of the nine values shown is £386. The averages for the rents and rates of purchases, so far as shown, are £111 and £4,445 respectively.

[6] Jn. Huckle purchased the Hundreds of Biggleswade and Clifton.

[7] P.S. No. 1 transferred to Oxford.

[8] Add. MS. 30208 records all the Hundreds.

[9] H. Kelsall bought Macclesfield Hundred.

[10] Capt. Wm. Braddon and Ensign Thos. Hancocke contracted for these.

[11] Appletree sold to R. Mortlock for £596·3, and Captain Dan. Henchman contracted for High Peak on behalf of Col. Hewson's regiment.

[12] Thos. Lea purchased St. George, etc., Hundreds.

[13] P.S. 4 distinguishes the County Courts from the Hundred Courts.

[14] P.S. 3 was addressed to " Mr. Webb att Mr. Webs an appothecary in Old Bayley ". The seven Hundreds of Cranbrook are there declared to be but six, with the Town of Tenterden. Nos. 5 and 7 reserved for Major Keyne, and No. 6 sold to Capt. Bowles, 1654.

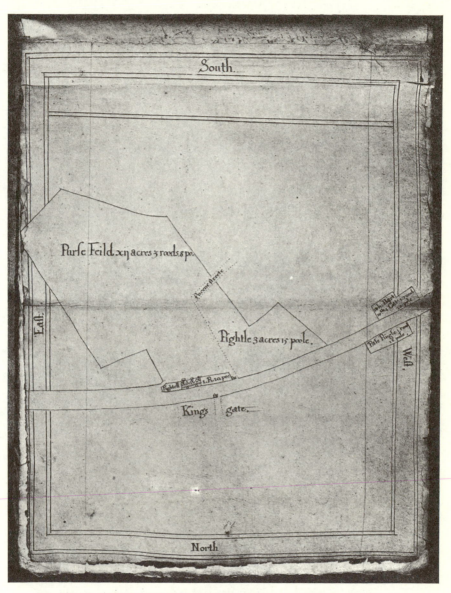

ST. GILES IN THE FIELDS, KING'S GATE, LONDON : PLAN, 1650

[face p. 384

		Annual Values.	
Counties.	Parl. Surveys.	Lowest.	Highest.
		£	£
Lancashire [1]	Nos. 1–5.	3·5	93·8
Leicester .	Nos. 1–5.	5·0	13·3
Lincoln .	Nos. 1–4.	5·0	127·0
Middlesex .	Nil.	—	—
Norfolk .	Nos. 1–7.	3·2	26·0
Northants .	Nos. 1–14.	0·3	15·5
Northumberland	Nil.	—	—
Nottingham .	Nos. 1–6.	24·0	194·7
Oxford [2] .	Nos. 1–7.	6·7	19·3
Rutland .	No. 1.	5·0	6·0
Shropshire .	Nos. 1–2.	0·1	1·5
Somerset .	Nos. 1–12.	1·4	11·9
Stafford .	Nos. 1–6.	10·8	14·6
Suffolk [3] .	Nos. 1–9, 12.	4·3	24·5
Surrey [4] .	Nos. 1–3.	7·0	13·4
Sussex [5] .	Nos. 1–9.	1·8	54·0
Warwick [6].	Nos. 2–7.	5·2	15·0
Westmorland .	Nil.	—	—
Wiltshire [7] .	Nos. 1–18, 42.	1·5	80·0
Worcester .	Nil.	—	—
Yorkshire [8] .	Nos. 1–14.	1·9	33·3
	Averages	£5·6	£33·4

Surveys of the Hundreds (Act of 11th Mar. 1649–50), are included in the Augm. Off. Series. They contain rentals, and notes on assart lands, boundaries, Courts, fines, leases, seizures, and townships. Spelhoe Hundred, Northants (No. 10), surveyed Nov. 1651, gives a list of " Certeinetye Mony or Sherriffes Yeild ", ranging from 1s. 4d. (Spratton) to £1 and £1 12s. in the case of Moulton and Great Billing. The total of these " Rents in Possession " came to £7 4s. 8d., and the clear Improved Value £4 ; so that the annual value of the rents and royalties of the Hundred sold to John Gifford, 16th Dec., 1651, came to £11 4s. 8d. Gifford also purchased the Hundreds of Barford and Stodden, Bedford, and Fawsley, Northants.

V. Sale Values of Crown Lands Classified

Note.—The amounts recorded include in some cases other premises in the same county, or even in different counties. Where no values are given there are no separate conveyances or counterparts of deeds of sale preserved, and the rates of purchase are then included in other amounts. Only the first name in a group of purchasers is here given. The enrolments on the Close Rolls should be examined to ensure accuracy in doubtful cases. See under Parks (Bedfordshire) and footnotes.

[1] Salford and West Derby were bought by Thos. Birch and J. Whitworth, and the latter acquired Blackburnshire for £3,297·2.

[2] P.S. 7 sold with the Manor of Woodstock to Lieut.-Gen. Fleetwood. There is a note referring to the Oxford Hundreds in Aug. Off. Misc. Bks., vol. 137, fol. 22b, the fourteen hundreds being indicated in the margins by the letters A to I, K to O.

[3] P.S. 4, 5, 8, and 9 have the Commonwealth arms in colour, but in No. 9 the left side (containing the cross in a circle) has been cut out. Sam. Chidley purchased Tedwestry for £367·2.

[4] P.S. 1–3, all endorsed " Sold to Major L. Awdley ". For Surrey hundreds see Aug. Off., Misc. Bks., vol. 137, fol. 41b (Letters A to N).

[5] P.S. 2 missing.

[6] No. 5 sold to Bolt, Jn. Rownd and Ric. Lambert. No. 6 discovered by and (sold to) Edw. Harrison.

[7] Several of these surveys are mud-stained owing to the fire at the Houses of Parliament in 1834. Nos. 10, 16, and 18, sold to Jn. Casbeard 22nd June, 1659 (a very late sale).

[8] P.S. 14a and 14b are the discoveries of Bernard Emott, and Ric. Clapham. The first was assigned to Matt. Scarborough, but it was overlooked by the surveyors.

	Counties.	Premises and Purchasers.	Yearly Rents. £	Sale Values. £
1.	BOROUGHS.[1]			
	Cheshire . .	Macclesfield : E. Southes . . .	22·4	634·9
	Cornwall . .	Crofthole : W. Menheire . . .	1·8⎫	
		Fowey : W. Menheire	2·3⎬	406·2
		Portpighan : W. Menheire . . .	3·2⎭	
		Lostwithiel : J. Menheire . . .	9·5	207·2
	Devon . .	Bradninch : S. Larke	203·3	19,517·6
		Lidford : W. Braddon	0·7	97·9
	Somerset . .	Milverton : R. Pratt	19·2	792·9
2.	BRIDGES.[2]			
	Surrey . .	Cobham Bridge	—	—
	Yorkshire .	Boroughbridge	—	—
3.	CASTLES.[3]			
	Cornwall . .	Launceston : W. Menheire . . .	38·1	1,376·0
		Tintagel : T. Herne	27·1	1,647·6
		Trematon : W. Braddon . . .	1·3	1,499·2
	Cumberland .	Carlisle : M. Dawson	52·0	1,433·9
		Penrith : M. Dawson	14·0	16,653·5
	Kent . .	Queensborough : J. Wilkinson . .	2·4	2,110·0
	Leicester . .	Leicester : J. Saunderson . . .	37·2	720·9
	Northumberland	Newcastle : P. Darell	2·0	463·8
	Notts . .	Newark : J. Nelthorpe . . .	103·9	3,830·2
	Warwick . .	Kenilworth : W. Combey . . .	127·2	18,775·2
	Yorkshire .	Tickhill : J. Northend	89·1	1,906·1
	Monmouth .	White Castle : W. Style . . .	51·6	3,334·6
	Pembroke . .	Haverford West : J. Warr . . .	2·0	42·0
4.	CHASES.[4]			
	Hereford . .	Ledbury : G. Ellis	31·9	574·6
	Huntingdon .	Somersham : V. Walton . . .	839·8	19,885·7
	Lancashire .	Bowland : J. Singleton . . .	82·7	2,429·2
		Trawden : A. Eyres	342·7	6,853·8
	Somerset . .	Exmoor : J. Strange	46·7	7,417·7
5.	CHURCH LANDS.[5]			
	Berkshire .	Martin Abbey : C. Whichcote . .	5·6	2,804·7
		Reading Abbey : R. Hammond . .	14·2	3,707·3
	Bucks . .	Burnham Abbey : W. Style . .	11·9	3,334·6
	Cornwall . .	Stratton Sanctuary : S. Lark . . .	7·8	536·5
	Herts . .	St. Albans Abbey : G. Ellis . .	52·5	1,824·6
	Northants .	Chalcombe Monastery : E. Southes	1·7	99·4
		Northampton (St. James's Monastery) :		
		S. Childley	1·3	132·4
	Somerset . .	Chantry Lands : R. Pratt . . .	6·3	792·9
	Surrey . .	West Sheen Monastery : A. Easton .	3·3	2,333·6
	Sussex . .	Bexley, etc. (Chantry Lands) : T. Kidder	80·7	1,645·0
	Warwick . .	Alvecote Priory : A. Evelyn . . .	80·2	3,023·1
	Yorkshire .	Beverley Chapter : S. Richardson . .	72·0	—
		Rosedale Abbey : N. Conyers . .	102·6	2,908·0

[1] The rent of the Borough of Thaxted, Essex, was £1·7. The Improved Values of the above boroughs (over the yearly rents) ranged from £7 to £1,673.

[2] Occur incidentally in connection with Farms, Houses, Rents and Tolls, and Waste lands ; for example, in Berkshire, Surrey, and Yorkshire.

[3] The honours and manors included. Improved Values from £16 to £413. Exeter, Gloucester, and Lincoln castles are incidentally recorded.

[4] Somersham and Enfield Chases are mentioned in connection with the Lodges (q.v). See also under Forests, No. 14 below.

[5] Improved Values, £11 to £218. Monastery lands are included with Kenilworth Castle (q.v). Tottenham Court (Prebend) was purchased by T. Harrison in two Conveyances of £4,633·7 and £5,163·6.

Counties.		Premises and Purchasers.	Yearly Rents. £	Sale Values. £
6. CONDUITS.[1]				
Middlesex	.	Westminster (Conduit Head) : W. Bell .	1·3	—
7. COTTAGES.[2]				
Bedford .	.	Ampthill : J. Huckle . . .	0·4	—
Bucks	.	Burnham : J. Byfield . . .	6·0	891·6
Derby	.	Eckington : R. Mortlock . . .	3·4	—
Kent	.	Newington : J. Brown . . .	0·5	—
Lancashire	.	Clitheroe : J. Whitworth . . .	0·1	—
Leicester .	.	Newbold Moor : M. Scarborough . .	9·0	144·8
Middlesex	.	Hyde Park : J. Hemsdell . .	2·4	—
Northants	.	East Cotten End : M. Bayley. .	0·7	36·1
Oxford	.	Cuddesdon : G. Herne . . .	5·0	70·0
Staffs	.	Anslow : T. Baker . . .	0·8	—
Suffolk	.	Layston : G. Sumpter . . .	1·0	—
Wilts	.	Calne : R. Stevens . . .	3·0	57·6
Yorkshire	.	Rossington : W. Farrar . . .	3·6	—
		Royston : J. Saunderston . .	5·0	—
		Tadcaster : W. Taylor . . .	8·2	196·8
Flint	.	Coleshill : T. Mackworth . .	1·8	—
8. DOCKS AND WHARVES [3]				
Kent	.	Maidstone (New Wharf) : W. Weaver .	0·2	40·3
Middlesex	.	London (Tower Dock) : D. Judd . .	0·1	—
		London (Tower Wharf) : G. Vaux . .	75·4	4,218·3
9. ENCLOSURES.[4]				
Middlesex	.	St. James (Swallow Close) : R. Scutt .	0·4	193·4
		St. James (Pell Mell Close) : J. Wakeford	184·3	1,912·4
		Whitechapel (Well Close) : D. Goldsmith	22·0	286·0
Northants	.	Greens Norton (Two Yard Lands) : G. Taylor	0·7	46·7
Surrey	.	Cheam : S. Chidley . . .	7·1	131·7
Yorkshire	.	York (Toft) : W. Webb . .	9·5	142·5
10. ENCROACHMENTS.[5]				
Cheshire .	.	Halton : S. Chidley . . .	0·5	—
		Macclesfield : E. Southes . . .	17·3	634·9
Derby	.	Eckington : R. Mortlock . . .	3·4	—
Herts	.	Cheshunt : R. Thorpe . . .	8·3	639·7
Leicester .	.	Newbold Moor : M. Scarborough . .	9·0	144·4
Notts	.	Hucknall Brecks, etc. : W. Sampson .	9·0	230·0
11. FARMS.[6]				
Berks	.	Clewer Farm : J. Floyd . .	23·0	1,650·3
		Frogmore Farm : C. Whichcote . .	28·8	2,804·7
		Talcotts Farm : W. Combey . .	13·8	621·7
Herts	.	Waltham Cross : W. Humberstone .	7·4	1,289·3
Kent	.	Eastcombe Farm : T. French . .	109·5	3,655·6
		Neats Court Farm : R. Downton . .	70·0	2,132·1

[1] The " Conduit Head " was the name of a shop in King Street, Westminster, in 1650.
[2] Several on encroachments or wastes, and here separately sold ; the values when included in manorial rentals are always small. The Improved values of the above range from £1 to £69.
[3] See also Harbours. The London references concern tenements and ground near the Tower. The improved values range from 2s. 6d. to £914 3s.
[4] Improvements from £8 to £70.
[5] Improved Values of Halton and Cheshunt, £5·5 and £7·8.
[6] Only selected (named) farms. See List of Manors, etc. Improvements range from £8 to £408. The Surrey farms are in Chertsey, Egham, Esher, Weybridge.

Counties.		Premises and Purchasers.	Yearly Rents. £	Sale Values. £
11. FARMS (*continued*).				
Lincs	. .	Pinchbeck : T. Gardiner . . .	16·0	1,864·9
		Spalding : J. Willesby, etc. . . .	113·8	7,505·7
		Yaddlethorpe (King's Farm) : J. Nelthorpe	1·2	7,553·2
Northants .	.	Aldrington (Travells Farm) : E. Southes	2·3 ⎫	793·9
		Aldrington (Ives Farm) : E. Southes .	1·0 ⎭	
Somerset .	.	Inglescombe Farm : J. Warr . .	12·0	1,055·6
		Widcombe Farm : S. Nash . ·. .	4·0	497·5
		Woolverton Farm, etc. : R. Magg . .	9·8	644·9
Surrey	. .	Bannisters Farm : E. Hannan . .	3·0	419·7
		Brookland Farm : M. Carleton . .	10·0	1,476·0
		Cobham Bridge Farm, etc. : A. Bickerstaffe	6·8	239·8
		Depenhams Farm : R. Scutt . .	12·7	1,352·8
		Inglefield Farm : T. Bartholomew . .	2·2	192·0
		Sayes Farm : S. Oram . . .	2·3	376·7
		Winter House Farm : J. Northend . .	3·7	557·0
Sussex	. .	Bexhill, etc., Farms : J. Warr . . .	132·0	3,055·0
		Colstable Farm : T. White . .	10·5	2,064·5
		Oldbury Farm : W. Cawley . .	20·4	1,196·6
Warwick .	.	Teddington Farm : R. Sankey . .	6·4	1,297·3
Wilts	. .	Cricklade Farm : R. Wagstaffe . .	52·6	2,351·2
Yorks	. .	Rosedale Farms : R. Heyborne . .	17·6	570·5
12. FERRIES.[1]				
Derby	. .	Willington : R. Knight . . .	7·7	122·7
Lincs	. .	Barton : J. Nelthorpe . . .	22·0	1,888·0
Surrey	. .	East Moulsey : R. Stevens . .	3·0	91·2
		Richmond : T. Rokeby . . .	167·7	13,562·0
13. FISHERIES.[2]				
Berkshire .	.	Wallingford (Northeights) : W. Cooke .	2·0	76·5
Cornwall .	.	Calstock (Weir) : E. Hoare . . .	140·0	2,030·0
		Fowey : F. Titon, etc. . . .	5·0	—
Lincoln	. .	Croyland (Fishing fields) : H. Thorpe, etc.	43·3	1,129·7
Northumberland		Aylemouth : E. Orpin	2·0 ⎫	
		Denton (Salmon) : E. Orpin . . .	2·0 ⎬	4,067·7
		Tweed : E. Orpin . . .	9·3 ⎭	
Wilts	. .	Avon : J. Dove . . ·. .	8·7	216·7
14. FORESTS.[3]				
Cumberland	.	Inglewood : M. Dawson . . .	357·5	16,653·6
Derby	. .	Duffield Frith : J. Munday . . .	22·0	484·0
Notts	. .	Bestwood : J. Grove . . .	457·8	6,953·4
15. FORFEITURES.[4]				
Lincs	. .	Cheyle's Lands : J. Nelthorpe . .	3·4	1,888·0
16. FORTS.[5]				
Kent	. .	Milton (The Blockhouse Field), etc. :		
		J. Browne	16·7	386·5

---

[1] Rivers Humber, Thames, and Trent. The ferry boats of East Moulsey and Richmond are included (with fishing) in the Manor purchase rates. The Surrey Improved Values amounted to £24.
[2] In the rivers of Lincolnshire and Wiltshire, with the Fowey, Tamar, Thames, Tweed, and Tyne.
[3] See under Chases and Lodges. The Manor of Penrith is included above. Refer also to the section on the valuation of the five forests or chases, Appendix V, ii, above.
[4] Forfeited by attainder. Improved value, £15·7.
[5] The improved value of £16 15s. doubled the rent of the land and tenements.

Counties.		Premises and Purchasers.	Yearly Rents. £	Sale Values. £
17.	GARDENS.[1]			
Berks	.	Windsor (King's Garden) : C. Whichcote	—	224·0
Middlesex		St. James (Mulberry Garden) : A. Deane	55·0	770·0
Surrey	.	Southwark (Pike Garden) : J. Hemsdell .	24·8	667·3
18.	GRANGES.[2]			
Cumberland	.	Norton Grange : R. Stafford . . .	36·0	504·0
Yorks	.	Barnsley : A. Holmes	4·3	2,866·1
		Meaux : J. Saunderson	21·0	2,812·1
19.	HARBOURS.[3]			
Devon	.	Dartmouth : E. Bagdale . . .	—	213·3
		Plymouth : E. Fowell	13·3	230·0
20.	HOSPITALS.[4]			
Kent	.	Dover (Maison Dieu House) : T. French	326·5 }	2,632·9
		Dover (Do., messuages, etc.) : T. French	13·0 }	
Middlesex		Islington (Spittle House) : W. Moore .	9·0	130·5
21.	HOUSES.[5]			
Bedford	.	Ampthill (Falcon) : T. Bussey . .	3·6	281·6
Berks	.	Wallingford (Dyehouse) : R. Angell .	1·5	202·5
		Windsor (King's Slaughter House) : C. Whichcote	1·5	2,804·7
		Windsor (King's Head) : R. Harris . .	4·3 }	232·7
		Windsor (The Rolph) : R. Harris . .	1·4 }	
Cambridge		Newmarket (Court House) : J. Okey, etc.	123·0	1,722·0
		Royston (King's Lodging) : L. Audley .	34·5	517·5
Cheshire	.	Northwich (Salthouses) : E. Southes .	3·4	344·4
Devon	.	Pyeworthy (Bradford), etc. : J. Warr .	1·8	893·6
Dorset	.	Eversholt (Northolt) : J. Warr . .	0·7	245·2
Essex	.	Havering (Wolves) : J. Searle . .	7·3	519·1
Hereford	.	Marden (Smith's forge) : S. Bayley .	2·7	113·2
Herts	.	Cheshunt (Falcon and Bells Inn) : R. Thorpe	11·9	639·7'
		Hemel Hempstead (Shambles) : R. Combe	1·0	95·5
Kent	.	Greenwich (Hobby Stables) : R. Tichborne	2·5	—
		Rochester (Slaughter House) : T. Kidder	15·5	310·0
Leicester	.	Leicester (High St. tenement) : W. Cowles	0·2	27·4
Middlesex	.	London (Crooked Lane messuage) : H. Boyce	0·2	200·0
		London (Red Cow Alley tenement) : E. Palmer	30·0	—
		London (Tower Hill messuages) : G. Vaux	37·7	4,218·3
		St. James (Suffolk Stables) : H. Edwards	1·0	2,246·7
		St. John's St. (Unicorn Inn and Hare and Hounds tenement) : J. Dickenson .	44·0	704·0
		Somerset Backyard (Two tenements) : H. Browne	—	—

[1] The improved value at Windsor was £28. In Millbrook Manor, Bedford, seven tenements with their gardens (rents, £1·4) were worth £2 8s. 8d. per annum ; they were sold for £59·6.

[2] The Yorkshire improved values were over £289.

[3] The office of Water Bayliff of Dartmouth, improved value £6·3. Sutton Pool in Plymouth improved value, £6·6. Knaresborough Manor included the royalties of waifs and wrecks of sea, etc.

[4] At Dover the improved value amounted to £126·8 on a rent of £13. The Spittle house was situated between Highgate and Holloway.

[5] Only houses with significant names, such as inns, etc., with certain mansions. For manor houses and farmhouses, see Manors, farms, etc. (App. V, sec. i, v. No. 11).

Counties.	Premises and Purchasers.	Yearly Rents. £	Sale Values £
21. HOUSES (*continued*).			
Middlesex (ctd.)	Strand (Duchy House) : R. Price . .	60·0	1,200·0
	Strand (King's Head Tavern) : H. Browne	0·7	722·0
	Strand (Jack-an-Apes) : F. Messervy .	0·7	272·0
	Strand (Sign of the three Pattens) : H. Browne	0·9	—
	Strand (Three Bells) : W. Bacon . .	1·0	224·0
	Westminster (King St. messuage) : J. Whitworth	5·0	340·0
	Westminster (St. Margaret's Lane tenements) : A. Wharton . . .	5·5	690·3
	Westminster (New Palace Yard, " three sheds ") : V. Overton . . .	7·0	196·0
	Westminster · (Charing Cross, Mermaid Tavern) : J. Hammond . .	2·0	164·0
	Westminster (Conduit Head, King Street) : W. Bell	1·3	—
	Westminster (Dog Tavern, New Palace Yard) : V. Overton	5·9	291·6
	Westminster (Ship Tavern, New Palace Yard) : J. Whitworth . .	3·0	186·0
	Westminster (Star Chamber House, New Palace Yard) : J. Hunt . . .	40·0	1,600·0
	Westminster (Stone Gatehouse, New Palace Yard) : T. French . .	3·0	—
	Westminster (Three Flower de Luces, St. Margarets) : R. Baldwin . .	1·3	167·7
Northants .	Grafton (King's Arms) : J. Haslerigge .	1·3	169·7
	Holdenby House : A. Baynes . .	552·9	22,299·3
Surrey . .	Chertsey (Walnut Tree House) : R. Wheatley	0·2	81·2
	Chertsey (Wagshotts tenement) : T. Milward	1·2	153·4
	Chertsey (Bowsers') : A. Washington .	2·9	354·2
	Chertsey (Chertsey Haw) : E. Southes .	4·4	173·1
	Chertsey (Depenham's Brewhouse) : R. Scutt	12·6	—
	Chertsey (Ampners Barns) : J. Baylye .	3·3	382·1
	Egham (Combes) : E. Dendy . . .	6·0	81·6
	Esher (Winter House) : J. Northend .	3·7	—
	Lambeth (Vaux Hall) : J. Trenchard .	75·0	—
	Mortlake (Tapestry House) : E. Bass .	59·0	826·0
	Southwark (King's Bargehouse) : W. Rowland	8·0	144·0
	Weybridge (Oatlands House) : R, Turbridge	3·5	4,933·9
	Weybridge (Dorney House) : R. Wagstaffe	1·3	—
	Weybridge (Hay's tenement) : T. Richardson	10·5	355·6
Sussex . .	Colstable House : T. White . . .	10·5	—
Worcester . .	Ribbesford (Ticknell House) : G. Ellis .	7·4	5,915·7
Yorkshire .	York (Dring Houses) : W. Webb . .	9·5	142·5
Denbigh .	Wrexham (Vicarage House) : R. Vaughan	3·0	—
22. ISLANDS.[1]			
Wilts . .	River Avon (Two Osier Islands) : J. Dove	8·7	216·7

[1] With the fishing in the River Avon. The Scilly Isles were separately surveyed but not sold : 17,000 A., rent roll £317 (and Crown lease £40), value under £6,000.

Counties.		Premises and Purchasers.	Yearly Rents. £	Sale Values. £
23. LODGES.[1]				
Cornwall	.	Liskerret Park Lodge : R. Knight .	20·0	—
Hunts	.	Somersham : V. Walton .	29·7	—
Middlesex	.	Enfield (Dighton's Lodge) : A. Evelyn	45·2	904·4
		Enfield (Norris's Lodge) : A. Evelyn	40·1	712·3
		Enfield (Potter's Lodge) : J. Nelthorpe	79·6	1,493·9
Surrey	.	Ash (Lynchford Lodge) : G. Wither	14·0	238·7
Wilts	.	Braden (Longhopshill Lodge) : H. Pretty	78·5	3,174·4
		Creekland (Slyfield Lodge) : G. Vaux, etc.	78·8	3,770·6
24. MARSH LANDS.[2]				
Essex	.	West Ham : J. Hawkridge	7·7	396·3
Gloucs	.	Fretherne, etc. : T. Constable, etc. .	3·8	311·3
Kent	.	Halstow : W. Bowler	30·0	816·3
Lincs	.	Moulton : W. Hobson .	4·5	1,523·8
		Moulton : D. Henchman	59·9	2,010·2
		West Fen : H. Jones	345·0	5,767·5
Middlesex	.	St. Giles : T. French	3·0	—
25. MEADOW LANDS.[3]				
Berks	.	Reading (King's Mead) : R. Hopton	140·0	5,100·4
		Wallingford (King's Mead) : R. Sykes	7·1	636·2
		Wallingford (Northeights) : W. Cooke	2·0	76·5
Dorset	.	Hammoon (Parker's Leaze) : J. Warr	1·3	132·3
Herts	.	Cheshunt : J. Townshend	3·9	—
		Cheshunt : J. Hemsdell .	3·9	—
		North Church : W. Lake	4·0	—
Lincs	.	Snitterby : J. Nelthorpe	3·0	—
Northants	.	Higham Ferrers : R. Knight .	4·4	—
Staffs	.	Tutbury (Stewards) : M. Scarborough	4·0	—
		Tutbury (Trenches) : R. Sankey	15·6	—
Surrey	.	Egham : E. Dendy	4·2	27·2
Warwick	.	Warwick (Earl's Meadow) : J. Bridges	17·0	272·0
Worcs	.	Bewdley (Lady Meadow) : J. Price.	3·1	751·1
York	.	Kippax : A. Baines	6·3	—
		Kippax Ings : J. Saville.	6·8	342·5
		Pickering : P. Pescodd .	14·2	—
Carmarthen	.	Llandingate : D. Morgan	2·2	—
26. MILLS.[4]				
Berks	.	Skippon : J. Hemsdell .	5·3	474·7
Cornwall	.	Lostwithiel : W. Kendall	2·0	126·0
Devon	.	Sidmouth : E. Raddon .	4·7	429·3
Dorset	.	Dorchester : R. Farr	5·0	405·0
Northants		Roade (Bosnam Mill) : N. Gauntlett	1·4	184·2
Northumberland		Newminster (two Fulling Mills) : E. Orpin	0·2	10·5
Shropshire	.	Ludlowe (Moiety) [5] : G. Clark	6·7	140·6
Suffolk	.	Layston : G. Sumpter .	1·0	—
Sussex	.	Ashley Mills : T. White	6·7	—

[1] Within the Chases named. The improved value of Liskerret is £90.
[2] Improved values, £13 to £282.
[3] These meadows have improved values ranging from £1·8 to £61.
[4] The windmill on Layston Coney Warren had already disappeared in 1650. Corn mills in Harlech (Merioneth), Rosemarket (Pembroke), and Glandestry (Radnor) were included in the manorial rents of £103, £16, and £11 respectively. There were two corn mills in Skippon, five in Ludlow, and seven in Brecknock, with Fulling mills as shown. Improvements of the above mills range from £4·9 to £115·3.
[5] Moiety of five mills : Rents, £6 13s. 4d. ; Improved Value, £20 12s. 8d.

Counties.	Premises and Purchasers.	Yearly Rents. £	Sale Values. £
26. MILLS (continued).			
Wilts	Malmesbury : W. Murford	33·5	535·5
Brecon	Brecknock Honour : D. Morgan	43·3	1,776·5
	Brecknock (Fulling Mill) : W. Phillips	4·5	72·0
Carmarthen	Eglwys-Cymmyn (Water Grist Mill) : J. Menheire	4·1	136·6
Pembroke	Milton (Water Corn Mill) : J. Warr	25·0	—
27. MINES.[1]			
Cheshire	Nantwich (" leads walling ") : W. Higgenson	16·0	400·0
	Northwich (salt houses) : E. Southes	3·4	344·4
Cornwall	Helston, etc. (tin) : A. Rous	20·3	465·3
Derby	High Peak (lead) : D. Henchman	11·3	—
	Wirksworth (lead) : T. Baynes	73·3	—
Durham	Softley (King's Colliery) : A. Holmes	20·0	—
Lancashire	Coal Mines, etc. : E. Green	6·2	—
Northumberland	Bebside, etc. : E. Orpin	0·5	10·5
	Denton : E. Orpin[2]	4·5	—
Westmorland	Casterton : J. Baynes	3·0	—
Worcester	Bewdley : J. Lloyd	7·2	278·0
Yorks	Barnsley : A. Holmes	21·0	—
	Knaresborough : J. Houghton	15·0	240·5
Denbigh	Abergele Gult (lead) : P. Eyton	0·1	—
Flint	Prestatyn (mines and quarries) : T. Mackworth	20·0	270·0
28. PARKS.[3]			
Bedford	Ampthill (Great Park) : R. Knight[4]	420·0	7,410·0
	Beckering : F. Thompson	300·0	8,311·0
	Brockborough : T. Bridge	392·8	11,208·1
Berks	Moat Park : H. Cannon	80·0	6,739·1
	Windsor (Little Park) : F. Thompson	309·2	—
	Windsor (Great Park) : E. Scotton	1371·0	22,755·0
Bucks	Olney : R. Wagstaff	100·3	2,568·7
Cornwall	Helston : J. Hollwell	16·7	1,247·6
	Kirribullock : Jn. Fathers, Clerk	8·0	—
	Liskerret : R. Knight	20·0	—
	Restormel : A. Trevill	28·3	2,081·0
Dorset	Gillingham : J. Kirk	32·5	1,673·2
Essex	Havering (3 parts) : R. Deane, J. Grove, W. Wood	306·3	13,051·3
Gloucester	Whitemead : J. Warr	22·2	795·2
Hants	Alice Holt (Goose Green and Old Close Parks) : J. Beale	60·0	1,747·3
	Binstead (Great Lodge Park) : J. Urlin	40·0	1,260·0

[1] All of coal except marked otherwise. Some amounts include the value of quarries, Bewdley includes the manor. Knaresborough includes mines, waifs, and wrecks. The mines of Abergele are stated to be lead, but those of Prestatyn are not indicated. The improved values vary from £8 to £400. The Lancashire mines were included in the contract for Newnham Manor, Bedford, etc., £7,361 18s. 3½d.

[2] In 1656.

[3] Including the " disparked parks " of Kirribullock, Liskerret, Restormel, Gillingham, and Mere. Hyde Park, Bowood, and Clarendon Parks were divided into five or more sections for sale. The improvements of the various parks range from £2·2 to £479·7. See the List of Manors, etc., for improved values. Potters Park, Surrey, was a coppice in 1650.

[4] This is an instance where, five items being combined in one conveyance of £24,237, I have separated the " rates " and entered them separately under Bedford, Cornwall, Hertford, and Northampton.

Counties.	Premises and Purchasers.	Yearly Rents. £	Sale Values. £
28. PARKS (*continued*).			
Hants (ctd.) .	Buckholt (East Park) : J. Saunderson .	40·5	946·5
	Caresbrook : W. Menheire . . .	160·0	3,200·0
	Somborne : J. Saunderson . . .	225·0	3,878·0
Herts . .	Cheshunt : W. Goff	504·8	33,528·9
	Berkhampstead : W. Lake . . .	34·0	—
	Berkhampstead : J. Alford . . .	45·0	5,220·6
	Theobalds : W. Disher . . .	1,549·3	35,873·6
Kent . .	Eltham (Middle Park) : T. French . .	223·7	—
Lancashire .	Myerscough : J. Whitworth . .	37·5	1,297·5
Middlesex .	Enfield (Old Park) : G. Lloyd . .	343·5	7,520·0
	Hampton Court (Bushey Park) [1] :		
	E. Blackwell	328·7	3,014·7
	Hyde Park (five parts) [2] : A. Dean,		
	T. Tracey, R. Wilcox	838·7	—
	Marylebone : J. Spencer . . .	628·2	13,215·3
Northants .	Grafton and Pury : R. Wakeman . .	426·4	18,228·3
	Higham : W. Raynborow . . .	2·7	5,498·8
Notts . .	Bestwood : J. Grove	457·8	6,953·4
Staffs . .	Barton (Sherholt Park) : P. Eyton . .	18·5	—
	Hanbury (New Park) : P. Eyton . .	35·9	—
	Hanbury Park : T. Morgan . . .	124·3	2,002·0
	Tattenhill (Heighlyns Park) : J. Hemsdell	114·6	5,540·4
	Tutbury Honour (Aggardsbury Park) :		
	O. Pretty	61·2	1,357·8
	Tutbury (Castle Park) : G. Ellis . .	71·0	1,709·4
	Tutbury (Castle Hay Park) : R. Sankey .	461·6	7,697·6
Surrey . .	Bagshot Park : C. Oxenbridge . .	94·6	3,911·3
	Nonsuch (Little Park) : G. Smythson, etc.	402·6	14,158·6
	Nonsuch (Great Park) : T. Pride . .	550·0	11,591·4
	Oatlands Park : H. Cerrier, etc. . .	200·0	8,209·2
	Potters Park : S. Oram	1·8	376·7
	Richmond (Little Park) : W. Broome .	220·7	7,884·9
Sussex . .	Sedgwick Park : R. Price . . .	55·2	2,573·7
Westmorland .	Troutbeck Park : M. Dawson, etc. . .	44·7	—
Wiltshire . .	Bowood (nine divisions) [3] : C. Barrett, J. Baynes, W. Cowles, H. Hales, W. Menheire, R. Ring, W. Sellers, H. Webb, etc.	457·5	2,729·6
	Clarendon (five divisions) : W. Dawgs, etc., J. Dove, W. Ludlow, L. Steele .	822·8	11,301·1
Yorkshire .	Pickering (Blandesby Park) : A. Eyre .	11·2	5,966·4
	Radholme Park : J. Halliday . .	17·3	896·5
	Sheriff Hutton Park : A. Baynes . .	8·7	1,668·5
	Sutton (New Park), etc. : G. Smithson .	364·0	—
29. PASTURE LANDS. [4]			
Cumberland .	Lazonby : M. Dawson	18·7	—
Lincoln . .	Pinchbeck : R. Brown	1·1	73·7
	Poynton : R. Margerye . . .	45·0	1,148·7
Northants .	Aldrington : S. Horton	1·2	59·3
Staffs . .	Hanbury : R. Adderley	4·3	577·1
30. QUARRIES. [5]			
Lancs . .	Burnley, etc. (Limestone) : E. Green .	0·3	33·5

[1] With Hare Warren (Rent £80).
[2] Conveyance not found at P.R.O.
[3] For three divisions only out of nine, under " Sale Values ".
[4] Creslowe Pastures, Bucks, are included with the Manor.
[5] Quarries in Knaresborough and Prestatyn are combined with mines (q.v.).

Counties.		Premises and Purchasers.			Yearly Rents. £	Sale Values. £
31. RENTS AND ROYALTIES.[1]						
Cambridge	.	Clare and Richmond : J. Blackley .	.	.	39·6	1,683·1
Kent	. .	Otford : J. Warr .	.	.	6·3	228·0
Lancs	. .	Burscough : H. Kelsall .	.	.	1·0	152·0
		Lancashire (Butlerage) : H. Kelsall .	.		15·0	—
Lincs .	. .	Sutton (Feodary) : W. Skepper	.	.	7·0	—
Northants .	.	Grafton (Feodarith) : G. Vaux	.	.	29·0	829·3
Suffolk	.	Clare Mandeville : G. Adams .	.	.	35·5	925·4
York	. .	Pontefract : J. Saunderson	.	.	109·6	2,672·0
		Whitgift : J. Saunderson	.	.	20·0	669·6
32. TOLLS.[2]						
Bedford	.	Camelton, etc. : R. Wagstaffe .	.	.	26·2	586·1
Cumb.	. .	Carlisle : M. Dawson .	.	.	2·0	—
Lincs	. .	Grantham : J. Nelthorpe	.	.	8·9	249·1
Norfolk	.	Kings Lynn : P. Skippon	.	.	6·5	104·0
Northants .	.	Old Stratford : G. Vaux	.	.	5·0	—
Wilts	.	Mere (Fairs) : J. Awbrey	.	.	7·7	—
Denbigh	.	Denbigh (Fairs) : P. Eyton	.	.	20·0	—
33. WARRENS.[3]						
Bedford	. .	Millbrook : N. Potts	.	.	7·0	266·0
		Ampthill : T. Bridge	.	.	14·0	—
Lincs	.	Bromby : J. Nelthorpe .	.	.	4·0	—
Middlesex .	.	Hampton Court (Hare Warren) :[4]				
			E. Blackwell		80·0	—
Norfolk	. .	Methwold : G. Lloyd .	.	.	30·0	680·0
Oxford	.	Ewelme : T. Butler	.	.	13·0	518·9
Suffolk	.	Layston : G. Sumpter	.	.	20·0	768·0
Surrey	.	St. Ann's Hill : E. Leigh	.	.	0·3	25·0
		Byfleet[5] : J. Reyner, etc.	.	.	1·0	—
34. WASTE GROUNDS.[6]						
Bucks	.	Eton : R. Aldridge	.	.	0·7	9·9
Essex	.	Romford : J. Reynor	.	.	2·0	134·0
Middlesex	.	Tower Dock : D. Judd[7]	.	.	—	—
		Westminster : J. Davis .	.	.	3·0	40·0
York	.	Langdale : R. Thorpe .	.	.	25·0	400·0
35. WOODS.[8]						
Bedford	. .	Steppingley : J. Styles .	.	.	0·2	11·6
Bucks	. .	St. John's Wood : J. Byfield .	.	.	40·0	622·5
		Lillingstone Darell : J. Urlyn .	.	.	85·7	—
Cornwall .	.	Highwood : R. Knight	.	.	4·6	—
Kent	. .	Gillingham : E. Orpin .	.	.	6·8	—
Lincs	. .	Bromby (Princes Wood) : E. Scotton .			1·0	62·4
		Whapload (Kits Grove) : J. Northend .			0·2	—

[1] See the List of Manors. Portreeve rents in Carmarthen (£6·4) were bought by Jn. Warr.

[2] The tolls of Barnsley, Presteigne, etc., are included among the Profits of Manors (q.v.).

[3] The improved values range from £6 to £92 above the rents.

[4] Bushey Park and Hare Warren (Rents, £328·7 plus £80), purchased for £3,014·7.

[5] With Messuage (total rents, £2·1 ; improved value, £30·6), purchase price, £319·8.

[6] The improved Value of Romford, including tolls, was £98, making £100 annual value. Another piece of waste in Westminster near Old Palace Yard, had a rent of 6s. 8d. It was bought by A. Garfield.

[7] Judd's portion, valued at 2s. 6d., improved rent, was near Lord Leicester's House.

[8] The range of improved values extends from £1 to £146.

Counties.	Premises and Purchasers.	Yearly Rents. £	Sale Values. £
35. WOODS (continued).			
Middlesex . .	Little St. John's Wood : R. Clutterbuck .	4·6	327·3
	Great St. John's Wood : W. Clark . .	64·4	3,645·3
Norfolk . .	Ellingham (King's Wood) : C. Fleetwood	0·8	136·7
Northants . .	Blisworth : W. Tibbs	9·3	342·1
	Roade : J. Urlyn	7·1	—
	Stoke Bruerne : T. Milward . . .	10·6	389·6
	Whittlebury : J. Urlyn	19·0	—
Oxford . .	Woodstock : N. Duncan . . .	66·6	3,450·8
Suffolk . .	Goswould : J. Nelthorpe . . .	1·7	332·7
Surrey . .	Chertsey : T. Milward	38·1	1,454·8
	Chertsey : T. Diason	9·3	567·9
	Egham (Sherwoods) : T. Brough . .	0·2	117·9
	Egham : T. Blackwell	1·3	—
	Long Ditton : H. Webb . . .	1·0	16·0
	Potters Park (Coppice) [1] : S. Oram . .	1·8	376·7
Warwick . .	Kenilworth : R. Sankey . . .	83·1	7,187·8
Wilts . .	Mere : J. Awbrey	4·7	—
Worcs . .	Bewdley : G. Ellis, etc. . . .	34·0	2,002·5
Yorks . .	Meaux : J. Saunderson	46·6	—
	Newton Dale : W. Storey . . .	6·0	124·0
	Pickering Beck : J. Singleton . . .	5·0	672·6
Radnor . .	Presteigne : G. Saunders . . .	37·1	—

VI. RECORD OF SALES ENDORSED ON PARLIAMENTARY SURVEYS, 1650–9[2]

1650. May 15.   Cornwall P.S. No. 40.[3]
1651. June 2.   Wm. Clarke : Mx.[4]
  Sep. 9.   Wm. Lenthall, Speaker [5] : Berks, Nos. 7, 8.
   „   23.   Sam. Row " for lo: President Bradshaw " : Wilts, No. 7.
  Oct. 14.   Wilts, No. 6.
  Nov. 5.   T. Gates (?) : York, No. 62.
   „   11.   Mr. Pawson : Hunts, Nos. 1, 2.
   „   25.   Jn. Urlyn : Northants, Nos. 2, 7, 12.
  Dec. 9.   Ric. or Lawrence Wollaston : Bucks, No. 6. Lieut.-Col.
     Thomlynson : Northants, No. 5. Jn. Urlyn : Sx.,
     Nos. 1, 3.
   „   16.   Jn. Gifford : Northants, Nos. 3, 10.
   „   17.   Wilts, No. 26.[6]
1652. Mar. 26.   Lt.-Col. Michell : Derby, Nos. 6, 8, 9. Chas. Bowles :
     Leic., No. 2. Wm. Burnet : Northants, Nos. 1, 6, 11.
   „   30.   Ric. Stephens for Thos. Dummer : Hants, No. 7.
  Apr. 6.   Walt. Urlyn : Bedf., Nos. 2, 5–8. Hy. Brandreth : Derby
     No. 7. Lt.-Col. Juxon : Herts, Nos. 1, 2.
  July 13.   Wm. Cox : Som., Nos. 1–3, 5–12. Ric. Wall : Som.,
     No. 4.

[1] With Farm (rent, £2·3 ; improved value, £47·7).
[2] With occasional notes recorded in the later Surveys.
[3] S.P. Dom., 1650, p. 164. Stoke Climsland manor " sold by the Contractors".
[4] Clarke Papers, Cam. Soc., vol. ii, pp. 227–8 (St. John's Wood).
[5] Inscribed, " Speaker of the Parliament."
[6] All divisions of Clarendon Park, except Hunt's sold (L.R. 2, Survey). Hunt's
division sold 1652.

Aug. 3. Jn. Hemsdell : Berks, No. 10.

„ 22. Col. Rob. Guybon : Kent, No. 3.

Dec. 14. Gabriel Taylor : Herefs., No. 1–3, 5–8.

Jan. 4. Edm. Denton : Bucks, No. 3.

„ 18. Lt.-Col. Juxon : Sx., No. 8.

Feb. 26. Capt. Dan. Henchman, on behalf of Col. Hewson's Regt. : Derby, No. 5.

1653. May 12. Capt. Geoff. Ellis (fee simple of Wm. Marstons) : Herts, No. 6b.

July 5. Edw. Allen : Staffs., Nos. 2, 3, 5, 6. Jn. Rownd and Ric. Lambert : Warw., No. 2. Bolt, Rownd and Lambert : Warw., No. 5.

Jan. 1. Col. Webb [1] : Ex., No. 9.

„ 12. Hy. Robinson : Suff., No. 3.

„ 17. Gyles Sumpter [2] : Dev., No. 4.

Feb. 2. Dawbeny Williams : Dors., No. 1.

„ 6. Jn. Mynheire, for Ric. Moore : Hants, No. 6.

„ 28. Edw. Harrison : Warw., No. 6.

1654. Apr. 25. Val. Knight for Wm. Ireland : Leic., No. 3.

May 9. Capt. Bowles [3] : Kent, No. 6.

1655. June 27. Owen Cambridge : Linc., Nos. 2, 4 ; Northants, No. 13.

1656. May 14. Wm. Wise : York, No. 12.

„ 21. Maj. Lewis Awdley : Surr., Nos. 1–3.

1657. June 10. Ric. Lee [4] : Surr., No. 2.

1658. Feb. 23. Jn. Singleton [5] : Norf., No. 6.

1659. June 22. Jn. Casbeard : Glouc., No. 1, Wilts, Nos. 3b, 10, 16, 18.

„ 29. Notts, No. 3 : Trustees Order as to Sale.[6]

[1] Added : " for Ric. Mullenex ".
[2] At twelve years' purchase.
[3] At thirteen years' purchase.
[4] Afterwards erased, with date 9th December, 1656.
[5] Part of Mitford Hundred.
[6] The following references are undated : Beauchamp (Sx. A.S. Coll., Sx. No. 6, vol. xxiii, p. 231). Bovey : Som., No. 36B. Brooke, Alice : Leic., No. 4. Collins (Clarke Papers, vol. ii, p. 227) : Mx. Col. Dove : Wilts, Nos. 5, 8. Col. Downe (Sx. A.S. Coll., Sx. No. 9, vol. xxiii, p. 242). Col. Arth. Evelyn : Berks, No. 31. Row. Hale : Herts, No. 3. Wid. Harris : Shrop., No. 3. Lt.-Col. Juxon (Sx. A.S. Coll., Sx. No. 28, vol. xxiv, p. 218). Maj. Keyne : Kent, Nos. 4, 5, 7. Mrs. Mallett or Mr. Perkins : Glouc., No. 4. Sir Greg. Norton : Surr., No. 47. Mr. Perkins : Glouc., No. 4, and Lincs, No. 42b. Sam. Richardson : Bucks, No. 1. Wid. Searle : Sx. No. 5. Walt. Strickland : Monm., No. 6. Thyn (?) or T. Hyll : Hunts, No. 8. Towcester : Northants, No. 4. Wheeler : Wilts, No. 18.

APPENDIX VI

THE AUDIT OF THE RESTORATION OFFICIALS, 1662

I. Abstract [1] of the Accounts Relating to the Sales of Crown Lands, 1649–1656

Exch. L.T.R., Pipe Off., Declared Accounts, No. 603. Taken 22nd March 1660–61, and declared 20th December, 14 Chas. II., 1662. m. 86.

Account of Sir John Dethicke, Kt., the surviving Treasurer appointed by a pretended Act of Parliament made *16th July, 1649*, for the sale of Crown Lands all which were by the said Act vested and settled in the real and actual possession and seisin of Thomas Coke of Pedmarsh, co. Essex, and divers others in the said Act named, and sold by several contracts, of the sums accruing and also for sums arising by virtue of another Act made *31st December, 1652*, and also of sums arising from the sale of divers lands within Endfield Chase and Ashdowne, and Needwood Chase sold by virtue of an ordinance of the late Protector Oliver dated *10th August, 1654*, and confirmed by a pretended Act of a parliament beginning and held at Westminster *17th September, 1656*.

As below :—

(a) *Sales under the Act of Parliament of 16th July, 1649*

		£	s.	d.
1.	Money from sales as appears by a book or certificate by John Wheatley, gent., deputy registrar of the Trustees paid to the Kings Remembrancer	1,423,710	18	3
2.	Money received by the said Treasurer from divers Receivers General	4,696	1	6½

m. 86*d.*

3.	Money received from farmers and tenants of divers manors, parks, lands, etc., due from them before the selling thereof	3,108	15	11¼
4.	Money received from woods before the selling thereof	2,762	19	8¾

	£	s.	d.
Total	£1,434,278	15	5½

(b) *Sales under the Act of 31st December, 1652.*

Money received by the said Treasurer from Sales as appears by a book of particulars in the Custody of the King's Remembrancer — 29,839 12 6

(c) *Sales under the Ordinance of 10th August, 1654.*

Money received by the said Treasurer from the sale of divers lands parcel of the Forest or Chase of Needwood and Ashdowne, and the Chase of Endfield under the ordinance 10 Aug. 1656 (*sic*), etc. — 290 17 8½

	£	s.	d.
Total	£1,464,409	5	8

From which :—

(d) *Payments under the Act of 16th July, 1649.*

The same accountant in payment of several sums of money from sales

---

[1] I have divided these abstracts into sections, with subdivisions, to facilitate reference to the items of each account.

under the Act *16th July, 1649*, and of the Act which authorized the sales by the said Trustees, namely :—

	£	s.	d.
m. 87.			
1. Deductions and defaults made upon several purchases :— Four amounts, King's Remembrancer, debentures, etc., viz. £1,292,802 6 9⅜ (q^{a}. di.) 26,887 9 3⅝ (ob. di. q^{a}.) 11,404 18 1¼ (q^{a}.) 7,852 6 11⅛ (di. q^{a}).	1,338,947	1	1⅜
2. For the salary of the accountant and his associates at the rate of 1*d*. per £1 and in like manner for any allowance made by default upon contract namely for £1,434,278 15*s*. 5½*d*. amounting to	5,976	3	10
3. For salary paid to Sir Wm. Roberts, Kt., and others appointed in the Act to be contractors at the rate of 3*d*. per £1 for all lands sold for the said sum of £1,434,278 15*s*. 5½*d*., namely for part of their fees beyond £3,926 3*s*. 5½*d*.	13,160	0	0
4. Paid to Thomas Coke, esq. and other Trustees at 3*d*. in the £1	13,130	0	0
m. 87*d*.			
5. Paid to Henry Colbron and John Wheatley Register and Keeper of Records for salary at the rate of £100 yearly for 7¾ years	775	0	0
6. Paid to Henry Robinson, controller at £300 by the year for 3 years	900	0	0
7. Paid to Colonel William Webbe, surveyor-general for the salary of himself and his clerks at £150 yearly for several years	1,457	2	7
8. Allowed to the said Acct^{t} for payment made to particular surveyors in England and Wales by warrant of the Trustees	30,487	17	10½
9. Paid to divers artificers and labourers for work done in and about Worcester House and for the purchase of "peristromata"[1] and other necessaries for the use of the Trustees, contractors and other officers	2,755	16	4½
10. Paid to two counsellors and other clerks attending the Trustees and others	12,218	15	5
m. 88.			
11. Paid to "lez debent^{rs}" and the Auditor for their services in making estates and examining salaries and the arrearages of several officers and other soldiers in the Army . .	5,858	0	8
12. Paid to the Committee of Accounts sitting at Worcester House	8,342	1	7
13. Repaid to persons who had paid into the Treasury at the rate of 2*d*. in the £ for money due upon their purchases, but who had not completed their purchases	176	17	10¼
14. Discharge of part of £84 5*s*. 1*d*. in the accountant's hands, etc.	63	3	9¾
Total allowances and payments[2]	£1,434,248	1	1⅜

(*e*) *Payments under Other Acts, 1652–6.*

Money paid by divers persons from the sale of the parks, lands, and tenements late of King Charles and Henrietta Maria his queen and sold by virtue of an Act of Parliament made 30th November, 1652, namely :—

	£	s.	d.
1. Paid to Richard Hutchinson esquire, Treasurer for the Navy by virtue of several ordinances of the Commissioners, authorized by a pretended Act of Parl^{t} published *1 Jany 1652*	12,453	3	2
2. Paid to John Hippesley by virtue of a pretended ordinance of Parliament dated *31 Dec. 1652 to wit* : on 13 December 1653, £300, and on 15 December 1653, £950	1,250	0	0

[1] Tapestry hangings, curtains, etc.

[2] Items 2–7 are added in the margin, giving a total of £35,398 6*s*. 5*d*. ; and items 8–13 similarly add up to £59,839 9*s*. 9½*d*. No. 14 allowed by Lord Ashley, 26 Sept. 1662.

<table>
<tr><td></td><td>£</td><td>s.</td><td>d.</td></tr>
</table>

3. Paid to Sidrack Brice and John Inwood on 3 March 1653 by virtue of a pretended Ordinance of the late Protector at Whitehall dated 24 Feb. 1653   1,390   0   0

m. 88d.

4. Paid to Edward Backwell 13 March 1653 by virtue of a like Ordinance dated 10 March 1653   6,210   17   0

5. Paid to John Parker 12 Augt. 1656 by virtue of a like Ordinance dated 29 July 1656   1,221   12   9

6. Paid to the Receipt of the Exchequer :—

           on 15 Feb. 1654 £3,473 5s. 0d.
           on 17 Mch. 1654 £3,000 0s. 0d.
           on 15 Aug. 1656 £478 7s. 3d.
                    Total   .   .   .   6,951   12   3

7. Paid to the Clerk of the Treasury called The Cashier of the numbered money (i.e. the Tellers) and his messenger for their labour and attendance and for books, bags, paper, pens and ink and other necessary things. This allowance is by virtue of a warrant of Anthony, Lord Ashley, chancellor and under-treasurer, dated 26th Sept. 1662 · . . .   334   2   10

         Total allowances and payments [1] £29,811   8   7
             Total allowances and payments, £1,464,059 9s. 8⅜d. (q^a di).
             Balance, £349 15s. 11⅝d. (ob. di. q^a).

(*f*) *Final Payments, 1662.*

Whereof there is paid to the Receipt of the Exchequer on 15 December, 1662, as by tallies thereof levied appear, £300 and there remains further £49 15s. 11⅝d. (ob. di q^a) which said sum is allowed to William Gwynn and Richard Aldworth, the auditors and their clerks for their labour in and about the taking of the account by the order of The Most Noble Anthony lord Ashley, chancellor and under treasurer of the Court of Exchequer, dated 11 December, 1662.

And so it balances.[2]

(*g*) This Account is taken by William Gwynn and Richard Aldworth two of the Auditors of His Majesty's Revenue by order of the right honorable Thomas Earl of Southampton, Lord High Treasurer of England, dated the xxij^th of March, 1660.

    Exd. by R. Aldworth, auditor.
    Exd. by Wm. Chislett: Dep^y.
    Exd. by Wm. Gwynn, auditor.

                         Declared 20th December, 1662.
                               ASHLEY

(*h*) The aforesaid John Dethicke, Kt., was sworn upon this Account 20 December 1662 before me,

                               EDW. ATKINS.

[1] This total is 7d. in excess of the added items.
[2] The balancing of this account involves the setting out of a complicated array of figures, of which the following may serve as a sample (in the order of the text above):—

<table>
<tr><td></td><td></td><td>l'</td><td>c'</td><td>m'</td><td>c'</td><td>li'</td><td></td><td>s.</td><td>d.</td></tr>
<tr><td>(m. 86)</td><td>m</td><td>iiij</td><td>xxiij</td><td>vij</td><td>x</td><td></td><td>xviij</td><td>iij</td><td></td></tr>
<tr><td>(m. 86d.)</td><td>m</td><td>iiij</td><td>lxiiij</td><td>iiij</td><td>ix</td><td></td><td>v</td><td>viij.</td><td></td></tr>
<tr><td>(m. 88d.)</td><td>m</td><td>iiij</td><td>lxiiij</td><td></td><td>lix</td><td></td><td>ix</td><td>viij</td><td>q^a. di.</td></tr>
</table>

See the note on these accounts in Appendix VI (iii), page 405.

II. Abstract of the Accounts Relating to the Sales of Fee-farm
Rents, 1649–1657

Exch. L.T.R., Pipe Office, Declared Accounts, No. 602. Taken
23rd March, 1660–61, and declared 20th December, 1662.

m. 89.

Account of Sir John Dethick, Knt., the surviving of four Treasurers
appointed by a pretended Act of Parliament (intituled An Act for selling
the Fee-farm rents belonging to the Common Wealth of England formerly
payable to the Crown of England, Duchy of Lancaster and Duchy of Cornwall made and promulgated *11 March 1649*, for all the money arising from
all the sales of all the Fee-farm rents, tithes or rents reserved in the name
of a tithe, rents-sec, hundreds, liberties, bailiwicks, reservations, conditions,
franchises and pensions issuing out of any manors, lands, tenements and
other hereditaments within England Wales and the town of Berwick upon
Tweed belonging to the republic of England and formerly due and payable
to any King or Queen of England, Prince of Wales, Duke of Lancaster,
Duke of Cornwall, Earl of Chester, or any of them and not from them
nor by them lawfully alienated according to the laws of this nation at or
before *1 January 1641* and by the said Act of Parliament held to be in the
real and actual possession of Thomas Coke of Pedmarshe, Essex, esquire,
William Bosvile, esq. and divers others as well by virtue of the Act aforesaid
as by another pretended Act intitled " An Act for the further explanation
of the former Act intitled An Act for the selling of the Fee-farm rents, &c.
(as above) " and by them sold to divers persons as well by virtue of the
same Acts as of a certain other Act intitled " An additional Act for the sale
of the Fee-farm rents and for the doubling of money thereupon ".

To wit :—

(*a*) (An account) of all the money received by the said Accountant
and other Treasurers from the said sale as well as of all payments made
to any person or persons by virtue of the said Acts.

As below :—

		£	s.	d.
1.	Recd. by the Accountant and other Treasurer from Sales	£239,206	4	5⅜
2.	Recd. de duplicacione £250,000	£288,031	16	2¼
3.	Recd. of divers purchasers who were overdue according to their contracts	£1,570	12	5
	Total	£528,808	13	0¼

m. 89*d*. *Against which* :—

Paid to divers persons for several uses as well by virtue of a pretended
order of Parliament as by several orders and warrants of the Trustees for
Sale authorized by another Act of Parliament :—

(*b*). Paid to the use of the Navy by virtue of a pretended Ordinance dated
30th March, 1650, namely :—

CROWN LANDS SALES : AUDIT, 1662

1. To Sir Henry Vane, knt., treasurer of the same " Classis " 5 June 1650
    by the warrant of the Committee of the Navy dated 3 May 1650   £10,000

2. To the same by like warrants :—

19 June, 1650	£10,000
6 Aug. „	£10,000
17 Sept. „	£10,000
3 Oct. „	£10,000
23 Oct. „	£10,000
2 Dec. „	£10,000
31 Dec. „	£10,000

3. To Rich. Hutchenson, Treasurer for the Navy on 13 Feb. 1650   £10,000
    To the same 4 March 1650   £10,000

Total .	£100,000

m. 90.

(c) Payments to the use of the Army by virtue of the pretended Ordinance 30 March, 1650.

To John Wollaston, Knt., and other Treasurers for War, namely to James Smith their cashier, by like warrants :—

20 June, 1650	£14,000
14 July „	10,000
22 Aug. „	12,000
25 Sept. „	4,000
9 Oct. „	14,000
21 Oct. „	100
16 Nov. „	8,000
21 Nov. „	3,280
31 Dec. „	14,620
3 March „	20,000
Total	£100,000

(d) Payments to the Treasurer for War at Guildhall, London :—

1. To James Smith, by like warrants :—

	£	s.	d.
1650, 3 Mar. .	7,300	0	0
25 „ .	1,346	16	11
25 „ .	2,481	18	2
1651, 12 Apr. .	500	0	0
12 „ .	700	0	0
12 „ .	850	0	0
12 „ .	514	3	8¼
12 „ .	888	17	4
12 „ .	500	0	0
14 „ .	813	6	8
15 „ .	450	0	0
16 „ .	1,000	0	0
21 „ .	300	0	0
21 „ .	283	7	11
22 „ .	500	0	0
22 „ .	500	0	0
23 „ .	400	0	0[1]
25 „ .	350	0	0

[1] Query this item and one or two others in the document. The amount of 12th April, 1651, was altered to £850.

m. 90 *d*.

		£	s.	d.
1651, 2 May	. . . .	1,406	18	0
6 ,,	. . . .	1,000	0	0
6 ,,	. . . .	350	0	0
10 ,,	. . . .	612	0	0
10 ,,	. . . .	350	0	0
13 ,,	. . . .	150	0	0
14 ,,	. . . .	209	7	0
21 ,,	. . . .	400	0	0
23 ,,	. . . .	350	0	0
26 ,,	. . . .	75,000	0	0
28 ,,	. . . .	1,500	0	0
29 ,,	. . . .	150	0	0
30 ,,	. . . .	150	0	0
30 ,,	. . . .	190	0	0
17 June	. . . .	100	0	0
23 ,,	. . . .	160	0	0
1 July	. . . .	400	0	0
10 ,,	. . . .	1,444	19	8
12 ,,	. . . .	11,000	0	0
12 ,,	. . . .	2,997	12	10
19 ,,	. . . .	400	0	0
29 ,,	. . . .	758	9	0
30 ,,	. . . .	800	0	0
8 Aug.	. . . .	400	0	0
20 ,,	. . . .	17,000	0	0
26 Sept.	. . . .	800	0	0
1 Oct.	. . . .	500	0	0
4 ,,	. . . .	7,000	0	0
15 ,,	. . . .	2,148	0	0
21 Nov.	. . . .	4,261	6	3
25 ,,	. . . .	27,244	12	6
1 Dec.	. . . .	18,000	0	0
1 ,,	. . . .	2,000	0	0
1 ,,	. . . .	3,160	0	0
19 Jan.	. . . .	12,000	0	0

m. 91.

		£	s.	d.
8 ,,	. . . .	1,000	0	0
21 ,,	. . . .	3,000	0	0
31 ,,	. . . .	300	0	0
2 March	. . . .	15,600	0	0
1652, 24 Apr.	. . . .	1,190	0	0
7 May	. . . .	10,000	0	0
20 ,,	. . . .	4,000	0	0
28 ,,	. . . .	3,000	0	0

2. To Joshua Watmough, for the Treasurer of War, by like warrants :—

		£	s.	d.
14 June, 1652	. . . . . .	2,500	0	0
8 July ,,	. . . . . .	2,500	0	0

3. To James Smith, by like warrants :—

		£	s.	d.
27 July, 1652	. . . . . .	2,600	0	0
13 Aug. ,,	. . . . . .	30,000	0	0
14 Aug. ,,	. . . . . .	400	0	0
20 Sept. ,,	. . . . . .	10,000	0	0
18 Mar. ,,	. . . . . .	4,000	0	0
11 July, 1653	. . . . . .	5,495	0	0
11 July, ,,	. . . . . .	55	0	0
5 Feb. 1654	. . . . . .	6,000	0	0

4. To Joshua Watmough, by like warrants :—

	£	s.	d.
22 Aug. 1656	284	16	8½
15 Oct. „	500	0	0
22 Feb. 1657	900	0	0
Total [1]	£317,396	12	7¾

(*e*) *Repayments to Purchasers, as follows* :—

	Names.	*Dates.*	£	s.	d.
1.	Thomas Symon	31 Dec. 1650	£12	0	0
2.	Francis Tyton, for Thomas Reynolds	11 Jan. „	6	0	0
3.	Joseph Hawkesworth	2 Nov. „	13	1	2¾
	Joseph Hawkesworth	30 „ „	75	10	10½
4.	Thomas Butler, captain	24 Feb. „	8	8	10½
5.	John Lisle, Esq.	8 March „	67	15	4¾
m. 91 *d.*					
6.	Roger Hill	9 April, 1651	362	18	1½
7.	Francis Collins	26 June „	33	17	1¼
8.	Alexander Popham, Esq.	12 July „	2	4	7¼
9.	Major Jervase Blackwall	23 July „	55	18	10¾
10.	Thomas Wortley	23 „ „	68	16	0½
11.	John Baker	27 „ „	5	3	8¼
12.	Major John Browne	27 Sept. „	8	6	3½
13.	David Morgan	7 Apr. 1652	8	7	10½
14.	John Pargiter	23 May „		14	9¾
15.	Adam Games, captain, and Richard Sikes	24 July „	71	1	4¼
16.	Algernon Sidney, Col.	8 Sept. „	12	19	2¾
17.	Francis Allen	21 Feb. „	283	14	3½
18.	Jervase Blackwell	4 May, 1653	25	3	7¼
	Jervase Blackwell	4 „ „	16	12	11½
19.	Major John Browne	9 March „	8	13	10¾
20.	Henry Vane, Knt., the elder	30 May 1654	40	5	0¾
21.	Jervase Blackwell	1 June „	26	8	4¾
22.	Abraham Browne for John Lisle	10 Jan. „	10	13	3¾
	Total		£1,224	15	11¼

(*f*) *Other Payments to Officials at Worcester House.*

		£	s.	d.
1.	Repaid to William Mynheire which he paid for the purchase of rents issuing out of the lands of Lord Herbert and the said lands were afterwards discharged by law from the payment of the said rents and are here allowed to him by virtue of the pretended Ordinance of the Protector	540	12	0
m. 92.				
2.	Paid to divers particular surveyors in the several counties of England and Wales by the warrants of the Trustees	3,458	10	0
3.	Paid to Robert Manwaringe esquire, "Register Accomptant" for the salary of himself and his clerks at £200 p.a. for one whole year ending 12 Feb. 1651	200	0	0
4.	Paid to Wm. Webbe esquire for divers paper books, paper, pens, ink and divers other necessaries	408	12	0
5.	Paid to Richard Graves, esquire, "jurisconsult" for his salary at £150 p.a. for 2 years	300	0	0
6.	Paid to Ralph Darnell another "jurisconsult" for his salary at above rate and time	300	0	0
7.	Paid to the said Richard Graves for his salary at £50 p.a. for 4¾ years	237	10	0
8.	A like payment to Ralph Darnell	237	10	0
9.	Paid to divers officials in attendance on the Trustees and Contractors for salaries and necessary expenses [2]	3,107	0	11

[1] Additions of later date on ff. 90*b* and 91 record totals of £194,743 5*s.* 3*d.* and £103,314 16*s.* 8½*d.*

[2] The amount has been altered. Items 3–9 have a separate total of £4,790 12*s.* 11*d.* recorded in the margin.

m. 92 *d.*

£ *s. d.*

10. Paid to officials of the Liberty of the Duchy of Lancaster, and of the parish of St. Clement Danes for divers parish duties at Worcester House 66 19 8

11. Paid to divers artificers and labourers for their services at Worcester House 196 8 9

Total [1] £9,053 3 4

(g) Exchequer Tallies.

Paid to the Receipt of the Exchequer by 2 tallies thereof levied as appears by virtue of a warrant *2 March 1657*, namely :—

10 March, 1657	1,000	0 0
12 ,, ,, ...	134	15 4

£1,134 15 4

Total Deductions. . . . £528,809 7 3

And remains nothing because he has a (surplusagium) deficit of 14 2¼

(h) This account is taken by order of the Rt. Honble Thomas Earl of Southampton, Lord High Treasurer of England, dated *23 March, 1660.* Exd. by R. Aldworth, auditor. Exd. by Wm. Hills, auditor.

Declared 20 Dec. 1662.

ASHLEY.

(i) The aforesaid John Dethick, Knt, was sworn upon this Account *20 Dec. 1662* before me,

EDW: ATKYNS.

III. ABSTRACT OF THE ACCOUNTS RELATING TO THE SALES OF FOREST LANDS, 1653–6

Exch. L.T.R., Pipe Office, Declared Accounts, No. 604, Taken 14th Feb., 1660–61, and Certified 10th July, 1662.

m. 202

Account of Mathew Sheppard and Charles Doyley nominated and appointed Treasurers in a certain pretended Act of Parliament promulgated *22 November, A.D. 1653* intituled An Act for the de-afforestation, sale and augmentation of the Forests ('Anglice' the Improvement) and of the Honours, Manors, lands, tenements and Hereditaments late to the King Queen and Prince belonging within the Kingdom of England as below follows :—

(a) Namely :—

£ *s. d.*

1. The same accountants are charged with the sums of money by them received 11 January A.D. 1653 from Theophilus Boughey citizen and baker of London upon this account as they say upon their personal oaths 2 May 13 Car. II. before Christopher Turner one of the Barons of the Court of Exchequer by virtue of the Warrant of Thomas Earl of Southampton now lord Treasurer of England bearing date 14 Feb. 1660 and in the Bag of particulars remaining as appears 328 0 0

[1] This total is not recorded in the document.

2. And also they are charged with the sums of money by them received £ *s. d.*
18 January 1653 from Laurence Wollaston of the town of
Northampton co. Northampton ironmonger as they say upon
their oaths aforesaid 201 5 0
3. And also they are charged with the sums of money 21 January 1653
of George Hooper of the City of Westminster as they say as
aforesaid 192 3 4
4. And also they are charged with the sums of money by them received
23 January 1653 from Walter Payne of the parish of " le Savoy in
le Strand ", co. Midd. gent as they say as aforesaid . .   12 10 0

Sum of the charge aforesaid £733 18 4

(*b*) *Against which* :—

The same accountants ask allowance and discharge of several sums of
moneys by them paid by virtue of a certain pretended Ordinance of Oliver
(late calling himself the Lord Protector) and of his Council dated 18th April,
1656, namely :—

(1) of £328, paid 14 May 1656 to the beforenamed Theophilus Boughey :
(2) and of £201 5*s.* paid on the same day and year to Laurence Wollaston :
(3) and of £192 3*s.* 4*d.* paid to the said George Hooper :
(4) and of £12 10*s.* paid to Walter Payne.

Total paid   £733 18 4
And so there remains   Nil.
because it balances.

(*c*) *10 July 14 Car. II, 1662.*

Mathew Sheppard the younger son of the said Mathew Sheppard
certifies that his said father is not of sound memory and therefore is not
fit to render his account.

Taken before,
THO. LEEKE.

Exd. by J. Blomley,
    Deputy Auditor.
10 July, 1662.

(*d*) *10 July 14 Car. II, 1662.*

The aforesaid Charles Doyley certifies on his personal oath that his
account is correct.

Taken before,
THO. LEEKE.[1]

---

[1] The items of these three accounts are set out in Roman numerals with great precision, the pounds being indicated in groups of scores, hundreds, thousands, and millions,
and the pence in halfpence, farthings, and halves of farthings as well. The " million "
proved difficult to set down, but was finally disposed of by arranging the figures in groups
of hundreds and thousand of *thousands*. See " The Use of Arabic and Roman Numerals
in English Archives " by Hilary Jenkinson, M.A., F.S.A. (the *Antiquaries Journal*, vol. vi,
272–4, July, 1926), who illustrates the method of stating the sum of £1,423,710 18*s.* 3*d.*
in Account No. 603. In the case of Tintagel, Cornwall, the rents add up to fractions of
" ¼ *plus* ¼ *plus* ⅛ " of a penny, the property being purchased for the sum of £1,647 11*s.* 11*d.*
" *plus* ¾ *plus* ⅞ " of one penny. It is worthy of remark that the only undetected error in
the accounts, which the auditors failed to notice, consists of *sevenpence* in No. 603 (*e*).
In regard to the balances, No. 604 alone shows no remainder. The balance in the case of
No. 602 is *adverse*, for the Exchequer officials have overpaid the account by 14*s.* 2½*d.*, and
presumably Charles II recovered this amount from the surviving trustee, Sir John Dethick.
But the largest account of all, No. 603, displayed a balance of £349 15*d.* 11*d.* and five-
eighths of a penny, of which £300 was paid into the Exchequer on 15th December, 1662,
and the rest given to two of the auditors and their clerks " for their labour in and about
the taking of the account ".

IV. Conveyances of £5,000 and Upwards, Disclosed at the Audit, 1662

Cambridge Univ. Lib. MS., Dd. xiii, 20, gives a list of 653 conveyances, ranging from 1s. (No. 632) to over £35,000 (No. 431). The present list is restricted to amounts above £5,000, tested and confirmed by reference to various lists of purchasers.[1] The number of the Conveyance is given below, with an indication of group-purchasers. The following lists and signs are used :—

Purchasers :—

* Single Purchasers and Counties.	IT. Immediate Tenants.
† Mixed Counties.[2]	OC. Original Creditors.
‡ Partially Confirmed.	AB. Assigned Bills.

Lists.	Conveyances.	Purchasers.	Counties.	£	s.	d.
* 1	OC.	521	1	Berkshire . . .	5,100	8	6
2	OC.	444	4	Somerset . . .	5,109	13	4
3	OC.	177	3	Cornwall . . .	5,166	1	11½
4	IT.	322	1	Hertfordshire . .	5,220	11	3
† 5	OC.	105	4	Derby, Nottingham .	5,414	18	10
6	OC.	25	1	Northamptonshire .	5,498	15	0
7	AB.	542	1	Staffordshire . .	5,540	8	4
† 8	OC.	353	4	Westmorland, Yorkshire .	5,766	4	5
‡ 9	— [3]	615	1	Lincolnshire . . .	5,767	10	0
10	OC.	396	3	Dorset	5,900	0	3
†11	OC.	560	3	Lancashire, Lincoln .	5,910	8	5
12	OC.	118	1	Worcestershire. .	5,915	14	0
12	AB.	496	2	Yorkshire . .	5,965	7	6
†14	OC.	324	2	Hereford, Radnor .	6,415	3	3¾
15	OC.	141	10	Lincolnshire . .	6,610	10	9
†16	OC.	420	2	Cheshire, Huntingdon .	6,618	16	9½
17	OC.	27	2	Berkshire . . .	6,739	1	2
18	OC.	515	2	Cornwall . . .	6,823	0	10½
19	OC.[4]	289	1	Lancashire . .	6,853	16	1+
†20	OC.	138	1	Lancashire, Yorkshire .	6,909	6	10
21	OC.	154	1	Surrey	6,952	11	4½
22	OC.	609	6	Nottinghamshire .	6,953	8	3
23	OC.	498	2	Yorkshire . .	6,967	8	2¼ .
24	OC.	308	1	Somerset . . .	7,151	8	2
25	OC.	607	7	Warwickshire . .	7,187	16	4
26	OC.	539	6	Bedfordshire . .	7,410	0	0
†27	OC.	509	1	Devon, Somerset .	7,417	14	6
28	IT.	369	1	Lincolnshire . .	7,505	15	0
29	OC.	423	4	Middlesex . . .	7,519	19	6
†30	OC.	383	6	Lincoln, Norfolk .	7,553	4	11¾
‡31	— [5]	505	2	Denbigh . . .	7,672	5	11
32	OC.	134	2	Staffordshire . .	7,697	13	0
33	OC.	50	1	Surrey . . .	7,884	18	11½

[1] Camb. Univ. Lib. MSS., Dd. viii, 30 (Nos. 4, 5, and 6).
[2] In smaller amounts, ranging from £91 to £4,669 (total, £70,123 17s. 7¼d.), there are thirty-six other items which relate to " Mixed Counties ", viz. Bedf., Berks, Bucks, Camb., Ches, Corn., Cumb., Derby, Dev., Dors, Dur., Ex., Hants, Herts, Hunts, Kent, Lancs, Lincs, Mx., Norf., Northants, Northumb., Notts, Oxf., Som., Staff., Suff., Sur., Sx., War., Wilts, Yorks, and Brecon, Card., Carm., Flint, Monm., Pembroke.
[3] Nos. 9 and 31 are missing in AB., IT., OC. lists.
[4] The amount of the Conveyance includes " 1d. *plus* one-third of 1d."
[5] Occurs in the Conveyance list only. See No. 9.

Lists.		Conveyance.	Purchasers.	Counties.	£	s.	d.
†34	OC.	40	6	Bedford, Yorkshire .	7,899	0	0
*35	AB.	544	1	Northamptonshire . .	8,120	0	0
36	OC.	343	2	Surrey	8,209	3	6
37	AB.	293	1	Northamptonshire . .	8,310	9	8
38	OC.	210	4	Bedfordshire . . * .	8,311	1	0
39	OC.	234	1	Wiltshire	8,393	0.	7
40	OC.	318	2	Warwickshire . .	9,159	15	6
41	OC.	427	2	Cardigan	9,898	10	9
42	OC.	451	17	Cumberland . . .	10,320	18	5½
43	OC.	371	6	Hertfordshire . . .	10,579	15	4
44	OC.	436	5	Hertfordshire . .	10,594	18	8
45	OC.	400	7	Bedfordshire . .	11,208	2	6
46	OC.	486	1	Surrey	11,591	8	8
47	OC.	523	6	Norfolk	12,107	13	3
48	OC.	219	6	Kent	12,583	5	3¾
49	OC.	637	5	Lincolnshire . .	12,857	16	11¾
†50	OC.	302	2	Stafford, Denbigh . .	13,171	2	6
51	OC.	112	3	Middlesex . .	13,215	6	8
†52	OC.	292	3	Middlesex, Surrey .	13,562	0	6
53	OC.	74	6	Surrey	14,158	12	0
‡54	OC.	576	1	Kent	16,615	13	1½
†55	OC. ¹	354	1	Cumberland, Westmorland	16,653	9	0¼
56	OC.	257	1	Surrey	16,825	17	8
57	OC.	455	4	Oxfordshire . .	17,214	19	9
58	OC.	126	2	Northamptonshire .	18,222	6	2
59	OC.	380	7	Warwickshire . .	18,775	3	9
60	OC.	266	2	Devonshire . .	19,517	11	10¼
61	OC.	551	1	Huntingdonshire .	19,885	14	0
62	OC.	216	1	Northamptonshire .	22,299	6	10
†63	OC.	150	6	Berkshire, Surrey .	22,755	0	0
†64	OC.	431	6	Hertford, Middlesex.	35,873	11	3

²Total . . £654,010 17 0½

¹ The entry is confirmed by reference to AB. and OC. lists—the latter accounting for £12,903 9s. 0¼d., and the former for the remainder (£3,750). The only items traced in the list of assigned Bills are Nos. 7, 13, 35, and 37 above. The list of Immediate Tenants contains two entries, viz. Nos. 4 and 28.

² The total includes "one-third of one penny" from item No. 19. The average of this list of conveyances exceeds £10,218.

INDEX

I. INDEX OF COUNTIES

NOTE.—Places are entered in alphabetical order under the counties to which they belong. Middlesex and Surrey retain the parishes which they lost after 1888. The cities of London and Westminster are separately grouped under " London and Middlesex ". Saints' names are dispersed under the principal names, e.g. St. Albans (Alban's, St.). Variant spellings occur in brackets. Only one reference to a name on a page is recorded; there may be more, both in the text and the notes. Where the name occurs on several consecutive pages, the first and last are given to show the limits. Footnotes (*n.*), unnumbered, are indicated only when a separate reference is needed, apart from the text. The tables and the Appendix are fully indexed, Roman figures being used for the Preface and tables, and Arabic figures for the text or the notes. The references under Duchies and Earldoms include records. *See* the General Index for Illustrations and additional names.

ENGLAND AND WALES

ANGLESEY.
County : 11, 138, 253, 317, 378.
Dindathway : 378.

BEDFORDSHIRE.
County : 5 n., 8, 9, 11, 35, 38, 39 n., 124, 131, 136, 137, 145 n., 180, 213, 214, 219, 223, 235, 252, 300, 309 n., 313, 315, 317, 340, 343, 344 n., 345, 346, 368, 383–5, 387, 389, 392, 394, 395, 406, 407.
Hundreds : 384.
Ampthill : 261, 368, 387 ; — The Falcon, 389 ; — Great Park, 392 ; — Honour, 383 ; — Warren, 394.
Barford : Hundred, 385 n.
Beckering : Park, 214, 392.
Bedford : 368.
Biggleswade : 368 ; — Hundred, 136, 384 n.
Brockborough : Park, 214, 392.
Campton (Camelton) : 368, 394.
Clifton : Hundred, 384 n.
Millbrook (Milbroke, Milbrooke) : 261, 368, 389 n. ; — Warren, 394.
Newnham : 347, 392 n.
Shefford : 368.
Steppingley : 222, 368, 394.
Stodden : Hundred, 385 n.

BERKSHIRE.
County : 5 n., 8, 11, 25, 35, 38, 39 n., 42 n., 127, 128, 130, 131, 145 n., 180, 185, 186 n., 187, 214 n., 215 n., 219, 223, 234, 239 n., 250 n., 252, 270, 273 n., 300, 309 n., 312, 313, 315, 317, 318, 325, 339 n., 340, 343–6, 368, 369, 384, 386–9, 391, 392, 395, 396, 406, 407.

BERKSHIRE (*continued*).
Hundreds : 384.
Abingdon : 243, 261.
Ashbury : 18.
Bray : 276, 277 n.
Clewer : 340, 368, 369 ; — Farm, 389.
Cookham : 369.
Frogmore : Farm, 387.
Garston, East : 368.
Maidencote (Maydencote) : 271.
Martin Abbey : *see* Windsor.
Moat Park : *see* Windsor.
Reading : 8, 369 ; — Abbey, 386 ; — King's Mead, 391.
Shippon (Skippon) : 368 ; — Mills, 391.
Tallcott : Farm, 387.
Wallingford : 243, 368 ; — Dyehouse, 389 ; — King's Mead, 391 ; — Northeights, 388, 391.
Windsor : 102, 113, 298, 366, 368, 369, 389 n. ; — Castle, 90, 103–5 ; — Deanery, 73 n. ; — Forest, 366 ; — Great Park, 212, 392 ; — King's Garden, 389 ; — King's Head, 389 ; — King's Meadows, 90 ; — King's Slaughter House, 389 ; — Little Park, 90, 392 ; — Martin Abbey (Pescod St., New Windsor), 386 ; — Moat Park, 369, 392 ; — New, 386, 392 ; — Office of Works, 90, 103 ; — Park, 214 ; — The Rolph, 389 ; — Timber Yard, 90, 103.

BRECKNOCKSHIRE.
County : 11, 146 n., 220, 238 n., 250 n., 253, 342, 378, 392, 406 n.
Brecknock : 378 ; — Forest, 304 ; — Fulling Mill, 392 ; — Mills, 391 n., 392.

COUNTIES 421

NOTTINGHAMSHIRE (continued).

Newark : 8, 155, 375 ; — Castle, 386.
Nottingham : 223-4.
Rufford : 381 ; — Waste, 381 n.
Sherwood Forest (Derby, Notts) : 27 n.,
  117, 119, 240-1, 321, 380 n., 381 ; —
  Billhay, 380, 381 n. ; — Birkland,
  381 ; — King's Hays, 381 ; — Noe-
  man's Wood, 381 ; — White Lodge
  (Birkland), 380 n,. 381 n.
Thoroton : 5 n.
Trent, River banks, 180.

OXFORDSHIRE.

County : 5 n., 8, 9, 11, 25, 35, 38, 39 n.,
  130, 145 n., 152, 155, 180, 214 n., 223,
  234-5, 253, 299 n., 313, 318, 325, 341,
  344-6, 368, 375, 384-5, 387, 394-5,
  406 n., 407.
Diocese : 73.
Hundreds : 385.
Chalgrove : Field, 48 n.
Cornbury : Park, 90, 102.
Cuddesdon : 18, 387.
Ewelme : 375, 384 ; — Warren, 394.
Manor Place (? Manor) : 235 n.
Oxford : vii, 133, 261, 291, 303 ; — All
  Souls College, 330 ; — Bodleian
  Library, see General Index : — St.
  John's College, 261.
Shotover : Forest, 111.
Stowood : Forest, 111.
Woodstock : 90, 103, 155, 375, 384, 385 n.,
  395 ; — Parks, 90, 103.
Wootton : Hundred, 384 n.

PEMBROKESHIRE.

County : 11, 56, 146 n., 253, 313, 342, 379
  386, 392, 406 n.
Earldom : 78.
David's, St. : Diocese, 73.
Florence : 379.
Haverford, West : 379 ; — Castle, 386.
Milton : Mill, 392.
Rosemarket : Mill, 391 n.

RADNORSHIRE.

County : 11, 138, 253, 273 n., 276, 379,
  395, 406.
Gladestry (Glandestry) : 379 ; — Mill, 391 n.
Ischoyd : 379.
Knighton : 277.
Knocklas ; 379.
Presteigne : 379, 394 n., 395.
Radnor : 379.
Rhayader (Royader) : 379.
Southagree : 379.
Southnethian : 379.

RUTLAND.

County : 5 n., 8, 9, 11, 33, 35, 38, 39 n.,
  136, 138, 194 n., 238 n., 253, 277 n.,
  312, 314, 345-6, 375, 385.

RUTLAND (continued).

Dukedom : 295.
Hundreds : 385.
Leighfield : Forest, 103.

SHROPSHIRE.

County : 5 n., 11, 35, 38, 39 n., 138, 151,
  152 n., 220, 253, 341, 345-6, 375, 385,
  391, 396 n.
Hundreds : 385.
Bromfield : Lordship (see Denbigh), 133.
Ludlow(e) : 375 ; Mills, 391.
Shrewsbury : 375.

SOMERSET.

County : 5 n., 6 n., 8-9, 11, 35, 38, 39 n.,
  56, 127-8, 131-2, 146 n., 186 n., 187,
  208 n., 215 n., 219, 253, 281, 294, 303,
  312-14, 317, 324-5, 341, 345-6, 349 n.,
  355 n., 370, 375-6, 385-6, 388, 395,
  396 n., 406 ; — Chantry Lands, 375,
  386 ; — Somerset House, see London.
Hundreds : 385.
Bath : 295 ; — Diocese, 73, 74 n.
Bristol : see Gloucester.
Chewton : 375.
Curry Mallet : 375-6.
Easton : 341.
Exmoor (Exmore) : Chase, 376, 386 ; —
  Forest, 273 n., 281.
Falconbridge : see Milton.
Farrington Gurney : 376.
Fosseway : 375.
Frome : 314.
Hampden : 376.
Harptree, West (Westharptree) : 375.
Inglescombe : 375 ; — Farm, 388.
Kilverdon : 314.
Laverton : 376.
Midsomer Norton : 375-6.
Milton Falconbridge : 376.
Milverton : 375, 386.
Norton : see Midsomer.
Stoke sub Hampden : 376.
Stratton on the Fosse : 375.
Wells : 295 ; — Diocese, 73.
West Harptree : see Harptree.
Widecombe : 355 n., 375 ; — Farm, 388.
Woolverton (Wolverton) : Farm, 388.

STAFFORDSHIRE.

County : 5 n., 8, 11, 35, 38, 39 n., 130, 131,
  151, 152 n., 180, 214 n., 220, 223, 234,
  239, 253, 312-13, 315, 318, 324-5, 341,
  344-6, 376, 380 n., 381 n., 384-5, 387,
  391, 393, 396, 406-7.
Hundred : 385.
Aggardsbury : Park, 393.
Anslow (Aynslow) : 381, 387.
Barton : 381 ; — Lodge, 380.

OTHER PLACE NAMES.

II. GENERAL INDEX

A

Abatement : Taxes, 247.
Abbeys : 18, 24, 274 n., 364, 386 ; — leases, 274 n. ; — Manors, 305.
Abnormal : values, 159.
Abolition : House of Lords, 63.
Abridgment : Records, 309 n.
Absolute : Ownership, 14, 24.
Abstracts and abstracting : 137, 141, 145, 148, 153, 178, 187–8, 213 n., 336, 339, 380 n., 381, 391 ; — Accounts, 332, 397–405 ; — claims, 322 ; — copyholds, 336 ; — Cornwall Duchy, 313 ; — Old Shoreham Manor, 188, Table liii *B* ; — patents, 337 ; — surveys, 128; — Values, 148, 187, 339.
Abuses : 50, 52, 54, 109, 321, 326 ; — abuse of State, 215.
Abutments : 146 ; — butting, 335.
Access : houses of, 61, 259 ; — London, 241 ; — records, 195.
Accommodation : Office, 114.
Accountancy : methods, 6, 33–8, 191.
Accountants (Accomptants) : 36, 283, 398, 400, 404–5 ; — associates, 398 ; — certificates, 113 ; — clerks, 100, 403 ; — fee farm rents, 100 ; — forest lands, 113; — instructions, 113 ; — methods, 33 ; — registrar-accomptant, 100, 111, 113–14, 229, 403 ; — salaries, 100, 111, 114.
Accounts (accompts) : 13 n., 38, 43, 77, 82–3, 87, 92–4, 113, 129 n., 140 n., 144,

Accounts (*continued*).
192 n., 196, 279–280, 313, 319, 322, 326–8, 330–2, 334, 352, 355, 362–3 ; — Abstracts, 332 ; — adverse, 405 n. ; alterations, 401 n., 403 n. ; — army, 193, 224 ; — arrears, 82, 94 ; — audit and Auditors, 38, 41, 255–6 ; — balance, 399, 405 ; — certified, 82 ; — committee, 93–4, 398 ; — Commissioners, 38, 86–7 ; — complicated calculations, 399 n. ; — Crown Lands, 279, 320, 322, 397–9 ; — declared, 41 n., 76 n., 192 n., 300 n., 301, 320, 322, 328, 397, 400, 404 ; — deductions, 87 ; — deficit, 404 ; — department, 92, 191 ; — discharged, 405 ; — errors, 405 n. ; — Escheators', 35 ; — examination, 82, 86 ; — Exchequer, 35, 300 n. ; — Fee farm rents, 231, 236, 322, 400–4 ; — foreign, 34–5, 37, 300 n. ; — forests, 35, 322, 404–5 ; — imperfect, 322 ; King's Revenue, 307 ; — Manors, 29 n., 32 n., 43 n., 279, 280 n., 281 n. ; — Ministers, 274 n., 283, 300 n. ; — miscellaneous, 35, 195 ; — missing, 279 ; — office, 38 ; — officials, 94 ; — original, 35, 283 ; — overpaid, 405 n. ; Parliamentary, 307 n. ; — public, 38 ; — Receivers, 283 ; — Regimental, 224 ; — revised, 82 ; — rolls, 34–5 ; — sales, 76, 256, 397–405 ; — Sheriff's, 33–4, 302 ; — stated, 93–4, 265, 320 ; — Sworn, 399, 404 ; — Treasury, 236 ; — Worcester House, 92, 94, 398.

427

GENERAL INDEX

435

C

Cadiz: expedition, 41.
Caedualla: King, 18.
Cæsar: Sir J., 298.
Cake: 268.
Calamity: public, 285.
Calculations: xvii (25), 20 n., 32 n., 51, 70 n., 71 n., 72 n., 73 n., 77 n., 157 n., 158 n., 165 n., 252, 262 n., 280 n., 356 n., 366 n., 399 n., 405 n.; — Abacus (Exchequer), 33 n.; — accounts 405 n.; — complicated, 399 n.; — dates, 3 n.; — double reckoning, 160, 165; — errors, 351 n.; — fractions, 405 n.; land valuation, 163; — measurement (q.v.), 157–8; — numerals, 303, 405; — precision, 224; — Statistics (q.v.); — values, 188.
Calendars (Kalendars): vii–viii, 3, 4, 6–7, 40, 123–132, 152 n., 194, 195 n., 198 n., 199, 203, 204 n., 208 n., 225 n., 227 n., 231, 236 n., 242 n., 244, 267, 313, 323–5, 348 n., 358 n.; — ancient, 306; — imperfect, 323; — new, 126 n.; — P.R.O. (q.v.).
Caley: John, 42, 243 n., 298, 312.
Callis: — 300 n.
Calthrope: C., 299.
Cam: H., 299.
Cambridge: Owen, 396.
Cambridge: University Library (MSS.), 77, 80 n., 99 n., 123, 131, 161 n., 196–7, 200, 203–4, 207 n., 208 n., 220 n., 221 n., 224 n., 231 n., 240–1, 243–4, 248, 251–2, 253 n., 254–5, 263, 292, 311 n., 312, 323, 325–6, 342 n., 344 n., 349 n., 353 n., 355 n., 357 n., 358 n., 368 n., 406–7; — Modern History, 63 n., 72 n., 75 n., 133 n., 308; — Surveys (q.v.), 123.
Camden: Society, 294, 395 n.
Camelot (Camelott, Camlet, Camlett): East, Hill, North, West, 382–3; — Camlet Moat (Moate), xvi (20), 382–3.
Camerarius: see Chamberlain.
Campbell (MSS.): — 161 n.
Cancellation: 202 n.
Cannon: Capt. H., xvi (17), 224 n., 229, 300 n., 392.
Canterbury: Archbishop, 18, 34; — Archbishops' Lands (q.v.), xvi (7), Elthorne, Mx.
Capitalists: London, 219.
Capital Messuage: xvi (25).
Capite: Tenures, xvi (11), 37, 178, 263, 301 n., 306, 338.
Capitular Lands: See Dean and Chapter Lands.
Capons: Rents, 144, 334.
Careless: Wm., 345.
Carew: — 110; — John, 342; — Lord, 299.
Carey (Cary): John, 342; — Thos., 340.

Carleton: Sir Dudley, 57; — M., 388.
Carlisle: Earl of, 295; — see xvi (10).
Carlyle: Thos., 247 n., 299.
Carriage (Carts): — 322; cartboots, 352; — carters, 180; — works, 144.
Carter: Henry, 345; — M., 299; — S., 299.
Carto-bibliography: 310.
Cartwright: — 126.
Casbeard: John, 385 n., 396.
Caser: John, 342.
Cashier: see Tellers (Exchequer).
Cassells: — 295.
Castle: Capt., 342.
Castles: xvi (9), 37, 49, 61, 69, 79–80, 85, 90, 96, 102–6, 119, 123, 143, 171 n., 180, 276, 369, 379, 386, 393; — castle-guard, 297; — castleward rents, 234; — decayed, 276; — garrisoned, 89, 103; — parks, 214; — royal, 29 n.; — Sales, 321, 328; — Surveys (q.v.), 316; walls, 174.
Casualties: 43; — receipts, 265; — revenues, 263 n., 307, 326.
Catalogues: 42 n., 125, 239 n., 291, 294–5, 306 n., 326.
Categories: Buyers, 210, 219, 221, 259.
Cater's Lodge: xvi (22).
Cathedrals: 43 n., 70, 136; — property, 145.
Catherine (of Braganza): Queen Dowager, 279; — furniture, 280.
Catholic Church: 40.
Cattle: 17, 26, 31, 183, 277; — Cattle Gate, xvi (20).
Causeways: 142, 179–180.
Cautions: Purchases, 327.
Cavalier Lands: 3 n.
Cave: — 308 n.
Caveat Emptor: 260.
Cavendish (Cavendishe): Sir Wm., 238 n.
"Cavy": John, 142, 179.
Cawley: W., 388.
Cecil: — 295; — Sir Wm., 40–1, 50–1, 53 n.; — Lord Hugh, 57 n., 287; — Cecil Street, xvi (10); — see Salisbury.
Cellar rents: 234.
Celtic period: 13–14.
Centuries: first twelve, 15 n.; — fourth to twentieth (q.v.).
Ceowulf: King, 18.
Cerrier: H., 393.
Certainty Money: 385; — offers, xvi (18); — payments, 144.
Certificates and Certification: xvi (1, 11, 18), 29 n., 40, 42 n., 52, 84–5, 94, 137, 192, 195, 198 n., 201, 203–4, 207, 232, 240 n., 242 n., 243 n., 244, 248, 251, 308, 314–15, 322–4, 326, 330, 344, 351–2, 355, 357–9, 380 n., 381 n., 405; — additional, 137; — arrears, 82, 86–7, 93; — auditors (q.v.), 307 n.; bills (q.v.), 242; — books, 256; — church lands, 308 n.; — claims (q.v.), 84;

Grounds (continued).
387 n.; — coarse, 155, 351, 361; —
common ways, 362; — coney, 146,
161–2; — enclosed, 109; — grubbed,
366–7; — leazow, 170, 348, 351, 361;
— meadow, 146; — mountainous,
xvi (22); — pasture (q.v.); — Poor's,
112; — plots, 213, 298; — rents
(q.v.), 284 n.; — strips, 282; — un-
even, xvi (22); — values (q.v.), 163; —
waste (q.v.), 163, 338; — woody, 167,
176.
Groups: Purchasers (q.v.); — sales, 194.
Grove: Capt. Jn., xvi (16), 223 n., 224,
388, 392–3.
Groves (Greaves): xvi (21), 175, 367, 394;
— rents, 235.
Growth: trees (100 years), 279.
Guard: Castle, 297.
Guides: Court Keeper's, 308; — guidance
(Lord Treasurer), 268; — official, viii;
— see Bird and Giuseppi (P.R.O.), 123,
126.
Guildhall: — 71; — Library, 131, 239,
293, 311 n.; — Treasurers for War,
227, 401–3.
Guilds: rents, 235.
Guilt: War Clause, 80 n.
Gult: 392.
Gunton: Nich., xvi (12), 139, 244 n., 344.
Gurdian: see Granger (alias).
Gurdon: Jn., 343.
Gurney: House, 229–230; — MSS.,
59 n., 216 n.
Gurton: T., 302.
Gutters: "lugges," 181.
Guybert: — 302.
Guybon: Col. Rob., 396.
Gwyn (Gewen, Gwynn): Thos., 270, 272;
— Wm., xvi (25), 399.

H

Haberdashers: 341 n.
Hackert: Col., 223.
Hackman: A., 294.
Haddock (Haddocke): Jn., 136, 346.
Haddon, East: Northants, xvi (21).
Hadley: Middlesex, xvi (20); — Common,
xvi (12, 20).
Hale (Hales, Hayle); — 300, 306; — H.,
393; — Sir M., 302; — Rowl., 396 n.;
— Wm., 340.
Hall (Halls): — 274 n., 308 n.; — Ezekiel,
344; — Dr. Hubert, vii–viii, 15–17,
22 n., 23 n., 25 n., 26, 27 n., 29 n.,
30 n., 33 n., 34 n., 48, 123 n., 278 n.,
291, 296, 298, 302, 309 n.; — Mr.,
232; — Ralph, 113, 193, 343; — Wm.,
245, 343.
Hallam: Hy., 58, 61.
Halliday (Holliday): J., 393; — Mr., 343.

Halliford Manor, Middx.: Survey and
sale, 348–367; — see Index I.
Hallowes: Nath., 343.
Halls: 90, 103, 172, 371, 376, 390; —
Guildhall (q.v.): — halmote, 304; —
Park hall, xvi (22); — rent, 235.
Halsey: Jn., 345.
Ham: Meadow, 366.
Hamers Wood Grove: 175.
Hammond: J., 390; — R., 386; — Ham-
mond's Hook, xvi (20.)
Hampden: Jn., 48 n.
Hamstall: 381.
Hanaper: 50 n.
Hancock (Hancocke): Ensign Thos.,
224, 384 n.
Hand: Manors in, 55; — see Possessions.
Handbooks: Records, 309.
Hangings: Tapestry, 398 n.
Hannan: E., 388.
Hanoverian Period: see George I, II, III,
IV, V, VI, William IV, Victoria,
Edward VII, VIII.
Harbert: see Herbert.
Harboard (Harbord): Sir Chas., 268, 275.
Harbours: 266, 387 n., 389.
Harby: Sir Job, 110, 114.
Hardres: Sir T., 302.
Hardy: Sir T. D., 300, 302, 304, 306; —
W., 129, 314; — W. J., 303.
Hare: Hounds, 389; — Warren, 90, 104,
393 n., 394.
Hargrave: — 294.
Harleian MSS. (Brit. Mus.): xvi (16, 17)
76 n., 161 n., 194, 222 n., 223 n.,
224 n., 238 n., 241, 294; — Charters,
274 n.
Harold: King, 22.
Harrington: Sir Jas., 78, 108, 343; —
Sir John, 302.
Harris: R., 389; — Thos., 364; — Wid.,
396 n.
Harrison (Harison): — 116; — Edw., 341,
385 n., 396; — Sir Geo., 302; — J.,
302; — Joan, 204; — John, 342–3; —
Sir John, 114; — Major Gen., 110,
268; — Ralph, xvi (21), 78, 80, 233,
243, 343, 358, 362; — Col. Thos., 204,
207, 223, 343, 357, 386 n.
Hart: — 132 n.; — Jas., 345; — Thos.,
351, 361; — W., 302; — Wm.,
341.
Harthacnut: King, 18.
Harts (Harte): 351, 361, 365; — Harte's
Eight, 351; — White Hart, xvi (24).
Harvest: value, 144.
Harvey: Col. Edm., 343.
Harwood: — 5 n.; — see Horwood.
Haslerigge (Hazlerigge): Sir Arth., 223–4;
— J., 390.
Haslewood: Nath., xvi (17).
Hassell: Ralph, 342.
Hasted: — 5 n.

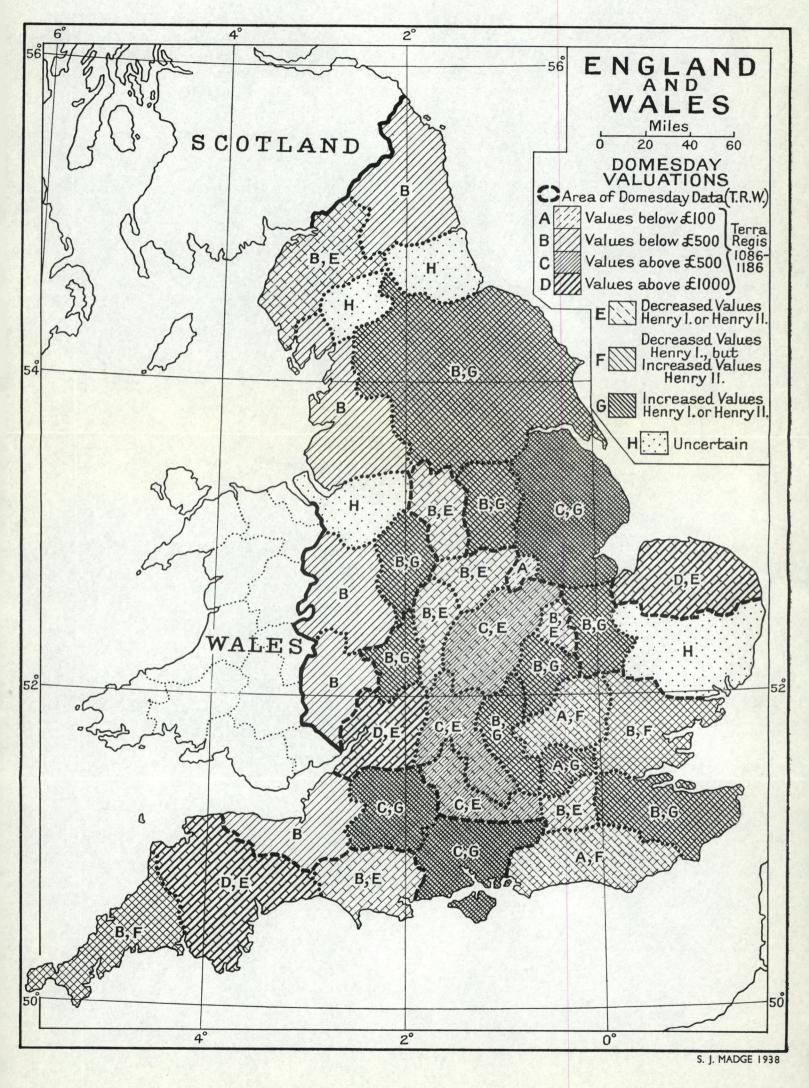

ENGLAND AND WALES

Miles

0 20 40 60

DOMESDAY VALUATIONS

⬭ Area of Domesday Data (T.R.W.)

A — Values below £100
B — Values below £500 } Terra Regis 1086-1186
C — Values above £500
D — Values above £1000

E — Decreased Values Henry I. or Henry II.

F — Decreased Values Henry I., but Increased Values Henry II.

G — Increased Values Henry I. or Henry II.

H — ⋯ Uncertain

SCOTLAND

WALES

B

B, E

H

H

B, G

B

H

B

B

B, E

B, G

B, G

B, E

B, E

C, E

B, G

C, G

A

B, E

B, G

B, G

D, E

H.

D, E

C, E

B, G

A, F

B, F

A, G

C, G

C, E

B, E

B, G

C, G

A, F

B, E

D, E

B, F

S. J. MADGE 1938

[face p. 16

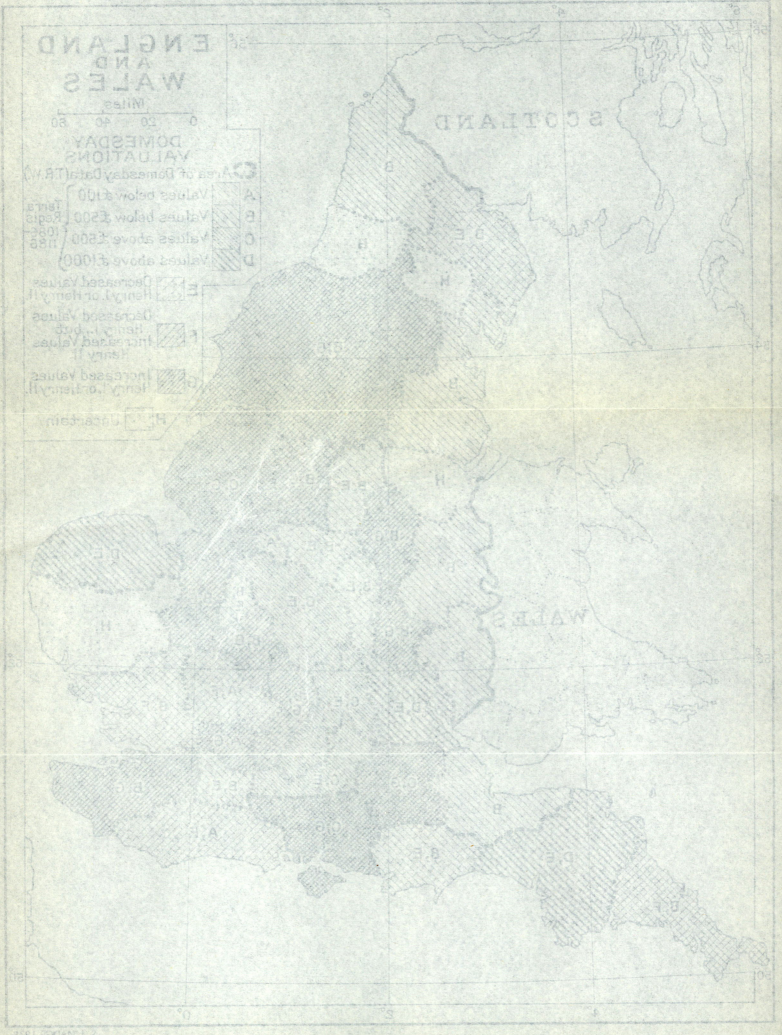

ENGLAND
AND
WALES

Miles

0   20   40   60

STUART LAND
VALUATIONS

A { Schedules of James I:
    Annual Values above £1000

B { Sales of Charles I 1626-1627:
    Counties unaffected

2-17 { Group Purchasers of
       Crown Lands:
       Commonwealth Sales

SCOTLAND

A,B 2-11

A,B 17   A 11

B 4

BORDERLANDS AREA
(NORTH)

A,B 2-3   A 2-11

B 2
2   B 2   2-4   B 2-6   A 2-10

A 2
2   EXTRA-METROPOLITAN AREA
                                                        (NORTH)
B
WALES   B   A 2-6

                    2-8   2   B

B 2   B 2   BORDERLANDS   2-8   A 2-11   A,B   B 2-10   A 2-5
                (CENTRAL)   2
              AREA
              2

B 2   2   4-10

6   6   2-4   2-7   A 2-6   A 2-5

B 2   B 2-7   2   METROPOLITAN AREA
                              (NORTH)

                                              2-6

        A 2-4   2-6

              2-10   2-10   METROPOLITAN AREA
EXTRA-METROPOLITAN AREA   (SOUTH)   A,B
        (SOUTH)   2-11

      2   6-10   B 2-3

BORDERLANDS   B 2-3
AREA
(SOUTH)

2-10

S. J. MADGE 1938

[face p. 256

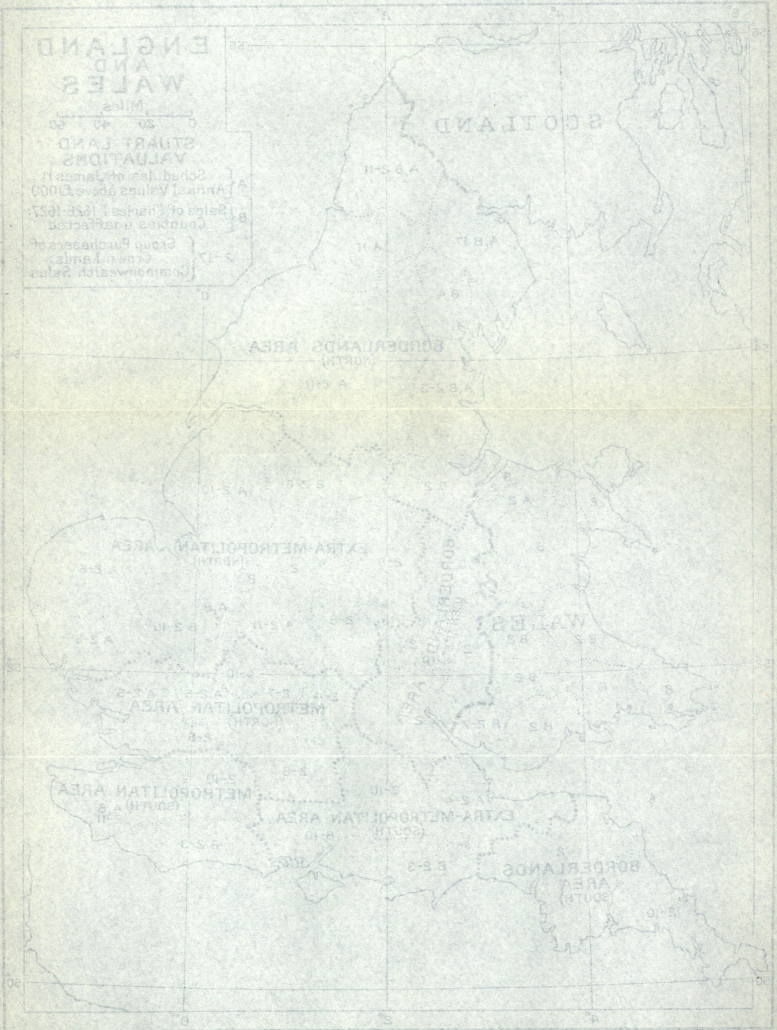